Pain, Penance, and Protest

In medieval England, a defendant who refused to plead to a criminal indictment was sentenced to pressing with weights as a coercive measure. Using peine forte et dure ("strong and hard punishment") as a lens through which to analyze the law and its relationship with Christianity, Butler asks: Where do we draw the line between punishment and penance? And, how can pain function as a vehicle for redemption within the common law? Adopting a multidisciplinary approach, this book embraces both law and literature. When Christ was on trial before Herod, he refused to plead, his silence signaling denial of the court's authority. England's discontented subjects, from hungry peasants to even King Charles I himself, stood mute before the courts in protest. Bringing together penance, pain, and protest, Butler breaks down the mythology surrounding peine forte et dure and examines how it functioned within the medieval criminal-justice system.

Sara M. Butler is the King George III Professor in British History at The Ohio State University. She is the author of three books: *The Language of Abuse: Marital Violence in Later Medieval England*, *Divorce in Medieval England: From One to Two Persons in Law*, and *Forensic Medicine and Death Investigation in Medieval England*.

T0384654

STUDIES IN LEGAL HISTORY

See the Studies in Legal History series website at
http://studiesinlegalhistory.org/

Studies in Legal History

EDITORS

Sarah Barringer Gordon, University of Pennsylvania
Lisa Ford, University of New South Wales
Michael Lobban, London School of Economics and Political Science
Reuel Schiller, University of California, Hastings College of the Law

Other books in the series:

Michael Lobban, *Imperial Incarceration: Detention without Trial in the Making of British Colonial Africa*
Stefan Jurasinski and Lisi Oliver, *The Laws of Alfred: The Domboc and the Making of Anglo-Saxon Law*
Sascha Auerbach, *Armed with Sword and Scales: Law, Culture, and Local Courtrooms in London, 1860–1913*
Alejandro de La Fuente and Ariela J. Gross, *Becoming Free, Becoming Black: Race, Freedom, and the Law in Cuba, Virginia, and Louisiana*
Elizabeth Papp Kamali, *Felony and the Guilty Mind in Medieval England*
Jessica K. Lowe, *Murder in the Shenandoah: Making Law Sovereign in Revolutionary Virginia*
Michael A. Schoeppner, *Moral Contagion: Black Atlantic Sailors, Citizenship, and Diplomacy in Antebellum America*
Sam Erman, *Almost Citizens: Puerto Rico, the U.S. Constitution, and Empire*

Pain, Penance, and Protest

Peine Forte et Dure in Medieval England

SARA M. BUTLER
The Ohio State University

CAMBRIDGE
UNIVERSITY PRESS

Shaftesbury Road, Cambridge CB2 8EA, United Kingdom

One Liberty Plaza, 20th Floor, New York, NY 10006, USA

477 Williamstown Road, Port Melbourne, VIC 3207, Australia

314–321, 3rd Floor, Plot 3, Splendor Forum, Jasola District Centre, New Delhi – 110025, India

103 Penang Road, #05–06/07, Visioncrest Commercial, Singapore 238467

Cambridge University Press is part of Cambridge University Press & Assessment, a department of the University of Cambridge.

We share the University's mission to contribute to society through the pursuit of education, learning and research at the highest international levels of excellence.

www.cambridge.org
Information on this title: www.cambridge.org/9781009065726

DOI: 10.1017/9781009067065

© Sara M. Butler 2022

This publication is in copyright. Subject to statutory exception and to the provisions of relevant collective licensing agreements, no reproduction of any part may take place without the written permission of Cambridge University Press & Assessment.

First published 2022
First paperback edition 2024

A catalogue record for this publication is available from the British Library

Library of Congress Cataloging-in-Publication data
NAMES: Butler, Sara M. (Sara Margaret), author.
TITLE: Pain, penance, and protest : peine forte et dure in medieval England / Sara M. Butler, The Ohio State University.
DESCRIPTION: Cambridge, United Kingdom ; New York, NY : Cambridge University Press, 2022. | Series: Studies in legal history | Includes bibliographical references and index.
IDENTIFIERS: LCCN 2021037180 (print) | LCCN 2021037181 (ebook) | ISBN 9781316512388 (hardback) | ISBN 9781009067065 (ebook other)
SUBJECTS: LCSH: Peine forte et dure – England – History. | Pleas (Criminal procedure) – England – History.
CLASSIFICATION: LCC KD8225.P45 B88 2022 (print) | LCC KD8225.P45 (ebook) | DDC 345.42/077–dc23
LC record available at https://lccn.loc.gov/2021037180
LC ebook record available at https://lccn.loc.gov/2021037181

ISBN   978-1-316-51238-8   Hardback
ISBN   978-1-009-06572-6   Paperback

Cambridge University Press & Assessment has no responsibility for the persistence or accuracy of URLs for external or third-party internet websites referred to in this publication and does not guarantee that any content on such websites is, or will remain, accurate or appropriate.

Contents

Tables

Acknowledgments

While writing a book may sometimes *feel* like the most solitary task in the world, it never actually is. In the seven years I have spent writing this book, I have accrued many debts. The funding for this project originated in the Gregory F. Curtin, S. J., Distinguished Professorship held at Loyola University New Orleans, as well as the King George III Professorship in British History at The Ohio State University. Many thanks to the staff at The National Archives for their assistance with manuscripts and to the wonderfully hard-working inter-library loan staff members at both Monroe Library (Loyola University New Orleans) and Thompson Library (The Ohio State University). For advice, insight, translation assistance, reading tips, and emotional support, many thanks to: Deanne Baker, Brian Butler, Lin Butler, Siobhain Bly Calkin, Deb Grayson, Huguette LaBine, Kenneth LaBine, Heather Mack, Jennifer Jahner, Leslie Joseph, Leslie Lockett, Geoffrey Parker, Ted Powell, John Sebastian, Karl Shoemaker, and Tina Sessa. Many thanks to Jordan Schoonover for her hard work indexing this book. Both Krista Kesselring and Cynthia Neville read early drafts of the book manuscript and gave invaluable advice; to both of you I express my gratitude for your support, encouraging critiques, keen eyes, and enduring friendship. One of the series' editors, Michael Lobban, spent hours reading multiple versions of this manuscript and offered superlative guidance to clarify and bolster the book's larger argument. The two anonymous reviewers for the press must also be thanked: their insightful reviews proved to be highly useful and I believe have made this a better manuscript. Finally, many thanks to my children: Cade, Genevieve, and Miranda. During the coronavirus pandemic we have spent much more time together than I suspect any teenager wants to spend with their mother, and we did it without driving each other mad. Finally, many thanks to my husband, Mark LaBine, for his patience, love of family, and weird sense of humor – this book could not have been written without you.

I dedicate this book to my mother, Carol Marie Butler (née Allen), who left a big hole in all of our lives when she passed away September 8, 2014 after a two-year battle with cancer. I was ten years old when my mother started passing along historical fiction for me to read. Little did she realize at the time she was feeding the passions of a budding historian. Her unending love and support gave me the confidence to pursue my dreams, the humor to laugh at my mistakes and not take myself too seriously, as well as the grounding to help me realize the importance of a balanced life and having a family to cherish. Mom, you are sorely missed.

Table of Statutes

Abbreviations

AJLH	*American Journal of Legal History*
Blackstone	Blackstone, William. *Commentaries on the Laws of England*, 4 vols. (1723–1780). In "The Avalon Project: Documents in Law, History and Diplomacy." New Haven. Online.
Bracton	Bracton, Henry of. *De Legibus Et Consuetudinibus Angliæ*, in *Bracton Online*. Cambridge, MA. Online.
C&C	*Continuity and Change*
CCR	*Calendar of Close Rolls, 1273–1485*. 45 vols. London 1911–63.
CFR	*Calendar of Fine Rolls, 1272–1509*. 22 vols. London, 1911–62.
CIPM	*Calendar of Inquisitions Post Mortem*. 26 vols. London, 1898–2009.
CPR	*Calendar of Patent Rolls, 1216–1509*. 55 vols. London, 1891–1916.
EETS	*Early English Text Society*
EHR	*English Historical Review*
JBS	*Journal of British Studies*
JUST 1	Justices in Eyre, of Assize, of Oyer and Terminer, and of the Peace
JUST 2	Coroners' Rolls and Files, with Cognate Documents
JUST 3	Justices of Jail Delivery: Jail Delivery Rolls and Files
L&HR	*Law and History Review*
LHP	Leslie J. Downer, ed., *Leges Henrici Primi*. Oxford, 1972.

ODNB	*Oxford Dictionary of National Biography*. Online.
OED	*Oxford English Dictionary*. Oxford, 2020. Online.
P&M	Frederick Pollock and Frederic Maitland, *The History of English Law before the Time of Edward I*, 2 vols. Cambridge, 1895.
P&P	*Past and Present*
PIMS	Pontifical Institute of Mediaeval Studies
RS	Rolls Series, also: *Rerum Britannicarum medii aevi scriptores*. 253 vols. (1858–1911).
SC	Special Collections, Ancient Correspondence of the Chancery and Exchequer
Seipp	Seipp, David J. "Seipp's Abridgement." Boston. Online.
SR	Alexander Luders, et al., eds. *Statutes of the Realm*. 11 vols. London, 1810–28.
SS	Selden Society
TNA	The National Archives, Kew (Surrey)
TRHS	*Transactions of the Royal Historical Society*
YB	Year Book
YLS	*Yearbook of Langland Studies*

Introduction

[S]he turned all things to her good, and sucked honey out of the cruelty of her enemies. They persecuted, and she thereby learned patience; they shut her up into close prison, and she learned thereby to forget and despise the world; they separated her from house, children, and husband, and she thereby became familiar with God; they sought to terrify her, and she thereby increased in most glorious constancy and fortitude, insomuch that her greatest joy was to be assaulted by them.

John Mush, "A True Report of the Life and Martyrdom of Mrs. Clitherow."[1]

In 1586, after prolonged deliberation and with great reluctance, Justices Clench and Rhodes, sitting in judgment at the Castle of the Common Hall in York, ordered the execution of the recusant, Margaret Clitheroe (also, Clitherow). Her offense was a distinctly post-Reformation one: she was charged with harboring Catholic priests, a crime for which she was most surely guilty, having constructed a hidden room in her neighbor's home where multiple well-known Catholic dissenters had taken refuge. Harboring of this kind was also a newly legislated felony, having been enacted at parliament a year prior. The evidence poised against her was slim,

---

[1] John Mush, "A True Report of the Life and Martyrdom of Mrs. Clitherow," in John Morris, ed., *The Troubles of Our Catholic Forefathers Related by Themselves*, 3rd ser. (London: Burns and Oats, 1877), 371–2.

resting principally on the confession of a young Flemish boy schooled in her home, whom city authorities had browbeaten and manhandled until he agreed to guide them to the concealed room. The presence of chalices and vestments there hinted at the enormity of Margaret's wrongdoing. Yet, not having encountered an actual priest in residence, authorities had only the boy's testimony to substantiate that Margaret had in fact sheltered priests there in the past. If she had been tried, in all likelihood, as the justices continually assured her, she would have been acquitted. The evidence left far too much room for doubt. Even if the jury did somehow find against her, once again the queen's justices pledged her mercy.

Nonetheless, her trial never quite got off the ground. At her arraignment, when Judge Clench asked Margaret how she wished to plead, she refused to tender an answer. Common law labeled this behavior as "standing mute," although as the hagiography admiringly penned by her private confessor and spiritual guide, John Mush, makes amply clear, she was anything but silent. When asked "how will you be tried?" her response was

'Having made no offence, I need no trial.' They said: 'You have offended the statutes, and therefore you must be tried;' and often asked her how she would be tried. The martyr [Margaret] answered: 'If you say I have offended, and that I must be tried, I will be tried by none but by God and your own consciences.' The judge said, 'No, you cannot so do, for we sit here,' quoth he, 'to see justice and law, and therefore you must be tried [by the country, i.e. a jury trial].' The martyr still appealed to God, and their consciences.[2]

Fervent attempts to extract some sort of plea continued all that day and the next. The justices extended every sensible opportunity to Margaret to cease her perilous resistance and accept a jury trial, at which they were certain she would be acquitted. They tried to reason with her by outlining in gory detail the penalty for her failure to cooperate. Those who refused to plead were habitually sentenced to peine forte et dure ("strong and hard punishment"). As one of the judges explained it,

If you do not put yourself to the country, this must be your judgment: You must return from whence you came, and there in the lowest part of the prison, be stripped naked, laid down, your back upon the ground, and as much weight

---

[2] Mush, "A True Report," 413.

laid upon you as you are able to bear, and so to continue three days without meat or drink, except a little barley bread and puddle water, and the third day to be pressed to death, your hands and feed tied to posts, and a sharp stone under your back.[3]

Still, she refused to concede defeat. Her bold impertinence in the face of death strikes just the right note for a saint's life. According to Mush, she declared, somewhat deliriously, "God be thanked all that He shall send me shall be welcome; I am not worthy of so good a death as this is."[4]

Weary and exasperated, the king's justices sent for the sheriff to escort her back to prison. Over the course of the following week, the city's authorities, loath to assist in Margaret's rise to martyrdom for the Catholic faith simply by following the dictates of the law, made several last-ditch attempts to coax her into a plea. Meeting failure at every turn, finally authorities had no choice but to make an example of her. Margaret, wife of a well-respected butcher, daughter of a former sheriff of York, stepdaughter of a man who ultimately rose to prominence as the city's mayor, mother of three who professed that she was likely pregnant again, was sentenced to death by the peine. Mush's description of her execution on Good Friday of that year underscores the city's efforts to make a public example of her. Rather than a solitary death in the deepest, darkest part of the prison, as described above by Judge Clench, she was brought out to the toll bridge on the River Ouse, not seven yards from where she had been imprisoned in the Tollbooth. Before a crowd of onlookers, in what Peter Lake and Michael Questier in their recent biography of Margaret Clitheroe have described as an "obscene, virtually pornographic, shaming ritual," she was stripped naked, stretched by the limbs with inkle strings "so that her body and her arms made a perfect cross." Under her back, "a sharp stone as much as a man's fist" was placed, while a door balanced on her chest.[5] Her spine instantly snapped when the four beggars assigned to the task began piling irons and stones on the door, "seven or eight hundred-weight ... breaking her ribs" and

---

[3] Mush, "A True Report," 417.   [4] Mush, "A True Report," 417.
[5] Peter Lake and Michael Questier, *The Trials of Margaret Clitherow: Persecution, Martyrdom and the Politics of Sanctity in Elizabethan England* (London: Continuum, 2011), 4; Mush, "A True Report," 432.

causing them to "burst forth of the skin."[6] The whole grisly ordeal took less than fifteen minutes. The inhumanity of her death and her venerable resistance to what her Catholic supporters saw as an unjust authority led to instant martyrdom and eventual canonization.

Any internet search for the phrase peine forte et dure will lead you straight to the story of Margaret Clitheroe. For many, her gruesome death is the archetype of the practice. However, as this book will argue, Margaret's experience of the peine very much represents the exception, not the rule. In Margaret's case, the peine functioned as a form of capital punishment, reprimanding her for rejecting the queen's law by witholding consent to be tried; although, as Mush reports, the sheriff of York, who was present at the end, tried in vain to persuade her that it was in fact her treasonous activities that prompted the execution.[7] Despite the celebrity of this example, Margaret's death was not a typical example of peine forte et dure in the medieval context, or afterwards, for that matter. Since its emergence in the early thirteenth century, the peine, or some variant of it, existed chiefly as an inducement to compel reluctant defendants to submit to jury trial. Time in prison under harsh conditions was hoped to incite a speedy change of heart, propelling the defendant back into the courtroom ready to plead. The coercive nature of the practice intimates that its usual application was much less rigorous in format than what we saw above with Margaret Clitheroe. Further, medieval defendants subjected to peine forte et dure sometimes languished for days and weeks at a time; thus, the form and nature of the punishments endured by Margaret could not have been conventional.

Given the horror and revulsion that Margaret's execution inspired in the English public, it should come as no surprise that peine forte et dure was never a popular option for defendants. Those who stood mute were in a distinct minority. For the medieval era, James Masschaele describes it best when he observes that silent defendants "were not common, but neither were they entirely rare."[8] For the fourteenth century, Barbara Hanawalt offers us a more precise assessment. In her *Crime and Conflict in England Communities,*

---

[6] Mush, "A True Report," 432.   [7] Mush, "A True Report," 431.

[8] James Masschaele, *Jury, State, and Society in Medieval England* (New York: Palgrave Macmillan, 2008), 82.

1300–1348, she includes an extensive statistical breakdown of indictments drawn from the jail delivery and coroners' rolls for eight counties.[9] In her analysis, she discovered that 0.8 percent of accused felons stood mute, leading her to describe it as a "very uncommon" practice.[10] Yet, it persisted as the legal punishment for those who stood mute on a felony indictment until the prison-reform movement of the eighteenth century took hold in Britain, leading to an urgently required overhaul of England's prisons and punishment procedures. The Felony and Piracy Act of 1772 declared that, in the future, refusal to plead would be treated as a guilty verdict: silence, then, left a defendant undefended and bound for the gallows.[11] After 500 years of coercion, peine forte et dure as a practice became obsolete overnight, jubilantly discarded by a humanitarian movement that considered physical coercion barbaric. Of course, the 1772 Act was not the end of the story. The Act of 1827 overturned the 1772 decision. The success of a burgeoning psychiatric movement in Britain brought new thinking to the subject of criminal behavior. The Act concluded that the courts would henceforth consider a failure to plead instead as a plea of not guilty, thus necessitating holding a trial with evidence and a jury verdict before deciding the defendant's guilt. This reversal is how we get to where we are today.

Despite the rarity of the practice and its long history, peine forte et dure has cast a dark shadow on medieval history. As recently as 2011, Lake and Questier referred to the peine as a "sickeningly barbaric medieval punishment."[12] Their statement is not a novel interpretation, nor is it inspired purely by the histrionic tone of Mush's overblown *vita*. For centuries, legal scholars and historians alike have roundly described peine forte et dure as a lingering manifestation of medieval barbarity. William Blackstone (d.1780) infamously dubbed it a "monument of the savage rapacity" of feudalism.[13] Frederick Pollock and Frederic Maitland, England's

---

[9] Essex, Herefordshire, Huntingdonshire, Norfolk, Northamptonshire, Somerset, Surrey, and Yorkshire.

[10] Barbara Hanawalt, *Crime and Conflict in English Communities, 1300–1348* (Cambridge, MA: Harvard University Press, 1979), 42.

[11] 12 Geo. III, c. 20 (1772), as cited in Andrea McKenzie, "'This Death Some Strong and Stout Hearted Man Doth Choose': The Practice of *Peine Forte et Dure* in Seventeenth- and Eighteenth-Century England," *L&HR* 23.2 (2005): 282.

[12] Lake and Questier, *Trials of Margaret Clitherow*, 4.   [13] *Blackstone*, vol. IV, ch. 25.

legal history giants, were somewhat more restrained in their derision, depicting it as "barbarous enough and clumsy enough."[14] Luke Pike decried the peine as both a "perpetuation of barbarism" and a "hideous cruelty."[15] Vic Gatrell called it "a relic of torture."[16] Historians' condemnations decrying peine forte et dure as a vestige of medieval barbarity are intended as a criticism not only of the practice, but also of the era. In this discourse, barbarity and civilization are binaries, sitting at opposite ends of a spectrum, intrinsically tied to the premodern–modern divide in a history that is linear and progressive. As Stuart Caroll opines, medieval man has become "the barbarian 'other' to our civilized 'self.'"[17] This critique is especially damning, given that what Margaret endured was not, in fact, typical of medieval practices. One of the goals of this book is to suggest that this discourse of medieval barbarity must be eradicated in order to better understand the "medievalness" of the peine.

Here, it is important to note that although peine forte et dure looks as if it was a method of torture, and is sometimes referred to as such by historians, technically it was not. Judicial torture in the context of medieval Europe was a fact-finding tool, devoted expressly to wringing a confession from an averse defendant. This was not the purpose of peine forte et dure, in which coercion was intended to extract consent to a trial, not a confession. The method of coercion differed also dramatically. Judicial torture relied on the application of short bursts of severe pain through stretching or searing the body, serious enough in nature that custom regulated the duration of its use to the length of time it takes to say a prayer, and required the presence of a physician in case things did not go as planned. The brutality was intended to produce immediate results. Peine forte et dure, however, was entirely different in nature and did not require any extraneous safety measures. Despite what we saw above with Margaret Clitheroe, more generally, peine forte et dure was a slow process, involving mostly deprivation and discomfort. It usually took days or weeks

---

[14] P&M, vol. II, 660.

[15] Luke Pike, *A History of Crime in England: Illustrating the Changes of the Laws in the Progress of Civilisation*, 2 vols. (London: Smith, Elder, and Co., 1876), vol. I, 211.

[16] Vic Gatrell, *The Hanging Tree: Execution and the English People* (Oxford University Press, 1994), 15.

[17] Stuart Carroll, "Thinking with Violence," *History and Theory* 55 (2017): 25.

before a defendant agreed to jury trial. More important still, the peine existed outside the trial altogether. As we discovered with Saint Margaret, a jury of her peers had not found her guilty of a felony. Instead, because she declined jury trial, the court deemed Margaret to have refused the common law. In consequence, her case never proceeded to trial; technically, she died unconvicted.

Law and Rationality

"Medieval barbarity" points to a primitiveness that has been especially problematic for legal historians, whose focus rests on the timing of the practice's appearance. Peine forte et dure emerged as a practice alongside the trial jury, the very symbol of modernity. Thus, with Frederic Maitland at the helm the more pressing concern has been to comprehend how peine forte et dure fits into the larger historical narrative which presents the development of the common law as a progression from unreason to reason, impelled by the rediscovery of Justinian's *Corpus Juris Civilis* in the eleventh century. While the English spurned the wholesale adoption of Roman law, the absorption of Romanism into the English legal system, particularly under the aegis of the great jurist Henry Bracton, led to the emergence of English "Rationalism," the ingenuity of this new phase signaled by Maitland's bold capitalization of the term.[18] Shedding the "archaisms" of the early medieval period – typically represented by the *wergeld* (which Maitland described as a remnant of "Welsh barbarism"), the ordeal, judicial combat, and compurgation – by 1272 English law could be described as "modern" and "enlightened," a "law for all men."[19]

The effective abolition of the ordeal by the Fourth Lateran Council (1215) and the subsequent emergence of jury trial stand as the apex of this transition from irrational to rational. Often referred to as the "palladium of justice," or the "palladium of our liberties," the trial jury is emblematic of the rationality and modernity of thirteenth-century common law. The English people no longer turned to God for a verdict, as they had done with the ordeal. Instead, in jury trial,

---

[18] Frederic Maitland, ed., *Bracton's Note Book: A Collection of Cases Decided in the King's Courts during the Reign of Henry the Third* (London: C. J. Clay and Sons, 1887), 9.

[19] P&M, vol. 1, 224.

the torch of justice passed into the hands of men, who reviewed the evidence and drew a reasonable conclusion. For legal historians of yore, then, the emergence of the jury trial heralded the death of the age of superstition. Common law arose from the ashes of the early Middle Ages, unconnected entirely with the law codes of the Anglo-Saxon kings that bear a striking resemblance to penitentials. In this version of history, the legal revolution of the long twelfth century (1085–1215), so heavily mired in the study and adaptation of Roman law, persuaded the English to strip God from their laws, amending them in accordance with the rationality of Roman precedent, and wisely to relegate churchmen to courts of their own. God's mystery overthrown (or perhaps, outgrown?), common law took on a new sense of authority and certainty. It is no surprise, then, that for this period historians begin to speak of the advent of the "science of law."[20]

Charles Radding's comments on Lombard law underscore just how deeply historians have associated Christianity with superstition and irrationality. He writes that Lombard law stands out from other barbarian law codes primarily because of its secular nature. The "virtual absence from the surviving *placita* of cases decided by judgments of God in any of its forms – compurgation, duel, or ordeal – has led some scholars to refer to the 'rationality' of Lombard procedures."[21] In this narrative, Christianity is not simply tied to irrationality; it is the *cause* of irrationality. One senses this also in Maitland's eagerness to weed out religion from law, seeing them as distinct realms of influence. One is highly irrational, relying on supernatural intervention as evidence; the other is comfortably, familiarly rational, manned by England's trustworthy elites. His perspective also reflects post-Enlightenment sensibilities that only when church and state are separate can modernity prevail. Recently, Christina Caldwell Ames has questioned whether we have achieved any progress in this respect, observing just how much trouble historians have with the idea that the medieval world was "governed

---

[20] Stephan Kuttner, "The Revival of Jurisprudence," in Robert Benson, Giles Constable, and Carol Lanham, eds., *Renaissance and Renewal in the Twelfth Century* (University of Toronto Press, 1982), 299.

[21] Charles Radding, *The Origins of Medieval Jurisprudence: Pavia and Bologna 850–1150* (New Haven: Yale University Press, 1988).

by a god who watches, torments, burns, and persecutes."[22] To Maitland, and to many other legal historians, severing the link between law and religion is a necessary precursor to understanding how the medieval world might have laid a solid foundation for modern legal practice. As a sign of this modernity, the character of the trial jury is inviolable; even though, as Rebecca Colman has complained cynically, "[t]he modern verdict of the jury in perplexing cases often has all of the inscrutability of a judgment of God," a sentiment with which I suspect most Anglo-Americans today would agree.[23]

For the purposes of this study, this surprisingly enduring narrative prompts an imperative question: how is it possible that the thirteenth century gave birth to the jury trial, a purported harbinger of modernity and enlightenment, at the same time as peine forte et dure, a practice regularly described as barbaric? While one speaks to progress, the other, by all appearances, is a step backwards. If this was a work of fiction, one suspects that my editor would gently remind me that the peine should be more appropriately situated in the irrational early Middle Ages. No wonder Maitland tried his best to steer clear of this question. In Pollock and Maitland's two-volume history of English law comprising 1,379 pages, only a page and a half is dedicated to peine forte et dure. The authors present it as an "expedient," borrowed from the Normans when justices could think of no better way to coerce defendants into submitting to jury trial.[24] Following Maitland's lead, most legal scholars have chosen simply to ignore peine forte et dure altogether; this is why so little has been written on the subject for the medieval period, with historians preferring to turn to Margaret Clitheroe or Blackstone for information about the medieval practice. Unfortunately, neglect is not going to get us any closer to answering this difficult question.

One of the overarching goals of this book is to establish that peine forte et dure is, in fact, not aberrant; it is not a hideous blight on England's march towards legal progress; it is not a resort to a primitive mentality when rationality fails. Rather, it was every bit

---

[22] Christine Caldwell Ames, "Does Inquisition belong to Religious History?," *AHR* 110.1 (2005): 37.
[23] Rebecca Colman, "Reason and Unreason in Early Medieval Law," *Journal of Interdisciplinary History* 4.4 (1974): 591.
[24] P&M, vol. II, 651.

as much a product of the evolution in common-law ideology as was the jury trial. In order to make sense of this development, peine forte et dure must be considered from the vantage point of the world that produced it. This book sides with Mirjan Damaška when he writes, "To be rational is to try to bring about the best result possible under the circumstances."[25] For that reason, this book first examines it with respect to contemporary legal process and jurisprudence. English justices imposed peine forte et dure upon individuals who refused to plead to a felony indictment. The severity of the court's reaction implies a need for a clearer understanding of conceptions of standing mute from both sides of the bar. What prompted an accused felon to choose silence? Was this a curial strategy exerted as a last-ditch effort to save one's neck from the gallows? Or, did the defendant exploit silence as a tool of resistance against what was perceived to be an unjust judicial process? What were the implications for English justices? Why did it matter so deeply whether the defendant pled to the accusations? Why didn't they simply proceed to trial without a plea? All of these questions are critical to our understanding of the function of peine forte et dure in the legal context. The premise of this book is that we cannot study the consequence without also studying the cause; that is, peine forte et dure cannot be properly understood until we peel back the various layers of meaning to the act of silence in the context of the medieval courtroom. It was not a one-way process in which the Crown held all the power. It is critical to recognize also the agency of the victims of peine forte et dure, and appreciate that silence might be a powerful weapon in which they attempted to bend the courts to their will.

Second, peine forte et dure must be interrogated in light of contemporary religious practices. The thirteenth century was not a watershed moment in the separation of church and state, as the traditional legal historiography implies. In fact, even with the influence and incorporation of Roman law in various manifestations across Europe, the era represents a deeper Christianizing of an already-entrenched religious judicial system. English justices wore multiple hats; or, at the very least, in the thirteenth century many of them also

---

[25] Mirjan Damaška, "Rational and Irrational Proof Revisited," *Cardozo Journal of International and Comparative Law* 5.25 (1997): 32.

wore a bishop's miter, and as Philippa Byrne summarizes eloquently, "There is no reason to assume that such individuals neglected their moral responsibilities as churchmen, or deliberately divorced their ecclesiastical and temporal identities."[26] Justices were not the only Christianizing element. English "jurors were [also] trained extracurially, in pew and confession."[27] Presumably, so, too, were defendants. A more nuanced appreciation of peine forte et dure, then, must see the act through the eyes of not only common lawyers, but also canonists and theologians. In this respect, it is helpful to remember that medieval salvation was hard-won, typically through acts of self-violence. Fasting, flagellation, hairshirts are the tools of the ascetic. They are also forms of violence that were prized for their efficacy rather than condemned for their barbarism. How might the Christian approach to cleansing violence have influenced popular perceptions of peine forte et dure, which employed many of the same tools?

Finally, this book chips away at the boundaries of English law to think about peine forte et dure in a broader geographical context. English legal history stands deeply mired in the myth of English exceptionalism. Yet, England's justices in the formative period of the thirteenth century were typically trained in canon law in Continental universities, and while the rediscovery of Roman law did not have the same kind of earth-shattering impact on English law as it had in many other places in Europe, it still seeped furtively into the holes and corners of common law.

Numbers and Sources

At the heart of this study lies a corpus of 481 cases drawn mostly from jail delivery rolls (JUST 3), with some supplementation also from assize rolls (JUST 1), coroners' rolls (JUST 2), as well as instances drawn from the year books. The fourteenth century is the focus for the statistical analysis in this study chiefly because of two landmark cases. The 1302 deaths of John of Darley and Sir Ralph de Bloyou (or, Bloyho), amply

---

[26] Philippa Byrne, *Justice and Mercy: Moral Theology and the Exercise of Law in Twelfth-Century England* (Manchester University Press, 2019), 7.
[27] Elizabeth Papp Kamali, *Felony and the Guilty Mind in Medieval England* (Cambridge University Press, 2019), 305.

described in the year books, make it clear that by this point pressing had emerged as part of the body of torments that came to define this practice.[28] On the other end of the spectrum, the celebrated 1406 case of two suspected robbers includes a dialogue in which justices declare that peine forte et dure had developed into a death sentence. Since the time of Blackstone, this case has been held up as a turning point in the history of peine forte et dure in which the practice transitioned from coercive measure to capital punishment. These two cases then are the bookends that frame the fourteenth century as the heyday of peine forte et dure as a coercive device.

Nonetheless, this study aspires to move beyond the parameters of just one century. For the thirteenth century, when this practice emerged, I have relied on the work of Henry Summerson, whose study on the subject of peine forte et dure has been foundational for this project. The thirty-five cases under examination from the thirteenth century, included in the 481 total cases, were uncovered through references in the footnotes of Summerson's chapter in *Law, Litigants and the Legal Profession*.[29] For the fifteenth century, reliance shifts instead to political chronicles and the year books, which record celebrated or instructive examples of actual cases and the courtroom discussions that accompanied them. The purpose of the year books was didactic. English common law was not learned through university training, but rather through spectatorship at the Inns of Court, and by studying the year books. As Maitland has suggested the dramatic nature of the year-book accounts can be quite gripping: "What they desired was the debate with the life-blood in it: the twists and turns of advocacy, the quip courteous and the countercheck quarrelsome. They wanted to remember what really fell from Bereford, C.J.: his proverbs, his sarcasms, how he emphasised a rule of law by *Noun Dieu!* Or *Par Seint Pierre!* They wanted to remember how a clever move of Sergeant Herle drove Sergeant Toudeby into an awkward corner, or how Sergeant Passeley invented a new variation on an old defence."[30]

---

[28] Alfred Horwood, ed., *Year Books of the Reign of Edward the First: Years xxx and xxxi (1302–1303)* (RS, no. 31, pt. A, vol. III, 1863), 510–11 (Seipp 1302.200rs).

[29] Henry Summerson, "The Early Development of the Peine Forte et Dure," in Eric Ives and Anthony Manchester, eds., *Law, Litigants and the Legal Profession* (London: RHS, 1983), 116–25.

[30] Frederic Maitland, ed., *Year Books of Edward II, vol. I: 1 & 2 Edward II (A.D. 1307–1309)* (SS, vol. XVII, 1903), xv.

The remarkably detailed and lively, in-depth conversations provide abundant insight into the multiple ways jurists might interpret and apply the law. The year-book format is also indispensable for tracing changes over time in the legal atmosphere as it relates to peine forte et dure and its implementation.

When it comes to the fourteenth-century material, in order to track the greatest number of relevant cases, this study surveyed every jail delivery roll for the fourteenth century housed at the National Archives. However, notation was made only in relation to cases of those who stood mute and/or peine forte et dure, not with respect to *all* felonies – such an endeavor might have taken another decade or two to complete. The benefit of this approach is that it provided me with a sufficiently large sample size to be able to trace patterns concerning peine forte et dure and draw some conclusions. The downside is that this study cannot offer a precise gauge of the proportion of felonies which this number represents. For this, I rely on the snapshot offered by Barbara Hanawalt's rigorous study for the first half of the fourteenth century, mentioned above, in which she notes that 0.8 percent of accused felons stood mute in that era.[31]

Admittedly, 481 cases is a small number, underscoring just how rarely individuals chose to stand mute when faced with a felony indictment. As this study demonstrates, the meaning of the act outweighed the numbers. Standing mute was an event that earned a person some notoriety and inspired others to emulate; when one defendant stood mute, others at the same jail delivery often chose to follow suit. The trial records reveal resistance to the common law by clusters of individuals at the same jail delivery. For example, on the Monday after Saint Gregory in the year 1316, Christina, wife of John Attehil of Mendham appeared before justices at the castle of Norwich accused jointly with her daughter Maud of feloniously slaying Olivia, widow of Henry Attehil (relationship unspecified). Maud failed to bring her paperwork to her trial; specifically she "forgot" a writ *de bono et malo*, authorizing justices to try her on felony charges. Hence, justices had no choice but to return her to prison until the next delivery. Her daughter Christina, however, refused to plead and so justices sentenced her to "prisone dure."[32] The same day – in fact, inscribed

---

[31] Hanawalt, *Crime and Conflict*, 42.   [32] TNA JUST 3/48, m. 27 (1316).

on the same membrane of the jail delivery roll – Beatrice le Say of Brandon also stood mute; so, too, did Alice, wife of Nicholas Tascy.[33] Presumably both were in court for Christina's arraignment and witnessed her silent refusal. As all three were women, there is also good grounds for assuming that they were housed together in prison and might have concocted the plan prior to their appearance in court. What is striking is that several other defendants present at the same delivery that day also refused to plead: Thomas, son of Geoffrey, Roger, son of Richard Carkeny, and John le Spenser of Besthorpe.[34]

Sometimes whole groups of individuals indicted for the same felony chose to stand mute. On December 6, 1306, at Stafford's jail delivery, William of Podmore was indicted for being an accomplice in the homicide of John de la Dolye, murdered by Robert Swyft and others. In addition, Thomas, son of Utte, William Clyde, William Stok, junior, William Stok, senior, John of Fenny Shaw, and Alexander of Bignall End (*de Bygenowe*) were also indicted for receiving the perpetrators. Each and every one of them stood mute and were returned to prison to undergo peine forte et dure, their chattels confiscated.[35] Given the small number of those who chose to stand mute, collective solidarity of this nature surely is meaningful. In the chapters that follow, I will attempt to unravel the various meanings of standing mute as well as the social and political experiences that incited defendants to make this choice. In the literature of the era, those who stood mute were represented as heroic martyrs: one cannot help but wonder if these men and women also became local legends for their willingness to buck the system and stand up to the king and his justices.

Marginal notations in the legal record afford yet another means to gauge the popularity of a refusal to plead, this time from the perspective of court officials. Scribes regularly used the margins of trial records to sum up a case, noting the pertinent data along the left-hand side of the membrane so that anyone looking back at the rolls could swiftly skim through the dense listing of cases to find what was needed. Soon after the abolition of the ordeals in 1215, scribes hastily established a marginal notation to identify those instances when

---

[33] TNA JUST 3/48, m. 31 (1316).   [34] TNA JUST 3/48, m. 27 (1316).
[35] See "Gaol Delivery for Staffordshire: 34 Edward I," in George Wrottesley, ed., *Staffordshire Historical Collections* (London: William Salt Archaeological Society, 1886), vol. VII, pt. 1, 154–72.

a defendant chose to submit to trial jury: "po[suit] se" (that is, "he put himself" upon the country). The very fact that "po' se" became a marginal notation implies that justices and scribes were aware of and troubled by those who *did not* submit to jury trial; otherwise, there would have been no need to create this new abbreviation. Its very existence emphasizes the wariness with which justices approached those who refused jury trial. Despite being in a distinct minority, their refusal to comply with the normal procedure of arraignment made them notorious, and a matter of great concern for royal justices.

Standing mute and peine forte et dure both assume a much broader cultural significance than the numbers might suggest. This study seeks to put the law in context of the era that produced it. In order to understand the practice within a legal framework, this study draws on legislation and statute law from England for the entirety of the Middle Ages, as well as legal treatises and handbooks, such as *Leges Henrici Primi* (*c.*1108–9), *Glanvill* (*c.*1187–9), *Placita Corone* (*c.*1274), *Bracton* (*c.* 1220s–60s), *Mirror of Justices* (*c.*1285–90),[36] *Britton* (*c.*12912), and *Fleta* (*c.*1290–1300). Legal treatises not only provide insight into contemporary practices, but as justices of jail delivery came to rely more heavily on them for reference in difficult cases, the treatises played a role in shaping the practice of the law. This fact is critical when studying a practice like peine forte et dure. Because defendants seldom opted to stand mute, one expects that justices faced with an uncooperative defendant turned to the legal literature for guidance. This study examines also Continental law where appropriate (especially Norman law and custom) and canon law, on the grounds that both Continental and canon law had a much greater influence on the construction of English secular legal practices than is sometimes recognized. As Peter Clarke has recently noted, medieval England "formed part of this European culture of the *ius commune*,"

---

[36] Maitland's dismissiveness of the *Mirror* relegated it to the backwaters of legal history for much of the twentieth century. Seipp's 1999 study, however, demonstrates that it was indeed the product of a legal mind, and that earlier authorities utilized the *Mirror* in the justification of legal arguments. David Seipp, "The *Mirror of Justices*," in Jonathan Bush and Alain Wijffels, eds., *Learning the Law: Teaching and the Transmission of the Law in England, 1150–1900* (London: Hambledon, 1999), 85–112.

the name typically awarded collectively to canon and civil law.[37] Thus, the English were far more in touch with Continental practices than is often credited. In doing so, this study works to integrate English law more closely with law as it was practiced by the church and on the Continent. In particular, the literature helps us to discover that peine forte et dure was not an exclusively English practice, but rather drew from ecclesiastical penal practices employed throughout Europe.

Undergirding this study is the notion that English law worked in concert with Christian morality; accordingly, this monograph also branches out to examine theological treatises, confessors' manuals, sermons, *exempla* (that is, sermon stories), and saints' lives. Despite the existence of distinct courts, church and state were not wholly separate in medieval England because the Christian faith permeated the processes and verdicts of both courts. Until the fourteenth century, they also sometimes shared personnel – bishops, whose dedication to God and natural law did not end the moment they removed the miters from their heads. The integrity of law and religion is emphasized in the era's literary texts. As John Alford writes, "[s]o intertwined historically are the vocabularies of law and theology that medieval writers found it impossible to explain certain doctrines of Christianity without recourse to legal terminology."[38] Recognizing the fundamental role of religion in law, this book hopes to draw out the penitential practice that lays at the base of common law.

Not only do we see a cross-over in personnel between the church and the Crown, many medieval writers supported their literary aspirations with day jobs as legal administrators and civil servants. Among Henry III's itinerant justices, for example, were "the satirist Walter Map and the chronicler Roger Hoveden; his treasurer Richard FitzNeal wrote the important *Dialogue Concerning the Exchequer* [*c*.1180]; and his justiciar Ranulf Glanvill is credited with having written the first classical textbook of English law."[39] This trend continued also into the fourteenth century. Geoffrey Chaucer studied

---

[37] Peter Clarke, "Canon and Civil Law," in Candace Barrington and Sebastian Sobecki, eds., *The Cambridge Companion to Medieval English Law and Literature* (Cambridge University Press, 2019), 31.

[38] John Alford, *Piers Plowman: A Glossary of Legal Diction* (Cambridge: D. S. Brewer, 1988), xiv.

[39] John Alford, "Literature and Law in Medieval England," *PMLA* 92.5 (1977): 941.

law at the Inner Temple and supported himself as a royal courtier and
civil servant, working as comptroller of the customs for the port of
London and occasionally as a justice of the peace. Thomas Usk was
a collector of customs for a while, then an undersheriff of London;
William Langland made a living copying legal documents; Thomas
Hoccleve was a clerk in the office of the Privy Seal.[40] John Gower
stands out as an exception here. Recent scholarship concludes that he
most likely gained his expertise in the law as a litigant rather than as
a lawyer. Yet, he, too, wrote extensively about the law. His *Mirour de
l'Omme* (before 1380) fulminates about the abject corruption of
lawyers and the judiciary, sheriffs, bailiffs, and even jurors. The dual
lives of England's civil servants extended into the early modern era
such that by the mid 1500s, the Inns of Court became "the chief center
of literary activity in England."[41] It is no wonder that legal vocabulary
and themes form the backbone of much of medieval literature. Thus,
for the social and political meaning of standing mute and peine forte et
dure, this study turns to the literary sources of the era, among others,
the annual mystery cycles, *The Pistil of Swete Susan*, *Chasteau
d'Amour*, *The Seven Sages of Rome*, and *Bevis of Hampton*. Paul
Strohm puts forward some useful advice in ferreting out the
historical meaning of fictional texts. He writes that texts are "all
finally composed within history – if not within a sense of what did
happen, at least within a sense of what might have happened, or what
could be imagined, of what commonly held interpretive structures
permitted a late fourteenth-century audience to believe."[42] As such,
fiction offers "crucial testimony … on contemporary perception,
ideology, belief, and – above all – on the imaginative structures
within which fourteenth-century participants acted and assumed that
their actions would be understood."[43] These texts allow us to share
a commoner's perceptions of standing mute and peine forte et dure; at
the same time, the popularity of these texts imbued the act of standing
mute with new meaning. Literary descriptions of peine forte et dure
also sometimes functioned as a means to challenge the Crown's
treatment of individuals whom the English people regarded as heroic.

---

[40] Alford, "Literature and Law," 941.   [41] Alford, "Literature and Law," 941.
[42] Paul Strohm, *Hochon's Arrow: The Social Imagination of Fourteenth-Century Texts*
(Princeton University Press, 1992), 3.
[43] Strohm, *Hochon's Arrow*, 4.

Breakdown by Chapter

The first three chapters of the book endeavor to overturn some long-held assumptions concerning the joint practices of peine forte et dure and standing mute by surveying the medieval evidence, drawn chiefly from the jail delivery rolls. Apart from Henry Summerson's excellent and thought-provoking 1983 article on peine forte et dure in thirteenth-century England, almost nothing has been written on the subject by a medievalist. The paucity of research has led medieval historians also to rely on the early modern source material, such as Margaret Clitheroe's experience and Blackstone's *Commentaries*, for information on the subject, leading to a number of misconceptions that these three chapters address.

If Margaret Clitheroe's experience was not typical of peine forte et dure in medieval England, then what was? Chapter 1 examines precisely what peine forte et dure entailed during the Middle Ages. Paying special attention to the vocabulary related to peine forte et dure in the legal record, this chapter argues that "hard prison" (prison forte et dure) should be considered an umbrella term that includes a wide variety of practices, such as fasting, cold and nakedness, seclusion, and sometimes pressing. The make-up of the punishment depended on the nature of the crime and the defendant's conduct at court. The traditional narrative sees an evolution in the practice from prison forte et dure, described as a starvation diet and miserable prison conditions, intended as a coercive measure to encourage the defendant to plead, gradually superseded by peine forte et dure, pressing with stones and irons unto death. The medieval evidence, however, does not corroborate this vision. Even in the fifteenth century, some silent defendants fasted while others were pressed, and while it was clearly used as capital punishment in some instances, at no point in time did the practice shed its coercive nature altogether. This chapter will also tackle the practice's origins. Not only does it push back the date at which peine forte et dure was first used in England, it also challenges the belief that it came to English soil from Normandy. Rather, this chapter contends that prison forte et dure springs from the church's penitential practices, specifically in the public penance (*poenitentia publica*) assigned to murderers, political rebels, and other serious crimes. By the high Middle Ages, public penance often translated to *murus strictus*, an especially harsh form of incarceration imposed on the sinful with the aim of rehabilitating the soul. Recognizing its origins and purpose permits us to contextualize the various ways in which the officials within the criminal justice system experimented with peine forte et dure as short-term punishment to reorient spiritually approvers, idlers, heretics, and petty thieves. It also fosters an appreciation for the fact that peine forte et dure was not a uniquely English phenomenon.

Technically, peine forte et dure was the sentence imposed on suspected felons who stood mute, that is, who refused to plead. Chapter 2 speaks to the process of standing mute in the courts of medieval England. Despite the nomenclature, as we saw with Margaret Clitheroe above, refusal to plead did not necessarily involve silence. Some accused felons feigned muteness with such remarkable authenticity that sheriffs organized an inquest staffed by the defendant's fellow prisoners to testify to whether the defendant was capable of speech, or was in fact naturally mute. Others, like Margaret, refused to offer a straightforward plea; a final category comprised individuals who chose to delay the process with multiple jury challenges. All of these various approaches constituted what justices referred to as "standing mute" (*nichil dicit*). The underlying goal of this chapter is to assess the challenges an accused felon faced in negotiating the legal process sufficiently to develop a solid defense strategy. Not only were there multiple means of standing mute, but silence only sometimes functioned as a refusal to plead. Distinctions were made based on venue, process, and the nature of the charge. For example, in the church courts, silence was viewed as an admission of guilt: this was also true in the king's courts when the defendant was accused of a trespass. In treason trials under the law of arms, defendants were not even extended the opportunity to plead. In the early modern era, justices did not permit silence upon appeal or for treason. It has often been assumed that these rules also applied in the Middle Ages. The medieval evidence demonstrates that these rules developed over the course of the period. To make matters even more perplexing, they were enforced only at the discretion of the justices assigned to try the cases. Gender also mattered in the formulation of a defense strategy: women rarely opted to stand mute, but those who did were in dire straits and probably saw it as a last-ditch attempt to prolong their lives. The one redeeming feature for the defendant is that the king's justices acted as counsel for the defendant, meaning, that they were tasked with explaining the intricacies of pleading procedure to the defendant so that he or she might make an informed decision.

Consent is the issue at the heart of Chapter 3. Peine forte et dure was necessary simply because the English court system required a defendant's consent before submitting the defendant to trial by jury. Without consent, justices could not proceed to trial. No other court system in Europe, not even the church courts, sought a defendant's permission to be tried, prompting James Masschaele to ask, "[w]hy was the principle of giving consent to a jury trial so highly cherished [by the English] that even torture was worth accepting to maintain it?"[44] This chapter seeks to respond to Masschaele's question by explaining why the English cared so deeply about consent. In part, the answer lies in their heritage. Consent was a traditional part of English legal culture, signaled by a defendant's choice of proofs (compurgation, ordeals, battle). In choosing a method of proof, an accused felon recognized the court's authority in the matter, and consented to abide by its decision. With the transition from proofs to trial (by jury) that began under Henry II and coalesced with Lateran IV's abandonment of the ordeal, a defendant's rights were gradually whittled away. Despite the appeal of jury trial to plaintiffs, some defendants resented the loss of choice and surely "voiced" their grievance by refusing to plead. Defendants were not the only ones unhappy with this turn of events. Justices and jurors also resisted the responsibility foisted upon them by this "new" method of trial. Where once God had been responsible for determining who was to be punished, now that decision belonged to the jurors who rendered a verdict and the justices who ordered the sentence carried out. When they sent a convicted felon to be hanged, what impact did that decision have upon their souls? Indeed, Margaret Clitheroe asserted that one of the reasons she refused to plead was because she did not want to burden the jurors' consciences with her homicide for a crime that was not properly a crime at all. A cooperative defendant who consented to the judicial process was the key to keeping one's conscience clean. Justices and jurors could then cling to the knowledge that they were

[44] Masschaele, *Jury, State, and Society*, 82.

simply doing their jobs. Prison forte et dure was the mechanism created to extract that consent when it was not immediately forthcoming, so that justices and jurors could proceed without dread for their own spiritual health.

The justices' decision was not as callous and self-centered as it might seem. In order to understand the English vision for prison forte et dure, it must be put in context of the legal climate that produced it. This coercive measure emerged at the tail-end of the legal revolution, which rethought radically the indictment and trial process. The burgeoning discipline of natural rights theorized the ideal relationship between king and his subjects, inspiring them to profess a broad range of enhanced protections for accused felons. While Magna Carta, with its emphasis on due process, is the flagship document for the English in this respect, it was not alone. All across Europe, charters of rights appeared asserting the same sort of protections. In this climate, a defendant had a better chance at a fair trial than ever before in the medieval period. This is the era that gave birth to prison forte et dure; the practice must be seen as part and parcel of this innovative jurisprudence. As hard as it may be to imagine, justices and jurors saw rigorous fasting and even pressing as measures that protected a defendant's right to a fair trial by preventing him from being tried against his will.

Chapter 4 represents the pinnacle of the book's argument, by asking us to rethink our perceptions of the criminal justice system in medieval England. Typically, historians have seen the purpose of punishment in the medieval context as both revenge for an affront to the king's dignity, and deterrent to other would-be criminals. Chapter 4 seeks to add a third dimension to this perception. Court records regularly refer to peine forte et dure as *penitentia* (penance). Taking a cue from this terminology, Chapter 4 seeks to reinstate God to our understanding of medieval law. Traditionally, the abolition of the ordeal has been interpreted as signaling a farewell to divine intervention in the administration of criminal justice. Yet all the evidence demonstrates that God played just as important a role in jury trials as He did in the ordeal. Medieval society blurred the lines between sin and crime, penance and punishment. Recognizing this distortion is how one makes sense of peine forte et dure. Pain as an experience is key to the performance of penance. Through physical pain, the disordered soul is righted and the sinner gains entrance to heaven. Fasting, seclusion, denial of luxuries – these are all ascetic practices with a long association with Christian penance. Even pressing with weights appears as a penitential practice in numerous sermon stories from the era. Exposing the uncooperative sinner to an ascetic lifestyle, even if it was against his or her wishes, was in the best interests of the defendant's soul. As a coercive measure, it helped to begin the process of purging sin before the defendant agreed to jury trial. As such, the defendant displayed to jurors a willingness to reform one's ways and reconcile with the Christian community before consenting to trial.

Chapter 4, then, argues in favor of recognizing the multifaceted nature of medieval justice. Its procedures and punishments were shaped to achieve multiple goals: vengeance and deterrence certainly, but also penitential justice with the ultimate goal of spiritual reform. One act could simultaneously satisfy all three of these goals. This finding is borne out by the statistics: if vengeance and deterrence were the ultimate goals of medieval justice, conviction rates hovering between 17 and 30 percent would seem to imply that its administrators failed miserably. Legal historians have long recognized that an acquittal in the medieval context was not the same thing as a declaration of innocence. This fact leads us to ask, why would jurors acquit an individual they knew to be guilty? The answer to that question is because they believed the defendant was contrite, eager to reconcile to the Christian community and to God, and prepared to begin the penitential process. Since it was God's responsibility alone to determine which souls were damned, rehabilitation was the goal even for those bound for execution. The medieval church believed that very few sins were so great that they could not be worked off in purgatory. Submitting the accused to peine forte et dure gave the defendant a head-start on the pain that one will eventually endure in purgatory; it also put the defendant in the right frame of mind to meet one's maker.

The final three chapters shift our lens from the Crown to the defendant, by asking, if peine forte et dure was such a horrific form of death, why would anyone choose to stand mute? In particular, these three chapters strive to recognize the agency of suspected felons, clarifying how they hoped family and friends might appreciate their actions. Chapter 5 looks to the evidence of the jail deliveries to re-examine the leading explanations put forward by historians. From at least the time of Blackstone, historians have rationalized a defendant's silence as a means to rescue his heir's birthright from felony forfeiture: if he dies unconvicted, his lands (although not his chattels) will be safe from the grasping paws of the Crown's escheator. Thus, a man who feared conviction chose silence in order to protect his family's welfare. The second most popular theory is tied inherently to the first because it, too, presumes that the defendant is in fact guilty. Knowing what awaits a felony conviction, the silent defendant opted for a more private form of death that was less humiliating personally and for his or her family. While both theories make sense, to date neither has been tested against the medieval evidence. This chapter explores these hypotheses while also investigating additional reasons why accused felons chose to stand mute. In particular, this chapter argues that for some standing mute was a practical delaying tactic, often combined with other means of postponing trial, such as: claiming benefit of clergy, challenging jurors, applying for the king's pardon, turning approver, and even sometimes pleading the belly. Standing mute was a useful means of buying time.

Of course, standing mute meant different things to different people at different times. While some exploited it as a tactic to delay trial, others saw it as an opportunity to make a political statement. Martyrdom is one thread that runs throughout this study. Margaret Clitheroe was a martyr to the Catholic cause; those who stood mute were martyrs to their families. None of this is coincidental. Chapter 6 turns its focus to the definitive Catholic martyr, Jesus Christ, whose stoic behavior at the Passion established a way forward for those who stood mute. When Herod summoned Jesus before him, the divine prisoner also stood mute. His silence functioned as a means of protest. Herod, like Annas, Caiaphas, and Pilate before him, engaged in overreach: in trying Jesus, he was attempting to extend the boundaries of his authority. Jesus' silence was an unwillingness to recognize the jurisdiction of any earthly authority to judge a god. In essence, Jesus was withholding his consent to be tried. This interpretation was well understood by English communities, who watched the drama unfold annually on the moving stages of the mystery plays, updated to resemble medieval England and its multiple systems of law (ecclesiastical, royal, and local), even appropriating the language of the common law, thus driving home the similarities between Christ's courtroom behavior and those who stand mute in the arraignment process. Similarly, depictions of the ancient martyrs who followed in Christ's footsteps, and of Susannah, an Old Testament heroine thought to prefigure Christ, also presented silence and passivity as models for resistance. These stories formed the base of countless sermons and homilies, as well as the saints' lives that were medieval bestsellers. These narratives shaped and reinforced the notion that only a heroic martyr stood mute. The world of literature is central to this analysis because it offers valuable insight into popular perceptions of peine forte et dure. While authorities worked on the ideal of peine forte et dure as penance, analysis of works such as *Chasteau d'Amour*, the *Seven Sages of Rome*, and *Bevis of Hampton* all clarify that in the popular mindset, hard prison was a sentence inflicted by an unmerciful, and often distinctly unChristian, authority, reminding us how judge and defendant might hold entirely different perceptions of the same act. In the end, these stories place the experience of peine forte et dure in a positive light: the intense suffering of such harsh incarceration supplies the falsely accused with the ideal surroundings to perform *imitatio Christi* (imitation of Christ), thus assuring his salvation.

Resistance to royal overreach is the theme of the final chapter and the logical conclusion to which the evidence has been leading. Among legal historians, there is a long tradition of seeing silence as a rejection of jury trial. Maitland and Plucknett once explained it as a popular response to a newfangled trial method adopted from a foreign source. While historians have since dismissed the "foreignness" of jury trial, it is clear that during the reigns of the Angevin monarchs, the regularization and proliferation of juries across England meant that they came to acquire a new meaning. Today, the jury stands as an emblem of rationalism and modernity. That is not how the medieval world saw it. After Henry II, the jury represented not freedom, equality, or modernity, but royal overreach. Standing mute was one among a number of weapons belonging to the peasantry's arsenal to voice disapproval of the growing power of the king, whose authority expanded at the expense of his subjects' rights. Passive noncooperation typified peasant strategies of resistance, which included also failure to perform labor services, ignoring summons to appear for jury duty, and rent strikes, as well as listening to outlaw tales, applauding the sermons of rebellious priests, and venerating at the shrines of political martyrs. These were the more usual weapons of popular resistance. Standing mute should take its place in this category.

I

Peine Forte et Dure: The Medieval Practice

They'll make you do penance [peine forte et dure], oh yes indeed – / And maybe you'll never get yourself freed. / That's why it's better to come live in the woods / Than lie chained up in the Bishop's slammer. / Such a long hard penance does nobody good – / You can get out from under, why wait for the hammer?

The Outlaw's Song of Trailbaston (fourteenth century)[1]

When an accused felon refused to plead at arraignment, the court was stuck in limbo. Without the defendant's consent to jury trial, implied in denial of guilt and a pledge to undergo jury trial, it had no other means to try the defendant. Contumacy derailed the entire system. What were they to do? In the minds of English jurists, the only *reasonable* alternative was to return the accused to prison and submit him or her to horrific treatment in order to coerce the accused into accepting the normal means of trial. Otherwise, medieval England's prisons – and there were not many of them in the early thirteenth century – would have been teeming with presumably guilty felons who chose to stand

---

[1] Carter Revard, ed., "*The Outlaw's Song of Trailbaston*," in Thomas Ohlgren, ed., *Medieval Outlaws: Ten Tales in Modern English* (Stroud: Sutton, 1998), 104. Although the translation takes some poetic liberties, it aligns with the meaning of the original: *E soffryr messayse e trop dure penaunce, / E par cas n'averez james delyveraunce. / Pur ce valt plus ov moi a bois demorer, / Q'en prisone le evesque fyergé gyser. / Trop est la penaunce e dure a soffrer. / Quy le mieux puet eslyre, fol est qe ne velt choyser?* Isabel Aspin, ed., *Anglo-Norman Political Songs* (Anglo-Norman Text Society, vol. IX, 1953).

mute knowing that any plea might well lead to an ignoble end. The peine's origin story is critical to remember: while it is often depicted in histories as a method of torture or execution, it was in fact a coercive measure designed to tackle contumacy and compel cooperation with common-law procedure. The moment the defendant agreed to submit to jury trial, conditions in prison improved. The coercive nature of peine forte et dure is underscored in the legal treatises of the thirteenth century. The author of *Fleta* (*c.*1290–1300) writes that peine forte et dure will continue "until he has learnt his lesson and asks leave to acquit himself of the charge according to the law."[2] *Britton* (*c.*1291–2) states simply, "he shall be put to penance, until he be prepared to answer better."[3]

To comprehend why the English adopted peine forte et dure, it is useful to examine it against the backdrop of coexisting practices with similar aims. Coercive measures akin to peine forte et dure had a long history in medieval law. Excommunication is the prime example. A formidable weapon forged in the fires of contumacy, it was the normal sentence for those who failed to reform their behavior or comply with the church's mandates. While people today tend to think of excommunication as expulsion from the church, in the Middle Ages its reach touched all walks of Christian society. Since interaction with an excommunicate resulted in spiritual pollution and further excommunication, the ban had sweeping consequences on business relationships, families, friendships, and even lodging and dining arrangements. The excommunicate was prohibited from entering a church as well as participating in the mass or any of the other sacraments, a pressing concern if one were to take ill and be denied anointing of the sick or last rites. Legal disability extended into the secular realm. An excommunicate had no legal protections or rights and, according to some canonists, all contracts with an excommunicate were declared null and void. No one could survive long in Christian society as an excommunicate, but that was the point. Excommunication was a temporary measure meant to make life so difficult that one capitulates and willingly rejoins the Christian

---

[2] Henry Richardson and George Sayles, eds., *Fleta* (SS, vol. LXXII, 1953), 86.
[3] Francis Nichols, ed., *Britton: An English Translation and Notes*, 2 vols. (Washington, DC: John Byrne and Co., 1901), vol. I, 85.

community. An excommunicate was only permitted to persist in excommunication for so long. After forty days, the church raised the stakes by mobilizing the secular arm of the law in a process known as caption to arrest and incarcerate the excommunicate (another coercive measure), until he or she assented to reconciliation.

Coercion was also a customary part of secular English law. Feudal lords had long relied upon distraint to deal with the nonperformance of services, by seizing a tenant's chattels and keeping them until performance of what was owed. This was not as extra-legal as it sounds; a lord had to obtain judgment in his own court before he might lawfully pursue this course of action.[4] Similarly, a tenant who was behind on rent sometimes discovered his or her lands seized as gage. The law prohibited the lord from profiting off the land – he was not permitted to harvest its crops, for example – and he had to be prepared to return it directly upon payment of the arrears. Coercion applied to not only a person's property, but also one's body. In the twelfth century, the Crown experimented with coercive imprisonment for securing payments into the exchequer on royal debts.[5] Similarly, incarceration as a coercive measure had a part to play in criminal pleas: as Glanvill (*c.*1187–9) observes, because felonies involve the interests of the king, an appellor is bound to prosecute. Thus, if the appellor fails to pursue the suit, he or she is immediately incarcerated and remains in prison "until he is willing to prosecute his appeal."[6]

The appeals process itself was one of the most popular forms of coercion. The Crown probably did not recognize it as such, but litigants certainly did. Victims or their families turned to the courts when they could not persuade the perpetrator into negotiation for an out-of-court settlement without the coercive power of the Crown. Despite *Glanvill*'s ominous statement above, the failure of most appellors to pursue their suits through to completion was due in large part to undocumented settlements: once faced with court-appointed damages (in civil pleas), or the looming possibility of execution (in crown pleas), arbitration and an out-of-court

[4] P&M, vol. I, 353–4.
[5] Ralph Pugh, *Imprisonment in Medieval England* (Cambridge University Press, 1968), 5.
[6] George Hall, ed., *The Treatise on the Laws and Customs of the Realm of England Commonly Called Glanvill* (Oxford: Clarendon Press, 1993), 21.

settlement suddenly seemed much more attractive. Englishmen and women recognized the value of an appeal as a form of blackmail with a good record for success.[7]

The twelfth and thirteenth centuries saw coercive practices expand in number and application, taking on a more extensive role in the everyday practice of the law. During this period, excommunication was refined to incorporate a greater number of variations (minor, major, *latae sententiae*/automatic, anathema/permanent) in order to produce a more flexible and awe-inspiring tool, and so that the degree of exclusion involved in the pronouncement more precisely reflected the nature of the offense. In England, the Crown imported excommunication as a concept into secular law and merged it with the existing practice of outlawry. Initially, much like the Scandinavians, the English employed outlawry as a punishment. Those believed to be guilty of a felony were ousted from the protections of the law so that killing an outlaw was not considered homicide. In Richard I's reign (r. 1189–99), an outlaw's head netted its hunter a reward of five shillings, as the government subcontracted law enforcement to private body hunters. During the thirteenth century, however, outlawry transitioned in status from a punishment to a process. It became "an engine for compelling the contumacious to abide the judgment of the courts."[8] After four consecutive failures to respond to a court summons, the sheriff passed a sentence of outlawry against the absent defendant. Once again, the purpose was to strong-arm the accused. Living on the fringes of society, without any legal standing, outlaws suffered similar disabilities as excommunicates, with the added injustice of felony forfeiture, the penalty for fleeing the scene of a crime. As a result, many outlaws eventually succumbed to coercion, turning themselves in and submitting to trial in the hopes of an acquittal and resumption of a normal life.

The myriad uses of incarceration in the thirteenth century reveal just how much the English Crown had come to appreciate its utility as a coercive measure. Incarceration was implemented to address contumacy in a wide variety of forms. Fine-breakers, that is, those

---

[7] Daniel Klerman, "Settlement and the Decline of Private Prosecution in Thirteenth-Century England," *L&HR* 19.1 (2001): 1–65.

[8] S. F. C. Milsom, *Historical Foundations of the Common Law* (London: Butterworths, 1969), 449.

who failed to pay amercements, found themselves in jail; payment of the overdue fine led to an immediate release. The most significant extension of the practice is apparent when it comes to statutes relating to debt. The Statute of Acton Burnell (1283) saw coercive imprisonment applied to the recovery of private debts by merchants who had the foresight to oblige clients to acknowledge their obligations publicly before city officials. If the appointed date came and went without repayment, the debtor's chattels were subject to distraint; if the debtor lacked goods to distrain, the solution was imprisonment until debts were paid in full.[9] The Statute of Merchants (1285) allowed creditors to bypass distraint altogether, authorizing immediate incarceration of a delinquent debtor.[10] Finally, a statute passed in 1352 simplified the process by eliminating any need for formal registration of the debt. This was a bold move that significantly empowered creditors. As Ralph Pugh explains, this "placed the common creditor in the same position as the crown and gave him the power of imprisoning his debtor's body until the debt in dispute should have been settled."[11]

These are not, by far, the only examples of coercive measures in medieval law. The *subpoena*, a writ commanding a defendant's appearance in court on pain of imprisonment, is an obvious if late example. Even judicial torture, reintroduced into European law in the aftermath of Lateran IV (1215), was envisaged as a coercive measure. Judicial torture was not a penalty, but a tool to pressure a reluctant defendant into supplying a confession. All of these developments are the necessary framework against which the practice of peine forte et dure must be examined. It was just one coercive measure among many that emerged over the course of the thirteenth century in order to compel a reluctant defendant into acknowledging royal authority. That medieval justices understood it in this fashion is emphasized not only in the legal treatises, but also in the arraignment of Adam le Walker of Garsington in 1315, which saw the king's justices drawing a conscious connection between peine forte et dure and another coercive measure: outlawry. When Adam stood mute in response to multiple appeals of felony, justices of jail delivery announced his silence as

---

[9] Statute of Acton Burnell, 11 Edw. I (1283), *SR*, vol. 1, 54.
[10] Statute of Merchants, 13 Edw. I (1285), *SR*, vol. 1, 99.   [11] Pugh, *Imprisonment*, 46.

a rejection of the common law. He was thus "outlawed to the penance [peine forte et dure]."[12]

This wider context is a valuable reminder that when examining peine forte et dure in the medieval setting, it needs to be approached afresh, without any preconceptions wrought by the more widely touted example of Margaret Clitheroe, whose infamous execution does not fit the model of the usual experience of peine forte et dure. As this chapter will outline, peine forte et dure should be conceived as a broad category that includes a range of coercive measures from fasting to pressing. Inspired by ecclesiastical penology, the primary goal behind the practice was spiritual reorientation, although as our comparison of hard prison with the more normal prison experience hopes to impress, the effectiveness of the practice likely had much to do with the degree of privation. Already accustomed to a subsistence lifestyle, the poor had less to fear from peine forte et dure than did the nobleman – and as we will see, nobility was no bar to sentences of peine forte et dure. While high rank typically functioned as a waiver to bypass the normal system of law for English subjects, this was not true at all when it comes to peine forte et dure. There were numerous spectacular cases of noblemen subjected to this coercive device. Moreover, while peine forte et dure was primarily a coercive measure, there were times when jailers or the courts imposed it punitively, and towards the end of the period, justices were more likely to see it as a form of capital punishment. Nonetheless, the practice never fully shed the trappings of its coercive origins.

Prison Forte et Dure v. Peine Forte et Dure

Prison forte et dure (that is, "strong and hard prison") is usually described as being the precursor to peine forte et dure. Mention of the practice appears first in a 1275 statute that recommends its use for notorious felons who refused to plead. Because written law regularly lagged a full step behind legal practice in medieval England, there is no reason to assume that the statute's drafting necessarily signals the birth of a new practice. More likely the legislation indicates instead that members of parliament believed an existing practice needed statutory justification in order to continue. Abuse of the practice, or excessive

[12] TNA JUST 3/75, m. 34 (1315).

reliance upon it by the king, may have prompted members of parliament to demand codification as a defensive move, as was the case with the Great Treason Statute of 1352. The specific language of the 1275 statute is edifying:

> It is provided also, that notorious felons, and which openly be of evil name, and will not put themselves in inquests of felonies, that men shall charge them with before the justices at the king's suit, [shall have] strong and hard imprisonment (*le prison forte & dure*), as they which refuse to stand to the common law of the land: But this is not to be understood of such prisoners as be taken [of] light suspicion.[13]

It is noteworthy that prison forte et dure was not originally intended for *all* those who refused jury trial, only "notorious felons, and which openly be of evil name." If this principle reflects early court practice, then England's justices who worried about the spiritual consequences of sentencing a person to death must have taken comfort knowing such an arduous torment was inflicted only on those who were guilty of some crime, if not necessarily the felony that brought the individual to court in the first place. Of course, the cautious approach dictated by this statutory provision did not last long. The court records indicate that prison forte et dure quickly came to apply to all those who stood mute.

What is absent from the statute is just as striking as what it includes. Nowhere does the legislation designate hard prison as a coercive measure intended to extract the defendant's consent to jury trial, as it was employed throughout much of the medieval period. Without this stipulation, hard prison might just as easily have been a judicially sanctioned death penalty for notorious felons. Indeed, the failure of the statute to define in even the vaguest terms what is meant by prison forte et dure has prompted notable commentary. Pollock and Maitland posited that "probably there was for many years much doubt as to the exact nature of the means that were to be employed in order to extort the requisite submission [to jury trial]."[14] The failure to identify exactly what "strong and hard prison" constituted in the minds of the legislators has left some to assume that the statute's ambiguity was purposeful, intended to grant the jailer *carte blanche*. However, it is

---

[13] Statute of Westminster I, 3 Edw. I, c. 12 (1275); *SR*, vol. I, 29.   [14] P&M, vol. II, 651.

more probable that this legislation held greater meaning for a medieval audience than for a modern one. The statute was not introducing prison forte et dure to English law; it was authorizing a pre-existing practice. No definition of the term was needed because its writers anticipated an audience already familiar with the practice. Furthermore, to dispel any budding suspicions that legislators framed the statute in a deliberately vague manner in order to slip judicial torture in without the king noticing, it should be clarified that this kind of imprecision was typical of the medieval English. In general, legislators and jurists preferred to name offenses and practices without explaining them. They were infinitely more concerned with procedure than with definition. As Richard Ireland observes, definitions materialized only when "lawyers attempt to hold the law, to give it form and substance," more often than not, in the midst of a legal challenge.[15]

Fixated on the wording of the statute, time and again historians have drawn a firm distinction between the "statutory penalty" of prison forte et dure, generally understood to mean spartan jail conditions and a starvation diet, and its derivative, the "nonstatutory" peine forte et dure, which added pressing with weights into the mix.[16] Yet, given the opacity of the statute and the medieval approach to legislation in general, these classifications, and the illegality implied by the descriptor "nonstatutory," are much more rigorous and distinct than the evidence would seem to support. Rather, this book adopts the standpoint that "prison forte et dure" and "peine forte et dure" should be used interchangeably to refer to a category constituting a number of discrete forms of deprivation that fluctuated depending on the nature of the alleged crime. Instead of two distinct procedures, one authorized by law, the other only by precedent, pressing was simply a more painful variation of the usual attributes of hard prison.

Nor do the records of law in practice give witness to the weighty connotations historians have attached to these two terms. While legal historians routinely use these two phrases, medieval scribes seldom

---

[15] Richard Ireland, "Law in Action, Law in Books: The Practicality of Medieval Theft Law," *C&C* 17.3 (2002): 310.

[16] Anthony Musson, with Edward Powell, eds., *Crime, Law and Society in the Later Middle Ages* (Manchester University Press, 2009), 142.

did. The phrase peine forte et dure surfaces intermittently in year-book dialogues between justices and sergeants, but it does not appear even once in the 481 cases drawn from jail deliveries under examination in this study. Why, then, is peine forte et dure the label that has come to dominate legal discourse? The popularity of the phrase among legal scholars seems to derive principally from its usage in the early modern era by such prominent jurists as Edward Coke (d.1634) and William Blackstone (d.1780). At 4.78 percent (or twenty-three of 481 cases), the phrase prison forte et dure was more common in the records of medieval England's jail deliveries, but still far from routine. However, the phrase does seem to have enjoyed fame among commoners as the Middle English "hard prison." The fifteenth-century Chancery petition of John Welles, vicar of Sparsholt, provides an instructive example when he complains of being kept "in hard prison in irons, as if he were a strong felon."[17] Similarly, when Thomas Payn of Glamorgan, former secretary to John Oldcastle, complained to parliament of his continued incarceration in 1422, he explained that he had been "detained a long time in hard prison, without indictment, impeachment, or other reasonable cause, but by suspicion, without being able to respond." He thus respectfully requested to be tried by members of parliament, as the law requires.[18] In these instances, though, "hard prison" would seem to refer simply to insufferable prison conditions rather than specifically a starvation diet or pressing.

If the scribes assigned to justices of jail delivery did not label this punitive measure as either prison forte et dure or peine forte et dure, which terms did they use? In practice, they employed a range of descriptors. As the records reveal, punishment (*pœna/pena* in Latin, or *peine* in French) dominates the pool, appearing 186 times, or in 38.7 percent of the 481 cases. The term is also incorporated into diverse phrases that appear multiple times, such as "punishment according to the ordinance" (*pœnam inde ordinatam*), or the "punishment of the statute" (*ad penam statuti*). *Pena* also appears regularly as a marginal notation: scribes typically provided an abbreviated summary of the key facts of a case (county; fate of

---

[17] TNA C 1/64/702, Welles v. The Sheriff of Hampshire (1475 X 1485). *OED*, "strong. adj.," no. 8g. "Of a malefactor: flagrantly guilty, habitually offending. Chiefly a strong thief."
[18] TNA SC 8/24/1186 (1422).

accused; monies owed to the king, scratched out if those monies had already been collected) in the margin of the roll so that the information might be retrieved at a glance. *Pena* regularly appears in those margins.

Jail delivery records routinely make note of a defendant sent back to prison and condemned "to the diet" (*ad dietam*): 150 of the 481 cases, or 31.2 percent, include sentences *ad dietam*. This label also appears as a common marginal notation, such as "to the diet" (*ad dietam*), or simply *dietam*.[19] The starvation diet is also the focal point of our earliest account of *prison forte et dure*, which comes from the late thirteenth-century legal treatise *Britton*.[20] In a dialogue on forgers "who will not put themselves upon their acquittal," *Britton* advises they be "put to their penance until they pray to do it." The author explains penance (*penitentia*) in the following manner:

and let their penance be this, that they be barefooted, ungirt and bareheaded, in the worst place in the prison, upon the bare ground continually night and day, that they eat only bread made of barley or bran, and that they drink not the day they eat, nor eat the day they drink, nor drink anything but water, and that they be put in irons.[21]

Britton mentions nothing about being pressed with irons; the author remarks instead that the accused felon be "put in irons," that is, chained to the wall, a standard practice in English prisons intended to deter escapes and referenced in *The Outlaw's Song of Trailbaston*, a fourteenth-century political poem protesting the corruptions of royal justices assigned to trailbaston.[22] Jailers allowed prisoners who swore an oath promising not to escape to pay a fee known as "le sewet" in order to be relieved of their chains.[23] The fee was so widespread that only those who could not afford to pay or were suspected of plotting a jailbreak wore fetters in prison. The implication in *Britton*'s treatise is

---

[19] For example, see the case of Richard of Crochill of Melton, TNA JUST 3/77/2, m. 6 (1336).

[20] For the dating of *Britton*, see David Seipp, "The *Mirror of Justices*," in Jonathan Bush and Alain Wijffels, eds., *Learning the Law: Teaching and the Transmission of the Law in England, 1150–1900* (London: Hambledon, 1999), 91.

[21] Nichols, ed., *Britton*, vol. I, 21–2.   [22] "*The Outlaw's Song of Trailbaston*," 104.

[23] Jonathan Rose, "*Feodo de Compedibus Vocato le Sewet*: The Medieval Prison 'oeconomy'," in Paul Brand, Andrew Lewis, and Paul Mitchell, eds., *Law in the City* (London: Four Courts Press, 2005), 72–94.

that the "mute by malice" forfeited the right to have one's shackles removed even if one might afford to pay the fee for their removal.

When it comes to descriptors, penance (*penitencia*) places a close third, with 117 of the 481 cases, or, 24.3 percent. More often than not, its usage adheres to the following pattern: in 1293 when John Blanke, indicted for the homicide of Brother Robert of Brierley of Rye House, stood mute before justices of jail delivery, they ordered him returned to prison to "have his penance" (*Et habeat penitentiam*).[24] Others were "sentenced to the penance" (*adiudicatur ad penam*), returned to prison "to endure the penance" (*ad penitenciam suam duratur*), and "committed to penance" (*commitatur ad penitentiam*). Penance also held pride of place in common parlance, translated into the Norman French as *penaunce* in *The Outlaw's Song of Trailbaston*.

Why did so many different terms exist for the same practice? Scribes using distinct vocabulary were most likely trying to denote different degrees of punishment. For example, a scribe assigned to royal justices in York noted that on August 2, 1352, Justice William Basset and his associates returned Thomas of Standon, accused of receiving, theft, and of being a common thief, to prison *ad penam*.[25] Just seven months later, and only five membranes apart in the same jail delivery roll (written in the same hand), Robert of Carleton stood mute before the exact same justices at the same castle, accused of two counts of theft and of being a common thief. This time, the scribe described his sentence as the diet (*ad dietam*).[26] While I cannot say for certain why different terms were employed, presumably, Justice Basset and his associates believed different degrees of punishment were warranted because of the different allegations against them, although given the vagueness of the term *pena*, it is impossible to discover whether this was the lighter or more severe of the two sentences.

Pressing with irons may have eventually come to define peine forte et dure, but that was not the case in the medieval era. Exactly *when* pressing as a practice joined the motley crew of deprivations is not clear. Historians typically point to Bartholomew Cotton's *Historia Anglicana* for the first documented evidence of peine forte et dure.[27]

---

[24] TNA JUST 1/1098, m. 72d (1293).   [25] TNA JUST 3/79/1, m. 9d (1352).
[26] TNA JUST 3/79/1, m. 14 (1352).
[27] First noted by Alfred Marks, *Tyburn Tree: Its History and Annals* (London: Brown, Langham and Co., 1908), 37–8.

Cotton's chronicle relates the 1293 Norfolk trial in which fourteen Englishmen stood accused of cruelly murdering sailors from Holland and Zeeland, stealing their goods, then setting fire to their ships – as one might imagine, a nightmare for international relations and trading partnerships, necessitating a swift and harsh judicial response. Justices sentenced thirteen of the accused to hang. The fourteenth refused to submit to jury trial. He was remanded to prison *ad dietam*, with the "cheapest bread" (*vilissimo pane*) and drinking only "putrid water" (*aqua putrida*). In addition, justices declared "that he should sit naked save for a linen garment, on the bare ground, and he should be loaded with irons from the hands to the elbows, and from feet to the knees, until he should make his submission."[28] In terms of the legal record, an indictment on charges of homicide just three years before Cotton's chronicle employs the phrase "severe pressing punishment" (*gravum pena constrictus*); it seems logical to assume that this was a reference to pressing with weights.[29] The year-book summaries of the 1302 trials of John of Darley and Sir Ralph de Bloyou (or, Bloyho) provide the first overt accounts of pressing in the legal record. Indicted of various felonies, the two separately refused to submit to jury trial and eventually died in prison. When justices returned Darley to jail, they commanded him to suffer his penance, describing it as being "put in a house on the ground in his shirt, laden with as much iron as he could bear," in addition to the usual diet of alternating days on meager rations of bread and water "that came neither from fountain nor river."[30]

However, a deeper survey of chronicle materials suggests that we might be able to push the date of the practice's emergence back even further in time. Let us consider two vignettes, detailing infamous, but instructive events drawn from chronicles regarding the reigns of two of England's most well-known Angevin monarchs, father and son. When Henry II (d.1189) entered into marriage with Eleanor of Aquitaine (d.1204). he acquired additional titles, becoming also count of Poitou and duke of Aquitaine. While Henry's heavy-handed ruling style

---

[28] Henry Luard, ed., *Bartholomaei de Cotton, Monachi Norwicensis, Historia Anglicana* (RS, vol. XVI, 1859), 227–8.

[29] See the indictment of Philip Lauweles of Ireland, TNA JUST 1/547A, m. 6d (1290).

[30] Alfred Horwood, ed., *Year Books of the Reign of Edward the First: Years XXX and XXXI (1302–1303)* (RS, n. 31, pt. A, vol. 3, 1863), 510–11 (Seipp, 1302.200rs).

encouraged submission in the northern part of his empire, his French subjects were vocal in their complaints about his contempt for regional traditions. His brash and domineering behavior prompted a series of noble revolts in defense of local political autonomy. In 1167, the counts and viscounts of Angoulême, March, Lusignan, Sillé, and Thouars rose up against the king, with the full and enthusiastic support of the French monarchy, with whom Henry was already engaged in open war. Henry's reaction was swift and brutal: he marched south with his army, razing towns and castles in his wake, crushing the rebel forces. While the leaders of the resistance were eventually forced into submission, even the exchange of a kiss of peace with a defeated party did not stop Henry from exacting his brutal revenge. According to the chronicle of Geoffrey de Vigeois, the Manceaux lord Robert de Seilhac bore the full brunt of the king's wrath. Henry had the rebel lord cast into prison, where he commanded that he be "cruelly clad in steel, with spare bread and little water to drink until he died."[31]

Flash forward forty-one years. Roger of Wendover relates that in 1209, soon after Innocent III's excommunication of King John (d. 1216) had been pronounced but not yet formally published, the news traveled swiftly throughout the kingdom, provoking a great deal of unquiet and growing alarm. Rumors about his excommunicate state became public at Westminster during a session of the exchequer one day, at which point Geoffrey of Norwich, an exchequer official, remarked to his colleagues that beneficed clerics were taking a pronounced risk by continuing to work in John's employ. He then departed the exchequer without troubling to ask the king's permission to do so. John soon became aware of the contentious Westminster quip. Not just a little annoyed, he sent one of his men to arrest the opinionated official. He had Geoffrey shackled and jailed. After several days languishing in prison, John ordered a cope of lead placed upon the prisoner. A short time later, "[f]or want of food and crushed by the weight of the cope, he departed to the Lord."[32]

---

[31] Geoffrey de Vigeois, *Chronica*, in Martin Bouquet, et al., eds., *Recueil des Historiens des Gaules et de la France*, 24 vols. (Paris: Victor Palmé, 1734–1904), vol. XII, 442. Robert de Seilhac is also known as Robert de Sillé and Robert Sillet.

[32] Roger of Wendover, *Flores historiarum*, ed. Henry Hewlett, 3 vols. (RS, 1886–9), vol. II, 53. Wendover makes several errors in the retelling of this story. First, he identifies the wrong Geoffrey of Norwich, assuming that it was Geoffrey de Burgh, archdeacon of

Neither of these chroniclers employed the term peine forte et dure; yet, that torment is exactly what these two noblemen forty-some years apart endured for their political crimes. Was the cope of lead in which Geoffrey of Norwich was dressed the very same one used by John's father on Robert de Seilhac all those years before? These events took place long before Bartholomew Cotton's account of the fourteenth rebellious sailor, confirming that the thirteenth century did not in fact witness the birth of the starvation diet and pressing as a punishment. Both Henry II and his son John reserved usage of starvation and the lead cope for their political enemies and in these two instances, it was plainly a means of execution, not a coercive measure. Henry's penchant for starving his opponents to death in prison was a trait inherited by both royal sons. Richard I and John brandished starvation as a weapon in wars on their enemies, too. Richard resorted to starvation chiefly as a vehicle for revenge. Upon returning to England after his crusade, Richard ordered one of the nobles who backed John's rebellion starved to death as punishment.[33] He similarly decreed the starvation of a man who had attempted to prevent his release from German captivity.[34]

John's approach was more politically astute: starvation as a coercive measure was his specialty. It was one among many "coercive measures

Norwich, when in fact it was Geoffrey of Norwich, justice of the Jews, who was involved in a conspiracy against the king with Robert Fitz Walter and Eustace de Vesci. Wendover also mistakenly dates the event to 1209 when it should be 1212. Despite these small inaccuracies, Painter sees no reason to doubt that the event actually took place. Sidney Painter, "Norwich's Three Geoffreys," *Speculum* 28.4 (1953): 808–13. Wilfred Warren, whose biography was intended to debunk the negative reputation of King John, sees the story as a fabrication to blacken John's name. Wilfred Warren, *King John* (London: Eyre and Spottiswoode, 1961), 12–15. The story also appears in Ralph de Coggeshall, *Chronicon Anglicanum*, ed. Joseph Stevenson (London: Longmans, 1875), 165; and in Henry Luard, ed., "Annales Prioratus de Dunstaplia (AD 1–1297)," in *Annales Monastici*, 3 vols. (London: Longmans, 1866), vol. III, 34; and Thomas Arnold, ed., *Memorials of St. Edmund's Abbey*, 2 vols. (London: Eyre and Spottiswoode, 1892), 25, although here, he is described simply as being dressed in iron (*ferro vestitus*). Marc Morris, author of *King John: Treachery, Tyranny and the Road to Magna Carta* (London: Hutchinson, 2015), mentions this episode most recently in his article "Starved to Death," *History Today* (January 29, 2016), www.historytoday.com /starved-death (accessed June 25, 2019).

[33] Ralph Turner, "England in 1215: An Authoritarian Angevin Dynasty Facing Multiple Threats," in Janet Senderowitz Loengard, ed., *Magna Carta and the England of King John* (Woodbridge: Boydell, 2010), 18.

[34] Morris, "Starved to Death."

of a peculiarly draconian kind" he exercised in order to bring his political machinations to fruition.[35] In 1202, in an effort to pressure his rival Arthur of Brittany into ending his rebellion, he had twenty-two of Arthur's noblemen incarcerated at Corfe. When Arthur refused to capitulate or desist, John had the noblemen slowly starved to death. In 1210, he experimented with starvation as a means to compel repayment of Crown loans and incite a return to loyalty. William de Briouze, fourth lord of Bramber and once John's favorite, owed a debt of £13,000 to the Crown for the Irish honor of Limerick in northern Munster. In an effort to get him to repay it, John seized his Welsh properties; William retaliated by raising a force to retake the confiscated castles, and when that failed, he burned Leominster to the ground and fled with his troops to Ireland. In order to pressure William into returning to England, John had his wife Matilda and son (also named William) flung into the dungeon at either Windsor or Corfe. When William neglected to reappear, his wife and son withered away without food or drink. Their deaths became one of the worst atrocities of John's reign, a close second to the secretive "disappearance" of his nephew Arthur, of course. John employed similar threats against the rebel baron Oliver d'Argentan in 1215 and a few months later with William d'Aubigné, another dissident baron.[36]

What these tactics tell us is that long before hard prison made its way into legislation, English kings were experimenting with similar practices on political enemies as both a means of execution and a coercive measure. These test runs provided the English Crown the opportunity to witness the horror with which such treatment was met, ensuring the tool's effectiveness as a coercive device. At the same time, the lurid retellings in chronicles and gossip circles ensured that starvation and irons were broadly understood to be the antidote administered to those who disrespected royal authority. Experimentation of this kind is probably also the reason why parliament eventually saw fit to legislate the practice, to rein in royal enthusiasm for starvation and pressing of those the king deemed his enemies.

---

[35] John Maddicott, "The Oath of Marlborough, 1209: Fear, Government and Popular Allegiance in the Reign of King John," *EHR* 126.519 (2011): 312.

[36] Morris, "Starved to Death."

Nonetheless, even after the formal appearance of pressing, there is no evidence to document the practice supplanting or even surpassing the more traditional method of the starvation diet. It seems noteworthy that there is no equivalent of the marginal notation *ad dietam* to refer to pressing with weights (perhaps something along the lines of *ad ferram?*); nor is it at all clear that *pena* or *penitencia* were meant to refer to pressing rather than simply hard prison. While 1290 marks the first documented incident of judicial pressing, long after that date the Crown issued pardons to men and women seemingly sentenced exclusively, or mainly, to a starvation diet. In April of 1357, the king pardoned Cecily, widow of John of Ridgeway, with the explanation that after forty days in a "narrow prison without food or drink," her continued survival was nothing short of a miracle.[37] A 1384 pardon issued to John atte Puttes of Bishopsden produced a similar justification: he had survived for so long on the diet it must be a miracle.[38] In 1390, the queen saw fit to intercede on behalf of Thomas Herry of Braunston, who also withstood death after enduring the peine for such a long time; he, too, was the beneficiary of the king's grace.[39] Admittedly, these examples are exceptional: royal officials did not typically leap to the conclusion of a miracle. They were more likely to finger the jailer for unlawfully and covertly assisting the condemned, as they did when William of Podmore, sentenced to undergo peine forte et dure at Stafford, December 6, 1305, was found still alive on July 15, 1306. Royal justices suspected the sheriff had improperly supplied him with food and drink.[40] What is perhaps most striking about William's case is that after seven months of incarceration, he finally agreed to jury trial and was acquitted.[41]

These instances confirm that long after authorities first experimented with pressing it had still not become routine for those sentenced to hard prison. If pressing had been imposed on any of these

---

[37] *CPR*, Edward III, vol. VII (1345–58), 529.

[38] *CPR*, Richard II, vol. II (1381–5), 373. The English calendar uses the term peine forte et dure; however, the Latin of the original explains that he was sentenced to the diet (*ad dietam suam poni*).

[39] *CPR*, Richard II, vol. IV (1389–92), 333.

[40] George Sayles, ed., *Select Cases in the Court of King's Bench*, 7 vols. (SS, 1936–71), vol. II, clv (also, TNA JUST 1/809, mm. 9 and 15).

[41] George Wrottesley, ed., "Extracts from the Plea Rolls, AD 1294 to AD 1307," in Wrottesley, ed., *Staffordshire Historical Collections*, vol. VII, 171.

men and women, they could not have survived for as long as they did. The chronicler of the *Vita Edwardi Secundi* (c.1326) acknowledges this point specifically in relating the prison death of Sir Robert le Ewer (or Lewer) in 1322. Accused of multiple felonies, including theft and sedition, when Ewer stood mute the king's justices sentenced him to both the diet and pressing "with as great a weight of iron as his wretched body can bear," remarking that "He who survives this punishment beyond the fifth or sixth day would have strength beyond that of normal human nature."[42] Admittedly, on its own, the starvation diet was a severe enough punishment that irons only hastened an already fast-approaching death. Sixty percent of the human body is comprised of water: without replenishment, the body typically begins to fail after only three or four days. A few mouthfuls of "cloudy and stinking water" every second day would soon take its toll.[43] Therefore, when a prisoner died just four days after being returned to prison, as was the case in the 1304 death of Robert de Talonse, a London cordwainer appealed for robbery, there is no reason to believe that weights should have been a part of his hard prison experience.[44]

There is no evidence to claim that the diet was a precursor of the pressing punishment, as is usually argued.[45] That justices of jail delivery were still sentencing men and women to the diet in the fifteenth century, over two centuries after pressing came into being, is evidence of the coexistence of practices rather than a clear evolution from one to the other. At the 1425 trial of John Norham of Harldsey, a shepherd accused of murdering his wife, when he refused to plead justices assigned him to penance, "namely to the diet" (*videlicet ad dietam*).[46] Even in the late fifteenth century, suspected felons who refused to plead continued to be incarcerated *ad dietam*.[47] It seems more likely that the diet remained the most common version of hard

[42] Wendy Childs, ed., *Vita Edwardi Secundi: The Life of Edward the Second* (Oxford: Clarendon Press, 2005), 216–18.
[43] Childs, ed., *Vita Edwardi Secundi*, 216.   [44] TNA JUST 3/38, m. 5 (1304).
[45] See Edward White, "Peine Forte et Dure," in his *Legal Antiquities: A Collection of Essays upon Ancient Laws and Customs* (St. Louis: Nixon-Jones Printing Co., 1913), 180.
[46] TNA JUST 3/199, m. 2d (1415).
[47] Anthony Fitzherbert, *La Graunde Abridgement* (London: John Rastell and Wynkyn de Worde, 1516), fo. 246, no. 65.

prison assigned by the courts, but if justices were faced with hardened criminals or political upstarts, pressing was an additional strategy that might be employed.

Margaret Clitheroe survived only fifteen minutes after the weights were piled onto the door balanced on her chest. The manner and swiftness of the saint's death may have been typical by the 1580s. Thomas Smith's *De Republica Anglorum* (1583) – predating Margaret's execution by three years – dubs peine forte et dure "one of the cruellest deathes that may be." He explains it accordingly: "he is layd upon a table, and another uppon him, and another weight of stones or lead laide upon that table, while as his bodie be crushed, and his life by the violence taken from him." Only "some strong and stout hearted man" chooses a death of this nature.[48] As he explains it, this methodology bears a striking similarity to that imposed upon Saint Margaret. It would seem that this was just the beginning of perfecting the process of using the peine as a particularly sadistic form of capital punishment. By the eighteenth century, prisons installed "press rooms," devoted exclusively to carrying out the sentence. The eighteenth-century defendant was loaded with a more modest weight of 350 pounds (the 700 pounds used in Margaret's case was probably overkill), and yet it was still rare for the accused to survive more than fifteen minutes.[49] None of this resembles the medieval peine forte et dure in which an accused felon survived for days, even months at a time.[50] The inescapable conclusion is that peine forte et dure in medieval England was a different beast altogether.

How much weight was involved in the medieval practice? If the objective was to make sure that a person made weak by malnourishment and dehydration could not remove the irons, it did

---

[48] Thomas Smith, *De republica Anglorum: A Discourse on the Commonwealth of England*, ed. Leonard Alston (Cambridge University Press, 1906), 97.

[49] McKenzie, "'This Death'," 281–7.

[50] Thomas Bernard took four days to die: he stood mute March 17, 1316 (TNA JUST 3/30/1, m. 35), and was found dead March 21, 1316 (JUST 2/94A, m. 5). John of Flexham took nineteen days to die: he stood mute July 31, 1344 (JUST 3/130, m. 90d), and was found dead August 19, 1344 (JUST 2/195, m. 13d). John Hoveden died twenty-three days after incarceration: he stood mute August 1, 1392 (JUST 3/177, m. 87), and was found dead August 24, 1392 (JUST 2/85, m. 2d). Robert Everard took forty-two days to die: he stood mute on July 23, 1323, and died September 3, 1323 (JUST 3/115B, m. 7).

not have to weigh more than a few pounds. The *Mirror of Justices* (*c.*1285–90) states specifically that it is an abuse of power to load a prisoner with more than twelve pounds in weight.[51] Did wardens adhere to this standard? And where on the body was that iron placed? The early modern evidence characteristically describes weights placed on a board or a door balanced on the defendant's chest. If enough weight was added to the board, it would crush the defendant's lungs, guaranteeing a quick death. But how much weight is too much? In this respect, Roderick Smith's and L. B. Lim's 1995 study of crush barriers, in which they draw an historical comparison with peine forte et dure, is instructive. The purpose of the study was to rethink safety guidelines at sports grounds. The two engineers from the University of Sheffield hoped to simulate the pressures of a crowd behind crush barriers at a sporting event in order to better understand just how much pressure a human body can safely endure. In their study, the subjects themselves operated a hydraulic jack with a hand pump and instantaneous release. Their findings are useful for our purposes. First, Smith and Lim argue that their subjects were most comfortable with flat barriers placed on the upper chest, suggesting that the addition of the board or door piled with weights might have actually helped to alleviate some of the defendant's pain. Second, the mean load of discomfort was 94 pounds of force, with a minimum of 25 pounds and a maximum of 174 pounds, experienced in 30-second increments.[52] All of this implies that if jailers adhered to the *Mirror*'s suggested twelve pounds in weight, the defendant might have been sufficiently "comfortable" (obviously a highly subjective term) to withstand the torment for some time.

Yet, balancing a board on the defendant's chest is not mentioned anywhere in the medieval evidence; therefore, it might have been a sixteenth-century innovation, as we see in the example of Margaret Clitheroe. The medieval instructions for the practice typically combined the diet with pressing: placing a board on the defendant's chest would prevent the defendant from eating or drinking, making the medieval dietary stipulations somewhat superfluous. Bartholomew Cotton described weights being loaded on the hands to the elbow

---

[51] William Whittaker, ed., *The Mirror of Justices* (SS, vol. VII, 1893), 160.
[52] Roderick Smith and L. Lim, "Experiments to Investigate the Level of 'Comfortable' Loads for People against Crush Barriers," *Safety Science* 18 (1995): 329–35.

and the feet to the knees, hinting that it might in fact have been seen as a variant of a pillory which limited movement in the four limbs.[53] If jailers followed this model, presumably lifting the weights off at least one hand for occasional eating or drinking, the suspect might endure peine forte et dure for an extended period, although not without serious physical, not to mention psychological, trauma. Prolonged interruption to blood flow would eventually cause the feet and hands to fester in self-amputation, but the defendant might still live for some time in this state.

In defining hard prison, the presence or absence of irons was not the only variation. Time in prison itself was seen as part of the punishment. It is striking that the York eyre of 1293 condemned multiple mute defendants to prison sentences,[54] others simply to the penance of prison,[55] some to both.[56] Life imprisonment – described as perpetual penance (*ad penitentiam suam perpetuo*), or penance until death (*penitentia ad mortem*) – surfaces as a possibility as early as 1327.[57] Incarceration under horrific conditions may also have been a loose interpretation of hard prison. *Dure prisoun* for Brother Thomas Dunheved (d.1327) was a deep pit in which he was cast after storming Berkeley castle where Edward II (d.1327) was being held, momentarily springing him from his prison. The *Annales Paulini* report that he died pitifully there, but only after he attempted to rally the other prisoners into a massive jail-break.[58]

---

[53] Luard, ed., *Bartholomaei de Cotton*, 228.

[54] For example, Richard Attestede of Pickill, TNA JUST 1/1098, m. 87d (1293).

[55] See Robert of Beeston, TNA JUST 1/1098, m. 81d (1293). Note: Richard Clerk of Ormskirk (*de Oskyrk*) was sentenced to the penance of prison for a period of six months. See TNA JUST 3/79/3, m. 2d (1377).

[56] See Simon le Conestable, TNA JUST 1/1098, m. 80d (1293).

[57] A man arrested on a felony indictment was placed in the prison stocks; while so engaged, another individual rescued him and the two broke out of prison. When the first man stood next before justices on the charge of prison break, he did not stand mute; he willingly agreed to undergo jury trial. However, as an accomplice in the escape, he could not be tried until the principal had been attainted and the principal had yet to be arrested. Thus, the presiding justice declared that he would "remain in the grace of the king," and "have perpetual prison, or another penance, according to what the king wishes." YB Trin. Term, 1327, fo. 16b (Seipp 1327.096).

[58] George Aungier, ed., *Croniques de London, depuis l'an 44 Hen. III jusqu'à 17 Edw. III* (London: Camden Society 1844), 58. William Stubbs, ed., "Annales Paulini," in *Chronicles of the Reigns of Edward I and Edward II* (London: Longman and Co., 1883), vol. 1, 337.

The conclusion to all of this is that when a suspected felon in a medieval prison was sentenced to what legal historians typically refer to as peine forte et dure, the punishment imposed did not necessarily include pressing to death. Rather, pressing belonged to a category of punishments that included also rigorous fasting, nakedness, and shackles.

Why Pressing? The Legal Historian's Perspective

Understanding why jailers decided to inflict pressing with irons and weights on their famished inmates is a question that has preoccupied legal historians for quite some time. William Blackstone was the first to propose that peine forte et dure (in his mind referring expressly to pressing with weights) was borne in error, a corruption of the scribal abbreviation for *prison*.[59] This notion has won plentiful support among legal scholars who cannot otherwise account for what they see as a transition from a starvation diet to pressing with weights. In the 2019 edition of his textbook, John Baker rehearses this venerable story, explaining that the peine derives from "a grisly misunderstanding" in which "the *prison* of the statute was inexplicably read as *peine* [that is, pain]."[60] Not only does this account conflict with the medieval evidence, cited above, in which the diet and pressing co-existed, it raises some additional concerns. First, in Anglo-Norman French "peine" does not translate to "pain," but to "penalty, penance, punishment."[61] While any one of these procedures might include pain, the ambit was much broader than corporal punishment: "penalties" at common law included amercements, "penance" sometimes referred to pilgrimage.[62] There is

---

[59] *Blackstone*, vol. IV, ch. 25.

[60] John Baker, *An Introduction to English Legal History*, 5th edn. (Oxford University Press, 2019), 549.

[61] John Baker, *Manual of Law French*, 2nd edn. (Aldershot: Scholar Press, 1990), 167. That "peyne" does not refer to "pain" is made clear from looking at the term in context. For example, the Statute of Winchester explains that a *peyne* will be enforced for the concealment of felonies; the context makes it clear that the *peyne* was an amercement, not corporal punishment. See "Statute of Winchester," 13 Edw. I (1285), *SR*, vol. I, 96.

[62] In Middle English, *peine* sometimes referred to physical pain; although it could just as easily refer to punishment, amercement, threats, torture, or time in purgatory; but the statutes are written in French not English. See *Middle English Dictionary* entry for "peine" (n), in "Middle English Compendium" (Ann Arbor: University of Michigan,

little reason to suppose such a misreading led to the Crown's historic decision to torment silent defendants by piling weights upon their naked bodies.

Second, a survey of the various abbreviations used by medieval scribes helps us to assess the potential for such an error in transmission. Because of the haphazard development of abbreviations across time and space, often multiple forms existed for the same term. Looking first to the Latin, the language of record for English law, it is hard to see how a scribe could have mistaken "prison" for "punishment." English scribes were disinclined to abbreviate *prisona*. More often than not, it is spelled out in full or it crops up in the marginal notation *r' pr* (returned to prison).[63] Often, the records use instead the word *gaola* (jail). Given the evidence, a misreading of *prisona* is not likely. For punishment (*pœna*, or *pena*), English legal documents make use of *p̄ᵃ*, *peᵃ*, *p̄eᵃ*, *pen'*, *p̄na*, or for the plural (*pœnae/penae*), *pē*. None of these look anything like *prisona* or its abbreviation *pr*. We see something similar when it comes to Latin abbreviations for penance (*pœnitentia*, or *penitentia*). Scribes abbreviated penance as *p̄nia*, *p̄nᵃ*, *p̄eia*, *p̄na*, *p̄n̄a*, *p̄nia*, *p̄nia*, *penᵗetia*, and for the plural (*pœnitentiae*), *p̄nie*.

Law French, employed in the writing of statutes and legal treatises, also presents few opportunities for error. For prison (*prisone*), the scribes who worked for royal justices regularly spelled the word out in full (*prison, pryson*), or abbreviated it as *prison, p'son*, or *p'sone*. The same holds true for punishment (*peine*): at only five letters *peine* rarely appears abbreviated. It is improbable that even a poorly qualified scribe might have confused *p'son* for *peine*. Penance (*penaunce*) also leaves little room for corruption: it was usually abbreviated as *penanc̄, penaunc̄, penāce, pen̄ce*, or spelled in full as *penaunce* or *penans*. Apart from the initial letter, there is not enough overlap to point to scribal corruption as the originator of a new practice.

2018), https://quod.lib.umich.edu/m/middle-english-dictionary/dictionary/MED32728/ track?counter=1&search_id=1138482 (accessed June 18, 2019).

63 Charles Trice Martin includes no abbreviations whatsoever for *prisona*. See his *The Record Interpreter*, 2nd edn. (1892; repr. Chichester: Phillimore and Co., 1999); nor does Adrian Cappelli, *The Elements of Abbreviation in Medieval Latin Paleography* (Lawrence: University of Kansas Libraries, 1982); nor does Olaf Pluta, *Abbreviationes* (1993–2015), www.ruhr-uni-bochum.de/philosophy/projects/abbreviationes/index.html (accessed June 1, 2015).

Abbreviations in French and Latin notwithstanding, it is even more difficult to imagine that England's small central corps of royal justices, responsible for preserving the judicial system's institutional memory, simply "forgot" the meaning of the statute. Work in the common law required a trained memory: serjeants-at-law typically memorized all of the statutes, so that they did not have to waste their time in court looking up legislation. Moreover, while standing mute was not common, justices did encounter it on a relatively regular basis. An analysis of the fourteenth-century jail delivery rolls by decade – indicating trial dates as opposed to date of crime – highlight that a small minority of defendants habitually stood mute:

TABLE 1.1 *Numbers of defendants who stood mute in fourteenth-century England by decade*

Decade	Defendants who stood mute
1300–9	75
1310–19	76
1320–9	67
1330–9	41
1340–9	74
1350–9	24
1360–9	23
1370–9	17
1380–9	18
1390–9	18

Blackstone's contention that the peine developed from a misreading of the legislation gives little credit to the institutional memory and legal literacy of England's royal justices. This hypothesis also, quite frankly, makes medieval justices seem like bumbling fools faking their way through justice – an impression that we know to be false.

Rather, pressing needs to be recognized as a conscious innovation. Both Henry Summerson and John Bellamy have proposed a hypothesis that makes good logical sense. They suggest that peine forte et dure came into existence as a coercive measure because of the need for speed. Justices of jail delivery hoped to bend an indicted felon's will and induce him or her to plead all while the court remained *in situ*.[64] English justices worked at breakneck speed; medieval prisons were habitually delivered in just one or two long, exhausting days of work, producing swift justice with individual trials of anywhere between fifteen and thirty minutes.[65] Pressing was part and parcel of that efficiency: the intensity of the pain produced a plea with much greater haste than did slow starvation and cramped surroundings. Indeed, the defendant might be prepared to plead before justices left town, thus helping to clear the prisons and make badly needed space available for the persistent overflow of prisoners.

Despite the inherent sensibility of this explanation, once again the evidence furnishes little support. In reality, justices were not so meticulous in their performance, driven to try each and every accused rather than simply returning the problematic cases to prison before moving on to deliver the next jail. Royal justices commonly ordered defendants returned to prison for one defect or another. The most popular deficiencies were: the nonappearance of key persons in the legal process (jurors summoned who failed to appear, an absent coroner); insufficient paperwork, especially a missing writ *de bono et malo* or indictment; incomplete process (accomplices could not be tried until the principal was sentenced or proof of the principal's outlawry was presented); and insufficient evidence (justices needed further inquiry before the trial might continue). In fact, at some deliveries, it was not at all unusual to see more prisoners returned to jail than actually tried. Perhaps the greater question to ask here is: why would royal justices feel any more sympathetic to the notorious felon who refused to plead by making sure he had access to swift justice when others did not? Again, none of this suggests that Bellamy's and Summerson's theory is incorrect; but given the evidence, it does not seem that speedy justice was their foremost concern.

A more likely explanation is that the English adopted the practice of pressing in cases where justices believed that the nature of the crime

---

[64] John Bellamy, *The Criminal Trial in Later Medieval England* (University of Toronto Press, 1998), 13.

[65] Ralph Pugh, "The Duration of Criminal Trials in Medieval England," in Eric Ives and Anthony Manchester, eds., *Law, Litigants and the Legal Profession* (London: RHS, 1983), 108.

justified escalating the horrors of prison forte et dure. The fact that those who stood mute for political crimes were usually subjected to pressing in addition to the diet, lends this theory some weight. Comforts in prison existed on a continuum: while the poor made do without bedding, the well-to-do paid for a drawing room and servants. Wouldn't it be fair to assume that the same might be said of hardship in prison? It, too, existed on a continuum: fasting, denial of necessities, darkness, dampness, solitude, and discomfort due to chains or weights were all possible weapons in the war on defiance of the king's law.

Origins of Prison/Peine Forte et Dure

Norman law has traditionally been understood as England's inspiration to adopt hard prison as a coercive device.[66] The Norman customals see a very similar usage of hard prison, chiefly in instances in which a suspected felon refuses jury trial. *L'Ancienne Coutume de Normandie* recommends hard prison for up to a year and a day for an individual rumored to be guilty of murder and "communally blamed," in the hopes of persuading him to submit to jury trial.[67] The same holds true for suspected receivers of felons who decline trial by sworn inquest.[68] The one deviation is that the Normans also prescribed a year and a day of hard prison (*forte prison*) as a punishment for wives strongly suspected of heinous activity.[69]

Nevertheless, the Normans did not transmit the concept of hard prison to the English; rather the Normans and the English adopted it from the same source. It is the contention of this book that the concept was harvested from ecclesiastical soil. The church's early forays into penal enclosure as a penitential practice led to the establishment of *murus strictus* (severe imprisonment), the forerunner of England's hard prison. Indeed, it would seem to be the common progenitor of hard prison also as it appeared in royal prisons across Europe. While English historians tend to associate hard prison chiefly with England, it was used as both a tool of punishment and coercion in a number of

---

[66] P&M, vol. II, 648.

[67] William de Gruchy, ed., *L'Ancienne Coutume de Normandie* (Jersey: Charles le Feuvre, 1881), 167.

[68] de Gruchy, ed., *L'Ancienne Coutume*, 184–5.

[69] de Gruchy, ed., *L'Ancienne Coutume*, 182.

European states. French letters of remission speak frequently of incarceration on a diet of bread and water for months at a time, occasionally resulting in the prisoner's early demise. The practice's penitential origins are hinted at by the Parisians' view that such a sentence was "a form of atonement, like a pilgrimage to be performed."[70] In Sweden, hard prison (*svårare fängelse*) also operated as a coercive measure. Jailers typically handcuffed suspects and hung them on the wall, administering lashes also to the most obstinate of prisoners, with the superior objective of forcing a confession.[71] Scotland also seems to have espoused a form of hard prison. In 1437, when Robert Grame was arrested for having stabbed King James I to death in conspiracy with Walter Stewart, Earl of Atholl, he was cast violently into "soore and fulle harde presune," wearing only a rough Scottish mantle.[72]

Scholars of penology have long recognized that the Catholic church's precocious experimentation with penal cloistering (*detrusio*), also referred to as "monastic exile," guided secular authorities in the eventual development of carceral theory and practice across Christendom.[73] In fact, prior to the twelfth-century English prison-building campaign, initiated by King Henry II's Assize of Clarendon (1166) and which mandated that sheriffs erect jails in every county, references to prisons in England invariably referred to either restraint within the stocks or a monastic cell.[74] At this early stage, the incarcerated were not ordinary sinners; the king's reach expanded also to include monastic space within his realm, thus many of those subjected to penal cloistering were in fact laymen accused of worldly crimes, more often than not political rebels or murderers. Confinement in a monastery was the most common form of public penance (*paenitentia publica*), so called because of the nature of the sin rather than the penance. Its

---

[70] Bronislaw Geremek, *The Margins of Society in Late Medieval Paris* (Cambridge University Press, 2006), 17.

[71] Heikki Pihlajamäki, "The Painful Question: The Fate of Judicial Torture in Early Modern Sweden," *L&HR* 25.3 (2007): 565.

[72] Margaret Connelly, ed., "The Dethe of the Kynge of Scotis: A New Edition," *The Scottish Historical Review* 71.191/192, parts 1&2 (1992): 67.

[73] Mayke de Jong, "Monastic Prisoners, or Opting Out? Political Coercion and Honour in the Frankish Kingdoms," in Mayke de Jong, Frans Theuws, and Carine van Rhijn, eds., *Topographies of Power in the Early Middle Ages* (Leiden: Brill, 2001), 293.

[74] Pugh, *Imprisonment*, 1.

purpose was in part punitive: sin is an affront to God's majesty, therefore, punishment in one form or another as compensation for that offense is compulsory. However, the ultimate goal was spiritual conversion. The monastery's sacred location was thought to sanctify its religious community; imprisonment in that space then, in conjunction with the deprivations that attended it, created the ideal conditions for the sinner's rehabilitation through suffering, contemplation, and a selfless existence.[75] The penitential nature of prison is emphasized in the term "penitentiary" (*penitentiarius* in Latin, or *penitenciarie* in Middle English), stemming from the word penitence (meaning contrition), which the medieval church employed to refer to its prisons.

The concept of gradations in penitential experiences according to the nature of the sin committed was a central part of the penology crafted by the church. This concept dates back as far as antiquity, although it is commonly believed that public penance fell out of favor during the early Middle Ages only to be revived by the Carolingian church during the penitential reform of 813.[76] The "Carolingian dichotomy" in penance promoted the idea that secret sins should be expiated by private penance, while public sins – that is, sins that had become scandals, and thus set a poor example for one's Christian neighbors – required public penance. Although, as Mayke de Jong has noted, apart from the solemn ceremony prior to incarceration or at the end of the term reconciling the penitent to his community, there was nothing public about the nature of public penance. Imprisonment in a monastery effectively meant withdrawing from the world.[77]

Public penance (in Old English, *opene dædbote*) was in place in England as early as the ninth century in association with crimes such as homicide and oath-breaking.[78] The pastoral letters of Ælfric, Abbot of Eynsham (d.1010) also repeat the necessity of public penance for public sins, and give us some insight into how the English believed

[75] de Jong, "Monastic Prisoners," 300.

[76] Mayke de Jong, "What was Public about Public Penance? *Paenitentia Publica* and Justice in the Carolingian World," *Settimane di Studio del Centro Italiano di Studi Sull'Alto Medioevo* 44 (1997): 867.

[77] de Jong, "What was Public about Public Penance?," 872.

[78] Sarah Hamilton, "Rites for Public Penance in Late Anglo-Saxon England," in Helen Gittos and Bradford Bedingfield, eds., *The Liturgy of the Late Anglo-Saxon Church* (Woodbridge: Boydell, 2005), 65–103.

time in prison should be spent.[79] According to Ælfric, the penitent assigned to public penance:

should not wash himself in a bath, nor shave, nor cut his nails, nor sleep under coverings, but on the naked ground. He should walk about in a hairshirt, unarmed and barefoot. Day and night he should bewail his sins and with tearful prayers seek grace from the Lord. He shall not enter the church, nor shall he accept the kiss of peace; he should abstain from meat and wine and copulation with his wife. He must not communicate as long as he is penitent, unless he should be stricken with terminal illness.[80]

Homo quidam (*c.*1155–65), an anonymous Anglo-Norman *ordines*, describes the nature of public penance needed to atone for homicide as seven years of fasting on water and bread without salt (*panem sine sale*) while sitting on the earth without a table; penitential whipping; and abstention from wine, mead, and malted ale.[81] It is undeniable that public penance of this nature shares a good deal with hard prison as it was employed in the king's prisons.

By the thirteenth century, public penance in a church-run prison had come to assume two distinct variations: *murus largus* ("light imprisonment") and *murus strictus* ("severe imprisonment"), sometimes described also as being placed *in stricto carcere* ("in severe prison").[82] *Murus largus* purportedly resembled life in a typical monastery. Institutional living with no license to leave, although prisoners were permitted to converse among themselves and move about inside the prison and there was a general willingness of authorities to permit visitors entry into the prison environment. Most importantly, the sentence was finite. *Murus strictus* was another beast altogether. It has been called the medieval equivalent of a maximum-security prison, or even solitary confinement. Bernard Hamilton explains that the practice was likely modeled on the lifestyle of the

[79] Bernhard Fehr, ed., "Teile aus Ælfrics Priesterauszug," in *Die hirtenbriefe Ælfrics in altenglischer und lateinischer fasung* (Hamburg: Verlag von Henri Grand, 1914), 243.

[80] Fehr, ed., "Teile aus Ælfrics Priesterauszug," 246; translated by Brad Bedingfield, "Public Penance in Anglo-Saxon England," *Anglo-Saxon England* 31 (2002): 235.

[81] Pierre Michaud-Quantin, ed., "Un manuel de confession archaïque dans le manuscrit Avranches 136," *Sacris Erudiri* 17.1 (1966): 23–4.

[82] Megan Cassidy-Welch, *Imprisonment in the Medieval Religious Imagination, c. 1150–1400* (Basingstoke: Palgrave Macmillan, 2011), 64.

stylite saints, early Christian ascetics who lived on pillars high up in the air and endorsed the notion that extreme mortification of the body offered a more expedient route to salvation.[83] *Murus strictus* typically involved life imprisonment, described as "perpetual penance," in a single cell "of the smallest size and worst description, dark and unsavoury," forbidden all visitors except spouses, and sentenced to chains and iron fetters binding the feet, the only sustenance on offer "the bread of sorrow and the water of tribulation."[84] *Murus strictus* was typically reserved for those whose offense had been particularly scandalous. For example, in 1226 a monk of Jouy found himself sentenced to perpetual imprisonment of the worst kind for threatening to kill his abbot with a razor.[85]

In Christian penitential theology, punishment of the body results in purification of the soul. Thus, the intent behind such a brutal form of incarceration was not so much revenge as reform, sacrificing the prisoner's earthly life in an effort to salvage the prospect of an afterlife in heaven. The spiritual overhaul envisioned by the creators of *murus strictus* was commendable, yet it was not without problems. Penance is most effective when undertaken voluntarily. To return to the case of Robert le Ewer mentioned briefly earlier, this is exactly what the anonymous chronicler of the *Vita Edwardi Secundi* was referring to when he declared that Robert's death by peine forte et dure was "a punishment fitting for his crimes and *healthy for his soul, provided that he bore it with resignation.*"[86] Christian penitential theology supports the notion that an individual cannot be compelled into penance against his will: one must accept one's fate, show contrition for past sins, and believe that the suffering one is undergoing will make one worthy of reconciliation with God. Forcing it upon the impious in the hopes of eventual acceptance and submission before God might well be an act in futility. However, the medieval English believed compelled penance might have some benefits. As *Homo quidam* acknowledges, "[a] sinner

---

[83] Bernard Hamilton, *The Medieval Inquisition* (New York: Holmes and Meier Publishers, Inc., 1989), 53.

[84] Arthur Turberville, *Mediaeval Heresy and the Inquisition* (London: C. Lockwood and Son, 1920), 215; Cassidy-Welch, *Imprisonment*, 64.

[85] Megan Cassidy-Welch, "Incarceration and Liberation: Prisons in the Cistercian Monastery," *Viator* 32 (2001): 30.

[86] Italics are mine. Childs, ed., *Vita Edwardi Secundi*, 218–19.

should hold back from inflicting such physical correction upon himself by his own initiative, for when it is imposed by someone else it provokes shame and this shame," so the text argues, "forms part of the penance."[87]

While *murus strictus* began as punitive incarceration with a penitential mission, in the hands of the Languedocian inquisitors desperately battling the Cathar heresy, it evolved into a coercive measure, not long before prison forte et dure made its first appearance in legislation. How else were they to pressure the uncooperative masses into providing evidence against friends and family who belonged to the Cathar heresy, or to confess themselves? Ecclesiastical authorities did not sanction the use of torture for interrogation until 1252 under Pope Innocent IV; yet even after this watershed moment, inquisitors were hesitant to employ torture except in extreme circumstances. They generally preferred to subject reluctant witnesses to extended periods of hard prison than rely on instruments of torture.[88] Inquisitorial treatises of the era acknowledge the psychological benefits of hard prison. *De inquisitione hereticorum*, penned by German mystic David of Augsburg (d.1271), recommends breaking the will of fractious witnesses through time in solitary confinement on a reduced diet, explaining that: "[t]he fear of death and the hope of life [will] quickly soften a heart that could otherwise hardly be moved."[89] In his *Practice Inquisitionis*, Bernard Gui (d.1331) made a similar observation: "Imprisonment – coupled if necessary with hunger, shackles, and torture – could ... loosen the tongues of even the most obdurate." Gui also endorsed solitary confinement to shake their confidence, because "suspects housed together could encourage one another to remain silent."[90] When imposed as a punishment, however, *murus strictus* was earmarked for heresiarchs and Cathar priests. This is reflected in the numbers. In early fourteenth-century Toulouse, 3.2 percent of penitents were sentenced to *murus strictus*; 57.6 percent to the more relaxed *murus largus*.[91]

---

[87] As cited in Rob Meens, *Penance in Medieval Europe, 600–1200* (Cambridge University Press, 2014), 211. *Homo quidam* can be found in Michaud-Quantin, ed., "Un manuel de confession archaïque," 5–54.

[88] James Given, *Inquisition and Medieval Society: Power, Discipline, and Resistance in Languedoc* (Ithaca: Cornell University Press, 1997), 54.

[89] Given, *Inquisition*, 54.   [90] Given, *Inquisition*, 54–5.

[91] Andrew Roach, "Penance and the Making of the Inquisition in Languedoc," *Journal of Ecclesiastical History* 52.3 (2001): 426.

Admittedly, detailed evidence of the practice of *murus strictus* in the English church in the period leading up to the 1275 statute that officially sanctioned hard prison is scanty, but it does exist. For example, a letter written by Roger, Bishop of Worcester to Gilbert Foliot, Bishop of London, in 1165 seeks advice regarding a group of heretics who had entered into his diocese. Foliot's response was to arrest them and put them in solitary confinement with imprisonment of "moderate severity" until they could decide exactly what should be done with them. "But in the meantime you should hold them separately, lest together they persevere in wicked conversation ... softening them with warnings, and scaring them with threats and fear of punishment, and in the meanwhile curbing with whips and lashings with moderate severity."[92] During his time in office as Archbishop of Canterbury, Boniface of Savoy (d.1270) recommended the "perpetual penance" of *murus strictus* for "ungracious clerks, taken in crime or convicted," who are "so malicious or incorrigible and so accustomed to mischief." Boniface was also responsible for requiring bishops to establish prisons in the first place; thus, the need for an environment conducive to *murus strictus* may well have been taken into consideration in the design and construction of episcopal prisons under his watch.[93]

It became the standard policy of the church that clerks who had confessed to a crime or were notorious or publicly defamed were banned from purgation; once delivered out of the hands of the king's officials, they were locked up in prison in perpetual penance.[94] A 1351 mandate issued by Simon Islip, Archbishop of Canterbury (d.1366), details the nature of the conditions under which they were to be incarcerated. They were to exist on a diet consisting solely of the bread of sorrow (*de pane doloris*) and the water of anguish (*aqua angustiae*), the same phrase noted above. When Islip explained what he meant by this, the phrase appears to translate out to six days of the week on bread and weak beer; but on the seventh day, because the

---

[92] Gilbert Foliot, *The Letters and Charters of Gilbert Foliot, Abbot of Gloucester (1139–48), Bishop of Hereford (1148–63), and London (1163–87)*, ed. Zachary Brooke, Adrian Morey, and Christopher Brooke (Cambridge University Press, 1967), 207–8.

[93] Pugh, *Imprisonment*, 135.

[94] This is spelled out in statute law in 1377; Pugh, *Imprisonment*, 49.

Sabbath should be honored, the prisoners might also partake in vegetables, providing they were contributed through alms or donations from their family members.[95] Those in bishops' prisons were also regularly shackled, and there does not seem to have been an ecclesiastical version of a *sewet*, that is, a fee paid in the king's prisons to have those shackles removed.[96]

These deprivations were not reserved solely for those sentenced to perpetual penance; indeed, they were shared also by the clergyman who was delivered to the ordinary as *clericus convictus*, that is a convicted clerk, having been tried by a jury in the king's courts and found guilty. Because clergymen were bound to be tried by the ordinary at a specially constituted ecclesiastical tribunal, the secular verdict was not considered valid. Yet, bishops did not hasten to command purgation (trial). As Alison McHardy has observed, it was normal to sit in a bishop's prison for years at a time awaiting one's purgation. Most often, terms of two, four, or six years were the norm; however, her study uncovered a number of individuals whose prison terms stretched out to seventeen, twenty-five, or even twenty-six years.[97] The length of time spent in prison before trial did not correspond to the nature of the crime; indeed, McHardy's study shows that the matter of punishment was "both illogical and haphazard." However, denying a cleric purgation upon entrance was deliberate. Time spent in prison was intended to be rehabilitative. Only after doing his time might a clergymen be considered eligible for purgation.[98] By 1352, perpetual penance applied also to all criminous clergymen who failed purgation, as mandated by the common-law statute *pro clero*.[99]

The English church also regularly employed some of the tactics of *murus strictus* as a coercive measure on the laity. Sanctuary-seekers

---

[95] David Wilkins, ed., *Concilia Magna Brittaniae et Hiberniae a Synodo Verulamensi anno 446 ad Londinensem 1717*, 4 vols. (London: R. Gosling, et al., 1685–1745), vol. III, 13–14.

[96] Margaret McGlynn, "Ecclesiastical Prisons and Royal Authority in the Reign of Henry VII," *Journal of Ecclesiastical History* 70.4 (2019): 760.

[97] Alison McHardy, "Church Courts and Criminous Clerks in the Later Middle Ages," in Michael Franklin and Christopher Harper-Bill, eds., *Medieval Ecclesiastical Studies in Honour of Dorothy M. Owen* (Woodbridge: Boydell, 1995), 172–3.

[98] McHardy, "Church Courts," 173 and 183.

[99] John Bullard and Chalmer Bell, eds., *Lyndwood's Provinciale: The Text of the Canons Therein Contained, Reprinted from the Translation made in 1534* (London: Faith Press, 1929), 144. *Statutum pro clero*, 25 Edw. III, c. 4 (1352), *SR*, vol. I, 316–18.

were permitted thirty-nine days of shelter in any church, chapel, or cemetery, at which point they were expected either to confess and undergo trial in the king's court or abjure the realm. For those who overstayed their welcome, the church turned to the deprivations of *murus strictus*. In its justification of the practice, *Bracton* asks what else might be done in this situation. "I see no remedy except that food be denied him that he may come forth voluntarily and seek what he has scornfully refused, and that he who supplies food to him be deemed the king's enemy and one contemptuous of the peace."[100] The fifteenth-century Chancery bill of the tailor John from Kent of Winchester clarifies that some laymen merited the full rigors of *murus strictus*. From a cell in the Bishop of Winchester's prison at Wolvesey castle, he complained that he was "most straightly kept," loaded with "as much irons as he may bear and more" and deprived of the company of his wife and friends, all "to the jeopardy of his life."[101]

Several points are critical here. First, the penitential origins of hard prison indicate that the practice is in fact much older than recognized to date. Incarceration in solitary confinement in nakedness, on a fasting diet, deprived of all comforts, with or without the addition of a hairshirt or shackles, was imposed on sinners and criminals long before the 1275 statute. Second, the objective of incarceration, as the church devised it, is spiritual rehabilitation. Recognizing this has a profound impact on historical interpretations of the function of prison/peine forte et dure. Again, this aspect will be explored in greater detail in Chapter 4. Finally, this history helps us to sever the psychological link between England and hard prison. In the minds of most legal historians, hard prison and peine forte et dure are integrally associated with English history. As such, these practices have presented a puzzle to historians who fail to understand how they align with thirteenth-century England's larger legal reform program. Acknowledging that hard prison did not originate in England, and that variations of it existed across Europe in ecclesiastical prisons and also in some secular prisons helps us to put England back into a European context and forces us to realize that English common law does not hold all the answers to this puzzle.

---

[100] *Bracton*, vol. II, 383.
[101] TNA C 1/184/22, Kent v. Bishop of Winchester (1493–1500).

Hard Prison in Context

How horrific was the experience of hard prison? Any assessment of hard prison must gauge its privations against the more typical experience of prison. This means first expunging the virulent mythology that surrounds medieval incarceration. In the Middle Ages we see regularly on the big screen, *all prison* is hard prison. Prisoners are cast into damp, dark dungeons, replete with shackles, gruel, and rats for company. If the normal prison experience in medieval England had been that horrendous, then hard prison would not have been all that effective as a coercive measure. Moreover, medieval prisons had a different purpose than do prisons today. In the modern West, most crimes are punished with incarceration. Prison thus exists chiefly as a form of punishment. This is not true of the European Middle Ages, in which the majority of prisoners were incarcerated awaiting trial. Convicted felons were never lodged in medieval jails because when a jury voted unanimously to convict, the defendant was escorted directly to the gallows for execution. Of course, prisons did contain some convicted petty thieves, vagrants, and debtors, but most inmates were suspects awaiting trial and likely to be acquitted. My point is that prisoners in general were not necessarily the kind of hardened criminals one might be inclined to lock up in a dungeon and throw away the key. Indeed, the fact that the vast majority of felons fled the scene of the crime implies that those who stuck around for trial were often innocent, or repentant and thus hopeful that their neighbors would give them a second chance and not convict.

That prison was *not* as horrific as movies and television make it out to be is substantiated by the fact that the French public insisted that prisoners be permitted to eat their meals at tables like ordinary human beings.[102] Evidently, there was a desire to maintain some semblance of normal life. Secular jails were housed in castles or city gates, the only highly fortified buildings in the English landscape. The setting meant that they did not have the same kind of institutional feel as prisons do today, but they were still rigorously organized. The Fleet prison in London in many respects represents the medieval ideal. The prison was divided into

---

[102] Patricia Turning, "The Right to Punish: Jurisdictional Disputes between Royal and Municipal Officials in Medieval Toulouse," *French History* 24.1 (2010): 11.

six wards: (1) the barons' ward (for the wealthy), (2) the women's ward,
(3) the two-penny ward (that is, where accommodations cost two penny
a night), (4) the beggars' ward (accommodations were free), (5) Bolton's
ward (the most fortified section of the prison where dangerous felons
could be bolted to walls or floors), and (6) the tower chambers (for
political prisoners).[103] Quality of life in prison differed considerably
depending upon the ward in which a person was housed. For the price
of two shillings, four pence per week, prisoners lodged in the barons'
ward had separate rooms with use of a parlor and servants to attend to
their needs; and friends could come and go as they pleased. Affluent
inmates might even find incarceration conducive to writing, as the
works of Sir Thomas Wyatt, Henry Howard Earl of Surrey, and Sir
Thomas More would seem to suggest.

Margery Bassett tells us, "[s]o 'unprisonlike' was the atmosphere
that the warden was forbidden to arm his officers unless he suspected
a plot to escape was brewing."[104] Excessive use of irons by prison
guards was also grounds for dismissal.[105] Guards shackled only two
types of prisoners: (1) those whom the jailer feared might escape, and
(2) those who could not afford to pay the *sewet*. Irons secured the legs,
but also sometimes the neck.[106] Regulations governing the practice
required wardens to charge a "reasonable *suwette*."[107] What was
considered reasonable though was not the same across the board.
The keeper of Winchester jail in 1358 charged a one-time fee of five
pence.[108] The prison code of Coventry issued in 1515, designated two
pennies as an acceptable sum, while the keeper of the county jail of
Somerset charged one shilling a week for his prisoners to be free from
irons.[109]

As these rates should suggest, the costs associated with prison were
the greatest hardship. The Crown's strategy for funding penal
institutions was to shift the burden of the expenses onto the backs of
those housed in the facilities. The Crown appointed sheriffs to assume
responsibility for the prisons within their jurisdictions. Sheriffs, in

---

[103] Margery Bassett, "The Fleet Prison in the Middle Ages," *The University of Toronto Law Journal* 5 (1944): 393.
[104] Bassett, "Fleet Prison," 398.   [105] Rose, "*Feodo de Compedibus*," 78.
[106] TNA C 1/64/356, Comford v. JPs of York (1475–80, or 1483–5).
[107] Rose, "*Feodo de Compedibus*," 80.   [108] Pugh, *Imprisonment*, 179.
[109] Pugh, *Imprisonment*, 170 and 180.

turn, retained jailers whose positions were either low-paid or unpaid. Jailers expected to support themselves out of the monies tendered by prisoners for a wide variety of fee payments, although select fees were funneled directly to Crown revenues. The costs associated with incarceration were multiple and varied. Prisoners doled out cash for every expense imaginable. There were entry fees, which included a round of drinks for prison personnel to celebrate one's arrival in prison and tips for the chamberlain, porter, and jailer, as well as fees for meals and bedding; wood for a fire; candles for light; a bond for good behavior, another for the removal of iron shackles; and of course a discharge fee upon deliverance. Rates were based upon one's ability to pay, with differential pricing for lords, knights, gentry, ordinary folk, and beggars. Indicted felons paid their expenses out of their confiscated properties – under rules of felony forfeiture, upon arrest indicted felons had their private property confiscated to the king. In practice, this meant that the king's escheator sold the movables and the monies garnered from their sale supported the inmate until trial. The remainder was returned upon acquittal, providing the defendant had never fled the king's justice.

Not everyone was happy with this system.[110] The *Mirror of Justices*, written on the heels of the crisis of 1289 that led to the wholesale dismissal of Edward I's array of justices and ministers, presents the most utopian vision of all the treatises. Its author rejects the notion that prisoners should be charged for anything other than basic amenities. In particular, it decries entrance and exit fees as an abuse.[111] *Britton* also speaks of the dangers of exit fees, grousing about prisoners whose sentences dragged on because they could not meet their financial obligations.[112] *Britton* advocates fees of a reasonable nature, declaring that prisoners should not be expected to pay more than four pence altogether, and that the poor should be exempt

---

[110] A late medieval sermon complains: "Now they are taken to the king's bench, now they are hurled into Marshalsea, and although they may be worth twenty or forty pounds before they come into their custody, these tricks and deceits shall bring such a writ of *Nichil Habet* on their heads that they are not left with a single penny." Patrick Horner, ed., *A Macaronic Sermon Collection from Late Medieval England: Oxford MS Bodley 649* (Toronto: PIMS, 2006), 182. *Nichil Habet* is a return made by the sheriff on a *scire facias* or other such writ indicating that the defendant has no property.

[111] Whittaker, ed., *Mirror of Justices*, 160.   [112] Nichols, ed., *Britton*, vol. I, 46–7.

entirely.[113] The treatise either proposed or reflected contemporary ideals: Newgate prison was limited to collecting four pence from its prisoners when regulation of fees began in 1346.[114] Periodic amendment to municipal guidelines concerning the scope of prison fees and their approved rates, as well as repeated attempts to eliminate entry and exit fees, substantiate that the regulation of prison fees was a widespread concern.

Inmates were not left to starve in prison because they could not afford to buy food. Poorer prisoners relied heavily upon charity. Because assisting prisoners fulfilled four of the seven Corporal Acts of Mercy (to feed the hungry; to give drink to the thirsty; to clothe the naked; to visit the imprisoned), regular charity was forthcoming. Assistance from bequests, parish fundraisers, royal alms, and individual donations were supplemented in a variety of ways. At times, jailers released impoverished prisoners to beg for alms in the marketplace during the day. For suspected felons who needed to be secured, prison wardens had to resort to unconventional practices. For example, in fourteenth-century Colchester, they chained prisoners to poles outside the moothall to beg during the day. Prisoners might support themselves in a variety of other ways. In Coventry, prisoners continued to work in their own trades at the prison to fund their upkeep.[115] The Fleet in London authorized some debtors to pernoctate, meaning, to go about their own business each day, spending only their nights in prison.[116] Charity on a larger scale was also sometimes organized by the city. In London, confiscated food that violated ordinances controlling weight, packing, and freshness was sent to Newgate to feed the poor.[117] The outcome is that few people starved to death in prison, although they may have survived by eating stinking fish, stale loaves of bread, and watery ale.[118]

---

[113] Nichols, ed., *Britton*, vol. I, 46–7.   [114] Pugh, *Imprisonment*, 170.

[115] Helen Carrel, "The Ideology of Punishment in Late Medieval English Towns," *Social History* 34.3 (2009): 314–15.

[116] Jean Dunbabin, *Captivity and Imprisonment in Medieval Europe, 1000–1300* (New York: Palgrave, 2002), 96.

[117] Margery Bassett, "Newgate Prison in the Middle Ages," *Speculum* 18.2 (1943): 245.

[118] Guy Geltner, *The Medieval Prison: A Social History* (Princeton University Press, 2008), 102; Christine Winter, "Prisons and Punishments in Late Medieval London," (PhD Diss., Royal Holloway, University of London, 2012), 238.

Most of the evidence regarding living conditions inside prisons comes from complaints, which centered on deteriorating buildings, access to fresh water, poisonous vapors (that is, miasmas) that endangered the prisoners' welfare, and jail fever, an illness that periodically ravaged the prisons. Though, too much weight should not be accorded to criticisms voiced by prisoners and their families as decrying prison conditions was a popular means of challenging the political leadership of local authorities.[119] Dirty prisons filled with starving prisoners made a mayor look bad to his constituents. Recent studies surprisingly offer a relatively positive assessment of medieval prison conditions. In Venice, Florence, Bologna, and London, prison death rates were low.[120] Few prison deaths imply that actual conditions could not have been as bad as petitions imply. Christine Winter goes a step further to emphasize "[t]he complete absence of any reference to a violence-related death in [Newgate] prison is remarkable, especially considering the close proximity, the conditions and the potential for confrontation."[121] The general conclusion is that life in medieval prison was a "tolerable if unpleasant experience."[122]

The intention of this discussion is not to present a rosy image of prison life in the medieval era. Obviously, for anyone elderly or suffering from a health condition, incarceration was no picnic; and during cold and flu season, the lack of available healthcare together with the dense living conditions must have made them feel as if they were sitting ducks. Nonetheless, the experience was not as dire as is often portrayed in the popular media. Indeed, the very public nature of prison life in the Middle Ages acted as a safeguard to thwart seriously deteriorating prison

---

[119] Carrel, "Ideology of Punishment," 310.

[120] Geltner, *Medieval Prison*, 102; Winter, "Prisons and Punishments," 238.

[121] Winter, "Prisons and Punishments," 221.

[122] Geltner, *Medieval Prison*, 102. Having a reputation for decent living conditions was a source of pride for some wardens. Because wardenships generally stayed within families, family honor turned on running a respectable institution. In her study of prison conditions in southern France, Patricia Turning remarks upon the dedication of jailers and guards to keeping up appearances. In order to maintain the public's respect, they needed to "present themselves as both disciplinarian and humanitarian." Patricia Turning, "Competition for the Prisoner's Body: Wardens and Jailers in Fourteenth-Century Southern France," in Albrecht Classen and Connie Scarborough, eds., *Crime and Punishment in the Middle Ages and Early Modern Age: Mental-Historical Investigations of Basic Human Problems and Social Responses* (Berlin: De Gruyter, 2012), 286.

conditions. Here, a comparison between modern and medieval approaches to prison as an institution and its relationship with society is useful to consider. In the modern-day West, prisons are typically situated in isolated locations, away from prying public eyes, with strict regulations limiting outsiders' access to a room within the prison appointed specifically for the purpose of visiting. The implications of this arrangement are twofold. First, society is capable of hiding all evidence of nonconformity and immorality, such that prisoners are merely statistics to the rest of society rather than real persons in need of rehabilitation. Second, the conduct of prison wardens and guards takes place in a world beyond public scrutiny, relying chiefly on the moral rectitude of the warden to keep an orderly and humane prison that adheres to state regulation between supervisory visits. The medieval world would have judged modern prison conditions as being ripe for misuse. The public nature of medieval prisons was deliberate, founded on the ideal that the shameful nature of prison life functions as a visible deterrent to crime. As a result, penal institutions were located in highly central, urban locations, and prison life had a "porous flow" with inmates and visitors moving back and forth between prison and city.[123] Indeed, male prisoners' wives sometimes opted to relocate to prison with their husbands rather than support a household on their own. Most prisons did not supply meals at all, relying instead on the inmates' family members to bring them in at appointed times throughout the day. The constant presence of outsiders as visitors in the prison meant increased scrutiny and a steady flow of complaints dispatched to municipal authorities and the king.

None of this is to suggest that abuses of power did not happen in the prison environment. Under the wrong leadership, or with the employment of inept or cruel jailers, abuses happened, and the Crown's oversight was not proactive but reactive: it relied on complaint, rather than taking an active stance and regularly monitoring the conditions in prison. Both *Fleta* and the *Mirror of Justices* acknowledge the problems engendered by this approach. The cruelties singled out by the author of *Fleta* are disturbing: hanging by the feet, tearing out nails, and loading with irons, the final element obviously associated most closely with peine forte et dure.[124] Yet, the treatises make it just as clear that such behavior

---

[123] Turning, "Competition," 286.   [124] Richardson and Sayles, eds., *Fleta*, 68.

was unacceptable and was strenuously discouraged and punished. The *Mirror* adopts a strong stance, declaring "[t]he law wills that no one be placed among vermin or putrefaction, or in any horrible or dangerous place, or in the water, or in the dark, or any other torment."[125]

How does any of this help us to better understand hard prison? First, it provides a sense of the disparity between normal prison experiences and that of hard prison. For the poorly clothed beggar, accustomed to sleeping on straw-laden floors and relying on charity for sustenance, the leap from prison to hard prison was not as great as it was for the gentleman debtor, who continued to employ manservants and entertain guests in a drawing room. For both, as accustomed as they were to seeing prison as a vital and regular part of the larger community in which they had constant access to a support network that expanded well beyond one's family, the greatest adversity presented by hard prison was its isolation. Solitude alone was probably enough to prompt many reluctant defendants into a swift change of heart. Isolation had other benefits: it signaled the Crown's intolerance of disobedience to the suspect's family and friends. Punishment in the Middle Ages was about legal performance: typically, it was carried out in front of a great audience. Therefore, the assumption was that any punishment that took place in private must be truly horrific. Why else would it need to be hidden from public view? All of this implies that as a coercive measure, hard prison was probably effective enough for most prisoners to change their minds without having to include pressing with weights.

Second, the numerous complaints over the course of the period signal that men and women had set expectations regarding the quality of life in prison. There were limits to what a prisoner might endure. *The Mirror of Justices* insinuates that this was true also of peine forte et dure. The treatise denounced the practice, stating that "it is an abuse that a prisoner should be loaded with iron or put in pain before he is attainted of felony."[126] The treatise's author also spells out the spiritual implications. The overzealous jailer who kills "a man in prison by excessive pains when he is adjudged to do penance [peine forte et dure]" falls into the sin of homicide.[127]

---

[125] Whittaker, ed., *Mirror of Justices*, 52.
[126] Whittaker, ed., *Mirror of Justices*, 160; this statement is repeated in slightly different words on 185.
[127] Whittaker, ed., *Mirror of Justices*, 24.

Prison/Peine Forte et Dure as Punishment

Up to now, this chapter has dwelt on the fact that prison/peine forte et dure existed as a coercive measure, thus the fact that justices insisted on referring to it as a punishment (peine) is more than a little perplexing. Technically, it was not a punishment. When the medieval English punished felony, the impact was intended to be permanent: death, mutilation, exile. As a coercive measure, peine forte et dure was only temporary. The practice also put ultimate control in the hands of the defendant. As soon as he or she agreed to jury trial, the suffering came to an end. Nonetheless, the distortion in function apparent in the judges' labeling should not be overlooked. Was peine forte et dure sometimes employed specifically as a punishment?

To be clear, the language of the legal record declares that one was *sentenced* to suffer peine forte et dure by justices of jail delivery (*adiudicatur ad penam*) for refusing to participate in judicial proceedings. As Chapter 2 will address, justices probably understood peine forte et dure as an appropriate punishment for contempt. In addition, recognizing the prompt efficiency of the practice as a coercive device, over time jailers and royal justices branched out in its usage beyond those who refused to plead in felony indictments. In the following instances, there is good reason to see that peine forte et dure functioned simultaneously as both coercive measure and punishment for individuals whom the judiciary and prison wardens, if not always the legislature, held in especially low regard.

(1) Approvers

A career felon who turned king's evidence provided a valuable service to the Crown. By voluntarily appealing all his former criminal associates in exchange for his life, an approver's confession enabled the king to put to bed numerous cold cases with a minimum of effort. Professional criminals often operated out of gangs; their appeals, then, were a valuable crime-fighting tool, affording the Crown the means to reduce a gang's numbers and even stomp it out of existence. The Crown was enormously supportive of approvement: in the twelfth century, for example, the Crown expended "huge sums of money" on special king's approvers retained on a professional basis.[128] Eager to please their employers, jailers were also keen to persuade notorious felons under their care of the merits of turning approver. Complaints about jailer behavior expressed in parliamentary petitions suggests that zealousness led some jailers to draw on familiar practices, specifically those associated with hard prison.[129] Prisoners' stories make clear that withholding food and drink was a common tactic used by jailers on this quest.[130] At his trial for larceny at Salisbury, Robert the chandler of Somerset maintained that his keepers not only denied him food and drink, they also tied his hands behind his back for three days and nights.[131] In his petition to the chancellor, John Hanger and his three fellow complainants imprisoned at Lydford (Devon), purportedly "without any cause reasonable," alleged that they were being held in "a great and horrible dungeon of the said prison," deprived of light and "kept under the most cruel" conditions. The jailer regularly shackled and starved them. At the time of their writing this had been going on for a period of thirty weeks. The four complainants urged the chancellor to act swiftly, for they "fear that they be likely to perish."[132] In her 1495 complaint to Star Chamber, Alice, widow of William Tapton of Thoverton (Devon) claims her torment continued for twenty-four weeks, or so. She relates that when city officials came to arrest her, they beat her, dragged her out of her home by her hair and imprisoned her at Exeter. There she was fettered in leg irons weighing thirty pounds and more and tied up with a chain. During her time in prison, her jailer forbid her clothes or straw to lie on. She had no choice but to sleep on bare boards and when she asked for a surgeon to dress her wounds, her request was denied.[133]

None of these complainants were in prison because they refused to plead to a felony indictment; yet, the nature of their treatment is eerily

---

[128] Anthony Musson, "Turning King's Evidence: The Prosecution of Crime in Late Medieval England," *Oxford Journal of Legal Studies* 19.3 (1999): 471.

[129] John Bellamy, *The Criminal Trial in Later Medieval England* (University of Toronto Press, 1998), 41.

[130] Musson, "Turning King's Evidence," 470.

[131] TNA JUST 3/156 m. 5 (1366), as cited in Musson, "Turning King's Evidence," 470.

[132] TNA C 1/319/23, Hanger v. Furse (1504–15).

[133] Isaac Leadam, ed., *Select Cases before the King's Council in the Star Chamber, Commonly Called the Court of Star Chamber* AD1477–1509, 2 vols. (SS, vols. XVI and XXV, 1903–11), vol. I, 51–2.

similar to what we see in sentences of peine forte et dure. Either they
fabricated their narratives with that experience in mind; or, they were
being tormented for other reasons with the methods a jailer already
had at his disposal. The Crown did not sanction this usage of prison
forte et dure. This is made clear in its response to prisoners' complaints.
In 1326–7, Edward II initiated an inquiry into jailers who manhandled
prisoners in order to persuade them to turn king's evidence. The Crown
not only listened to prisoners' grievances, but it assigned commissions
to investigate instances in which prison forte et dure was imposed
without judicial sanction. In December of 1379, a commission of
oyer and terminer was tasked with inquiring into the complaint of
John of Kingston, prior of Sandwell, who complained that he had been
assaulted, held hostage, and subjected to prison forte et dure against his
will by eight of his fellow clergymen. The purpose of the attack was
extortion: once he agreed to renounce his estate and possessions and
revoke all proceedings in Court Christian against the abbot of
St. Peter's, one of his attackers, and bind himself over in the sum of
£200 should he retract his consent, his jailers permitted him to go
free.[134]

What is not clear is whether the judiciary covertly supported this
behavior. Presumably, when jailers' unorthodox methods resulted in
a conviction without complaint, they were approving. However, there
is good reason to think that justices wanted penance applied with
restraint. The 1290 conviction of Richard of Harlow (*de Herlawe*)
makes this point. As a servant to the jailer John Gille (since
deceased), Richard was held responsible for the death of one of his
prisoners, Philip Lauweles of Ireland. Richard kept Philip in such
"grave pressing penance" (*gravum pena constrictus*) that he died
his second day in prison. Richard was immediately arrested for
homicide and imprisoned also at Newgate, presumably a dreadful
experience for a former prison guard.[135] Despite being incarcerated
for suspected homicide, Richard sought bail on the grounds that he had
been indicted out of hate and spite (*de odio et atya*). The investigation
into his claim resulted in one of the rare instances in which the jury
dissented with the prisoner who footed the bill for the inquest. The jury
declared that Richard was wholly guilty:

---

[134] *CPR*, Richard II, vol. 1 (1377–81), 423.   [135] TNA JUST 1/547A, m. 6d (1290).

he held the prisoner out of malice and true ferocity with chains and iron devices, to the extent that the neck of the aforesaid Philip was broken by the extreme pressure and constriction of those chains and devices, and the bones of the back of the aforesaid Philip were broken through the middle. They [the jurors] say also that the aforesaid Richard, in order to produce a greater injury in the aforesaid Philip and in order to hasten his death more greatly, seated himself on the neck of the aforesaid Philip.[136]

The jury's verdict was not the final word on the matter; it merely resulted in Richard being denied bail. Given the jury's uncommonly tough stance, it comes as no surprise that Richard's trial jury also found him guilty, and he was hanged. Richard of Harlow's punishment makes clear that a sentence of peine forte et dure was not an excuse for prison wardens and their officials to torture a prisoner mercilessly. Both justices and jurors expected prison staff to adhere to standards that did not include such inhumane treatment as sitting on the prisoner's neck.

Nonetheless, it is critical to acknowledge the elephant in the room: when immoral jailers employed these practices to coerce accused felons into confessing and turning approver, their activities were deemed reprehensible. Yet, when a defendant stood mute, the decree of a royal justice made that very same conduct commendable.

(2) Idlers

While the Crown did not endorse prison forte et dure as a punishment for approvers, idlers were another matter altogether. Legislators found infractions of the labor laws in the period after the Black Death so disconcerting that they turned to prison forte et dure as a solution. One of the unexpected outcomes of the pandemic was a serious workforce crisis in which laborers were in such great demand they could exploit their bargaining power by holding out for higher wages, regular pay, and better working conditions. When the aristocracy realized they had lost control of the workforce and risked either paying what they deemed to be excessive wages or having fields remain unplowed, they turned to the law, drafting the Statute of Laborers (1349), followed soon after by the Ordinance of Laborers (1351).

---

[136] C 144/30, no. 16 (August 1, 1290). Many thanks to Leslie Lockett of The Ohio State University for her assistance with this transcription and translation.

The objective of this two-pronged legislative attack on the newly empowered laborer was to return English labor relations to the pre-plague status quo. As Lawrence Poos writes, the laws were "enacted by a Parliament comprised of magnates and gentry with strong vested interests in maintaining an assured supply of cheap labour for production on their own manorial demesnes."[137] Doing so required an "unprecedented intervention" by the Crown in labor relations, traditionally left to the local courts to regulate.[138] Although the legislation of 1349 preserved the authority of local elites, the 1351 follow-up handed jurisdiction to the central courts. Expansion of the Crown's dominion into a hitherto private area of law was greatly resented by the English populace. The "unmistakable tone of moral guardianship" evident in the legislation signaled also the early stages of a new social policy in which the English Crown began to intrude heavy-handedly into the daily lives of its subjects, including the kinds of clothes and food permitted according to social rank (sumptuary laws of 1336, 1337, 1363, 1463, and 1483), the variety of games and sports in which they engaged (the prohibition of tennis, quoits, dice, skittles, and football in legislation of 1351, 1388, 1410, and 1478), the kind of dogs they might own (a ban on hunting dogs by persons of low status in 1390), etc.[139]

Active resistance to the labor legislation resulted in widespread refusals to swear the compulsory oath to abide by the statutes' expectations. Constables compiled long lists of "rebellious" and "disobedient" laborers unwilling to take the oath.[140] Early enforcement efforts show the Crown intent on making its authority known. Between the years 1349 and 1359, the Crown appointed 671 men as "justices of labourers."[141] The vast majority of the penalties

---

[137] Lawrence Poos, "The Social Context of Statute of Labourers Enforcement," *L&HR* 1.1 (1983): 28.

[138] Paul Booth, "The Enforcement of the Ordinance and Statute of Labourers in Cheshire, 1349 to 1374," *Archives* 127 (2013): 1.

[139] Chris Given-Wilson, "Service, Serfdom and English Labour Legislation, 1350–1500," in Anne Curry and Elizabeth Matthew, eds., *Concepts and Patterns of Service in the Later Middle Ages* (Woodbridge: Boydell, 2000), 34–5.

[140] Bertha Putnam, *The Enforcement of the Statutes of Labourers: During the First Decade after the Black Death, 1349–1359* (New York: Longmans, Green and Co., 1908).

[141] Putnam, *Enforcement*, 20.

imposed for violations were fines, somewhere between forty pence and one pound, although the total amounts amassed per county per year are striking.[142] Colchester evidence for the year 1352 records 7,556 violations of the statute in the shire, amounting to a total collective fine of £719 10s.[143]

Members of parliament were particularly contemptuous of those who spurned offers of employment in search of something better. Hence, compulsory service for all under the age of sixty was one of the many requirements of the 1349 statute. Anyone who refused to work was to be incarcerated, "under strait keeping" until one might find a surety to guarantee one's future hard work.[144] What exactly was meant by "straight keeping" is not clarified in English law, although as the petition of the tailor John from Kent of Winchester above suggests, when he used the phrase to describe the conditions in the Wolvesey prison, it very much resembled peine forte et dure.[145] Here, the literature of the period helps us to fill in the gaps in the legal record. The "Plowing of the Half Acre" in William Langland's fourteenth-century poem *Piers Plowman* also hints that straight keeping was most likely peine forte et dure. Langland's poem is an extended commentary in narrative form on the new labor legislation by which Langland hoped to communicate his distaste for parliament's heavy-handed treatment of the poor. The 1349 statute effectively criminalized begging and homelessness. At the same time, it stipulated that charity must be qualified: anyone giving alms to the able-bodied poor risked imprisonment. Through satire, Langland aspired to remind his audience that hunger is no basis for a solid work ethic and that giving to the poor (*all* the poor, able-bodied or not) is a Christian duty. That "Piers Plowman" became a rallying cry and "in-group code language" for the rebels in the 1381 English Rising indicates that Langland's apprehensions were shared by a larger group.[146]

Passus VI begins with Piers and his new companions eager to see his half acre plowed so that they might embark on their collective pilgrimage. Everyone pitches in. Even the knight, who knows nothing

[142] Booth, "Enforcement," 7.   [143] Poos, "Social Context," 44.
[144] "The Statute of Labourers," 23 Edw. III, c. 1 (1349), *SR*, vol. I, 307.
[145] TNA C 1/184/22, Kent v. Bishop of Winchester (1493–1500).
[146] Michael Johnston, "William Langland and John Ball," *YLS* 30 (2016): 29.

about farming. Everything is going well – some are digging, others are pulling weeds – and then Piers spies some of his workers lazing about, cheering on the plow with a "ho trolley-lolley" while gulping down their ale. Piers instructs them to get back to work, but instead the wasters begin boldly to feign disabilities: some pretend to be blind; others claim to have missing limbs – an uncanny analogy to those who "feign muteness" before the courts. But Piers will not be fooled:

"If it be soth," quod Pieres, "that ye seyne, I shal it sone asspye. / Ye ben wastoures, I wote well, and Treuthe wote the sothe, / And I am his [holde] hyne and [aughte] hym to warne / Which thei were in this worlde his werkemen appeyred. / Ye wasten that men wynnen with travaille and with tene. / Ac Treuthe shal teche yow his teme to dryve, / Or ye shal ete barly bred and of the broke drynke."

   ("If what you say is so," said Piers, "I'll soon find out. / I know you're ne'er-do-wells, and Truth knows what's right, / And I'm his sworn servant and so should warn him /

   You waste what men win with toil and trouble. / But Truth shall teach you how his team should be driven, Or you'll eat barley bread and use the brook for drink[.]")[147]

With this passage, Langland is mocking the perception embraced by England's elites that vagrants and beggars are frauds: that is, they only pretend to be disabled because they prefer begging to hard work. Yet, in doing so, his passage sketches out what punishment awaits the waster: a diet of barley bread and brook water, an unmistakable allusion to the fasting diet reserved for those in hard prison.[148] Straight keeping, it would seem, was merely another term for prison forte et dure.

   A 1376 petition to parliament provides evidence to substantiate this link. Complaining of reluctant laborers, "staffstrikers"[149] and "fugitive servants whose names are not known," the petition demands that the punishment of the statute and ordinances be imposed; although, it is striking that in this instance, punishment is

---

[147] B.6. 129–35. William Langland, *Piers Plowman*, trans. Talbot Donaldson, ed. Elizabeth Robertson and Stephen Shepherd (New York: W. W. Norton and Company, 2006), 102–3.

[148] For a reference to "brook water," in particular, see Chief Justice Robert Danby's response to Robert Eypton in Chapter 3 of this book.

[149] According to *OED*, "a sturdy beggar, tramp."

described as *la penance*, as was typical of peine forte et dure. More important still, in describing what needs to be done with them, the petition encourages parliament to order their arrest and incarceration until they are prepared to return to their homes and labor according to the legislation. If they refuse to identify themselves by name, their masters by name, and also the hundreds and counties from which they had come, they should remain in prison on bread and water (*payne et ewe*).[150]

If members of parliament did indeed intend to inflict hard prison upon idlers and vagabonds, their scurrilous plans were undermined by officers of law enforcement, who only occasionally saw fit to sentence offenders to prison. For example, Putnam came across one instance of an offender incarcerated after a second infraction of receipt of excess wages who was adjudged to prison for forty days.[151] A similar reluctance to impose the full rigors of the law is evident also with the 1361 statute, in which parliament declared that monetary fines for violations were to be abolished (although reinstated the following year) and replaced with imprisonment and branding on the forehead with the letter "F" for falsity. No evidence exists to suggest that this brutal form of mutilation was ever carried out.[152] As a result, the legislation was never as effective an "instrument of social control" as members of parliament envisioned.[153]

(3)   Heretics

The rising popularity of Lollardy, an evangelical proto-Protestant sect energized by the writings of Oxford theologian John Wycliffe (d.1384), persuaded parliament to turn once again to hard prison. In 1382, in the aftermath of the English Rising, and believing the kingdom to be overrun by heretics openly preaching sacrilegious doctrine "to the great emblemishing of the Christian faith, and destruction of the law, and of the estate of the Holy Church, to the great perils of the souls of the people, and of all the realm of England," parliament recommended the arrest and incarceration of heretics in strong prison (*forte prisone*)

---

[150] John Strachey, et al., eds., *Rotuli Parliamentorum: ut et petitiones, et placita in parliamento*, 7 vols. (London: HMSO, 1767-77), vol. II, 340-1.
[151] Putnam, *Enforcement*, 83.   [152] Given-Wilson, "Service, Serfdom," 27-8.
[153] Poos, "Social Context," 36.

until "they will justify themselves according to the law and reason of Holy Church."[154] This was a short-lived experiment: the subsequent parliament nullified the statute, presumably because of the number of high-status individuals in good standing with the king who were drawn to the idealism of this dynamic sect.[155] However, even if it was not sanctioned by statute, there is reason to believe that justices and jailers alike continued to see hard prison as appropriate to inflict on suspected Lollards. Thomas Payn of Glamorgan, a clerk and the chief counsellor to John Oldcastle, leader of a rebellion in the name of Lollardy, was imprisoned between 1419 and 1422. In his petition to parliament complaining of his treatment, he asserted that he had been "detained for a long time in a hard prison without indictment, impeachment or other reasonable cause, but by suspicion without being able to respond."[156]

(4)   Petty Thieves

The Statute of Westminster I (1275) was the first to define petty larceny, setting twelve pence, roughly the value of a sheep, as the firm boundary marking the distinction between trespass and felony.[157] One week's incarceration for every penny stolen was the most frequent penalty, although Ralph Pugh observed that forty-day sentences, mirroring the Lenten period, were also common.[158] The statute says nothing about the nature of the prison conditions tied to the sentence. Yet, it is noteworthy that the penitential language normally reserved for hard prison also appears in the legal record for myriad petty thefts of an egregious nature, implying that the judiciary interpreted parliament's measures as approving prison forte et dure, at their discretion. At the 1394 Nottingham jail delivery, John, servant of Walter Derlyng of South Carleton was tried for having stolen seven-penny worth of goods and chattels from Agnes Perker, also of South

---

[154] 5 Ric II, Stat. 2, c. 5 (1382), *SR*, vol. II, 25–6.
[155] Strachey, et al., eds., *Rotuli Parliamentorum*, vol. III, 141, item 53.
[156] TNA SC 8/24/1186, as cited in Maureen Jurkowski, "Henry V's Suppression of the Oldcastle Revolt," in Gwilym Dodd, ed., *Henry V: New Interpretations* (York Medieval Press, 2013), 125.
[157] Statute of Westminster I, 3 Edw. I, c. 15 (1275), *SR*, vol. I, 30.
[158] Pugh, *Imprisonment*, 27 and 30.

Carleton. Although the indictment described him as having done so "feloniously," at seven pence his offense did not rise to the level of serious crime. When the jurors delivered a guilty verdict, they also recognized the small value of the goods he had stolen. For his punishment, justices declared that he should be returned to prison, "to have his penance" (*pro penitentia sua habenda*).[159] Justices may have meant simply that he should use his time in prison to think carefully about his misconduct and strive to lead a more Christian life. This perception, however, is undermined by usage: in the jail delivery rolls, when scribes inserted the term penance it invariably refers to hard prison. This case is not an anomaly. Justices sent many others off to prison "to have their penance" in similar cases of petty theft.[160]

Why would petty thieves have been candidates for hard punishment? Medieval society particularly despised any act that incorporated premeditation and secrecy. Those characteristics pushed a killing over the edge from simple homicide into the realm of murder. For jurors, an assault turned fatal in hot blood might easily be justified as an impulsive act, quickly regretted, and unlikely to reoccur; whereas, a planned homicide, in which the perpetrator lay in wait for his victim under the cover of night betrayed a calculating and disturbed mind that might not easily be rehabilitated. Jurors' fear of secret crime and their desire to thwart recidivism led them to convict murderers at a much higher rate than regular homicides. Theft was much more likely than homicide to involve premeditation and secrecy. With the dense living of medieval society, a good thief had to choose his time well in order to carry it out without witnesses. Not to mention, selling the proceeds of thievery added yet another layer of deception. While the offense was not egregious enough to reach the level of a felony, justices wanted a stiff punishment to discourage future lapses in behavior. If his short-lived stint in jail included elements of hard prison – presumably just enough to nudge him into a spiritual reform without also endangering his life – surely he

---

[159] TNA JUST 3/177, m. 52 (1394).
[160] Among others, see: TNA JUST 3/177, m. 68 (John of Howden, 1389); JUST 3/177, m. 76d (William Clerk, 1391); JUST 3/164, m. 17d (John Mason, 1378); JUST 3/164, m. 22 (John Stodham, 1382); JUST 3/185, 18 (Thomas Stede of Willougby, 1398).

might think twice before pocketing his neighbors' possessions in the future.

Peine Forte et Dure as Capital Punishment

Blackstone contends that the fifteenth century saw peine forte et dure morph from coercive measure to capital punishment. Specifically, he dates the transition to the 1406 arraignment of two indicted felons accused of robbery, a case that appears in the year books with an animated courtroom discussion full of conflict and lawyerly banter. Blackstone sees this moment as a turning point in the history of hard prison; instead of "continuing until he answered, it was directed to continue until he die."[161] After 1406, pressing became an especially gruesome form of execution, but one that suspected felons willingly endured to protect their heirs. It is only recently that historians have begun to question Blackstone's timeline. Andrea McKenzie, for example, observes that pressing retained both functions in eighteenth-century England: while justices sometimes assigned pressing as a form of capital punishment, they also continued to employ it as a coercive measure, when the situation called for it.[162] This leads us to question whether the 1406 case was in fact the defining moment that it has traditionally been regarded to have been.

While Blackstone may have inflated the impact of the 1406 arraignment, he was correct in seeing the case as groundbreaking. The dialogue between sergeants and pleaders represents the first serious deliberation of hard prison as a form of capital punishment that made its way into print. Faced with two indicted felons who adamantly refused to plead, Chief Justice William Gascoigne ordered the marshal to send them to their penance, and return the goods to the appellor. Here, we are fortunate enough to have Gascoigne define what precisely he meant by penance: the defendants should be placed

in various low dungeons and that they should lie on the ground naked except for their arms, and that they should put upon each of them as much iron and weight as they could bear, so that they could not lift it, and that they should have no food or drink except the worst bread that could be found and from the worst place near the gaol door running water, and on the days they had bread

---

[161] *Blackstone*, vol. IV, ch. 25.   [162] McKenzie, "'This Death'," 279–313.

they would have no water and *vice versa*, and that they should lie thus *until they were dead.*[163]

This grim sentence launched the assembled justices and pleaders into a debate about the role of hard prison in the English judicial system. Sergeant Robert Hill saw the suspected thieves' refusal to plead as contempt of court; accordingly, he declared that "penance unto death, so that it is a judgment of life and limb" should be their punishment. At this point, the older and wiser chief justice interjected to clarify that peine forte et dure "cannot be called a judgment of life and limb, for it may happen that they stay alive for several years, despite such a penance."[164] Moreover, as Sergeant Richard Norton reminded his colleagues, only felony merits a judgment of life and limb and disobedience to the law was not a felony, nor had these two, in fact, been convicted of a felony.[165] As such, he reminded his colleagues that peine forte et dure was not a punishment in the traditional sense.

Why Blackstone and other legal scholars after him saw this case as a watershed moment is easy to understand. Even if the assembled lawmen concluded that hard prison was not a death sentence, the dialogue makes it clear that this was merely a technicality: whether it was death on the gallows or death in prison, the end result was all the same. When exactly this change in policy occurred is not clear, but there is reason to believe justices had come to see the potential for peine forte et dure to function as a death penalty long before 1406. As early as 1329, the year books include an instance of justices condemning an accused felon to penance "unto death." In this instance, the defendant did not stand mute: in fact, he agreed to jury trial, but then immediately began challenging the composition of the jury. Chief Justice Scrope warned him that if he refused three full arrays he would be condemned to both the fasting diet and pressing with weights, and that this punishment would "continue until he died." Of course, this is exactly how it all played out.[166] Language of this type appears also in the

---

[163] Italics are mine. Alfred Kiralfy, ed., *Source Book of English Law* (London: Sweet and Maxwell Limited, 1957), 15. YB, Mich. 8, Hen. 4, fos. 1b-2b (Seipp 1406.101).

[164] Kiralfy, ed., *Source Book*, 16 (Seipp, 1406.101).

[165] Kiralfy, ed., *Source Book*, 14–16 (Seipp, 1406.101).

[166] Donald Sutherland, ed., *The Eyre of Northamptonshire, 3–4 Edward III (1329–1330)*, 2 vols. (SS, vols. XCVII and XCVIII, 1983), vol. I, 179 (Seipp 1330.325ss).

formal records from the same era. A 1336 London coroner's roll remarks that Hugh le Bevere (or Benere) died in Newgate prison after refusing to plead to charges of uxoricide. The justices assigned to his case remanded him to prison to "remain in penance until he died."[167]

Yet, there exists also evidence to the contrary. Deaths in prison were subject to coroners' inquests, but very few investigations seem to have centered on deaths brought about by peine forte et dure.[168] Naturally, because the primary task of these inspections was to exonerate the warden of abusive behavior, it is possible that coroners' reports failed to mention the circumstances of the prisoner's death because they were not relevant to his mission. Thus, the myriad deaths in prison tersely recorded in the coroners' rolls may conceal examples of deaths by penance. Coroners may also have recorded the cause of death as natural: after all, death is the natural result of a starvation diet. Of course, it is equally possible that justices appreciated both functions of peine forte et dure: as capital punishment and as coercive device. There are numerous examples of hard prison as coercive measure after 1329. As late as September of 1373, the Crown permitted John Tailor of Monmouth to turn approver after his brief exposure to the horrors of *penitentia*.[169] Presumably in instances like this, the decision was made at the justices' discretion, much as Andrea McKenzie discovered in her eighteenth-century sample.

Conclusion

When the English adopted prison forte et dure in the thirteenth century, they did so out of a sense of necessity. Without a means to coerce suspects into pleading at their arraignments, the prisons risked dangerously filling beyond their capacity. Prison forte et dure, then, was a coercive measure, existing within a system founded on the concept that coercion is the normal means to enforce compliance with the law. Isolation, confiscation of property, and bodily restraint were all standard tools of justice, and the necessary context into which hard prison must be inserted. When the practice first emerged, the

---

[167] Reginald Sharpe, ed., *Calendar of Coroners' Rolls of the City of London, AD 1300–1378* (London: R. Clay and Sons, Limited, 1913), 177–8.

[168] This study uncovered only fourteen instances in the coroners' rolls.

[169] TNA JUST 3/161, m. 11 (1373).

focus was on deprivation along penitential lines in order to turn the mind: fasting, isolation, and a loss of all comforts formed the corpus of tactics employed by jailers. Over time, pressing with weights (in moderation) was added to the mix of possibilities. In this respect, there is no rigid distinction between prison forte et dure and peine forte et dure, nor is one a scribal corruption of the other. The terms themselves were rarely used in the period and were probably considered interchangeable.

The penitential origins of the practices employed in hard prison are critical. Chapter 4 will return to this discussion, to underscore that hard prison was a form of public penance in a world where penitential justice was the norm. Yet, peine forte et dure might have different meanings to different people. Legislators may have viewed the peine as a form of penance with a public utility; jailers, however, may have been more attracted to its punitive role. This is especially apparent in those instances in which justices and jailers experimented with usage of peine forte et dure outside the normal parameters, specifically for approvers, idlers, heretics, and petty thieves. By the fourteenth century, hard prison grew also into a form of capital punishment. However, the evidence implies that justices, upon their own discretion, continued to use peine forte et dure as a coercive measure when it best suited them.

2

Standing Mute in the Courts of Medieval England

> Which bed, because it shall not speak of your pretty encounters, /
> Press it to death: away.
>
> Pandarus, in William Shakespeare's *Troilus and Cressida*,
> 3.2.206

> O, I am pressed to death through want of speaking.
>
> The Queen, in William Shakespeare's *Richard II*, 3.4.72

In *The Regement of Princes*, devised as a mirror for the future Henry V while he was still a boy, Thomas Hoccleve (1368–1426), a poet whose day job was as king's clerk in the office of the Privy Seal, held silence in the highest regard.

Who so þat hatiþ mochil clap or speche, / Qwenchiþ malice; and he þat his mouth kepiþ, / Keepith his soule, as þat þe bookës teeche. Vnbridlid wordës oftë man by-weepiþ; / Prudencë wakiþ whan þe tongë sleepiþ, / And slepith oftë whan þe tongë wakiþ ... Silence of tunge is wardein of good fame.

(Whosoever that has much noise or speech quenches malice; and he that keeps his mouth closed, keeps his soul, as the Bible teaches. Unbridled words often make man weep; prudence wakes when the tongue sleeps and sleeps often when the tongue is awake ... A silent tongue is the warden of a good reputation.)[1]

---

[1] Thomas Hoccleve, *Hoccleve's Works*. III. *The Regement of Princes* AD 1411–12, *from the Harleian MS. 4866, and Fourteen of Hoccleve's Minor Poems from the Egerton MS. 615*, ed. Frederick Furnivall (EETS, e.s., vol. LXI, 1897), 88.

Another clerk turned poet, George Ashby (c.1390–1475), clerk of the signet to King Henry VI (r. 1422–61, and 1470–1), and later steward to his wife, Queen Margaret of Anjou (d.1482), tendered similar advice. In a manuscript of his collected poems, composed towards the end of his life, he articulated carefully its benefits:

To be stille is more profit / Thanne to speke; & harme to speke more damage / Thanne to be stille, & grettir discomfit. / To speke litil, is knowen a man sage; / To speke meche, is knowen a man in Rage. / Whan a man spekith, his wit is knowen, / To be stille, doubte is how it shal be blowen.[2]

(To be silent is more useful than to speak; and speaking does more harm and damage, and greater discomfort, than to be silent. A wise man is known to speak little; an angry man is known to speak much. When a man speaks, everyone knows how smart he is. To be silent, there is still doubt.)

The message in these poems is clear: when in doubt, remain silent. With such high praise for silence coming from the pens of two Crown administrators, one of whom intended his advice specifically for the ears of a prince, it seems astonishing that the same does not hold true also in a court of law, at exactly that moment when speaking might well endanger one's soul, as Hoccleve alludes. If a defendant indicted of a felony confesses one's guilt at the arraignment, one's options are limited: (1) execution, or (2) turning approver, that is, trading knowledge of fellow accomplices for one's life, yet in doing so one risks dying an even more gruesome death through trial by combat. If one chooses deceit instead, denying involvement in the crime, one risks also eternal damnation by adding perjury, a serious crime and sin, to one's already overtaxed soul. Caught in this moral quagmire, silence would seem to be the best option. Yet, the English courts were averse to permitting a defendant to remain silent. For the king's justices, standing mute was the equivalent of refusing to plead, and without the defendant's consent to be tried by a jury of one's peers – signified by a denial of guilt and choice of jury trial – the court languished in a state of paralysis. The needs of the court, then, worked at cross-purposes with those of the defendant.

---

[2] Mary Bateson, ed., *George Ashby's Poems, edited from Two Fifteenth-Century Manuscripts from Cambridge* (EETS, e.s., vol. LXXVI, 1899), 98.

Peine forte et dure was the punishment for standing mute. Thus, we cannot understand how the English felt about peine forte et dure unless we better understand what it meant to stand mute and in what circumstances it applied. Many of our learned assumptions, founded on the legal treatises of the early modern era which are much more verbose on the subject of standing mute than their medieval counterparts, do not fit the medieval paradigm as neatly as we have come to expect. For example, while many have assumed that Blackstone's definitive statement that a suspect may not stand silent on appeal or when accused of treason can also be applied to the medieval era, the evidence of the medieval records suggest instead that these limitations were not in place from the very beginning, and although they had begun to develop by the end of the period, their application was erratic and subject to judicial discretion. Nonetheless, even if standing mute on charges of treason was permitted, it is clear that justices associated standing mute with contempt of the king.

The overarching purpose of this chapter is to outline the medieval process and underscore just how challenging it must have been for defendants to navigate the criminal justice system. For an Anglo-American audience accustomed to the adversarial criminal trial in which counsel for the prosecution and the defense star in a larger-than-life courtroom drama, the premodern criminal trial seems unfairly, perhaps even unconscionably, stacked against the defendant. A suspected felon had no right to assigned counsel; nor, it seems, could he or she call witnesses in defense.[3] A successful defense relied chiefly on the defendant's behavior in court. As John Beattie has written for a later era, "if he *were* innocent he ought to be able to demonstrate it for the jury by the character and quality of his reply."[4] One assumes the same logic applied in the medieval context. While suspected felons may not have had assigned counsel to assist them in planning a defense strategy, that does not mean they didn't have any strategy: because our silent suspects were intentionally deviating from the usual path, their digressions must be recognized as being part of a larger plan.

---

[3] John Baker, *An Introduction to English Legal History*, 5th edn. (Oxford University Press, 2019), 550–1.

[4] John Beattie, *Crime and the Courts in England, 1660–1800* (Oxford: Clarendon Press, 1986), 341.

What Does It Mean to "Stand Mute"?

Today, common-law courts treat standing mute on a felony indictment as a plea of not guilty. Not so, in medieval England. Pleading was a vital prerequisite; in its absence, the case could not proceed to trial. The author of *Fleta* (*c.*1290–1300), a thirteenth-century legal treatise, indicates that the defendant's plea plays a central role in arraignment procedure.

[A]nd if he will say nothing else by way of defence and the appellor pray judgement, then he will stand without defence for indeed no man may be constrained or instructed by the court [to choose] some particular defence. He shall not, however, be condemned to death but shall be committed to gaol, there to be safely kept, on a regimen, until he has learnt his lesson and asks leave to acquit himself of the charge according to the law. And this shall be his condition: he shall be clad in a single garment and be unshod and lying upon the bare earth, he shall for food but a quartern of barley bread every second day, not so that he shall eat daily but only every other day, nor shall he drink daily, but on the day when he does not eat, he shall drink only water. And this regimen shall be enjoined on all who refuse to abide by the law, until they seek that which formerly they contemned . . . . And if anyone of the aforesaid ask leave to answer and come to judgement, he must deny all felony and refute the words uttered against him in the order in which they were spoken in the appeal, and then he shall say 'And [to prove] that I am not guilty thereof, I put myself on a jury for good and ill.'[5]

Silence necessitated coercion because justice was at a standstill until the defendant willingly submitted to jury trial. The passage above also explains why this was the case: in essence, the court's refusal to proceed without explicit guidance from the defendant was intended as a protection of the defendant's legal rights.[6] No one can choose a defense for the defendant; that is the defendant's prerogative. Of course, the court's patience was not infinite. The defendant could not be permitted to buck the system and refuse the law altogether.

The author of *Fleta* also supplies the defendant with practical instructions on the proper means of pleading. Putting the author's advice in context of a typical arraignment helps to visualize the medieval process. England adhered closely to the ensuing model. The

[5] Henry Richardson and George Sayles, eds., *Fleta* (SS, vol. LXXII, 1953), 85.
[6] Chapter 3 will discuss in more detail the subject of a defendant's legal rights.

jailer escorted a suspected felon to court. A court in the medieval context
was not a place, that is, a room or even a hall appointed exclusively for
that purpose; rather, a court was an event held anywhere a judge sits.
Upon this occasion, the accused should look appropriately penitent:
barefooted, bareheaded, unbelted, wearing only a tunic. *Britton*
(*c.*1291–2) tells us that the accused was also to appear "without irons
or any kinds of bonds, so that [he] may not be deprived of reason by
pain, nor be constrained to answer by force, but of [his] own free will."[7]
Next, the king's justices, who bore a commission from the king to
deliver the jail of its involuntary occupants, summoned the prisoner to
the bar by calling his name. It was the defendant's responsibility to prove
his or her identity by raising a hand, a process that came to be known as
"evidence of the person," or *constat de persona*. One of the king's
justices then proceeded to read the indictment aloud in English, the
language of the masses, despite the fact that the majority of the court
proceedings would in fact transpire in insular French, England's
language of the law. As *Fleta* suggests above, the defendant needed to
grasp fully the charges levied against him or her, because the defendant
had to repeat the accusations word for word in denial. The defendant
was then asked, "how do you wish to acquit yourself?" At this moment,
the king's justices hoped to hear only one response: a flat denial of all
culpability, what was apparently known as a *thwert-ut-nay*, followed by
an expression of willingness to yield to jury trial. In the trial report
recorded in the jail delivery rolls, "he puts himself upon the country for
good or ill" is the phrase scribes traditionally employed to indicate the
defendant's readiness to be tried by jury.

The least popular option was to stand mute, an action that came to
be known as *nihil dicit* ("he says nothing"). Despite the nomenclature,
as we saw with the example of Margaret Clitheroe in the introduction
to this book, the act incorporated a number of potential responses,
expanding the scope well beyond silence. *Nihil dicit* broke down into
three categories of behavior:

(1) The defendant might choose to stand silently, feigning muteness
    with such efficiency that the sheriff was compelled to assemble

---

[7] Francis Nichols, ed., *Britton: An English Translation and Notes*, 2 vols. (Washington,
DC, 1901), vol. I, 29.

a jury of prisoners who had been housed closest in the jail to inquire whether they had heard the accused speak earlier that day while incarcerated and thus was now standing mute purposefully, or, he or she was in fact naturally mute (*mutum de natura*). The distinction was significant because standing mute out of malice (*ex malicia*) earned the accused time in prison subject to peine forte et dure, until the defendant decided to plead. Muteness by nature was another matter altogether, one that required leniency, not coercion.

(2) Standing mute might also imply failing to answer properly according to the common law. At a jail delivery in 1474, the king's attorney, William Hussey explains it in the following manner: "it is as if he [the defendant] said nothing, because it is all the same when he pleads a plea which is no answer according to the order of the law."[8] This was precisely what happened with Margaret Clitheroe. Margaret was anything but mute; rather, she contended that she had done nothing wrong and that whatever she had done it was for God alone to judge, thus rejecting altogether the monarch's role as God's anointed representative here on earth. Medieval men and women also pursued this tactic. John Norham of Harldsey, a shepherd accused of murdering his wife in 1415, told justices of jail delivery that he was in no way guilty of the crime, but that he altogether refused to verify this by a jury of the country according to the law and custom of the kingdom. Asked again how he wished to respond to the charges in a lawful way, he replied that he wished to say nothing. The scribe remarked that because he did not respond sufficiently at law to the question he was to be remitted to prison to peine forte et dure.[9]

(3) Since at least 1335, *nihil dicit* included also the excessive use of jury challenges.[10] Under common law, the defendant might challenge up to thirty-five jurors on the grounds of insufficiency. The need for a juror to be "free and lawful, impartial and disinterested,

---

[8] YB Trin. 14 Edw. IV (1474), fo. 7a (Seipp 1474.019).

[9] TNA JUST 3/199, m. 2d (1415).

[10] Richard of Beyton, a hatter, was in 1335 accused of slaying a man at New Salisbury. His accomplice was acquitted; but Richard instead began challenging jurors. After thirty-six, justices ordered him remanded to prison to endure peine forte et dure. TNA JUST 3/120, m. 6d (1335).

neither the enemies nor the too close friends of either litigant"
meant that jury challenges were a normal and wholly acceptable
part of the judicial process.[11] A defendant did not need to explain
the reason why he or she chose to dispute the legitimacy of
a particular juror. Nonetheless, defendants who challenged more
than thirty-five jurors were seen as simply trying to avoid trial
altogether, once again effectively refusing to submit to jury trial.
It was this avoidance of the law that led justices to categorize
defendants who challenged jurors in an undue manner as standing
mute.

Of course, judges only *sometimes* construed silence as a refusal to
plead. The nature of the crime as well as the venue in which it was tried
played a vital role in the court's interpretation of silence. In the
common-law courts, silence as a failure to plead was tied exclusively
to serious crime (*felonia*). In accusations of assault or petty theft –
despite the quasi-criminal nature of the acts, both were sued at law as
a species of trespass, a civil suit – justices considered a defendant's
silence to be an admission of guilt.[12] The same holds true with civil
suits in general. The year books record a 1316 suit of false judgment, in
which Sergeant Denom expounds that "he who keeps silence and will
not answer, will be held by the Court to have assented."[13] By 1481,
a pithy but memorable legal maxim had emerged. A suit in Common
Pleas centering on an annuity relating to a parish vicarage sees Justice
Guy Fairfax throwing about the phrase "silence presumes consent"
(*qui tacet consentire videtur*).[14] Naturally, the difference here lay in the
scope of the suit's consequences. A losing defendant in a civil suit is on
the hook for payment of a fine and damages; an indicted felon risks life
and limb. If either situation commanded lenience, surely it was the
latter.

To complicate matters further, the English church also read silence as
a confession. The Crown shared criminal jurisdiction with the church.[15]
Ecclesiastical tribunals regularly addressed crimes committed by or

---

[11] P&M, vol. II, 621.
[12] William Whittaker, ed., *The Mirror of Justices* (SS, vol. VII, 1893), 99.
[13] YB Mich. Edw. II (1316), fo. 52 (Seipp 1316.059ss).
[14] YB Pasch. 21 Edw IV (1481), fos. 33b–36b (Seipp 1481.060).
[15] Richard Helmholz, "Crime, Compurgation and the Courts of the Medieval Church,"
    L&HR 1.1 (1983): 1–26.

against the clergy, as well as those of a sexual nature (rape, sodomy, bestiality), and intra-familial crimes. Yet, unlike what occurred in the courts of common law, a sinner before the church courts who "contumaciously refused to answer" the charges leveled against him found his silence treated as an acknowledgment of guilt. The one minor qualification upon which canonists insisted is that it must be an "informed silence" if it was to be accepted as a confession.[16] Of course, the church also taught its members that electing to remain silent in a court of law is a mortal sin. Thomas Aquinas (d.1274) laid out the rationale behind this pronouncement by disclosing that a man who knew he was guilty, then "stood silently at the docket," committed a mortal sin because he did not admit to the truth.[17] The obligation stands even when doing so might lead to self-incrimination. Aquinas holds firm, noting that:

[w]hen the judge requires an accused person to respond to a charge against him, he is bound to reply, if it is done in accord with law, even though the response will convict him; his obligation to obey his superior overrules the obligation that he has against self-incrimination.[18]

As Aquinas explains it, silence in court is permissible only when the judge neglects to follow proper procedure, for example, if he attempts to prosecute a crime in the absence of an accuser or public infamy.[19] This loophole, of course, was critical given the number of Christian martyrs, including the faith's central figure, whose silence in court functioned as resistance to tyranny and a rejection of the court's or the judge's jurisdiction.

As the phrasing above implies, canonists grouped silence with contumacy, such that standing mute was considered a form of nonattendance at court. Hence, a man who stood mute in an ecclesiastical court was treated as if he had failed to appear in answer to a summons. In canon law, flight was also construed as a confession of guilt.[20] In this aspect Continental judges tended to follow suit. Those

---

[16] Ansgar Kelly, "The Right to Remain Silent: Before and After Joan of Arc," *Speculum* 68.4 (1993): 998.

[17] Charles Nemeth, *Aquinas on Crime* (South Bend, IN: St Augustine's Press, 2008), 117.

[18] Kelly, "Right to Remain Silent," 1002.   [19] Kelly, "Right to Remain Silent," 998.

[20] Paul Cavill, "Heresy, Law and the State: Forfeiture in Late Medieval and Early Modern England," *EHR* 129.537 (2014): 282.

who chose not to appear in court to defend their good names were considered guilty and convicted *in absentia*. Again, this position conflicts with English common law. In England, repeated failure to respond to a court summons led to outlawry. An outlaw was guilty only of flight from the law. Many assumed that an outlaw was probably also guilty of the crime for which he was accused (why else would he have fled?); but the law did not convict him in his absence, and if he chose to turn himself in at a later date, he was then put on trial. Given the high rates of acquittal in the era, in all likelihood, he might still be acquitted.

It is doubtful whether the typical medieval Englishman or woman was aware of the discrepancy between Continental, canon, and common-law approaches to silence and absence. Such technicalities were fodder for academic dialogues at the Inns of Court, where the subtle differences between "our law" and "church law" generated heated debate. However, the inconsistency in meanings of silence *within* England must have been perplexing to the illiterate and unschooled suspected felons who sometimes opted for silence. To make matters worse, the process itself as it was administered in court sent its audience mixed messages. To offer an example: one night at the end of September in 1357, purportedly John, son of Thomas Symson of Braham, furtively and feloniously stole three cows from William Wynter of Tadcaster, who later appealed him of the crime. At his trial, John said nothing, but held mute. Justices dispatched him into the custody of Peter of Nutley, the sheriff of York, tasked with punishing him with the regimen spelled out so clearly by the author of *Fleta* above. The record concludes by stating that John has no chattels, no tenements, etc. to be confiscated by the king. As an afterword, it notes that William reclaimed his cows.[21] If the king's justices did not see John's silence as an admission of guilt, how did they know that those cows, presumably in John's possession, in fact belonged to William? The answer to this question will be explored in the section below – but for the spectators at that trial, unfamiliar with the ins and outs of the law, surely most left court that day believing that John's silence was equated with a confession of guilt.

[21] TNA JUST 3/141a, 34d (1357).

Exceptions to the Rule?: Appeals

Common law was not uniform in its approach to standing mute even when it applied to felony charges. The means of prosecution, that is, whether the individual being arraigned was charged by appeal (private prosecution), or by indictment at the king's suit (public prosecution), seemingly dictated whether a defendant had the right to stand mute. The distinction is thought to be reflected in the first Statute of Westminster (1275), which is the only medieval legislation to address the matter of those who refuse to plead. It pronounced that men charged at the king's suit who "refuse to stand to the common law of the land" and who are "notorious felons" and "openly be of evil name," are to be subject to "strong and hard imprisonment" (prison forte et dure).[22] In actual practice, the notorious-felons clause was obsolete soon after it was put in writing. By at least the early fourteenth century, justices saw strong and hard prison as a cure-all for indicted felons who refused to plead regardless of their notoriety. Yet, what is striking about this statute is its emphasis on the king's suit. No mention is made about the process justices should pursue when a defendant stands mute upon appeal, although the wording of the statute would seem to imply that differential treatment existed according to the means by which an accused felon made his way into court.

In attempting to understand why this distinction existed, traditionally historians have turned to *Doctor and Student* (1528), an instructional text on equity in the common law penned by sixteenth-century lawyer and polemicist Christopher Saint German (d.1540). As is the case with most primers in the scholastic era, the book was written in the format of a dialogue, in this case between a doctor of divinity and a student of English common law. The aim was to probe the relationship between common law and conscience, but in doing so it furnishes a convenient introduction to the rudiments of English common law. Quite helpfully, Saint German also articulates the reason why standing mute was not deemed acceptable in appeals, although his answer is not quite as straightforward as we might prefer. Chapter 41 sees the teacher muse aloud that in the *Summa Angelica*, a fifteenth-century dictionary of

---

[22] Statute of Westminster I, 3 Edw. I, c. 12 (1275); *SR*, vol. I, 29.

moral theology, a mercenary can be executed summarily providing he has first been proven in a court of law to be a mercenary. He adds that anyone can slay such a man with impunity if he does so with a "zeal of justice." The teacher then asks his student if the same applies also to an English outlaw, a man who has abjured the realm, or a convicted felon. The student's deliberative response acts as our guide here. He explains that in sixteenth-century England no such law exists. The English do not convict based on criminal identities (i.e., *being* a hired killer), only criminal acts. Thus, if it can be proven that the mercenary has in fact slain someone, he will be convicted and punished for his crime. The student continues, outlining the arraignment and trial process. If a mercenary kills a man, he will be indicted and then arraigned for murder. If he confesses or is found guilty by a jury of twelve honest and lawful men, he will be executed and have his lands and goods confiscated by the king.

It is at this point that his explanation at last touches on our subject of interest. He explains that on appeal of murder, if:

he stande dombe & wyll nat answer to the murdre: he shall be attaynted of the murdre and shall forfeyte lyfe landes & godes but if he be arrayned of the murdre vpon an Indytement at the kynges sute: & there vppon he standeth dombe & wyll not answer: there he shall not be attainted of the murdre but he shall haue peyn forte & dure (that is to saye) he shall be pressyd to dethe and he shall there forfeyte his goodes and not his landes. But in non of these cases (that is to saye) though a man be outlawed for murdre or felonye or be abiured or that he be otherwyse attaynted: yet it is not laufull for no man to murdre hym or slee hym ne to put hym in execucyon but by auctoryty of the kynges lawes. In so moche that yf a man be aiuged to haue peyn forte & dure & the offycer byhedyth hym or on the contrary wyse putteth hym to peyn forte & dure where he sholde byhede hym: he offendeth the law.

(he stand dumb and will not answer to the murder: he shall be attainted of the murder and shall forfeit life, lands, and goods, but if he be arraigned of the murder upon an indictment at the king's suit: and there upon he stands dumb and will not answer: there he shall not be attainted of the murder but he shall have peine forte et dure (that is to say) he shall be pressed to death and he shall there forfeit his goods and not his lands. But in none of these cases (that is to say) though a man be outlawed for murder or felony or be abjured or that he be otherwise attainted: yet it is not lawful for no man to murder him or slay him, nor to put him in execution, but by authority of the king's laws. In so much that if a man be adjudged to have peine forte et dure and the officer beheads him, or on the contrary wise puts him to peine forte et dure where he should behead him: he offends the law.)²³

Among other points of law that Saint German is trying to underscore in this passage, he is reminding us of the fundamental discrepancy between private and public prosecution. While the king's indictment filled an important gap in the system by rescuing abandoned appeals, it did not replace private prosecution. An appeal always took precedence: the king's indictment could not deprive the victim of his or her rights to sue. Subsequently, the normal rules did not always apply to private accusations. For example, a pardon issued by the king exonerated the felon only for the offense to the king; it could not pardon the offense to the victim or the victim's family, who might still prosecute the recipient of a pardon for the very same felony. In terms of method of trial, an appeal also opened up combat as a viable option, and appellors had to seek pledges to prove the truth of their accusations. When convicted upon appeal, stolen goods returned to the appellor (as was the case with William Wynter of Tadcaster, above), whereas indictments at the king's suit led to felony forfeiture in which the king stood as beneficiary for the goods in question, specifically all the felon's chattels (in perpetuity) and lands (for a year and a day). When it comes to standing mute, silence on the king's indictment for felony charges left a defendant unconvicted. The same was not true of an appeal, where justices considered silence merely a failure to defend oneself against serious allegations. In this instance, it was an admission of guilt, or a very poor decision that ended at the gallows.

Given the slavish adherence to the law meticulously outlined by Saint German above, as well as the language of the 1275 statute, the usual presumption is that an appellee had no right to stand mute in medieval England. Period. Yet, in practice, medieval justices only sometimes applied this distinction. Granted, they seem to have had little guidance on the matter. Even the medieval legal treatises do not agree on whether a defendant has the right to stand mute on appeal. *Glanvill* has naught to say on the matter. *Bracton*'s message is far from straightforward. Its authors do not address either standing mute or peine forte et dure, but the treatise does speak to the reluctant appellee,

²³ Christopher Saint German, *Doctor and Student*, ed. Theodore Plucknett and John Barton (SS, vol. XCI, 1974), 264–5.

and in doing so, one might argue that its authors side with Saint German. In a section entitled "How those appealed ought to make their defence," *Bracton* underscores the appellee's responsibility to choose a method of trial. The choice lay between jury trial and trial by combat, and the appellee *must* choose:

> If he simply says that he wishes to defend himself as the court of the lord king decides, unless he says more he will be without defence, because it is not for the king's court to show him how he ought to make his defence. And so if he says, 'I am ready to make my defence either by my body or by the country as the king's court decides,' because the king's court ought not to compel him to one rather than the other, nor to impose his form of defence on him in any way, since the choice is his own [and] it is evident that he thereby deprives himself of the choice. If he is unwilling to adopt either he will remain undefended and *quasi-convicted*.[24]

Yet, *Fleta* and *Britton*, two of the three late thirteenth-century abridgements of *Bracton*, unequivocally adopt the opposite position. Both treatises tackle the subject of standing mute outright, most likely reflecting the later dates of their composition at a point when refusal to plead had gained a measure of popularity. Both works also state plainly that in an appeal of homicide, an appellee who is unwilling to answer or who refuses a jury merits peine forte et dure "until he be prepared to answer better."[25]

The medieval legal treatises, then, do not support Christopher Saint German's unflinching assurance that an appeal was an exception to the rule when it comes to standing mute. Nor does the evidence of the medieval jail delivery rolls. Of the 481 individuals sentenced to peine forte et dure for standing mute, fully 100 (or, 20.8 percent) stood on appeal rather than indictment at the king's suit. In this respect, a chronological breakdown of peine forte et dure by means of prosecution is instructive (see Table 2.1).

What is striking from an analysis of the numbers is that even in the thirteenth century when parliament issued the Statute of Westminster, the courts applied the same process to silent defendants regardless of means of prosecution. The evidence points to the likelihood that later jurists read a distinction into the 1275 statute that was not intended by

---

[24] *Bracton*, vol. II, 390.
[25] Nichols, ed., *Britton*, vol. I, 85; Richardson and Sayles, eds., *Fleta*, 85.

TABLE 2.1 *Standing mute: Private versus public prosecution*[26]

	Appeal	Indictment
THIRTEENTH CENTURY	10	25
1300–9	4	71
1310–19	23	54
1320–9	23	44
1330–9	6	35
1340–9	6	68
1350–9	4	20
1360–9	8	15
1370–9	7	10
1380–9	10	9
1390–9	7	11
FIFTEENTH CENTURY	4	7
TOTALS	112	369

its original authors. And while fewer appeals resulted in peine forte et dure over time – most likely reflecting the decline of the appeal, more than anything else – the fact that some fifteenth-century justices continued to overlook the distinction suggests the nature of the process was not particularly meaningful for most justices in the medieval period.

If this change does result from a misreading of the statute, when did that fateful error first occur? There is sound reason to believe that differential treatment as it applied to appeals and indictments commenced in the mid-fourteenth century. A year book case from 1347 recounts how an unnamed appellee who refused to plead to a charge of robbery at Common Bench was quickly made aware of the flaw to his legal strategy. Justice Richard Willoughby sentenced him to hang because he stood undefended on appeal and the stolen goods returned to the appellor. Willoughby explained his decision carefully, remarking that "if this had been at the suit of the king, he

---

[26] Please note that a comprehensive search of the jail delivery rolls was not performed for the thirteenth or fifteenth centuries. However, I have included those few cases that I have come across for those eras to demonstrate that standing mute on appeal occurred also in both those centuries.

would have his penance."[27] A similar decision in a 1352 case is also included in the year books.[28] Finally, a 1406 arraignment of two appellees who stood accused of robbery likewise includes the express statement that according to the Statute of Westminster, in the case of an appeal if one stands mute he will be convicted of felony and forfeit his goods.[29] This final case is significant merely because Blackstone (d.1780) in the eighteenth century cited it as evidence that standing mute on appeal must result in execution, not peine forte et dure.[30]

Because these cases appeared in the year books, read voraciously by those aspiring to careers in law, one might think that the 1347 decision should have brought an end to sending appellees to prison to suffer peine forte et dure (and if not the 1347 decision, then that of 1352, or 1406). Yet, as the numbers in the table above indicate, working justices continued to send some appellees to peine forte et dure even as late as 1474, although it is not at all clear why some appellees merited peine forte et dure while others were convicted. Nor is there any indication that justices saw themselves as acting mercifully in sending those few silent appellees to prison.[31] And despite Christopher Saint German's firm statement, confusion over this issue persisted well into the early modern era. Edward Coke's *Institutes of the Laws of England* (1628–44) remarks that even though the Statute of Westminster authorized peine forte et dure only in instances of indictments at the suit of the king, "the judgement of *paine forte et dure* was at the common law, both in appeales, and in indictments."[32]

Exceptions to the Rule?: Treason

In his *Commentaries*, Blackstone identifies one additional exemption. He declares, "if it be on an indictment of high treason, it is clearly settled that standing mute is equivalent to a conviction, and he shall receive the same judgment and execution."[33] Although he does not explicitly state

---

[27] YB Pasch. 21 Edw. 3 (1347), fo. 18a (Seipp 1347.071).
[28] YB 26 Edw. III (1352), fo. 122b (Seipp 1352.080ass).
[29] YB Mich. 8 Hen. IV (1406), fos. 1b-2b (Seipp 1406.101).
[30] *Blackstone*, vol. IV, ch. 25.
[31] YB Trin. 14 Edw. IV (1474), fo. 7a (Seipp 1474.019).
[32] Edward Coke, *Institutes of the Lawes of England*, 4 vols. (London: E. and R. Brooke, 1797), vol. II, 177.
[33] *Blackstone*, vol. IV, ch. 25.

the reasoning, it seems clear that Blackstone's logic is founded on the exceptionality of the crime. In many respects, treason stands out from other felonies. Treason is the only felony in medieval English history in which thoughts or words, rather than acts, were deemed criminal.[34] It was also not a clergyable offense, meaning that men indicted of treason were prohibited from claiming immunity to secular prosecution because of their clerical status, as they could for most serious crimes. Closing the loopholes that might allow a traitor to escape punishment highlights the extraordinariness of the crime. It was one of the few crimes deemed so horrific "as to mark the point at which law is, or should be, completely merciless."[35] Treason differed from other felonies also in its punishment. Medieval execution rites for traitors were truly horrific: being drawn to the site of execution, disemboweling, beheading, quartering. Quite frankly, who wouldn't stand mute if it meant escaping such an agonizing and ignominious death? In this light, Blackstone's pronouncement makes sense: treason should be an exception.

Once again, Blackstone's confident statement seems to reflect better the state of law in the eighteenth-century rather than the Middle Ages. In fact, one of the earliest recorded instances of pressing involved a notorious traitor, Robert le Ewer (or Lewer), once the king's waterbearer, later a royal sergeant, whose checkered career and "lax morals from his youth" brought him into conflict repeatedly with the king.[36] In 1311, he was appointed constable of Odiham Castle, signifying his close relationship with King Edward II, whom he had accompanied on a trip to France to attend the knighting of the queen's three brothers.[37] The *Vita Edwardi Secundi* offhandedly remarks that some years later he "killed a good man, and made off with his wife, with whom he had previously committed adultery."[38] This episode explains why in February of 1320, Edward asked Robert to step down from his position to be replaced by Hugh

---

[34] Isobel Thornley, "Treason by Words in the Fifteenth Century," *EHR* 32.128 (1917): 556–61.

[35] Neil Cartlidge, "Treason," in Candace Barrington and Sebastian Sobecki, eds., *The Cambridge Companion to Medieval English Law and Literature* (Cambridge University Press, 2019), 84.

[36] Wendy Childs, ed., *Vita Edwardi Secundi: The Life of Edward the Second* (Oxford: Clarendon Press, 2005), 218.

[37] *CPR*, Edward II, vol. I (1307–13), 580 and 584 (Robert Lewere).

[38] Childs, ed., *Vita Edwardi Secundi*, 219.

Despenser the younger.[39] Robert did not cooperate in his dismissal: instead, as it is reported in the official record, he "threatened some of the king's faithful subjects with [loss of] life and limb, ascertaining that he would slay them and cut them up limb by limb wherever he should find them, either in the presence or the absence of the king, in contempt of the king's order and in rebellion." Not surprisingly, the king's letter commanding his arrest declared it necessary "lest others should be encouraged to perpetrate the like or worse things against the king by the example of such public disrespect and disobedience against the king's faithful subjects by so vile a person."[40] Nonetheless, the tension between the two seems to have dissipated swiftly, likely because the king urgently required Robert's military expertise in his campaign against the Scots. By May of 1321, newly reappointed as constable of Odiham castle, Robert headed off to war with pardon in hand, while his wife and friends were released from prison.[41] Their reconciliation had lasted less than a year when Robert deserted his king in the midst of battle and refused to explain why.[42] Presumably another clash with the Despensers had impelled Robert into full-out rebellion. The *Vita Edwardi Secundi* recounts how Robert attacked Hugh Despenser the elder's manors, carrying off "victuals and other necessities as he liked," before visiting the tenants of two recently hanged rebels (Henry Tyes and Warin de Lisle) to distribute the proceeds of his theft as alms.[43] He then went into hiding. He was arrested while attempting to flee to France. At his trial on December 27, 1322, Robert refused to plead and was sentenced to peine forte et dure. The *Vita Edwardi Secundi* remarks that after a few days in prison, "he died as he deserved."[44]

As Ewer's example discloses, standing mute was originally conceived as an option available to those accused of treason and it remained a possibility throughout the Middle Ages, even if suspected traitors seldom chose this path. However, few silent rebels were as scandalous as Ewer, or committed crimes that were so personally

---

[39] *CFR*, Edward II, vol. III (1319–27), 15 and 18.

[40] *CCR*, Edward II vol. III (1318–23), 260.

[41] *CPR*, Edward II, vol. III (1317–21), 586, 596; *CCR*, Edward II, vol. III (1318–23), 312 and 394; *CFR*, Edward II, vol. III (1319–27), 64.

[42] *CCR*, Edward II, vol. III (1318–23), 597; *CPR*, Edward II, vol. IV (1321–4), 206.

[43] Childs, ed., *Vita Edwardi Secundi*, 217.   [44] Childs, ed., *Vita Edwardi Secundi*, 219.

offensive to the king. More often than not, they stood accused of counterfeiting the king's money.[45] At times, what made a defendant's actions treasonous was not spelled out, but the indictment was littered with the language of sedition. For example, in 1318, Robert of Appleton stood before Justice Henry Spigurnel at York castle's jail for having notoriously and treasonously (*proditore*) committed diverse robberies, arsons, homicides, and felonies against the peace, when, with strength and arms (*vi et armis*) he stole goods and chattels worth £3,000 (the equivalent of £1,380,261.30 in today's currency!) from a wide number of named individuals.[46] The impressive value of the goods stolen was certainly enough to make his perpetrators wish him dead, but was Robert actually a traitor? Did he consort with the enemy while carrying out these actions? Up north, when crimes were committed by a team of English and Scottish perpetrators, jurors saw their actions move beyond felony into treason. We see this clearly in the indictment of John Bell Clerk of Birley, born at Birley (an Englishman), indicted for having during a three-year period adhered to the enemies of the king (that is, the Scots), during which time, in the company of the enemy and thus treasonously against the king, he came to Birley and stole two bullocks from Thomas Porter of Bromley, and then he feloniously and treasonously set fire to two homes in the village. At his arraignment before justices William of Skipwith and William Rise at the jail of Newcastle upon Tyne in 1362, he refused to speak, and was sent to the diet.[47]

Even by the fifteenth century, the law's position on suspected traitors standing mute had not changed. The era witnessed a publicly humiliating verbal attack on King Henry VI that resulted in peine forte et dure. Admittedly, the fact that the perpetrator was a woman may have guided justices in their decision to opt for a private prison death rather than a public execution that might have inflamed crowds against a king whose grip on the throne was somewhat tenuous. In 1442, Juliana, daughter of William Quick, reportedly spoke contemptuously of the king in his presence when she encountered him at Blackheath, saying

---

[45] For example: TNA JUST 3/106, m. 4 (William of Danbury, 1306); TNA JUST 3/130, m. 76 (Thomas of Sherbourne (*Shirburn*), a chaplain, 1347).
[46] TNA JUST 3/74/4, m. 3 (1318); TNA's "Currency Converter: 1270–2017," www.nationalarchives.gov.uk/currency-converter/#currency-result.
[47] TNA JUST 3/145, m. 24 (1362).

"Harry of Windsor, ride soberly, thy horse may stumble and break thy neck." When asked to whom she was speaking, she explained "To that proud boy in red, riding on horseback," pointing her finger directly at the king. She then followed up by saying, "It becometh thee better to ride to thy uncle, than that thy uncle should ride to thee; thou wilt kill him, as thou hast killed thy mother: send to thy uncle's wife, whom thou keepest from him. Thou art a fool, a known fool throughout the whole kingdom of England."[48] Another source tells us that she also "reviled hym vngoodly and vnwisely" for his treatment of Dame Eleanor Cobham (d.1452), duchess of Gloucester, recently imprisoned for treason and sorcery. Juliana informed him that "he shuld haue hir hoom [home] ageyn to hir husbond." Incensed by her impertinence, the king ordered her arrest for her "vngoodly langage, and fole-hardynesse to speke so to hir liege lorde, the Kyng." At court, she refused to plead, asking instead for the king's grace (a pardon). Justices initially returned her to prison, then summoned her back to court where she was re-examined; once more she refused to plead. In light of the highly public and incendiary nature of her crime, justices ordered her to "stand in a cart upright," travelling throughout London, Southwark, and Blackheath so that all might see her with a "paupire [paper] about hir hede, of hir proude and lewed langag." Upon completion, the king's justices sentenced her to peine forte et dure, to have "as moche yron vpon hir body till she be dead: and thus she ended in this world, for hir proude langage to hir Kyng and souerayn lord."[49]

In effect, it was not until the reign of Henry VIII (d.1547) that jurists stated definitively that an individual suspected of treason should not be permitted to evade a traitor's death by a failure to plead. A statute of 1541–2 declares that when it comes to treason, misprision of treason, murder, manslaughter, or blood shed in the king's palace, those who refuse to answer or stand mute "shalbe convicte judged and demed guyltie of the thinge whereof he or they ys or shalbe so indicted [or] arraigned."[50] In general, Henry's reign was a watershed moment for

---

[48] Thomas Howell, ed., *A Complete Collection of State Trials*, 21 vols. (London: T. Hansard, 1816), vol. III, 360, no. 132. Many thanks to Ted Powell for bringing this case to my attention.

[49] Friedrich Brie, ed., *The Brut or the Chronicles of England*, 2 vols. (EETS, vols. CXXXI and CXXXVI, 1908), vol. II, 483–4.

[50] 33 Hen. VIII, c. 12, iv (1541–2), *SR*, vol. III, 847.

how those who stood mute were treated under the law. Despite its title, "An Acte for stondyng muet & peremptoritie challenge," the 1533–4 statute was focused chiefly on clergyable offenses, strictly narrowing the number of crimes for which a defendant might claim benefit of clergy. However, the statute also reduced the number of juror challenges available to a defendant from thirty-five to twenty and declared that those who "wyll not or doo not aunswere directly to the same indytment and felony [where apon] he is soo arrayned," are no longer eligible to claim benefit of clergy.[51] Granted, in general practice once a prisoner had been subjected to peine forte et dure, the likelihood was small that he was going to then declare himself to be a member of the clergy. However, the statute barred the possibility altogether.

Silence As Contempt for the Crown

Not only were suspected traitors able to stand mute on arraignment, but the records intimate that justices typically interpreted standing mute as a form of resistance to the king. Scribes pronounced the defendant's conduct a rejection of common law, or a refusal of jury trial; common law was the king's law, and the jurors, known collectively as "the country," were envisioned as representing the kingdom and its king. Thus, it should come as no surprise that justices construed silence as a form of contempt of court. This association is underscored by a number of courtroom discussions in the year books which center on the defendant's disobedience. A 1366 note recounts the arraignment of an unnamed man who had been appealed for a homicide committed within the past year. The man stands mute, thus justices adjudge "him to his penance, as one who had refused the common law." The justices then go on to explain why they interpret his actions in this light. They remark that he could not be tried or executed within the year because the king granted an appellor a year and a day with which to appeal. They conclude that "when he did not speak, he refused every advantage that was given to him, and for his *disobedience* he would have his penance," at which point the defendant grew cooperative. He put himself upon a jury, "and nothing was done."[52]

---

[51] 25 Hen. VIII, c. 3 (1533–4), *SR*, vol. III, 439.
[52] Italics are my own. 40 Edw III (1366) (Seipp 1366.157ass).

The very same 1406 year book case, discussed in Chapter 1, which had legal historians pondering whether peine forte et dure had transitioned from coercive device to death penalty also incorporates discussion of peine forte et dure as punishment for contempt. Two men stood accused of robbery on appeal and yet both refused to plead. In the ensuing debate between justices and pleaders as to who should benefit from the defendants' confiscated properties (the appellor or the king), Sergeant Richard Norton declares that "When they were mute they did not answer for the felony, so it may not be assumed that they were convicted of the felony, but only put to their penance for their *disobedience to law*, and not for felony." He then passes the torch to Sergeant Robert Hull, who explains that "When the felons were mute and it was found that they had been speaking on that same day, it was of their own malice that they did not speak, and a *contempt of the law*, which malice and *contempt* are a trespass for which their goods were forfeited, and for no other reason."[53]

In an article written in 1921, John C. Fox put forward the hypothesis that hard prison existed precisely as a punishment for those convicted of contempt of court.[54] To make this argument, Fox drew principally from Edward Coke, writing in the seventeenth-century:

But what should be the reason of this so terrible a judgement? This act answereth, because he refuseth to stand to the common law of the land, that is, lawfull and due triall according to law, and therefore his punishment for this contumacy without comparison is more severe, lasting, and grievous, then it should have beene for the offence of felony it selfe; and for the felony it selfe, it cannot be adjudged without answer.[55]

In Fox's perspective, the inquest into muteness was a trial itself. If the defendant was "convicted by a jury of standing obstinately mute," the punishment was peine forte et dure.[56]

[53] Italics are my own. This interpretation may have been favored because it awarded the confiscated goods to the king instead of the appellor. YB Mich. 8 Hen. IV (1406), fo. 1b–2b (Seipp 1406.101). See Kiralfy, ed., *Source Book*, 16. Describing the defendant as mute by malice dates back to at least 1317. See the trial of Robert of Appleton, TNA JUST 3/74/4, m. 3.
[54] John Fox, "The Nature of Contempt of Court," *Law Quarterly Review* 37.2 (1921): 191–202.
[55] Coke, *Institutes*, vol. II, 179.   [56] Fox, "Nature of Contempt of Court," 200.

Since that time, Fox's theory has not garnered any support among legal historians; but as the year books confirm, it finds strong backing in the medieval evidence. Contempt was a popular theme in intellectual circles of the high and late Middle Ages. Thanks to Peter Abelard (d.1142), after the twelfth century contempt was considered the distinguishing characteristic of sin. In his *Ethics*, Abelard writes, "sin is scorn for the creator, and to sin is to scorn the creator – not to do for his sake what we believe we ought to do for his sake, or not to renounce for his sake what we believe ought to be renounced."[57] Abelard's treatise marks the entrenchment of the interiority of sin typical of the era. In Abelard's mind, sin did not need to be active. An emotion or a thought on its own was sufficient to constitute sin, and each and every sin was an act of *lèse majesté* against the divinity. While intention had always been critical in determining the severity of a sin, under Abelard and his fellow theologians, it became the exclusive concern.[58]

This development in ideology appears also in English law and reflects the distance between legal treatises of the twelfth century and those of the thirteenth. *Glanvill* explains contempt of court (*contemptus curiae*) as an act: specifically, its author defines contempt narrowly as contumacy, that is, failing to show up to court when summoned. *Bracton*, on the other hand, adopts a much broader perspective. His gaze rests not upon an act, but a temperament. He aligns contempt most closely with disobedience: "There is no greater crime than contempt and disobedience, for all persons within the realm ought to be obedient to the king and within his peace."[59] This fuller interpretation enlarged the scope of contemptuous behaviors in the thirteenth century. Fox records the following variations on the theme to be found in the legal record: "plaintiff in mercy for false claim"; "a county in mercy for false judgment"; "mistake in pleading"; "complaining to the King that his

[57] Paul Spade, ed., *Peter Abelard: Ethical Writings: Ethics and Dialogue between a Philosopher, a Jew, and a Christian* (Indianapolis: Hackett Publishing, 1995), 3.

[58] Jean Porter, "Responsibility, Passion, and Sin: A Reassessment of Abelard's *Ethics*," *Journal of Religious Ethics* 28.3 (2000): 385. Anglo-Saxon scholars have noted quite rightly that it is incorrect to argue that early medieval penitentials concerned themselves only with an outward expression of contrition. See Rob Meens, *Penance in Medieval Europe, 600–1200* (Cambridge University Press, 2014), 203.

[59] George Hall, ed., *The Treatise on the Laws and Customs of the Realm of England Commonly Called Glanvill* (Oxford: Clarendon Press, 1993), Book I, ch. 33; *Bracton*, vol. I, 7.

justices have failed to do justice"; "parties coming to an agreement without licence"; "defendant failing to appear after being seen in court"; "a party's claim inconsistent with his own deed"; "producing a deed with an erasure"; "deceiving the court"; and "a party having denied that he spoke words against the jury in court, a jury finds that he spoke them in contempt of the King."[60] It is easy to see how refusing to plead might fall squarely into this category. These scenarios give priority to an uncooperative and/or dishonest litigant. An accused felon who stood maliciously mute was both. It is worthy of note also that the standard punishment for contempt was imprisonment – at times even perpetual imprisonment – and sometimes also a fine, although financial penalties seem to have been reserved either for contempt exhibited by officers of the law or in civil suits.[61] While hard prison was a more severe form of punitive incarceration, given that the defendant was thought to be rejecting the king's jurisdiction, the punishment would seem to fit the crime.[62]

Recognizing that justices associated silence with contempt of the king's law helps us to place silence within the rubric of protest against the encroachment of an ever-expanding centralizing monarchy, a topic which will be discussed further in Chapter 7. Effectively, silence was a defendant's means of asserting that the king did not have jurisdiction over his trial. Indeed, a year book note from the year 1423 makes this connection explicit: the writer explains that when a defendant pleads, he is giving jurisdiction to the court; silence, then, is emphatically a rejection of the Crown's jurisdiction.[63]

Every now and then, the jail-delivery rolls also provide a case in which an uncooperative defendant was eager to point out to justices

---

[60] Fox, "Nature of Contempt of Court," 195.

[61] Fox, "Nature of Contempt of Court," 198.

[62] The naturalness of strong prison as a punishment for disobedience is underscored in a passage from *Piers Plowman*. "That yif Do-Wel [and] Do-Bet did ayein Do-Best, / [And were unbouxome at his biddyng and bolde to don ille], / Thanne [sholde] the kynge come and castem hem in [prisone, / And puttehm hem there in penaunce without pité or grace," / But if Do-Best bede for hem, thei to be there forever" (That if Do-Well and Do-Better did anything against Do-Best, / And were disobedient to his bidding and bold to do evil, / Then the king should come and cast them in prison, / Put them there in penance [peine forte et dure] without pity or grace, / Unless Do-Best recommends mercy, to remain there forever.) B.VIII. 102–6. Langland, *Piers Plowman*, 126.

[63] YB term Pasch, 1 Hen. VI (Seipp 1423.009abr).

that they had no jurisdiction to try his case. For example, in 1318, Andrew Le Pottere was arraigned before justices of jail delivery at York castle for consorting with the Scots. When he refused to plead, he explained that he did so because he did not recognize the authority of the jurors to pass judgment on him. The record does not elaborate why he believed this to be true. He may have felt that a case of treason should go before a higher tribunal. Perhaps, he thought a cross-border case of this nature belonged instead to the jurisdiction of the warden of the march. There is also a distinct possibility that he was in fact a subject of the Scottish Crown and expected his case should be tried in the Scottish kingdom. In any event, justices in attendance determined that he had repudiated the common law and sentenced him to the diet.[64] A similar situation arose in 1362 in another possible instance of cross-border crime. A clerk who stood accused of felony "refused to put himself on the verdict of a jury comprised solely of Northumberland men." He expressed his concern through jury challenges, but exceeded the acceptable number, leading justices to condemn him to peine forte et dure. His stance may have been premised on the fact that he was on trial for a march-related offense; in such a situation a mixed jury of Englishmen and Scots was appropriate.[65] As a member of the clergy, he may also have hoped to be transferred to ecclesiastical jurisdiction. In all of these cases, what is striking is that defendants' uncooperativeness was voiced specifically as a denunciation of the court's jurisdiction.

Right of Reply in the Law of Arms

The links between silence and treason were cemented further through the trial of traitors under the international law of arms as it played out in fourteenth-century England. When it came to treason trials, in this venue, summary procedure – without formal indictment, right of defense, or the empaneling of a jury – was the norm. By the time of King Edward III (r. 1327–77), such trials typically took place in the court of Chivalry, which sat in the white chamber at Westminster

---

[64] TNA KB 27/238, m. 109 (1318).
[65] TNA PRO JUST 3/145, m. 24 (1362), as cited in Cynthia Neville, *Violence, Custom and the Law: The Anglo-Scottish Border Lands in the Later Middle Ages* (Edinburgh University Press, 1998), 60.

under the aegis of the Lord High Constable of England and the Earl Marshall, who presided as judges. The court had jurisdiction over all cases arising from acts of war carried out within the English realm. Before that time, however, the law of arms was typically administered by summary courts assembled in an *ad hoc* manner by royal commanders. What is striking about these trials, however, is that the public seems to have had little understanding of the process involved, and widely disapproved of their summary nature, equating the refusal to allow the defendant to speak with injustice. Indeed, cases of this nature may have erroneously led early modern commentators to believe that treason was exempt from common-law rules regarding those who stand mute.

The early fourteenth century witnessed a series of treason trials under the law of arms in which the defendants were denied right of reply, beginning with the beheading of Thomas, second Earl of Lancaster, also second Earl of Leicester and Earl of Lincoln (*c.*1278–1322). News of his execution sent shockwaves across the English kingdom. Despite numerous uprisings and civil wars, he was the first English earl executed at the king's command since Waltheof, Earl of Northumbria (d.1076), over two centuries earlier.[66] He was also one of the first English rebels to be labeled a traitor. As Neil Cartlidge has noted, prior to the fourteenth century, rebellion was not considered a form of treason.[67] Lancaster was of Plantagenet stock, grandson to Henry III and first cousin to Edward II; he was also the richest man in England next to the king. Most importantly, he was an advocate for restructuring government, becoming the spokesman for the Lord Ordainers, the baronial representatives who presented the king with the Ordinances of 1311, a series of demands for reform reminiscent of the Provisions of Oxford, singling out especially the ungovernable behavior of Edward's favorite, Piers Gaveston. While Edward initially agreed to abide by the ordinances, going so far as to exile Gaveston to France, by January of 1312 he revoked them and restored his favorite to his lands and titles. In violation of the king's wishes, Lancaster and a group of magnates took it upon themselves to arrest

---

[66] Andy King, "False Traitors or Worthy Knights? Treason and Rebellion against Edward II in the *Scalacronica* and the Anglo-Norman Prose *Brut* Chronicles," *Historical Research* 88.239 (2015): 35.

[67] Cartlidge, "Treason," 86–7.

Gaveston, stand as judges at his trial, and have him beheaded, prompting all-out civil war. Edward's inglorious defeat at Bannockburn in June of 1314 represents a crossroads in his reign; popular sentiment saw the hand of God intervene to see Edward defeated, persuading him to resign himself to rule by Lancaster and the other barons. For the next two years, Lancaster took the lead in reforming government along the lines laid out in the ordinances, becoming the king's chief councilor in 1316. Yet, within a year, Edward and Lancaster were quarreling once again over the removal of corrupt advisors; this time Lancaster hoped to see the Despenser family ousted from court. Exasperation with the king's favorites eventually provoked Lancaster into taking part in the writing of the *Modus Tenendi Parliamentum* (1321), a manifesto for reform of parliamentary procedure, which would see the House of Commons take on much greater authority, including the right to depose a king who lost the support of his subjects. By 1322, Lancaster had taken up arms against the Despensers in a short-lived offensive that resulted in Lancaster's defeat at the Battle of Boroughbridge, then incarceration until trial.[68]

His trial was conducted by Hugh Despenser the elder, Earl of Winchester, who actively stage-managed the event in order to emphasize the heinousness of Lancaster's crimes. The chronicles that describe the event all zero in on the denial of right of reply; yet, none of them highlight that the trial in fact belonged to the jurisdiction of the law of arms and thus demanded an unusual set of procedures unfamiliar to the vast majority of Englishmen and women. The pro-royalist *Vita Edwardi Secundi* remarks that Lancaster, "wishing to speak in mitigation of his crimes, immediately tried to make some points; but the judges refused to hear him." The chronicle attempts to explain the judge's decision as springing from Lancaster's manifest guilt: "because the words of the condemned can neither harm nor be of any profit." The earl's response seems to justify their decision: "This is a powerful court, and great in authority, where no answer is heard, nor any excuse admitted."[69] *The Brut*, a pro-Lancaster chronicle offers

---

[68] John Maddicott, "Thomas of Lancaster, Second Earl of Lancaster, Second Earl of Leicester, and Earl of Lincoln, (c. 1278–1322)," *ODNB* (January 3, 2008).

[69] Childs, ed., *Vita Edwardi Secundi*, 212–15.

a different persective entirely. Eager to exploit this episode as evidence
of the king's unfitness for his post, the chronicle underscores the
scandalous injustice of Lancaster's trial, declaring that he was denied
"iugement of his peris" (judgment of his peers), brought before the bar
"bare-heauede as a þef," "excludeþ" from "al maner ansuere"
(bareheaded as a thief ... excluded [from] ... all manner of answer).[70]
The validity of the trial under the law of arms does not seem to have
diminished the horror expressed by contemporaries. Denying these
accused traitors the right to plead or defend their actions in any way
incited widespread outrage. More to the point, for those court factions
who eventually transferred their allegiance to Queen Isabella (d.1358)
and Roger Mortimer (d.1330), it provided solid justification that Edward
II had overstepped his bounds and that something drastic needed to be
done to rein in his swelling tyranny. As one Westminster monk describes
it, Edward II "hated all the magnates with such mad fury that he plotted
the complete and permanent overthrow of all the great men of the realm
together with the whole English aristocracy."[71] Surprisingly, given the
overblown rhetoric of this passage, historians seem to agree. John
Gillingham observes that "[t]he bloodshed of Edward II's reign marked
a violent turning point in English political life."[72]

Given the handling of the trial in the chronicles, it is no wonder that
historians have conventionally interpreted Edward's distinctly un-
English act in trying men without their consent as an attempt to
emulate contemporary French legal practice in its early flirtation with
absolutism.[73] The fourteenth century saw accused traitors in the French
context, such as Bernard Saisset in 1301 and Enguerran de Marigny in
1315, also denied the right to defend themselves at court.[74] Lancaster's
"show" trial was thought to set a dangerous precedent. Between the

---

[70] Brie, ed., *Brut*, vol. I, 221–2.
[71] Henry Luard, ed., *Flores Historiarum*, 3 vols. (*RS*, 1886–9), vol. III, 200; as cited in
    John Gillingham, "Enforcing Old Law in New Ways: Professional Lawyers and
    Treason in Early Fourteenth Century England and France," in Per Anderson,
    Mia Münster-Swendsen, and Helle Vogt, eds., *Law and Power in the Middle Ages*,
    (Copenhagen: Djoef Publishing, 2008), 199–220.
[72] Gillingham, "Enforcing Old Law," 201.
[73] Edward may have been inspired to do so by his in-laws. Three of Isabella's brothers
    ascended the French throne during her marriage to Edward II: Louis X (1314–16),
    Philip V (1316–22), and Charles IV (1322–8).
[74] Gillingham, "Enforcing Old Law," 217.

executions of Lancaster and Roger Mortimer, a broad swathe of the nobility fell victim to the same fate, "put to death arbitrarily and without either right of reply or lawful conviction."[75] Maurice Keen in 1996 was the first to argue that Lancaster's trial makes sense chiefly if it was enacted under the law of arms, rather than common law.[76] While Keen is undoubtedly correct, the chroniclers' unease implies that the English population were not content to see a suspected traitor refused the right to offer a defense.

Edward II's orchestrated disappearance from public life after 1326 saw a turning of the tides. The trial of Hugh Despenser the elder again confirms that chroniclers did not understand the law of arms and simply viewed denial of a defendant's right of reply as unjust. The author of the *Annales Paulini* explains that his judges sought revenge for Lancaster's mock trial by similarly depriving him of the right of reply. They declared that "This court denies you any right of answer because you yourself made a law that a man could be condemned without right of answer."[77] The two Despensers, father and son, were sentenced to five years of perpetual imprisonment in the Tower. However, the fact that they were condemned without arraignment was held as the grounds for annulment of the judgment once Edward III came into power in January of 1327 – hinting that it was not only the chroniclers who were uncomfortable with the nature of the trial. That same year, Robert Mablethorpe, the judge who prohibited Lancaster from pleading, sought a pardon for violating his responsibilities as a judge.[78] The following year, the Crown spearheaded the annulment of Lancaster's sentence, making a formal declaration that he had been convicted unjustly and against the common law.

Regardless, it would seem that the English Crown was not yet ready to learn any lesson from Lancaster's and the Despensers' trials. The trial of Roger Mortimer and his uncle, Roger Mortimer of Chirk (d.1326), took place without right of reply. After his uncle had died in perpetual imprisonment and he had duly escaped the Tower of London, Mortimer petitioned the king to have the judgments served

---

[75] P&M, vol. ii, 502–8.

[76] Maurice Keen, *Nobles, Knights and Men-at-Arms in the Middle Ages* (London: Hambledon, 1996).

[77] William Stubbs, ed., "Annales Paulini," in *Chronicles of the Reigns of Edward I and Edward II*, 2 vols. (RS, 1882–3), vol. I, 317.

[78] Gillingham, "Enforcing Old Law," 209.

against the two men affirmed void. His petition declared boldly that he and his uncle had been tried without arraignment or without even being "permitted to answer to any of the matters charged against them, which is contrary to the law and custom of the realm, etc, and therefore the proceeding to judgement against them was erroneous."[79] The Crown revoked both judgments, and Mortimer saw his lands temporarily reinstated, before eventually being condemned once more, tried again without right of reply, and then executed. Finally, parliament intervened and pronounced the judgment erroneous because he had been tried without right of reply.[80] As a result of parliament's intervention, the Crown's experimentation with summary justice for treason trials drew to an end.

These experiences serve chiefly to emphasize the sanctity of the arraignment process. Disregard for a defendant's right to reply to the charges imputed against him demonstrated to the elite the dangers of law without justice under a dictatorial government. What is most striking is how this episode affected the people at large. In death, Lancaster found the celebrity he was denied in life. A cult grew up around the beleaguered earl. During his lifetime, Lancaster had attempted to paint himself as "political heir" to Simon de Montfort, assisted by the fact that he had inherited the de Montfort land and titles.[81] The cult that instantly took root around "Saint Thomas" hints at his success in this respect.[82] Within a week of his execution, miracles were being attributed to the martyr.[83] In September of 1323, Archbishop Melton of York tried to put a stop to local veneration of Lancaster at Pontefract (Yorkshire), the site of his execution, with no success. Two guards were killed when the thousands of pilgrims from Kent, Essex, and Lancashire present at the shrine rioted in response to

---

[79] *CPR*, Edward III, vol. 1 (1327–30), 32.

[80] Luke O. Pike, ed., *Year Books of the Reign of King Edward the Third*, Year XIX (London: HMSO, 1906), xliii.

[81] James Robinson, "Pilgrimage and Protest: Badges at the British Museum Relating to Thomas of Lancaster and Isabella, Queen of Edward II," in Sarah Blick, ed., *Beyond Pilgrim Souvenirs and Secular Badges: Essays in Honour of Brian Spencer* (Oxford: Oxbow Books, 2007), 171.

[82] John Theilmann, "Political Canonization and Political Symbolism in Medieval England," *JBS* 29.3 (1990): 249.

[83] Danna Piroyansky, *Martyrs in the Making: Political Martyrdom in Late Medieval England* (New York: Palgrave Macmillan, 2008), 24.

requests to leave.[84] The cult even spread to London where a tablet meant to memorialize the Ordinances of 1311 became a popular site of veneration for Lancaster, cementing his personal connection with the legal reforms in popular memory.[85] Pro-Lancastrian chronicles took these miracles as a sign that God supported Thomas, not the king. The *Anonimalle Chronicle* explained the miracles as a product of God's grace "to show that the *gentil* earl of Lancaster died in a just cause to uphold the estate of the realm."[86]

Lancaster was never actually canonized, although there were numerous attempts to make this happen. After Edward II's death in 1327, a petition in parliament called for the king to reach out to Rome to have Thomas of Lancaster canonized. Edward III's first letter to the pope on Thomas' behalf is dated to February 28, 1327; he wrote again repeating the request in 1330 and 1331, although the pope never responded.[87] Regardless, there was widespread popular belief that he had been canonized, leading Thomas Walsingham (incorrectly) to claim that Thomas was in fact canonized a saint in 1390.[88] The absence of a formal ceremony meant little to those who traveled from far and near to his shrine at Pontefract. Nor did his cult remain exclusively English. His martyrdom was well known in Gascony and Cologne.[89] Unlike the veneration of "Saint" Simon de Montfort, Lancaster's cult persisted well into the Reformation era. In 1359, his blood was seen to be flowing from his tomb; in 1361, a chantry chapel was built in his memory on top of the hill where he was executed.[90] His cult was revived in the reign of Henry IV, when William of Norfolk of Pontefract made his will, leaving twelve pence for the upkeep of a light for the Guild of Blessed Thomas of

---

[84] John Edwards, "The Cult of 'St.' Thomas of Lancaster and its Iconography," *Yorkshire Archaeological Journal* 64 (1992): 113.

[85] Theilmann, "Political Canonization," 249.

[86] Wendy Childs and John Taylor, eds., *The Anonimalle Chronicle, 1307–34* (Yorkshire Archaeological Society Record Series, vol. CXLVII, 1991), 112; as cited in King, "False Traitors or Worthy Knights?," 40.

[87] Edwards, "Cult of 'St.' Thomas of Lancaster," 107.

[88] David Preest, ed., *The Chronica Maiora of Thomas Walsingham, 1376–1422* (Woodbridge: Boydell, 2005), 277.

[89] Piroyansky, *Martyrs in the Making*, 33.

[90] Edwards, "Cult of 'St.' Thomas of Lancaster," 107.

Lancaster.[91] Two hundred years after his death, women still used Lancaster's belt to assist during their lying-in, and his hat to heal headaches.[92] When it comes to political implications, in the short term, Thomas of Lancaster's cult "gave opponents of Edward II a convenient stick with which to beat the king and legitimize the cause that Thomas has championed."[93] As John Edwards writes, "saints ranked higher than kings," a fact that no one in medieval England would have missed.[94]

What the example of Thomas of Lancaster and others who were refused the right of reply in this era tells us is that it was technically legal under the law of arms; however, the chroniclers, parliament, common-law justices, and certainly the people of England were all uncomfortable with denying the accused the right to plead and offer a defense on his behalf. Indeed, the "injustice" of Lancaster's trial made him a political martyr of pan-European celebrity. Moreover, as we will discuss at greater length in the second half of this book, Lancaster's execution highlights a special relationship between silence and attacks on the king in the English mindset.

Was Standing Mute a Gendered Practice?

Did women stand mute? Andrea McKenzie's award-winning study of peine forte et dure in seventeenth- and eighteenth-century England sees that standing mute was a choice few women elected. On the odd occasion, a woman summoned to the bar initially refused to plead, but after her thumbs were fastened tightly together with a whipcord – an excruciating practice initiated after the Restoration in order to induce a willingness to plead without having to resort to the severity of peine forte et dure – she soon capitulated. Remarkably, Margaret Clitheroe is the only woman that McKenzie has come across in the early modern era who persisted in her refusal so that she was subjected to peine forte et dure.[95] Hence, McKenzie contends that pressing came to acquire a masculine tenor, reflecting the lives of the principally

---

[91] Nicholas Rogers, "Appendix: The Continuation of the Cult in the Fifteenth Century," *Yorkshire Archaeological Journal* 67 (1995): 190.

[92] Piroyansky, *Martyrs in the Making*, 29.

[93] Theilmann, "Political Canonization," 250.

[94] Edwards, "Cult of 'St.' Thomas of Lancaster," 109.

[95] McKenzie also uncovered an Old Bailey arraignment from 1676 in which a woman was sentenced to be pressed, but she found no evidence that the sentence was carried out. Andrea McKenzie, "'This Death some Strong and Stout Hearted Man Doth

lower-class men lost to the press room, a chamber designed exclusively for the purpose of pressing defendants who remained contumacious. She recognizes that these men stood mute in protest against an elite system of justice that punished brutally the crimes of desperation perpetrated by the poor, while ensuring that the affluent's more substantial crimes would go unpunished. In doing so, the popular literature describing their deaths "invoked a discourse of manly courage and resolution," imagining these men dying privately in the press room to protect family property and honor.[96] McKenzie is not the only historian to note the absence of women from these practices. James Cockburn has made a similar observation.[97] In order to appreciate the defense strategies available to suspected felons, we need to ask: was this the case also in the Middle Ages?

Royal justices in medieval England undoubtedly considered a woman capable of standing mute. The year books contain a 1321 arraignment in which Justice Passeley urges Isabel of Bury not to persist in her muteness because if she then decides to speak she will be prevented from challenging jurors.[98] Even if this case represents one of the few instances in which a woman opted for silence at her arraignment on felony charges, its regular duplication in the year books ensured that England's rapidly expanding cadre of professional lawmen was perfectly aware of the prospect that a woman might refuse to plead. All the same, evidence from the practice of the law is heavily weighted towards men. Of the 481 cases of those who stood mute, only twenty-nine (roughly 6 percent) were women. Granted, this figure cannot be taken merely at face value. It must be examined against the backdrop of women's overall participation in serious crime. Medieval women, much like their modern

---

Choose': The Practice of Peine Forte et Dure in Seventeenth- and Eighteenth-Century England," *L&HR* 23.2 (2005): 286n.

[96] McKenzie, "'This Death'," 294.

[97] James Cockburn, ed., *Calendar of Assize Records. Home Circuit Indictments, Elizabeth I and James I: Introduction* (London: HMSO, 1985), 72. One voice of dissent comes from the law reports of Arthur Turnour, a barrister of the Middle Temple from the summer of 1616. His notes indicate that the long clerk of the peace of Middlesex explained that women were equally eligible for peine forte et dure, and that he had seen women accordingly subjected "often at Newgate." John Baker, ed., "Criminal Justice at Newgate 1616–1627: Some Manuscript Reports in the Harvard Law School," *Irish Jurist* 8 (1973): 316.

[98] "Rex v. Bury," in Helen Cam, ed., *Year Books of Edward II, pt. 1: The Eyre of London, 14 Edward II v.26 (1321)* (SS, vol. LXXXV, 1968), vol. I, 73–4 (Seipp 1321.124ss).

counterparts, were a distinct minority when it comes to perpetuating felonies. James Given's study of homicide in thirteenth-century England saw women accused in 8.6 percent of cases.[99] Barbara Hanawalt's study of felony indictments in the years 1300–48 for three English counties reveals an 11 percent participation rate.[100] The figure of 6 percent, then, is low, but not that far out of proportion with women's typical involvement in felony behavior.

Yet, those women who refused to plead were not your typical criminals. Keeping in mind that acquittal was the usual judgment in medieval England, it is striking that most of these women seemed destined for conviction. Five were caught red-handed (*cum manuopere*). Alice Rout of Gissing (Norfolk) was arrested in possession of a cow belonging to her appellor, whose home she had burgled.[101] So, too, was Alice, wife of Nicholas Tascy.[102] Indicted felons detained with stolen goods in their possession and with a questionable reputation fell into the category of a violent presumption of guilt. Where in an earlier period, hand-having (*handhabbende*) or back-bearing (*bacberende*) thieves were hanged on the spot, by *Bracton*'s era mere possession of stolen goods was deemed insufficient to proceed directly to a conviction. Evidently, for a time between the abandonment of trial by ordeal and the adoption of jury trial, mainour combined with a refusal to plead resulted in hanging. This brief recital of the history is intended to clarify that, despite the absence of set rules of evidence, jurors and common-law justices saw possession of stolen goods as solid proof of guilt. All five of these women, if they had pled, were most likely bound for the gallows.

Another six were described in their indictments as common thieves (*communes latrones*). Once again, by the fourteenth century, being a common thief was no longer grounds on its own for a formal accusation. A proper indictment must contain a specified crime, with a named victim in an identifiable location, tied to a particular date and time. Still, presenting jurors continued to insert language of this nature into indictments in order to call attention to the defendant's criminal

---

[99] James Given, *Society and Homicide in Thirteenth-Century England* (Stanford University Press, 1977), 134.

[100] Barbara Hanawalt, "The Female Felon in Fourteenth-Century England," *Viator* 5 (1974): 254.

[101] TNA JUST 3/48, m. 24 (1315).   [102] TNA JUST 3/48, m. 31 (1316).

background. In doing so, they made it amply clear to the jurors assigned to her trial that this was not a one-time offense; rather, the felony belonged to a string of crimes perpetuated by a professional criminal. Bandying about the phrase "common thief" was not the only means to achieve this goal. For other defendants, indictments included meticulous details relating to multiple crimes, leaving no doubt to the accused's status as a career criminal.[103] For example, Beatrice, wife of John Hodecook of Corpusty stole four sheep worth three shillings from Alexander Pitecook before moving on to the home of William, son of Reginald of Felmingham where she carried off another four.[104] Cecily, daughter of Emma Attehirne was charged with three separate burglaries, pilfering goods of a total value of nineteen shillings and four pence, while Maud Mese burglarized the home of Alice, niece of the vicar of Deopham (Norfolk), stealing goods valued at forty shillings, followed up with the remark that she was responsible also "for many other thefts" (*per pluribus aliis latronicii*).[105] Though jurors were inclined to acquit, John Bellamy notes that the inclusion of language to indicate the notoriety of a defendant's career substantially increased the accused's chances of being convicted. For the fifteenth century, he observes a conviction against acquittal ratio for common felons of one to three compared to one to eight in those instances where the accused was not described as common.[106] Thus, these six women were also likely to have been convicted.

Status as a career criminal might also be indicated through association. Felise Duffield and Isote la Smale, for example, were arrested while working in partnership (*in societate*) with William le Taillour, a convicted felon.[107] Christina atte Sewe Hous had two strikes against her. Arrested while in the company of the common thief John of Runcton, she was also in possession of stolen goods

---

[103] Bellamy found a 62 percent conviction rate for those accused of multiple felonies at Hertfordshire in the period 1573–1624, compared to an overall conviction rate of 23 percent. See John Bellamy, *The Criminal Trial in Later Medieval England* (University of Toronto Press, 1998), 124.

[104] TNA JUST 3/48, m. 23d (1315).

[105] TNA JUST 3/49/1, m. 52 (1323); TNA JUST 3/106, m. 1 (1305).

[106] Bellamy, *Criminal Trial*, 30.

[107] TNA JUST 3/1/6, m. 4d (1334). They died, alongside William le Taillour and three others in prison the following year. The coroner's finding suggests that they starved to death on the diet. TNA JUST 3/1/7, m. 1d.

(*cum manuopere*), seven-shillings' worth of wool and linen cloth.[108] In at least three instances, presenting jurors drew attention to the premeditated nature of the crime by writing that it had taken place at night (*noctanter*). Again, the term *noctanter* belongs to a pool of terms described by Bellamy as words or phrases of afforcement, which jurors included in the indictment with the sole purpose of signaling that the defendant deserved conviction.[109]

An appeal pursued all the way through to completion was also markedly more likely to end in conviction than an indictment at the king's suit.[110] The reason why is not difficult to fathom. Trial jurors appreciated the strenuous nature of the appeals process that required raising the hue and cry; notification of the coroner and subsequent interrogation before the inquest jury; multiple (up to four) appearances at the county court for the reading of the summons; followed by a final appearance at the trial in which the appellor normally conducted his or her own prosecution. Such heavy demands on an appellor's time and energies meant that few persisted through to the end. Appellors were also expected to memorize their count word-for-word; the inability to recite it appropriately resulted in a failed appeal. Throughout this process, the appellor continued to reside among neighbors who might well interpret his or her actions as hostile or incendiary. Finally, the appellor also risked being imprisoned and fined for a false appeal if the suit ended in acquittal. With so many deterrents along the way, jurors likely felt that the appellor who committed to seeing a suit through to the end persevered out of righteousness. Five of those women who stood mute were appealed of their crimes.[111]

Finally, certain crimes were substantially more likely to end in conviction. Petty treason, that is, homicide of one's husband, was one of them.[112] Five of the twenty-nine women who stood mute were

---

[108] TNA JUST 3/49/1, m. 8d (1318).   [109] Bellamy, *Criminal Trial*, 29.

[110] Musson found a 60 percent conviction rate for those prosecuted on appeal. See Anthony Musson, *Public Order and Law Enforcement: The Local Administration of Criminal Justice, 1294–1350* (Woodbridge: Boydell, 1996), 171.

[111] TNA JUST 3/48, m. 24 (Alice Rout of Gissing, 1315); JUST 3/1/3, m. 5 (Alice Gynego, 1321); JUST 3/49/1, m. 32d (Joan daughter of Galsum de Brannerthorp, 1321); JUST 3/49/1, m. 52 (Cecily daughter of Emma Attehirne, 1323); JUST 30/130, m. 52 (Isabel atte Pile, 1346).

[112] In fourteenth-century England, 22 percent of men suspected of killing their wives were convicted, compared to 35 percent of women accused of petty treason.

accused of petty treason.[113] Granted, two of these women eventually received pardons from the king and were released from prison. Here it is worthy of note that because the murder of one's husband fell under the category of treason, a woman convicted of the crime faced burning rather than hanging as a means of execution, a much more painful and prolonged form of death. It is not hard to imagine that fasting in a cell with or without weights may have seemed preferable to those women who knew conviction was in their future. Arson, closely associated with popular protest in medieval England and widely feared because of the potential for spread, was also likely to lead to conviction. Three of the twenty-nine women were indicted also on charges of arson.[114]

In total, twenty-four of the twenty-nine indictments point to an impending conviction. These women refused to plead because undergoing trial more than likely would have resulted in their executions. While men also sometimes refused to plead out of fear of conviction, as will be discussed at greater length in Chapter 5, it was not the prime motivation for them. Women who stood mute before the king's justices, then, were women who valued silence as a means to prolong their lives.

Self-Incrimination

Those who stood rightfully accused of felony found themselves in a distasteful predicament. A defendant signaled his consent to a jury trial with an exculpation oath – that is, by denying his guilt (a guilty plea, of course, simply hastened execution). Yet, in doing so predictably the defendant multiplied the number of sins for which one needed to atone. Falsely denying one's guilt did not open the defendant up to a charge of perjury. Not because justices deemed the lie defensible, but rather because there was no need to pursue the issue

---

Sara Butler, *The Language of Abuse: Marital Violence in Later Medieval England* (Leiden: Brill, 2007), 91.

[113] TNA JUST 3/87, m. 8 (Maud Kene de Cradebrugge, 1292); JUST 3/39/1, m. 22 (Maud wife of Hugh of Kinsham, 1305); JUST 3/140, m. 18d (Cecily, widow of John Gereson of Ekyngton, 1357); *CPR*, Edward III, vol. IX (1350–4), 175 (Katherine, widow of John Lakford of St. Edmund, 1351); *CPR*, Edward III, vol. X (1354–8), 529 (Cecily wife of John of Ridgeway 1357).

[114] TNA JUST 3/1/6, m. 4d (Felise Duffeld and Isote le Smale) and JUST 3/130, m. 57 (Isabel atte Pile).

at law: the defendant was already on his way to the gallows. The matter was better left to God at that point. An appellor who lost his case was another matter entirely. The appellee's acquittal doubled as the appellor's conviction: the appellor was guilty of perjury and faced jail time and a financial penalty. One might also lose one's standing for law-worthiness in the community. Swearing a false oath was a grievous matter. Oaths performed a pivotal role in medieval society, employed in a variety of circumstances and venues outside the court: civic oaths or oaths of office; oaths of fealty; contracts, including marriage; initiation into a tithing group or a guild; religious ordination; political alliances, the list goes on. An oath-swearer called on God or a saint to stand as witness to the oath-swearer's truth. At times, oaths were performed in the presence of a Bible or a relic acting as a point of contact between spiritual and material world, adding substantial credibility to an oath-taker's sincerity. God would surely strike down anyone who abused His trust in such an impetuous and arrogant manner. The invocation of God or His saints meant that false oaths and breaches of contract were spiritual concerns, belonging to ecclesiastical rather than secular jurisdiction.

Given the centrality of oath-taking to medieval society, it is no wonder that preachers railed against sinners who presumed to swear false oaths. Doing so was blatant disrespect for the eighth commandment: "You shall not bear false witness against your neighbor." The early fourteenth-century preacher's handbook, *Fasciculus Morum*, has much to say on the subject. The author warns that "a person who knowingly lies with perjury first of all commits himself to the devil; and when he touches the Book or some sacred object with his hand, by this hand the devil holds him until he returns to penance." He decries a perjurer as being "worse than the devil, who with God's permission dares commit every evil but does not dare to swear." Finally, he writes, "according to Augustine: even if it is permissible to swear, every oath is dangerous: hence one must always beware and fear lest one fall into perjury, because for whatever reason a man swears, he ties a rope around his neck and binds himself to danger."[115] For the guilty defendant standing at the bar, Augustine's

---

[115] Siegfried Wenzel, ed., *Fasciculus Morum: A Fourteenth-Century Preacher's Handbook* (University Park, PA: Pennsylvania State University Press, 1989), 165, 167, 169.

cautionary note surely struck a familiar chord. In his *Mirror of Mankind*, John Gower (d.1408) sketches for us the place of perjury in the hierarchy of sins. He explains that

> He who perjures himself commits great sin ... Perjury is by nature worse than homicide, for one might perchance see an occasion when one man might kill another, but no one could contrive to justify perjury. ... It is one of the most feared vices, which is expressly forbidden by divine commandment ... Whoever puts hand on the Book to swear falsely for mark or pound, by holding out his hand to perjure, separates himself from God, withdraws his fealty, and refuses thereafter to belong to Him; and now he swears his homage for the rest of his life to the devil, who rejoices at the covenant and has him inscribed in hell.[116]

An accused felon had much more to fear from God than from a jury of men. As a Middle English sermon expounds, "For God is suche a domes-man þat þou may not flee from hym" (For God is such a lawman that you cannot flee from him.)[117] In court, justices evoked this sentiment with the oft-repeated proverb: "once forsworn [perjured], ever forlorn."[118]

Knowing the consequences, if a suspect chose silence in court, the motivation may have been to avoid self-incrimination, perhaps not in the eyes of the court, but in God's. Typically, legal historians have traced the emergence of the privilege against self-incrimination in England to the quarrels between church and state developing in the seventeenth century. It did not arise earlier because the privilege made little sense in the medieval context. As John Langbein articulates it, in the Middle Ages, "[t]he right to remain silent when no one else can speak for you is simply the right to slit your throat, and it is hardly a mystery that defendants did not hasten to avail themselves of such privileges."[119] The central thrust of Langbein's point is well taken. The medieval courts did not recognize the privilege against self-incrimination; however, even

---

[116] John Gower, *Mirour de l'Omme (The Mirror of Mankind)*, trans. William Wilson (East Lansing: Colleagues Press, 1992), 89–90.

[117] From the sermon "De muliere Chananea," in Woodburn Ross, ed., *Middle English Sermons; edited from British Museum MS Royal 18 B. xxiii*, (EETS, vol. CCIX, 1940), 68.

[118] YB Mich. 18 Edw III (1344) (Seipp, 1344.226rs).

[119] John Langbein, "The Historical Origins of the Privilege against Self-Incrimination at Common Law," *Michigan Law Review* 92.5 (1994): 1047 and 1054.

if the English did not adopt the privilege until much later, the concept was hatched in the jurisprudence of medieval canonists. The maxim that "no one is obliged to accuse himself" (*nemo tenetur prodere se ipsum*) was expressed first in Pope Gregory IX's *Decretals* (1234), but repeated also in the writings of Pope Innocent IV (d.1254), Bartolus de Saxoferrato (d.1357), Panormitanus (d.1445), and Antonius Gabrielus (d.1555).[120] Justification for the maxim springs from Saint John Chrysostom (d.407)'s commentary on Saint Paul's letter to the Hebrews, in which he wrote "I do not say to you that you should betray yourself in public nor accuse yourself before others, but that you obey the prophet when he said, 'Reveal your ways unto the Lord.'"[121]

The rule grew up in response to the emergence of the church's oath *de veritate dicenda*, also known as the *ex officio* oath, required of witnesses in church court proceedings from the thirteenth century onward. Witnesses swore to answer all questions truthfully before they knew what questions might be asked, prompting fears that inquisitors tempted witnesses into committing perjury, a mortal sin.[122] This oath was also administered to sinners in ecclesiastical courts, although the church made no commitment to tender the articles sued against them before swearing. At the very least, canonists insisted that a sinner could not be asked to take the oath unless there existed "something like a prima facie case."[123] The right to remain silent intruded also into the *ius commune*, finding articulation in the *Speculum iudiciale* (1271) of William Durantis who declared that "no one is compelled to bear witness against himself, because no one is bound to reveal his own shame."[124] Thus, while the seventeenth-century Puritans are often credited with

---

[120] John Langbein, "Bifurcation and the Bench: The Influence of the Jury on English Conceptions of the Judiciary," in Paul Brand and Joshua Getzler, eds., *Judges and Judging in the History of the Common Law and Civil Law: From Antiquity to Modern Times* (Cambridge University Press, 2013), 67–82.

[121] As cited by Richard Helmholz, "The Privilege and the *Ius Commune*: The Middle Ages to the Seventeenth Century," in Helmholz, et al., eds.,*The Privilege against Self-Incrimination: Its Origins and Development* (University of Chicago Press, 1997), 26.

[122] Michael McNair, "The Early Development of the Privilege against Self-Incrimination," *Oxford Journal of Legal Studies* 10.1 (1990): 71.

[123] Richard Helmholz, *The Spirit of Classical Canon Law* (Athens: University of Georgia Press, 1996), 156.

[124] As cited in Helmholz, "Privilege and the *Ius Commune*," 26.

devising the privilege, they were in fact seizing on a pre-existing concept of Catholic design to which English subjects had been exposed for hundreds of years through the church courts.

The *ius commune*'s position on forced self-incrimination was well known and respected among the medieval English. Some few English litigants brandished the rule as grounds for refusing to answer questions before ecclesiastical justices. The most spectacular instance occurred in the mid thirteenth century, when Robert Grosseteste (d.1253), Bishop of Lincoln, endeavored to compel the laity in his diocese into taking an oath to reveal their secret faults. Not only did they fail to comply, they turned to the king for a writ of prohibition, "end[ing] this experiment in pastoral control."[125] In a 1532 heresy trial, John Lambert, a priest, declared that canon law protected him from answering incriminating questions under oath because "no man is bound to betray himself."[126] What is important about these examples is that they demonstrate a broader concern for public self-incrimination that was not respected by the courts of common law's pleading requirements. While it is impossible to gauge how many suspected felons preferred silence to self-incrimination, surely the oath's impact upon their souls was one of the many factors they needed to take into consideration.

The Right to Counsel

For a suspected felon, the greatest impediment to navigating the criminal justice system of medieval England was having to do so without the aid of counsel. The prohibition on legal counsel has long been thought to be grounded in Chapter 47 of the *Leges Henrici Primi,* which declares that in serious crimes, "no one shall seek counsel"; rather, the accused must respond immediately to the charges levied against him.[127] Of course, it is important to acknowledge that while the defendant did not have a professional pleader to assist him in formulating a defense, nor did he have a slick, fast-talking man of law with a weighty fee and knightly pretensions employed by the

---

[125] Helmholz, "Privilege and the *Ius Commune*," 32–3.
[126] Kelly, "Right to Remain Silent," 994.
[127] Italics are my own. *LHP*, ch. 47, subsection, 1, 156–9. Baker, *Introduction*, 5th edn., 546.

prosecution steering the jury to convict. Before the development of the adversarial system of trial in the eighteenth century, criminal trials in England were intended to be lawyer-less affairs.[128] Eliminating the need for counsel on either side was supposed to keep the law on an equal footing. It also leveled the playing field in terms of expenses: the impoverished defendant was not at a disadvantage because he could not afford the services of the *best* lawyer.

The trial process itself was designed to avoid prejudicing those in attendance. The king's justices simply read the prisoner's indictment aloud. Much to the chagrin of the legal historian, English indictments are brief, formulaic affairs, devoid of the kind of emotional language that might incite violence or anger. The defendant was then asked how he wished to acquit himself. Admittedly, after the defendant denied his guilt and agreed to rest his fate in the hands of the jury, things get more than a bit fuzzy. Transcripts of courtroom proceedings do not exist for medieval felony trials. In particular, whether witnesses presenting evidence in court was part of the process on either side is still a bit of a mystery. Anthony Musson has uncovered a number of cases which explicitly remark that the defendant called on witnesses to give evidence in his favor.[129] Yet, given that medieval felony trials typically lasted somewhere between fifteen and thirty minutes, trials must have centered on the testimony of the defendant, and if he had been appealed, also the appellor's count.[130] While the logistics of such a trial may be hard to imagine for a modern audience, it should be remembered that medieval juries were intended to be self-informing. They were expected to arrive at the trial knowing how they were going to vote, because another jury had already completed the legwork of the investigation and communicated those results to the trial jurors.[131] That is not to say that the verdict was fixed: as Musson writes, "[t]he reputation of the accused and the way he or she handled themselves in court could be

---

[128] John Langbein, *The Origins of the Adversary Criminal Trial* (Oxford University Press, 2005).

[129] Musson, *Public Order*, 202–5.

[130] Ralph Pugh, "The Duration of Criminal Trials in Medieval England," in Eric Ives and Anthony Manchester, eds., *Law, Litigants and the Legal Profession* (London: RHS, 1983), 108.

[131] Daniel Klerman, "Was the Jury ever Self-Informing?," *Southern California Law Review* 77 (2003): 123–49.

a vital factor leading to acquittal."[132] From this vantage point, the defendant actually dominated trial proceedings. One might argue that equipping him with legal counsel would unjustly give him a leg up.

Early modern jurists, also laboring under a lawyerless system of criminal justice, proposed additional justifications for not involving legal counsel in felony trials. In his *Institutes of the Lawes of England* (1628), Edward Coke reassured his audience that any systemic partiality was not deliberate: the legal process itself made counsel for the defense superfluous. High evidentiary standards are the key. A defendant might only be convicted if the evidence was "so manifest, as it could not be contradicted."[133] Under these circumstances, Coke reports, the unjustly accused had nothing to fear. The simplicity of the process that Coke describes had additional perquisites. As William Staunford (d.1558) observed a century earlier, pleaders with their fondness for verbal sparring and legal strategy would unnecessarily complicate and prolong the proceedings. They would be "so wary in their speech that it would be too long before the truth became apparent."[134] Further, keeping the defendant in the dark as to the nature of the evidence to be presented meant that a jury had a better chance of assessing the defendant's guilt or innocence by permitting its members to witness the accused's unmediated response. As William Hawkins' 1721 treatise remarked, "the very speech, gesture and countenance, and manner of defence of those who are guilty, may often help to disclose the truth, which probably would not so well be discovered from the artificial defence of others speaking for them."[135] Denying a suspected felon counsel, then, maintained the integrity of the process, ensured a speedy trial, and preserved the authenticity of an innocent person's incredulity.

In addition, it was the responsibility of the justices to see that "the indictment, triall, and other proceedings be good and sufficient in law; otherwise they should by their erroneous judgement attaint the prisoner unjustly."[136] Here, Coke hints at what was later articulated

---

[132] Musson, *Public Order*, 204.   [133] Coke, *Institutes*, vol. III, 137.
[134] William Staunford, *Les Plees del Coron* (London, 1557; repr. 1971), 151v.
[135] William Hawkins, *A Treatise on Pleas of the Crown*, 2 vols. (London: Elizabeth Nutt, 1721), vol. II, 400.
[136] Coke, *Institutes*, vol. III, 137.

as the legal maxim, "the court is counsel for the prisoner." The judge was not an umpire, but he was tasked especially with looking out for the defendant's welfare. This does not imply that he strategized with the accused on the best defense; but when it comes to points of law, such as defective indictments, or illegal procedure, the responsibility fell to the king's justices to inform the defendant of his or her rights and to advocate for a fair trial. If they failed to do so, and the defendant was executed, that death lay on their consciences. Coke spread the blame to an ever wider group by pointing out that "it is lawfull for any man that is in court, to informe the court of any of these matters, lest the court should erre, and the prisoner unjustly for his life proceeded with."[137]

How applicable are these statements to the medieval trial process? The medieval evidence presents a number of distinct stumbling blocks. First, the presumption that jurors would not convict without evidence of an incontrovertible nature is hard to sustain for an era in which the rules of evidence were unwritten and undefined. Legal treatises attempt to establish high standards. The *Leges Henrici Primi*, for example, pronounces that judges must not believe allegations "unless they can be established by unassailable proofs."[138] Admittedly, much changed in the era after the creation of this text. It is reassuring that the sentiment is echoed also in the *Mirror of Justices*, which declares that "it is an abuse to adjudge a man to death for felony on the testimony of suitors, except in cases so notorious that there is no need or room for any answer or jury."[139] Of course, neither treatise gives any indication as to what constitutes an indisputable proof. In a discussion regarding charters, *Bracton* employs language no doubt borrowed from the *ius commune* regarding full proofs and half proofs; he also quotes Matthew 18:16, that "in the mouth of two or three witnesses, every word may be established."[140] *Bracton*'s frequent borrowings from Roman law have often been interpreted as wishful thinking. In no medieval English treatise do we get a firm sense of just how high that bar was set. Criteria for proof very much remained in the hands of the jury; although the exceptionally low conviction rates of the era point to a high benchmark.[141]

---

[137] Coke, *Institutes*, vol. III, 137.   [138] *LHP*, ch. 5, subsection 18, 90–1.
[139] Whittaker, ed., *Mirror of Justices*, 159, no. 44.   [140] *Bracton*, vol. II, 120.
[141] Conviction rates for fourteenth- and fifteenth-century England hovered between 12.5 and 21 percent. Bellamy, *Criminal Trial*, 69.

Second, the problem with the "court-as-counsel rubric" is the simple fact that the king's justices held their offices at the pleasure of the Crown. They were also presiding over cases in which the Crown (their employer) stood as victim. The king's role as a party to the suit was *ex officio* – the defendant was indicted at the king's suit – but the king's participation in that suit was not fictitious, nor was it peripheral. In serious crimes, the *king's* peace had been breached; thus, the king was in fact the identifiable victim of every crime committed during his reign. Nor was his victimization merely rhetorical: a violation of the king's peace undermined his authority, stained his reputation, and endangered his standing as king. A king incapable of keeping the peace in the realm was likely to be overthrown. That each felony was interpreted as a personal attack on the king is underscored also by the fact that the king's peace died with him. Accordingly, upon his death, all those imprisoned awaiting trial on felony indictments were released.[142] One might argue then that expecting justices of jail delivery to act as counsel for the defendant placed them in a serious conflict of interest.[143]

Bracton would also seem to place the onus for preparing a defense squarely on the defendant's shoulders: "If he simply says that he wishes to defend himself as the court of the lord king decides, unless he says more he will be without defence, *because it is not for the king's court to show him how he ought to make his defence.*"[144] Naturally, this statement cannot be taken entirely at face value as it follows directly on the heels of the treatise's detailed instructions on how an accused felon ought to defend him/herself. A passage in *Britton* implies that the accused must be granted time to weigh options: "To the intent that no one may be unprepared with his answer, let those who are so taken have fifteen days at least, if they pray it, to provide their defence, and in the meantime let them be safely kept."[145] How the defendant was expected to use that time is not spelled out: but surely fifteen days

---

[142] This process, naturally, builds on and mirrors the appeal: when an appellor dies, his appeal also dies with him.

[143] John Langbein, "The Prosecutorial Origins of Defence Counsel in the Eighteenth Century: The Appearance of Solicitors," *Cambridge Law Journal* 58. 2 (1999): 316. In its long list of abuses, the *Mirror* speaks directly to this problem, stating "[i]t is an abuse to suffer judges to be plaintiffs for the king." Whittaker, ed., *Mirror of Justices*, 161, no. 64.

[144] Italics are my own. *Bracton*, vol. II, 390.   [145] Nichols, ed., *Britton*, vol. I, 26.

was sufficient to consult with a serjeant-at-law, or someone with at least a rudimentary understanding of the law.

Evidence from the courtroom practice, however, demonstrates that justices did act as counsel for defense. To clarify: they did not see it as their jobs to assist the accused in planning a defense; yet, they took it upon themselves to explain the proceedings to the defendant, much like a legal consultant, so that when the defendant pled, he or she did so in an informed manner, cognizant of the options available and of the possible outcomes. There are numerous examples from the existing record to corroborate this perspective. *Placita Corone* (*c.* 1274), a form book for English students of law, provides an instantly recognizable example of a judge guiding the defendant through the legal process. Suspected of stealing a mare, Nicholas de E. stands before the bar with little confidence in his comprehension of the law. When prompted to answer the allegations against him, Nicholas replies: "Sir, God knows, I am an unlettered man and have scarcely ever made a plea: hence I feel scarcely able to defend myself, and for this reason, sir, I beg you to let me be advised by some learned person as to how I can best defend myself in this case." The justice's reply clarifies that he cannot provide the defendant with hired legal counsel because to do so was unlawful; yet, he notes that it is also unnecessary, "for who can tell us more about your doings than you yourself? Do as a wise man, and as a good and law-abiding man should do; keep God before your eyes and tell us the truth of this matter, and we shall be as merciful as we can, according to the law."[146] The trial that ensued was effectively a dialogue between judge and defendant. While the accused was ultimately sentenced to hang, he had ample opportunity to defend his actions and have his case heard.

Standing mute had procedural implications of which a defendant needed to be aware when planning a defense. Justices of eyre in the homicide investigation of Isabel of Bury, accused of killing a man while in church, took their responsibility as counsel seriously to make certain that she did not box herself into a corner through poor legal decision-making. Although Isabel initially claimed sanctuary, because the homicide transpired in the very church in

---

[146] John Kaye, ed., *Placita Corone, or La Corone Pledee devant Justices* (SS, supplementary series, vol. IV, 1966), 17.

which she took refuge, the ordinary rejected her plea. She was ejected from the church, imprisoned, and then brought to trial before justices of eyre, at which point she kept silent.

So the court demanded what her name was and whence she came, and she did not answer.

[JUSTICE] BEREFORD: Enquiry had better be made whether she is dumb or not, and when she last spoke.

Thereupon twelve came and took oath to tell the truth thereupon and went out to speak together. And then (said)

PASSELEY, J. You would do better to speak, for if we hold an inquest and find that you can speak you will not be permitted to challenge the jurors. So speak and put yourself on a jury and you will be acquitted.

ISABEL. Sir, mercy for God's sake!

PASSELEY, J. Recall the jurors, for she is speaking.

Then she was charged with the death, as above, and she said 'Sir, he struck me'.

PASSELEY, J. Did you kill him or not?

ISABEL. Sir, I did it in self defence.

PASSELEY, J. How do you wish to acquit yourself?

ISABEL. Sir, I could do no other.

PASSELEY, J. Then do you wish to say that you did not kill him?

ISABEL. Sir, I did it in self defence.

PASSELEY, J. You should deny the felony.

And so she did, and said that she did not kill him, and put herself (on the country) and so she was hanged.[147]

In Isabel's case, she was not able to convince a jury of her innocence, and we have no idea of knowing why. Even still, this dialogue underscores the uncertainty that existed regarding pleading. It reveals also how the king's justices were enthusiastic guides in the legal process, navigating defendants through a sea of choices. Admittedly, Justice Passeley was more confident in Isabel's chances of acquittal than he should have been; given the high acquittal rates of the period, his assurance would seem to have been appropriate.

---

[147] Cam, ed., *Year Books of Edward II*, 73–4 (Seipp 1321.124ss).

Even the most prepared defendant relied on the extensive knowledge of the king's justices as a guide through the process. This is apparent in a 1292 presentment for rape, in which the accused felon, identified only as Hugh, initially claimed benefit of clergy; however, one of the justices balked at turning him over to the ordinary because Hugh, presumably a member of minor orders, had contracted marriage to a widow, making him a bigamous cleric and therefore ineligible for the privilege. The defendant then objected to the composition of the jury as his accusers were also sitting on the trial jury. Further, as a knight, Magna Carta guarantees that his peers, not his social inferiors, stand as jurors. Justices complied with his request, summoning twelve knights to sit in judgment. Still, he refused to plead. One justice warned him of where his obstinacy would lead: peine forte et dure. At this point, Hugh switched tactics and asked to challenge particular members of the jury. He was asked to put his objections down in writing, and so Hugh requested the assistance of legal counsel, prompting one of the judges, whose patience was surely starting to wear thin, to remind him that a defendant might not consult legal counsel during a felony trial. Hugh explained that he could not read (or write, presumably), despite having already claimed benefit of clergy at a time when *clericus* (clergy) and *litteratus* (literate) were interchangeable terms. Uncertain exactly how to proceed, Hugh stood quietly, confused. Exasperated, the same judge cried, "I don't know why you are speechless, now is the time to speak!" Taking matters into his own hands, the judge appointed Lord Nicholas of Leicester to write down Hugh's challenges. When it came time for the accused to read out the names, the judge ordered Lord Nicholas to read them in private to the defendant so that Hugh might repeat them, because the challenges "must come through his own mouth" (*quia per os suum debent exsumi*). Having removed those individuals from the jury, they finally proceeded to trial.[148]

Of course, the ban on counsel for the defense was not absolute. When the defendant stood on appeal, both appellor and appellee had the right to legal representation. The intent was to maintain a sense of symmetry and fair play. If the appellor has the right to a serjeant to

---

[148] Horwood, ed., *Year Books of the Reign of Edward the First*, 529–32 (Seipp 1295.003rs).

present his count, the appellee should be similarly equipped. Given the "greater heat and spleen" that typically motivates a private accusation, leaving the accused unassisted against a trained serjeant-at-law likely did not seem amenable to producing a just outcome.[149] Further, because trespass belonged to civil jurisdiction, and thus was deemed by the law to be a personal matter, a defendant in a case of assault had every right to defense counsel. The irony of this situation did not go unnoticed by Blackstone, who opined: "For upon what face of reason can that assistance be denied to save the life of a man, which yet is allowed him in prosecutions for every petty trespass?"[150] Indeed, the absurdity of providing legal counsel to the perpetrator of an assault, but refusing it to one whose assault turned fatal begs the question of whether this was in fact the plan from the beginning.

Informed Silence

Justices sometimes feared that a defendant's silence sprang from ignorance of the legal system. This concern was voiced openly by the author of the *Mirror of Justices*, who fretted that "some folk make themselves guilty by not answering in court or answering badly or insufficiently."[151] This may have been particularly true in the thirteenth century when pleading procedure was becoming increasingly more complicated. When God was the anticipated audience of the defendant's plea, there was no concern that He might not appreciate the circumstances surrounding the crime, or the defendant's state of mind. Yet, when a jury of twelve mortal men replaced God as judge, a denial of the charges alone was insufficient to explain the defendant's position.[152] In this transitional context, surely some confusion existed regarding both the need to plead and how to plead. How else do we explain the 1286 trial of Walter le Monner of Histon at Cambridge? He was one of a number of persons who stood indicted of the death of Benedict del Howes. Because Walter would not submit to jury trial the king's justices returned him to prison to suffer

---

[149] Hawkins, *A Treatise on Pleas of the Crown*, vol. II, 401.
[150] *Blackstone*, vol. IV, 349.
[151] Whittaker, ed., *Mirror of Justices*, 90.
[152] S.F.C. Milsom, *Historical Foundations of the Common Law* (London: Butterworths, 1969), 30–2.

peine forte et dure. Some time afterwards, he reappeared in court and informed the judge that he had not agreed to jury trial because Justice Southfleet and his associates had already acquitted him of this homicide. After a review of the records, the court agreed and ordered him acquitted (again).[153] The fact that he did not mention the acquittal in the first place can only be rationalized as a defective understanding of legal process. The process became even more convoluted with the development of pleading at bar. In these instances, when asked how the defendant wished to acquit him- or herself, instead of a direct denial of the accusation the defendant put forward an exception against the appeal (*exceptiones contra appellum*). Exceptions might include: that the appeal was fabricated out of hate and spite (*de odio et atya*); the indictment was spoiled because it failed to identify the defendant properly; or, that the defendant had in fact been defending against an attack initiated by the "victim."

Nonetheless, the Crown was attentive to the legal needs of its subjects. The reforming years of the mid thirteenth century saw the king's justices embrace the ideology of "fair treatment of everyone regardless of their status."[154] Providing fair treatment translated into the proliferation of resources available to the lower orders to better equip themselves to fight their battles in court. Parliament and the judiciary organized diverse forms of "legal aid" to offset the expenses of litigation for the poor. Full-time, professional pleaders date back as early as the 1220s or 1230s, and the late medieval era witnessed an upsurge in numbers and affordability.[155] Litigants too impoverished to hire a pleader in their defense were sometimes provided one by justices at no charge. Petitions to parliament sought to reduce the costs associated with purchasing an original writ and action initiated by bill (that is, an oral complaint) became gradually more common for those who sought justice at King's Bench.[156] The move to adopt English as the language of pleading, initiated first by the City of London in 1356 and legislated for the rest of England just six years

---

[153] TNA JUST 1/92, m. 12d (1286).

[154] Anthony Musson, *Medieval Law in Context: The Growth of Legal Consciousness from Magna Carta to the Peasant's Revolt* (Manchester University Press, 2001), 164.

[155] Paul Brand, *The Origins of the English Legal Profession* (Oxford: Blackwell, 1992), 55.

[156] Musson, *Medieval Law*, 164–7.

later, spoke directly to this concern.[157] Parliament cautioned that conducting court proceedings in French, a language that is "much unknown" in England, meant that litigants "have no knowledge nor understanding of that which is said for them or against them by their sergeants and other pleaders."[158] The increasing frequency of court sessions over the course of the thirteenth and fourteenth centuries must also have provided the English population with myriad opportunities to become familiar with the workings of the law.

The trial of Robert Eypton provides an instructive example of a royal justice determined to prevent the defendant from making a bad decision with fatal consequences. On July 23, 1463, Thomas Armethorpe came before royal justices assembled at Nottingham for jail delivery to appeal Robert Eypton, a Yorkshire weaver, of having stolen forty sheep from Armethorpe's land. When asked how he would acquit himself, Eypton offered a rather cryptic response, declaring that he would do so "by God and Our Lady Saint Mary and by the Holy Church."[159] With Margaret Clitheroe in our hindsight, it is possible that Eypton's reply hints at a heretical leaning; yet justices at the time were merely puzzled by his nonsensical plea. One of the justices dutifully informed the defendant that his was not a proper answer, that he needed to respond according to the form and process of the law and to do as the law provided, otherwise he would not do well. Still Eypton would give no other answer. Justices prodded him gently on the matter, advising him to say "according to the law of the land," and yet again for the next hour Eypton remained silent.

In the meanwhile, a second appellor appeared with a complaint of robbery against Eypton; then a third. With three appeals of felony lodged against him, Eypton needed to submit an admissible plea, yet his performance remained unchanged: he continued to plead as he had before and refused to plead otherwise. Seeing the danger imminent in this stubborn refusal to comply with the law, Chief Justice Robert

---

[157] Reginald Sharpe, ed., *Calendar of Letter Books of the City of London: G, 1352–1374* (London: HMSO, 1905), 73; also cited in Musson, *Medieval Law*, 168.

[158] 36 Edw. III, Stat. 1, c. 15 (1362), *SR*, vol. 1, 375.

[159] His peculiar response is far more reminiscent of a will than a plea, as English wills at that time commonly opened with the phrase "I bequeath my soul to Almighty God, and to our Lady Saint Mary, and to all the saints in Heaven." In his *Grande Abridgement*, Fitzherbert also mentions this case. Anthony Fitzherbert, *La Graunde Abridgement* (London: John Rastell and Wynkyn de Worde 1516), fo. 246, no. 27.

Danby took it upon himself to counsel the defendant. In laymen's terms he explained to Eypton that according to the common law, his response was the same as giving no response at all. Indeed, the law interpreted his actions as contumacy or a refusal to plead. Choosing this course of action would result in his death and jeopardize his soul. Danby advised him to give up his folly, to enter his plea, and "to place his life in the mouth of the jury." Once again Eypton replied that he would be acquitted "by God, Our Lady, and the Holy Church."

Surely on the verge of losing his patience, Danby wished Eypton to know exactly where his failure to conform to legal expectations would lead. He cautioned Eypton that he would be the cause of his own death. This reply would land him in prison where they would weigh down his body with as many stones and irons as he could bear and more, feeding him on a diet of brown bread one day and water the next, the water drawn from whatever brook or stream stood closest to the prison, and he would remain in this state until he was dead. Thus, it was in the defendant's best interests to tender a different response to the court's query of how he wished to acquit himself. With counsel for the plaintiff hounding him to hang the defendant for his silence, Danby and his fellow justices adjourned court for dinner, requesting the sheriff in their absence assign the defendant a confessor who might offer him some valuable advice. When justices returned, they discovered the defendant had experienced a change of heart: he pleaded "not guilty" to each of the charges; and on one charge after another, the jury found him guilty. Justices sentenced Eypton to hang for his crimes.[160]

Chief Justice Danby was convinced that Eypton failed to plead because he did not understand the legal proceedings; he also went to great lengths to remedy Eypton's ignorance of the law, not only through his own lectures on the subject, but also by asking that the prisoner be permitted access to a confessor, presumably as both spiritual and legal counsel. In any event, Danby was not content to have Eypton sent to peine forte et dure without understanding full well the implications of a refusal to plead. Because Eypton was bound for death either way, the modern reader might not appreciate the value of Danby's intervention in the case. First, it must be acknowledged that with such high rates of acquittal in the Middle Ages, Danby could not

[160] YB Pasch. term, 1464 (Seipp, 1464.021).

have known definitively that the jury was going to convict. Second, even if he did somehow realize Eypton was facing certain conviction, surely he appreciated that hanging was a much swifter and more dignified form of death. His counsel, then, was critical in making sure that if Eypton persisted in his refusal to plead then he did so in an informed manner.

The law set a high bar for judges. *Bracton* regularly likens the seat of judgment to the throne of God. The man who ascends to this throne must be wise, learned, and experienced. Above all, he must keep his eye on the prize: justice, lest "by judging perversely and against the laws, because of prayer or price, for the advantage of a temporary and insignificant gain, he dare to bring upon himself sorrow and lamentation everlasting." *Bracton* pulls no punches in warning judges how the Lord will take revenge on evil judges on the day of wrath. "Who shall not fear that trial, where the Lord shall be the accuser, the advocate and the judge? From his sentence there is no appeal, for the Father has committed all judgment to the Son; he shuts and there is none to open; he opens and there is none to shut. O how strict shall that judgment be, where we shall give account not only of our acts but even of every idle word."[161]

Justices of jail delivery were concerned to protect the legal rights of the defendant by advising him on all of his options. This is evident more than ever when indicted felons pled insufficiently. Justices were uncertain whether their intent was to refuse to plead, or if they merely did not know what they were doing. Eypton's case is mirrored in the 1378 trial of John Tyglere, arrested with goods in hand (*cum manuopere*) for breaking into the parish church of Wells (Sussex) and stealing a missal worth ten pounds as well as two decorated silver chalices worth nine marks. At trial, when asked how he wished to acquit himself, Tyglere disavowed the goods and declared he wished to place himself in the grace of the king (*quod se ponere in gratiam domini Regius*). One of the king's justices subtly corrected Tyglere, pointing out that he needed to put himself upon the country, not the king, but Tyglere would in no way assent to a jury trial. Twice more he petitioned to place himself in the grace of the king; one can only assume this was an unconventional, last-ditch attempt to obtain a pardon for

---

[161] *Bracton*, vol. II, 21.

his crimes without paying for it. Yet, this was neither the time nor the place to initiate that process. Following the third round of explanations about proper pleading procedure, justices conceded that Tyglere's tenacity must be deliberate. They sentenced him to the starvation diet.[162]

The decision to provide the defendant multiple opportunities to plead also springs from justices' eagerness to confirm that the defendant was in fact refusing trial. In the eighteenth century, Blackstone explained that an accused felon must receive a third warning (*trina admonitio*) then a "respite of a few hours" in which the sentence was once against read to the defendant "so he may know his danger."[163] It is not clear exactly when this procedure began to be employed, but most medieval felons were given an opportunity to rethink their position. For example, the scribe in Nicholas of Cerne's 1293 appeal of homicide commented specifically that he was asked once, twice, and a third time (*ipse primo secundo tercio*) whether he wished to plead.[164] Justices at Oxford jail in 1319 also asked Ellen Kyteben once, then again and a third time (*iterum et tercio*).[165] Others offered four[166] or five[167] opportunities to plead. Some justices clearly went overboard: when John of Greete of Rowley stood accused of homicide and burglary in 1354, the record explains how justices of jail delivery ordered three separate inquests just to be certain about whether he could speak.[168] Given the feverish pace at which justices of jail delivery worked, it seems unlikely that each silent defendant was afforded a few hours to consider the consequences of his actions. However, these examples attest to the dedication of royal justices to follow a generous procedure that allotted the defendant numerous opportunities to rethink the decision to stand mute and plead before being condemned to peine forte et dure.

---

[162] TNA JUST 3/163, m. 12 (1378).   [163] *Blackstone*, Book IV, ch. 25.
[164] TNA JUST 3/91, m. 15d (1293).   [165] TNA JUST 3/115B, m. 4d (1319).
[166] In 1323, William Rokeley of Bromham was given four chances. TNA JUST 3/1/4, m. 4d (1323).
[167] Robert of Carleton in 1352 was accorded five opportunities to plead. JUST 3/79/1, m. 14 (1352). Arraigned in 1309, justices asked Richard Faber of Sinethecote "often" how he wished to plead; in 1394, Nicholas Reyron of Chilton was also asked "often at the required intervals" how he wished to plead. TNA JUST 3/122, m. 10 (1309); JUST 3/179, m. 19d (1394).
[168] TNA JUST 3/131, m. 22 (1354).

Conclusion

If standing mute was a tactic belonging to a grander defense strategy employed by a defendant upon arraignment for felony charges, it is critical to understand the challenges of navigating the judicial process. Without access to a legal advisor, whether friends who had witnessed other trials or had been burned by the law themselves, it is hard to imagine that an untaught suspect might easily determine when refusing to plead would lead to peine forte et dure versus execution. The venue mattered: yet, it is important for us to ask how easy it was for men and women of the time to discern the nature of the court, given that the location was not always set in stone, and the justices presiding might be the same whether the law being administered was criminal, civil, canon, or the law of arms. Over the course of the era, justices became more and more convinced that standing mute should not be permitted in instances of appeal or in accusations of treason; and yet, judicial discretion meant that cases slipped through the cracks despite their illegality. Defendants also stood at a disadvantage as standing mute was clearly aligned with contempt of court in the minds of late medieval English justices. What is clear is that the law's requirement for a plea stood at cross-purposes with a defendant's desire not to self-incriminate. Nor did suspected felons avail themselves equally of this tactic: women rarely stood mute, but those who did made the choice out of desperation.

The one positive note is that justices of jail delivery saw themselves as legal consultants for the defendant, and made an effort to explain the inner workings of the justice system when needed. When a defendant fumbled through the arraignment process, they feared he or she did so through misinformation and justices intervened to share their knowledge of the judicial system in order to guide the defendant towards the appropriate choices. The cases in this chapter, then, show us that Justice Clench's behavior when confronted with Margaret Clitheroe's persistent obstinacy was not necessarily exceptional. The determination of justices to steer defendants through a complex process in fact reflects a broader jurisprudence that prioritized the rights of the defendant to a fair trial, which will be addressed in the following chapter.

3

Due Process and Consent to Jury Trial

[L]et me know by what lawful authority I am seated here, and I will answer it; otherwise I will not answer it.

> King Charles I, at his trial (January 20, 1649).[1]

Presumably, common-law justices never intended to grant a defendant license to stand mute. Rather, the accused's liberty to do so was a predicament generated by the court's arraignment process in which English justices asked the accused: "*how* do you wish to acquit yourself?" The original intent behind the question was to uncover which method of proof the defendant favored: compurgation, fire, water, or combat. That the choice belonged to the defendant is emphasized in *Bracton* in his instructions for "[h]ow those appealed ought to make their defence." The author writes, the defendant "will then have the choice [*electionem*] of putting himself on the country or of defending himself by his body." If he chooses jury trial, he must say "that he is not guilty thereof he puts himself on the country for good and ill." If he prefers combat, he should say that "he is ready to defend himself against him by his body as the king's court decides."[2] Naturally, the full range of options was not available to every defendant; one's status in the community and the manner in which one had been brought to trial dictated the means of proof available. A trustworthy individual

---

[1] Krista Kesselring, ed., *The Trial of Charles I* (Toronto: Broadview Press, 2016), 36.
[2] *Bracton*, vol. II, 390.

of good standing in the community earned the right to prove his or her innocence through compurgation. For the less trustworthy, compurgation was not an option, but there were still choices. The accused was permitted to select battle (on appeal) or the ordeal, making one feel as if one was at least partly in control of one's fate. It was the judges' responsibility to counsel the accused in this matter. This is demonstrated amply in *Placita Corone*. When a man impleaded of felony was asked how he wished to acquit himself, he opted for combat. However, because he was indicted at the king's suit, rather than on appeal, the judge gently informed him that combat was not an option: "My good friend, no man makes suit against you except the king, and the king does not wish to do battle." Thus, he asked him again, "how do you wish to acquit yourself of such a theft?" Eventually, the accused settled on jury trial, declaring "By the country, to be sure."[3]

The question itself, "how do you wish to acquit yourself," today is seen only as a request for a plea. Nonetheless, it very much encapsulates a foundational concept in medieval English criminal justice: the defendant's right to choose the method of trial. From the perspective of the Crown, the implications of a defendant's choice were not simply procedural. A note in a year book from 1423 explains that "by pleading not guilty, [the defendant] gives jurisdiction to the court."[4] Consent, then, represented the defendant's recognition of the king's jurisdiction, but also consent to be tried, and a willingness to abide by the outcome of the trial.

This book is not the first to argue that some defendants withheld their consent because of loss of choice. Theodore Plucknett writing in 1929 made this point; it was reiterated most recently in a 2003 article by Benjamin Berger.[5] Yet, what neither scholar seems to have noticed is the full extent of the changes which took place over the course of a fifty-year period, dramatically reducing the customary rights of the accused. A defendant's right to choose his method of trial came under fire beginning in the twelfth century with what is commonly referred to

---

[3] John Kaye, ed., *Placita Corone, or La Corone Pledee devant Justices* (SS, supplementary series, vol. IV, 1966), 23-24.

[4] YB Pasch 1 Hen. VI (1423), fos. 80r–80v (Seipp 1423.009abr).

[5] Theodore Plucknett, *Concise History of the Common Law*, 2nd edn. (London: Butterworths, 1936), 118; Benjamin Berger, "*Peine Forte et Dure*: Compelled Jury Trials and Legal Rights in Canada," *Criminal Law Quarterly* 18.2 (2003): 205–48.

as the "Angevin leap forward." The legal reforms of Henry II (d.1189) and his descendants in the process of centralization and expansion of royal power included a multi-step process. First, the era saw the emergence of "felony" as a coherent category, defined chiefly as a breach of the king's peace, thus becoming a matter solely for royal adjudication.[6] Not only did this mandate remove the power to try a broad array of criminals from noble hands, it entailed also effectively the criminalization of homicide. As Tom Lambert has noted, prior to the late twelfth century, English law equated crime chiefly with offenses against property, namely theft, but also unjust seizure of property, what a later era would describe as disseissin.[7] For a feud culture, the secretive and dishonorable nature of theft was intolerable: the hidden identity of the offender left the victim with no recourse for compensation, no means to strike back and restore his honor. English law codes thus adopted a hard line on the matter. As early as the seventh century, execution and felony forfeiture had become the twin punishments implemented to deter and stigmatize theft. Homicide, along with other offenses against the person, was not subject to the same kind of prohibitions. It was considered a private offense for which compensation, not execution, was the prescribed remedy. Compensation in the form of *wergeld* was paid directly to the victim's family; while the victim's lord and the king both stood to gain, their shares (*manbot* and *fihtwite* respectively) were negligible.[8] Indeed, by Cnut's time (r. 1016–35), the king had minimized his involvement in adjudicating homicide cases, leaving it chiefly to local lords to administer. Thus, when the Angevin kings forged a monopoly on serious crime, and included homicide within

---

[6] John Hudson, *The Formation of the English Common Law: Law and Society in England from King Alfred to Magna Carta*, 2nd edn. (London: Routledge, 2018), 16. The term "felony" appears in the 1176 Assizes of Northampton to mean a "serious wrong" (150).

[7] Tom Lambert, "Theft, Homicide and Crime in Late Anglo-Saxon Law," *P&P*, 214.1 (2012): 3–43. Patrick Wormald was the first to observe that "theft" of property was also treated as a serious crime in the Anglo-Saxon era. See his "Anglo-Saxon Law and Scots Law," *Scottish Historical Review* 88.2 (2009): 194.

[8] Wormald suggests that we can only label an offense a crime if the element of royal punishment dominates the settlement. See Patrick Wormald, "Giving God and King their Due: Conflict and its Regulation in the Early English State," in Patrick Wormald, ed., *Legal Culture and the Early Medieval West: Law as Text, Image and Experience* (London: Hambledon, 1999), 341–2.

that category, this "post-Conquest development" was nothing less than "revolutionary."[9]

Second, the revision of the accusation process for felony, prompting the creation of the jury of presentment, fundamentally transformed the accusation process by empowering the ordinary man and woman to protect themselves through anonymous complaint. This transition also entailed an abandonment of compurgation, the dominant means of proof. Again, the radical nature of this change suggests an extraordinary measure for extraordinarily violent times. Paul Hyams lays the blame on Henry's predecessor. King Stephen (d.1154)'s lax rule in which he had permitted the nobility greater freedom led to higher levels of private warfare and internecine crime. Initially, Henry probably envisioned presentment as "a one-time exercise" to get England's soaring crime levels under control and assert his dominance over the peerage. Yet, once he and his administrators discovered the advantages of a process that leveled the playfield for accusers, they decided to transform an expedient measure into a permanent process.[10]

For the suspected felon, Henry's reforms represented a serious reduction in choice and control over the nature of trial. These options diminished even further with Lateran IV's 1215 pronouncement that priests were no longer permitted to preside over ordeals of water or fire. Battle continued to be available, but only in private prosecution – a much less popular choice after the introduction of the jury of presentment made anonymous accusation the norm. By 1217, the number of choices a defendant had to prove his or her innocence had effectively narrowed to one: jury trial, which had come to replace the ordeals. For the Crown, this transition had multiple benefits. Not only did it assure the Crown superior control of the peace-keeping process, thus helping to secure the king's reputation and his grip on the throne, it also held the promise of greater financial returns. However, from the defendant's perspective, the stakes had risen tremendously. The man who killed another in what many would have seen to be a fair fight was now deemed a criminal

[9] Lambert, "Theft, Homicide and Crime," 5.
[10] Paul Hyams, *Rancor and Reconciliation in Medieval England* (Ithaca: Cornell University Press, 2003), 164.

who risked execution (rather than compensation), in a nontraditional trial, in which men, rather than a merciful God, decided his fate.

The justices' request to know how the accused wished to acquit himself, then, existed both as a relic from the past when a defendant had multiple options, as well as an ongoing charade that those choices continued to exist. In this early phase, for some defendants, asking how they wished to plead was probably a perpetual irritant, reminding them of all that they had lost in the Crown's efforts to centralize criminal justice. In addition, failure to rephrase the question meant that English justices made it *sound* like a defendant might refuse jury trial and hold out for something better, when in reality no one had come up with an alternative to the trial jury. Of course, peine forte et dure would have been wholly unnecessary if the courts had simply imposed trial jury on accused felons as justices did on the Continent, rather than pausing to ask permission before trying them. In doing so, the English put themselves in an impossible bind, officially eschewing judicial torture and yet condoning (at times) equally brutal behavior when defendants were uncooperative and refused to plead. Thus, this book asks, as James Masschaele has: "Why was the principle of giving consent to a jury trial so highly cherished that even torture was worth accepting to maintain it?"[11]

That is the question this chapter endeavors to answer. The following pages zero in on that moment of transition to elucidate why some defendants withheld their consent to be tried, but also to understand the thought processes of the justices who refused to move forward without it. Consent was critical because justices viewed a defendant's right to a fair trial as paramount. The long twelfth century (1085–1215) marks the emergence of a pan-European natural rights discourse that championed the notion that an accused felon was entitled to a public trial with due process. While the theologians who pioneered the discipline of natural law were the first to promote this new jurisprudence, almost at once enthusiasm for an individual's rights at law infused also canon law, Europe's *ius commune*, and England's common law. This atmosphere is the necessary background in which to deconstruct the common law's approach to those who stood mute. Agreement to jury trial became pivotal because it represented consent,

---

[11] James Masschaele, *Jury, State, and Society in Medieval England* (New York: Palgrave Macmillan, 2008), 82.

and in an era which prized a defendant's right to a fair trial, justices were reluctant to move ahead when the trial's central actor was an unwilling participant.[12]

The transition to jury trial exacerbated the judiciary's disinclination to proceed in the absence of consent. In the days of the ordeal, the fate of the accused was left in the hands of God. With jury trials, the jury handed down a verdict, while justices ordered it carried out. The weight of this transition bore heavily on both justices and jurors, who balked at the notion of sending an uncooperative defendant to the gallows. Consent became central, then, for multiple reasons. Not only was it necessary to protect a defendant's right to justice in an era preoccupied with natural rights; it was also necessary to assuage justices and jurors alike, who saw that a defendant's consent relieved them of the spiritual burden of homicide. Indeed, the judiciary's preoccupation with extracting consent can be traced in a number of ways. England's brief experimentation with writs *de bono et malo* were an attempt to set consent in stone by requiring written evidence of a defendant's consent to trial. When that failed, justices put renewed emphasis on oral consent, not only insisting that they must hear it directly from the lips of the accused, but also emphasizing that the defendant was (1) capable of consenting, and (2) making an informed decision when he or she chose to withhold consent to trial. In this context, the emergence of the category of prison (or peine) forte et dure as a body of coercive measures begins to add up: a defendant's consent was so badly needed, justices would do almost anything to get it.

Consent and the defendant's right to due process are the keys to comprehending the Crown's reliance on peine forte et dure. Withholding consent put the defendant in the driver's seat: through silence the accused gained control over his or her life (and death), simultaneously debilitating the courts. In order to move forward, justices had to turn the tables and reclaim their position of authority, all while respecting a defendant's right to be tried in a just manner.

---

[12] Please note: the goal here is to uncover what the medieval world interpreted as a fair trial, not whether they implemented a fair trial in the modern sense. For example, we cannot complain that they did not implement an appeals process in medieval England. The appeals process was an invention of the mid nineteenth century – how was the medieval world supposed to know that an appeals process was a hallmark of justice when they had never before encountered such a system?

Coercion through prison forte et dure was the answer: it allowed them to extricate "voluntary" consent from the defendant, compelling the accused into submission so that they might proceed to a lawful trial.

Transitioning from Proofs to Jury Trial

Standing mute as a practice emerged in the wake of this transition, such that historians have typically interpreted the practice as a rejection of jury trial. As Maitland once opined, "one hears talk of trial by jury as of an obviously just institution. Our ancestors did not think so."[13] Plucknett declared that "if such a prisoner could have spoken the language of modern constitutional law he would very likely have raised a doubt whether trial by jury in criminal cases was due process of law, for the time-honoured methods of trial were the ordeals, and the petty jury was a new-found device of very recent origin."[14] Admittedly, much of the discomfort both Maitland and Plucknett detected in the medieval reception of jury trial was premised on the belief that jury trial was some new-fangled experiment borrowed from the Norman tradition and imposed on the English people from above when the pope's prohibition of ordeals left them without any normal means of trial. Maitland and Plucknett saw the medieval English reacting strenuously to an unfamiliar adjudicatory process. Since that time, historians have clarified that jury trial was not in fact a foreign import, but a homegrown institution of long duration.

In any event, it is easy to see why both Maitland and Plucknett set their sights on jury trial. The legal record itself offers this impression. When a suspected felon stood mute, court scribes remarked that "he refused to put himself upon a jury." The willingness of some defendants to choose hard prison over jury trial belies the notion that medieval men and women saw jury trial as "the sacred personal right of the accused," a description drawn from the exultant narrative of the modern world concerning the trial jury.[15] Appreciating what jury trial meant to the English people means exploring the context in which it developed as

---

[13] Frederic Maitland, *The Constitutional History of England. A Course of Lectures* (Cambridge University Press, 1909), 131.

[14] Plucknett, *Concise History*, 118.

[15] Chester Oppenheim, "Waiver of Trial by Jury in Criminal Cases," *Michigan Law Review* 25.7 (1927): 702.

a mechanism for criminal adjudication. The reason why Henry II is regarded with such admiration by legal historians is because it is during his reign that a recognizable English common law came into existence; or, as Paul Brand puts it, "both a set of national legal institutions bringing law and justice to the whole of England, and a body of legal rules applicable over the whole or almost the whole of England."[16] Thus, it is not the institutions for which he is given credit, but the widespread dissemination of royal law and the greater availability of royal justice throughout England's counties. Victims of crime are also consumers of justice, a fact that Henry shrewdly recognized and exploited in the centralization and expansion of common law. Henry sold an ideal of royal justice to the English public with the promise of speedy, impartial, and nonviolent resolution; affordability; and the availability of trials over proofs. The anonymity of the indictment process also held great appeal to those who feared that speaking out might launch a cycle of intra-familial bloodshed. Where many had once found themselves excluded from compurgation because of their disreputability or foreign background, trial by jury, at least on the surface, is highly democratic: most defendants undergo the same process, regardless of rank, provenance, or gender (with the obvious exceptions of the nobility and clergymen). With these changes, Henry not only constructed an ideal of the king's justice as desirable justice, he also seemingly leveled the playing field. And most people were happy with these changes. Suspected felons, however, had little to celebrate. The dissipation of traditional means of trial, in many respects, was a violation of their customary rights. Standing mute was one means of expressing discontent with this new process.

Empathy with the defendant's perspective requires delving deeper into the nature of the transition from proofs to jury trial. The scope of the transition should not be underestimated. These were entirely distinct processes. Proofs put less emphasis on investigation. Of course, no matter the means of proof, the verdict was ultimately left up to God. This is true even in compurgation which medieval men and women understood as a form of ordeal. With the abolition of the ordeals and

---

[16] Paul Brand, "Henry II and the Creation of the English Common Law," in Christopher Harper-Bill and Nicholas Vincent, eds., *Henry II: New Interpretations* (Woodbridge: Boydell, 2007), 215.

the adoption of jury trial, the Crown effectively removed God's hand from the verdict. In doing so, it made the judicial process much more onerous. Jurors were drawn from the defendant's home community and they could not formulate a verdict about an individual's guilt, potentially leading to death, without securing information about what precisely had transpired. This necessitated inquiry on a scale that had never before been demanded when justices relied on God to determine whether a suspected felon had earned conviction. Given the nature of this transition, it should not be surprising that some accused felons groused at the loss of choice, most likely believing that they would have fared better at the hands of a merciful god than being subjected to the petty vengeances of their long-suffering neighbors.

A brief examination of the various forms of proofs, their dissolution, and the process that led to the adoption of jury trial will help to outline why some defendants resented the shift, what they lost in the process, and why they may have felt compelled to withold their consent to trial.

Compurgation

Compurgation was the normal means of proof for much of the period leading up to the thirteenth century. The proof involved being asked to affirm one's innocence on oath, supported not only by the saint upon whose relic one swore, but also an assigned number of oath-helpers.[17] Typically, justices commanded that proof of innocence be set upon a number of hands corresponding to the severity of the allegations as well as the individual's standing in the community. Oath-helpers were not simply character witnesses, but nor were they eyewitnesses. Rather, they were honorable men of good standing in the community, willing to put their reputations on the line. By demonstrating their faith in the accused, they helped restore his or her good name.

---

[17] Oaths "were treated as if they were 'ritual charms,' which would lose their virtue if changed in the least; a wrong word used would cause the oath to 'burst' thus allowing the adversary to win." The act was not merely symbolic. Swearing a false oath on a relic would result in the saint taking revenge. The accused would be "stricken down senseless or rendered rigid and motionless." William Shack, "Collective Oath: Compurgation in Anglo-Saxon England and African States," *European Journal of Sociology* 20.1 (1979): 8.

As a means of proof, compurgation was ideally suited to those living in small villages where everyone was broadly familiar with each other's moral past, and honor and faith were vital components of daily life. Because trust was at the heart of compurgation, those deemed untrustworthy were prohibited from participating, while the less trustworthy were required to find a greater number of oath-helpers to speak out on their behalf. A person's trustworthiness, as one might expect, aligned closely with one's place in the social hierarchy. The *Leges Henrici Primi* (*c.*1108–9), for example, includes a detailed and extensive description of the value of each oath by rank, those who are not permitted to clear their names through oaths, and the process required depending on the nature of the offense.[18] It also decried "evil men and the conspiracy of perjurers" who had so abused the system that judges had no choice but to resort more frequently to ordeals as a means of proof.[19] Tom Lambert has argued that the accessibility of compurgation had also become an issue for royal justice. Manipulation of the system by professional criminals simply made the Crown look weak and ineffectual; clamping down on who was permitted to prove their innocence through wager of law was vital to maintaining the Crown's reputation for successful peace-keeping.[20]

With Henry II's Assize of Clarendon in 1166, compurgation disappeared altogether from the menu of proofs available to those charged with a felony.[21] Eager to abolish opportunities for manipulation, Henry required all those not taken *cum manuopere* to go to the ordeal. At the same time, he authorized the creation of the jury of presentment, which by the nature of the process itself eliminated any need for compurgation. This group of twelve to twenty-four lawful and well-respected men drawn from local communities responded to the king's "articles of the eyre," a constantly expanding list of questions regarding a broad array of subjects. Juries presented on all crimes that had transpired since the justices' last perambulation

---

[18] *LHP*, 203–7.   [19] *LHP*, ch. 64, subsection 1f, 203.

[20] Tom Lambert, *Law and Order in Anglo-Saxon England* (Oxford University Press, 2017), 261.

[21] That compurgation persisted as a means of trial in manorial and ecclesiastical courts (as canonical purgation), as well as civil suits in the king's courts especially for debt and covenant, long after it vanished from felony trials is a testament to the confidence which medieval men and women had in the act.

(during the era of the grand eyre, every seven years). They were also expected to investigate and report on financial matters, such as escheats, wardships, marriages, treasure trove, and wine sold contrary to the assizes.[22] The intermingling of the various category acts as a reminder that what in fact unites all the articles is a violation of the king's rights and laws (hence, "crown pleas"). The purpose of presentment was to produce actionable items for the justices. When it comes to the relatively new category of crown pleas, their presentment acted as an indictment. In essence, the jury of presentment made compurgation redundant: as men of standing within their communities, jurors took the place of oath-helpers. As such, they subjected all accusations to a "pre-indictment sorting process," in which they determined whether an accusation was baseless, or it had some merit and should be formally registered. They also offered a preliminary verdict on each indictment.[23]

The Assize of Clarendon, then, prompted substantial change to the criminal process, that was not particularly welcoming from the perspective of an accused felon. It eliminated compurgation in felony trials, the normal means of trial up to that point and a key part of the English legal identity. In English parlance, when a man "waged his law," he did so through compurgation. Indeed, when Magna Carta speaks of "the law of the land," the charter was referring explicitly to compurgation.[24] Both phrases emphasize just how quintessential compurgation was to the English legal process. Compurgation also had much appeal for the accused. One selected one's own oathhelpers. Doing so gave the defendant faith in the system: as Richard Helmholz has argued, "[t]his put the defendant's fate into the hands of men he could himself select."[25] Accordingly, Daniel Klerman has described compurgation as having been "extremely pro-defendant."[26] In order

---

[22] A sample version of the "Articles of the Eyre" can be found in Helena Chew and Martin Weinbaum, eds., *London Eyre of 1244* (London Record Society, 1970), 5–10.
[23] Roger Groot, "The Jury of Presentment before 1215," *AJLH* 26.1 (1982): 1–24.
[24] Thomas McSweeney, "Magna Carta and the Right to Trial by Jury," in Randy Holland, ed., *Magna Carta: Muse and Mentor* (Eagen, MN: Thomson Reuters, 2014), 146.
[25] Richard Helmholz, *The Ius Commune in England: Four Studies* (Oxford University Press, 2001), 87.
[26] Daniel Klerman, "Jurisdictional Competition and the Evolution of the Common Law: An Hypothesis," in Anthony Musson, ed., *Boundaries of the Law: Geography, Gender and Jurisdiction in Medieval and Early Modern Europe* (Aldershot: Ashgate, 2005), 155.

to garner the wholehearted support of one's oath-helpers, one needed to be credible and persuade them of one's innocence before they were willing to jeopardize their own reputations. The performative nature of the defendant's oath provided the accused an opportunity to stage-manage the production, again granting some sense of control.[27] Indeed, the "ready availability of oath helpers for hire" meant "a defendant willing to perjure himself or suffering from a self-serving bias could prevail, regardless of the strength of the evidence against him."[28] More important still, losing compurgation as an option meant losing an opportunity to affirm one's standing as a freeman in the community. It is no wonder that not everyone complied with the demands of the Assize. The city of London, for example, saw compurgation as too valuable a privilege to abandon. Long after 1166, the city retained compurgation as an option for certain members of society.[29]

Trial by Battle

Trial by combat existed as an option only on appeal. An appellor had to be prepared to risk life and limb to defend the veracity of his accusation through an offer of battle, although the choice itself remained in the hands of the appellee, who might prefer to defend himself by another form of proof instead. The rigors of battle meant that it was not an option available to all appellors or appellees. Women, clerics, the elderly, the disabled, and children constituted one category of exclusion. By charter, exceptions existed also for the inhabitants of a number of England's most populous urban centers where a more peaceful resolution was deemed compulsory: Bedford, Canterbury, Lincoln, London, Newcastle, Norwich, Oxford, and Winchester, among others.[30] Trial by battle was off limits as well

---

[27] Richard Helmholz's study of compurgation in the church courts demonstrates the extraordinary appeal of the proof: those defamed of criminal acts eagerly sought out compurgation as a means to demonstrate publicly their innocence. They also tended to be successful – almost every person in Helmholz's study who came before the ecclesiastical courts defamed of theft, murder, or some other secular offense was successfully purged of the allegations. Helmholz, "Crime, Compurgation and the Courts," *L&HR* 1.1 (1983): 19–21.

[28] Klerman, "Jurisdictional Competition," 155.   [29] Plucknett, *Concise History*, 116.

[30] Michael Russell, "I. Trial by Battle and the Writ of Right," *Journal of Legal History* 1.2 (1980): 118–19.

when the appellor and appellee were brothers, men of widely differing status, or in a position of immediate authority, such as master and servant, or lord and tenant.[31] The appellee might also sidestep combat altogether by charging the appellor of appealing out of hate and spite (*de odio et atya*), sending the matter instead to a jury. If the jury determined that the appellee's allegation was in fact true, the appeal was quashed altogether.[32] Nonetheless, despite the restrictions and alternatives, battle remained an option regularly exercised by men accused of theft and homicide who saw it as their right to challenge their accuser to open combat.

This was no longer the case after the Assize of Clarendon. The emergence of the jury of presentment ushered in the decline of the appeal, thus robbing the accused of the right to defend himself by means of his body where he stood accused on the king's indictment. Public prosecution made the entire process anonymous: seeing a crime as a breach of the king's peace made the king the accuser, when in reality everyone knew an anonymous complainant stood behind the indictment. Perhaps not surprisingly, the initial reception of the presenting jury was fraught. Paul Hyams argues that Englishmen and women likely understood the presenting jury as a new practice "pressed on them as a coward's way to deny men the ancient right to face off their accuser ... Many will have deemed the assize a highly radical, even unwanted step."[33] Again, this was particularly meaningful for free men, who conceived of battle as a privilege associated with status. Scott Taylor writes the "larger public ... were imbued with the concept of battle as the franchise of the *francus homo* [free man]."[34]

---

[31] Russell, "I. Trial by Battle," 120; Michael Russell, "II. Trial by Battle and the Appeals of Felony," *Journal of Legal History* 1. 2 (1980): 139. If the appellee had been caught red-handed, justices also deemed it inappropriate to imperil the appellor by allowing judicial combat to proceed. In felony appeals, the parties were required to wage battle themselves; champions were strictly forbidden. Russell, "II. Trial by Battle," 139.

[32] Roger Groot, "Teaching Each Other: Judges, Clerks, Jurors and Malefactors Define the Guilt/Innocence Jury," in Jonathan Bush and Alain Wijffels, eds., *Learning the Law: Teaching and the Transmission of Law in England 1150–1900* (London: Hambledon, 1999), 21.

[33] Hyams, *Rancor*, 163.

[34] Scott Taylor, *"Judicium Dei, vulgaris popularisque sensus*: Survival of Customary Justice and Resistance to its Displacement by the 'New" *Ordines iudiciorum* as Evidenced by Francophonic Literature of the High Middle Ages," in Albrecht Classen and Connie Scarborough, eds., *Crime and Punishment in the*

Although battle remained on the books until common-law courts discontinued the felony appeal altogether in 1819, in criminal law, after 1166 it become closely associated with the approver, that is, a confessed felon who chose to appeal and then battle his accomplices one by one rather than be put to death. Therefore, as a result of Henry's reforms, battle swiftly lost its customary standing as a right exerted chiefly by free men to become a punishment imposed on convicted felons.

Trial by Ordeal

Trial by ordeal was reserved exclusively for those who were known to be guilty, or for whom a substantial body of evidence implying guilt existed.[35] Known technically as *judicium Dei* (judgment of God), the ordeal existed chiefly in two formats in the English context: trial by water and trial by fire. Surviving illustrations of trial by water explain how the process worked. Tied in a fetal position in order to restrict bodily movement, officials either dunked the accused in a giant cistern, or rowed him out into a body of water and released him over the side of the boat. Founded on baptismal ideology, the ordeal functioned on the premise that God works through the elements of His creation, therefore if one sank it is because the water accepted one's body, meaning that God recognized a worthiness for reform. The coxswain then yanked the accused from the water before he or she drowned and the court followed through on a formal declaration of acquittal. Floating was evidence of God's rejection; justices then might confidently proceed to a conviction. When it comes to the ordeal by fire, there were two distinct variations. The accused felon either plunged a hand into a cauldron of boiling water or directly into the fire with the purpose of retrieving a piece of iron blessed by a priest, then walked nine paces before depositing the iron. The hand was bandaged for three days following the ordeal, at which point the dressing was removed and the hand examined closely. Festering indicated God's desire to see the individual punished. If the hand was

---

Middle Ages and Early Modern Age: Mental-Historical Investigations of Basic Human Problems and Social Responses (Berlin: De Gruyter, 2012), 119.

[35] Margaret Kerr et al., "Cold Water and Hot Iron: Trial by Ordeal in England," *Journal of Interdisciplinary History* 22.4 (1992): 577.

free of infection, God was announcing instead the defendant's reconciliation with the Christian community.

In 1215, the Fourth Lateran Council under the auspices of Pope Innocent III took the dramatic step of issuing legislation barring clerical participation in judicial ordeals. The ban was not wholly unexpected. Criticism of the ordeal among theologians and intellectuals had been building for some time prior to Lateran IV. The prevailing concern was that the ordeal operated as a miracle on demand and theologians pondered whether mere humans had the power to force God's hand. There was also mounting disbelief among the educated elite that the ordeal in fact expressed God's judgment rather than a measure of how callused were an individual's hands, or how adept one was at expelling the air from one's lungs. God's presence was not the church's only concern: in officiating the ordeals, clergymen were participating in the shedding of blood, as ordeals might result in mutilation or execution. The church had long prohibited clergy from inflicting or causing bloodshed, alleging that it defiled a priest and made him an unworthy vessel for handling the sacrament. Since the eleventh century, the church had issued bans on the clergy commanding soldiers or practicing surgery in the hopes of severing the links between bloodshed and the clergy.[36] Extricating priests from the ordeal process was just one more attempt by the top echelons of the church to enforce this prohibition.

The church's decision was not a welcome one. The abolition of the ordeal left justices across Europe scrambling. Hesitant to impose the death penalty without the approval of a higher authority, Continental courts placed their trust in Rome's stringent evidentiary requirements, experimenting with torture to extract confession and introducing expert testimony by medical practitioners in order to achieve a high degree of certainty with their verdicts. Judges then could take comfort in knowing that when they sentenced an individual to death, they did so confident that the accused had earned that fate. In England, where the common-law courts did not adopt Roman rules of evidence (or indeed any rules of evidence), their quest for license and assurance led

---

[36] English synods also joined in this barrage of legislation. As early as 1075, a London council barred clergymen from participating in pronouncing sentences of death or mutilation. Julius Goebel, Jr., *Felony and Misdemeanor: A Study in the History of Criminal Law* (Philadelphia: University of Pennsylvania Press, 1976) 412.

them instead to deliver authority out of God's hands into humanity's through the establishment of the trial jury.[37]

At the level of the ordinary people, the loss of the ordeal was no less traumatic. Trial by jury was in no way equivalent to the ordeal. How do you replace an omniscient deity? God's role was not simply to pass judgment on the accused. Those sent to the ordeal were already deemed guilty – they did not need God to confirm that. Rather, they wanted God to look into the accused's heart to determine whether he or she was truly penitent and thus deserving of His infamous mercy. As Bernard Gui (d.1331) pronounced so memorably in his inquisitorial manual, mere mortals are limited in this respect: "one cannot establish anything about the mind, for deep is the heart of man, and inscrutable."[38] Through the ordeal, God could compensate for humanity's limitations. English society had long relied on the ordeal to determine how to handle the most troublesome offenders in their communities, and they were satisfied with its results. As Peter Brown articulates it, the ordeal was "an instrument of consensus;" it "applied a discreet massage to the ruffled feelings of the group" and was "reassuring and peace-creating."[39] Scott Taylor makes a similar point when he writes that they appreciated the "communal input into imposition and interpretations of ordeal;" they "felt comfortable with their customary justice, the spectacle of an ordeal with the prospect of a good castration and blinding or drawing and quartering being as dear to their hearts as public hangings were in nineteenth-century

---

[37] Despite decades of passionate debate about the origins of the jury, particularly whether it was a Frankish or Scandinavian invention, historiographical consensus has finally formed around the belief that the jury was in fact an institution with solid Anglo-Saxon roots. Thus, when the king's justices turned to the trial jury after Lateran IV it was a "natural development." Ralph Turner, "The Origins of the Medieval English Jury: Frankish, English, or Scandinavian?," *JBS* 7.2 (1968): 1–10. For its Anglo-Saxon roots, see Michael McNair, "Vicinage and the Antecedents of the Jury," *L&HR* 17 (1999): 537–90. Elizabeth Papp Kamali and Thomas Green, "A Crossroads in Criminal Procedure: The Assumptions Underlying England's Adoption of Trial by Jury for Crime," in Travis Baker, ed., *Law and Society in Later Medieval England and Ireland: Essays in Honour of Paul Brand* (New York: Routledge, 2018), 52.

[38] Peter Biller, "'Deep is the heart of man, and inscrutable': Signs of Heresy in Medieval Languedoc," in Helen Barr and Ann Hutchinson, eds., *Text and Controversy from Wyclif to Bale: Essays in Honour of Anne Hudson* (Turnhout: Brepols, 2005), 267–80.

[39] Peter Brown, "Society and the Supernatural: A Medieval Change," *Daedalus* 104.2 (1975): 137–8.

England."[40] The English were not alone in this respect. Across Europe, ordeals were abandoned only with the greatest of reluctance. Indeed, King Philip IV of France (d.1314) eventually succumbed to popular pressure and restored the practice to the royal courts.[41] Throughout the Holy Roman Empire the church's directive was ignored entirely; the ordeals continued unabated through to the end of the Middle Ages.

From the perspective of the accused felon, the demise of the ordeal meant the loss of a valuable procedural advantage. At times, justices granted an appealed felon the option to shift the burden of proof to the appellor, compelling him to carry the iron rather than engage in the ordeal himself. For example, at the Lincolnshire Assize of 1202, when Astin of Wispington appealed Simon of Edlington of assault and blinding, the court granted Simon the choice (*in electione*) of whether he or Astin would carry the iron. Of course, he opted for the appellor. Not surprisingly, Astin baulked when asked to carry the iron. Instead, the two opted for private settlement.[42] At the same assize, Walter, son of William of Clixby appealed Ralph the freeman of premeditated assault and maiming, such that his arm was broken and bones had to be extracted from the wound in his head. Once again, the court offered Ralph a choice as to whether he wished to carry the iron himself, or have Walter carry it. He, too, chose the appellor. When the appointed day for the ordeal came around, Walter could not go through with it. Ralph was acquitted, and Walter stood in mercy to the court.[43] As these examples demonstrate, the ordeal played an important role in keeping the peace. An astute defendant might employ it tactically to push for an out-of-court settlement, which suddenly seemed like a much more attractive option to the appellor when faced with carrying the iron.

Finally, as Theodore Plucknett has observed, the defendant's rank defined the nature of the ordeal: in England, hot iron was associated

---

[40] Taylor, "*Judicium Dei*," 119.   [41] Taylor, "*Judicium Dei*," 127.

[42] Doris Stenton, ed., *The Earliest Lincolnshire Assize Rolls*, AD 1202–1209 (Lincolnshire Record Society, vol. XXII, 1926), 106, no. 595.

[43] Stenton, ed., *Earliest Lincolnshire*, 143, no. 851. Another similar case: Alan Pigun appealed Gosse of Immingham of assault and wounding. The record specifically states that because Gosse had passed fighting age, they settled on the ordeal, however the court gave Gosse the option of carrying the iron himself, or having Alan do it. He chose Alan. Afterwards, Alan returned to court and withdrew himself, and was in mercy for three marks. Stenton, ed., *Earliest Lincolnshire*, 142, no. 843.

with freedom, cold water with unfreedom.[44] Gender also mattered. For women, hot iron was sanctified by its association with Emma of Normandy, Teutberga of Lotharingia, and the legendary Isolde – all queens who defended their sexual honor through the ordeal; it afforded women a dignity that was absent in the ordeal of cold water, which required parading about in a wet and clingy linen shift. The integral association between rank, gender, and method of proof was a defining feature of English law. As we have come to see, a person's choice of proofs was tied to social standing. A freeman might defend himself by his word (compurgation), by his body (battle), or by iron (ordeal), while the unfree had only cold water to defend his good name. In this respect, jury trial was a leveling force: regardless of rank or gender everyone had access to the same means of trial. Today, we might think the English should have embraced happily such a democratic revision to the criminal justice system. Victims of crime generally did. When it comes to those accused of crimes, however, the freeman had much to criticize. He lost the few perquisites afforded by his rank in a relatively brief period of time.

All of these changes relate chiefly to the process of criminal law, which existed within a much larger framework. When it comes to civil dispute resolution, trial by ordeal had never been an option. For disputes over land, though, battle remained a viable and honorable option alongside the Grand Assize. So, too, did compurgation, the time-honored means by which an Englishman might "wage his law," remain an option in civil suits (both in the king's courts and the local courts), as well as the ecclesiastical courts until the end of the Middle Ages. The preservation of compurgation in civil suits underscores that there was no popular loss of confidence in the procedure; nor, did the king take a definitive stance on the trustworthiness of compurgation, permitting it in civil suits in royal courts, just not in criminal matters. Thus, traditional defense procedures persisted as options in civil suits and yet were now denied to the criminal defendant (that is, of course, unless he happened to be in London, in which case, compurgation continued to be an option). To a criminal defendant eager to avoid the gallows, the law's baffling inconsistency must have seemed a deliberate ploy by the crown to jeopardize his defense.

[44] Plucknett, *Concise History*, 114.

Redefining Crime

Lateran IV's pronouncement cast the final blow to England's customary system of justice. The array of choice that had once characterized English criminal justice in just fifty short years had been whittled away. The Assize of Clarendon in 1166 eradicated compurgation altogether as a means of proof, and drastically diminished opportunities for trial by battle. Then in 1215, the only remaining proofs were abruptly abandoned. More important still, all of this was happening at the same time that the category of felony effectively was being defined for the first time in English history. The Angevin enthusiasm for classification saw the term applied to a much broader collection of offenses than it had been during the Anglo-Saxon era when crime was synonymous with theft and other offenses against property.[45] From the time of Æthelred (d. 871), these belonged to a larger category of *bótleas* (or bootless) offenses, that is, "wrongs so serious that redress may no longer be taken by private agreement with the wronged."[46] Treason, arson, attacks on houses, open theft, persistent robbery, and coining were reserved to episcopal supervision; the convict was subjected to forfeiture of property and execution, "placing God and the king ahead of the victim's kin."[47]

Homicide, along with other offenses against the person, was a private offense, not a crime, leading to compensation, rather than forfeiture of property and execution. The one exception was "murder" (*morð*) – a rather ill-defined term for the era. Under Old English law, Bruce O'Brien sees that it was defined to mean either (1) a homicide that could only be amended by feud, or (2) a betrayal of one's lord.[48] O'Brien argues that under Cnut, it came also to include the slaying of a Dane by an Englishman. While II Cnut 64 would seem to have made murder a *bótleas* offense, II Cnut 56 explains that the slayer should be given to the kin of the slain, "in some rude calculus of sympathetic punishment," while the king collects his fine.[49] Once again, as Tom

---

[45] Hudson, *Formation of the English Common Law*, 150.

[46] Paul Hyams, "Feud and the State in Late Anglo-Saxon England," *JBS* 40.1 (2001): 17.

[47] Naomi Hurnard, "The Anglo-Norman Franchises," *EHR* 64.252 (1949): 291; Hyams, "Feud and the State," 17.

[48] Bruce O'Brien, "From *Morðor* to *Murdrum*: The Preconquest Origin and Norman Revival of the Murder Fine," *Speculum* 71.2 (1996): 346.

[49] O'Brien, "From *Morðor* to *Murdrum*," 336.

Lambert writes, it seems fair to say that murder was simply not "a legislative priority" for the early kings.[50] It is under Henry II that homicide was recast unmistakably as a felony. The new categorization was not merely academic: it had meaningful consequences. Felonies were to be adjudicated within the king's (rather than one's feudal lord's) court. They were also punishable by death or mutilation, not compensation.

For the suspected felon, then, the late twelfth century represents a virtual sea of change. As Scott Taylor writes,

[t]he criminal defendant of the thirteenth and early fourteenth centuries was often worse off than he would have been in the day of the ordeal. He was all but presumed guilty, afforded no meaningful examination of witnesses, provided no real procedural protections, and given no means either by wit or divine intervention, to escape with his life and body parts intact.[51]

It is no coincidence that this moment also marks the beginnings of the practice of standing mute. The pleading process is the one aspect of the legal system that did not change as a result of the transition from proof to trial. Defendants had always had the opportunity to refuse to plead if they had chosen to do so, but for one reason or another, they had not opted for silence. Why then? For the defendant newly stripped of his customary rights, especially the freeman who resented the loss of his privileged position within the justice system, silence was a powerful form of noncooperation meant to signal his protest.

Legal Culture of the Long Twelfth Century

Understanding the response of English justices to those who stood mute requires immersing ourselves in the legal culture of the long twelfth century, not just of England, but of medieval Christendom. The renewed interest in Roman law led to the creation of the *ius commune*, which "provided medieval Christendom with a common conception of law and common legal language that transcended the boundaries of European politics."[52] While the ways in which Roman

---

[50] Lambert, "Theft, Homicide and Crime," 26. *Morð* appears only three times in the law codes of the Anglo-Saxon kings.
[51] Taylor, "*Judicium Dei*," 119.
[52] Ada Maria Kuskowski, "*Lingua Franca Legalis?* A French Vernacular Legal Culture from England to the Levant," *Reading Medieval Studies* 40 (2014): 157.

law interacted with traditional law codes and legal structures varied
tremendously across the European landscape, no European polity
remained untouched, including England. The vast gulf that separates
the Anglo-Saxon law codes from Glanvill's *Tractibus* (c.1187–9) in
terms of the latter's sophistication is a testimony to the profound
impact of this new legal thinking. Nor was this a short-term
experience. The rise of what Ada Maria Kuskowski has termed
a *lingua franca legalis* – that is, French as a common legal language –
stretching from England to Outremer over the course of the thirteenth
and fourteenth centuries facilitated the spread of a common legal
culture and jurisprudence, despite minor variations in judicial practice.

Protecting the rights of the accused to a fair trial was one of the
central tenets of the legal culture that emerged from the academic
debates of the high and late Middle Ages, sparked by the recently
rediscovered *Corpus Juris Civilis*. Roman law articulates plainly the
belief that the rights of the accused in a criminal trial are a priority for
jurists. In Justinian's *Novellae*, especially novel 90, there is an explicit
statement that a defendant has the right to be present at all legal
proceedings against him. Equally, his accuser has the obligation to
state the charges against him and produce the necessary evidence in
the presence of the accused.[53] Roman law also set a high bar for
evidentiary standards: a full proof required two eyewitnesses. As
Ulpian (d.228) declared in the *Digest*, "it is better to let the guilty go
unpunished than to punish the innocent," a phrase that was eventually
reformulated by Johannes de Pogiali, a late fourteenth-century
Franciscan inquisitor, into the more familiar it is "better to leave
a crime unpunished than to condemn an innocent person."[54]

Roman law was only partly responsible for "new" ideas on natural
rights.[55] Enthusiastic and meticulous analysis of the *Corpus Juris
Civilis* in a university environment provoked new thinking on the

---

[53] Samuel Scott, ed., *The Novels of Justinian* (Cincinnati: The Central Trust Company,
1932), novel 90 (chs. 1, 2, and 9 especially).
[54] As cited in Kenneth Pennington, "Innocent until Proven Guilty: The Origins of
a Legal Maxim," *Jurist* 63 (2000): 118.
[55] While Roman law contained some of the essential facets of human rights discourse,
the role of the judge was to act as an extension of the coercive powers of the state.
Legislation intended to protect litigants, defendants in particular, from those coercive
powers were developed by medieval canonists. Anders Winroth, "The Legal
Revolution of the Twelfth Century," in Thomas Noble, et. al, eds., *European*

subject of natural law and its relationship with man-made (or what is typically referred to as "positive") law. The medieval discourse on natural law was deeply rooted in Christian interpretation. Natural law is God's law. It functions on the premise that nature is a manifestation of God's will. As *Bracton* (*c.*1220s–60s) writes, "[n]atural law is that which nature, that is, God himself, taught all living things."[56] Because God created the natural world, studying it provides us with the opportunity to access and interpret God's intentions. When it comes to inferences concerning the divine plan for earth's human inhabitants, we are thus required to turn to Genesis, the account depicting the moment when God first created man and woman.[57]

In an assuredly familiar story but with a markedly legalistic retelling, the canonists affirm that justification for due process (or in medieval parlance, *ordo iudiciarius* – the order of law) can be traced back to the time of Adam. God set down the law that Adam and Eve were not to eat from the tree of knowledge. This newly minted legislation was personally communicated to Adam so that when he plucked a piece of fruit from the forbidden tree and consumed it he knowingly violated the law. Adam was the principal offender: Eve may have been the first to eat from the tree, but her dependent status as Adam's wife made her only an accomplice to the crime. God issued a summons (a citation): He called out to Adam, asking "Where art thou?" When Adam finally appeared before God, He explained the charge (*objectio*) against him, and asked Adam how he wished to defend himself. Adam instantly denied his guilt, but raised a formal objection (*exceptio*). Initially, he claimed entrapment: the wife God had chosen for him offered him the fruit. When that defense fell flat, he shifted tactics and blamed instead the serpent. Always the attentive judge, God listened courteously to Adam's defense, no matter how half-hearted and self-serving, before offering up a final verdict and sentence. Their punishment? Exile from the Garden of Eden as well as corporal punishment: Adam (and all men after him) were punished

---

Transformations: The Long Twelfth-Century (South Bend, IN: University of Notre Dame Press, 2011), 345.
[56] *Bracton*, vol. ii, 26.
[57] Brian Tierney, *The Idea of Natural Rights: Studies on Natural Rights, Natural Law, and Church Law, 1150–1625* (Grand Rapids, MI: Eerdmans, 1997).

with the pains of manual labor, while Eve (and all women after her) must suffer the pains of reproductive labor.

From the medieval canonist's or theologian's perspective, what is striking about this story is that God bothered to hold a trial at all. God, of course, is omniscient. Consequently, He not only *knew* the circumstances that prompted Adam to commit the crime before He even asked Adam to explain himself, but He also instantly recognized Adam's guilt. Nonetheless, rather than bypassing a formal trial and moving directly to sentencing and punishment, God still permitted Adam an opportunity to defend himself. Why? Because he was adhering to natural law. As canonist Johannes Monachus (also, Jean Lemoine; d.1313) wrote in his *Glossa Aurea* (1301), "God could not condemn Adam without a trial because even God must presume that Adam was *innocent until proven guilty.*" This bold assertion gave birth to a recognizable legal maxim with a long and powerful history.[58] Just as all men after Adam shared in his punishment, so too, in this canonist's assessment, must the expectation of innocence be applied universally, without exception. Johannes maintained the pervasiveness and rigidity of the rule by asking, "could the pope proceed against a person without a summons?" The answer to that question is, no. While the pope may rise above positive law, no one is above natural law.[59] Johannes Monachus was not the first canonist to introduce the biblical paradigm of Adam and Eve's expulsion into theoretical discussions of natural law. What is original in Johannes' work is that he outlines clearly the implications of this provision for the "prince": if God could not dispense with natural law when it was inconvenient, neither could his representatives here on earth.

Using the Bible as a vehicle to access God's expectations of law played a fundamental role in devising canonical procedures as they relate to trials both civil and criminal within the church. For example, while excommunication traditionally required a three-fold admonition, because God issued only one peremptory admonition to Adam, the canon law adopted this as the standard.[60] The Bible also vindicated

---

[58] Italics are my own. Pennington, "Innocent until Proven Guilty," 115.

[59] As cited in Kenneth Pennington, *The Prince and the Law, 1200–1600: Sovereignty and Rights in the Western Legal Tradition* (Berkeley: University of California Press, 1993), 161.

[60] Richard Helmholz, "Fundamental Human Rights in Medieval Law," *Fulton Lectures* (University of Chicago Press, 2001), 14–15.

proceedings springing from public fame (*fama*). *Clamor* about the immoral lifestyles of those living in Sodom and Gomorrah prompted God's investigation; why should human authorities need more? Canon law's rules of evidence may be drawn from Roman law, but biblical rationale provided their justification. Moses decreed that the truth can be found in the testimony of two or three witnesses (Deuteronomy 19:5). Canon law was not alone in seeing an infusion of biblical reasoning.

It is noteworthy that a biblical flavor permeates also English law at this time. Chapter 5, 7a of the *Leges Henrici Primi* declares:

> Nothing shall be done in the absence of an accuser; for God and our Lord Jesus Christ knew Judas was a thief, but because he was not accused, he was therefore not cast out, and whatever he did among the apostles remained credited to the dignity of his office.[61]

Apparently, the law cannot cut corners in trying criminals even when it comes to Judas. More commonly, men of law used a different biblical passage to justify the rule that a person cannot be condemned without a lawful accuser. For example, the *Mirror of Justices* turns to the passage in the Gospel of John in which Jesus speaks to a woman accused of adultery. When he asks the woman who are her accusers, she replies "No one, Lord." Jesus, too, fails to condemn her. He tells her to go and sin no more. In referencing this story, the author of the *Mirror* writes that we must heed

> the example God gave when he constituted himself judge in consistory, and called for the accuser of the woman who had sinned. And to give us a perpetual example that there can be no lawful judgment without three persons – judge, plaintiff, defendant – God told her to go without day, since it does not pertain to a judge to act as both judge and party.[62]

Even English jurists saw the Bible as an exemplar of natural law.

The scope of rights attributed to individuals under natural law guided the development of policies regarding the treatment of accused felons. A number of the era's legal maxims, which played a key role in the pan-European transmission of this new jurisprudence, succinctly express the law's commitment to protecting the defendant from biased treatment. Both "the burden of proof lies with the accuser, not the defendant," and

---

[61] *LHP*, ch. 5, subsection 7a, 86–7.
[62] William Whittaker, ed., *The Mirror of Justices* (SS, vol. VII, 1893), 43–4.

"in doubtful matters the defendant is favored, not the plaintiff" were pervasive in medieval law.[63] In this respect, lawyer-pope Innocent III's contributions were critical. In *Venerabilem* (1202), a decretal addressed to a German duke, he pronounced that "if a defendant had not been cited, witnesses could not present testimony against the defendant."[64] Five years later, in *Dudum* (1207), a decretal written to the provost of Milan, Innocent expounded that a cleric who carried a papal mandate did not have to prove himself worthy, because "he may be presumed worthy unless the contrary may be shown."[65] It may not have been Innocent's express purpose to establish the firm foundations for a general presumption of innocence in the law, but later jurists heartily credited him with having done so through statements of this nature.[66] Innocent III's crowning achievement, the seventy canons produced by the Fourth Lateran Council (1215) in under just three weeks, went further than a presumption of innocence to stipulate that no plaintiff can attempt to "fatigue the accused with labor and expenses" by summoning the accused to a court farther than a two-day journey from home (canon thirty-eight); there must be due process even in sentences of excommunication (canon forty-seven, "Prelates are not to excommunicate subjects without a previous warning and without reasonable cause"); and finally, those excommunicated unjustly must have a right of appeal (also canon forty-seven).

Johannes Monachus' affirmation that "the law is more inclined to absolve than to condemn" confirms the development of a legal tradition focused on protecting a defendant's natural rights to order of law.[67] Stephen of Tournai (d.1203) in his commentary (c.1165) on Gratian's *Decretum*, defined order of law accordingly:

the defendant shall be summoned before his own judge and be legitimately called by three edicts or one peremptory edict. He must be permitted to have legitimate delays. The accusation must be formally presented in writing. Legitimate witnesses must be produced. A decision may be rendered only after someone had been convicted or confessed. The decision must be in writing.[68]

---

[63] As cited in Pennington, *Prince and the Law*, 156.
[64] Pennington, *Prince and the Law*, 145–6.   [65] Pennington, *Prince and the Law*, 157.
[66] Pennington, *Prince and the Law*, 157.   [67] Pennington, *Prince and the Law*, 162.
[68] As cited in Melodie Eichbauer, "Medieval Inquisitorial Procedure: Procedural Rights and the Question of Due Process in the Thirteenth Century," *History Compass* 12.1 (2014): 74.

At no point in time, even after conviction, does a criminal surrender his or her natural rights. Henry of Ghent (d.1293) argued passionately that a convicted felon has property rights in his own body: he possesses a natural right to preserve his life and do what he must to acquire the necessities of life. The judge at his trial has only the "use" of a criminal's body, allowing him to arrest, imprison, and execute the criminal. However, because ownership always overrides use, a criminal's right to preserve his life takes priority over the judge's right to take it away. More important still, the condemned's authority over his own body is "equitable," "licit," "right," and "necessary."[69]

While this new philosophy of law sprang from the Continent's university classrooms, the English Channel did little to brake the progress of its influence on developing English jurisprudence. Canon law had a secure home in the courts of the English church, which applied the same law and procedure as their Continental counterparts. The twelfth century saw many of England's devoted scholars travel to Bologna, Paris, and Tours for law degrees. England also produced some of the era's most celebrated canonists: Honorius of Kent (d.1210), John of Tynemouth (d.1221), and Simon of Southwell (d. c.1205), who were among the first instructors of canon law at Oxford University, which eventually became one of the pre-eminent places to study canon law in all of Europe, luring students from Continental Europe.[70] Because canon law existed as the "only truly international system of law the West has ever known," Richard Helmholz tells us that in situations "where the local law was incomplete or insufficient, English lawyers felt no shame in drawing upon the vast resources of the Roman and canon law for inspiration."[71] Indeed, in his analysis of year-book dialogues, David Seipp argues that "common lawyers paid more attention to canon law than to civil law."[72]

---

[69] Henry of Ghent, *Quodlibet IX*, ed. Raymond Macken, *Henrici de Gandavo Opera Omnia*, vol. XIII (Leuven: Brill, 1983); also cited in Virpi Mäkinen and Heikki Pihlajamäki, "The Individualization of Crime in Medieval Canon Law," *Journal of the History of Ideas* 65.4 (2004): 528–9.

[70] William Bassett, "Canon Law and the Common Law," *Hastings Law Journal* 29 (1977–8): 1400.

[71] Bassett, "Canon Law," 1384. Richard Helmholz, "Magna Carta and the *ius commune*," *Chicago Law Review* 66.2 (1999): 305.

[72] David Seipp, "The Reception of Canon Law and Civil Law in the Common Law Courts before 1600," *Oxford Journal of Legal Studies* 13.3 (1993): 390.

The key factor in transmission is the long-standing involvement of clergymen in the design and administration of English secular law. Until the fourteenth-century rise of professional lawyers, the king's courts were staffed largely by English clerics. The great jurist Henry de Bracton (d.1268), whose name is used as shorthand for medieval England's most well-known legal treatise, was both a professional judge employed as a justice of assize in England's southwestern counties and a member of the clergy, at various points rector of Combe-in-Teignhead, rector of Bideford, archdeacon of Barnstaple, and chancellor of Exeter Cathedral.[73] Other well-known justices of the bench also did double-duty as prelates within the English church, to name a few: Walter Map (d.1210), Martin of Pateshull (d.1229), and William Raleigh (d.1250). A meaningful cross-over existed also between the upper ranks of England's clergy and the king's sheriffs. During his appointment as joint sheriff of the counties of Nottingham and Derby, Walter Giffard (d.1279) was also Archbishop of York.[74] Roger de Meyland (d.1295) stood as bishop to two dioceses (Coventry and Lichfield) while he was simultaneously sheriff for the counties of Oxfordshire and Berkshire.[75] Indeed, while the fourteenth century marks a key period in the "laicisation of the English civil service," as W. Mark Ormrod writes it was a long and drawn-out process.[76] It did not come to an end until well after the Middle Ages. Throughout the medieval era, the position of chancellor, the highest office in royal administration, responsible for passing down verdicts in England's court of Chancery, was almost always filled by an English prelate, and prelates continued to play a role as judges in parliament and the royal council.[77] It is hard to imagine that these men of the cloth put aside their teachings on natural law (again, *God's* law) while working in the king's courts. The overlap between personnel reflects a blurring

---

[73] Plucknett, *Concise History*, 265–8.

[74] *List of Sheriffs for England and Wales from the Earliest Times to A.D. 1383, Compiled from Documents in the Public Record Office* (London: HMSO, 1898; repr. Kraus, 1963), 102.

[75] *List of Sheriffs*, 107.

[76] W. Mark Ormrod, "The Politics of Pestilence: Government in England after the Black Death," in W. Mark Ormrod and Phillip Lindley, eds., *The Black Death in England* (Stamford: Paul Watkins, 1996), 151.

[77] Gwilym Dodd, "Reason, Conscience and Equity: Bishops as the King's Judges in Later Medieval England," *History* 99.335 (2014): 213–40.

of the lines between sacred and secular typical of the era. This is true of law in general. As Manlio Bellomo has noted, in the Middle Ages, the judicial realm was effectively a branch of theology.[78] As such, the clergyman was "a divine judge and a terrestrial judge; he was a theologian, a 'jurist,' a rhetorician, and a 'notary'; he knew and judged harmful human acts and illicit thoughts as 'sins' but at the same time as 'illegal' civil or criminal behavior."[79]

As a result, English jurists did not see natural law as some "exotic foreign import, but rather as a legitimate source of English law."[80] The view of natural law as foundational aligns with Aquinas' assessment of positive law, which he, too, reasons emanates from natural law, and thus it is not possible for the two to contradict: "Every human law has just so much of the nature of law as it is derived from the law of nature. But if, in any point, it deflects from the law of nature [i]t is no longer a law but a perversion of law."[81] Because natural law is God's law, at no point in time can it be merely waived or dismissed as irrelevant without solid justification. English common lawyers, Helmholz maintains, were in firm agreement. They saw the two laws as "harmonious, that the natural law stood behind and supported the English common law."[82] "All law is one law" and the English people had a "profound faith in law as the tie that binds all things in heaven and in earth."[83]

English Law and Respect for the Rights of the Accused

Of course, a strong sense of congruence between natural and common law did not lead to wholesale adoption of canon law by England's able corps of common lawyers. Nor did the English jettison existing laws that seemingly stood in contradiction. Rather, English justices interpreted law creatively in order "to avoid clashes with natural law

---

[78] Manlio Bellomo, *The Common Legal Past of Europe, 1000–1800,* trans. Lydia G. Cochrane (Washington, DC: Catholic University of America Press, 1995), 47.

[79] Bellomo, *Common Legal Past,* 47–8.

[80] Richard Helmholz, "Natural Law and Human Rights in English Law: From Bracton to Blackstone," *Ave Maria Law Review* 3.1 (2005): 11.

[81] For further discussion, see Daniel Westberg, "The Relation between Positive and Natural Law in Aquinas," *Journal of Law and Religion* 11.1 (1994–5): 1–22.

[82] Helmholz, "Natural Law," 21.

[83] John Alford, "Literature and Law in Medieval England," *PMLA* 92.5 (1977): 942.

principles." Natural law was inherently useful. It helped justices to fill in the gaps in common law, for which "the lawgiver had no provision, but for which judges had to find answers."[84] Most importantly, natural law set limits on the acceptability of some legal practices. Helmholz maintains that this was "particularly effective in securing procedural safeguards for litigants." Natural law afforded the suspected felon a panoply of what we might term "human rights." In medieval England, "[r]ules and statutes were interpreted so as to protect these rights."[85] In this legal culture, it is hard to imagine the success of legislation intended to undermine or eradicate those basic, God-given rights. As Helmholz explains it, "[i]f one assumes that the sovereign wishes to have statutes read in light of natural law, that the legislator could not have intended to deviate from its paths, then there is rarely a need to invalidate the statutes themselves."[86] Thus, judges felt comfortable reading exceptions into laws in order to reconcile common with natural law.

The impact of the natural rights vogue on English jurisprudence is easily traceable at law. The Anglo-Saxon law codes have little to say about the legal rights of the accused. That is not surprising. The early codes follow the same format typically as the tariffs of the early penitentials: for each crime they include a punishment. The law codes take on the appearance of a laundry list of criminal scenarios rather than a treatise on morality. Every now and then they include gestures towards a sense of fairness. For example, in III Edgar the law declares that "every man, rich or poor, obtain the benefit of the public law and be awarded just decisions."[87] There are also protections for the individual who has been falsely accused, although the burden of proof lies principally on the defendant. III Edgar 4 states that if the defendant manages to clear himself of the charges, his plaintiff will lose either his tongue, or if he can pay, his *wergeld*.[88] V Æthelred 3 is the most directly pertinent. It speaks to the need to keep punishments proportionate, explaining that "men shall not be condemned to

---

[84] Helmholz, "Natural Law," 17–18.   [85] Helmholz, "Natural Law," 19.
[86] Helmholz, "Natural Law," 17–18.
[87] III Edgar 1, in Agnes Robertson, ed., *The Laws of the Kings of England from Edmund to Henry I* (Cambridge University Press, 1925), 24–5.
[88] III Edgar 4, Robertson, ed., *Laws of the Kings*, 24–5. This appears also in II Canute 16, Robertson, ed., *Laws of the Kings*, 182–3.

death for too trivial offences, but, on the contrary, merciful punishments shall be determined upon for the public good, that the handiwork of God, and what he purchased for himself at a great price, be not destroyed for trivial offences." The consensus behind this statement is punctuated by its reappearance almost verbatim in the prefatory remarks of II Canute and the So-Called Laws of William I.[89]

In the works of the long twelfth century, however, an English passion for natural law and its advocacy of a defendant's rights flourishes. The *Leges Henrici Primi* marks the beginnings of this transition. Here, we see a bold articulation of the rights of the accused much more in keeping with what was transpiring in the university environment. The preface to the *Leges* is positively euphoric in its commitment to a broad application of the law, which:

ought to be manifest, just, honourable, and capable of application, in the case of every rank, profession, and class, of every kind and condition of causes, of every dispute whether simple or complex, of all law, whether natural law or customary, and of every place, whether near or far; and it ought to be appropriate to the place, the time, and the person, serving above all no private advantage but seeking the increase of truth and justice, not the wretched accretion of wealth.[90]

The *Leges* abounds with protections: "Each person is to be judged by men who are of equal status and from the same district as himself";[91] as well as "[n]o judgement shall be given in a doubtful case or when the accused is absent";[92] and, "[n]o one should be judged or condemned before he has lawful accusers personally present and the opportunity to offer a defence for the purpose of clearing himself of the charges."[93] These bold clauses, with no Anglo-Saxon precedent, mirror the newfound sense of entitlement integral to the discussions taking place in philosophical circles regarding individual rights in natural law. They also strike at the heart of modern concerns about due process: defendants must be given a right to know their accusers, to know the charges raised against them, and be permitted to offer a defense on their behalf.

---

[89] v Æthelred 3, Robertson, ed., *Laws of the Kings*, 80–1. See also II Canute 1, Robertson, ed., *Laws of the Kings*, 176–7 and the So-Called Laws of William I 40, Robertson, ed., *Laws of the Kings*, 270–1.
[90] *LHP*, ch. 4, subsection 5, 82–3. [91] *LHP*, ch. 31, subsection 7, 134–5.
[92] *LHP*, ch. 5, subsection 2a, 84–5. [93] *LHP*, ch. 5, subsection 9a, 86–7.

Remarkably, the *Leges* also enshrines a defendant's right to silence as a means of protesting the legal process: "A person accused before a judge of his own choosing shall plead his defence, if he wishes, and if he is not accused before a judge of his own choosing, he shall, if he wishes, remain silent."[94] Here, "not of his own choosing" should perhaps be interpreted to imply the defendant sees the judge as insufficiently qualified, biased, or inept. This clause, especially, hints at one of the reasons why English defendants may have opted for silence; it also explains why England's judiciary sometimes interpreted silence as protest. In another applicable statement on the subject of silence, the *Leges* claims that "[g]ood people very often remain silent and tolerate evils of which they are aware because they lack proofs and they cannot establish these things before the judges; for however true they are, they are not to be believed by a judge unless they can be established by unassailable proofs."[95] Both statements clarify that the accused's right to justice was very much at the heart of jurists' thinking.

While the *Leges Henrici Primi* represents the inauguration of this movement in an English setting, Magna Carta (1215) has come to be the touchstone for its progress in terms of the rights of the accused. Pressed on the king not long before the drafting of Innocent III's canons of Lateran IV, the charter was intended as a check on princely sovereignty.[96] Originally conceived as a peace treaty to quell hostility between King John (d.1216) and his oppressed baronage before it resulted in conquest by the French king, the charter is awash with resolute declarations about the rights of freemen. For the purposes of this study, two in particular stand out. Chapter 39 of the 1215 version declares, that "[n]o freeman shall be taken or imprisoned or disseized or outlawed, or in any way destroyed, nor will we go upon him nor send upon him, except by the lawful judgment of his peers or by the law

---

[94] *LHP*, ch. 5, subsection 13, 86–7. Another interesting statement on silence: the *LHP* declares that if a defendant appears in court to answer multiple charges laid against him, but responds to only some of those accusations, his silence on the other matters will be treated as an admission of guilt. *LHP*, ch. 49, subsection 3, 163. In this instance, selective denial is seen as a devious legal strategy.

[95] *LHP*, ch. 5, subsection 18, 90–1.

[96] The English barons presented King John with the Magna Carta at Winchester on June 15, 1215. The Fourth Lateran Council was a three-week council that began November 11 of the same year.

of the land."[97] As John Baker has noted, this chapter was the "chief legal weapon deployed against growing absolutism." It was repeated and expanded in a series of statutes over the course of the Middle Ages, climaxing in a 1354 statute that references for the first time "due process of law."[98] Chapter 40 of the 1215 version promises "To no one will we sell, to no one will we refuse or delay, right or justice."[99] The import of this particular chapter is signified by the fact that in the year 1278 it was incorporated into the oath of appointment undertaken by each of the king's justices, who swore that they would not "prevent or delay justice by any trick or device against right or against the laws of the land."[100] Moreover, the charter's reputation for protecting the rights of the subject against a predatory Crown only grew with time, such that legal remedies developed to address some of these issues came to be "retrospectively linked to Magna Carta." By the fourteenth century, Chapter thirty-nine was understood as a guarantee that "no one could lawfully be sentenced to death without a specific accusation followed by a trial before twelve sworn members of the public." Similarly, various protections developed to safeguard a subject's property from unlawful seizure by the Crown, such as the petition of right, over time came to be integrally associated with the famed charter.[101]

---

[97] Charles Mont, ed., *Chartes des libertés anglaises (1100–1305)* (Paris: Alphonse Picard, 1892), 33. At the time Magna Carta was written, "law of the land" likely referred to compurgation. See Thomas McSweeney, "Magna Carta and the Right to Trial by Jury," in Randy Holland, ed., *Magna Carta: Muse and Mentor* (Eagen, MN: Thomson Reuters, 2014), 148.

[98] John Baker, "Human Rights and the Rule of Law in Renaissance England," *Northwestern University Journal of International Human Rights* 2 (2004): 11; 28 Edw. III, c. 3 (1354), and 42 Edw. III, c. 1 (1368), *SR*, vol. 1, 388.

[99] Mont, ed., *Chartes des libertés anglaises*, 33. Of course, the English have always sold justice. Those who wanted to take a case to the king's courts had to obtain a writ from chancery. While writs for the poor were often issued free of charge, a sealing fee of six pence (roughly the equivalent of two days' wages for a skilled tradesman) still had to be paid for the chancery clerk's labor. For why this phrase appears in the Magna Carta, see Helmholz, "Magna Carta," 342.

[100] As cited in Paul Brand, "'To None Will We Sell, to None Will We Deny or Delay Right or Justice': Expedition and Delay in Civil Proceedings in the English Medieval Royal Courts," in Remco van Rhee, ed., *Within a Reasonable Time: The History of Due and Undue Delay in Civil Litigation* (Berlin: Duncker and Humbolt, 2010), 57.

[101] John Baker, *The Reinvention of Magna Carta 1216–1616* (Cambridge University Press, 2017), 43–4.

Magna Carta exemplifies how deeply the concept of a defendant's right to a form of due process was embedded in the legal culture of medieval England. Again, it would be wrong to assume that Magna Carta existed in a class by itself. Across Europe, the troubled aristocracy who saw their customary authority being eroded by an aggressively expanding monarchy adapted the language of liberty and individual rights to their own purposes. The era was thus transformed into "a great age for grants of fundamental liberties and for statements of fundamental laws."[102] The Statutes of Pamiers (1212), Simon de Montfort's charter promising protections for his Occitan subjects in the midst of the Albigensian crusades, contains a number of provisos paralleling (presaging?) Magna Carta, including the provision of free justice and an assurance that no man will be imprisoned if he can find sufficient pledges to guarantee his appearance in court. The Hungarian Golden Bull of 1222, often referred to as "Hungary's Magna Carta," also contains similar safeguards to what appears in the great charter. King Andrew pledged that "neither we nor our successors shall detain or oppress the nobles on account of any powerful person, unless they be first summoned and sentenced by due process of law."[103] Other thirteenth-century constitutions include the German *Statutum in favorem principum* (1231) as well as Frederick II's Constitutions of Melfi (1231), and the thirteenth-century *Fueros de Arágon*. The assertion of a defendant's rights that appears in the Magna Carta, therefore, is not an example of English exceptionalism; nor was it an "infection spreading from one country to another; they [liberties] were part of the very atmosphere."[104]

This era gave birth also to a prolific tradition of complaint literature which centered on giving a voice to the voiceless and restricting the monarch's capacity to abuse its subjects by means of the law.[105] The *Mirror of Justices* (c.1285–90) very much belongs to this genre, making liberal use of the same kind of allegory, satire, and biblical rhetoric.[106]

---

[102] Helmholz, "Magna Carta," 363.
[103] Arminius Vámbéry, *The Story of Hungary* (New York: G. P. Putnam's Sons, 1886), 130.
[104] James Holt, *Magna Carta*, 3rd edn. (Cambridge University Press, 2015), 92–3.
[105] See Wendy Scase, *Literature and Complaint in England, 1272–1553* (Oxford University Press, 2007).
[106] Jennifer Jahner makes this connection. See her "The *Mirror of Justices* and the Arts of Archival Invention," *Viator* 45.1 (2014): 221–46.

Philippa Byrne sees it as a "product of a particular late 13th-century English concern for abuses of law – and a cry for their proper investigation and immediate extirpation."[107] The book presents itself as a legal treatise in the same vein as *Glanvill* and *Bracton*; in reality, it was much more of a "reformist textbook on law," presenting law as it should be, by turning to scripture for guidance in moving forward during an era of moral decay.[108] This is particularly true in respect to safeguarding the rights of accused felons. As David Seipp notes, "the author's special concern and constant advocacy are for criminal defendants and prisoners."[109] Book 5 of the *Mirror* is dedicated exclusively to listing abuses of the law; in fact, it is in this section that the author includes a gloss of the Magna Carta, which he makes clear did not go far enough in its reforms for his liking. Encapsulating the reforming spirit of the era, it is noteworthy that the first spot on the list was reserved to the king: it is an abuse "that the king is beyond the law, whereas he ought to be subject to it, as is contained in his oath."[110] Much of Book 5 is relevant to expectations of due process and preserving the rights of the accused. Abuse number 115, for example, denounces justices who will not permit the defendant to read the written indictment, and thus have a full understanding of the charges.[111] The right to a speedy trial is addressed as well, somewhat enigmatically, in number five: "it is an abuse that nowadays right is longer delayed in the king's court than elsewhere."[112] Book 5 also touches on a number of elements critical to the treatment of accused felons not mentioned elsewhere. Multiple abuses on the list address the handling of prisoners awaiting trial: being illegally stripped of their personal effects by the jailer or his superiors (number fifty-two), being required to pay fees to enter or leave jail (number fifty-three), being shackled or loaded with iron prior to conviction (number fifty-four), and suffering an unnecessary delay of the delivery of the prison after the king has issued the appropriate commission (number fifty-five).

[107] Philippa Byrne, "Medieval Violence, the Making of Law and the Historical Present," *Journal of the British Academy* 8.s3 (2020): 134.

[108] David Seipp, "*The Mirror of Justices,*" in Jonathan Bush and Alain Wijffels, eds., *Learning the Law: Teaching and the Transmission of Law in England 1150–1900* (London: Hambledon, 1999), 112.

[109] Seipp, "*Mirror of Justices*," 100. [110] Whittaker, ed., *Mirror of Justices*, 155, no. 1.

[111] Whittaker, ed., *Mirror of Justices*, 172, no. 115.

[112] Whittaker, ed., *Mirror of Justices*, 156, no. 5.

Number fifteen decries the practice of forfeiting the movable goods of a fugitive before he or she has been formally outlawed or convicted of a felony (a standard practice well into the early modern era).[113] Myriad complaints lampoon approvers' appeals. *The Mirror* protests the very existence of approvers: why should untrustworthy criminals be permitted to make appeals at all? The author was especially incensed with the practice that permitted "clerks, women, children, and others who cannot fight" to turn approver, when the only means an approver has to prove the truth of his appeal is through trial by combat (number seventeen). The author also criticizes the heavy-handed judge who pushes for jury trial instead of trial by battle (number nineteen), fails to show his commission when asked (number 107), upholds false judgments that result in capital punishment (number 108), manipulates jury verdicts through incarceration and deprivation of food (number 134) or puts words in the jurors' mouths (number 135).[114] Certainly, the *Mirror of Justice* leaves the reader with the distinct impression that the rights of the defendant were near and dear to the hearts of thirteenth-century jurists.

Devising a Plan for Those Who Stand Mute

Standing mute as a practice emerged at the tail end of the long twelfth century's zeal for natural rights and its impassioned advocacy of the rights of the accused. It also coincided with the abolition of the ordeal in 1215, at a point when justices were already struggling, and were not equipped to deal with those who refused to cooperate. Those few defendants who chose to stand silent thrust them into a dilemma, and they had no guidance as to how to proceed. Examining the various ways in which justices moved forward helps to shine a light on the compromises they made in order to meet the needs of the judicial system, while still respecting the rights of the defendant in an era that prized natural rights. It also gives us an opportunity to understand what defendants might have been thinking in choosing silence. These cases, although few in number, also help us to understand why justices eventually chose hard

---

[113] Whittaker, ed., *Mirror of Justices*, 157 no. 15.
[114] Whittaker, ed., *Mirror of Justices*, 157, no. 19; 166, nos. 107 and 108; 173, nos. 134 and 135.

prison as a response to standing mute. The eyre of 1221 provides multiple examples from this transition period, all in neighboring shires, of defendants who refused to plead. Desperation led to creativity, prompting royal justices to devise three distinct solutions to the problem.

In Gloucestershire, the king's justices were eager not to impose trial juries on accused felons against their will. In Gloucester, eleven defendants in eight cases refused to put themselves upon jury trial. The court's solution was either to permit them to abjure, or find pledges for future good behavior.[115] Only one individual ended up dead. At his arraignment for the murder of Robert the Merchant, Roger Wulmangere ("woolmonger") denied the crime but refused to submit to jury trial. Jurors reported that they had not seen Roger enter or exit Robert's home, yet they still strongly suspected Roger of the death. Royal justices ordered Roger returned to prison, where he masterminded a jailbreak, then fled to the church of Hope in Herefordshire to claim sanctuary. Locals raised the hue and cry and pursued Roger to the church, where a debate arose as to whether he should be permitted to claim sanctuary since he had just broken out of prison. Ultimately, church officials handed Roger over to secular authorities. Justices still had no plea; but what they did have was irrefutable proof of his guilt for jailbreak, also a felony. Thus, they were justified in according him much the same treatment as a thief caught in possession of the goods – that is, summary justice. They proceeded directly to sentencing and Roger was hanged.[116]

Roger Groot has argued that the experience of the contingent of defendants who refused jury trial at Gloucester is important. "Gloucester defendants learned that there was a new convicting jury, that it could be refused, and that refusal generally resulted in a relatively favourable outcome."[117] This knowledge was passed on informally, encouraging others to emulate this pattern. Yet, the tolerance shown towards defendants at Gloucester was not repeated at subsequent eyres.

In Worcestershire, justices chose to treat silence as a confession. John Alfolc, the brother of a hanged murderer, was arrested because of ill fame as a possible accomplice to his brother's crime. When he utterly

---

[115] Groot, "Teaching Each Other," 28.
[116] Frederic Maitland, ed., *Pleas of the Crown for the County of Gloucester* (London: Macmillan, 1884), 75–6, no. 316.
[117] Groot, "Teaching Each Other," 29.

refused to put himself upon the country, justices did not know how to proceed. Initially, they hoped to persuade his lord to coerce him into pleading through seizure of goods, but as the record indicates, "[he] has no lord who will replevy him." Uncomfortable with trying and potentially executing an uncooperative defendant, their final solution was to presume some degree of guilt (why else would he refuse to plead?), but stop short of implementing the full rigors of the law. Rather than execution or mutilation, they drove John into exile and confiscated his goods.[118]

At Warwickshire, they decided instead to bring in the heavy guns by empaneling a special jury of knights. Two cases required this approach. The first was an appeal by Agnes, widow of Robert of Boscombe (*de Bosco*) who accused Thomas, son of Hubert of murdering her husband. Because she had since remarried and her new husband did not appear jointly in court with her, the appeal was quashed, but the case was picked up by the Crown and pursued at the king's suit. At his arraignment, Thomas denied having committed the crime but he declined to submit himself to jury trial. Justices instructed the jury to proceed regardless. The jury found Thomas guilty, but justices hesitated to follow through with a sentence. Despite having an appellor determined enough to have persisted to the end of the process, without a plea from the defendant, they felt the jury's verdict was inadequate on its own to send a man to his death Therefore, they commanded the sheriff to empanel a special jury of twenty-four knights to render judgment; they, too, found him guilty and Thomas was ordered to hang.[119] At the same eyre, Thomas de la Hethe, arrested on charges of theft, receiving malefactors, and "other evil deeds" (*aliis nequitiis*), also spurned jury trial. Justices carried on just as they had in the case of Thomas, son of Hubert. Two juries were assigned: the usual twelve free and oathworthy men of a jury trial followed by a special jury of twenty-four knights. Both declared him guilty and this Thomas was also sentenced to hang.[120]

[118] Frederic Maitland, ed., *Select Pleas of the Crown, Vol. 1: AD 1200–1225* (SS, vol. I, 1888), 93.

[119] Maitland, ed., *Select Pleas of the Crown*, 99; also in Doris Stenton, ed., *Rolls of the Justices in Eyre in Eyre being the Rolls of Pleas and Assizes for Gloucestershire, Warwickshire and Staffordshire, 1221, 1222* (SS, vol. LIX, 1940), 332–3, no. 728.

[120] Stenton, *Rolls of the Justices in Eyre*, 346, no. 767.

These four instances show royal justices tackling an unanticipated problem, but resolute, through experimentation, to locate a solution that was beyond reproach. In doing so, they had to perform a balancing act, satisfying the needs of the Crown while respecting the rights of the people. The final two cases discussed above, in which the defendants were effectively tried twice, demonstrates just how desperate they were to find an equitable solution. What is clear is that even at this early stage in the transition, justices had come to accept that a jury had the power to convict and send a man to his death; yet, they were not so eager to see a man lose his life on the basis of a jury trial to which he had not consented.[121] At any rate, the solutions fashioned in these four examples were unworkable in the long run. Sending defendants back to prison without a plan for how to proceed was not viable given that medieval prisons were designed for short-term occupancy. If abjuration of the realm became an option extended to all those who stood mute, would any guilty man ever have stood trial in England again? Ordering a special jury of twenty-four knights was similarly impracticable: sheriffs had enough difficulty getting jurors to court already, and the elite were notoriously reluctant to be pressed into service. The wealthy readily purchased exemptions from jury service from the Crown.[122] If the sheriff now had to assemble thirty-six jurors, twenty-four of which must be knights, for all those who stood mute, many of those men were going to be returned to prison anyway because of deficiencies in the juries.

Over a decade later, justices were still struggling for an answer to the problem of silent defendants. The fact that they had not yet established a solution implies that silent defendants were few and far between in this era. At the 1235 Essex eyre, when two defendants refused to put themselves upon the country, justices decided simply to ride roughshod over the defendants' objections and proceed to jury trial without consent. So, too, did they at Canterbury in 1251 when encountering a foreign merchant who would not consent to jury trial.[123] The justices' brash policy fulfilled the needs of the Crown by ensuring

---

[121] See McSweeney, "Magna Carta and the Right," 150–2.

[122] Scott Waugh, "Reluctant Knights and Jurors: Respites, Exemptions, and Public Obligations in the Reign of Henry III," *Speculum* 58.4 (1983): 937–58.

[123] TNA JUST 1/230, mm. 2d and 10 (1251); TNA C 145/5, no. 25; as cited in Henry Summerson, "The Early Development of the Peine Forte et Dure," in

efficient justice, yet it did not sit well with everyone involved. Discomfort with this policy eventually prompted a retraction: by 1256, they initiated the practice of returning defendants to prison until they agreed to undergo jury trial. As such, justices settled firmly in favor of tradition: the defendant's consent was requisite for trial, no matter how it must be extracted.[124]

What can we learn from this era of experimentation? First, justices saw a defendant's rights to a fair trial (or at least, as fair a trial as they could make it in the absence of a cooperative defendant) was a pressing concern. If punishing criminals was the justices' only priority, an obstinate defendant would have been no cause for alarm, nor would it have been grounds for deviation from the normal process. That they resorted to commandeering twenty-four knights in order to validate the process demonstrates just how uneasy justices were with moving forward without consent. In the English tradition, a defendant's consent to be tried, signaled by his choice of trial method, was requisite for what they considered to be a "fair trial." Entrenched in a legal culture that essentialized protecting the rights of the accused, an English judge could not confidently proceed without a defendant's willingness to undergo jury trial.

England's long history requiring an accused felon's consent to be tried is pivotal. James Masschaele's query that began this chapter could easily be turned around. Instead of asking why England was so focused on consent, one might well ask why Continental authorities were not? The reason quite simply is that it was not a part of their heritage. Englishmen and women saw the need to consent to trial as a quintessentially English right of a long-standing nature. It was part of the English legal identity. While the entire system of criminal justice might have been changing around them, in an atmosphere that championed the rights of the accused, eliminating the need for a defendant's consent was not a viable option.[125]

Eric Ives and Anthony Manchester, eds., *Law, Litigants, and the Legal Profession* (London: RHS, 1983), 116.

[124] Summerson, "Early Development," 117.

[125] It is no surprise, then, that Normandy stands out as an exception to the Continental rule. Like the English, the Normans prescribed hard prison as a coercive measure for a suspected felon who refused jury trial. Their shared heritage gives us good reason to believe that the Normans also felt uneasy eliminating a right that men and women believed was fundamental.

Second, justices worried specifically about sending a convicted criminal to death when he or she had not consented to trial. Historians have long recognized that judges struggled with the moral implications of capital punishment. This issue was particularly sensitive with the shift from proof to trial when responsibility for ending the life of the accused shifted from God alone to a group of exceedingly human justices. Without God's sign of approval was a death sentence homicide? What were the implications for a judge's soul? This concern is brashly articulated in a wide variety of English sources. As early as the twelfth century, the *Leges Henrici Primi* delivered a cautionary note warning the judge that "any judgment we pass on others is held in store for ourselves."[126] The *Mirror of Justices* seeks to reassure judges that capital punishment is not a form of homicide, providing "lawful judges ... kill by right judgment and holy conscience." Yet, it also provides an extensive discussion of how *false* judgment in a capital case is in fact homicide, including forty-four examples drawn from the reign of King Alfred to confirm that justices in these instances should be put to death.[127] Even John Fortescue's fifteenth-century *De Laudibus* touches on this subject. He held all judges morally responsible for whatever actions they ordered in court.[128] In the era after Lateran IV, James Whitman has argued persuasively that justices assuaged their consciences by clinging to one of St. Augustine's maxims: those who follow the order of the law cannot be held responsible for the results of its actions.[129] In Augustine's mind, a rigorous adherence to legal process alleviates any moral responsibility. On the Continent, "rigorous adherence" entailed the development of the "reasonable doubt formula." While today this formula is understood as a protection for the defendant, in its earliest manifestation it was intended instead to shield the souls of judges who would not perform the duties of the state otherwise.[130] Low execution rates were tied to judicial certainty: to avoid the taint of sin, justices

---

[126] *LHP*, ch. 28, subsection 5, 130–1.

[127] Whittaker, ed., *Mirror of Justices*, 135–6. *LHP* calls it a "homicide without sin." See *LHP*, ch. 72, subsection 1c, 228–9; Whittaker, ed., *Mirror of Justices*, 166.

[128] John Fortescue, *De Laudibus Legum Angliae*, ed. Stanley Chrimes, 2nd edn. (Cambridge University Press, 2011), 69.

[129] James Whitman, *The Origins of Reasonable Doubt: Theological Roots of the Criminal Trial* (New Haven: Yale University Press, 2008), 39–40.

[130] Whitman, *Origins of Reasonable Doubt*.

only sent a criminal to the gallows when they were certain beyond a shadow of a doubt that he or she was indeed guilty. In England, where justices shared this anxiety also with a group of twelve good men and true, the focus instead shifted to obtaining a defendant's consent.

Written Consent

A defendant's consent ensured more than cooperation. It was an explicit recognition that the accused acknowledged the court's jurisdiction and would voluntarily comply with its decision. Thus, no judge might find himself in the troubling situation of sending an individual to death who did not even recognize his authority as a judge to do so. Prioritizing consent meant the development of a number of safeguards within the common law to certify that consent was voluntary and genuine. It is for this reason that, in parallel with the transition from proof to trial, the English judiciary developed the writ *de bono et malo* (for good and ill), introduced exclusively for homicide trials. This writ functioned as an individualized commission of jail delivery, addressed to named justices, ordering them to deliver a named prisoner who could be found in a named prison. Justices had no power to try a suspect for homicide without one.[131] The court charged the prisoner (or more likely, someone on the prisoner's behalf) with the responsibility of acquiring the writ and bringing it to trial. In its absence, the trial could not proceed; justices simply remanded the prisoner to jail until the next eyre. Accordingly, the writ functioned as written proof that the prisoner accepted jury trial, that "he placed himself upon the country for good and ill" (the formulaic language used to indicate the accused had chosen to submit to jury trial), as chancery only issued the writ upon condition that he or she pled.[132]

The writ, then, was intended to pave the way for a smooth trial; by securing consent before arraignment, justices hoped to make it difficult for a defendant to retract that consent at a later date, specifically when standing before the justices.[133] Of course, the best laid plans sometimes

---

[131] Ralph Pugh, *Imprisonment in Medieval England* (Cambridge University Press, 1968), 25.

[132] Naomi Hurnard, *The King's Pardon for Homicide Before AD 1307* (Oxford: Clarendon Press, 1969), 355.

[133] Summerson has argued the court's intention was "to ensure that suspected killers did not hold up proceedings by standing mute." Summerson, "Early Development," 123.

go wrong. Some of those who appeared at trial with writ in hand still refused to plead, while others opted to claim benefit of clergy.[134] Because oral proceedings took precedence over anything written on parchment, a refusal to plead, even when the defendant arrived in possession of a writ *de bono et malo*, left justices with no choice but to resort to hard prison. The silent defendant who later decided to plead added further delays. He or she was then required to seek out a second writ *de bono et malo*, as each writ was tied to a particular delivery.[135]

In this end, writs *de bono et malo* were a failed experiment. Chancery ceased issuing them in the mid fourteenth century because of the sheer inconvenience. Far too many prisoners could not be tried because they failed to follow proper procedure.[136] Particularly astute prisoners delayed their trials by conveniently "forgetting" to follow through in obtaining the proper paperwork. The experience of a Norfolk woman, Agnes Roger, offers an instructive example. Indicted for homicide, she stood before justices of jail delivery in June of 1325, at which point she challenged the jury sitting to try her and then was returned to prison because the sheriff did not have enough qualified men to assemble a new jury. A month later, she appeared again before royal justices, although this time she reported that she had neglected to obtain the writ *de bono et malo* required to initiate her trial. In December of 1325 she turned up once more empty-handed.[137] What Agnes' example demonstrates is that a clever felon could prolong her life for months, maybe even years, if she played the system right. The prisons spilling over with those awaiting trial, royal justices conceded that the process desperately needed simplification. After 1335, only a generalized commission of jail delivery was necessary to try all individuals from a named prison indicted or appealed of felony, taking the responsibility of remembering the paperwork out of the defendant's hands altogether.

---

[134] Edmund, son of Gilbert of York of Oakley appeared before royal justices at the castle of Norwich in 1315 on charges of homicide. Even though he produced his writ *de bono et malo*, he refused to put himself upon the country. He was sentenced to the diet. TNA JUST 3/48, m. 23d (1315).

[135] John Kaye, "Gaol Delivery Jurisdiction and the Writ *de Bono et Malo*," *The Law Quarterly Review* 93 (1977): 263–4.

[136] Kaye, "Gaol Delivery Jurisdiction," 271.

[137] As cited in Anthony Musson, *Public Order and Law Enforcement: The Local Administration of Criminal Justice, 1294–1350* (Woodbridge: Boydell, 1996), 196.

Despite the relatively short-lived nature of this experiment, the writ's function as proof of consent reminds us just how critical consent had become under English law. Moreover, the fact that it appeared contemporaneous with jury trial emphasizes that consent was central to the trial process from the very beginning of this new phase in English legal history.

Oral Consent

When the writ *de bono et malo* was required, oral pleading was the second stage in the process for those accused of homicide; after 1335, it came to be the only stage. With so much riding on this particular moment, the English insisted that a defendant must plead for himself and he must do so orally in the presence of the king's justices because "only words from his mouth were authentic."[138] The need for an explicitly verbal statement aligns with the general orality of medieval legal culture. Today we think of law primarily in terms of written documents: legislation, commentary and interpretation, citations, case law, written contracts. Not so in the Middle Ages. The medieval common law was a noisy affair: the hue and cry; proclamations, summons, and exactions; *fama*; presentments; testimony extracted from witnesses who swore to tell the truth regarding only what they had seen or heard; oral pleading; oaths; statutes recited from memory; the oral debates of justices and pleaders; compurgation; confession; judges pronouncing verdicts.[139] When a defendant chose to trust jury trial, as the author of *Bracton* writes, "he puts himself for good and ill upon the *words* of [the jurors'] mouths."[140] Common law itself was unwritten; it was the responsibility of judges and pleaders to administer it from memory, with some assistance from the legal treatises, pocket statute books, and the instructions included in their written commission. Contracts were also chiefly oral in nature well into the early modern era despite the existence of an entire corpus of written legal devices.

---

[138] Michael Clanchy, *From Memory to Written Record: England 1066–1307*, 3rd edn. (Malden: Wiley-Blackwell, 2012), 270.
[139] See Gwen Seabourne, "'It is Necessary That the Issue Be Heard to Cry or Squall Within the Four [Walls]': Qualifying for Tenancy by the Curtesy of England in the Reign of Edward I," *Journal of Legal History* 40 (2019): 44–68.
[140] Italics are mine. *Bracton*, vol. II, 405.

Somewhat counter-intuitively, the courts' dedication to speech only increased over time. Legal authorities of the later Middle Ages saw the need to protect the authenticity of speech by criminalizing inappropriate uses of it, such as barratry, scolding, gossiping, cursing, taking false oaths, blaspheming, defaming, perjuring, spreading false rumors, engaging in treasonable speech, and speaking heresy.

The weight accorded to speech in the late medieval courtroom derives also from the church's renewed emphasis on oral confession in the thirteenth century. Royal justices saw an explicit link between a defendant's plea and the sacrament: pleading was a "natural extension" of one's religious duty.[141] Given that many of thirteenth-century England's justices were also bishops, they were already wearing the appropriate hats for the job of hearing confession. In church, they sat as judges in the internal court of conscience; in court, their jobs were merely more public in nature. That England's insistence on spoken consent comes also at the time when annual confession became mandatory across Christendom is not merely coincidental. *Britton* draws attention to the religious undertones of pleading when its author writes of the need to establish ideal conditions in which the penitent defendant can confess freely. Accused felons should be brought to court "without irons or any kind of bonds, so that they may not be deprived of reason by pain, nor be constrained to answer by force, but of their own free will."[142] This sentiment is echoed in a year book from 1292, which states "nor ought [a prisoner] be brought to the bar in irons: because while he is in irons he is in prison; and while he is in prison he can not make any admission or give any answer."[143] Shackles undermine the sincerity of a plea.

The intrinsic orality of medieval legal culture is the context into which the court's insistence on spoken consent must be considered, as well as the implications of standing mute.[144] For the king's justices, they were not willing to go forward with a trial until they heard a plea

---

[141] Anthony Musson, "Turning King's Evidence: The Prosecution of Crime in Late Medieval England," *Oxford Journal of Legal Studies* 19.3 (1999): 469.

[142] Francis Nichols, ed., *Britton: An English Translation and Notes*, 2 vols. (Washington, DC: John Byrne and Co., 1901), vol. I, 29–30.

[143] Alfred Horwood, ed., *Year Books of the Reign of Edward the First: Years xx and xxi (1292–1293)* (RS, no. 31, part A, vol. I, 1866), 244 (Seipp 1292.228rs).

[144] None of this implies that legal records and texts did not exist – legal texts date well back to the Anglo-Saxon era and they played a key role in legal culture; however, at

directly from the accused's lips. The foundational relationship between speech and consent is spelled out in *Bracton* in a discussion on land acquisition. The treatise explains that an individual who is deaf and "dumb" "cannot consent, because he is completely unable to hear the words of the stipulator, and since he cannot hear or speak at all, he cannot express his will and consent either by words or signs," thus he cannot legally acquire land.[145] In terms of criminal justice, where the defendant's words might result in loss of life, the court's insistence on spoken pleas as a form of consent meant that royal justices were not content to proceed without one.

Naturally, felons knew that muteness might save their lives. This explains the plentitude of cases of those who feigned muteness, even those few who resorted to self-harm. When John Maughan of Brokenheugh,[146] a yeoman in the county of Northumberland stood accused of cattle theft in 1434, the jurors tasked with explaining his silence reported that he had voluntarily bitten off his own tongue (*lignam suam dentibus suis propris voluntare momordit et abscidit*) in order to simulate natural muteness in the hope of being acquitted on an exception. His ruse did not work. Justices ordered him sent to prison to endure peine forte et dure where he died two years later.[147] Maughan may well be the only accused felon who devised such an extreme solution – certainly, this study did not uncover any similar examples. However, his desperation tells us that he believed mutilation might save his life.

The Inquest into Muteness as a Test of Competence

For those of us living in the twenty-first century, subjecting a suspected felon to hard prison does not seem like a protection of a defendant's right to a fair trial. However, modern expectations of a fair trial and humanitarian treatment in prison are far different from the medieval

no point was orality overshadowed by the centrality of legal documents in the Middle Ages.

[145] *Bracton*, vol. IV, 309.
[146] A hamlet in the parish of Haydon Bridge, Northumberland.
[147] TNA JUST 3/208, m. 31d (1434); discussed first in Cynthia Neville, "Common Knowledge of the Common Law in Later Medieval England," *Canadian Journal of History* 28 (1994): 1–18. Maughan's example may lie behind the apocryphal man who stands mute because he cut out his own tongue mentioned by *Blackstone*, Book IV, ch. 25.

ideal. The medieval era gave birth to a concern for the rights of accused felons, but that concern did not end there. In the eight hundred years since then, a plethora of legal remedies have evolved to protect defendants and ensure that their time in prison is unpleasant without denying them what we would see as the basic comforts of life (food, clothing, warmth, a bed, a toilet). The distance in time and moral principles makes it more challenging for us to appreciate the medieval approach. In this respect, there are a number of factors to consider. First, as Chapter 1 made clear, coercion was a normal part of medieval English law. Common law contains myriad devices to coerce an uncooperative defendant into complying with the dictates of the law. In particular, employing prison as a form of coercion was common – indeed, even the church saw incarceration as a valuable tool for bring excommunicates back to the faith. English justices would have felt no moral twinge incarcerating a suspected felon as a coercive measure, especially when the prize was consent. Second, most aspects of hard prison (fasting, denial of comforts, some degree of suffering) were reminiscent of the normal penitential process, and thus court and church alike could justify hard prison as being in the best interests of the defendant (or at least, in the best interests of his or her soul). Therefore, when the defendant finally agreed to trial, as most eventually did, he or she could proceed with all of the normal safeguards in place. There was only one flaw to the plan: what if a defendant stood mute, not out of discontent with the system, but because he didn't understand what was being asked of him?

The inquest into muteness developed to address specifically this fear. Most inquests aligned with the following scenario: on July 17, 1357, Simon Hande of Hanslope, an alleged cattle thief, was asked how he wished to acquit himself by justices of jail delivery. In response, he said nothing but always held mute (*nichil dicere set se semper tenet mutum*). Fearing Simon might be naturally mute and thus physically incapable of denying the allegations, Northamptonshire's sheriff, a man named Walter Parles (whose name somehow feels ironic) assembled an inquest of twelve honest and lawful men of the jail (*xii proborum et legorum homines gaole*) housed closest to the prisoner and asked whether Simon was simply feigning his muteness; that is, was it possible that he could speak, but did not wish to do so. The jurors replied on oath that Simon was capable of speech and had

spoken earlier that day, therefore he was simply pretending to be mute
(*se fingit mutum*) before the king's justices.[148]

Inquests of this nature should be recognized as another example of
how the courts guaranteed the defendant a fair trial. The king's justices
stood firm against proceeding until they were in full possession of
information relating to the defendant's competence. Justices could
not advance to trial with a genuinely mute defendant; nor did they
wish to apply coercive measures to compel the defendant to plead if
one was incapable of doing so. As the inquest above implies, sheriffs
took the obligation to organize an inquest into the defendant's ability
to speak seriously, making an effort to empanel eyewitnesses to the
accused's time in prison. When this practice first evolved is not entirely
clear. No statute exists mandating the inquest, but the first recorded
instance comes from the year 1300, some time after standing mute had
become an established alternative to pleading.[149] Further, while today
we might be uncomfortable with the notion of a jury composed of
prisoners (i.e. convicted felons), it is worth remembering that prisoners
in the medieval context were either awaiting a trial (and thus not
necessarily guilty – in fact, given the high rates of flight, there is an
argument to be made that at least some of these individuals stuck
around for trial precisely because they were innocent), or convicted
debtors. Such a group would seem to be as qualified to act as jurors in
this scenario as any other.

Organizing an inquest into the defendant's ability to speak became
a regular part of the sheriff's job when it comes to dealing with
defendants who stood mute. In the 481 cases of peine forte et dure
here under examination, 106 of them, or 22 percent, necessitated juries
of inquest to examine the accused's fitness to speak. Over time, the
inquest became *pro forma* – sheriffs held them even when they were
unnecessary. For example, in March of 1361, William, son of William
Elison Wright of Broughton told justices at his arraignment that he did
not wish to speak and so he stood mute (*dicit nec vult loqui set se tenet
mutam*). There should have been no confusion about whether William
was able to speak (after all, he *told* them he did not wish to speak), but
standing mute called for an inquest and so the sheriff clung to process.
He assembled a jury whose members reported that William was indeed

[148] TNA JUST 3/140, m. 7d (1357).   [149] Summerson, "Early Development," 124.

capable of speech and justices followed up by sentencing him to peine forte et dure.[150]

Every so often royal justices encountered a legitimately mute defendant. When John Raven of Oxborough (Norfolk) and his brother Henry were arrested with thirty stolen sheep in tow, John immediately claimed benefit of clergy, abandoning his brother to fend for himself. At his trial at Norwich castle in 1315, Henry remained silent. An inquest determined that he could not speak due to a physical disability (*pro debilitate corporis*). Justices remanded him to prison, although the record offers no indication of what ultimately happened to Henry.[151] Richard Undyrwode, rector of the church of Gedding (Suffolk), also suffered from an infirmity, although of a more short-term nature. When he was accused of slaying William Clerk of Gedding and his servant, he stood mute before the court. Jurors found that he did so because of a certain natural infirmity which prevented him from speaking. Not only had he not spoken that day, but he was not able to speak before he was incarcerated. Justices returned him to prison in the hopes that he might be fully recovered by the date of the next delivery.[152]

At times, justices suspected the defendant's silence was a product of mental disability. This is hinted at in the account of William Gibberish (*Gyberyssh*), indicted by the coroner of Surrey for homicide in 1337. Contrary to the moniker by which they referred to him, the inquest concluded that he was able to speak, presumably coherently, and thus he was sentenced to the starvation diet.[153] Justices' concerns about the defendant's mental aptitude were more pronounced in two other instances. In 1384, Roger Frere of Canterbury, a butcher, stood mute before the court when indicted of stealing nine sheep and five lambs from William Haningfeld of Fulburne. After asking him at intervals if he wished to respond and receiving no reply, justices ordered an inquest which determined not only that he was capable of speech, but that the defendant was in his right mind (*compos mentis sue*). Justices also sentenced him to the diet.[154] Similarly, in 1390, royal justices at Hertford castle arraigned Henry, servant of Thomas Ledes,

---

[150] TNA JUST 3/145, m. 16 (1361).   [151] TNA JUST 3/48, m. 28d (1315).
[152] TNA JUST 3/212, m. 9 (1440).   [153] TNA JUST 3/135, m. 55d (1337).
[154] TNA JUST 3/164, m. 21d (1384).

a cordwainer (a shoemaker who works in leather) living in Hertford and accused of petty treason for killing his master as well as his master's wife and daughter then stealing their goods. The indictment reflects the community's distaste for such an odious crime through the inclusion and repetition of the term traitorously (*proditorie*) which appears four times in the short record. In court, Henry said nothing. Justices assembled an inquest of his fellow prisoners who remarked that Henry could speak if he wished. They also noted that he was sane and in his right mind (*compos mentis sue et sane memorie*). Asked once more how he wished to plead, Henry persisted in his silence. The fasting diet of prison forte et dure was also his fate.[155] A study of the widely recognized link between mutism and mental illness in the modern world explains it as a product of this history: defendants feign muteness because they know that jurors have a tendency to interpret it as mental illness. In the modern West, feigning mutism takes pride of place among the most commonly faked symptoms of mental illness in those defendants hoping to hoodwink the courts into a verdict of not guilty by reason of insanity.[156]

Assembling an *impromptu* inquest was a normal part of the process; it was also an inconvenience, needlessly prolonging the arraignment and wasting the justices', sheriff's, and jailer's time at a point when everyone was working on a tight schedule. Justices of jail delivery hoped to deliver a prison of all its accused in a period of a day or two; they worked at breakneck speed in order to accomplish this goal, with each trial lasting somewhere between fifteen and thirty minutes.[157] Unnecessary delays by those pretending to be naturally mute must have tried everyone's patience. Irritation explains some of the hints of hostility that crop up in the legal record towards those who stood mute. To offer a few examples: the portrayal of Thomas Frend, a carpenter from Potesgrove (Buckinghamshire) held for burglary and sheep-stealing, points to an impudent demeanor. The scribe noted that "he did not care to respond"

---

[155] TNA JUST 3/178, m. 3 (1390).
[156] Anasseril Daniel and Phillip Resnick, "Mutism, Malingering, and Competency to Stand Trial," *Bulletin of the American Academy of Psychiatry and the Law* 15.3 (1987): 301–8.
[157] Ralph Pugh, "The Duration of Criminal Trials in Medieval England," in Eric Ives and Anthony Manchester, eds., *Law, Litigants and the Legal Profession* (London: Hambledon, 1983), 108.

(*nichil respondere curat*) at his 1370 trial but always held himself mute. The inquisition found that Thomas' refusal of the common law was "voluntary" (*voluntarie*).[158] More pointedly, a man accused of homicide in 1366 who refused to speak was sentenced to penance "for his disobedience" (*et pur sa disobedience il avera sa penance*).[159] The records regularly describe silent defendants as being mute by malice (*per malicia tenet se mutum*), or "maliciously pretend[ing] to be mute" (*set maliciose fingit se mutum*).[160] William the Chapman, indicted of homicide at Bedford in 1316, was described as having "maliciously and feloniously pretended to be both mute and deaf" (*fingit se mutum et surdum*).[161] At times, the terminology employed in trial records make it clear that jurors believed the defendants were driven by wicked intentions to cheat the system. John Hobbe of Hartford was described as standing mute "to escape the common law" (*tenet se mutum causa communis legis evitandem*).[162] John, son of Andrew, William, son of Nicholas, and John of Craven "did not wish to speak but maliciously held mute to prolong their lives" (*noluit loqui set ad elongationem vitae sua maliciose se tenet mutus*).[163] John Richard of Laceby (*Lanckeby?*) "maliciously pretended to be mute when he could speak in order to prolong his life," (*maliciose se fingit mutum ubi loquie posset sez prolongendum vitam suam*) and William Systegale "maliciously hoped to prolong his life and avoid the law" (*maliciose pro vita sua elongatus et legem evitandem*).[164] Despite the many and varied instances of those who pretended to be mute, sheriffs continued to arrange inquests, because no matter how irritating it must have been to arrange inquests for men who were perfectly capable of speech, obtaining the defendant's consent was the top priority.

---

[158] TNA JUST 3/152, m. 35d (1370). A certain facetiousness is evident also in the arraignment of William Parlebien ("speaks well") of Alphamstone in 1355, whose efforts to feign muteness were evidently unsuccessful. TNA JUST 3/18/4, m. 4d (1355).

[159] YB 1366, fo. 250a (Seipp 1366.157ass).

[160] See TNA JUST 3/74/4, m. 1 (1318), John of Cleasby.

[161] TNA JUST 3/1/1, m. 15/1 (1316). Feigning a physical disability did not actually constitute a felony, but it was fraudulent behavior: when two indicted felons stood mute in 1470 before the court of Common Bench, jurors described them as doing so by fraud (*par fraude*). YB Mich. 1470, fo. 19b (Seipp 1470.086ss).

[162] TNA JUST 3/22/2, m. 5d (1324).

[163] TNA JUST 3/128, m. 4d (1335); JUST 3/132, m. 4d (1338).

[164] TNA JUST 3/51/3, m. 14d (1321); JUST 3/222, m. 27 (1324).

Conclusion

As John Langbein has remarked, in the premodern era, "the
fundamental safeguard for the defendant in common law criminal
procedure was not the right to remain silent, but rather the
opportunity to speak."[165] When the king's justices inquired how
a defendant wished to plead, they were granting the accused
a moment in the spotlight to make his or her voice heard, to reject
the charges, and clear his or her name. In a world with such a deeply
entrenched social hierarchy, it is striking that all defendants, regardless
of rank or birth, were awarded this very same privilege.

Historically, when justices asked a defendant how he wished to
acquit himself, they were asking the defendant to make a choice.
Before Henry's reforms, English criminal justice included a wide
array of proofs: compurgation, battle, ordeals. Not every option was
open to each defendant. Trustworthiness, often defined by rank,
shaped the availability of one's options. Freemen of good reputation
were best poised to take advantage of the full slate. While
compurgation was the normal means of trial, in the quest to restore
his honor, a freeman whose reputation was still smarting from insult
might prefer the glorious spectacle of a battle; or, if he was not so
handy with a sword, the miracle of carrying iron. With Henry's
reforms, some of those choices vanished. Compurgation was
eliminated altogether from the list of options, while the establishment
of the jury of presentment dramatically reduced the opportunities for
battle. The transition from proofs to trial was complete when Lateran
IV issued a ban prohibiting priests from participating in ordeals,
prompting the English to adapt juries for the purposes of trial. The
vastness of the change was exacerbated by a simultaneous redefinition
of felony as a category under the law. Where serious crime was once
associated chiefly with theft, under Henry II the scope expanded
considerably to include a wide variety of offenses. Most importantly,
homicide transformed from a personal offense resolved through
compensation to a felony subject to capital punishment. Henry II is
regularly lauded for the creation of a highly efficient judicial system,
but for suspected felons, almost overnight their legal world had turned

---

[165] John Langbein, "The Historical Origins of the Privilege against Self-Incrimination at
Common Law," *Michigan Law Review* 92 (1994): 1047.

upside down. Behavior that was once anti-social and costly, now risked their lives rather than their purses; and they had no ability to manipulate the judicial system to their best advantage. Standing mute was one means, approved by the *Leges Henrici Primi*, to express discontent with a system that Englishmen and women considered overly stringent and alienating.

Even though a defendant's options for method of trial realistically had shrunk to just one (jury trial), justices continued to ask defendants how they wished to acquit themselves. They did so because of what that choice traditionally represented: consent. When a man accused of a felony agreed to place his case before a jury of twelve men for consideration, he gave them permission to determine whether he would live or die; he also agreed to abide by their decision. For the English, consent to trial was a time-honored, elementary right. Systems might change; but such a right so fundamental to the English identity could not be easily eradicated. This is particularly true because of the legal currents of the age. These transitions took place against the backdrop of a European-wide legal reform in which natural rights theorists issued vehement defenses of the rights of an accused felon. Among others, they prioritized the defendant's right to know the nature of the accusations, to confront his or her accuser, and to have a speedy trial conducted according to an established process in which one was presumed innocent until proven guilty. In the English context, consenting to trial became part and parcel of this package of protections accorded a defendant under the law. By the fourteenth century, rhetoric about natural rights led English jurists to develop even more protections for the rights of the accused, beginning with the indictment process. Since at least 1311, the jury process ensured that no one stood indicted of a crime without reasonable evidence. It was not sufficient to accuse an individual of criminal behavior (for example, being a "common thief"). Rather, the indictment must include details relating to a specific crime on a named date tied to a precise location and an identifiable victim.[166] The 1413 "Statute of Additions" stipulated also that a formal indictment was not valid unless it identified the accused with utter certainty. Therefore, the

---

[166] John Baker, *Introduction to English Legal History*, 5th edn. (Oxford University Press, 2019), 546.

defendant's full name, estate, profession, and place of residence must be included, so that no John Smith of London might be confused with another.[167] Imprisonment or trial without a formal indictment filed with the king's justices was prohibited. And as Magna Carta makes clear, indictment was the result of a fixed process, involving presentment by jury, the findings of a coroner's inquest, or an appeal by a private citizen.

Over time, the medieval trial process included just as many precautions designed to safeguard the rights of the accused. An accessory could not come to trial until the principal had been either convicted or outlawed. An individual who committed a crime while in the throes of insanity was not held accountable for that crime: one was declared *non compos mentis* and imprisoned only if one was a danger to oneself. The defendant had the right to challenge up to thirty-five jurors if they were in any way biased against the defendant, even more if there was an overlap between indicting and trial juries. While double jeopardy per se did not exist, by 1300 there were at least four pleas in existence that resembled it (former acquittal, former conviction, dismissal, and issue preclusion) and achieved the same goal, to ensure that a person could not be tried twice for the same crime. All of these developments tell us that the right of the accused to a fair trial was at the forefront of everyone's minds.

The practice of the law, more than anything, reinforces the pro-defendant stance of medieval criminal justice. Convictions were in a distinct minority: Bellamy offers a meager conviction rate of 23 per cent for late medieval felons.[168] The multiplicity of loopholes by which defendants were capable of avoiding or delaying execution (sanctuary, benefit of clergy, purchasing a pardon, pleading the belly) are a useful reminder of the various forms of mercy built into the criminal justice system precisely so that the Crown did not have to impose the full rigors of the law. Speaking of the inadequacy of medieval law enforcement, John Bellamy has written that "a felon could consider himself distinctly unlucky if he were captured by the

---

[167] "Statute of Additions," 1 Hen. V, c. 5 (1413), *SR*, vol. II, 131.

[168] John Bellamy, *The Criminal Trial in Later Medieval England* (University of Toronto Press, 1998), 124. Please note: I am not arguing that civil law was pro-defendant. The ability to forum shop as well as jurisdictional competition very much inclined English civil jurisdiction to be pro-plaintiff.

authorities."[169] This statement is equally applicable to the unlucky felon actually convicted in a medieval court of law.

This merciful environment is the backdrop against which justices formulated a response to reluctant defendants who chose to stand mute. The plan they formulated was a product of the times and reflects thirteenth-century views of what constitutes a fair trial. Obtaining a defendant's consent to be tried became a priority: in their minds, there was no such thing as a fair trial in which the defendant was an unwilling, silent nonparticipant. A wide array of safeguards developed to ensure that a defendant's consent was also sincere. Writs *de bono et malo* and a firm insistence that consent come directly from the defendant's lips are best explained by justices' persistence to ensure consent was genuine. Similarly, when a defendant stood mute, they sought to determine whether one was naturally mute, or even mentally disabled. Despite the inconveniences of additional inquests, they persevered because they could not proceed to trial without consent. Prison forte et dure, then, emerged as a coercive measure intended to fulfill multiple needs: in thwarting the defendant's attempts to derail the legal process, it upheld the king's reputation as the ultimate peacemaker. At the same time, it protected a defendant's right to due process and a fair trial by making it difficult for the accused to refuse it when offered. Finally, it assuaged the guilty consciences of justices and jurors who feared that sentencing criminals to death jeopardized their chances of salvation.

Returning briefly to James Masschaele's question cited in the introduction to this chapter: "Why was the principle of giving consent to a jury trial so highly cherished that even torture was worth accepting to maintain it?"[170] Consent was central because it was the quintessentially English means of protecting a defendant's right to a fair trial.

---

[169] John Bellamy, *Crime and Public Order in England in the Later Middle Ages* (University of Toronto Press, 1970), 201.

[170] Masschaele, *Jury, State, and Society*, 82.

4

Peine Forte et Dure as Barbarity? Putting the Practice in Context

> Wo to that flesch that has not been maystrede and ouercomen in this worlde!
>
> Attributed to Cassiodorus, *Speculum Christiani*[1]

> For penalties are devised to control men, so that those whom the fear of God will not turn from evil may at least be restrained from wrongdoing by a temporal penalty, as it is written: "Good men hate to err from love of virtue; the wicked hate to err from fear of pain."
>
> *Fleta*[2]

Not only has peine forte et dure regularly been depicted as a relic of medieval barbarism, the "grand narrative" of legal historical tradition has long reviled it as a stain on the common law's march of progress. Two statements, similar in tone but roughly 200 years apart in time, make the point. In 1765, William Blackstone described peine forte et dure as "a monument of the savage rapacity, with which the lordly tyrants of feudal antiquity hunted after escheats and forfeitures."[3] In 1941, George Woodbine echoed Blackstone, calling

---

[1] (Woe to that flesh that has not been mastered and overcome in this world.) Gustaf Holmstedt, ed., *Speculum Christiani: A Middle English Religious Treatise of the Fourteenth Century* (EETS, vol. CLXXXII, 1933), 68.

[2] Henry Richardson and George Sayles, eds., *Fleta* (SS, vol. LXXII, 1953), 34.

[3] *Blackstone*, vol. IV, ch. 25.

peine forte et dure "the hideous custom of pressing a man to make him plead," noting how it "cast its blight on English criminal procedure for hundreds of years."[4] The sentiment, if not the overwrought expression, is still found in some twenty-first century studies of the common law. In this tradition, peine forte et dure – typically described as a form of judicial torture – exists as an anomaly in an otherwise linear story of legal innovation and achievement, dating back to that imposing intellectual edifice of the twelfth-century legal revolution. Spurred on by the rediscovery of Justinian's *Corpus Juris Civilis*, the revival of the study of Roman law in the period 1085–1215 has been seen fundamentally as a crossroads in the history of the law. When confronted with the logic, efficiency, and judiciousness of Roman law, over a period of time Continental states jettisoned the archaic law of talion, which functioned on the premise of law as balance – an eye for an eye – and instead embraced law afresh as a science, setting Europeans on the road to modernity. This is true even of England where judges and jurists vetoed the wholesale adoption of Roman law, yet the intellectual momentum generated by the legal revolution inspired a budding English jurisprudence and sweeping changes in legal procedure and methodology, many of which mirror devices or strategies belonging to the *ius commune*.

To capture the tenor of this transformation, historians typically point to the abandonment of the old "irrational" proofs such as the ordeal, compurgation, and trial by combat; in their place, new "rational" methods of proof arose. In much of Europe, the two-eyewitness rule of Roman law was adopted; in England, the trial jury prevailed. In this account, rationality is tied wholly to an elimination of the influence of the Christian faith on the law's search for knowledge: irrational proofs rely on God's judgment (*vox Dei*); rational proofs rely on man's (*vox populi*). The jury takes top billing among the qualities that historians contend make late medieval law modern. As Raoul van Caenegem wrote in the year 2000, after the abolition of the ordeal, law was "based, not on some supernatural sign but on a rational enquiry by

---

[4] George Woodbine, review of Doris Mary Stenton, ed., *Rolls of the Justices in Eyre for Gloucestershire, Warwickshire and Staffordshire, 1221–1222*, in *The Yale Law Journal* 50.4 (1941): 731.

freemen from the neighbourhood"; as such, for the English, jury trial has become the emblem of modernity.[5]

Peine forte et dure is just one of the incongruities marring this narrative. The practice's chronology is all wrong. It seems far more reminiscent of the so-called barbaric and primitive methods of the early Middle Ages than the sophistication and rationality of the later phase that actually gave birth to it. It is a piece of the puzzle that does not fit, no matter how hard we try to force it. It is no wonder that scholars waste little time contemplating it.[6] In fact, most historians have solved the problem by omitting discussion of the practice altogether.

For some time now, this grand narrative has been under fire: critics have exposed the dubious framework propping up this Whiggish chronicle. In 2011, Anders Winroth denounced it as a fiction, a "triumphalist" chronology which sees "the twelfth century as the first modernizing century," when "rationality and order replaced chaos and arbitrariness."[7] The misappropriation of history stands at the heart of critiques by Winroth and others. Too often, medieval law is interpolated with an eye to the present. Analyzing medieval laws and legal practices simply as the precursors of their modern counterparts is a road littered with obstacles and diversions. This approach necessitates a modern interpretive framework and a narrow focus. As a result, the process helps us to better understand the meaning and trajectory of contemporary laws and practices by ignoring the medieval context in which they developed and thrived. In this respect, the aberrancy of peine forte et dure is a clear signpost. The fact that peine forte et dure does not fit neatly into the grand narrative should tell us that it is the wrong narrative.

Peine forte et dure may be the most obvious flaw in the traditional account, but it is not the only one by far. A linear interpretation of the

---

[5] Raoul van Caenegem, "The Modernity of Medieval Law," *Legal History Review*, 68.3 (2000): 323. The language of rationality is still employed in twenty-first century studies. See Francisco Appellàniz, "Judging the Franks: Proof, Justice, and Diversity in Late Medieval Alexandria and Damascus," *Comparative Studies in Society and History* 58. 2 (2016): 351.

[6] To offer an example, in Baker's widely used textbook on English legal history, peine forte et dure takes up one page in a book of 600. John Baker, *An Introduction to English Legal History*, 5th edn. (Oxford University Press 2019), 549.

[7] Anders Winroth, "The Legal Revolution of the Twelfth Century," in Thomas F.X. Noble, et al., eds., *European Transformations: The Long Twelfth Century* (South Bend, IN: University of Notre Dame Press, 2011), 348-51.

medieval history is predicated on a total break with the past after the twelfth century, but as numerous studies over the last twenty years or so have helped us to appreciate, that version of history is simply not accurate. The reality is a story of continuity rather than across-the-board change. Research on the legal system of the early Middle Ages has done much "to recuperate the period before 1200 as an actual society rather than a Lord of the Flies anarchy," as Daniel Lord Smail has so cleverly described it.[8] Law prior to the twelfth century was not irrational; it very much had its own consistent rationale, even if nineteenth- and twentieth-century legal historians frowned upon its inherent religiosity. More important still, the Angevin law reforms and those of Lateran IV do not represent a wholesale desertion of so-called irrational proofs: compurgation and trial by combat did not vanish from the legal world. While compurgation disappeared from criminal justice, it remained significant in both ecclesiastical and local courts throughout the era. Trial by combat may have gone into an appreciable decline, but appellees did sometimes demand to prove their innocence through battle, and it lingered on as a method of tackling approvers' appeals throughout the period. Even the abolition of the ordeal has been overrated; while ordeal by water and fire disappeared from England, ordeals continued unabated in various regions of Europe up to the very end of the Middle Ages. Finally, the trial jury, once thought to be the brainchild of Henry II (d.1189), the very symbol of modernity representing a turn away from the English legal past, was not an innovation at all; it was in fact a borrowing from traditional Anglo-Saxon practices.[9] None of this is to suggest that the movement known as the legal revolution was not significant in terms of the degree of change it ushered into law and society: *it was*. However, there was far more continuity with earlier periods than was once recognized, and the nature of the change had more to do with systematization and professionalization than a move towards rational methods and jurisprudence.

---

[8] Daniel Lord Smail, "Violence and Predation in Late Medieval Mediterranean Europe," *Comparative Studies in Society and History* 54.1 (2012): 10.
[9] See Ralph Turner, "The Origins of the Medieval English Jury: Frankish, English, or Scandinavian?" *JBS* 7.2 (1968): 1–10; Michael McNair, "Vicinage and the Antecedents of the Jury," *L&HR* 17 (1999): 537–90; and Patrick Wormald, "Neighbors, Courts, and Kings: Reflections on Michael McNair's *Vicini*," *L&HR* 17 (1999): 597–601.

If everything we thought we once knew about the impact of the legal revolution on the practice of the law has been called into question, this is even more applicable to our understanding of the much less studied relationship between English law and the church. Recent studies by Philippa Byrne and Thomas McSweeney have demonstrated that the clergy did not retreat from the administration of criminal justice because of Lateran IV's canons.[10] The ordeal was just one facet of priestly oversight of law enforcement. English prelates played a key role as sheriffs and justices in eyre at least through the end of the thirteenth century and in the king's court of Chancery they sat in judgment as chancellors on a wide variety of quasi-criminal cases well into the early modern era.[11] Ecclesiastical courts and specially constituted tribunals shouldered the burden of investigating and adjudicating crimes committed by clergymen, as well as against the clergy, requiring them to cast judgment in a multitude of instances of homicide, larceny, and rape. After Boniface of Savoy's 1261 mandate requiring each diocese to establish its own prison, all bishops became prison wardens of sorts, although episcopal prisons were distinct from secular ones in that convicted clerics often earned life sentences for their crimes.[12] The church also regularly intervened to protect criminals from the rigors of the common law with sanctuary rites, respected equally by king and his subjects. The administration of sanctuary, both temporary and chartered, required close cooperation between the county coroner, the local clergy, and the community watch. Contrary to traditional wisdom that once argued for late medieval sanctuary as "an obsolete relic of earlier conceptions of law, punishment, and the role of the church," as Shannon McSheffrey has demonstrated, in fact the practice continued in great health and vigor until the dissolution of the monasteries during the

---

[10] Philippa Byrne, *Justice and Mercy: Moral Theology and the Exercise of Law in Twelfth-Century England* (Manchester University Press, 2019), and Thomas McSweeney, *Priests of the Law: Roman Law and the Making of the Common Law's First Professionals* (Oxford University Press, 2019).

[11] Ralph Turner, "Clerical Judges in English Secular Courts: The Ideal Versus the Reality," *Medievalia et Humanistica*, n.s. 3 (1972): 159–79; Gwilym Dodd, "Reason, Conscience and Equity: Bishops as the King's Judges in Later Medieval England," *History* 99.335 (2014): 213–40.

[12] Margaret McGlynn, "Ecclesiastical Prisons and Royal Authority in the Reign of Henry VII," *Journal of Ecclesiastical History* 70.4 (2019): 750–66.

time of Henry VIII (d.1547).[13] More to the point, because kings claimed to rule by the grace of God, they could not divorce themselves or their courts entirely from the church: they needed to heed the church's advice on law and legal matters, and as one of God's two swords, appear to work in concert with rather than in opposition to the church.

Because "irrationality" is so closely linked with "divine" in the grand narrative, we need to ask: and what of God? Did the English see His hand vanish entirely with the abolition of the ordeal? Ordeals functioned on the principle of God's immanence: God is present everywhere in His creation. His participation in the ordeals is just one example among many of "the routine operation of an active divine providence in everyday life."[14] While the pope might bar the clergy from officiating at ordeals, he could not outlaw God's worldly presence (nor one suspects would he have wanted to do so). When it comes to the ordeal and its standing among English subjects, there is no evidence of a crisis of faith over God's participation. Rather, as both Trisha Olson and Paul Hyams have remarked, jury trial eventually became the new *judicium Dei*. Juries were thought to function as a form of trial by oath. Each juror swore the following oath on the Gospels or a relic: "Hear this, ye justices, that I will speak the truth as to that on which you shall question me on the lord king's behalf, and I will faithfully do that which you shall command me on the lord king's behalf, and for nothing will I fail so to do to the utmost of my power, so help me God and these holy relics."[15] God would not tolerate perjury; thus, jurors had no choice but to tell the truth about what happened. Accordingly, Englishmen and women imbued trial juries with the same divine aura once attributed to the ordeal. In Olson's words, "[t]hirteenth and early fourteenth century England kept faith with the idea that the Divine manifested when an accused in humility and contrition, perfected his bond with his country and his god by throwing himself upon the community's judgment of his character."[16]

---

[13] Shannon McSheffrey, "Sanctuary and Legal Topography of Pre-Reformation London," *L&HR* 27.3 (2009): 513. The purpose of McSheffrey's article is to refute this traditional view.

[14] Paul Hyams, "The Legal Revolution and the Discourse of Dispute," in Andrew Galloway, ed., *The Cambridge Companion to Medieval English Culture* (Cambridge University Press, 2011), 60.

[15] *Bracton*, vol. II, 329.

[16] Trisha Olson, "Of Enchantment: The Passing of the Ordeals and the Rise of the Jury Trial," *Syracuse Law Review* 50 (2000): 113.

The twelfth and thirteenth centuries also represent the apex of power for the medieval church. The rediscovery of Justinian's *Corpus* was not the only stimulus prompting the legal revolution; it was tied closely also to the so-called Gregorian reform in which law was wielded as a weapon against a "world turned upside down." Pope Gregory VII (r. 1073–85) and his successors – especially the lawyer popes Alexander III (r. 1159–81), Innocent III (r. 1198–1216), and Innocent IV (r. 1243–54) – employed the law to great effect in pursuit of spiritual and institutional reform. Canon law's impact can be traced in the growth of papal power and the development of the ideology of papal monarchy, the monasticization of the secular clergy, the widespread campaign for the instruction and indoctrination of parish clergy and parishioners, as well as the behavioral modification of an errant, and sometimes heretical, laity.

Regardless, the traditional legal historical narrative contends that jurists, exhilarated with Roman law's potential as a science, began to see law and religion as separate and discrete entities. God was edged out of the practice of the law: He was no longer the driving force behind legislation nor its ultimate judge, replaced by human judges, lawyers, and jurors, in addition to man-made rules of evidence and sophisticated, rational procedures. To a post-enlightenment audience, accustomed to practicing religion chiefly on weekends and believing that reason and faith, as well as church and state, are always in conflict, such a process must be easy to envisage. But for the medieval historian, to posit the secularization of the law at a time when all of society was becoming more deeply entrenched in Christianity seems wildly out of place.

Admittedly, the grand narrative owes much to the seminal work of Frederic Maitland (d.1906), whose celebrated account of the foundations of the common law still maintains an iron grip on medieval English legal history. In his lively and spirited writing, Henry II appears as "the hero of Maitland's narrative," single-handedly responsible for developing the procedures that have since come to define common law (such as, Westminster's permanent court of professional judges, the perambulations of itinerant judges, introduction of the inquest, and the original writ).[17] *Glanvill*

---

[17] John Hudson, "Maitland and Anglo-Norman Law," *Proceedings of the British Academy* 89 (1996): 24.

(*c.*1187–9), penned at least in part by Henry II's chief justiciar, Ranulf de Glanvill (d.1190), is the testament to Henry's spectacular achievements. Maitland saw the writing of the treatise as "the moment when English law becomes articulate [and] we become the nation whose law may be intimately known."[18] Of course, Maitland was also a lawyer working in nineteenth-century Britain, a more secular age which cherished the hard-fought separation of church and state and held Catholicism in low regard, associated chiefly with old régime monarchs and the Irish. Maitland himself has been described as having held "somewhat agnostic religious views."[19] In Maitland's mind, such a solid foundation for modern legal practice could not be the product of a world in which law and religion entwined. Maitland was trained in the law, not in medieval history. The limits of his lens permitted him to view law in evolution separate from the society in which it existed. None of this critique is meant to diminish the scope of Maitland's achievements; but as Henry Summerson once wrote, "Maitland did not breathe late twentieth-century air, though we treat him as if he did."[20] Just as Maitland's assessment of Henry II has undergone substantial rethinking since his time, so, too, should the relationship between law and faith in medieval England be revisited.

This chapter proposes a different narrative. Instead of law as science it sees law as penitential process. The Angevin law reforms and the adoption of the trial jury do not represent the secularization of law. Under the Anglo-Saxons, Christianity was deeply ingrained in English law; the twelfth-century legal revival did nothing to alter this state of affairs. Common law was just as firmly Christian in its outlook and mission, and during the formative period of its medieval history, administered by "priests of the law."[21] The religious nature of the law is overt everywhere in the legal texts of the period. Think of the *Dialogue Concerning the Exchequer* (*c.*1180), whose opening lines clarify the centrality of faith to the medieval worldview: "It is

---

[18] Patrick Wormald, "Maitland and Anglo-Saxon Law: Beyond Domesday Book," *Proceedings of the British Academy* 89 (1996): 18.
[19] Hudson, "Maitland," 21.
[20] Henry Summerson, "Maitland and the Criminal Law in the Age of *Bracton*," *Proceedings of the British Academy* 89 (1996): 115.
[21] McSweeney, *Priests of the Law*.

necessary to subject one's self in all fear to the powers ordained by God, and likewise to serve them. For every power is from God the Lord."[22] Accepting the inherent religiosity of medieval law offers new insight into peine forte et dure. In this perspective, the practice does not represent barbarity or irrationality. Nor is it an anomaly; it only appears that way because it has been taken out of context. This chapter seeks to retrieve that context by exploring the role of pain and penance in the medieval mentality. This chapter builds on Esther Cohen's research on pain as a cultural expression in late medieval Europe. Coining the phrase *philopassianism*, she describes the development of a unique perception of pain peculiar to late medieval Christianity, in which pain was regarded as an "avenue to knowledge. Knowledge of the body, of the soul, of truth, or reality, and of God."[23] Pain was considered "a vehicle of grace, to be ardently sought."[24] Both Esther Cohen and Mitchell Merback have addressed how conceptions of the usefulness of pain for salvation lays the foundation for the medieval legal system's implementation of judicial torture and execution.[25] While their studies are emphatically Continental, Cohen's focus is on the French legal system while Merback concentrates on the Holy Roman Empire, both have drawn out the positive value of pain in the medieval mindset. The following pages hope to explore physical pain as a means to reorient the disordered mind, in order to offer a new vision of the purpose of peine forte et dure in the medieval legal system.

Law and punishment correspond with the needs of the system, and they can have multiple purposes at once. From the medieval vantage point, punishment acts as vengeance for the crime a person commits, deterrent for those who might be inclined to follow that example, and moral reform so that the defendant might be reconciled to the human

---

[22] Ernest Henderson, ed., "The Dialogue Concerning the Exchequer, circa 1180," in *Select Historical Documents of the Middle Ages* (London: George Bell and Sons, 1910), 20.

[23] Esther Cohen, "Towards a History of European Sensibility: Pain in the Later Middle Ages," *Science in Context* 8.1 (1995): 52–3.

[24] Cohen, "Towards a History," 57.

[25] Esther Cohen, *The Modulated Scream: Pain in Late Medieval Culture* (University of Chicago Press, 2010); Mitchell Merback, *The Thief, the Cross and the Wheel: Pain and the Spectacle of Punishment in Medieval and Renaissance Europe* (University of Chicago Press, 1998).

community and to God after atoning for one's crime. Because execution was the normal punishment for convicted felons, it is typically assumed that rehabilitation was not a medieval judicial ideal. This chapter will argue that spiritual reform, even for those about to be executed, was yet another dimension of the medieval judicial system that we need to take into account. Peine forte et dure was a means to activate that reform. None of this perspective diminishes the degree of pain or appearance of barbarism when it comes to peine forte et dure; however, one might argue that the term 'barbarous' should be reserved for when pain is imposed simply for the sake of causing pain. In this instance, pain had a higher meaning.

In Chapter 1, we learned that medieval jurists spoke of peine forte et dure as *penitentia*; they did so because they saw it as a form of penance. Understanding the penitential side of the English judicial system helps us to explain the role of peine forte et dure within it; but that is not all it does. It also guides us to a better appreciation of the overall system in general. Historians who apply the benchmarks of the modern era to the medieval judicial system have tended to view it as a failure. High acquittal rates, excessive pardoning, and sanctuary rites leave us with the distinct impression that murder regularly went unpunished; barbaric penalties, not just peine forte et dure, but also mutilation and hanging, seem cruel and heartless. Yet, if jurors and justices were focused chiefly on the reconciliation of a wayward sinner, and they understood that reconciliation cannot be achieved without pain, their system is no longer a failure. Indeed, from a medieval assessment, all of their goals were being met.

Crime and the Penitential Process

Trial reports drawn from jail delivery rolls permit us to glimpse only part of the defendant's judicial experience. The medieval world understood crimes also as sins and remedying sin fell squarely within ecclesiastical jurisdiction. The court's verdict addressed the defendant's physical fate, but his or her spiritual well-being remained in the hands of the church. Thus, there were two halves to the defendant's experience of the law. While the prisoner's aftermath is absent from Crown records, the centrality of the penitential process to late medieval pastoral care ensured that parish priests were responsive to the spiritual needs of their parishioners. As canonists were quick to remind the clergy, their souls depended on it: "if they allowed a sinner to escape uncorrected they would themselves share some degree of his guilt."[26] This decree was taken quite seriously: even Robert Grosseteste (d.1253), one of the era's most industrious writers of *pastoralia*, feared that his failures in pastoral care might redound negatively on his own soul upon Judgment Day.[27] In her study of thirteenth-century Welsh law, Catherine McKenna sees that this larger vision of the defendant's experience as penitent was a normal part of the process when it comes to serious crimes:

> Crimes like perjury and murder, always among those that the church treated most seriously, were regarded by lawyers as sins needing to be expiated through penance as well as crimes requiring redress through compensation. But that is to make too much of a distinction between the sacred and the secular, which in these cases operated as aspects of what was felt to be a *single* mechanism for reestablishing the equilibrium of a society disrupted by misconduct.[28]

While McKenna speaks to the Welsh approach to the law, as this chapter will argue, the same held true beyond Offa's Dyke. It would be wrong to see secular courts administering law that is wholly secular. In such a religious era, God's influence was felt everywhere.

Even in the event of an acquittal, one suspects the relieved defendant's first stop was a visit to the local parish priest as spiritual director. In a felony trial, because execution was the only available punishment, medieval men and women saw an acquittal less as a declaration of innocence (as we might see it today) than as a recognition that the defendant's actions were not so egregious that they merited capital punishment. As a result, acquittal and release from prison, while surely welcome stages in the process, did not represent the end of the defendant's ordeal. There were still several steps that needed to be taken before full reconciliation to neighbor, church, and God. First, one needed to appear contrite and sorrowful before the parish priest and the Christian community. It was not enough simply to

---

[26] Richard Helmholz, "Crime, Compurgation and the Courts of the Medieval Church," *L&HR* 1.1 (1983): 6.

[27] Philippa Hoskin, *Robert Grosseteste and the 13th-Century Diocese of Lincoln: An English Bishop's Pastoral Vision* (Leiden: Brill, 2019), 160.

[28] Catherine McKenna, "Performing Penance and Poetic Performance in the Medieval Welsh Court," *Speculum* 82.1 (2007): 84.

apologize for one's past behavior and to pledge to become a better person. From an early stage, theologians emphasized the theatricality of the penitential performance. "[A]uthentic sorrow for sin" was enacted dramatically by "looking downcast, lying prostrate, sitting sideways, kneeling, weeping, and blushing."[29] The penitent's vivid physical performance was key to expressing one's inner remorse and desire for reform. Weeping stood out as the focal point, but it was not merely for show. For the penitent, tears were intended to bring forth and animate one's contrition: tears lead the penitent to shame and sorrow.[30] As one eleventh-century author observed, "Whoever blushes for Christ shall be worthy of mercy" (*Qui erubescit pro Christo, fit dignus misericordia*).[31] For the penitent's audience, self-presentation sent a vital message: tears were a necessary prerequisite to reconciliation so that the community understood fully that the penitent was remorseful and ready for a fresh start.

Second, the penitent must make amends within the Christian community. This was true even if one's sin did not directly impact one's neighbors, because as Alain of Lille (d. 1202) explained, there are no "victimless crimes." Every time we sin our neighbors suffer through our bad example.[32] Medieval Christianity envisioned sin as a disease, easily communicated to others. Sinful behavior thus needs to be addressed before it infects the discipline and commitment of an entire community. Making amends within the community also involved multiple phases. Peter of Poitiers (d. c.1215) in his *Sententianum libri quinque* explained that one must begin by asking forgiveness from one's neighbors.[33] Penance to one's neighbors typically included the giving of alms. This might involve the donation of goods to the parish itself, such as the embroidered towel fashioned by Elizabeth Sharp and donated to

---

[29] See Karen Wagner, "*Cum aliquis venerit ad sacerdotum*: Penitential Experience in the Central Middle Ages," in Abigail Firey, ed., *A New History of Penance* (Leiden: Brill, 2008), 209.

[30] Allen Frantzen, "Spirituality and Devotion in the Anglo-Saxon Penitentials," *Essays in Medieval Studies* 22 (2005): 122.

[31] From the pseudo-Augustinian tract *De vera et falsa paenitentia*; as cited in Bernard Poschmann, *Penance and the Anointing of the Sick* (Freiburg: Herder and Herder, 1964), 141.

[32] Mary Mansfield, *The Humiliation of Sinners: Public Penance in Thirteenth-Century France* (Ithaca: Cornell University Press, 1995), 43.

[33] Mansfield, *Humiliation of Sinners*, 42.

the church of St. Ewen in Bristol to be used as a houseling-cloth, marking her husband John's reconciliation in 1464.[34]

Next, the penitent must seek forgiveness from the victim or the victim's family. Borrowing from the formalities associated with homage, this constituted a publicly enacted ritual of submission. As Paul Hyams explains it, at a minimum, seeking forgiveness involved the classic kiss of peace.[35] More commonly, submission rituals involved the sinner kneeling before the victim (or his/her family), "head bent forward to expose naked neck, and hands between those of his new lord" in a posture of "ostentatious vulnerability."[36] This pointed ritual was an attempt to transform a relationship of *inimicitia* into one of *amicitia*, marked by the lack of weapons (forbidden to a penitent),[37] as well as the penitent's open defenselessness and public deference. In return, the victim (or his/her family) must declare publicly that all of the aggressor's transgressions have been forgiven, and renounce any future plans to appeal. Ideally, the sinner should also communicate his or her contrition financially, by funding the entrance of one of the victim's relatives into the religious life, paying for the singing of masses, or some such charitable act. Almsgiving of this nature was beneficial to the welfare of both parties: it created a "lasting corporate memory to remember the peace publicly and so deter any resumption of hostilities."[38]

Forgiveness and submission were only one facet of this stage. In instances of theft, even if a group of twelve jurors chose to acquit out of pity, absolution was beyond the penitent's reach until he or she made restitution of the stolen goods to the victim. Many theologians considered restitution a necessary prerequisite to the penitential process. As Gratian explains, "sin is not remitted unless restitution of

---

[34] Mansfield, *Humiliation of Sinners*, 42; Daniel Thiery, *Polluting the Sacred: Violence, Faith, and the 'Civilizing' of Parishioners in Late Medieval England* (Leiden: Brill, 2009), 66.

[35] Paul Hyams, *Rancor and Reconciliation in Medieval England* (Ithaca: Cornell University Press, 2003), 201–2.

[36] Hyams, *Rancor*, 203.

[37] Sarah Hamilton, "The Unique Favour of Penance: The Church and the People, c. 800– c. 1100," in Peter Linehan and Janet Nelson, eds., *The Medieval World* (New York: Routledge, 2001), 239.

[38] Hyams, *Rancor*, 200.

the stolen item is made."[39] Not only was this an essential part of penitential theology, it had been enshrined in English law since the Anglo-Saxon era. Requirements for restitution appear in both the *Leges Edwardi Confessori* (*c.*1170) and the *Leges Henrici Primi* (*c.*1108–9).[40] According to the latter, a murderer can be buried in consecrated ground only if he had taken the oath, paid *wergeld* to the relatives of the dead, and paid *manbot* to the lord – meaning that he had shown contrition, made restitution, and been reconciled to the Christian community before his death.[41] The common law as it developed under the Angevin monarchs also prioritized and facilitated restitution, such that in an appeal of larceny, the appellor could purchase a writ for the restitution of stolen goods.[42] Restitution applied even to sanctuary-seekers and those who were executed.[43] As Mary Mansfield describes it, "[t]he victims were literally the dying penitent's 'creditors,' and the church would see them repaid before the heirs could collect."[44] If the victim of those thefts had died and had no family, it was still incumbent upon the thief to make reparations by donating the same sum originally stolen to those in need.

In canon law, restitution applied chiefly in instances of theft, although some canonists like John Duns Scotus (d.1308) envisioned a broader application, arguing that it might also be expected in instances of a damaged reputation, for example.[45] Traditionally in English secular law codes, compensation (long described as *wergeld*) in homicide was also the norm. It was once thought that compensation disappeared with the arrival of the Normans, at which point execution and mutilation took its place as the sole means of punishment for felonies. Henry I's 1130 pronouncement that if he pardoned a killer, the kin still reserved the right to pursue their claim for compensation

---

[39] *non remittitur peccatum nisi restituatur ablatum.* Gratian, *Decretum,* II, C. 14. Q. 6. C. 1, cols 1411–14; see also Emil Friedberg, ed., *Corpus iuris canonici,* 2 vols. (Graz: Akademische Druck, 1959), vol. I, 742.

[40] Bruce O'Brien, ed., *God's Peace and King's Peace: The Laws of Edward the Confessor* (Philadelphia: University of Pennsylvania Press, 2015), 177; *LHP,* ch. 24, subsection 3, 126–7.

[41] *LHP,* ch. 74, subsection 1c, 231–2.

[42] In 1529, the Crown ceded the right also to victims whose evidence had secured conviction upon the king's indictment; 21 Hen. VIII, c. 11 (1529). Spike Gibbs, "Felony Forfeiture at the Manor of Worfield, c.1370–c.1600," *Journal of Legal History* 39.3 (2018): 263.

[43] O'Brien, ed., *Laws of Edward the Confessor,* 163.

[44] Mansfield, *Humiliation of Sinners,* 85.   [45] Mansfield, *Humiliation of Sinners,* 56.

makes it clear that that was not the case.[46] Bruce O'Brien has argued the king's pardon was originally conceived as a mechanism "for preserving the wergeld system's ability to compensate aggrieved victims or their relatives by freeing the offender from death so that he might pay compensation for his misdeed to those whom he had injured."[47] Moreover, as Edward Powell and Anthony Musson have established, the myriad appeals that ended in arbitration represent the persistence of out-of-court compensation payments to the grieving families.[48] Musson has even described medieval England as a "compensation culture," while Krista Kesselring has documented how the popular custom of compensation extended well into the early modern era, with a strong sense of empathy for the plight of the widow.[49] Presumably, penitential theology's emphasis on the need for restitution served only to strengthen ideas of compensation as a vital part of the penitential process.

Contrite, forgiven by victim and community, and having made restitution, the penitent was finally prepared to undertake the assigned penance in order to receive absolution, a process referred to as *poenitentiam accipere* ("to accept penance"). When it comes to paying for sins against the self, *poentientiam agere* ("to perform penance"), theologians advocated in favor of the value of fasts, vigils and penitential prayers, although in reality there was substantial variation in regional approaches to penance.[50] For example, in France, authorities were often content to rely on almsgiving and pilgrimage as means of working off one's sins, whereas in England, corporal punishment was the norm.[51] England's approach was probably most economical – almsgiving and time off work for a pilgrimage might be out of reach for the impoverished sinner. It

[46] Hyams, *Rancor*, 85.   [47] O'Brien, ed., *Laws of Edward the Confessor*, 83.

[48] Edward Powell, "Arbitration and the Law in Late Medieval England," *TRHS* 33 (1983): 49–67; Anthony Musson, *Public Order and Law Enforcement: The Local Administration of Criminal Justice 1294–1350* (Woodbridge: Boydell, 2001), 169–71.

[49] Anthony Musson, "Wergeld: Crime and the Compensation Culture in Medieval England," (video lecture, Gresham College, October 5, 2009), www.gresham.ac.uk/lectures-and-events/wergeld-crime-and-the-compensation-culture-in-medieval-england; Krista Kesselring, *Making Murder Public: Homicide in Early Modern England, 1480–1680* (Oxford University Press, 2019), Chapter 3.

[50] Joseph Goering, "The Internal Forum and the Literature of Penance and Confession," *Traditio* 59 (2004): 198.

[51] Mansfield, *Humiliation of Sinners*, 107.

also fit best with medieval theologians and their ideas of penance, who taught that "baptism alone was free but thereafter forgiveness of the temporal penalty due must be paid for by suffering." Satisfaction for sins was intended to "share in and imitate Christ's satisfaction."[52] Pain, in one form or another, was therefore a necessary component of penance.

Pain and Penance

The authority of pain as a means to salvation in Christian theology has solid biblical foundations: according to Saint Paul, we are the heirs of God, but only if "we suffer with him, that we may be also glorified together" (Romans 8:17). This scriptural basis was bolstered by the absorption of Platonic ideals regarding the union of body and soul into early Christian thought. Plato explained that a disordered soul is best restored through the pain of punishment.[53] Pain provides the means to subordinate the physical to the spiritual. As Thomas Aquinas advocated, pain is a function of the soul: the bodily sensation is a consequence of the soul's striving towards goodness, such that "[w]ithout pain, penance is not possible."[54] A late medieval English preacher made a similar point, purportedly quoting Augustine: "Poenitere est poenam tenere, 'That is true repentance,' says he, 'to hold oneself ever in some pain.'"[55] Medieval theologians endorsed the notion that bodily suffering "atoned for past sins and trained the soul to shun future ones."[56] Positive endorsement of the value of pain led the church to sanction bodily suffering in ways that today seem incongruous to Christian sensibilities. For example, Saint Anselm advocated rigorous physical discipline of children, not out of cruelty, but out of love, administering blows with the intention of extirpating

---

[52] Mansfield, *Humiliation of Sinners*, 57.

[53] As noted in Ariel Glucklich, *Sacred Pain: Hurting the Body for the Sake of the Soul* (Oxford University Press, 2001), 18.

[54] As discussed in Karl Shoemaker, "The Problem of Pain in Punishment: Historical Perspectives," in Austin Sarat, ed., *Pain, Death, and the Law* (Ann Arbor: University of Michigan Press, 2001), 30.

[55] Ferdinand Holthausen, ed., *Vices and Virtues, Being a Soul's Confession of Its Sins with Reason's Description of the Virtues* (EETS, vol. LXXXIX, 1888), 120.

[56] Christine Caldwell Ames, "Does Inquisition Belong to Religious History?," *AHR* 110.1 (2005): 20.

the anarchic will.[57] Heroic asceticism is founded on these ideals, its adherents participating in a competition of self-injury that makes it clear the goal is more than *imitatio Christi*, because Christ's experience of pain on the cross seems almost inconsequential in comparison. Men like Henry Suso (d.1366), an esteemed doctor of the church, embody an inimitable role model for medieval sanctity. Suso's contempt for the body and its human desires is expressed in his strategies of suffering. For eight years, Suso wore a life-size imitation of the True Cross tied to his body with exposed nails pricking continuously into his flesh. To rip the skin from his back, he whipped himself with a hook, then rubbed salt and vinegar into his wounds. Only after twenty-two years of bodily torments of this nature did God see fit to grant him permission to lead an easier life.[58] The example of mystics like Henry Suso meant that pain assumed a central place in redemption theology and practice in the medieval period. For the reader, Suso's actions are also a measure of the distance between medieval and modern perceptions of pain. Framing Suso's self-injurious behavior as both purifying and praiseworthy is simply incomprehensible to the modern mind. Today, we regard pain as an unnecessary horror to be eliminated at all costs. Indeed, this intolerance of pain has generated a multi-billion dollar industry of pain relief, attempting to eradicate an experience that the medieval world understood as a path to redemption. Our mental distance must be kept in check when examining peine forte et dure.

The utility of pain for human salvation is key to understanding the medieval world's penitential process. The kinds of penance assigned by clergymen did not simply entail acts of satisfaction such as the recitation of prayers or pilgrimages; it included also fasting, bodily deprivation (the wearing of hairshirts or sackcloth, denunciation of shoes and head coverings), and, always a favorite of English bishops, being whipped in procession around the parish church three Sundays in a row. The 1202 penance assigned to Lumberd, a Scotsman who violently assaulted the Bishop of Caithness in northern Scotland, drives home the demanding physical burden imposed on the penitent

---

[57] Gregory Sadler, "Non modo verbis sed et verberibus: Saint Anselm on Punishment, Coercion, and Violence," *Cistercian Studies Quarterly* 45.1 (2010): 40.

[58] See Chapter 12 of Jerome Kross and Bernard Bachrach, *The Mystic Mind: The Psychology of Medieval Mystics and Ascetics* (New York: Routledge, 2005).

hoping to atone for his sins. Pope Innocent III's instructions detail a grueling pilgrimage on foot from Rome to the scene of the crime, at which point he was to don penitential garb, enjoin a fast of fifteen days on bread and water, followed by a public performance of prayer and physical punishment. Only at that time was the bishop permitted to offer the penitent remission of sins, conditional upon Lumberd's promise to continue weekly fasts and three years of crusading in the holy land.[59]

Remedies of this nature derive in part from the notion that punishing the errant body purifies the soul.[60] This viewpoint helps us to appreciate also why the medieval church authorized and employed judicial torture. As Isidore of Seville's *Etymologiae* (*c.*600–25) explains, it is called torture because it involves "the twisting of the mind: since, by the suffering of the body, the mind is therefore turned."[61] As pain became more central to penitential practice, so, too, did it acquire a more prominent role in criminal justice. Esther Cohen writes, judicial violence "was not a sign of brutalization; it was merely the other side of the coin of the spirituality of pain."[62] Quite frankly, this is the moment when Michel Foucault goes astray in his understanding of pain and its place in the judicial process of the premodern world. Foucault has argued in favor of a transition in the eighteenth century between a premodern state bent on punishing the body to instill terror to a modern state determined to punish the soul in order to inspire reform.[63] What he is missing is the fact that in

---

[59] As discussed in Cynthia Neville, "'No Remission without Satisfaction': Canonical Influences on Secular Lawmaking in High Medieval Scotland," in Jonathan M. Wooding and Lynette Olson, eds., *Prophecy, Fate and Memory in the Early and Medieval Celtic World* (Sydney University Press, 2020), 208.

[60] One sermon describes "works of penance" as "fastynge, wakynge, wolwarde werynge, barefoot goynge, harde lyuinge, scharpe disciplines, and many suche oþer" (fasting, waking, hairshirt wearing, barefoot going, hard living, sharp disciplines, and many such other). Gloria Cigman, ed., *Lollard Sermons* (EETS, vol. CCXCIV, 1989), 103.

[61] As cited in Edward Peters, *Torture* (Philadelphia: University of Pennsylvania Press, 1996), 55.

[62] Esther Cohen, "The Expression of Pain in the Later Middle Ages: Deliverance, Acceptance and Infamy," in Florike Egmond and Robert Zwijnenberg, eds., *Bodily Extremities: Preoccupations with the Human Body in Early Modern European Culture* (New York: Routledge, 2003), 217.

[63] Michel Foucault, *Discipline and Punish: The Birth of the Prison*, trans. Alan Sheridan (New York: Vintage Books, 1995).

the Middle Ages, the body was the vehicle to correct the soul. Thus, what might look like revenge pure and simple is in fact vengeance (in the positive sense of demanding satisfaction for offenses against God), as well as spiritual reform. One cannot preclude the other: one act simultaneously has multiple meanings. And because life on earth was just one stage in the soul's journey, the process of rehabilitation, through reconciliation to the Christian community and God, did not stop simply because the body was shed through the execution ritual.

Above all, pain is *imitatio Christi*, the ultimate goal of a good Christian. As Jody Enders writes, "[t]he foundational moment of Christianity is a moment of torture, a moment that transformed an empty pagan method of mangling bodies into an ennobled model of exemplary behavior to be imitated by the faithful."[64] This is especially true after the thirteenth century. Inspired by exposure to Byzantine artwork, Saint Francis (d.1226) and his brothers minor brought the life and death of the human Christ rather than the majesty of the divine Christ back to the forefront of everyone's minds in Western Europe. In art history, this transition in focus is explained as a passage from the *Christus Triumphans* of the early Middle Ages to the later medieval *Christus Patiens*; that is, the transition between images of the triumphant Christ, a divine Christ who "transcends suffering and is victorious over death" to the human Christ who embraces suffering in order to save humanity, best represented in images of the Man of Sorrows.[65] Penance is modeled on Christ's sacrifice: inevitably, then, physical suffering is a necessary element of the penitential process. These ideals lay a solid foundation for the ideology that gave birth to peine forte et dure.

Penance, Punishment, and the Law

Not only were crimes sins, but mortal sins were often crimes or the root causes of criminal behavior. The sinful nature of crime meant that theologians as well as canonists have had much to say on the subject – frankly, even more than secular jurists who drafted legal

---

[64] Jody Enders, *The Medieval Theater of Cruelty: Rhetoric, Memory, Violence* (Ithaca: Cornell University Press, 1999), 45.

[65] Anne Derbes, *Picturing the Passion in Late Medieval Italy: Narrative Painting, Franciscan Ideologies, and the Levant* (Cambridge University Press, 1996), 5.

treatises. The connections between sin and crime, penance and punishment thus deserve greater attention, chiefly because we today see a much greater distinction between them than did our medieval ancestors. Although the late medieval period saw a tightening of jurisdictional lines, for the majority of the Middle Ages what separated an ecclesiastical cause from a secular one was not always well articulated; moreover, penitential theology infiltrated every aspect of English criminal law, irrespective of the nature of the court in which it was administered. The blurring of the lines between crime and sin springs from their interconnectedness. Before the twelfth century, there was no distinction between crime and sin. The word *crimen*, meaning "sin," was used to refer to both homicide and adultery, for example. The same fuzziness of categorization is true of penance and punishment. As the anonymous author of the Anglo-Norman penitential treatise *Homo quidam* (c.1155–65) wrote, "It is called *poenitentia* (penance) such that *punitentia* is from 'punishing,' because by it man is punished."[66] In his *Sentences*, the standard university textbook on the subject of theology throughout much of the medieval period, Peter Lombard (d.1160) reiterated their shared qualities by explaining, "[i]t is called penance from punishment, for by it a man punishes the sins which he has committed."[67]

In England, the intermixing of law and theology persists as a legacy of the early Middle Ages in which bishops and ealdormen worked side by side in the moral correction of the kingdom's inhabitants.[68] The reign of King Alfred (d.899) was fundamental in this respect. Confronted with the insidious infiltration of pagan ideology from an occupying force, coupled with the need to rebuild a war-torn society, Alfred bolstered the Christian identity of his people by consciously borrowing from biblical tradition and penitential texts in the writing of his *Domboc* (lawbook). Indeed, the code's prologue reproduces lengthy excerpts from Mosaic code; tidbits from Exodus are

---

[66] Pierre Michaud-Quantin, ed., "Un manuel de confession archaïque dans le manuscrit Avranches 136," *Sacris Eruditi* 17.1 (1966): 10.

[67] Peter Lombard, Book Four of his Sentences, Distinction xiv, ii pt. ii, as translated in Elizabeth Rogers, ed., "Peter Lombard and the Sacramental System," (PhD Diss., Columbia University, 1917), 151.

[68] Patrick Wormald, *The Making of English Law: King Alfred to the Twelfth Century.* Vol. I: *Legislation and its Limits* (London: Blackwell, 2001), 212.

sprinkled throughout. The result is a distinct penitential edge to his legal reforms, which "put emphasis on the interior condition of the offender," shifting the focus from act to intention, and requiring compliant judges to inquire into what today is referred to as *mens rea* before passing sentence.[69] The focus on intention is evident in Alfred's treatment of homicide:

He who kills a man deliberately, let him die the death. But he who kills him out of necessity [or "under compulsion"] or unwillingly or unintentionally, as God put it in his hands, and he did not lie in wait for him, let him be worthy of life and of [the opportunity for] amends by folk-right [or "customary law"], if he should seek asylum. But if someone with desire and intent should kill his neighbor, remove him from my sanctuary so that he may die the death.[70]

Alfred may have been the first of the Anglo-Saxon kings to draw on the penitentials in the formation of a law code, but he was far from the last. As Stefan Jurasinski observes, from this point onwards, royal and ecclesiastical law "became progressively intertwined."[71] By the time of Archbishop Wulfstan (d.1023), known best in legal circles for having drafted royal law codes for both kings Æthelred II (d.1013) and Cnut (d.1035), penance appears there "inseparable" from secular punishments, reflecting a coalition approach to tackling the sinful acts of a delinquent laity.[72] Admittedly, for Wulfstan, moral integrity was not merely a religious concern: it was also political. He saw penance as the "central plank" in his battle strategy against the Viking onslaught. Only through spiritual regeneration of the English might they hope for God's favorable intervention.[73] Under his watch, Englishmen and women spent three full days in prayer and fasting in an attempt to win God's favor.

The Norman Conquest (1066) did little to alter this picture. This is exemplified by a Norman bishop's ordinance to all those who fought at the Battle of Hastings. Penance was the top priority:

---

[69] Stefan Jurasinski, *The Old English Penitentials and Anglo-Saxon Law* (Cambridge University Press, 2015), 59.
[70] Translated by Jurasinski, *Old English Penitentials*, 57.
[71] Jurasinski, *Old English Penitentials*, 34.
[72] Carole Hough, "Penitential Literature and Secular Law," *Anglo-Saxon Studies in Archaeology and History* 11 (2000): 136.
[73] Catherine Cubitt, "Bishops, Priests and Penance in Late Saxon England," *Early Medieval Europe* 14.1 (2006): 53.

Anyone who knows that he killed a man in the great battle must do penance for one year for each man that he killed. Anyone who wounded a man, who does not know whether he killed him or not, must do penance for forty days for each man he thus struck (if he can remember the number) either continuously or at intervals. Anyone who does not know the number of those he wounded or killed must, at the discretion of the bishop, do penance for one day in each week for the remainder of his life, or, if he can, let him redeem his sin by a perpetual alms, either by building or by endowing a church.[74]

It is no wonder the conquest ushered in an era of church building. Nor were there any changes in the administration of penance in England. While it was once thought that William the Conqueror (d.1087) mandated the creation of ecclesiastical courts, this was not in fact the case. Church courts as such did not come into being until around the year 1200. Rather, through his edict of 1072/6, King William endeavored to fortify the customary rights of the bishops (*episcopales consuetudines*), hoping to recover "that part of it which had fallen into lay hands," namely the hundred courts, where even if bishops typically sat in judgment, lay authorities profited from the fines imposed for spiritual offenses.[75] The conjunction of church and Crown persisted: for more than a century after the conquest, bishops and sheriffs sat cheek by jowl in adjudication at the shire courts. In line with the Continent, ultimately, the church synod branched off from the shire court, prompting also a gradual transference of spiritually-charged cases from shire to synod; yet even still, the synod continued for some time to replicate royal procedure as if it remained a branch of the king's jurisdiction.[76] This was a measured but steady development that, in some crucial ways, remained incomplete even at the close of the Middle Ages, at which point some essentially spiritual aspects of the law (such as sanctuary and benefit of clergy) continued to be governed by the Crown rather than the church.

Penance in the Long Twelfth Century

The legal and spiritual reforms of the long twelfth century served chiefly to consolidate penitential practices and clarify penitential ideals. This is

---

[74] Colin Morris, *The Discovery of the Individual, 1050–1200* (University of Toronto Press, 1987), 71.
[75] Colin Morris, "William I and the Church Courts," *EHR* 82.324 (1967): 450–1.
[76] Morris, "William I," 461.

apparent in a number of basic ways. With the emergence of church courts, theologians and canonists hammered out appropriate jurisdictional boundaries in the administration of penance. The church court prioritized treatment of the external forum; that is, it addressed the "public and manifest transgressions of the Church." The court of penance – a term used to describe the confessional experience – addressed the internal forum, that is, one's conscience. Heeding the dictates of the church court was mandatory: an adulterer who failed to appear in response to a court summons risked excommunication, even imprisonment. Confession, on the other hand, was voluntary, although the adulterer who tried to skip this stage of the process was ineligible for absolution. Bishop and confessor, then, represented complementary aspects of the penitential process, working hand in hand "to restrain vice and foster virtue in the Christian community."[77] The one exception was when it came to notorious or serious sins, such as arson, murder, sacrilege, or forgery, those sins requiring public penance. These belonged to a special category of reserved cases destined for judgment by the bishop's confessor-general (*penitentiarius*), the diocesan expert in penitential law and theology. The development of this critical position in the thirteenth century marks growing concern for the structured administration of the penitential process.

Before Peter Lombard's *Sentences*, what precisely constituted a sacrament and exactly how many existed was defined in a variety of ways. However, Lombard's enumeration of sacraments at seven (baptism, confirmation, Eucharist, penance, unction, orders, and marriage) is what stuck. By including penance among them, Lombard gave renewed emphasis to the centrality of penance in daily life. The *Sentences* laid the groundwork for Innocent III's Fourth Lateran Council (1215) in which he mandated that all the faithful of both sexes (*omnis utriusque sexus fidelis*) above the age of reason should confess at least once a year to one's proper priest. With the council's passionate endorsement of the sanctity of the confessional seal, one might also do so without fear that one's sins might be revealed to the community. The scope of the impact of this canon has often been underestimated. Confession, one of the integral components of the penitential process, became one of the key ways in which the laity practiced the Christian faith. The confessional mandate applied universally: to men and women, clergy and laity alike, regardless of wealth or status, such that both the pope and the lowliest Christian slave were expected to obey this decree upon pain of excommunication. By underscoring the centrality of confession, the penitential process became a regular part of the daily experience of men and women across Europe.

How penance was assigned was also undergoing a transition during this period. With the broad proliferation of early medieval penitentials from diverging regional traditions, priests engaged in pastoral care had often been required to mediate widely conflicting recommendations. The emergence of schools and universities, where penance was studied as a branch of theology, led to the creation of a "common tradition through a common curriculum of study where they developed common methods of thinking about and of teaching about penance."[78] One of the most important was a transition away from tariff penance to "arbitrary" or "discretionary" penance, in which greater onus was placed on the confessor to use his own judgment to determine the appropriate degree of penance to assign. Of course, all of this made the confessor's job much more difficult. As Arvind Thomas writes, "the canonically trained cleric was now expected to compute satisfaction not by mechanically selecting the penances recommended by the penitential canons but by exercising discretion diligently to temper justice with mercy, i.e., by increasing or decreasing the quality and quantity of satisfaction according to the sinner's ability to bear them."[79] The church facilitated this transition with an explosion in the production of penitential literature to act as a guide for confessors. In England, *summae* by men like John of Kent (*c.*1220) and Thomas of Chobham (*c.*1215–17) were integral.[80] Each diocese had multiple

---

[78] Joseph Goering, "The Scholastic Turn (1100–1500): Penitential Theology and Law in the Schools," in Abigail Firey, ed., *A New History of Penance* (Leiden: Brill, 2008), 219.

[79] Arvind Thomas, *Piers Plowman and the Reinvention of Church Law in the Late Middle Ages* (University of Toronto Press, 2019), 202.

[80] John of Kent was a canonist of the Anglo-Norman School who composed a *Summa de penitentia* modeled on Robert of Flamborough's *Liber penitentialis* around the year 1220. It is likely that he was chancellor of St. Paul's and master of the schools there. See Joseph Goering, "The 'Summa de penitentia' of John of Kent," *Bulletin of Medieval Canon Law* 18 (1988): 13–31. Thomas of Chobham was one of Peter the Chanter's students. Among other jobs within the church, he was subdean at Salisbury,

penitentials and guides for confessors which their clergy might consult in order to judge wisely. These guides also made it clear that it was not sufficient for a confessor to identify the penitent's sin; he must inquire also into the circumstances surrounding that sin so that he might better evaluate the sinner's intent. As Walter of Cantilupe (d.1266), Bishop of Worcester, intoned "if a murderer fails to confess that the murder took place in a church, or that it was done by slow torture rather than quickly with a sharp knife ... the sin takes on a different and more serious aspect."[81]

Theologians also had much to say about the meaning of sin. Perhaps reflecting the feud culture in which he lived and worked, in his *meditatio redemptionis humanae*, Anselm of Canterbury (d.1109) described sin as a dishonor to God. He writes that we need to defend the honor of God, "stolen by human sin: 'to sin is to dishonor God, and no man ought to do this.'"[82] Building on this theology, Peter Abelard (d.1142), one of the first authors to "systematize the theology of penance," in his *Ethics* took this a step further to explain how this works:[83]

What is mental vice, and what is properly called "sin"? So it is vice that makes us disposed to sin – that is, we are inclined to consent to what is inappropriate, so that we do it or renounce it. This consent is what we properly call "sin," the fault of the soul whereby it merits damnation or is held guilty before God. For what is this consent but scorn for God and an affront against him? God cannot be offended by injury but he can by scorn. For he is the ultimate power, not diminished by any injury but wreaking vengeance on scorn for him.

Thus our sin is scorn for the creator, and to sin is to scorn the creator – not to do for his sake what we believe we ought to do for his sake, or not to renounce for his sake what we believe ought to be renounced.[84]

---

and a prolific writer. See Joseph Goering, "Chobham, Thomas of," *ODNB* (September 23, 2004).

[81] Frederick Powicke and Christopher Cheney, eds., *Councils and Synods: With Other Documents Relating to the English Church*, 2 vols. (Oxford: Clarendon Press, 1964), vol. II, 1069–70; as cited in Goering, "Internal Forum," 195, note 63.

[82] Christina Heckman, "*Imitatio* in Early Medieval Spirituality: The Dream of the Rood, Anselm, and Militant Christology," *Essays in Medieval Studies* 22 (2005): 146.

[83] Sarah Hamilton, "Penance in the Age of Gregorian Reform," *Studies in Church History* 40 (2004): 52.

[84] Peter Abelard, "Ethics," Book I, c. 7 and 8; in Paul Spade, ed., *Peter Abelard: Ethical Writings, Ethics and Dialogue between a Philosopher, a Jew, and a Christian* (Indianapolis: Hackett Publishing, 1995), 2–3.

Abelard's synthesis clearly articulates the priority of intention. He sees sinful acts as symptoms of sin, not sins themselves. Action is not compulsory to sin; the thought or inclination alone is sufficient (i.e. failing to renounce that which one should renounce). That is not to say that there is no appreciation for the act: the act itself is tangible evidence of a sinful mind. Yet, theologically speaking, the act is the lesser part of the problem.

It is important to note that focus on the interiority of sin was replicated also in the punishment of crime. This is substantiated by a long tradition, dating back to the Anglo-Saxon era, in which murder was considered distinct from simple homicide. Jurors were much more inclined to punish premeditated crimes than those committed in hot blood. The fact that indictments often remark that a felony had been committed with felonious intent, that the mentally disabled were found to be *non compos mentis,* that self-defense warranted a pardon not execution, all this indicates that *mens rea* mattered greatly in medieval England.[85] Of course, in practice, jurists recognized that proving intent, especially in the absence of a criminal act, was not an easy matter. The internal forum of penance then functions as a natural extension of the process, picking up where the court system leaves off. Confession, freely given, opens a window into an individual's heart, permitting the penitential process to aspire to loftier goals when it comes to criminal reform, but also reminding us just how closely the two systems were meant to interact. Law enforcement and penitential process were meant to be two halves of one whole.

Theologically speaking, there are two parts to each sin: guilt (*culpa*) and penalty (*poena*). On its own, the guilt is enough to condemn an individual to hell; however, through the sacrament of penance, God in His mercy expunges a penitent Christian's guilt. The penalty (*poena*), though, cannot be so easily absolved. As Abelard underscores in the passage above, the penalty of sin arises from contempt for God. His honor has been affronted. Just as satisfaction is required when one person dishonors another, so too does God demand satisfaction in the

---

[85] Elizabeth Papp Kamali, "*Felonia felonice facta*: Felony and Intentionality in Medieval England," *Criminal Law and Philosophy* 9.3 (2015): 397–421. Felony convictions offer perhaps the best evidence for the centrality of intention: those whom jurors chose to convict were typically repeat or professional criminals, the replication of the act functioning as evidence of a criminal mind.

form of penalty. God cannot forgive a person's sin freely, because to do so would give that person license to sin. A king, in emulation of God's mercy, may pardon a crime, and in doing so, reconcile a felon to both Crown and community; yet, the king's pardon does not repair an individual's relationship with God. The penitent must still undertake the penitential process to compensate God for having dishonored Him, and restore oneself to God's good graces. Mortal sins cut the soul off from God. In the absence of reconciliation, damnation is the only outcome. Reconciliation is the key term here, and in many ways is the defining feature of Christianity. Through original sin, Adam and Eve broke faith with God; it was only through Christ's sacrifice on behalf of humankind that they were able to achieve reconciliation. This pattern repeats itself over and over again in the larger Christian narrative. Reconciliation is also the term that was used by medieval theologians to refer to participation in the Eucharist. As Robert Grosseteste, Bishop of Lincoln, argued, "the sacrament of penance should reconcile the sinner to the Church and precede the Eucharist, which in turn reconciled to God."[86]

As terms, sin and crime, punishment and penance were often used interchangeably in the medieval context. Even the thirteenth-century English legal treatises are not immune to this elision. In the *Mirror of Justices*, the author picks up on the terminology of penance by defining punishment as "satisfaction for a trespass or a sin." In surveying the various kinds of punishment available at common law, the treatise employs the language of penitential theology, explaining that some corporal punishments are mortal, some venial; mortal sins demand mortal punishments.[87] Penitential language also pervades *Fleta* (c.1290–1300)'s discussion of punishments, which sees the king's justice complementing God's: "For penalties are devised to control men, so that those whom the fear of God will not turn from evil may at least be restrained from wrongdoing by a temporal penalty, as it is written: Good men hate to err from love of virtue; the wicked hate to err from fear of pain."[88] Penitential language also crops up in the jail delivery rolls

---

[86] William Campbell, "Theologies of Reconciliation in Thirteenth-Century England," in Kate Cooper and Jeremy Gregory, eds., *Retribution, Repentance, and Reconciliation* (Woodbridge: Boydell, 2004), 89.

[87] William Whittaker, ed., *The Mirror of Justices* (SS, vol. VII, 1893), 132–3.

[88] Richardson and Sayles, eds., *Fleta*, 34.

at times. When John the Carpenter of Bridgwater (*Bruggewater*) was arraigned on suspicion of theft and prison-break at Salisbury on December 20, 1318, the court scribe who wrote up the trial summary noted that he was arrested on manifest suspicion of sins (*pecarrum*), and because of this he was returned to prison, where he remained in penance.[89] At William Basingthorp of Abingdon's 1407 arraignment at the castle of Lincoln in the third week of Lent, jurors explained that he was guilty of petty larceny, having stolen goods worth eight pence from William Fesedyk, a blindman. Justices determined that he had already undergone sufficient penance (*sufficiente penitencia*) for the crimes that he had perpetrated while awaiting trial. Thus, he was released from prison.[90]

Despite the conceptual overlap, theologians distinguished carefully between punishment and penance in order to indicate the superior nature of penance. An eleventh-century tract entitled *Concerning True and False Penance* explains punishment (*poena*) as "a hurt which punishes and avenges what one commits"; penance (*poenitentia*) is instead "avenging, always punishing in one's self what he is sorry to have done."[91] The obvious distinction here is the voluntary nature of confessional penance. In both punishment and penance as it is addressed in the church courts, authorities takes vengeance on behalf of God; in the internal forum, the sinner undertakes self-vengeance in the hopes of attaining spiritual purification to make oneself worthy of salvation. In its teachings on contrition, the church articulated that penance was effective only if undertaken willingly because one must acknowledge one's guilt and experience remorse in order to obtain God's forgiveness. Through the confessional experience, the church also fostered techniques of self-discovery and self-revelation, equipping the penitent with the spiritual tools necessary to begin this process. Nonetheless, it was broadly recognized that punishment at the hands of judicial authorities still has spiritual benefits. What begins involuntarily might become voluntary: virtue is a habit waiting to be adopted by the penitent. Contrition begins with the soul: punishment functions as an

---

[89] TNA JUST 3/114, m. 5 (1318).   [90] TNA JUST 3/188, m. 130 (1407).
[91] As cited by Harold Berman, *Law and Revolution: The Formation of the Western Legal Tradition* (Cambridge, MA: Harvard University Press, 1983), 172.

expression of the soul's contrition. As Esther Cohen writes, "[i]n a world that eulogized and enshrined suffering, infliction of pain upon blameless people could not be considered wrong."[92]

Aquinas saw earthly justice as a complement to God's justice from which it derives. Proverbs attribute to God the statement: "Through me kings rule and the framers of laws decree what is just" (Prov., 8:15), a passage that Aquinas (d.1274) quotes with confidence as proof that the connection between the two is incontestable. Human law is inevitably the lesser of the two, but they share the same aim. As is also true of God's law, "[h]uman law intends to bring men to virtue." They differ principally in the nature of the process. In human law, it must be done "not suddenly but gradually." Human law

> does not impose immediately upon the multitude of imperfect men those things which the virtuous already possess, namely, that they abstain from all evils, otherwise these imperfect men, being unable to bear such precepts, would break forth into worse evils, as is said in (Prov. xxx, 33), 'He who blows his nose too violently, brings forth blood,' and in (Matt. ix, 17), 'If wine is put in old skins,' i.e., if the precepts of a perfect life are imposed on imperfect men, 'the skins would break, and the wine would flow out,' i.e., the precepts would be contemned and men would break out into worse evils.[93]

Helping men and women to attain salvation is the underlying objective of both laws, but the final say ultimately belongs to God: no one can escape Judgment Day, a fact that medieval men and women had plentiful opportunity to contemplate. The proliferation of murals of the Last Judgment in the decoration of late medieval churches, positioned ominously in one of two places, either on the tympanum above the front entrance or over the nave from the chancel arc, acted as a constant reminder. Kings needed to tow a hard line in preparation for the final judgment because, as *Fleta* made clear, "the Son of God ... is a judge terribly strict and intolerably severe, offended beyond measure and vehemently angered, whose sentence none can commute, from whose prison there is no escape, whose punishments are without end.

---

[92] Cohen, *Modulated Scream*, 59.
[93] Aquinas, *Summa Theologica*, I–II, q. 96, art. 2; Robert Henle, ed., *Saint Thomas Aquinas. The Treatise on Law [Being Summa Theologiae, i–ii, QQ.90 through 97]* (South Bend, IN: University of Notre Dame Press, 1993), 313.

Who then shall not fear that trial where the Lord shall be the accuser, the advocate and the judge?"[94]

As uncongenial as it is to modern thinking, vengeance lies at the center of all discussions of punishment and of penance. The appeals process itself originated as a means to curb blood-feud, providing victims' or their families a court-approved, nonviolent means of taking vengeance in the hopes of bringing cycles of violence between families to an end. Vengeance for the victim or the victim's family, as well as the king whose majesty has been insulted, is thus an essential part of punishment in the royal courts. Execution is a form of vengeance for the convicted felon's breach of the king's peace. The same is true of penance. Medieval men and women were accustomed to the idea of a vengeful God who punishes His creations through pain and violence. Burchard of Worms (d.1025) attempted to deter participation in blood feuds by making vengeance an exclusively divine right: "Vengeance is mine; I will repay," saith the Lord" (Romans 12:19).[95] It is worth remembering that in common parlance, Judgment Day was referred to as the Day of (God's) Wrath (*dies irae*). God experiences no remorse in striking down sinners, even destroying the bulk of His creation when humans fail to live up to His expectations. Yet, God's anger manifests to our own benefit. As the *Leges Henrici Primi* extolls: "It is not only an angry God but also a compassionate God who casts out sinners; they are cast out in two ways: like the Sodomites, so that the people themselves may be punished for their own sins, or like the Ninevites, so that the sins themselves of the people may be punished and destroyed."[96] Christian salvation especially is tied intrinsically to violence and pain: Christ's own torment and execution – experienced through pain, suffering, and copious bloodshed – won salvation for the entire human race. A good Christian, then, expected salvation to be earned by pain, if not during one's lifetime, then in purgatory where bodily

---

[94] Richardson and Sayles, eds., *Fleta*, 37.
[95] Greta Austin, "Vengeance and Law in Eleventh-Century Worms: Burchard and the Canon Law of Feuds," in Wolfgang Müller and Mary Sommar, eds., *Medieval Church Law and the Origins of the Western Legal Tradition* (Washington, DC: Catholic University of America Press, 2012), 70–3.
[96] *LHP*, ch. 5, subsection 20, 92–3.

torment might feel as if it lasts an eternity. Penance, the path to salvation, was paved in violence, pain, and suffering.

Christianity and the Criminal Soul

Sin is a universal experience – with a couple of celebrated exceptions, all human beings sin, and through sin we are brought to Christ. As Robert Grosseteste constantly reminded his parishioners, there is benefit in sin: if we do not sin, we cannot be the recipients of God's mercy.[97] As humans, sin is an experience that unites us. Christian perceptions of the sinfulness of humanity provide an instructive reminder that all humans exist somewhere on a continuum of sin. Not only did this encourage empathy towards the sinful; it also fostered a distinct understanding that it is up to God (not humans) to determine how much sin is too much to enter heaven. This was true even when it comes to the deadly sins. Contrary to the gloomy nomenclature, deadly sins only *threaten* the soul with damnation. Both the early penitentials and the later confessors' manuals make it clear that absolution still remains within the realm of possibility. Even the worst sinners, such as Mary Magdalene, thought to have been a prostitute, or Dysmas, the "good thief" crucified by Jesus' side, might overcome their sins and reap the highest rewards as saints. Catholicism is a religion of second chances (and third, and fourth). Penance does not even need to be constrained by the limits of one's mortal life, as purgatory offers the perfect escape clause, granting the penitent additional time. Thus, there is little reason to believe the English judicial system treated the criminal soul as a lost cause; or that medieval Englishmen and women, schooled in an understanding of Christianity as fraternity, would willingly abandon a fellow parishioner's soul, no matter how corrupt the sinner's actions.

There was also a distinct understanding that while the judicial process might inflict some of the suffering needed to atone for one's sins, its function was limited. A death sentence on earth would help satisfy some of the sinner's penalty, but it was up to God to determine whether an individual's soul was damned, or redeemable.[98] From the

---

[97] Hoskin, *Robert Grosseteste*, 54
[98] Neville, "No Remission without Satisfaction," 213.

time of Jerome (d.420), intellectuals pondered how judicial sentence fit within the penitential process. Jerome argued that God does not punish the same crime twice. Thus, upon Judgment Day, He assessed just how effective judicial punishment had been in effacing a penitent's sin. Sometimes judicial punishment itself was sufficient penance; if not, it was God's prerogative to assign an additional, but complementary eternal punishment.[99] Peter of Poitiers (d. *c.*1205–15) made the link between God and king even more explicit by arguing that judicial punishment is a test by which a sinner is granted the opportunity to repent. If the sinner truly regrets a sin, it will be absolved.[100] Execution mandated by an earthly authority, however, in no way constrained God's actions. Judges and jurors knew nothing about a convicted felon's eternal fate. Execution did not entail damnation; it was merely an earthly punishment merited by an earthly crime.

This is key: felons' souls mattered to the Christian community. By its very nature, medieval Christianity was a communal religion. Redemption of the collective soul was the ultimate objective. Medieval strategies for salvation call attention to its communal nature, including the mass (collective prayer); parish bede rolls and prayers for the (parish's) dead; prayer guilds and confraternities (praying for each other's souls); pious bequests (prayer for one's own soul, as well as prayer for the souls of fellow parishioners past and present). Confession and communion, the main forms of religious participation for lay Christians after Lateran IV, merged into annual events occurring in time for Easter each year. These seemingly solitary experiences were undertaken jointly as everyone queued up before the nave to wait their turn with the priest. The fact that confessional boxes had yet to be invented helped to transform confession into a "fundamentally collective enterprise": the words exchanged between parishioner and priest were private, but the conversation itself transpired publicly in whispered tones just feet away from one's neighbors.[101] Rogationtide, days of prayer and fasting in which

[99] As discussed in Raphaël Eckert, "Peine judiciare, pénitence et salut entre droit canonique et théologie (xiie s. – début du xiiie s.)," *Revue de l'histoire des religions* 228.4 (2011): 489.

[100] Eckert, "Peine judiciare," 496.

[101] Ellen Rentz, *Imagining the Parish in Late Medieval England* (Columbus: Ohio State University Press, 2015), 35.

the parish as a community asked (*rogare*) God to forgive their transgressions, involved all parishioners walking in concert the boundaries of the parish on three consecutive days. Group perambulations of this sort marked out the liturgical year for its parishioners, such that "[w]alking was one of the most defining features of parochial worship" in medieval England.[102] Even the rosary, which today tends to be a very solitary activity, was then typically prayed in guilds. Therefore, "many medieval preachers taught Christianity as fraternity and community," drawing on Mark 12:31, "you shall love your neighbor as yourself."[103] The policy of "no soul left behind" tended to privilege the parish, but medieval theologians worked hard to undermine pride in parish and parish competition by stressing the concept of Christendom as a mega-church in which all of God's people are parishioners.[104]

The communal nature of Christianity also had its drawbacks. The biblical experience of the Flood sent two key messages to medieval Christians: one, God communicates his anger with Christian immorality through natural disaster; two, their own salvation depends precariously on their neighbors' moral behavior. As a result, a good Christian does not respect a neighbor's privacy by dismissing his sex life as his own business because turning a blind eye to fornication, especially when it becomes a cultural habit, might lead God to eradicate His creations and start over once again. The impact of this mentality is most evident in the aftermath of the Black Death when fears of further provoking God's anger prompted community elders to organize late-night home invasions and shotgun weddings when sin threatened to undermine their communities' spiritual wellbeing.[105]

---

[102] Rentz, *Imagining the Parish*, 64.
[103] Katherine French, "Localized Faith: Parochial and Domestic Spaces," in John Arnold, ed., *The Oxford Handbook of Medieval Christianity* (Oxford University Press, 2014), 167.
[104] Saint Bernard of Clairvaux (d.1153), sometimes sentimentally referred to as the theologian of love, argued magnanimously that even Jews and heretics have a place in the universal church. See John Sommerfeldt, *On the Spirituality of Relationship* (New York: Newman Press, 1997).
[105] Shannon McSheffrey, "Men and Masculinity in Late Medieval London Civic Culture: Governance, Patriarchy and Reputation," in Jacqueline Murray, ed., *Conflicted Identities and Multiple Masculinities: Men in the Medieval West* (New York: Garland, 1999), 243–78.

An environment of collective Christianity founded on the Golden Rule in which individual salvation was predicated on one's efforts to release fellow parishioners from the chains of purgatory is the backdrop against which the place of a felon's soul in medieval Christendom should be contemplated. In this atmosphere, it is hard to imagine that any soul, even that of a convicted felon, was simply written off as damned without great reluctance. Nonetheless, this is exactly what some historians have contended. Historians have long argued that it was not until the fourteenth century that prisoners were permitted the opportunity to confess to a priest prior to execution. At the Council of Vienne in 1312, Pope Clement V (r. 1305–14) issued a bull forbidding the denial of confession and absolution to the condemned.[106] To many historians, Clement's legislation is evidence of a changing climate in penology, representing new approaches to justice, salvation, and punishment forged in the fourteenth century.[107] Clement's prohibition signals the introduction of "a strong religious element into what had hitherto been a secular ceremony."[108] Building on this hypothesis, Paul Friedland explains that the ritual of repentance symbolized by the *amende honorable*, an elaborate public performance in which the defendant begged God's forgiveness, only became part of the French execution process after its king fell in line with papal policy and issued legislation in 1396 mandating religious confession to felons awaiting capital punishment.[109] Speaking explicitly to the situation in England, Katherine Royer writes that "[p]rior to the fourteenth century the condemned were often denied the sacrament of penance because their severance from both society and community of Christians was intended to be permanent."[110]

Many of these scholars draw heavily from Aquinas' theory of the Common Good to support their theses. Thomas Aquinas was a staunch supporter of capital punishment, which he believed was

---

[106] *Corpus iuris canonici*, vol. II, 1190, tit.IX, cap. I.
[107] Madeline Caviness, "Giving the 'Middle Ages' a Bad Name: Blood Punishments in the *Sachenspiegel* and Town Law Books," *Studies in Iconography* 34 (2013): 221–2.
[108] Esther Cohen, *The Crossroads of Justice: Law and Culture in Late Medieval France* (Leiden: Brill, 1993), 198.
[109] Paul Friedland, *Seeing Justice Done: The Age of Spectacular Capital Punishment in France* (Oxford University Press, 2012), 96–101.
[110] Katherine Royer, *The English Execution Narrative, 1200–1700* (London: Pickering and Chatto, 2014), 52.

mandated biblically in the passage "And if your right hand causes you to sin, cut it off and throw it away. For it is better that you lose one of your members than that your whole body go into hell" (Matthew 5:30). In his justification, Aquinas also applied a surgical analogy. In a manner strikingly reminiscent of Aristotle's *Politics,* Aquinas explained:

> every part is directed to the whole, as imperfect to perfect, wherefore every part is naturally for the sake of the whole. For this reason we observe that if the health of the whole body demands the excision of a member, through its being decayed or infectious to the other members, it will be both praiseworthy and advantageous to have it cut away. Now every individual person is compared to the whole community, as part to whole. Therefore if a man be dangerous and infectious to the community, on account of some sin, it is praiseworthy and advantageous that he be killed in order to safeguard the common good, since "a little leaven corrupteth the whole lump" (1 Cor. 5:6).[111]

In Aquinas' statement, it is implicit that execution was absolutely a last resort. Amputation was a risky business in medieval Europe: it might save the patient's life, but it might also precipitate the patient's death. An astute surgeon eager to maintain his reputation amputated cautiously and only when a raging infection threatened the patient's overall wellbeing.

In arguing that a criminal soul be sacrificed for the common good, Aquinas offers the impression that the criminal soul is beyond redemption. In fact, this was not his position. He argued that execution itself might propel the soul towards repentance. He noted that "death inflicted by the judge profits the sinner, if he be converted unto the expiation of his crime; and, if he be not converted, it profits so as to put an end to the sin, because the sinner is thus deprived of the power to sin anymore."[112] Aquinas' harsh stance on criminal culpability derives principally from his Aristotelian appraisal of human intellect. Aquinas endorsed a relatively optimistic position on human nature. Intellect is what separates humans from other mammals, and in human beings intellect rules supreme. Our capacity to reason, a gift from God, makes us naturally inclined to goodness. As

---

[111] Thomas Aquinas, *Summa Theologica*, trans. Fathers of the Dominican Province (New York: Benzinger Brothers, 1947), II–II, q. 64, art. 2.
[112] Aquinas, *Summa Theologica*, II–II, q. 25, art. 6.

a result, from Aquinas' perspective, no one falls into a criminal lifestyle. His criminology is "one of personal responsibility." A criminal deliberately and consciously chooses immorality, knowing that it is wrong, that it is against one's best interest and the interests of one's community, and one must overcome the goodness of one's own human nature in order to commit that crime.

This is one of those instances when medieval England stands out from the rest of Europe. Even if the pope did not urge protection of a prisoner's right to confession until the fourteenth century, in England concern for doing so can be traced back as early as the ninth.[113] The church laws of Edward the Elder (d.924), king of England, and Guthrum (d.890), king of the Danes in East Anglia, declare that "if a person condemned to death wishes to confess, it shall never be refused him."[114] The laws of Cnut (d.1035) repeat this injunction, instituting a fine of 120 shillings for those who prevent a convicted felon from confessing, an amount that far surpassed the spending capacity of most Englishmen and women, indicating that its chief purpose was as deterrent.[115] The defense of a felon's right to confess survived the Norman Conquest, appearing in the same format in the *Leges Henrici Primi.*[116] It is striking that while access to confession was sacrosanct, the *Leges* spells out that protections did not extend also to communion. Convicts were excluded from participation in the Eucharist.[117] The *Libri Sententiarum VIII* of the English cardinal Robert Pullen (d.1146) provides an explanation for why criminals should not be granted the Eucharist. In consuming the consecrated host, the criminal becomes the Temple of God. How can a judge then order the convict's execution? "Better then that the criminal should forego the consolation of Holy Communion than that men should lay

---

[113] The English were not "going rogue" in mandating confession for convicted felons prior to Clement V's 1312 bull. Peter Lombard's *Sentences*, which eventually replaced Pullen's *Libri Sententiarum* as the church's official textbook of theology, stated emphatically that emergency penance AND reconciliation (communion) must not be denied to any Christian, including the thief. Peter Lombard, Distinction xx, v, 209.

[114] David Wilkins, ed., *Concilia Magna Brittaniae et Hiberniae a Synodo Verulamensi anno 446 ad Londinensem 1717*, 4 vols. (London: R. Gosling, et al., 1685–1745), vol. I, 203.

[115] Wilkins, ed., *Concilia Magna Brittaniae*, vol. I, 307.

[116] *LHP*, ch. 11, subsection 9, 112–13.   [117] *LHP*, ch. 5, subsection 18a, 90–1.

violent and sacrilegious hands on one who is the tabernacle of Christ."[118] Under Peter Lombard, however, the church reversed its stance and agreed that neither confession nor Eucharist might be denied a penitent felon waiting for execution.

The 1260s were a defining moment in underscoring just how horrific the English church believed it was to deny a prisoner the opportunity to repent. In 1261 Boniface of Savoy, the Archbishop of Canterbury, presided over a council at Lambeth in which he denounced the practice of refusing confession to prisoners as inhumane (*inhumaniter*), unChristian (*infideliter*), and worthy of excommunication.[119] Seven years later, the English legatine synod declared that keepers who obstructed confessions would be denied canonical burial.[120] While some jailers may have been negligent in their duties, there is good reason to believe that the English Crown took seriously the need to instruct royal justices on their spiritual responsibilities towards felons.[121] In practice, incarceration in English prisons provided many opportunities for confession. In some regions, prisoners were released on their own accord to go to mass outside the prison. A London ruling of 1431 required Newgate's jailer to allow all freemen of the city, as well as "other honest persons" to attend mass on condition that they provide surety. Elsewhere, chapels were built into the prisons themselves.[122] The

---

[118] Francis Courtney, *Cardinal Robert Pullen: An English Theologian of the Twelfth Century* (Rome: Pontifical Gregorian University, 1954), 243. In France, denial of the sacrament to prisoners was seen to be a deterrent to crime. See Jules Corblet, *Histoire du sacrament de l'eucharistie*, 2 vols. (Paris: Paris société générale de librarie Catholique, 1885), vol. I, 335.

[119] Wilkins, ed., *Concilia Magna Brittaniae*, vol. I, 754.

[120] The 1287 statutes of Exeter repeat this prohibition. Powicke and Cheney, eds., *Councils and Synods*, vol. II, 750 and 994–5. *Lyndwood's Provinciale* (1496) reiterated Boniface's earlier provision for prisoners' to have the space and opportunity to confess. John Bullard and Chalmer Bell, eds., *Lyndwood's Provinciale* (London: Faith Press, 1929), tit. 16, ch. 2, 146.

[121] *Placita Corone* (c.1274) includes numerous examples in which convicts were granted the opportunity to confess to a priest before being hanged. John Kaye, ed., *Placita Corone, or La Corone Pledee devant Justices* (SS, supplementary series, vol. IV, 1966).

[122] A chance discovery in the will of a burgess' widow makes it clear that this was the case at the town jail of Bury Saint Edmunds: she left a bequest to pay for a priest to say mass in the prison chapel on Sundays and holy days. Samuel Tymms, ed., *Wills and Inventories from the Registers of the Commissary of Bury St Edmunds and the Archdeacon of Sudbury* (Camden Society Original Series, vol. XLIX, 1850), 77. Noted in Helen Carrel, "The Ideology of Punishment in Late Medieval English Towns," *Social History* 34.3 (2009): 316.

English also respected the right of executed felons to a Christian burial, a necessary prerequisite for those aspiring to enter heaven. It was denied only to those convicts who failed to show signs of repentance, emphasizing once again that spiritual rehabilitation was not closed to convicted felons.[123] From the thirteenth century, the Knights Hospitallers in England made it their special mission to retrieve hanged felons and bury them.[124] The English even buried the remains of traitors in hallowed ground rather than risk God's ire.[125]

Accepting that medieval men and women did not see felons' souls as lost, nor did they deny felons those rites needed for a soul's safe passage to heaven, helps us to realize that secular punishment cannot be separated out easily from penance. Rather, it must be conceived as being part of the penitential process. Each member of the Christian community has a part to play in each other's salvation. In this respect, a contract exists between fellow Christians. No sin is so horrific that it excludes a sinner from salvation, providing he or she is willing to embark on the penitential process. It is the responsibility of one's fellow Christians, and God's representative on earth especially, to ensure that a sinner has the opportunity to commence this process.

Sacred Kingship, Common Law and Penitential Justice

Just as the law administered in secular courts was far from secular, so, too, should we imagine kings as quasi-religious figures who were responsible for the souls of all their subjects, regardless of their proclivity to crime. As Ernst Kantorowicz long ago argued, the

---

[123] In 1352, Archbishop Zouche of York made this point explicitly: "ecclesiastical burial is not to be denied to those hanged on the gallows as long as they died penitent." As cited in Henry Summerson, "Attitudes to Capital Punishment in England, 1200–1350," in Michael Prestwich, Richard Britnell, and Robin Frame, eds., *Thirteenth Century England* VIII (Woodbridge: Boydell, 2001): 131.

[124] Ralph Pugh, "The Knights Hospitallers of England as Undertakers," *Speculum* 56.3 (1981): 566–74.

[125] Robert Pullen's *Libri Sententiarum* warns that the one who denies burial in consecrated ground to a criminal who had confessed and/or participated in communion, commits a grave sin and endangers one's own soul. Courtney, *Cardinal Robert Pullen*, 243.

"language of christological exemplarism" was put to work throughout European society by both church and state alike in order to "proclaim the king a *typus Christus*."[126] Well before the pope usurped the title, kings referred to themselves as vicars of Christ in order to cement the association, a title that appears repeatedly in *Bracton* (*c.*1220s–60s).[127] In a section entitled "The King Has No Equal," *Bracton* makes the comparison explicit for his reader:

Since he is the vicar of God, and that he ought to be under the law appears clearly in the analogy of Jesus Christ, whose viceregent on earth he is, for though many ways were open to Him for his ineffable redemption of the human race, the true mercy of God chose this most powerful way to destroy the devil's work, he would use not the power of force but the reason of justice. Thus he willed himself to be under the law that he might redeem those who live under it. For He did not wish to use force but judgment. And in that same way the Blessed Mother of God, the Virgin Mary, Mother of our Lord, who by an extraordinary privilege was above law, nevertheless, in order to show an example of humility, did not refuse to be subjected to established laws. Let the king, therefore, do the same, lest his power remain unbridled.[128]

As *Bracton* clarifies, sacral kingship of the late Middle Ages was not the semi-magical in-dwelling divinity of the earlier period; rather, kings aspired to the wisdom of Solomon to rule responsibly in the name of God.[129]

In England, the sanctity of kingship was enhanced by a blessed lineage, comprising numerous Anglo-Saxon monarchs (Æthelberht of Kent, Æthelberht II of East Anglia, Alfred, Edmund the Martyr, Edwin of Northumbria, Oswine of Deira) venerated regionally as saints although not formally beatified, but it was the canonization of Edward the Confessor (d.1066) in the twelfth century that cast "an aura of holiness" on the entire monarchy.[130] Royal families in medieval Europe perpetuated the notion of *beata stirps* (holy stock),

---

[126] Ernst Kantorowicz, *The King's Two Bodies: A Study in Medieval Political Theology* (1957; repr., Princeton University Press, 2016), 88.

[127] For example, *Bracton*, vol. II, 305 and 419.   [128] *Bracton*, vol. II, 33.

[129] Nicholas Vincent, "The Pilgrimages of the Angevin Kings of England, 1154–1272," in Colin Morris and Peter Robert, eds., *Pilgrimage: The English Experience from Becket to Bunyan* (Cambridge University Press, 2002), 43.

[130] John Theilmann, "The Miracles of King Henry VI of England," *The Historian* 42.3 (1980): 458.

that sanctity might be transmitted through the bloodlines.[131] While most kings deliberately cultivated a broad-based patronage of the cults of English saints for nationalistic purposes, Edward the Confessor always took centerstage because an astute monarch realized that "association with a saintly predecessor brought an aura of religiosity to the dynasty."[132] Nor did Edward the Confessor's canonization represent the end of English attempts to produce new royal saints. At various points, Henry III (d.1272), Edward II (d.1327), and Henry VI (d.1471) were all put forward as candidates for canonization, without success.

Sacral kingship began with the coronation ceremony, in which the Archbishop of Canterbury anointed the king, thereby investing him with the mediatory powers necessary to act as moral guide for his people. The Crown engaged multiple strategies in royal mythmaking. Royal seals depicting the king sought to recall the image of Christ enthroned so familiar to medieval audiences.[133] Through royal pardons, kings established and enacted their own penitential process, employing the king's grace to erase the earthly consequences of sin. When Pope Boniface VIII (d.1303) rejuvenated Leviticus' concept of jubilee, convoking a special year of remissions of sins and universal pardon for all those who went on pilgrimage to Rome to be held at fifty-year intervals, he inspired the English kings. Thus, when Edward III (d.1377) turned fifty years of age in 1362, he held his own "jubilee" of sorts by issuing a general pardon to his subjects. Then when he reached his fiftieth year of rule in 1377, he issued yet another general pardon in an ostentatious display of royal grace.[134] Much like Christ among the lepers, with the royal touch they healed the sick, a practice that extends back to the time of King Henry II (d.1189), although the

---

[131] Anna Duch, "Chasing St Louis: The English Monarchy's Pursuit of Sainthood," in Elena Woodacre, et al., eds., *The Routledge History of Monarchy* (London: Routledge, 2019), 330.

[132] Paul Webster, "Faith, Power and Charity: Personal Religion and Kingship in Medieval England," in Woodacre, et al., eds., *Routledge History of Monarchy*, 196.

[133] Johanna Dale, "*Christus Regnat*: Inauguration and Images of Kingship in England, France, and the Empire c.1050–c.1250," (PhD Diss., University of East Anglia, 2013).

[134] W. Mark Ormrod, "The English Monarchy and the Promotion of Religion in the Fourteenth Century," in Ludger Körntgen and Dominik Waßenhoven, eds., *Religion and Politics in the Middle Ages* (Berlin: De Gruyter, 2013), 216.

granting of coins as a souvenir likely did not begin until the pomp and circumstance of the reign of Henry III. The utility of this custom in presenting the king as God's representative here on earth was such that it survived the ravages of the Protestant Reformation, with Queen Anne being the last English monarch to heal by touch. Medieval monarchs applied themselves assiduously to this task to the benefit of their subjects.[135]

As all of this suggests, kings took their religious responsibilities seriously. Since at least the twelfth century, the royal almoner has played a key role in the king's household, responsible for coordinating and administering the king's charitable activities.[136] From distributing the leftovers ("broken meats") of the king's dishes to the poor after mealtimes, to funding the building of monasteries, the almoner was responsible for setting aside available monies and disbursing them accordingly. Long-term, a king's building projects memorialized his piety; short-term, the impact upon his subjects came from charitable acts on a much smaller scale. For example, Henry III seems to have spent much of his time feeding the poor. Upon the death of his sister, Isabella of England (d.1241), Holy Roman Empress through her marriage to Frederick II, Henry fed 50,000 paupers in her honor. Two decades later, when his half-brother, Aymer de Lusignan (d.1260), bishop-elect of Winchester, passed away Henry fed 20,000 paupers in his honor.[137] His son, Edward I (d.1307), also was renowned for his generosity to the poor. His financial records demonstrate daily charitable acts. In the year 1283–4, on a daily basis he provided food for thirteen paupers, totaling £36 19s 4.5d for the year. In addition, every Saturday, he fed fifteen paupers (£4 17s. 6d.); every Sunday, forty paupers (£14 15s);

---

[135] For example, between December of 1340 and November of 1341, Edward III carried out no fewer than 355 healings by the royal touch. W. Mark Ormrod, "The Personal Religion of Edward III," *Speculum* 64.4 (1989): 863.

[136] See Lawrence Tanner, "Lord High Almoners and Sub-Almoners 1100–1957," *Journal of the British Archaeological Association*, 3rd series, 20–1 (1957–8): 72–83.

[137] Katie Philipps, "Devotion by Donation: The Alms-Giving and Religious Foundations of Henry III," *Reading Medieval Studies* 43 (2017): 83. Henry also personally engaged with the poor. In emulation of Christ's washing the feet of his disciples at the Last Supper, at Maundy Thursday in 1237, he washed the feet of 200 paupers, supplying them also with new tunics and shoes – a tradition that continued well beyond the Middle Ages. Philipps, "Devotion by Donation," 84.

every Monday, Tuesday, and Friday throughout the year, fifty paupers (£46 17s. 6d.); and while the numbers of paupers vary, he participated in similar acts for saints' days and festivals throughout the year (£69 6s. 3d.).[138] Nor did his charitable inclination trail off over time. Royal alms and oblations for the year 1299–1300 reached a grand total of £1,166 14s. 6d.[139] Piety of this nature attested to the king's concern for his subjects and his moral responsibility for their physical and spiritual wellbeing, as royal alms offered spiritual rewards to both the king and his kingdom.[140]

That the king's piety was not just a ceremonial show to augment the prestige of his kingly office is evidenced by the centrality of devotion in the daily calendar of the king's activities. Kings traveled with a portable chapel, which included a substantial collection of relics, as well as the fingerbone of Saint Bernard acquired by Henry II in 1178.[141] Daily mass was obligatory, and failure to attend resulted in self-imposed penitential alms, such as the one hundred paupers fed by King Edward I for each missed daily mass.[142] The itinerant lifestyles of the English kings afforded frequent visitation to England's multiplicity of saints' shrines, such that Nicholas Vincent argues historians should see medieval kings as "near-perpetual pilgrim(s)."[143] English kings regularly visited shrines in thanks for recovery from illness. While multiple English kings vowed to take up the cross, two actually did (Richard I and Edward I). As a young man, Henry IV (d.1413) was the only English king to visit the Holy Sepulcher in Jerusalem, and to make offerings there and at the Mount of Olives. He dreamed of going on a penitential crusade later in life in order to be forgiven for his cousin's death, but ill health prevented him from doing so.[144] The power of

---

[138] Arnold Taylor, "Royal Alms and Oblations in the Later Thirteenth Century: An Analysis of the Alms Roll of 12 Edward I (1283–4)," in Frederick Emmison and Roy Stephens, eds., *Tribute to an Antiquary: Essays Presented to Mark Fitch* (London: Leopard's Head Press, 1976), 97.

[139] Taylor, "Royal Alms and Oblations," 94.

[140] Philipps, "Devotion by Donation," 83.

[141] Vincent, "Pilgrimages of Angevin Kings," 34.

[142] Similarly, King John fed the poor as an act of contrition for those times he failed to observe the dietary requirements of holy days. Charles Farris, "The Pious Practices of Edward I, 1272–1307," (PhD Diss., Royal Holloway College, University of London, 2013), 112.

[143] Vincent, "Pilgrimages of Angevin Kings," 21.

[144] Debbi Codling, "Henry IV and Personal Piety," *History Today* 57.1 (2007): 24.

prayer was recognized also for its military benefits. Edward I regularly sought prayers and mass said on behalf of English troops while away on campaign. When he set out for his first expedition to Wales in 1277, he wrote to the abbot of Bury St. Edmunds requesting a program of 3,000 masses and 800 psalters as well as other prayers and devotion to be said on behalf of the kingdom each year the army was in Wales.[145]

For the historian, recognizing the religious aura of medieval kingship is critical to appreciating how monarchs grasped the broader context in which their justice was exercised. Because of their dual position, kings embodied both secular and spiritual concerns. As the leaders of their people, they were responsible for the physical safety of their subjects, but as God's representatives they were equally answerable for their subjects' spiritual well-being. Royal cure of souls is expressed best through the king's justice, where crime and sin, punishment and penance converge. Those guilty of mortal sin who escaped the long arm of the law found themselves condemned to hell; but those who commenced the process of penitence through earthly judicial punishment reopened the possibility of salvation, even if they were in fact executed. The welfare of the realm depended on the king's success: sin has pollutant properties that might be expiated only through penance. The unrepentant sinner thus endangered the salvation of the entire kingdom whose inhabitants risked pollution through association. The king who harbored an unrepentant sinner also jeopardized the kingdom's place in God's favor.[146]

Royal paternalism is deeply embedded in English law. Kings made certain that they had done their part in preparing their criminal subjects to meet their maker. The penitential process includes three defined stages: contrition (*contritio in corde*), confession (*contritio in ore*), and satisfaction (*satisfactio in opere*). Contrition was the sole responsibility of the accused; however, the king employed the coercive conditions of prison to nudge a suspected felon towards it. The arraignment and trial also provided the Christian community an opportunity to witness for themselves whether a suspected felon was

---

[145] David Burton, "Requests for Prayers and Royal Propaganda under Edward I," in Peter Coss and Simon Lloyd, eds., *Thirteenth Century England*, vol. III (Woodbridge: Boydell, 1989), 26.
[146] Tom Lambert, *Law and Order in Anglo-Saxon England* (Oxford University Press, 2017), 218–20.

contrite. The signs of true sorrow that crop up repeatedly in confessional manuals would have been familiar enough that a defendant hoping to play on jurors' heartstrings must have known how to emulate it. Kings were also partly responsible for the final part of the penitential process: satisfaction. In order to compensate God for the affront to His majesty, the sinner must pay for his or her sins. Typically, works of penance in medieval England were physical in nature, centered on the concept that punishing the body purifies the soul. In a sermon on the nature of penance, Robert Mannyng writes, "Penanunce pyneþ þy flesh þe fende / And pleseþ god & makþ hym frende" (penance pains the flesh [which is] the fiend, and pleases God and makes him [a] friend).[147] Pain pleases God – this ideology is central to understanding the medieval mindset when it comes to justice. What a modern world has labeled as barbarism, then was intended to right the mind through punishment of the body. It was critical that the priest accurately calculated the necessary penance, because if he did not, he would be responsible for working off the surplus sin in purgatory.[148] This responsibility was also incumbent upon the king: "Not to punish the wrongdoer in the here and now would entail spiritual peril to the king."[149] The physical pain and bodily deprivations suffered at the hands of the king's officials through time in the stocks, prison sentences, peine forte et dure, even execution, thus represent not only vengeance and deterrence, but also satisfaction.

The extent a king participated in the penitential process is measured by the fact that sometimes, much like a confessor, he mandated penance rather than punishment for his criminal subjects. In 1285, arrested for harboring his son after he slew two brothers, William Dun stood mute at his trial and was sentenced to peine forte dure. Upon the intercession of Queen Eleanor, Edward I pardoned the man, only on the condition that he leave the realm within the next forty days to go on pilgrimage to the Holy Land, where he was required to remain until he was granted special license to return.[150] The following year, a similar tactic was used to address the misdeeds of one of his tenants-in-chief,

---

[147] Robert Mannyng of Brunne, in Idelle Sullens, ed., *Handlyng Synne* (Binghamton: Medieval and Renaissance Texts and Studies, 1983), 270.

[148] Cardinal Robert Courçon addresses this subject in his *Summa de paenitentia*. Thomas, Piers Plowman, 185.

[149] Thomas, Piers Plowman, 171.   [150] *CPR*, Edward I, vol. II (1281–92), 194.

William de Monte Caniso of Edwardeston, whose sins are categorized elusively as "certain trespasses charged against him before the justices in eyre in the county of Essex, for which he fled and was put in exigent." He, too, was granted a pardon, contingent on traveling to the holy land before the Midsummer twelvemonth and remaining there "in God's service for ever."[151]

Peine forte et dure as Penance

Peine forte et dure played multiple roles within the medieval judicial system. As we have already seen, it was a coercive device designed to encourage a defendant to submit to jury trial. For those like Margaret Clitheroe, sentenced to death by peine, it functioned as a form of vengeance. Simultaneously, peine forte et dure was the ultimate form of penance. Peine forte et dure bears all the hallmarks of the penitential process: fasting, physical deprivation, solitary confinement, enforced periods of prayer. Prison also presented the ideal space to carry out one's penance, recognized by the appearance of the term "penitentiary" to refer to a prison by the fifteenth century.[152] The blurring of the lines between punishment and penance identifiable in peine forte et dure was not an anomaly. The anonymous chronicler of the *Vita Edwardi Secundi* (1326) made a telling remark when the traitor Robert le Ewer was pressed to death in 1302. He reflected that it was "a punishment fitting for his crimes and *healthy for his soul, provided that he bore it with resignation.*"[153] This unambiguous statement on the transcendent nature of peine forte et dure confirms that historians should take a cue from the medieval terminology. Peine forte et dure was commonly referred to as penance because medieval authorities considered it as such.

---

[151] CPR, Edward I, vol. II (1281–92), 247. Huw Pryce notes something similar in medieval Wales. He writes of a provision for secret killing in which the penalty might be mitigated if the offender produced a letter from the pope to prove that he had gone on pilgrimage to Rome. Huw Pryce, *Native Law and the Church in Medieval Wales* (Oxford University Press, 1993), 37–65. As noted in McKenna, "Performing Penance," 82.

[152] By 1433, the prison in Norwich was called "pentency," a form of penitentiary. Ralph Pugh, *Imprisonment in Medieval England* (Cambridge University Press, 1968), 365 n. 7. *OED* notes that the term "penitentiary" appeared sometime between 1421 and 1500.

[153] Italics are mine. Wendy Childs, ed., *Vita Edwardi Secundi: The Life of Edward the Second* (Oxford: Clarendon Press, 2005), 218–19.

The medieval penchant for symbolism and ritual in the performance of law helps us to better understand the multi-faceted nature of peine forte et dure and its objective. In penitential theology, the form and degree of penance was expected to align with the nature of the sin. Thus, the function of penance was twofold. Privately, it served as both punishment and a corrective for the penitent; but publicly, it acted as a deterrent, visually linking sin and penance for others hoping to stay on a righteous path. Public sins required public penance so that the laity might appreciate the church's vigilance and come to accept that no sin goes unpunished. This ideology carried over into secular law. Punishment varied according to the severity of the crime: petty offenses warranted fines, time in the stocks, or other forms of public humiliation; felonies warranted hanging or mutilation. For particularly heinous crimes, the courts became more creative in their means of execution in order to send a powerful message to the onlookers regarding the unacceptability of the offender's conduct. Heretics and petty traitors were burned to death. In this ritual, fire acted as a purgative, implying that diabolical incitement was required to lead Christians so far astray. The most symbolic means of execution was reserved for those guilty of high treason, in which the Crown hoped "to obliterate the criminal and remind the onlookers of the perils of such behavior."[154] When Hugh Despenser the Younger was executed in 1326, the text of his judgment explains that he was to be drawn and quartered for treason, hanged for robbery, beheaded for daring to return to court while outlawed, and disemboweled for sowing discord in the royal family.[155] His death underscores also that criminals guilty of multiple crimes deserved multiple deaths.

In peine forte et dure, the accused suffers weight, famine, and cold. These three means of torment are worthy subjects of analysis in order to discover what more they can tell us about both the church and the Crown's position on those who reject its authority. Interpreting the symbolism attached to weight, famine, and cold is not as easy in the absence of a text like the one for Hugh Despenser. Nor is it spelled out anywhere in the legal treatises. Nonetheless, religion, law, and medicine

---

[154] Susan Dwyer Amussen, "Punishment, Discipline, and Power: The Social Meanings of Violence in Early Modern England," *JBS* 34.1 (1995): 7.

[155] Danielle Westerhof, "Deconstructing the Identities on the Scaffold: The Execution of Hugh Despenser the Younger, 1326," *Journal of Medieval History* 33 (2007): 93.

combine to offer a number of practical clues to help piece together this legal puzzle, beginning with the starvation diet. Fasting was a standard penance assigned by medieval confessors, such that the term "penance" on its own was often thought to refer to fasting (that is, "penitential fare").[156] Fasting was also not at all unusual in the context of the medieval prison: a proband preparing for the ordeal typically fasted for three days in advance in order to demonstrate to God that he or she had already psychologically embarked on the penitential process.

The central purpose of fasting is spiritual purification through self-sacrifice in imitation of Christ. Purification is also a necessary process to make a penitent worthy of salvation by shedding the trappings of a sin-filled world. As Clement of Alexandria (d. *c.*215) explained, "Fasting empties the soul of matter and makes it, with the body, clear and light for the reception of divine truth."[157] Fasting was thought to be especially efficacious when it came to alleviating sin. An English treatise on the vices and virtues written around the year 1200 extols the benefits of fasting. It "has often cooled God's wrath." This was precisely the strategy employed by the inhabitants of Nineveh when they feared that their beloved city might encounter the same fate as Sodom. They fasted for three days, and it "assuaged" God's wrath. "All the people that dwelt therein were to be destroyed through God's right doom, if they had not fasted." The treatise-writer tells us that "Christ Himself hallowed this fasting when He fasted forty days in the wilderness, [away] from all men." Moses and Elijah also fasted for forty-day periods. But most importantly, "God is ever fasting."[158]

The medieval conception of fasting was not abstinence from food altogether. The penitent partook in one meal each day (normally in the evening), but meat, dairy, eggs, and alcohol were prohibited. Admittedly, the fasting involved in peine forte et dure was of a severe nature, but it adhered to these basic rules: it minimized the amount of food consumed and restricted it to bread and water of a particularly

---

[156] Middle English Dictionary, "penaunce" (n), no. 6. https://quod.lib.umich.edu/m/middle-english-dictionary/dictionary/MED32802/track?counter=1&search_id=1138482

[157] As cited in Caroline Walker Bynum, *Holy Feast and Holy Fast: The Religious Significance of Food to Medieval Women* (Berkeley: University of California Press, 1988), 36.

[158] Holthausen, ed., *Vices and Virtues*, 136.

disagreeable kind. For the purposes of this study, the nature of that diet is meaningful. Barley bread or rye bread, as is typically stipulated in the legal record for prison forte et dure, was the staple foodstuff of the peasantry. Barley, oats, and rye, in the forms of bread, gruel, and ale, were the basis of an English peasant's diet. The wealthy in medieval England ate white bread – they reserved rye bread for their trenchers.[159] Rye also has its uses in forming a compliant prisoner: the medical treatises claim it produces "weak blood" and provides little energy.[160] The absence of meat in a fast was only partly to do with self-sacrifice. Meat was associated with *luxuria* (lust), a perhaps too-literal interpretation of the "sins of the flesh." *Luxuria* was most closely associated with the wealthy. So, too, was meat. Access to meat in the medieval world was an expression of power and wealth. Hence, the starvation diet was not simply about starving an obstinate defendant into submission: it was also about disparagement, indignity, and disengagement with the material world.

Sermons also include multiple references to the bread or loaf of penance, seeing bread as the gateway to the penitential process. One sermon explains that "þis breed of penaunce, to him þat etiþ it willfully and gladly, doþe many goodis" (this bread of penance, to him that willfully and gladly eats it, it has many benefits). In particular, "it getiþ of god forȝyuenes of synnis" (it gets from God forgiveness of sins), as Peter demonstrates in the Deeds of the Apostles, when he says: "Doþe penaunce, and beeþ conuertid, þat ȝoure synnis be done awey" (Do penance and be converted, so that your sins will be [washed] away). Also, through penance "a soule is recounsilid to his heuenly spouse" (a soul is reconciled to his heavenly spouse [God]), as we learn from the prophet Jeremy, to whom God said "Þou, forsoþe, hast done fornicasion wiþ many louers; neþeles, turne aȝeyn and I shal receyue þee" (You, forsooth, have done fornication with many lovers; nevertheless, turn again and I shall receive thee). Finally, by eating the bread of penance, we "geten þe kyngdome of heuen" (get the kingdom of heaven), as Christ said to John the Baptist, "Doþe

---

[159] Melitta Weiss Adamson, *Food in Medieval Times* (Westport: Greenwood Press, 2004), 4. White bread was integrally associated with the host. Jacob Baum, "Sensory Perception, Religious Ritual and Reformation in Germany, 1428–1564," (PhD Diss., University of Illinois at Urbana-Champaign, 2013), 45.
[160] Adamson, *Food in Medieval Times*, 3.

penaunce; þe kingdome of heuen shal ny3e" (Do penance; the kingdom of heaven shall be nigh).[161]

Death by cold as a sentence can also be dissected for meaning. Temperature was evocative in both law and medicine. In humoral theory, a hot-blooded individual is choleric: angry, excitable, and impetuous. In law, a crime committed in hot blood was an irrational crime, the body's rise in temperature drives out reason and clouds the mind. As Thomas Aquinas remarked, "the passion of anger forestalls the perfect judgment of reason" because of "the commotion of the heat urging to instant action."[162] While common law of the early modern age was willing to forgive anger as a natural human reaction to provocation, the medieval world was more likely to take seriously the place of wrath among the seven deadly sins.[163] Jurors might find it in their hearts to excuse a spontaneous fistfight in an alehouse that unexpectedly turned deadly. The wrong kind of anger, though – long-held hatreds, vitriolic disputes simmering just below the surface, anger as the habit of a spiteful personality – led to condemnation. The simple whiff of anger ruined one's chances of obtaining a pardon.[164] The English monk Robert Mannyng's fourteenth-century penitential manual encapsulates best the medieval approach. He describes anger as "Þe deuyls doghter of helle fyre" (the devil's daughter of hell fire).[165]

Cold is the obvious antidote for hot blood. The medieval physician prescribed foods with cold properties to bring balance to the body's humors. Water to quench anger's fires. Both oats and barley were particularly effective in this respect. As a coarse food, physicians routinely prescribed oats to "coarse people" (that is, the lower ranks). It was said to have a "cooling and constipating effect on the body."[166] Barley bread, because it produces wind in the body, was especially cooling in its impact, and accordingly was thought to be the

[161] Cigman, ed., *Lollard Sermons*, 187.
[162] Aquinas, *Summa Theologica*, I–II, q. 48, art. 3; discussed in Elizabeth Papp Kamali, "The Devil's Daughter of Hell Fire: Anger's Role in Medieval English Felony Cases," *L&HR* 35.1 (2017): 175.
[163] Krista Kesselring, "No Greater Provocation? Adultery and the Mitigation of Murder in English Law," *L&HR* 34.1 (2016): 199–225.
[164] Kamali, "Devil's Daughter of Hell Fire," 171.
[165] Mannyng, *Handlyng Synne*, 94, line 3706; as discussed in Kamali, "Devil's Daughter of Hell Fire," 170.
[166] Adamson, *Food in Medieval Times*, 4.

ideal medicine for fever.[167] Thus, as a coercive measure, the penitent's diet in prison should have helped to cool tempers, uncloud the mind, and bring one closer to God.

Stripping the accused of his clothing is also a powerful way to strip him of his identity. As the creation of clothing laws imply, attire in the medieval context had meaning. Medieval sumptuary laws hoped to make one's rank immediately discernable through one's dress. Fur was reserved to those with an annual income of forty shillings or greater; only esquires or gentlemen were permitted to wear cracows, the shoes with points or spikes exceeding two inches in length that were all the rage in the fourteenth century.[168] Sumptuary laws reinforced the subtle distinctions in the visibility of class, preventing a wealthy merchant from being mistaken for a gentleman of noble birth. The nakedness of prison forte et dure thus acted as a class leveler: one's rank had no meaning, no influence in the prison cell.

The prisoner was not only naked; he was also barefoot and bareheaded.[169] This language brings to mind images of the penitent: Emperor Henry IV (d. 1106) at the gates of Canossa in January of 1077, kept waiting for three weary days in the snow wearing only a woolen robe, his head and feet bare. King Henry II in July of 1174, walking barefoot and bareheaded to Canterbury, where he was whipped at Becket's tomb by the monks. The penitential implications of the bare head and feet cannot be dismissed. The cold, starving prisoner was stripped of identity – we are all peasants in prison; humility was the order of the day, presumably in reaction to the pride that kept the mute defendant from complying with the expectations of the law. And hopefully, soon, cooler minds would prevail.

The meaning of weight as a punishment is not as easy to interpret. *Exempla*, the sermon stories that Joan Young Gregg has described as the mass media of the Middle Ages, offer a number of indications of the links between weight and sin. This would seem to be the message inherent in the *exemplum* of a pious lay brother, who, on his deathbed, declared that the "world was like a stone pressing on his

---

[167] Adamson, *Food in Medieval Times*, 4.
[168] A Statute Concerning Diet and Apparel, 37 Edw. III (1363), SR, vol. I, 378–83.
[169] Francis Nichols, ed., *Britton: An English Translation and Notes*, 2 vols. (Washington, DC: John Byrne and Co., 1901), vol. I, 26–7.

chest."[170] Iron weights were sometimes assigned as penance. Caesarius of Heisterbach speaks of two lovers who strive to make amends and put their sinful lives behind them. They both join religious orders and wear rings of iron around their waists as penance. Upon his death, the man's ring is removed; the woman's bursts of its own accord while lost in fervent prayer.[171] Caesarius also remarks on a devout nun named Clementina. In the hopes of atoning for a past sin, she secretly donned nine bands of iron that she wore around her waist for the remainder of her life. Only in death did her sisters discover her earnest penance.[172] The twelfth-century miracle collection of the monastery of Ste-Énimie in southern France also includes an instructive story. Intent on reforming his sinful ways, a man embarked on a "grand tour" of pilgrimage shrines, including not just the usual sites such as Jerusalem and Bethlehem, but hoping to journey as far afield as India. He bound "penitential iron bands" around his arms prior to departing on pilgrimage in the "expectation that the breaking of his bonds would signify that his sins had been forgiven."[173] The discovery of a body with an iron band around its stomach in an archaeological excavation at Llandough monastery in Wales hints that real devotees may also have pursued this penitential model.[174]

The overall conclusion must be that peine forte et dure – *penitentia* – was penitential in design. As such, it was the ideal penance for those in need of humbling, especially for men who overreached their station and the hot-blooded. As we saw in Chapter 2, those who stood mute were regularly described as disobedient and contemptuous of authority – surely justices saw them in need of a little chastening. This image was reinforced in contemporary hagiography. In the life of Saint Thomas Becket (d.1170), included in the *Early South English Legendary*, the narrator has Henry II cast Thomas into prison "in strongue warde . . . In penaunce and in pine i-nou3, his sunnes for-to amende" (in strong ward

---

[170] Frederic Tubach, ed., *Index Exemplorum: A Handbook of Medieval Religious Tales* (Helsinki: Suomalainen Tiedeakatemia Akademia Scientiarum Fennica, 1969), 351, no. 4631.

[171] Tubach, ed., *Index Exemplorum*, 217, no. 2760.

[172] Tubach, ed., *Index Exemplorum*, 284, no. 3672.

[173] Marcus Bull, "Pilgrimage," in John Arnold, ed., *The Oxford Handbook of Medieval Christianity* (Oxford University Press, 2014), 203.

[174] Christopher Daniell, *Death and Burial in Medieval England, 1066–1550* (New York: Routledge, 1996), 174.

in penance and in pain enough, to amend for his sins). In doing so, Thomas was being treated "as a lewd [lay] man."[175] Henry may have hoped to put Thomas in his place through hard prison, but the reader knew better. This viewpoint does not undermine the notion of peine forte et dure as a coercive device intended to induce a reluctant defendant to plead. If the defendant was going to return to court for trial, he or she needed first to embark on the penitential process in order to exhibit a credible willingness to reform.

Towards the end of the medieval period, a final harrowing ritual, intended to emphasize the penitential nature of the peine, joined the repertoire of deprivations. In 1474, justices at a Newgate jail delivery remanded an uncooperative accused felon to prison with the following sentence:

That the defendant be put in a room, and there defendant would be bare without any bedding or shirt or any other clothes or things, but only on the bare ground, and that he will be naked lying on his bare back without any other clothing around him except something to cover his member, and that his head be covered and the feet covered, and that one arm be pulled toward one corner of the room with a rope and the other arm toward another corner, and that the one foot be pulled toward one corner and the other foot toward the other corner, and that on the defendant's body be put a piece of iron as heavy as he can suffer, and borne on him, and more, and the first day afterward the defendant will have three morsels of bread made of barley without any drink, and the second he will drink three times as much as he can of water that is nearest the prison door, not running water, without any bread, and this will be his diet until he be dead.[176]

With this directive, the defendant's body is transformed into a living representation of the True Cross, the ultimate form of *imitatio Christi* (imitation of Christ).

Peine forte et dure and Torture

Seeing peine forte et dure as a form of penitential justice helps us to dismiss the view of peine forte et dure as an example of "lingering

---

[175] *St. Thomas Becket* (Laud) 432 in Carl Horstmann, ed., *Early South-English Legendary* (EETS, vol. LXXXIX, 1887), 119.

[176] YB Trin. 1474, fo. 8a (Seipp 1474.026). This is almost identical to the language employed in Edward Coke, *Institutes of the Lawes of England*, 4 vols. (London: E. and R. Brooke, 1797), vol. II, 178.

medieval barbarism." Next, we turn to another misconception: peine forte et dure as a form of judicial torture. While the English were content to appropriate some of the church's legal trappings, they stopped short of torture. The English were vocal opponents of the practice as it was employed on both the Continent and in the church. English justices took great pride in their ability to prosecute felons without needing recourse to torture. One might even argue that this attribute was an integral part of medieval English identity. Larissa Tracy maintains that the English overcame the challenge of their mixed linguistic and cultural heritage by fashioning an English identity defined in opposition to French torture, such that the denunciation of the practice had a "special iconic importance in English law."[177] Abstention from the practice permitted the English to proclaim loudly their moral and legal superiority over the French and other Continental nations. The strength of their position is evidenced in Edward II's repeated refusal to sanction the use of judicial torture on English soil in the interrogation of England's Templars in 1309.[178] The fifteenth-century Lord Chief Justice of England and Wales, John Fortescue (d.1479), also the author of a well-known legal treatise, articulated the quintessentially English response to torture when he described it as "A Practice so inhuman, [it] deserves not indeed to be called a Law, but the high Road to Hell."[179] Sir Thomas Smith (d.1577), Elizabeth's Secretary of State, wrote the following statement in his *De Republica Anglorum* (published in 1583):

Torment or question, which is used by the order of the civill lawe and custome of other countries, to put a malefactor to excessive paine, to make him confesse of him selfe, or of his fellowes or complices, is not used in England, it is taken for servile ... The nature of our nation is free, stout, haulte, prodigall of life and blood: but contumelie, beatings, servitude, and servile torment and punishment it will not abide.[180]

---

[177] Larissa Tracy, *Torture and Brutality in Medieval Literature: Negotiations of National Identities* (Woodbridge: Boydell, 2012), Chapter 4.

[178] Ultimately, constant pressure applied by papal authorities saw the king capitulate and issue his reluctant approval; yet most torture took place only after the Templars had been transported to the county of Ponthieu.

[179] John Fortescue, *De Laudibus Legum Angliae*, ed. Stanley Chrimes, 2nd edn. (Cambridge University Press, 2011), 69.

[180] Thomas Smith, *De Republica Anglorum*, ed. Leonard Alston (Cambridge University Press, 1906), 105.

Such passionate denunciations lead us to recognize that in no way did these individuals equate peine forte et dure with torture, as modern-day commentators are wont to do.[181]

The peine's existence independent of the regular legal process may be the explanation. Judicial torture had a formal place in the *ius commune* as a normal part of the legal process. Much like peine forte et dure, judicial torture was also a coercive device, implemented as a means of fact-finding, admittedly only in certain prescribed circumstances, that is, when the evidence was sufficiently damning to warrant such intrusive methods. Entire treatises were dedicated to the subject of when and how to employ torture appropriately as well as what safeguards needed to be put in place to protect the integrity of the process. The English use of peine forte et dure was different. Only one statute acknowledged its existence, and jurists were seemingly reluctant to discuss the matter in all but the barest detail. In part, this is because the practice existed outside the legal process. The trial proper began only once the defendant agreed to plead, not before. Nor was the peine used as a means of fact-finding. One might comfortably argue then that it was not a problem for England's jurists, but instead a matter best left to the jailers. Additionally, peine forte et dure was a relatively rare experience, at a rate of four to five individuals per year across the kingdom. The practice's extra-legal nature, coupled with its infrequency, might have granted Fortescue and other English jurists plausible deniability; or at the very least, these factors made it easier for them to maintain their ethical high ground by turning a blind eye.

Perhaps what is most striking is that there are no French or Continental authorities, tired of England's frank insistence upon their superior moral fiber, writing about the hypocrisy of England's anti-torture, pro-peine stance. That no one did is telling. It suggests that medieval jurists and writers generally understood hard prison and torture to be two distinct entities, rather than categorizing them together as historians glibly do. Heikki Pihlajamäki's study of hard prison in the Swedish context here provides a useful guide to how we

---

[181] See Theodore Plucknett, *Concise History of the Common law*, 2nd edn. (London: Butterworths, 1936), 119; Barbara Hanawalt, *Crime and Conflict in English Communities, 1300-1348* (Cambridge, MA: Harvard University Press, 1979), 451; James Masschaele, *Jury, State, and Society in Medieval England* (New York: Palgrave Macmillan, 2008), 82.

might think about answering the larger question. Premodern Sweden shared a comparable distaste for judicial torture, and yet also resorted to hard prison as a coercive measure when the circumstances warranted it, although their version of hard prison was more drastic than what existed in the English setting. Swedish jailers chained suspects to the wall and whipped them. They justified the practice by imposing it chiefly on individuals who represented a danger to the kingdom. In this respect, Swedish hard prison more closely resembled Continental approaches to torture: it was applied as a coercive measure in the hope of extracting a confession. Yet, legal commentators in Sweden saw also no inconsistency in approving hard prison but disapproving of torture. Indeed, until the late eighteenth century, the law maintained a firm distinction between the two.

In seeking to understand the medieval perspective, Pihlajamäki asks: "Why was the concept of torture in the traditional thinking restricted only to certain gruesome legal questioning practices while at the same time permitting other forms of harsh treatment defined as hard prison?" Insightfully, he notes that this is effectively an unanswerable question because it is one that "only a modern person would ask."[182] Medieval authorities recognized a firm line between hard prison and torture, and as Pihlajamäki explains: "[w]here exactly the line ... was drawn is ... not the point; the point is that the line was continuously drawn in legal practice."[183] To a modern audience, hard prison bears an uncanny resemblance to torture; not so to a medieval audience, and pursuing such anachronistic thinking produces an ethical turmoil that simply did not exist for contemporary jurists.

Penitential Justice and Other Peculiarities of the Law

Refocusing the lens on the penitential side of medieval justice not only helps us to better understand the place of peine forte et dure in the medieval legal system, it also illuminates and indeed vindicates some of medieval England's other legal curiosities. In the process, it helps to cement our impression that penitential justice is the superior narrative

---

[182] Heikki Pihlajamäki, "The Painful Question: The Fate of Judicial Torture in Early Modern Sweden," *L&HR* 25.3 (2007): 582.
[183] Pihlajamäki, "Painful Question," 576.

that draws together the various strands of medieval judicial practice to make a coherent picture. To offer some examples:

(1) Mutilation

Like peine forte et dure, mutilation as a punishment for felony in the form of blinding, castration, and amputation has long been chalked up as evidence of the system's cruelty and barbarity. Instead, the Old English *Consolation of Philosophy* (late ninth or early tenth century) makes a strong case for arguing that mutilation springs from compassion. Not only is it a much milder penalty than death, a factor often overlooked by historians, but corporal punishment as it is depicted in the *Consolation* performs "a sort of spiritual cleansing that purges an offender of his sins and allows his soul to be saved."[184] The author writes: "Just as a sick person needs to be brought to the doctor so that he can take care of him, so a person who commits evil needs to be brought to the judge so that his wrongs can be cut out and burnt."[185] In point of fact, mutilation came into the law precisely because the Crown feared for the souls of its subjects. Cnut's laws evince concern that execution might lead to damnation. Thus, in the case of a backsliding thief, II Cnut 30 (1020–3) recommends blinding, amputation of the nose, ears, and upper lip, or scalping, "whichever of these they may decide who must make the judgement; thus one can punish and also save the soul."[186] The Angevin monarchs were equally keen on mutilation. Henry I (d.1135) is best known for commanding all the minters in England castrated and deprived of their right hands for debasing the currency.[187] Early thirteenth-century royal justices regularly imposed blinding and castration as punishment for convicted criminals.[188] While mutilation in

---

[184] Nicole Marafioti, "Earthly Justice and Spiritual Consequences: Judging and Punishing in the Old English *Consolation of Philosophy*," in Jay Paul Gates and Nicole Marafioti, eds., *Capital and Corporal Punishment in Anglo-Saxon England*, (Woodbridge: Boydell, 2014), 117.

[185] As cited in Marafioti, "Earthly Justice," 117.

[186] As cited in Katherine O'Brien O'Keefe, "Body and Law in Late Anglo-Saxon England," *Anglo-Saxon England* 27 (1998): 217.

[187] C. Warren Hollister, "Royal Acts of Mutilation: The Case against Henry I," *Albion* 10.4 (1978): 330–40.

[188] Klaus Van Eickels, "Gendered Violence: Castration and Blinding as Punishment for Treason in Normandy and Anglo-Norman England," *Gender and History* 16.3 (2004): 595.

the form of amputation seems to have gone out of style by the late Middle Ages, it reappeared in the form of branding, brought in during the fourteenth and fifteenth centuries to address infractions of the labor laws as well as multiple assertions of benefit of clergy.[189]

Late medieval churchmen also supported mutilation. Thomas Aquinas, for example, favored dismemberment, explaining it as "a wise application of judicial power."[190] A castrated rapist is incapable of reoffending; so, too, is a pickpocket whose hand has been amputated. Branding meant a convicted criminal wore evidence of his crime on his body for all to see, eliminating any need for paperwork. When it comes to spiritual regeneration, mutilation relies on the unity of body and soul. Blinding, castration, and branding act not only as a permanent reminder of one's sinful past for both penitent and the Christian community, it compels the body to follow the soul into reformation. Maiming "forever after forces the body to confess its guilt as part of the process of salvation."[191]

(2) Imprisonment until Trial

Imprisonment while awaiting trial was a key part of the penitential process, not just for those who stood mute, but for all suspected felons. Even before the church prohibited the ordeal, God's role as judge required the defendant to begin the penitential process while in prison, to signal one's intention for reform in the hopes of persuading God to take mercy on one's soul. Guy Geltner has argued that the medieval mind viewed prison as "a place of penance," an "earthly purgatory" in which one's bodily suffering and mental anguish purified the soul and better prepared a defendant for judgment.[192] The parallels between prison and purgatory are no coincidence; rather, they grew out of a central ideal of Christian spiritual reform and developed in parallel. Medieval Christians considered purgatory an indispensable part of the ascent to heaven;

---

[189] John Bellamy, *Crime and Public Order in England in the Later Middle Ages* (University of Toronto Press, 1973), 112.

[190] Charles Nemeth, *Aquinas on Crime* (South Bend, IN: St Augustine's Press, 2008), 141.

[191] O'Keefe, "Body and Law," 217.

[192] Guy Geltner, "Medieval Prisons: Between Myth and Reality, Hell and Purgatory," *History Compass* 4.2 (2006): 265.

only the saints are able to omit this step in the process. In doing so, an essentially good Christian endures horrifying physical torment but with laudable aims: to cleanse one's soul before meeting one's maker. The pain endured there is wholly beneficial. All those whom God selected for purgatory were assured eventual salvation. Purgatory was not a test one might fail.

The close links between prison and purgatory meant that "imprisonment had a positive spiritual value in medieval culture."[193] In hagiography, imprisonment was often represented as the form of meritorious suffering that transformed an individual into a martyr for God.[194] Saint Paul, for example, saw his time in prison as "'training' to gain salvation."[195] Saint Peter's miraculous liberation from imprisonment was celebrated with a feast (Saint Peter in Chains) and there are numerous churches named for this experience across Europe and North America. Alongside myriad European pilgrims, the English journeyed to the Middle East on a regular basis to visit Christ's prison at the Holy Sepulcher.[196] With such eminent prisoners, jails were rarely presented in a negative light in Christian narrative. Saints' lives and sermon stories depict it as a site of revelation and miracle, where "Christ appears, where angels visit, where rays of light suddenly break through stone walls."[197] Christians across the West celebrated numerous saints, like saints Ninian of Whithorn, Leonard of Noblac, and Martin of Tours, for their penchant for liberating prisoners from chains.[198] All of these ideas imbued medieval attitudes towards prison. Medieval men and women were encouraged to see time in prison as a spiritual investment: "prison exchanged future for present suffering: if 'to live in that place taste[s] to you of death,' then 'the death that you suffer there [will] grant you eternal life.'"[199] The influence went both

---

[193] Anthony Bale, "God's Cell: Christ as Prisoner and Pilgrimage to the Prison of Christ," *Speculum* 91.1 (2016): 4.

[194] Megan Cassidy-Welch, *Imprisonment in the Medieval Religious Imagination, c. 1150–1400* (New York: Palgrave Macmillan, 2011), 37.

[195] Julia Hillner, *Prison, Punishment and Penance in Late Antiquity* (Cambridge University Press, 2015), 263.

[196] Bale, "God's Cell," 4.   [197] Cassidy-Welch, *Imprisonment*, 38.

[198] Michael Penman, "'Sacred Food for the Soul': In Search of the Devotions to Saints of Robert Bruce, King of Scotland, 1306–1329," *Speculum* 88.4 (2013): 1036; Cassidy-Welch, *Imprisonment*, 37–8.

[199] Ames, "Does Inquisition Belong to Religious History?," 21.

ways: the more purgatorial prison became, the more carceral purgatory appeared in both artwork and sermon stories.[200] For those awaiting trial, prison offered the kind of penitential experience to provide a jury of Christians a sense that a repentant sinner was on the path to reform.

(3) Acquittal Rates

What Foucault has missed in his vision of law and punishment in the service of state-building is that royal displays of cruelty are less effective in a Christian setting than displays of mercy. This is made abundantly clear by medieval England's high acquittal rates for felony. Some examples: James Given's research into homicide in thirteenth-century England uncovered an acquittal rate of 82.6 percent.[201] Thomas Green's study of the fourteenth-century trial jury produced a relatively consistent rate of 85 percent for homicide.[202] Barbara Hanawalt's analysis of English communities 1300–48 falls in line with 77.6 percent for larceny and 87.6 percent for homicide.[203] Finally, Edward Powell's figures for felony acquittal in the Midland circuit, 1400–29, came in slightly lower, at seventy percent.[204] When employed as a barometer of the efficiency of medieval England's criminal justice system, these figures would seem to be an embarrassing indictment of royal law enforcement.

Historians of the law have produced a number of astute explanations for such high rates. The legislated punishments for felony were out of step with popular perception: where common law called for execution, medieval juries were content to see the defendant harassed and inconvenienced by indictment and detention pending

---

[200] Andrew Skotnicki, "God's Prisoners: Penal Confinement and the Creation of Purgatory," *Modern Theology* 22.1 (2006): 85–110.

[201] James Given, *Society and Homicide in Thirteenth Century England* (Stanford University Press, 1977), 133.

[202] Thomas Green, *Verdict According to Conscience: Perspective on the English Criminal Trial Jury, 1200–1800* (University of Chicago Press, 1985), 22.

[203] Hanawalt, *Crime and Conflict*, 59.

[204] Edward Powell, "Jury Trial at Gaol Delivery in the Late Middle Ages: the Midland Circuit, 1400–1429," in James Cockburn and Thomas Green, eds., *Twelve Good Men and True: The Criminal Trial Jury in England, 1200–1800* (Princeton University Press, 1988), 100.

trial. The lack of gradations in punishment, in particular, encouraged leniency. Knowing that death was the inevitable consequence of a felony conviction, jurors uncomfortable with that sentence preferred acquittal. The disparity between law and popular conceptions of justice is most apparent in pardons for self-defense. Common law imposed stringent requirements permitting self-defense only after flight, cornering, and the surprise discovery of a weapon lying about that "just happened to hit vital spots"; however, juries considered such cowardly and unmanly behavior unnecessary in order to exonerate the accused on grounds of self-defense.[205] High rates of flight (72 percent) are also pertinent: it is entirely possible that those individuals who chose not to flee, but to stay and stand trial, did so because they were innocent.[206] Finally, given the speedy process of investigation, jurors may well have felt the evidence was insufficient, and as a result were more "convinced of their own ignorance . . . than the suspects' innocence."[207]

Through a penitential lens, high rates of acquittal are not a sign of failure but of resounding success. Granted, this conclusion requires acknowledging that acquittals in medieval England did not represent only findings of innocence; rather, they represented contrite defendants prepared to reconcile themselves to God and the community. The king and his representatives thus modeled themselves on Christ's willingness to show mercy to those He had condemned. Inevitably, in an ultra-Christian society, public displays of mercy are a more powerful tool of state-building than terror because these acts paralleled more closely those of Christ the King. Even pardons take on a new life when examined in a penitential light. Where pardons were once disparaged as evidence of corruption or a "defect in law," money-making tools that simply release criminals back into the general population to reoffend, when recast as Christian mercy granted by

---

[205] Naomi Hurnard, *The King's Pardon for Homicide Before* AD *1307* (Oxford: Clarendon Press, 1969), 267.

[206] Bernard McLane, "Juror Attitudes toward Local Disorder: The Evidence of the 1328 Lincolnshire Trailbaston Proceedings," in James Cockburn and Thomas Green, eds., *Twelve Good Men and True: The Criminal Trial Jury in England, 1200–1800* (Princeton University Press, 1988), 56.

[207] Ralph Pugh, "The Duration of Criminal Trials in Medieval England," in Eric Ives and Anthony Manchester, eds., *Law, Litigants and the Legal Profession* (London: RHS, 1983), 110.

God's earthly steward, the pardoned are merely rueful Christians enjoying God's grace.[208] This is reflected also in the language of pardons: the documents themselves are replete with "Christian notions of forgiveness."[209]

(4) Execution

Even the execution ritual belonged within the realm of penitential justice. The execution was the last public step in an unfolding penitential drama in which the crowd appeared as witnesses to the felon's desire for forgiveness and reform. It is worth remembering that medieval execution was not painless: hanging was not accomplished by a quick drop, but by the slow raising up of the body and eventual strangulation. In this fashion, a convict was not only aware of dying; it was painful, if short-lived. While judicial sentence had no impact on the state of the felon's soul, the manner in which a person died did much to reunite communities torn by sin. This pain, both visible and audible, was a critical part of the process, by opening "the possibility for the condemned to be transfigured in the eyes of the spectators into a holy vessel whose suffering signaled his entry into heaven and his reconciliation with his community."[210] The felon's body, twisting at the end of the rope, was a visual metaphor for Christ's execution on the cross with a thief on each side. Medieval audiences were "taught to see execution victims as suffering Christs and to weep for them, like Mary."[211] That audiences viewed hanged felons almost as martyrs is emphasized by the afterlives of their corpses: medieval men and women traded in the body parts of the executed as relics for medicinal purposes.[212]

---

[208] Helen Lacey, *The Royal Pardon: Access to Mercy in Fourteenth-Century England* (York Medieval Press, 2009), 3. The act of pardoning itself was a form of alms. See Thomas McSweeney, "The King's Courts and the King's Soul: Pardoning as Almsgiving in Medieval England," *Reading Medieval Studies* 40 (2014): 159–75.

[209] Lacey, *Royal Pardon*, 35.

[210] Trisha Olson, "Medieval Blood Sanction and the Divine Beneficence of Pain: 1100–1450," *Journal of Law and Religion* 22.1 (2006–7): 66.

[211] David J. Eshelman, "'Great mowrning and mone': Modeled Spectatorship in the Towneley Scourging," *Baylor Journal of Theatre and Performance* 2.1 (2005): 24.

[212] Byrne, *Justice and Mercy*, 193.

Conclusion

The penitential process is a mighty weapon in the hands of a Christian. As Isidore of Seville purportedly exclaimed: "O penaunce, that art more precyus than golde! Deth es destroyed be the, the deuil es fled, lyf es founde, god es nere by grace, helle es schette, heuen es opyn" (Oh penance, that is more precious than gold! Death is destroyed by you, the devil is chased away, life is found, God's grace is nearby, Hell is shut, Heaven is open.). And to Augustine of Hippo: "Penaunce geteȝ life to the ded man and delyuerez fro deth at the laste ende" (Penance gives life to the dead man and delivers [him] from death at the last end).[213] When Isidore and Augustine spoke of "life" they refer not to the life of the body, but that of the soul, because as they recognized, the soul is what really matters. Medieval kings also understood this. Criminal justice, then, punished the body: but the ultimate goal was always to correct the soul.

Historians who have labeled peine forte et dure a medieval barbarity or a form of torture have not only misunderstood the peine's place in the legal system, they have failed to recognize the overarching religiosity of medieval justice. The legal revolution of the long twelfth century does not represent a secularization of the common law; nor does the abandonment of the ordeal imply that God was ousted from the courtroom. While we today feel comfortable in distinguishing clearly between sin and crime, penance and punishment, that is because we live in a world committed to a church–state divide. Just because the medieval world also had church courts does not mean that Christianity was restricted to that venue: Christian values infiltrated every aspect of medieval society, and every court of law.

Christianity, especially in the medieval context, was taught and practiced as a collective faith in which salvation was a communal effort. For those whose immoral behavior saw them ousted from the community, the objective was reconciliation, not execution, or even Hell. A religion of second chances, Christianity willingly endures a plenitude of sinful acts before a sinner finds himself permanently excluded. Peine forte et dure must be understood within this context. It was not a barbarity marring the progress of England's march towards modernity; rather, it was a path to salvation.

---

[213] Gustaf Holmstedt, ed., *Speculum Christiani: A Middle English Religious Treatise of the Fourteenth Century* (EETS, vol. CLXXXII, 1933), 104.

5

Why Stand Mute?

But notwithstanding these terrors, some hardy delinquents, conscious of their guilt, and yet touched with a tender regard for their children, have rather chosen to submit to this painful death, than the easier judgment upon conviction, which might expose their offspring not only to present want, but to future incapacities of inheritance.

Blackstone, *Commentaries*[1]

When Margaret Clitheroe refused to plead at her arraignment, she accepted that her silence would land her in prison subject to peine forte et dure and probably also lead to her death. She deliberately chose that path, in part, out of a maternal instinct to protect her children, who otherwise would have been put in the morally compromising position of testifying about their mother's activities before Crown authorities. As her martyrdom and her eventual canonization (in 1970) attest, commentators have interpreted her self-sacrificing behavior as heroic. Margaret's experience of peine forte et dure was not typical, but others like her who elected to undergo pressing rather than plead have also regularly been labeled as heroes and martyrs, although most have been credited with exhibiting paternal rather than maternal concerns.[2] Blackstone (d. 1780) in his *Commentaries* explains

---

[1] *Blackstone*, vol. IV, ch. 25.
[2] This tradition continued well into the twentieth century. Plucknett also described peine forte et dure as heroic. He wrote, "[f]elons whose guilt was obvious sometimes

that "some hardy delinquents" who reject jury trial do so "with a tender regard for their children."[3] Because of his refusal to stand trial, the court could not find the defendant guilty; thus, his lands and goods were exempt from felony forfeiture, the burdensome financial penalty that awaited convicted felons and their families.

William Blackstone blamed felony forfeiture for giving birth to peine forte et dure. Desperate lords eager to collect their escheats, he believed, acted as the motivating force behind the court's desire to force a plea.[4] As a punishment, felony forfeiture has a long and oppressive history in England. Springing from the concept that a breach of the king's peace required payment of compensation to the king (not just the victim), felons lost their chattels permanently to the Crown, and lands for a year and a day before they passed into the hands of their feudal lords.[5] The impact of felony forfeiture, in many ways, was dreaded even more than execution, as the family of the dead was left not only without a father, but also destitute. Medieval law deemed a felon's bloodline corrupted: a convicted felon had no heirs. Treason remained the only exception to the rule. The heinousness of the crime meant that the king confiscated permanently both a traitor's goods and lands. Felony forfeiture remained on the books until it was abolished by statute in 1870; however, criticism of this miserly practice that seemed to rub salt into the wounds of a family already smarting from the antisocial behavior of one of its members was persistent. In the Middle Ages, jurors' sympathies with the family of the accused meant that lands and chattels were often intentionally underappreciated. Most felons were said to own nothing, apparently not even the clothes on their backs or the shoes on their feet. Even more curious, the king's justices were generally content not to challenge jurors' improbable appraisals. Of course, this does not mean that felony forfeiture was a dead letter: far from it. Jurors were not willing to take on the risk of a procedural amercement for all felons; and in some

---

heroically chose to die in this manner rather than plead, be convicted and hanged, for a prisoner who died under *peine forte et dure* had never been tried and never convicted, and consequently his goods and chattels could not be forfeited to the crown" (italics are my own). Theodore Plucknett, *Concise History* (1956; repr. Union: The Lawbook Exchange, 2001), 119.

[3] *Blackstone*, vol. IV, ch. 25.   [4] *Blackstone*, vol. IV, ch. 25.

[5] Krista Kesselring, "Felony Forfeiture in England, *c.* 1170–1870," *Journal of Legal History* 30.3 (2009): 203.

cases, it was simply not feasible to claim a defendant owned nothing when appearance and reputation indicated just the opposite. Rather, over the course of the period medieval men and women became much more astute at safeguarding their property through entails and uses, so that one fateful mistake might not ruin the entire family.[6]

For the guilty defendant, execution may have seemed an unavoidable part of the immediate future, regardless of whether he or she pleaded; but for the defendant's children, a failure to plead meant a man might still provide financially for his children, as a good father should, and in doing so secure their futures. The concept of heroic paternalism has helped generations of scholars to make sense of peine forte et dure as a legal strategy: why else would anyone chose to endure such a horrific means of death when they had an alternative? Integral to this explanation is the firm assumption of the defendant's guilt. Knowing that death was in the cards, destiny was controlled by the defendant, who chose the method of execution: pressing over hanging. This argument has been so persuasive that John Langbein in his 1977 book refers to standing mute as a "special kind of guilty plea."[7] This argument resonates also with scholars of the Middle Ages. In the only medieval study of peine forte et dure, Henry Summerson observes that the records offer the distinct impression that "[t]hose who stood mute were frequently people arrested in circumstances in which standing trial would have meant certain conviction, killers caught literally red handed, thieves arrested in possession of stolen goods."[8] He concludes that their refusal to plead was the "product of desperation, a frantic attempt to defer execution."[9]

Understanding why a defendant chose to stand mute is pivotal to making sense of this practice. Chapter 3 argued that silence emerged in order to protest a legal system that increasingly alienated accused felons by eliminating or reducing the availability of time-honored

---

[6] The 1285 statute of *De Donis Conditionalibus* stipulated that land held in fee tail was exempt from felony forfeiture, except in the instance of treason. Statute *De Donis Conditionalibus*, Statute of Westminster II, c. 1 (1285), *SR*, vol. I, 71; Kesselring, "Felony Forfeiture," 206.
[7] John Langbein, *Torture and the Law of Proof: Europe and England in the Ancien Régime* (University of Chicago Press, 1977), 76.
[8] Henry Summerson, "The Early Development of the *Peine Forte et Dure*," in Eric Ives and Anthony Manchester, eds., *Law, Litigants, and the Legal Profession* (London: RHS, 1983), 124.
[9] Summerson, "Early Development," 124.

methods of legal defense. Yet, this explanation surely had an expiration date tied to the legal memory of the typical Englishman or woman. So why did defendants continue to stand mute? Two elements have dominated analyses of those who stand mute: (1) heroic paternalism, and (2) a presumption of guilt. This chapter will explore both factors, but also a number of other possible explanations for why medieval men (and sometimes women) refused to plead.

Safeguarding Property

Because the bloodline remained uncorrupted until a judge had passed sentence, a man who refused to plead defended his landed property from royal confiscation. The same did not apply to his chattels. English kings were keen to lay their hands on the goods of indicted felons, whether they were convicted or not. As a result, members of the clergy, abjurers of the realm, outlaws, unrepentant usurers, as well as general fugitives, even if they ultimately turned themselves in and were acquitted by a jury, typically all lost their chattels. Medieval common law endorsed a broad interpretation of moveables. An accused's chattels might include outstanding loans (now owed to the king), leases, chattels owned jointly with others, recognizances, obligations or simple contracts, monies due upon accounts, growing crops, sometimes even stolen goods.[10] Thus, the loss of chattels was not insubstantial. Neither statute law nor legal treatises clearly spell out the reason why the king maintained the right to confiscate chattels of those who stand mute, but it is not hard to imagine. For abjurers of the realm who had confessed their guilt, forfeiture of chattels functioned as punishment for breaking the king's peace. For fugitives and outlaws, even if they proved to be innocent of the crime, they still showed the king contempt by failing to heed his summons, thus forfeiture of chattels was a fitting punishment. One suspects that a similar argument can be made for those who stood mute "out of malice." In refusing the common law, they became outlaws; like outlaws, they, too, saw their chattels confiscated.

---

[10] Kesselring, "Felony Forfeiture," 208. When Adam of Peshale was beheaded for rebellion, felony forfeiture meant that his loans transferred to the king. Thus, the close rolls record John Sutton being asked to repay his debt of £170, originally owed to Adam, now to the king. See CCR, Edward III, vol. VIII (1346–9), 176.

When it comes to felony forfeiture, the king's approach to chattels in fact is not supported by the medieval legal treatises, which maintain that conviction is a necessary prerequisite for confiscation of a suspect's lands *and* goods. *Fleta* (c.1290–1300), for example, encapsulates this ideal as early as the thirteenth century, stating that "no one who is arrested shall be disseissed of his lands, tenements, or chattels until he has been convicted of the felony charged against him."[11] *Britton* (c.1291–2) makes a comparable statement.[12] The reason to hold off on confiscation until conviction was pragmatic: an accused felon sat in prison for up to six months while awaiting trial, and prison life was riddled with miscellaneous fees and surcharges. Among others, prisoners paid for their accommodations, including a bed, meals, and drinks, and candles for light. Common law permitted prisoners and their families, who sometimes relocated to prison with their spouses or parents until trial, to support themselves out of their own goods.[13] *Bracton* (c.1220s–60s) states emphatically that if a prisoner dies in jail before conviction, his lands remain to his heirs, his chattels to his kinsmen and friends, "even though it is obvious that [he] would have been convicted had [he] survived to judgment, in accordance with the statement that if a man dies in chains or under sureties while the outcome of his case is uncertain his goods are not to be confiscated, nor, though a man has been cast into prison is it necessary to despoil him of his goods; [that is proper] only after conviction."[14] Together, the passages drawn from the legal treatises build a strong case to argue that a man who dies unconvicted should lose neither his lands nor his chattels.

Nonetheless, royal justices formally aligned themselves with their employer. Regardless of what it says in the legal treatises, as far back as 1330, the year books declare that the chattels of a mute defendant were forfeit to the king.[15] Attempts to justify the king's prerogative, however, shine a light through the holes in the judiciary's united

---

[11] Henry Richardson and George Sayles, eds., *Fleta* (SS, vol. LXXII, 1955), 67.
[12] Francis Nichols, ed., *Britton: An English Translation and Notes*, 2 vols. (Washington, DC: John Byrne and Co., 1901), vol. I, 38.
[13] Nichols, ed., *Britton*, vol. I, 38.   [14] *Bracton*, vol. II, 346.
[15] *Catalla eius sunt forisfacta.* Donald Sutherland, ed., *The Eyre of Northamptonshire, 3–4 Edward III (1329–1330)*, 2 vols. (SS, vols. XCVII and XCVIII, 1983), vol. I, 166 (Seipp 1330–302ss).

front. In practice, it seems that justices were not entirely sure why those who suffered peine forte et dure forfeited their chattels; they just knew that they did. Their dissent comes through most clearly in a 1406 courtroom debate, in which a man appeals two others of robbery before justices of King's Bench. The appellees proceed to stand mute, inducing the marshal to assemble a panel of jurors from among his officers and others to testify whether they stood "mute out of malice to delay their death, or by act of God." When the inquest returns that malice was indeed the cause, the king's justices order the silent men to suffer penance until death, while the appellor is to regain possession of the stolen goods. The question then arises over what exactly should be done with the accused felons' goods once they are in the Crown's custody. A rumor that one of the bailiffs in the employ of the bishop of London had taken them into his possession leads justices to compose a hasty letter demanding their return. Later that same day, an imposing contingent of the bishop's bailiffs arrives in court, royal charter in hand, asserting that the accused felons' goods rightfully belong to the bishop. Throughout the Middle Ages, the Crown regularly granted franchises to select lords to collect the chattels of felons (among other privileges) within their own manors or liberties.[16] The careful wording of the charter, included in the year book, suggests that the bishop had thought long and hard about how to maximize his profits from the privilege. The charter stipulates that the bishop should have:

the chattels of felons and fugitives, etc., so that if any man ought to lose life or limb for any trespass or other derelict, or shall have fled or *been unwilling to stand to judgment*, or done any other trespass whereby he ought to lose his chattels, wherever justice ought to be done on them, whether in our court or that of our heirs or in other courts, the chattels shall be the bishop's and he may seize the same into his hands by his officers.

Turning their backs on the bailiffs momentarily, the king's justices and sergeants launch into a lengthy impromptu debate on the subject of mute felons and their chattels, airing a great diversity of legal opinions. At least one sergeant argues that their chattels are due to the king because without a trial, the appellees are not convicted felons. This fact excludes the bishop as supplicant because his grant entitles him

---

[16] Spike Gibbs, "Felony Forfeiture at the Manor of Worfield, c.1370–c.1600," *Journal of Legal History* 39.3 (2018): 254.

specifically to the "chattels of felons and fugitives." Moreover, it is the king's prerogative to claim the chattels of mute defendants; the bishop does not share in this prerogative, once again, nullifying the bishop's claim. Yet another explains that standing mute is disobedience to law. While not a felony, it is in fact a trespass, and peine forte et dure is its punishment; but no one loses life or limb for a trespass, therefore the wording of the bishop's charter again makes him ineligible. Their goods must be forfeit to the king. Taking another tack entirely, Chief Justice Gascoigne reminds them that all goods in England that belong to no one in reality belong to the king. And when an accused felon stands mute, in effect, he is refusing to have ownership of any goods, and thus his goods belong to the king under his own prerogative.[17] Sergeant William Skrene takes the final word, explaining to his listeners that in appeals of felony (as opposed to indictments at the king's suit), those who stand mute are in fact convicted of the crime, as if it is a case without a defense, and thus their goods are forfeit to the king. Regrettably, the year book does not disclose their final decision on the matter, so we cannot be certain whether Skrene's sound reasoning won the support of his peers.

With such stalwart defenders of the king's rights and revenues, it is no wonder the phrase "profits of justice" held such powerful meaning in medieval England. What this remarkable exchange reveals is a profound uncertainty about the appropriate process when it comes to a defendant's chattels. Thankfully, the position on a mute defendant's lands seems much clearer in the surviving evidence. Once again, there is no statute or statement in the legal treatises to guide historians on this matter; however, a complaint from an indignant bishop of London to the king in January of 1294 is edifying. He writes that royal officials had seized lands in Temesford, recently held of him by Nicholas of Cerne, after his death in Bedford prison, "as if Nicholas had been convicted of homicide," even though, having stood mute and been sentenced to peine forte et dure, he died unconvicted.[18] The bishop's outrage leaves us with the distinct impression that from an early stage, common law protected an

---

[17] Italics are my own. Alfred Kiralfy, ed., *Source Book of English Law* (London: Sweet and Maxwell Limited, 1957), 14–16 (Seipp, 1406.101).

[18] *CIPM*, vol. III, 126–44.

unconvicted felon's lands from escheat. The year books offer some corroboration of this inference, but from a much later date. A brief note from 1464 explains that a writ of escheat is not granted to a defendant's lord when he dies as a result of peine forte et dure because his lands are not in fact subject to escheat.[19] This sentiment is reconfirmed ten years later at an appellee's arraignment on felony charges at Newgate prison. When the defendant refused to plead, a debate erupted on the subject of whether he should be hanged or subjected to peine forte et dure. Justice Richard Choke quoted the Statute of Westminster in an urgent defense of peine forte et dure, which he declared "benefits [the defendant's] children, for if he is put to his penance he will only lose his goods, and his lands and tenements are saved for his heirs."[20]

Despite what appears to be a coherent policy on the matter, the evidence of the plea rolls indicates that royal officials implemented it at their own discretion. Indeed, coroners sometimes carried out an investigation into both the lands *and* chattels of the accused, insinuating that they were prepared to have both confiscated, thwarted only by the poverty of most defendants. Trial records of convicted felons usually conclude with a list of the felon's goods and properties forfeit to the king and their value. It is striking that at least twenty records of prisoners subjected to peine forte et dure conclude with the statement: "he has no lands or tenements, nor goods or chattels" (*nulla habet terras seu tenementas, bona seu catalla*). William Belle of Ashby (*de Askeby*) is one of the few assigned to the penance who actually owned lands to confiscate: the inventory of his escheated lands include three acres planted with barley and oats, worth thirteen shillings and three pence.[21] Why even mention lands or tenements if they were not due to the king? It is possible that officials investigated both types of property on the assumption that the defendant would eventually capitulate and plead. Yet, the fact that the value of William's property was crossed out in the margin, indicating that felony forfeiture of both kinds had already transpired, without also an update on his status, leaves the distinct impression that justices made their own decisions about what was appropriate.

---

[19] YB Pasch 1464, fos. 19a–19b (Seipp, 1464.040).
[20] Kiralfy, ed., *Source Book*, 16 (Seipp, 1474.019).
[21] TNA JUST 3/135, m. 14d (1343).

The court's inconsistency may spring from the reality that felony forfeiture was not a common occurrence. Of the 481 cases in our sample, only 68 (or 14 percent) resulted in forfeiture. Despite the small numbers, the profits to the Crown from felony forfeiture might be substantial. For example, when Simon le Conestable, lord of Halsham and Burton, was pressed to death in 1293, his indictment reports that he had goods and chattels worth £366 8s. 7d. in York and another nine marks in the same county; as well as £73 12s. 10d. in Lincolnshire; and £28 19s. 9d. in Nottinghamshire.[22] Presumably, Simon stood silent in order to preserve his vast landed estates. Indeed, the inquisition post-mortem into his lands, dated to March 1, 1294, corroborates that his lands passed intact to his twenty-nine-year-old son and nearest heir, Robert.[23] Other forfeitures of goods and chattels leave the distinct impression that silence prevented the king from obtaining lucrative profits from landed estates: William of Podymore, 111s. 3d; John of Fenny Shaw, 22s. 9d;[24] Robert, son of Benedict of Butterton on the Moors (*de Boterdone*), 52s. 3d;[25] Roger of Norden, 42s. 1d;[26] Thomas Grene of Aston, £10.[27] The surviving inventory of goods for Hugh le Bevere (or Benere), the London vintner accused of uxoricide who died in hard prison in 1336, also reveals an impressive array of goods, valued in total at £12 18s. 4d.[28] All of these men surely had good reason to stand

---

[22] TNA JUST 1/1098, m. 80d (1293).

[23] William Brown, ed., *Yorkshire Inquisitions* (York: Yorkshire Archaeological Society, 1898), 160–2.

[24] George Wrottesley, ed., *Staffordshire Historical Collections* (London: Harrison and Sons, 1886), vol. VII, pt. II, 162.

[25] Wrottesley, ed., *Staffordshire Historical Collections*, vol. VII, pt. II, 171. Later that same day, Robert agreed to be tried. He was convicted and hanged. The value of his land and tenements is not included in the account.

[26] TNA JUST 3/129, m. 56.   [27] TNA JUST 3/185, m. 59.

[28] Included in the inventory was: one mattress, value 4s.; six blankets and one serge, 13s. 6d.; one green carpet, 2s.; one torn coverlet, with shields of cendale, 4s.; one coat and one surcoat of *worstede*, 40d.; one robe of perset, furred, 20s.; one robe of medley, furred, one mark; one old fur, almost consumed by moths, 6d.; one robe of scarlet, furred, 16s.; one robe of perset, 7s.; one surcoat, with a hood of ray, 2s. 6d.; one coat, with a hood of perset, 18d.; one surcoat, and one coat of ray, 6s. 1d.; one green hood of cendale with edging, 6d.; seven linen sheets, 5s.; one table-cloth, 2s.; three table-cloths, 18d.; one camise and one *savenape*, 4d.; one canvas, 8d.; three feather-beds, 8s.; five cushions, 6d.; one haketone, 12d.; three brass pots, 12s.; one brass pot, 6s.; one pair of brass pots, 2s. 6d.; one brass pot, broken, 2s. 6d.; one candlestick of *latone*, and one plate, with one small brass plate, 2s.; two pieces of lead, 6d.; one

mute. So, too, did Ralph de Bloyou (or Bloyho), indicted of multiple felonies in 1302, who died in prison after ten days of suffering under peine forte et dure.[29] That his son and heir, Alan, went on to inherit his father's fees in Treuual, Polrode, and Donnant confirms that Ralph's death was not in vain.[30] Similarly, when his sister-in-law appealed him of viciously murdering his brother while he slept, Robert de Hastang also stood mute.[31] As first baron of Hastang, Robert had much to lose if he did speak.[32] In Robert's case, he made the right decision; while this study was not able to uncover evidence of a pardon, the fact that Robert reappears in the calendar of the patent rolls the following year suggests that for him, penance was not unto death.[33]

If anyone was going to stand mute to protect their children's inheritances, one would expect those accused of treason to do so. Convicted felons lost their chattels permanently and their lands escheated first to the king for a year, day, and waste, then to their lords; convicted traitors, however, lost both chattels and lands permanently. As such, there was no possibility for the ousted heir to renegotiate with his felonious father's lord for a renewed tenancy.

---

grate, 3d.; two *aundirons*, 18d.; two basins, with one washing-vessel, 5s.; one iron herce, 12d.; one tripod, 2d.; one iron headpiece, 12d.; one iron spit, 3d.; one frying-pan, 1d.; one *tonour*, 1d.; one small canvas bag, 1d.; seven *savenapes*, 5d.; one old linen sheet, 1d.; two pillows, 3d.; one cap, 1d.; one counter, 4s.; two coffers, 8d.; two curtains, 8d.; two remnants of cloth, 1d.; six chests, 10s. 10d.; one folding table, 12d.; two chairs, 8d.; one aumbrey, 6d.; two *anceres*, 2s. Also, firewood, sold for 3s.; one mazer cup, 6s.; six casks of wine, six marks, the value of each cask being one mark. Total, £12 18s. 4d. The same John [Fot, citizen and vintner of London] also received, of the goods of the said Hugh, from Richard de Pulham, one cup called *note* with a foot and cover of silver, value 30s.; six silver spoons, 6s. Also, of John Wytsand, one surcoat and one woman's coat, value 8s., which were pledged to the said Hugh by Paul le Botiller, for one mark. Total, 44s. Henry Riley, ed., *Memorials of London and London Life in the 13th, 14th and 15th Centuries* (London: Longmans, Green, 1868), 195–202.

[29] YB 1302 (Seipp, 1302.200rs); as it appears in Alfred Horwood, ed., *Year Books of the Reign of Edward the First: Years XXX and XXXI (1302–1303)* (RS, no. 31, pt. A, vol. III, 1863), 510–11.

[30] Thomas Taylor, "Blohin: His Descendants and Lands," *The Ancestor* 9 (April, 1904): 26.

[31] Wrottesley, ed., *Staffordshire Historical Collections*, vol. x, 22–4.

[32] Robert de Hastang was made baron by writ December 19, 1311. See Bernard Burke, *A Genealogical History of the Dormant, Abeyant, Forfeited and Extinct Peerage of the British Empire* (London: Harrison, 1866), 266.

[33] Hastang appears in a mandate to deliver a castle to John Darcy le cousyn. See *CPR*, Edward II, vol. III (1313–17), 616.

Under these circumstances, as Jack Lander has described it, attainder represents the "legal death of the family."[34] In 1317, when John of Cleasby, a knight from Richmond, banded together with Gilbert of Middleton to rally the northern populace into rebellion against Edward II, "devastat[ing] the district, plundering, robbing, and wasting at his own and his people's pleasure," he took an enormous risk. "[B]y God's ordinance," so the *Lanercost Chronicle* tells us, they were soon arrested. Gilbert endured the summary justice of a military trial: his body quartered and dispersed throughout England as a warning to others with similar ambitions. John stood mute; he was put to his penance, and died soon afterwards in prison.[35] John's silence paid off. The Scrope of Bolton cartulary records a quitclaim dated to June 17, 1340 in which his son, also named John of Cleasby, surrendered his rights to the manors of Ellerton, Downholme, Dishforth, Yafforth, and Walborn, with their appurtenances, to William Lescrop.[36] Ellerton and Downholme, at the very least, were manors he inherited from his father, who was once their lord.[37]

Oddly enough, evidence from just a few years after John of Cleasby's death in prison suggests quite the opposite. Despite refusing to plead and his subsequent death by pressing, Robert le Ewer (d.1322), the seditious constable of Odiham castle, had both his landed estates and chattels confiscated by the Crown.[38] Two years after the fact, Isabel, widow of Hugh Bardolf was still in court fighting for return of the manor of Emsworth (Hampshire), of which she claimed Robert le Ewer had wrongly disseised her and her heirs; however, when Robert died as rebel, the manor was taken into the king's hands among his other forfeitures.[39] Once again, the evidence

---

[34] Jack Lander, "Attainder and Forfeiture, 1453–1509," *Historical Journal* 4.2 (1961): 119.

[35] Herbert Maxwell, ed., *The Chronicle of Lanercost, 1372–1346: Translated with Notes* (Glasgow: J. Maclehose, 1913), 218.

[36] Brigette Vale, "The Scropes of Bolton and of Masham, c.1300–c.1450: A Study of a Northern Noble Family with a Calendar of the Scrope of Bolton Cartulary," 2 vols. (PhD Diss., University of York, 1987), vol. II, 96.

[37] William Page, *A History of the County of York North Riding: Volume 1* (London: Constable, 1914), 225–32.

[38] Wendy Childs, ed., *Vita Edwardi Secundi: The Life of Edward the Second* (Oxford: Clarendon Press, 2005), 219.

[39] *CIPM*, vol. II, 347–53. When it comes to his chattels, a commission in the calendar of patent rolls explains that the men of the town of Southampton had hidden all of

would seem to imply that the king's justices did not follow the rules in a consistent manner.

In the vast majority of cases, the indictments claim that the defendants owned nothing.[40] This finding is fundamental: it echoes observations made by both Henry Summerson for the thirteenth century and Andrea McKenzie for the early modern era.[41] For these men, who had nothing to save for their children, it is difficult to maintain that heroic paternalism was the primary motivation for refusing to plead. Moreover, the Crown's inconsistency when it comes to felony forfeiture hints that Crown officials complicated the process for defendants: even if they did stand silent, their efforts may have been in vain.

Given the evidence, it seems unlikely that the fiscal well-being of their families was the chief priority for *all* those who chose to stand mute. Granted, this does not mean that altruism should be dismissed as a motivation altogether. Even if dying heroically did not necessarily salvage the defendant's properties, concern for one's family members might still have acted as the driving force behind the defendant's actions. The form book, *Placita Corone* (c.1274), points to this possibility, explaining frankly that "if he is a thief or if he is doubtful of the jury, [the defendant] will say, if he is sensible, that for reasons of family pride he would rather die in prison than be hanged."[42] The lives of medieval men and women hinged on their reputations, both individually and collectively as a family. Living in a mainly cashless society where deferred payments for goods and wages was the norm, the medieval English relied on an elaborate system of credit. This became

Robert's goods. The king assigned three men to empanel a jury to inquire into those concealed goods. *CPR*, Edward II, vol. v, 142.

[40] As the 1315 petition of Joan of Brigmerston (Wiltshire) shows, some of those forfeitures were not permanent. In her entreaty to the king, Joan reports that her husband Stephen, who had refused to plead, perished in prison as a result of peine forte et dure. After his death, the county sheriff confiscated all his goods and chattels, rendering it impossible for her to pay off her husband's debts or execute his will. She begged the king for assistance. TNA SC 8/91/4524 (1315). As an act of clemency, the king ordered the sheriff to return her husband's goods and chattels at once. *CCR*, Edward II, vol. II (1313–18), 182.

[41] Summerson, "Early Development," 124; Andrea McKenzie, "'This Death some Strong and Stout Hearted Man Doth Choose': The Practice of Peine Forte et Dure in Seventeenth- and Eighteenth-Century England," *L&HR* 23.2 (2005): 283.

[42] John Kaye, ed., *Placita Corone, or La Corone Pledee Devant Justices* (SS, supplementary series, vol. IV, 1966), 23.

even more critical over time, especially during the bullion famine of the fifteenth century, an era often described as "the Great Depression" of the Middle Ages. Creditworthiness was synonymous with one's communal reputation: immoral or criminal behavior by an individual, or someone within his or her family, jeopardized a person's ability to participate and survive in a credit economy. In this world, those who chose to die by penance spared their families the humiliation of a felony conviction and the impact it might have upon their family's reputation. Dying in penance might even earn the dead admiration for putting their family first. Death by the peine avoided public execution by hanging. Medieval society regarded hanging as a humiliating death. Slow strangulation produced a number of unpleasant but involuntary bodily responses, such as the release of the bladder and bowels, the bulging of the eyes from the head, the blackening of the lips; some individuals doubtless preferred to spare their families the public spectacle of such a shameful and indecorous end. Death through peine forte et dure had the added benefit of associations with martyrdom, as one sermon made explicit: "if any bodily harm beo doon to þe, of bodily persecucion, or los of catel or of frendes (for alle þese been scorgyngis to mannes bodi)" (if any bodily harm is done to you, of bodily persecution or loss of chattel or of friends (for all these are scourgings to man's body)), reminiscent of Christ's scourging before the ultimate martyrdom.[43]

Manifest Guilt

With or without concern for one's family, manifest guilt remains one of the most persuasive theories put forward by historians to explain why defendants chose to stand mute and risk being sent to peine forte et dure. For the manifestly guilty, what was the point in subjecting one's self to a highly public and degrading trial when the outcome was predetermined? Arrested with stolen goods in their possession (*cum manuopere*) and with a questionable reputation, there existed a violent presumption of guilt. In an earlier period, a court hearing was not even thought necessary. Hand-having (*handhabbende*) or back-bearing (*bacberende*) thieves were subject to summary justice for much of early English history, hanged on the spot, but by *Bracton's* era

---

[43] Gloria Cigman, ed., *Lollard Sermons* (EETS, vol. CCXCIV, 1989), 107.

possession of stolen goods on its own was often thought insufficient to proceed straight to conviction.[44] As Richard Ireland explains it, one had to make allowance for "the simpleton who, in defiance of common sense and of his obligation to raise the hue and cry, picked up the bloody knife to admire its design."[45] For a short time after the abolition of the ordeal, mainour combined with a refusal to plead resulted in hanging, not peine forte et dure, reminding us that the law continued to interpret possession of stolen goods as solid proof of guilt. Even once a trial became requisite, it was little more than a charade. The manifestly guilty typically hanged. Given the predictability of the conclusion, those destined to hang presumably saw standing mute as the most reasonable option, permitting them to skip the humiliation of both trial and public execution.

The theory of manifest guilt also aligns most closely with the premise of hard prison as punishment under statute law. Thirteenth-century lawmakers endorsed the usage of prison forte et dure only for notorious felons with criminal reputations who refused to plead. The statute deemed the practice inappropriate for all other suspected felons.[46] Without any later legislative corrective, one might argue that English justices sent only those who were strongly suspected of guilt, if not manifestly guilty, to suffer peine forte et dure. This conjecture might explain also why the statute does not label the practice a coercive measure: perhaps legislators preferred to think of it as a punishment for manifest guilt.

In any event, the manifest guilt theory does not take into account the pain awaiting the defendant with each form of execution. This scenario

---

[44] A year-book enrolment for 1302 indicates just how slow the transition was to requiring a trial. A man named only as John was arrested *cum manuopere* and delivered into the custody of a local tithing group to be held until the sheriff's *tourn*. Because felony belonged to the sheriff's jurisdiction, they should have indicted him and delivered him into the custody of the sheriff. However, the tithingmen saw John as a felon, not an accused felon; thus, they saw indictment as unnecessary. Their error in judgment empowered the defendant with choice: at his arraignment, he stood mute. Justices noted that if he had been properly indicted before being taken into custody, they could have proceeded directly to hanging. But since they had not, his silence gave them no choice: peine forte et dure was their only option. Horwood, ed., *Year Books of the Reign of Edward the First*, 502–3 (Seipp 1302-191rs).

[45] Richard Ireland, "The Presumption of Guilt in the History of English Criminal Procedure," *Journal of Legal History* 7.3 (1986): 248.

[46] Statute of Westminster I, 3 Edw. I, c. 12 (1275); *SR*, vol. 1, 29.

has the rightfully accused trading one horror (hanging) for another (famine/pressing). The real question to ask then is which horror was the most horrific? As suggested above, if the defendant was thinking chiefly of his family's reputation, standing mute saved them from public humiliation. However, if family was not a consideration, it is hard to imagine why anyone would willingly choose days or months of slow starvation and pressing with weights over hanging. All things considered, hanging was the gentler form of execution. In medieval England, the practice of hanging involved a process of slow strangulation as the body was hoisted into the air, rather than a swift break of the neck. Even still, the convict's experience of hanging was short-lived; oxygen deprivation would have the defendant drifting out of consciousness within three minutes. When compared to other English means of execution, such as burning at the stake, being drawn and quartered, or the peculiarly southern traditions of drowning, burial alive, or being flung from the cliffs of Dover, hanging would seem to be a relatively speedy and painless means of death. Hanging had the added benefit that the English did not employ professional hangmen; instead, the court hired or appointed its hangmen on an ad hoc basis. They were notoriously bad at their jobs, such that a surprising number of hanged felons revived, were pardoned of their crimes, and lived to tell the miraculous tale.[47]

Bear in mind that hard prison arose as a coercive measure because legislators deemed it a fate worse than death. That accused felons agreed with this assessment is made clear by those cases in which judges, eager to just get on with the trial, dangled peine forte et dure as a scare tactic to motivate reluctant defendants to plead. At a Yorkshire trial for rape, the judge instructed his silent defendant on the pains of peine forte et dure, here described as the starvation diet, saying "it would not be good to die in that manner and [it] would be much better to consent to the jurors."[48] Granted, the judge's intent to scare an individual straight presented the worst-case scenario; in practice, he might well prefer a more lenient version of hard prison. However, defendants had no way of knowing a judge's inclinations,

---

[47] See Robert Bartlett, *The Hanged Man: A Story of Miracle, Memory, and Colonialism in the Middle Ages* (Princeton University Press, 2004).

[48] Horwood, ed., *Year Books of the Reign of Edward the First*, 531 (Seipp, 1295.003rs).

and one suspects that most men and women in medieval England knew what it meant to be hungry and were not eager to go down that path needlessly. The year books provide two other examples. A man indicted of felony in 1330 stood mute before royal justices. Chief Justice Scrope therefore impaneled six members of the castle staff to assess his capacity to speak. When the jury affirmed that the defendant had spoken the same day, Scrope made a show of directing the sheriff to condemn him to peine forte et dure. Overhearing his fate, the prisoner all at once found his voice; he placed himself in the hands of the jury who pronounced him guilty and hanged him for his crimes.[49] Likewise, addressing a defendant who had just challenged an entire jury, Scrope dissuaded him from pursuing further this tactic by pointing out that challenging three juries was treated as the equivalent of refusing to plead. He might soon find himself in prison subjected to peine forte et dure. The accused hastily desisted in his obstructive behavior; he, too, hanged.[50] These examples testify amply to the terror that peine forte et dure stirred in the popular imagination. All of this is a useful reminder: for those suspected felons who chose to stand mute to protect their families, the sacrifice they were making on their family's behalf was sizeable.

Even the manifestly guilty did not relish the prospect of slow death through starvation or pressing. Apart from the cases regarding women who stand mute (discussed in Chapter 2), the evidence of the plea rolls does not make a strong argument for manifest theft. Only 44 of the 481 cases (or 9.15 percent) describe the accused being taken in possession of stolen goods. This is not an exceptional finding. To offer some comparisons: in a 1317 Kent jail-delivery roll, 10 percent of felony indictments remark that the accused was taken *cum manuopere*; a Northamptonshire jail delivery roll for the same year produced similar results at 9.3 percent.[51] A theory of widespread manifest guilt also does not take into account the defendants who, like Walter le Monner of Histon, finally agreed to submit to jury trial and were acquitted. The king's men arrested Walter for homicide in 1286 along with three others. One of his accomplices claimed benefit of clergy; the

[49] Sutherland, ed., *Eyre of Northamptonshire*, 177–8 (Seipp 1330-323ss).
[50] Sutherland, ed., *Eyre of Northamptonshire*, 179 (Seipp 1330-327ss).
[51] John Bellamy, *The Criminal Trial in Later Medieval England* (University of Toronto Press, 1998), 43.

other two pleaded and were acquitted. Initially, Walter stood mute; justices instructed the sheriff to return him to prison to suffer penance according to the statute. An addendum to the record tells us that Walter later returned to court, submitted to jury trial, and was acquitted.[52] The positive verdicts awarded to his two accomplices might have inspired Walter's change of heart. Granted, the jury's temperature could not always be taken so easily, as in the case of Richard Pely, detained alongside Walter le Spicer and William of Risbury in 1291 for many robberies and thefts. Walter and William both claimed benefit of clergy. The trial that followed found the two guilty and delivered them to the ordinary as convicted clerics. At the outset, Pely also claimed clerical status, but the archbishop through his ordinary pronounced that he was in fact a layman (*laicus*). Pely then refused to plead altogether. Eventually, Pely returned to court and stood trial: remarkably, the jury voted to acquit.[53] Walter le Monner and Richard Pely were not the only mute defendants eventually acquitted. Regrettably, because the research for this study focused on those subjected to peine forte et dure rather than recording the trials of every felon for the fourteenth century, it is not clear how often those who elected to undergo *penitentia* broke down under the strain of the diet and eventually pleaded. Yet, at least fifteen suspected felons (including Walter and Richard) did, and they were acquitted. An additional fifteen enjoyed the king's pardon. These outcomes undercut the feasibility of the thesis of manifest guilt. Indeed, turning once again to Barbara Hanawalt's evidence for the early fourteenth century, she observes that most of those defendants who stood mute in the eight counties under her evaluation eventually gave in and agreed to plead.[54]

Nor is there any evidence in the plea rolls to indicate that a specific kind of criminal chose to stand mute. A comparative analysis of the nature of this study's silent defendants' purported crimes shows nothing unusual. The table below examines the crimes of the 481 felons. Many of those felons were accused of multiple crimes; thus, 481 accused felons were suspected of committing 654 crimes in total. When breaking down the crimes by felony and analyzing the percentages, they are consistent

---

[52] TNA JUST 1/92, m. 12d (1286).   [53] TNA JUST 3/89, m. 1d (1291).

[54] Barbara Hanawalt, *Crime and Conflict in English Communities, 1300–1348* (Cambridge, MA: Harvard University Press, 1979), 42.

TABLE 5.1 *Breakdown by felony type*

Felony (654)	Percentage of overall felonies	Hanawalt: Percentage of overall felonies
Theft: including robbery, burglary, and larceny (457)	69.9	73.5
Homicide (138)	21.1	18.2
Receiving (10)	1.5	6.2
Arson (9)	1.4	0.8
High treason, including counterfeiting (9)	1.4	0.8
Prison-break (6)	0.92	-
Rape/ravishment (3)	0.46	0.5
Poaching (1)	0.15	-
Unknown (21)	0.21	-

with those found by Barbara Hanawalt in her fourteenth-century study of English criminal indictments, but with a slightly higher concentration of homicides.[55]

Rather than the hardened crowd of thugs and scoundrels whose scandalous reputations for truly monstrous crimes destined them for the gallows, our statistical analysis instead reveals a rather unexceptional group.

Needless to say, even if manifest guilt was not the motive behind a defendant's silent stance, a deep-seated fear of conviction might still be relevant to the defendant's decision-making. In order to answer this query, we must first scrutinize whether these particular suspected felons were any more deserving of conviction than the usual lot. In this instance, the language of the indictments is instructive. Common law required trial jurors to be self-informing, meaning they were expected to arrive at court the day of the trial fully versed in the evidence and prepared to cast their votes in the absence of anything more than a cursory courtroom presentation of the evidence or

[55] See Hanawalt, *Crime and Conflict*, 66. Hanawalt's study looks at jail delivery rolls for the following counties: Essex, Hereford, Huntingdon, Norfolk, Northampton, Surrey, Somerset, and York, in the years 1300 to 1348.

interrogation of witnesses. In theory, placing the responsibility for criminal investigation into the hands of those most affected by the case's outcome saved time and money. It also guaranteed acceptance by that same community, bringing a necessary sense of closure after a serious rift in communal peace. In practice, though, trials did not run as smoothly as the Crown envisaged. Jurors regularly ignored court summonses (for a wide variety of reasons, some licit), leaving sheriffs to cobble together a jury from whoever attended that day's jail delivery. In this chaotic reality, it is unlikely that all trial jurors possessed in-depth knowledge about the case at hand (although some surely did). Recognizing the inadequacy of the system, jurors solved the problem by developing coded communication inserted into the indictment to signal their intentions. For example, language emphasizing the heinousness of the crime by claiming it was premeditated (*premeditato*), committed by night (*noctanter*), carried out treacherously (*proditorie*), or belonged to the category of secret homicide (*murdravit*) were overt signs that jurors of presentment favored a guilty verdict. Declaring that the accused was a common or notorious thief accomplished much the same goal. So, too, did an indictment in which the defendant stood accused of multiple crimes simultaneously. "Phrase of afforcement" is the term that John Bellamy coined to describe coded communication of this nature between juries.[56] A final element included in our analysis in the table below is the number of defendants who ultimately confessed and turned approver. In these instances, we do not need to look for indications of guilt; we *know* that these individuals carried out the crimes for which they were accused (see Table 5.2).

The figure of 270 refers to indications of guilt, not guilty individuals. At times, one indictment includes multiple clues for the same individual. Wading through the overlap, it is clear that 211 of the 481 individuals (or 43.87 percent) were described in such a way as to indicate culpability. By all accounts, this is a high percentage, indicating that fear of conviction was a very real motivation for many of those who refused to plead.

Naturally, just because the jury who indicted the defendant believed he or she was guilty of the crime and deserved punishment, did not

---

[56] Bellamy, *Criminal Trial*, 29

TABLE 5.2 *Indications of guilt*

Indications of guilt	
Accused of multiple crimes	115
Common or notorious thief	59
Cum manuopere	44
Noctanter	25
Confessed & turned approver	17
Proditorie	6
Premeditated	2
Murder	2
TOTAL:	270

mean that he or she was bound for conviction. Trial juries in medieval England were inclined to acquit, seeing the indictment process itself as adequate penalty for most felonies. Phrases of afforcement, though, tended to produce substantially higher conviction rates. Bellamy observes that medieval juries convicted common or notorious felons at a rate of one to three, compared to the ratio of one to eight in cases where the accused was not so described.[57] Yet, nothing was guaranteed. Trial jurors were content to acquit common thieves and murderous villains when they felt so inclined.

The unpredictability of English verdicts arises from the nature of England's criminal trial process. Unlike the Continent, where a rigid law of evidence requiring two eyewitnesses prevailed, medieval England had no formal law of proof. All that was needed for a conviction was a unanimous verdict of the jury and how they reached that verdict is generally unknowable. Justices invited jurors to testify to the truth, although, as Richard Firth Green has argued persuasively, their definition of truth seems to have had little to do with the facts of the case. "Truth" instead spoke to a defendant's reputation for moral integrity.[58] In these circumstances, a defendant might technically have been innocent of the charges, but a jury still opted

---

[57] Bellamy, *Criminal Trial*, 30.
[58] See Chapter 4 of Richard Firth Green, *A Crisis of Truth: Literature and Law in Ricardian England* (Philadelphia: University of Pennsylvania Press, 2002).

for a guilty verdict because of the flagrant and persistent disregard for communal standards of morality with little hope of rehabilitation. Even with little concrete evidence to connect a defendant to the crime, if society deemed the felony itself as abhorrent and inexcusable the defendant might well predict the worst. Such vigorous distrust likely inspired Richard, son of William Boneclune of Wyke's silence at his 1308 arraignment. Arrested on suspicion of being a thief, the indictment draws attention to the testimony of the constable of the castle of Marlborough, as well as the mayor and a coterie of burgesses who described Richard as a common and notorious thief, guilty of many thefts in the counties of Dorset and Wiltshire.[59] Medieval Europeans were famously intolerant of secret crime; theft by its very nature belonged to this category. While a jury might rationalize stealing goods for survival, professional thievery, as the indictment's characterization implies, was especially repugnant. Further, the elite respectability of the witnesses involved projected the likelihood of a guilty verdict. Similarly, Thomas Lissell, arrested in 1398 and depicted by jurors as a common thief of farmers and a highwayman who plunders feloniously the king's subjects (*communis latro de populator agrorum et insidiator viarum ad depredandum felonice populum domini Regis*) surely had little hope of acquittal.[60] This is emphasized by the fact that he died the following day in prison, most probably having been subjected to pressing.[61] Twelve respectable and law-abiding men were just as unlikely to turn a sympathetic eye to serious transgressions of the social hierarchy. In such a patriarchal world where fathers ruled their households as kings, Richard of Thorpe, accused of patricide, had little chance of acquittal at his 1310 delivery.[62]

Buying Time

Fearing conviction, a shrewd defendant might also see a refusal to plead as a useful delaying tactic, buying time until one had a better

[59] TNA JUST 3/108, m. 4 (1308).   [60] TNA JUST 3/185, m. 4 (1398).
[61] TNA JUST 2/61, m. 15/1 (1398).
[62] TNA JUST 3/30/1, m. 3 (1310). Assuredly, the same realization by John Scot of Muskham, indicted for slaying his master at Tuxford in le Clay (Nottingham) in 1374, accounts for his silence. TNA JUST 3/162, m. 6d (1374).

sense of whether jurors from one's home community were inclined to convict. With this approach, a failure to plead offered a short respite while tempers cooled and memories faded, promises for reform were hastily made, and/or family members filed petitions for pardon on the accused's behalf.[63] For a suspect awaiting trial, time is a precious commodity, and given the speed with which the medieval English resolved criminal suits, often it was a commodity that needed to be manufactured creatively. Historians have long recognized the skillful manipulation of a wide variety of legal provisions by suspected felons in the hopes of prolonging the legal process. Sanctuary, for example, provided an individual an additional thirty-nine days in which one might marshal sureties to attest to one's good character, build a case for self-defense, or wait for saner heads to prevail. Indeed, the purchase appeal of the form book *Placita Corone* rests in part on the sound advice it offers as to "what delays [the accused] will be able to cause before having to reply."[64] Many of those who failed to plead did so only after they had already experimented with myriad strategies to delay the inevitable, from benefit of clergy to pleading the belly. Standing mute was just one among several implements in an accused felon's toolbox to defer trial to a later date.

(1) Benefit of Clergy

The courtroom behavior of the accused emphasizes the theatrical nature of a good defense in medieval England. Keen to avoid public execution, defendants refusing the law pretended to be mute. How far they went in this pretense – quiet repose, feigned deafness, sign language, gripping the throat in visible distress – is not clear, but for a sheriff to hold an inquest, presumably the performance had to be credible. For a select group (17 out of 481, or 3.5 percent), the show began with a different opening: when escorted to the bar, they chose instead to impersonate a member of the clergy. This was true of Richard Pely (1291) above. Standing in court before the king's justices, accused of multiple robberies, his first instinct was to follow

---

[63] After the 1278 Statute of Gloucester, all defendants were expected to stand trial before receiving a pardon. Statute of Gloucester, 6 Edw. I, c. 9 (1278), *SR*, vol. I, 49.

[64] Kaye, ed., *Placita Corone*, 22.

the lead of his associates and claim benefit of clergy, despite the fact that he had taken no vows, nor received ordination. By all indications, Richard was no priest. His false assertion was foolhardy, and it backfired: the ordinary outed him as a member of the laity.

Yet, it is easy to understand why some defendants were willing to throw caution to the wind. The reward was substantial. Clerical status did not excuse one's crimes; rather, it removed the defendant's case from royal to ecclesiastical jurisdiction. Since the early Middle Ages, clergymen had been exempt from secular laws because the hierarchical relationship between clergy and laity meant impartiality in a royal court was implausible. For that reason, the church supplied clergymen with a special tribunal in both civil and criminal causes before an ecclesiastical judge. When it comes to punishment, the church courts had to work within the constraints of canon law, which prohibited clerics from participating in bloodshed. Therefore, while a convicted felon in the king's courts hanged, a guilty verdict in a church court translated to degradation from orders and a prison sentence (sometimes even life in prison). The regularity with which complaints about the church's leniency cropped up in the medieval era hints that medieval Englishmen and women saw a meaningful discrepancy in punishments awarded by the two authorities. The English Crown kept the church courts in check by trying many (although by no means all) felonious clerks in the king's courts before they were released to the ordinary, a practice that in fact worked to the benefit of the accused. Acquitted clerics were simply discharged, without any notification to their superiors or the church in general. Those found guilty were delivered to the ordinary as convicted clerics. It was within the bishop's purview to ignore the Crown's verdict, but doing so made an undesirable statement about the church's unwillingness to cooperate in matters of public safety. It also undermined the good faith that existed between Crown and cross in an era when cooperation was central to the smooth functioning of a well-ordered Christian kingdom.

Not just anyone could masquerade as a member of the clergy. Women – even religious women – were excluded from the privilege until the seventeenth century. The logic behind this prohibition rests on the fact that crimes of the regular clergy (that is, those who follow a rule or *regula*) received discipline within the monastic environment.

Only secular clergy, whose movements were not restricted by an order, might commit the sort of public crime that would lead to criminal charges in a king's court. Since women religious were barred from entry into secular orders, benefit of clergy was technically of no use to them. As a result, women could not hope to get away with pretending to be a member of the clergy. Yet, even for men, impersonation presented obstacles. It was the bishop's ordinary, not the king's justices, that defendants had to deceive. In the twelfth and thirteenth centuries, the ordinary relied on one of a number of signs of status: tonsure, clerical garb, certification of orders, or a literacy test.[65] As the 1293 Bedfordshire arraignment of Nicholas of Cerne indicates, the church eventually had to tighten its standards, acknowledging that a tonsure was the least reliable of all the tests. Under arrest for the premeditated assault and homicide of Henry de la Leye, Nicholas pronounced his clerical status the moment he arrived in court. As proof, he paraded his freshly shaven tonsure before justices. The faithful judges were not hoodwinked by this cheeky performance: they reported that Nicholas had "fraudulently and maliciously and in deception of the court" shaven his head just three or four days previously in order to pose as a cleric. The assistance of a corrupt jailer facilitated Nicholas' dishonesty. They asked Nicholas once, twice, three times how he wished to acquit himself of homicide. Nicholas refused to abandon the ruse, persisting in the charade that he was in fact a member of the clergy. Justices ordered him returned to prison to suffer the punishment of the statute (peine forte et dure). The record concludes with some satisfaction that because of his protracted flight prior to arrest, his goods valued at £8 19s. and 8d. were forfeit to the king.[66]

By the fourteenth and fifteenth centuries, literacy assumed pride of place as the normal test of clergy. When the church first devised this strategy, it was founded on sound reasoning. For most of medieval history, the clergy were the only literate people in Europe. The church could not have foreseen the rapid expansion of literacy rates that was to take place over the course of the late Middle Ages, facilitated by the spread of paper mills and the development of the printing press. At the

---

[65] Leona Gabel, *Benefit of Clergy in England in the Later Middle Ages* (New York: Octagon Books, 1969), 64
[66] TNA JUST 3/91, m. 15d (1293).

very least, the king's justices recognized the risk increased literacy held for benefit of clergy. It had the potential to unwittingly expand the privilege to all literate men, thus well beyond the priesthood (as it eventually did). They endeavored to counteract this unwanted corollary by insisting on literacy in conjunction with other evidence of clerical status. For example, at an arraignment in 1352, Chief Justice William Shareshull reminded the court that literacy on its own was insufficient to meet the court's requirements. Rejecting the defendant's request to send for the ordinary, Shareshull repeated the Latin maxim, "that literacy does not make a clerk, unless he has a monk's tonsure."[67] Granted, the high bar set by the king's justices did not deter some frantic defendants, hoping to postpone their trial dates. At his arraignment at Appleby jail on August 18, 1365, John, son of Thomas Dennyson Trotter, senior, arrested on multiple appeals ranging from homicide to armed robbery, declared boldly that he was a member of the clergy and therefore the king's justices were not entitled to try him. However, when examined by the ordinary, it became immediately apparent that he did not know how to read. His claim rejected, Thomas refused to plead at all and was sentenced to the diet.[68] Some decidedly nonclerical prisoners were still able to fake their way through a literacy test. A Cumbrian jail delivery exposed two young boys caught teaching a prisoner the basics of reading in preparation for the test.[69] By the end of the Middle Ages, ordinaries unaccountably lowered the bar, making it easier for felons to cheat the system. The reading test consistently employed involved just one passage, Psalm 51, "Oh God, have mercy upon me, according to thine heartfelt mercifulness." Popular audiences referred to it as the "neck verse" because reading this compassionate plea might save a man's neck from the gallows. From time to time, royal officials disciplined jailers who were guilty of reciting the neck verse to prisoners for a price.[70] For the purpose of felony trials, all of these tactics ultimately extended clerical status to all literate (or quasi-

---

[67] YB 26 Edw. III (1352), fos. 122b–123a (Seipp 1352.083ass).

[68] TNA JUST 3/145, m. 57d (1365). See also the case of Hugh, son of Henry, Chapter 3 (Seipp 1295.003rs).

[69] Cynthia Neville, "Common Knowledge of the Common Law in Later Medieval England," *Canadian Journal of History* 28 (1994): 473.

[70] Neville, "Common Knowledge," 473.

literate) men, but it was not until the time of Henry VII (r. 1485–1509) that the judiciary began reluctantly to accept that the provision existed for all lettered people, regardless of their clerical status.

Ordinaries rejected other claims on the grounds of bigamy. Medieval law defined bigamy differently than do we today. A clergyman who married more than one time in succession, or had married a widow or non-virgin, was guilty of bigamy. Bigamy itself was not a crime; however, it acted as a bar against a cleric being ordained a priest, or rising above the rank of subdeacon. It also made him ineligible "to seek the milder justice of ecclesiastical courts."[71] Robert of Hardrow, imprisoned at Newgate for the death of Thomas Duffard of London, came before justices of jail delivery in June of 1290. When asked how he wished to acquit himself, Robert explained that his clerical status prevented him from pleading before royal justices. Therefore, they summoned Roger of Canterbury, a priest from the church of Saint Andrew at Holborn, and Thomas of Beccles, vicar of the church of St. Sepulcher outside Newgate, in order to test his clergy. The two men of the cloth professed that Robert's admittedly clerical status was negated because he had married a widow, making him guilty of bigamy, a fact that Robert conceded was true. Again, justices asked Robert how he wished to acquit himself and he replied that he in no way wished to proceed to jury trial. Thus, the court sentenced him remitted to prison to be burdened with the weight of sufficient iron and to subsist on an alternating diet of coarse bread and water.[72]

(2)   Challenging the Jurors

Assembling a jury was always a more complicated process than one might imagine. Jury service was not open to everyone. Although it probably goes without saying, all jurors had to be male, a condition that excluded half of the available population from the very beginning. Next, a juror had to be local. The self-informing nature of medieval juries made provenance the top priority: only residents from the vicinity of the crime might profess first-hand knowledge of its

---

[71] Sara McDougall, *Bigamy and Christian Identity in Late Medieval Champagne* (Philadelphia: University of Pennsylvania Press, 2012), 22.
[72] TNA JUST 3/87, m. 1d (1290).

particulars with any integrity. Yet, because felony trials were held at the county jail as opposed to the crime scene, members of the local community were not readily on hand for the trial. The county sheriff had to summon groups of potential jurors in advance of a delivery. Failure to send sufficient jurors to court resulted in an amercement of the entire village. However, given the expense of travel and absence from work (none of which was reimbursed by the Crown), some of those called to court took their chances and stayed home. Sheriffs regularly filled their seats with less appropriate jurors, often the very coroners, constables, and bailiffs who directed the original investigation and were required to be at court anyway.[73] Concerns to keep trial jurors local crop up at regular intervals in English legislation, implying just how difficult it was for sheriffs to enforce attendance at jail delivery. In the preamble of a statute from 1360, complaints abound of sheriffs and others who select jurors who are corrupt or who hail from distant counties. Hence, the statute reiterates that sheriffs, coroners, and other ministers must empanel only "the next people, which shall not be suspect nor procured."[74] That sheriffs attempted to adhere to the dictates of the law in this respect is confirmed by the fact that, even with officers of the court, sometimes sheriffs were incapable of assembling a jury. Each jail delivery witnessed an impressive number of defendants sent back to prison until the next delivery because of a "defect in the jury," meaning, the sheriff did not have sufficient numbers from the locality to constitute a proper jury.

Common law also imposed income requirements: jurors must own lands and/or tenements with an annual value of forty shillings (or two pounds), which was worth much more at the time than it sounds.[75] In 1290, two pounds was the cost of purchasing two horses, or 200 days of wage labor for a skilled tradesman.[76] Medieval jurisprudence linked wealth with knowledge. As the 1304 Articles of Lincoln explained, the

[73] Sara Butler, *Forensic Medicine and Death Investigation in Medieval England* (New York: Routledge, 2015), 95.
[74] 34 Edw. III, c. 4 (1360). *SR*, vol. II, 479.
[75] "The Statute of Persons to be Put in Assises and Juries," 21 Edw. I (1293), *SR*, vol. I, 113.
[76] "Currency Converter: 1270–2017," (Kew, Surrey: The National Archives), www.nationalarchives.gov.uk/currency-converter/#currency-result (accessed July 21, 2020).

"poor men" are those "who know nothing." Jurors should be drawn instead from "the better men ... who know better the truth."[77] In some vills, finding twelve men who met these qualifications was well-nigh impossible. This brings us to our final criterion: indicting jurors (that is, jurors from the coroner's inquest, or sheriff's tourn) were not permitted to sit as trial jurors on the same case.[78] This particular eligibility requirement was seldom enforced. For many vills, sheriffs were scrambling to find twelve men who met all of the above criteria; finding *twenty-four* such men left sheriffs at wits' end. No matter how much they wanted to, they could not enforce the statutory requirement. As a result, overlap between the two juries was so common that it was often hard to distinguish one from the other.[79] What this means is that clever defendants looking to exploit jury challenges as a means to postpone the judicial process had plenty of grounds for an objection.

When it comes to jury challenges, the accused had two options. First, the accused might challenge the array, meaning the entire panel of jurors. In this situation, the objection lies with the sheriff for arranging the panel in a manner that reveals his partiality. Second, the defendant might make exceptions to individual jurors, what later came to be known as a "challenge to the polls." The law permitted a defendant to oppose jurors on a number of grounds: they are personal enemies motivated out of hate and spite, friends or family members of the victim, or members of the presenting jury responsible for the original indictment. Justices allowed each defendant two challenges to the array, or up to thirty-five individual challenges. Upon the third challenge to the array, or the thirty-sixth individual challenge, the common law interpreted the defendant's behavior as a refusal to submit to jury trial, as if the defendant had stood mute. Peine forte et dure was the punishment.

A perceptive defendant who feared conviction challenged enough jurors to delay trial, but not enough to be considered in contempt of court. For example, when William Coupere of Harleston arrived at

---

[77] Francis Nichols, ed., "Original Documents Illustrative of the Administration of Criminal Law at the Time of Edward I," *Archaeologia* 40 (1866): 103.

[78] 25 Edw. III, c. 3 (1351–2), SR, vol. I, 320.

[79] Daniel Klerman, "Was the Jury ever Self-Informing?," *Southern California Law Review* 77 (2003): 128.

Norwich castle during Lent of 1373, arraigned on charges of sheep stealing, he exhausted the local jury pool within fifteen challenges. Justices had no choice but to return him into the custody of the sheriff until the following jail delivery, when a new pool of local jurors might be summoned to trial.[80] It is not hard to imagine that defendants who challenged thirty-six jurors were hoping to do just that, but the size of the jury pool foiled their plans. Unable to deplete the supply of locals, their return to prison involved peine forte et dure rather than simply waiting six months for the next delivery. The number of defendants who individually challenged thirty-six jurors –a rather time-consuming process, especially when justices expected to complete most trials in a fifteen-minute window – points in this direction.[81]

Admittedly, this strategy was not popular: the vast majority of accused felons went ahead with their trials and simply hoped for the best, even when the trial jury bore an uncanny resemblance to the indicting jury, even when sheriffs invited the coroners and bailiffs who headed the criminal investigation to fill an empty seat. Some adopted William Coupere's plan, and ended up reincarcerated, waiting for a future delivery of the prison. A minority abused the privilege: of the 481 cases of those who rejected the common law drawn from plea rolls, 21 (or 4.37 per cent) challenged 36 jurors, and found themselves back in prison, but under much more rigorous conditions. William Sherwynd of Flamborough arrested on appeal for stealing just about everything not nailed down at the home of Richard atte Hall of Morton in 1368, opted for this route. At his Lincolnshire arraignment, he challenged thirty-six jurors; justices sentenced him to the diet.[82] So, too, did Richard of Houghton of Ferriby, a shoemaker, at his arraignment for grand larceny at Lincoln in 1384. Similarly, he was sentenced to his penance.[83]

By the late fifteenth century, English justices seem to have lost their patience with jury challenges. Matters came to a head in 1487, when a defendant arraigned before justices at Newgate challenged thirty-six jurors in succession. Chief Justice of King's Bench, William Huse, explained that in the time of Edward II it had been common practice

---

[80] TNA JUST 3/152, m. 40 (1373).
[81] For example, see the arraignment of William of Holland, TNA JUST 3/177, m. 63d (1391).
[82] TNA JUST 3/142, m. 48 (1368).   [83] TNA JUST 3/167, m. 63 (1384).

to send the accused to his penance in such a situation. However, upon the unanimous agreement of the justices of King's Bench and Common Pleas, they agreed that henceforth the defendant would be hanged.[84] Of course, by the following year this unanimity had already been forgotten when a challenge in an appeal of felony resulted in sentencing the defendant to peine forte et dure.[85]

(3) Awaiting a Pardon

Pleading is the key moment in an arraignment in which the defendant has the opportunity to deny involvement in any criminal activity and bring forward exceptions that might prevent the trial from moving forward. In many of the trials here under consideration, it was at precisely this moment that a suspect chose to claim benefit of clergy, asked to speak to the coroner and turn approver, declared that the principal had still not been convicted (and thus, the defendant, as an accessory, could not be tried), or handed over a charter of pardon from the king. Monarchs rarely exonerated prisoners sentenced to the peine: only 15 of the 481 individuals (or 3.12 percent) received pardons for their crimes. Yet, that did not prevent others from stating falsely that they had been promised a pardon, but were still anxiously awaiting the arrival of their paperwork. At the Nottingham arraignment of John Kylnehurst in 1389, the indictment revealed that he had been arrested on the appeal of Thomas Smyth of Waterfall for having by night feloniously stolen cattle worth five marks. Rather than submit his plea, John disclosed that a friend named Ralph Bassett, a clergyman, had secured a pardon from the king on his behalf, but the charter still remained in the royal hanaper. Giving John the benefit of the doubt, justices ordered him remitted into the custody of the sheriff of Nottingham until the following week. At that time, it became painfully obvious that no pardon was forthcoming. His options narrowed, John opted for silence. With the assent of the appellor, justices called for an inquest to discover if John could speak. The jury determined that he voluntarily (*voluntarie*) pretended to be mute, that he could speak and had done so earlier that day. John returned to

---

[84] YB 1487, Mich., 3 Hen VII, fo. 12a (Seipp 1487.035).
[85] YB 1488, Hil. 3 Hen. VII, fo. 2a (Seipp 1488.005).

prison once more, this time on a starvation diet, and Thomas Smyth reclaimed his horse.[86]

Sometimes it worked in the reverse: standing mute was a maneuver employed by individuals buying time until the pardon was safely in hand. This was the strategy embraced by William le Firmager de Wychase, John Jowe, John Kyng, Stephen Stikebe, and Thomas Rotenhering of Hull when accused of robbery in 1301. Having all refused to plead before justices of jail delivery at Norwich they were sentenced to peine forte et dure. The record gives no indication of how long they suffered in prison before the king granted them pardons.[87] More commonly, the king granted a pardon as recognition of the defendant's overlong suffering, a medieval equivalent of "time served." This was the case with Thomas Harry of Braneston when he was appealed in 1390 by William Pekke for horse thievery. Silence was his first delaying tactic, leading to an inquest, and then prison on a starvation diet. Eventually Harry reappeared before royal justices with a pardon from the king. The charter itself makes the case that justices had sentenced him to death, but because he had suffered for such a long time, the king wished to recognize his agony and pardon him for his crime.[88] In 1369, the king also took pity on two monks from the abbey of St. Edmund, John of Grafton and William of Blundeston. Presumably harboring a grudge against his fellow monk, John of Norton, by night while everyone was asleep in the dormitory, John of Grafton stabbed him to death with a knife, in William's presence. Next morning, scandalized by what he discovered in his dormitory, the abbot ordered the body buried immediately without view of the coroner. Then, when hearing what had happened, he had William and John of Grafton put in prison forte et dure as punishment for the offense. When the event came to the king's attention, he not only pardoned the abbot for concealing the body, but "considering that the said felony was done in hot conflict and not of malice aforethought, and that the said John and William have long sustained the *peine forte et dure* of imprisonment," the king issued a pardon for the two prisoners.[89]

The king's pardon was not mercy without limits. Technically, it extended only to publicly prosecuted crimes; he was not entitled to

---

[86] TNA JUST 3/177, m. 42 (1389).   [87] TNA JUST 3/47/3, m. 5d (1301).
[88] TNA JUST 3/177, m. 4 (1390).   [89] *CPR*, Edward III, vol. XIV (1367–70), 186.

diminish his subjects' right of appeal by issuing a pardon. Of course, as was the case with Thomas Harry above, in practice there were always exceptions to the rule. John atte Puttes of Bishopsden was arrested on the appeal of William atte Chambre of Toneworth, bailiff to Thomas of Bishopsden, for stealing nine oxen worth £4 10s. held in William's custody at Lapworth (Warwickshire). At his arraignment on July 21, 1382, John stood mute and was sentenced to the diet, at which point, William reclaimed his oxen.[90] On February 9, 1384, the king issued John a pardon, at the insistence of the Earl of Warwick. John had lived so long on the diet that it seemed a miracle.[91] It seems likely that because William had recovered his oxen, he was content not to quibble with a miracle. John Hilton's pardon also stands out. He was appealed of having stolen a coverlet, coat, and gown, together worth forty shillings from William Colyere of Astley (Worcestershire) on March 24, 1384. He became the recipient of a Good Friday pardon from the king on May 1 of the same year.[92] In this instance, the nature of the pardon might have made John Hilton's case another exception.

A firmer line in the sand was drawn when it comes to the timing of pardons: the king's mercy did not extend to future crimes. Sir Ralph de Bloyou (or Bloyho) of Cornwall learned this after a long drawn-out feud with his cousin, Sir Henry of Bodrugan. In 1302, accompanied by Thomas le Arcedekne, an innkeeper, Ralph forcibly entered William Beyon's house where his cousin was residing with his (unfortunately unnamed) ward. They pressed Henry to hand over the boy, which he utterly refused to do. Incapable of accomplishing their goal with threats, the atmosphere then turned violent: Ralph and Thomas beat and wounded Henry before abducting his ward and transporting the boy to Thomas' home where he remained for the next three days. Ralph's and Thomas' crimes, as horrific as they were, did not reach the level of felony: abduction, assault, and wounding were all trespasses to be sued at King's Bench as civil pleas. Henry's complaint before the king's justices registered his desire to seek revenge: he asked for damages in the amount of 100 marks.[93] Luckily for Ralph, because of his recent service in Scotland, he held

---

[90] TNA JUST 3/167, m. 50/1 (1382).   [91] *CPR*, Richard II, vol. II (1381–5), 373.
[92] TNA JUST 3/172, m. 2d (1383); *CPR*, Richard II, vol. II, 392.
[93] Horwood, *Year Books of the Reign*, 106–11 (Seipp, 1302.065rs).

the king's favor. On January 22, 1302, Ralph received a pardon from the king for robbery and trespasses committed against Henry at Glasney, presumably a reference to the ill-fated home invasion. The pardon was renewed within a fortnight to include also receipt of felons.[94] In retaliation, Henry of Bodrugan and his retinue, which included his brothers John and Peter, robbed Ralph de Bloyou and three others at Bodmin (Cornwall), for which they received a pardon on September 15, 1302, at Henry's petition and in consideration of their service in Gascony and Scotland on behalf of the king.[95] Soon after, Ralph was back in court on felony charges, although the exact nature of those charges are unclear. At his arraignment, he chose silence and was adjudged to peine forte et dure. After ten days of suffering, his friends approached the king's justices, bringing the pardon issued to Ralph on January 22, 1302. The justices did not bend: because he was indicted for felonies committed since the date of the charter, they refused to recognize the pardon's validity. Ralph was sent back to prison to endure peine forte et dure, where he eventually died.[96]

(4)   Turning Approver

Approvement was one of the king's most powerful weapons in the battle against the criminal underworld. Turning king's evidence existed chiefly for career felons and/or members of organized crime. The Crown heartily, even heavy-handedly, encouraged approvement because it was understood to be effective in breaking down the bonds of loyalty between members of criminal companies.[97] Approver status did not function as a "get out of jail free card," even if it was often advertised as such. Confessed felons who turned king's evidence were expected to appeal each and every one of their former criminal associates. Judicial combat was the standard mode of proof, with the approver assuming the role of king's champion. A day would be appointed in which both combatants, clothed in leather and armed with shields and clubs pointed with horn or iron, provided at the king's

---

[94] *CPR*, Edward I, vol. iv (1301–7), 20.   [95] *CPR*, Edward I, vol. iv, 63.
[96] Horwood, *Year Books of the Reign*, 498–9 (Seipp 1302.188rs).
[97] Frederick Hamil, "The King's Approver: A Chapter in the History of English Criminal Law," *Speculum* 11.2 (1936): 239.

expense, would meet on the battlefield. The duel continued until death or surrender.[98] The prospect of battle alone was surely sufficient to discourage some would-be approvers who feared being cut down on the battlefield more than hanging from the gallows. Over the course of the fourteenth century, judicial combat became less popular as a mode of trial, aided in large part by the moral censure of ecclesiasts and the judiciary's marked preference for the speed of a jury trial. The choice of trial method belonged to the appellee, not the approver, and the appellee might well choose jury trial over battle. For the approver, it was enough to have assisted in securing the appellee's conviction. If each one of his myriad appeals resulted in a guilty verdict, an approver's freedom, although not in England, was his reward. He was permitted to abjure the realm safely. However, the Crown seldom lived up to its side of the bargain. Instead, as remuneration for betraying their accomplices, most approvers lived out the rest of their days in prison.[99] This was certainly a step up from hanging, but far from the life in France they had been promised. Granted, for those few who secured their liberty, it is hard to imagine how they escaped the enmity of those they had betrayed. Certainly, not all did. In 1277, one former approver, Roger le Barewer, made a short-lived attempt to reintegrate into society. After turning king's evidence and implicating his accomplices, he claimed benefit of clergy, underwent purgation, and was released. His former accomplices then hunted him down and murdered him.[100] Most approvers ended up hanging from the gallows. Jurors recognized that their appeals were designed principally to save their necks, and treated them accordingly. Conviction rates on approvers' appeals were notoriously low.[101] It is no surprise, then, that becoming an approver was very much a last resort. For most defendants, the risks far outweighed the likelihood of reward, making approvement an unappealing option.

---

[98] Hamil, "King's Approver," 245.

[99] Anthony Musson, "Turning King's Evidence: The Prosecution of Crime in Late Medieval England," *Oxford Journal of Legal Studies* 19.3 (1999): 471.

[100] TNA JUST 3/85, m. 10d (1277); cited in Henry Summerson, "The Criminal Underworld of Medieval England," *Journal of Legal History* 17.3 (1996): 217. A clergyman who turned approver could not be denied the privilege of the church; Articles of the Clergy, 9 Edw. II (1315–16), *SR*, vol. I, 174.

[101] Musson, "Turning King's Evidence," 477.

The option to turn approver was limited in its availability. Women, the disabled, and the elderly were prohibited from engaging in trial by combat; therefore, even though their appellees might prefer battle to jury trial, it was out of the question. Outlaws, abjurers, and anyone who had ever claimed benefit of clergy were excluded as well. The means of accusation was also relevant: only an accused felon on the king's indictment qualified to turn approver. Those appealed by a private accuser did not.[102] Nonetheless, for eligible men who were desperate to stay alive, or frantically clinging to the hope of a pardon or a prison-break, turning king's evidence was the perfect delaying tactic. This is even recognized in a statute of Henry IV (d.1413), which decried the "mischief of pardons granted to approvers." The statute explains that "divers common and notorious felons," at their arraignments, "for safeguard of their lives they become provers, to such intent, that in the mean time by brokage, [grants, and gifts to be made'] to divers persons, to pursue and have their charters, and then after their deliverance, they become more notorious felons than they were before." In the hope of putting an end to this nefarious practice, the king declared that anyone who brokered a pardon for an approver stood surety for his future behavior. If the approver returned to a life of crime after his release, his surety owed the king £100, a fine so exorbitant it was out of the realm of possibility for the vast majority of sureties.[103]

The approvement process was highly time-consuming. If the defendant waited until his arraignment to turn approver (after potentially months in prison awaiting trial), asking to confess to a coroner itself gained the defendant a delay of up to three days plus whatever time it took to extract a writ of approvement from the king (perhaps several weeks).[104] The expectation that approvers appeal

---

[102] Hamil, "King's Approver," 240. There are in fact instances when those appealed by an approver also became an approver. In 1329, Hugh Snow of Dunhull was taken on an approver's appeal, accused of having broken into the home of John Shepherd of Haynes at Haynes in the hundred of Flitton, where they stole linen and woolen cloth worth two shillings, and slew the said John. Hugh confessed to the felony before the coroner Richard of Merston and became an approver. We are told that he appealed many men. Superimposed on the entry in the jail delivery rolls is the statement that he held himself mute and it was found by an inquest that he could speak on that day. And so he was hanged. Chattels worth fifteen shillings, eleven pence, for which the vill of Flitwick will respond. TNA JUST 3/124, m. 20 (1329).
[103] 5 Hen. IV, c. 2 (1403–4), SR, vol. II, 144.
[104] Musson, "Turning King's Evidence," 472.

multiple former accomplices then drew out the process for months, sometimes even years at a time. Tracking down and arresting thirty to forty accomplices was a laborious process. Some approvers appealed and even greater number. In 1389, William Rose of Hampshire appealed fifty-four individuals.[105] Another *probator regis*, Robert Nurry, indicted at Gloucester in 1300, accused seventy-three of his former partners in crime.[106] Of course, the danger in appealing such an impressive number is that it upped the stakes significantly. One failed appeal might result in the approver's hanging; with seventy-three appeals, the odds were not in his favor.

To complicate the sheriff's investigation further, criminal associates might enjoy a string of aliases. Martin Budde, a thief convicted at Norwich in 1440, sometimes went by the name of William Neweman; John Spicer, one of Edmund Castelyn's associates, appealed in 1397, was also known by the surnames Silvestre, Flemyng, Drapere, and Leche.[107] Tracing a man's whereabouts when you were not entirely certain which name he was living under was not a simple task. Sheriffs were also limited by the geographic boundaries of their office. When an appellee fled outside the shire, their hands were tied. They could not barge into another county with a posse in tow. Rather, justices of jail delivery had to issue a writ to the sheriff of the relevant county ordering him to arrest the appellee and bring him to answer before justices.[108] Many fugitives evaded the law altogether, but the law did not abandon hope until outlawry had been pronounced. The process of outlawry required exaction before four successive county courts, typically held at three-week intervals. Thus, the process of outlawry alone added another three months' onto the approver's life. Here, it is important to recognize that with death looming, approvers had good incentive to lie. The allegations of John Kyroun of Norfolk sent Crown officials on a two-year "wild goose chase," at which point the county sheriff conceded that the approver had fabricated both the appellees and (remarkably) also the locations of the crimes.[109] Surely, many other approvers adopted this strategy in an effort to extend their lives.

---

[105] Musson, "Turning King's Evidence," 472.
[106] Summerson, "Criminal Underworld," 204.
[107] Summerson, "Criminal Underworld," 217–18.
[108] 28 Edw. I (1300), *SR*, vol. I, 141.
[109] TNA JUST 3/48, m. 20d (1314), as cited in Musson, "Turning King's Evidence," 472.

Only seventeen of the 481 who stood mute in the plea rolls (or, 3.5 percent) were approvers, most of those who turned king's evidence did so after time spent starving in prison had convinced them that there must be a better alternative. For a number of defendants, turning approver and standing mute were merely two distinct phases in a larger strategy of staying alive. The record of Henry Hedelowe of Worcester makes this clear. On November 29, 1390, Henry Hedelowe opted to become an approver, as the record states, of his own free will and in good faith. He confessed to multiple felonies, implicating his accomplices in the process. Among others, he admitted to being the principal offender in the burglary of John Come's homestead, alongside John Neweburgh, tailor, John Pixstoke, wheeler, and Jenan Walshman of Kempsey. In this instance, they targeted chiefly agricultural goods and implements, stealing twelve and a half bushels of wheat, estimated value of twenty-one pence; two axes, at twelve pence; two weights, at four pence; one spokeshave, at one penny; and a chimney iron, at two pennies. In addition, the approver admitted that the said John, John, and Jenan accompanied him also to burglarize the home of John atte Ree at Cleeve (*Clayves*) where they stole one brass pot worth five shillings. Oddly enough, after making these appeals, Henry clammed up and stood mute. He was returned to prison, one assumes (although the record does not actually say it) that he was hitherto subjected to peine forte et dure for rejecting the law.[110]

From the perspective of the king's justices, Henry's silence was not a problem. Even if an approver withdrew his appeal, the courts could still pursue the case upon the king's indictment. Why Henry chose to stand mute after his confession must remain a matter of speculation. Summerson argues persuasively that, for many approvers, the act of confession itself was meaningful: "[i]n a society in which confession was a religious duty, a detailed admission of past crimes may sometimes have eased a charged conscience."[111] In the English legal system, the only way to confess without inviting execution was to turn king's evidence, or abjure. There are other possible explanations for Henry's belated silence. Anxiety at the thought of engaging in judicial combat may also have been to blame. Anthony Musson writes of numerous approvers who withdrew their appeals when the prospect

---

[110] TNA JUST 3/180, m. 40 (1390).   [111] Summerson, "Criminal Underworld," 203.

of battle became too real.[112] Henry may also have come to regret
fingering his friends, appreciating the danger he brought to their
lives. Through his silence he might have hoped to retract or
undermine the credibility of his appeals.[113]

If unburdening his soul before he died was the goal of John of
Blackstone's bid for approvement, he managed to do it without
bringing his accomplices down with him. At his arraignment on
August 29, 1395 at York castle, the charges read out against him
were myriad. He had stolen six shillings and eight pence sterling from
the home of William Goldhouse of Hayton; he had burglarized the
home of William Wryght of Watton and stolen goods worth six marks
sterling; he took fifteen silver shillings in money from John Nude of
Pocklington; and he had stolen nine marks in silver and gold also from
William Wryght. With the cards stacked against him, surely John
realized the seriousness of his situation. When he arrived in court for
his arraignment, he immediately asked for the coroner, signaling his
intention to turn king's evidence. John did not appear in court again
until the following year during the fifth week of Lent. As an approver,
John was brought before justices to begin making his appeals, but he
said nothing. Simon of Elvington and John del More, two of the king's
coroners, reported that they had approached John many times during
his incarceration to ask him if he wished to make an appeal, but he
always refused. The justices asked John whether he knew that his
confession to the felonies would result in his execution, but he
continued to stand mute. Intent to ensure that he was mute for the
right reasons, justices assembled an inquest composed of jailers and
others nearest him in prison who concluded that John could speak and

---

[112] Musson, "Turning King's Evidence," 473.

[113] Other approvers trod a similar path. On March 1, 1326, Ralph Spatheman of
Poleshill confessed before Laurence of Acle (*Attele*) and Roger of Godshill
(*Godesseld*), coroners of Hertfordshire, that he had participated in many thefts,
including absconding with a mare from the home of John Knape of Litlington at
Litlington, worth four shillings. He petitioned to become an approver; but when he
came next before the court to initiate a series of appeals against his former criminal
associates, he stood mute and did not wish to speak. The trial record tells us that an
inquest was made with jurors from the inhabitants of Litlington and Hertfordshire
to see if he was mute by nature, but they declared his silence was malicious. Despite
his status as a confessed felon, justices followed the usual protocol for defendants
who stand mute: they sentenced him to the peine. TNA JUST 3/22/2, m. 1 (1326).

had done so that day. Rather, he pretended to be mute. Justices ordered him returned to prison to suffer the diet.[114]

As confessed felons, approvers bore a great risk when they chose to stand mute. Justices of jail delivery had every right to sentence them to execution on the basis of their confessions. Their unwillingness to do so most likely springs from their discomfort with executing a man without a proper trial. It is worth remembering that it was rare for medieval felons to confess spontaneously. Those who did either turned approver and fought for their lives on the battlefield, or they were sanctuarymen who abjured the realm. Defendants who stood trial invariably denied their guilt. Our silent approvers, then, obliged the king's justices to foray into unfamiliar territory, and in the absence of a jury verdict obtained through the usual channels, they hesitated to sentence a man to death.

Nonetheless, by the fifteenth century, the sense of the judiciary began to turn against approvers who stood mute. A 1406 case from King's Bench contains a courtroom dialogue concerning the options available to justices when faced with just such a situation. The case also demonstrates how a clever defendant employed a broad panoply of tactics in order to prolong his life. An abjurer discovered and arrested within the realm was brought before justices at bar. He was asked if he knew any reason why they should not immediately execute him. His first stratagem was to hide behind the sanctity of the church. His presence in England did violate the terms of his exile. Yet, when he was arrested, he was in a church, and brought out against his will; he prayed to be restored to the same church. The king's attorney swore the contrary; thus, an inquest needed to be assembled to inquire into the matter. When the king's attorney returned later the same day with a writ of *venire facias* to assemble an inquest, the defendant instantly switched tactics. Now, he stood mute. Chief Justice of King's Bench Gascoigne coached him, explaining that he was in danger, that he would be put to his penance if he did not speak. This statement launched an instructive debate among justices and pleaders. Justice Huls responded to Gascoigne's point, stating that "in this case, since he has confessed to a felony before the coroner, and he has made a true declaration, as it is shown, and now he stands mute, thus he will hang

---

[114] TNA JUST 3/183, m. 3 (1395).

because he cannot not be attaint of felony, but rather was attaint before by the confession." Huls went on to say that if he had been arraigned as a felon and agreed to jury trial, *then* stood mute, it would be as if he had said nothing; "but in this case he has confessed to felony before the coroner . . . in which case, he is hangable." Gascoigne disagreed, seeing that the defendant's silence mandated the assembling of an inquest to determine his capacity for speech. At this point, an unnamed clerk at the delivery piped up with a recent analogous case in the hopes of breaking a stalemate. He noted that when Justice Thirning was at the last delivery of Northampton, he sentenced a silent approver to hang, without assembling an inquest because he had already confessed the felony. Justice Gale (one suspects, heaving a sigh of relief) agreed that his action fell within the parameters of the expectations of the law.

The following day, the inquest returned with its results. First, the jurors noted that the defendant had indeed been escorted outside a church against his will, as he had said. Next, as to the matter of speech, they said that he spoke the day before, and that he now stands mute by fraud. Content to ignore the violation of sanctuary, or more likely resolved to accept that an abjurer was no longer eligible to claim the church's protection, Gascoigne announced that, on the advice of his fellow justices, he had determined that the felon was attaint by his confession; thus, penance was inappropriate. He would hang. The defendant suddenly found his voice. He claimed benefit of clergy, with one caveat: he could not read. Justices declared that he would thus not enjoy the privilege.[115]

In 1421, justices of jail delivery at Newgate encountered a similar case, but this time with a different result. At his arraignment, an unnamed man alleged that he had been arrested in a field belonging to the fee and ancient lordship of the church of Saint John, to which he hoped to be restored. His assertion provoked an interesting discussion of exactly which part of Saint John's lands might properly be considered part of the sanctuary. Justice Babington maintained that the houses with the crosses on their backs belonged to the sanctuary, but not the adjoining fields. At that, Justice Hankford interrupted with a relevant personal experience. He told the court how he had once attended the arraignment of a man apprehended in one of those houses and they had an inquest to determine whether the house in fact

---

[115] YB Mich. 8 Hen. IV (1406), fos. 1b–2b (Seipp 1406.104).

belonged to the sanctuary, or whether someone had put a cross on the house in collusion. It was found that sanctuary included the houses, and thus the man was restored; but, as Hankford noted, the current case was not about the houses, but about the fields, for which "the felon" must respond "to his peril." One can only imagine what the defendant was thinking at this point: labeled a felon even before conviction, warned of imminent danger, his carefully planned strategy crumbling around him, the man asked to speak to the coroner. He confessed to the charges against him, and swore on the Bible that he would appeal all of those who were guilty, and not be deterred by any favor; nor would he knowingly appeal anyone who was not guilty out of malice. He was given three days to make his appeals. When the sheriff and the coroner came to see him the following day to begin making his appeals, he said that he did not wish to speak; and so he was put to his penance.[116]

Fifty years later, a note by Justice Littleton inserted into the year books offers some clarification as to the judiciary's revised stance. He writes that in the case of

one who has abjured the realm or an outlaw for felony is taken and led to the bar, there shall be demanded of them what they can say wherefore they should not be put to death, and if they stand mute it shall be inquired into whether this be by reason of fraud, or by the act of God, etc. But if a felon plead not guilty, and is found guilty, and the justices give a respite of execution for some reason, and then he is led before them and stands mute, then no inquiry shall be made as above etc., but if he have matter to free him from the execution he must plead it at his peril etc. And the difference is that he has been all the time in their prison, and so it is clear to them that he is the same person who was attainted etc., but of the man who has abjured the realm or the outlaw it can be said that he is not the same person etc. and it may be that they are other persons etc.[117]

(5) Pleading the Belly

A woman's capacity to delay execution was constrained by her sex. As this book has already observed, female felons were barred from claiming

---

[116] Ralph Rogers, ed., *Year Books of the Reign of King Henry the Fifth* (Wurzburg: Privately Printed, 1948), 22 (Seipp 1421.102rog).

[117] Nellie Neilson, ed., *Year Books of Edward IV: 10 Edward IV and 49 Henry VI* (SS, vol. XLVII, 1930), 169.

benefit of clergy or turning king's evidence. A woman might petition for a pardon or flee to sanctuary; however, both choices were fraught with difficulties. When it comes to pardons, contemporary attitudes raised psychological barriers against women. The common law singled out felonious women for harsher treatment. Although significantly fewer women were indicted of crimes than were men (and the reasons why have been hotly debated), those few who stood before the courts were more likely to be convicted than the usual (male) criminal. Sermons and courtesy literature promoted a discourse that described the ideal woman as quiet and passive; *ergo*, a criminal woman was unnatural in her aggression and action, although not her disobedience (*vide* Eve). Pardoning a woman in this rhetorical atmosphere bore its pitfalls. That is not to say that the king's mercy fell short of extending to women; of course women were eligible to apply for pardons. Yet, the medieval world was much more comfortable with women who followed Mary's example and interceded with the king on behalf of criminals, rather than behaving as criminals themselves. These attitudes are reflected in fourteenth-century petitions for pardons: women were supplicants in only 29 of 500 (or 5.8 percent) existing petitions, although not all of those women were petitioning to have their own crimes exonerated. Of those twenty-nine, only fifteen received the king's pardon. These women were not typical: most belonged to England's elite, some were even members of the titled nobility.[118] The tiny percentage of petitions emanating from female supplicants implies that most felonious women saw it as a pointless endeavor. They knew they were wasting their time even asking for a pardon.

When it comes to sanctuary, again, women could flee to a church and request to be taken into the church's protection, but few did. Sanctuary principally housed male criminals.[119] Why women shied away from claiming sanctuary is not obvious. One can only hazard a guess. Perhaps residing within the precinct of a church surrounded by an all-male clergy did more harm than good to a woman's reputation. If she was planning to stand trial eventually, this consideration would

---

[118] Helen Lacey, *The Royal Pardon: Access to Mercy in Fourteenth-Century England* (York Medieval Press, 2009), 28.

[119] In her sample of 1,800 cases, only 1 percent of sanctuary-seekers were women. Shannon McSheffrey, *Seeking Sanctuary: Crime, Mercy, and Politics in English Courts, 1400–1550* (Oxford University Press, 2017), 19.

be particularly pertinent. Abjuration, the follow-up to sanctuary for many sanctuary-seekers, was probably not a viable option for most women. It is doubtful whether a woman could easily integrate herself into a new, foreign community as an exile and a single woman. The difficulty of relocating for women explains also why so few female felons became fugitives and stayed beyond the reach of the law. Outlawry – called "waivery" when it involved a woman – was also an "overwhelmingly male" activity.[120]

One of the few times that a woman had a legal advantage over a man is when it came to pregnancy: a female convicted felon might plead the belly in order to defer execution until after the birth of her child. Admittedly, the reprieve was only temporary. Despite the claims of some legal scholars who have bandied about the phrase "benefit of the belly" to imply that pregnancy saved a woman from the gallows, this was emphatically not true of the Middle Ages. Pregnant felons were typically executed after they had given birth.[121] Nonetheless, for those women capable of feigning pregnancy convincingly, pleading the belly might extend their lives for at least a few months before the jailer caught on to the ploy. Others might hope to get pregnant in prison. Very few women combined pleas of the belly with standing mute. Only two women in this study followed that path. When Mabel, wife of Roger Norman of Filby was arraigned on June 19, 1315, her prospects did not look good. Not only had she burglarized a home by night, implying premeditation, she targeted a member of the church. Her victim was the local chaplain, Robert of Salthouse Wroxham, from whom she had stolen an ox worth one mark. When asked how she wished to plead, she explained that she would not submit to jury trial. Justices ordered her subjected to hard prison (*prisone dure*).[122] Mabel appeared next before the king's justices on January 5, 1317, implying that after a year and a half on a starvation diet, she had decided to

---

[120] Jennifer Brewer, "Let Her Be Waived: Outlawing Women in Yorkshire, 1293–1294," in Alexander Kaufman, ed., *British Outlaws of Literature and History: Essays on Medieval and Early Modern Figures from Robin Hood to Twm Shon Catty* (Jefferson, NC: McFarland 2011), 29.

[121] See Sara Butler, "Pleading the Belly: A Sparing Plea? Pregnant Convicts and the Courts in Medieval England," in Sara Butler and Krista Kesselring, eds., *Crossing Borders: Boundaries and Margins in Medieval and Early Modern Britain. Essays in Honour of Cynthia J. Neville* (Leiden: Brill, 2018), 131–52.

[122] TNA JUST 3/48, m. 21 (1315).

plead. This time, she vehemently denied any criminal involvement before placing her fate in the hands of the jury. The jury rendered a verdict of guilty, at which point Mabel came forward and professed that she was pregnant. The sheriff assembled a jury of six matrons, who confirmed Mabel's pronouncement. She was sent back to prison to await the baby's delivery.[123] At that point, Mabel disappears from the records, so it is not entirely clear what happened to her in the end.

It is hard to imagine that Mabel survived a year and a half on a diet of bread and puddle water on alternating days. It is even harder to imagine that someone so malnourished managed to get pregnant, in prison, while she was in isolation. Mabel must have persuaded her jailer to pursue a less rigorous form of penance. That is exactly what happened in the case of Alice la Droys (also de Droys). On April 9, 1303, Richard atte Haghe (also atte Hawe), constable of the prison at Oxford castle, appeared before justices of jail delivery to respond to allegations that he had relaxed a sentence of peine forte et dure on a prisoner without authorization. The indictment notes that Alice had been detained in prison for burglarizing the home of William of Beresford at Brightwell, yet at her trial she had chosen to stand mute. Justices condemned her to peine forte et dure in Richard atte Haghe's prison, but he had rendered the sentence ineffective as a coercive measure when he "willingly relaxed" the punishment and "she was held softly in free prison," an act that they interpreted as contempt of court. A jury found him guilty and he was returned to prison. The record does not give any sense of how long his sentence lasted, but it was not long before he was reinstated in his position as constable of the castle prison.[124]

Three months later, on July 30, 1303, Alice appeared before the court charged with the same crime, but this time the indictment included further details. Purportedly, she had stolen a mazer (a bowl of maple-wood), one golden ring, and a sterling silver fork, appraised at a total value of half a mark. The items had been in the possession of William of Beresford at Brightwell, but they actually belonged to Geoffrey Blome, her appellor. At her arraignment, she denied any culpability, and agreed to put herself upon the country; but fewer than twelve lawful men from Brightwell and Whitney had come to

---

[123] TNA JUST 3/48, m. 40d (1317).   [124] TNA JUST 3/104, m. 1d (1303).

court so they could not assemble a proper jury. Alice was returned to prison once more. On September 5, 1304, she stood before the court again. On this occasion, the sheriff had no trouble putting together an appropriate jury. They found her guilty, and valued her goods and chattels at twenty shillings. In response, Alice pled her belly. A jury of matrons was brought in to examine her; the trustworthy (*fidedignes*) women confirmed her assertion. Justices granted her a delay, and Alice was returned to prison once again.[125]

Nothing more is heard from Alice, but Richard penned a petition to the king in 1307 begging his mercy. He explained that he had been imprisoned for the past three years on two charges. One, that he and others detained the castle at Oxford against Walter of Gloucester, escheator this side of Trent, sent by the king to take the castle into his possession. Since that time, his co-conspirators had all been released from prison. Two, that he had assisted in Alice la Droys' prison-break from the castle at Oxford, where she had been remitted by Roger le Brabanzun and his fellow justices of oyer and terminer after discovering she was pregnant. In his defense, Richard was quick to deny any culpability, claiming that after she had given birth he had obeyed the court's judgment, and refused to let her exit or give her permission to dwell elsewhere.[126] The king reopened the case in response to Richard's petition. In September of 1307, Richard was brought before the Marshalsea for trial, but he and the jury did not see eye to eye. The jurors placed the blame chiefly on Henry atte Berie, one of Richard's servants at the prison, who feloniously helped Alice to exit and escape the castle, but they stated unequivocally that Richard knew and consented and was thus an accessory to the crime. At this point, Richard pleaded his clergy.[127] What happened then is not entirely clear, but the king's private correspondence for December 6, 1307, includes an order for Richard's release.[128]

Alice la Droys clearly falls into the same category as the others discussed in this chapter: sheer desperation to avoid execution led her to stand mute, then plead the belly, and finally escape from prison. Her relationship with Richard atte Haghe is wholly suspicious. He put his job and health on the line for her not once, but twice, and did so even

---

[125] TNA JUST 3/104, m. 15d (1304).   [126] TNA SC 8/219/10921 (1307).
[127] TNA SC 8/219/10922 (1307).   [128] *CCR*, Edward II, vol. 1 (1307–13), 16–17.

after he learned that being a constable did not in fact secure him immunity from punishment for disregarding judicial mandates. Was Richard the father of her child? Or, was Henry atte Berie? Alice could not have been pregnant in April of 1303 when Richard first materialized in court, otherwise he would have cited her pregnancy as an excuse for why he flouted a court order and eased up on the court's mandate of peine forte et dure. No one would have blamed him for judging the life of her unborn child more important than following a court order. One also suspects that Alice would have pled pregnancy initially rather than refuse to plead at all if she had had that option. The most likely explanation is that, like Mabel Norman above, she became pregnant during her incarceration, and Richard's foolishly heroic efforts to keep Alice alive hint that he may have been to blame. With Mabel and Alice, pleas of the belly take their place among the legal loopholes manipulated by reluctant defendants to prolong their lives. The difficulty of faking pregnancy, especially for a sustained period, explains why the plea was seldom used for this purpose.[129]

Saving an Accomplice

In his *Commentaries,* when discussing the arraignment process, William Blackstone remarks that from the very beginning, English common law tied an accessory's fate closely to the principal's. He explains:

---

[129] The Carkeny family's experience before the courts demonstrates the various inclinations of defendants who feared the worst. On March 15, 1316, Richard Carkeny and his sons John and Roger, as well as his daughter Margaret and her son John, were all arraigned before justices of jail delivery at Norwich castle. Taken in possession of stolen goods, namely eleven sheep and twelve wool fells, they all responded in different ways. Richard and his son John explained that they were priests, and thus did not need to answer. Accordingly, the deacon of Norwich reported that he needed to inquire into the truth of the matter. The remaining three defendants, Roger, Margaret, and John, the grandson, all denied any participation in the alleged act. Roger refused to place himself upon the jury; justices returned him to prison on the diet. Margaret and John agreed to jury trial. After some deliberation, the jury put forward a verdict on the four Carkeny family members. They declared Richard was innocent; his clerical status, then, was irrelevant. He was released from prison. They found John, Richard's son, guilty; he was delivered to the deacon *clericus convictus.* Margaret and her son John were also found guilty. Margaret pled her belly, a claim corroborated by a jury of matrons; she was returned to prison to await delivery. Her son John was hanged. TNA JUST 3/48, m. 27 (1316).

By the old common law the accessory could not be arraigned till the principal was attainted; and therefore, if the principal had never been indicted at all, had stood mute, had challenged above thirty-five jurors peremptorily, had claimed the benefit of clergy, had obtained pardon or had died before attainder, the accessory in any of these cases could not be arraigned: for *non constitit* [not evident] whether any felony was committed or not, till the principal was attainted; and it might so happen that the accessory should be convicted one day, and the principal acquitted the next, which would be absurd.[130]

Blackstone's assured remarks have led many to conclude that a principal who stood mute in premodern England did so with the foreknowledge that a refusal to plead barred one's accomplice(s) from being arraigned.[131] While silence would not save one's own neck, it would save those of one's associates. This explanation bears a marked similarity to the notion that those who chose pressing did so to protect their families' financial prospects. Both interpretations place the defendant in the best possible light: a defendant's actions are selfless and heroic. In essence, the silent defendant becomes a martyr, self-sacrificing to save others. Logically, the reasoning behind the assertion is sound. Although an argument can be made for equality in guilt between the principal and the accomplice, an idea that dates back to Roman law and explains why their crimes, although different in degree, were still thought to warrant the same punishment, yet common law always prioritized the principal. The principal's acquittal functioned as a positive declaration of the absence of crime. No crime had taken place: thus, the accessory was released without trial. Justice William Thirning made this point clear in a 1406 statement:

in every case of felony where a man is indicted as principal, and is acquitted by a charter of pardon, clergy, or forswearing the realm, or in any other manner, the accessory in this case will not be arraigned, because when the principal is given his life by law (in whatever manner this be), this felony is extinct in his person, and consequently acquitted, and for the same reason the accessory is

---

[130] Blackstone, vol. IV, ch. 25.

[131] This was a concern in the case of Robert Crichton of Sanguhar (d.1612), executed for the murder of a fencing instructor. See Krista Kesselring, "Marks of Division: Cross-border Remand after 1603 and the Case of Lord Sanquhar," in Sara Butler and Krista Kesselring, eds., *Crossing Borders: Boundaries and Margins in Medieval and Early Modern Britain. Essays in Honour of Cynthia J. Neville* (Leiden: Brill, 2018), 272.

acquitted. For it cannot be that the principal is acquitted, and the accessory not.[132]

Of course, the reality of the courtroom experience is never quite as straightforward or as colorful. While an accessory could not be arraigned until the principal was convicted, the sheriff took no chances that the accomplice might duck out of town in the meantime. He ordered the arrest, indictment, and incarceration of the accomplice while awaiting the principal's trial and conviction. Accordingly, even if an accomplice might never be tried, his or her life did not remain untouched by the experience. Both one's reputation and one's finances took a serious hit. This process held even when the principal fled the scene of the crime and the sheriff was still optimistic about the outcome of the investigation. Nor did formal announcement of the principal's outlawry after the required number of exactions lead to the accomplice's release from prison; rather, in these circumstances, the law interpreted flight as a confession. The declaration of outlawry acted as a conviction, permitting them to proceed directly to trial for the accomplice. It is worth restating that common law did not normally equate outlawry with conviction. Indeed, the fact that a principal who turned him- or herself in to the sheriff still needed to be tried and might even be acquitted (regardless of the accessory's fate) underscores the utter absurdity of treating outlawry as a conviction when it comes to accomplices.

Outlawry was one of the few scenarios in which English justices were in firm agreement as to the necessary process. The year books outline a number of other plot twists that generated ceaseless debate between justices and pleaders about the proper course of action. To offer some curious examples: what if both principal and accessory were convicted, but following conviction (and prior to execution) the principal was awarded a pardon from the king? Was the accessory pardoned by association? As a 1341 homicide arraignment at King's Bench indicates, justices must consider the circumstances leading up to a pardon. A chaplain indicted as an accessory to homicide refused to plead at bar because he alleged that the principal in the crime had already been acquitted. A search of the relevant roll corroborated his story. Justices

---

[132] YB Trin. 7 Hen. IV (1406), fo. 16a (Seipp 1406.066).

learned that the principal had slain in self-defense and received a charter from the king as a result. One of the justices laid out the necessary course of action, stating that the principal was acquitted since "by law [homicide in self-defense] was not a felony"; thus, they could not arraign an accessory when there had been no crime.[133] Naturally, self-defense warranted a pardon *de cursu* because it was an excusable homicide. The king also regularly pardoned unexcusable homicides simply because the petitioner sought and paid for one. In that situation, shouldn't the accessory be required to seek his own pardon? Sir Geoffrey le Scrope, fourteenth-century chief justice of King's Bench, cited in Fitzherbert's *Graunde Abridgement*, vociferously agreed.[134]

Did the means of prosecution guide the process? That is, should trial procedure vary in accordance with whether principal and accessory stood accused on indictment at the king's suit, or through private appeal? The normal rules often did not apply to private prosecution. This was true of pardons, which exonerated felons of crimes for which they stood indicted at the king's suit, but not by appeal; the means of prosecution also defined one's right to legal representation, and the confiscation of stolen goods. Hence, it should not be surprising that Chief Justice of King's Bench, Thomas Byling, believed it made a difference when it came to the prosecution of principal and accessory. In a 1473 appeal, Byling asserted that the court must treat principal and accessory separately, because in an appeal "no one (defendant) will have advantage of the other (defendant's release)."[135] Appeals highlight the pro-plaintiff bias undergirding the common law. The law disconnected the trials of principal and accessory when it worked to the appellor's benefit, that is, when doing so prevented a criminal from evading prosecution. Otherwise, private prosecution saw the fates of principal and accessory tied more closely than usual. This is manifest in an appeal of felony from 1452, in which John Fortescue (d. 1479) and others argued that as soon as the principal is outlawed, the accessory's arraignment acts as an attainder

---

[133] Luke Pike, ed., *Year Books of the Reign of King Edward the Third: Year* xv (RS, no. 31, part B, vol. VI, 1891), 262–3 (Seipp 1341.155rs).

[134] Fitzherbert, *Graunde Abridgement*, section *Corone*, no. 151, fol. 214.

[135] *nul avera avantage d'auter.* YB Mich. 13 Edw. IV (1473), fo. 1b–2b (Seipp 1473.009).

of the principal. Thus, if the principal ever returns, there is no need for a trial. He or she is immediately hanged.[136]

What if the principal claimed benefit of clergy after both the principal and the accessory had been convicted of the crime? Should the principal, who bore the greater burden of guilt, receive the lighter sentence just because he could read? A 1488 discussion from the exchequer chamber concludes that the accessory was at a distinct disadvantage, but such was the law. Arguing by analogy, Justice Hussey noted that if the accessory is made to answer when the principal is outlawed, it stands to reason that the same should apply here, that is, the court should proceed with the accessory's hanging. Nonetheless, as the case reporter clarifies, timing is everything. If the principal confessed and then claimed benefit of clergy, the accessory could not be arraigned at all because judgment was not given on the principal.[137] When the same case reappears in Fitzherbert's *La Graunde Abridgement*, it includes also the first mention of what happens to an accessory when the principal stands mute. Fitzherbert embellishes the scope of the deliberation process by recounting how justices spent two days debating the larger question. Ultimately, all the justices except Townshend agreed that the accessory should hang "because the law had done all that could be done." Attempting to debunk the celebrated myth that the court must attaint the principal before an accomplice might be arraigned, Justice Hussey enumerates the various circumstances in which the legal maxim "the accessory follows the principal" (*accessorium sequitur suum principale*) does not apply. He states, "if the principal was outlawed, the accessory will be arraigned, and again if it is that the principal will reverse the outlawry and will be found not guilty, and if the principal stands mute, the accessory will be arraigned." At this point, Justice Bryan remarks on the one exception: that "if the prisoner would pray his clergy at the beginning [that is, during pleading], there is nothing [to be done] but he will be put to his penance."[138]

---

[136] YB Pasch 30 Hen. VI (1452), fo. 5a (Seipp 1452.010).

[137] YB, Hil., 3 Hen. VII (1488), fo. 1b (Seipp 1488.003). This case also appears in the reports of Sir John Caryll (dating to 1501–22). Caryll has Hussey musing haughtily, "it was amazing law to charge the same inquest with the principal and the accessory at the same time," noting "that he would never allow it to be done before him." John Baker, ed., *Reports of Cases by John Caryll* (SS, vol. cxv, 1998), 8.

[138] Fitzherbert, *Graunde Abridgement*, section *Corone*, no. 58, fo. 210v.

Fitzherbert's *Abridgement* would seem to be the only medieval source to address the fate of the accessory when a principal stands mute, and it implies that a principal's refusal of the law did nothing to save an accomplice's life. This ruling fits in well with the general jurisprudence exhibited by England's judiciary in the year books. The one unifying thread to emerge is a general reluctance to let an accessory walk free simply because the principal, for one reason or another, managed to evade the full rigors of the law. England's medieval judiciary was not going to let a loophole stand in the way of justice. Bryan's expectation that an accomplice be sent to peine forte et dure when the principal claimed benefit of clergy prior to conviction also reflects the unwillingness to permit felons to manipulate the law to their own benefit. Better to leave a prisoner in an indefinite state of limbo fasting in prison, than to let a criminal go free without a trial.

The records themselves offer little guidance to help us understand just how much justices and jurors cared about apportioning guilt. Jail delivery rolls seldom indicate which of the multiple participants in a felony was the principal. If the judiciary conferred on the issue, court scribes did not see it relevant enough to include in the trial reports. When they do include mention of the principal, it is usually because the accessory brought it up, objecting to trial on the grounds that the principal had already been acquitted. Nor were the trials of principal and accessory necessarily separate. Because they were included in the same indictment, if the sheriff had arrested both participants, they appeared in court together. The trial report states specifically that they were asked separately (*separatim*) how they wished to plead; yet it is clear that they were tried immediately one after another, in each other's presence, standing mere feet apart. While a medieval court labeled these "separate" trials, a modern court might quibble with that definition.

There are numerous examples of criminal partners tried jointly in which one refused to plead while the other hanged. In 1358, William Boone of Flitcham, Vincent Wynch of Flitcham, Henry Forster of Lillington and William Wriselee, tailor, were arrested and tried for having broken into the home of Richard de la Rokele at Appleton and stolen measures of linen and wool, a silver pot, and other valuables worth £100, in addition to 200 marks in cash. To make matters worse, they also set fire to the house. Not surprisingly, their indictment describes them as common thieves. They were asked independently how they wished to acquit themselves. William Boone and Vincent challenged so many jurors that they ended up in prison sentenced to the diet. Henry and William Wriselee submitted to jury trial and were found guilty; they hanged.[139]

Multiple fates also awaited the partners involved in the 1342 burglary of Farnham castle, the bishop of Winchester's seat of power. Eight men, all described as common thieves, stood indicted at the king's suit: Richard Sturrye, John of Woodford senior, Walter atte Mede of Weekley, John of Peckham, John of Daventry, John Bysshop of Romsey, John of Bristol, and John Waleys, the servant of Richard Sturrye. The indictment reports that they broke into William of Barkston's chamber at the castle, and stole goods from his custody worth ten pounds, namely two silver pots, twelve dishes, twelve silver salt-cellars, and two silver goblets. At their trials, Walter, John of Daventry and John Bysshop immediately and altogether declared that because they were members of the clergy, they might not respond without the ordinary. The vicar of Chertsey sent his ordinary to examine the claimants. Before they were released into his custody, jurors first passed sentence. They declared the men guilty, thus they were delivered *clerici convicti*. Of the remaining five accused, John of Woodford and John Waleys opted for jury trial; they were also found guilty, and the marginalia implies that they were subsequently hanged. Richard Sturrye, John of Peckham, and John of Bristol denied any involvement in the crime, but refused to put themselves upon a verdict of the country. They were committed to prison to endure peine forte et dure.[140] At no time, did the court make a point to designate one individual as being any more or less guilty than the others; nor is there any reason to believe that anyone's arraignment relied on the outcome of another. Even our master and servant duo, Richard Sturrye and John Waleys, defy the usual expectations. One suspects a jury might assume the existing hierarchy would bleed over into their criminal relationship. Yet, the two were arraigned at the same time; Richard's silence did not in any way deter justices from trying his servant.

What is most significant is that no medieval authority argues that when a principal stands mute he does so to save his accomplice's skin.

---

[139] TNA JUST 3/139, m. 32d (1358).   [140] TNA JUST 3/130, m. 43 (1342).

In the absence of evidence, it seems likely that this notion developed in the post-medieval age.

Conclusion

While Margaret Clitheroe's example hovers at the edges of any history of peine forte et dure, what the medieval evidence reveals is that her experience of martyrdom is the most central aspect. Standing mute has often been associated with martyrdom, a fact that will be explored in more depth in the following two chapters. Although the cause for individual sacrifice might vary, it has long been supposed that those who chose peine forte et dure did so to save their family's inheritance and reputation. The medieval evidence offers some evidence to support this assertion. Nonetheless, it is clear that most silent defendants had no lands or goods to pass on to their heirs. Martyrdom may have had more to do then with reputation than inheritances. Theories concerning manifest guilt are also not immediately substantiated by the medieval record, although many of those awaiting trial had good reason to fear that a jury might convict. What the records do substantiate is that standing mute was just one of a multitude of tactics manipulated by suspects to draw out the trial process. Some mute defendants also claimed benefit of clergy, challenged jurors, fed justices stories of charters of pardon being drawn up by the king, turned approver, or pled their bellies. All of these strategies smack of desperation, suggesting that a deep-rooted fear of conviction motivated some men and women to choose silence.

What this chapter has not addressed is protest against jury trial as a means of judgment, the very reason that scribes believed most defendants chose silence, and which they wrote time and again in the formal record of the arraignment. Chapter 6 will turn to that subject next.

6

Standing Mute as *Imitatio Christi*

> And Herod, seeing Jesus, was very glad; for he was desirous of a long time to see him, because he had heard many things of him; and he hoped to see some sign wrought by him. And he questioned him in many words. But he answered him nothing. And the chief priests and the scribes stood by, earnestly accusing him. And Herod with his army set him at nought, and mocked him, putting on him a white garment, and sent him back to Pilate.
>
> Luke 23: 8–11.

An anonymous Middle English sermon from the fifteenth century walks its audience through the process of arraignment. The writer tells us that one of the goals of this exercise is to instruct the audience of listeners how court procedure is founded on biblical exemplars, even in the king's court because all law comes from God's law. The sermon tells us that when a man is accused of any crime, he has four lawful choices for how he might respond. First, "he may put hym to witteneshyng of is countre, as þe gospel techeþ vs: 'In ore duorum vel trium stet omne verbum,' Mathei 18" (he may put himself to witnessing of his country [that is, jury trial], as the gospel teaches us: 'That in the mouth of two or three [witnesses] every word may stand.' Matthew 18:16). Second, he may claim benefit of clergy ("preuilige as ȝiff he be a clerke"). This, too, the sermon-writer advises us is grounded in scripture. The clerical exemption springs from Joseph's time in Egypt. When the Egyptians sold land to Joseph during the famine,

303

"þe clerkes lyvyd vppon þe kynges cost and sold not þer livelod, but were preuileged" (the clerks lived upon the king's cost and sold not their livelihood, but were privileged). The fourth is the option to which the sermon strives with little subtlety to guide us: confession, which elsewhere in this collection of sermons is described as the spiritual equivalent of the "lapis philosophorum" (philosopher's stone).[1] Confession also originates in a biblical passage, this time in Psalms, when David acknowledges before God his adultery with Bathsheba. "'Tibi soli peccaui, et malum coram te feci' ... I haue synned and afore þe I haue don wickednes" ('To thee only have I sinned, and have done evil before thee' (Psalm 50:6) ... I have sinned and before you I have done wickedness).

It is the third option that is most pertinent for this study. The sermon declares that "a man þat is acused, in ys examinacion he may stond dombe with-owten answere" (a man that is accused, in his examination he may stand dumb without answering). For this choice, the sermon's author tells us that we also have holy scripture to thank, specifically the parable of the marriage feast from Matthew 22: 1–14. Jesus tells his disciples that the kingdom of heaven is much like a king who prepares a feast for his son's wedding. When the king notices that one of the guests is unsuitably dressed (hinting that he had not in fact been invited to the wedding), the king asks: "Friend, how camest thou in hither not having a wedding garment?" In response, the man stands silent, speechless. The king's command in response to his silence is reminiscent of peine forte et dure: he has his servants escort the man outside, feet and hands tied together, cast into darkness, there to weep and gnash his teeth. The moral of the story? "For many are called, but few are chosen."

This illuminating sermon does not stop there. Understanding the process of arraignment is vital to all of us, its author explains, because with our "synneful lyvynge" (sinful living), someday we will all have to defend ourselves before God. And when we do, the sermon assures us that the first three approaches will not be "prophetabull" (profitable). For those who hope to put their fate in the hands of the jury, realize that the "queyste" (jury) is composed of the twelve apostles, and "on þat

---

[1] Woodburn Ross, ed., *Middle English Sermons: Edited from British Museum MS Royal 18 B. xxiii* (EETS, vol. CCIX, 1940), 286.

oþur side, we be all defawtyfe: Si dicimus quia peccata non habemus, nosmetipsos seducimus et veritas in nobis non est." (on that other side, we are all faulty:"If we say that we have no sin, we deceive ourselves, and the truth is not in us." 1 John 1:8). The apostles will surely judge rightly and present the truth, and "dowtelis þis is no vey for vs" (doubtless this is no way for us). As to the second option, benefit of clergy is not available in heaven: "for þer no man shall haue preuilege afore anoþur" (for there no man shall have privilege before another). Again, Psalms comes to the rescue to help us understand why this is the case: "Quia reddet ibi vnicuique iuxta opera sua" (because [God] will repay each one according to his deeds. Psalms 28:4). And what about the third way? Is it "prophetabull to vs to be still and sey not" (profitable to us to be still and say nothing)? No, "trewly þis vey is verstt of all" (truly this way is worst of all)! Because when the unwelcome guest stood silent, God bade that he be bound hands and foot and cast into "vttrest derkenes, whereas is wepynge and knastynge of tethe" (utter darkness, where there is weeping and gnashing of teeth). Who would want that? The sermon's writer then leaves us with the only reasonable choice: "'ʒiff þou wilt be Goddes childe, speke, oþur apeell.' But whom shalt þou apeell? I sey þi-selfe" ('If you will be God's child, speak or appeal.' But whom shall you appeal? I say, yourself).[2]

Of course, in reality, when it comes to choosing the appropriate response, venue matters. Before God, confession is the only rational choice – there is no point in a strategic defense when your judge is omniscient. But in the king's court, one suspects that even our sermon-writer would have opted for benefit of clergy. Nonetheless, the author's attempt to locate the genesis of standing mute is illuminating, yet truthfully, somewhat puzzling given the multitude of other biblical and hagiographic examples with seemingly greater relevance from which he might have chosen. Because the objective of his homily is to dismiss every option other than confession, he needs to cast the first three in a negative light. For standing mute, the parable of the marriage feast undoubtedly achieves that goal. There is nothing to admire in the dumbstruck party-crasher who, as the analogy implies, is destined for

---

[2] Ross, ed., *Middle English Sermons*, 269–70.

hell. The real question is whether the sermon-writer's audience would have found this origin myth convincing.

The sermon-writer presents standing mute as an option for fools and cheats. No doubt, the purpose of the sermon was to encourage in its audience a dutiful compliance with the law. By deriding those who do not comply, and questioning their potential for salvation, the sermon hopes to glorify obedience to the law as being in the best interests of a sinner's spiritual welfare. The sermon's narrative, however, is very much at odds with the image of Margaret Clitheroe's heroic martyrdom. Margaret's epic performance makes one point clear: silence is power. As Carolin Behrmann writes, under these circumstances, it is much more than mere silence. It is "a sign of utmost self-control under agonizing torture" and as such "forms the passive non-action tantamount to an act. Instead of extorted speech, the martyr opposes silently, withholding information as strategic action. Thus, the silence of the martyr, his denial of communication and resisting body becomes a sovereign act."[3] Margaret's choreographed rite of resistance was not unique: rather, it was modeled on that of Jesus Christ, who also stood mute when facing trial before unjust authorities in order to communicate the message that they held no power over him. So popular was this trope in medieval literature that her silence would have been instantly recognizable as *imitatio Christi*.

This chapter proposes to interrogate intersections of law and literature as they relate to standing mute and hard prison, relying on Bruce Holsinger's concept of "vernacular legality" as a guide. Holsinger defines vernacular legality as "the self-conscious use of a medieval vernacular in order to explore a specialized realm of authoritative legal knowledge and practice whose documentary and discursive apparatus is confined primarily to Latin."[4] Medieval literature presented its audiences with a unique opportunity to demystify controversial legal processes. As the law became more specialized and esoteric, "the provenance of legal technicians rather than legal actors," literature

---

[3] Carolin Behrmann, "On *actio*: The Silence of Law and the Eloquence of Images," *Zeitschrift für Kunstgeschichte* 76.1 (2013): 65–6.

[4] Bruce Holsinger, "Vernacular Legality: The English Jurisdiction of the *Owl and the Nightingale*," in Emily Steiner and Candace Barrington, eds., *The Letter of the Law: Legal Practice and Literary Production in Medieval England* (Ithaca: Cornell University Press, 2002), 157.

became the means by which ordinary citizens learned about and made sense of the law. This approach resulted in a proliferation of legalistic writing that has prompted literary critics to wonder why "law figures so much more heavily in medieval literature than in the literatures of later periods."[5] Law in medieval literature functioned in multiple ways. Sometimes literature hoped to incite support of, and ease tensions surrounding, existing law; Wendy Matlock sees *The Owl and the Nightingale* as responding precisely to that objective. The poem's underlying message is that "the legal system represents the best means to resolve conflicts, and legal action is a way to avoid violent action."[6] Elsewhere, as this chapter will examine, the legal imagination of literature served as commentary on, or in resistance to, the law. As Richard Firth Green explains, law and literature functioned as "parallel forms of discourse, each with its own conventions and traditions."[7] Literature conceptualizes legal practice often in a manner dissimilar to the legal treatises; taken together, the two provide a more holistic understanding of the law and the distinct legal cultures in which it existed.

With this in mind, the following pages seek to explore the various ways in which popular audiences encountered and shaped the concept of refusing to plead through the drama and literature of the period. Christ's trials before Caiaphas and Annas, Pilate, Herod, and then Pilate again will form the core of this chapter. Medieval England's literature adapted the Passion, setting it in a contemporary atmosphere, and employing the language of the common law so that spectators could appreciate better Christ's experience. As such, Christ's silence was presented as and equated with suspected felons who refused to plead. This is true also of other popular biblical characters, such as Susannah from the Book of Daniel, who functioned as a type of Christ and also chose silence when confronted by her accusers. Analyzing the ways in which authors staged these

---

[5] Emily Steiner and Candace Barrington, "Introduction," in Steiner and Barrington, eds., *Letter of the Law*, 9.

[6] Wendy Matlock, "Law and Violence in *The Owl and the Nightingale*," *Journal of English and Germanic Philology* 109.4 (2010): 448.

[7] Richard Firth Green, "Medieval Literature and Law," in David Wallace, ed., *Cambridge History of Medieval English Literature* (Cambridge University Press, 1999), 407.

defiant and spirited figures helps us to appreciate how a medieval audience reacted when more typical Englishmen refused to plead. In addition, these biblical fragments offer a glimpse into the minds of defendants who opted for silence over a plea: deeply entrenched in a legal vernacular culture in which Christ was the ultimate example of standing mute, surely some of them understood their actions as a form of *imitatio Christi*. Indeed, a Christ-like legacy is most likely what they hoped to leave behind them.

Finally, this chapter will investigate literary representations of hard prison. Historians have often been astonished to see the medieval English vociferously condemn judicial torture and yet remain silent concerning peine forte et dure; yet, in the literature, one unveils the anxiety that is absent from the legal treatises. While English authorities saw peine forte et dure as meritorious violence, putting a suspected felon firmly on the path to spiritual reform, there is no doubt that ordinary Englishmen and women believed the Crown's usage of hard prison was sometimes unjust. Literature was the means by which this sentiment was conveyed to the Crown.

Christ as a Model for Silence

A defendant's right to silence was recognized by the *Leges Henrici Primi* (*c.*1108–9) for those situations in which defendants found their judges objectionable. Why did the medieval English chose silence as the licit response? Why not verbal protest? What does silence symbolize? The answer to this question lies in Christ's defiant muteness before Herod, as recounted in Luke 23:8–11, reminding us that, he, too, declined to cooperate with the system when the law interfered where it did not properly belong. The political undercurrents of his story were not lost on a late medieval audience. In fact, the annual mystery cycles, funded, staged, and performed by local guilds in a number of towns (Chester, Penryn, Wakefield, York) across late fourteenth- and fifteenth-century England, depict a medievalized version of Christ's passion, which rendered his rebelliousness more evocative to contemporary audiences. Albeit, this kind of blatant anachronism was standard fare in medieval culture where the church touted religious art as the Bible of the illiterate. As a teaching aid, the fine arts were infinitely more meaningful when pertinent to the life experiences of parishioners. Portrayals of biblical scenes regularly depict men and women in medieval garb, inhabiting contemporary housing, consorting in European marketplaces or princely courts, and handling the tools of medieval tradesmen. As William Tydeman has noted, English cycle plays:

> had to declare both openly and tacitly their affinities with the life of the market place, the backstreet, the farmyard, and the language, both verbal and visual, had to convince onlookers that the men and women of the Bible looked, and even more importantly, spoke as they did themselves.[8]

The cycle plays were intended *for* and written *about* the commoner. Except for depictions of Pharaoh and King Herod, there are no extant cycle plays intent to relate the lives and experiences of aristocrats and kings.[9]

The updated settings provide valuable insight into how contemporary audiences of commoners viewing the annual mystery plays constructed an ideal of passive resistance to a lawful authority inappropriately expanding its jurisdiction. In doing so, they draw on the English common law to represent a defiant Christ, failing to plead sufficiently before ecclesiastical or royal authorities (respectively, Caiaphas and Pilate), and then standing mute when arraigned by local authorities (Herod) where he not only refused to plead, he even neglected to confirm his own identity. Accordingly, they paint a clear-cut image of the silent defendant as virtuous hero, victimized by a cruel and unreasonable state. The mystery cycles were not atypical in linking a trial that took place in biblical times to contemporary procedures. Representations of the Passion were deliberately suggestive of the late medieval penal system; as a result, they offered medieval audiences a venue to voice grievances about procedural biases, unjust laws, and even national politics.[10] As Theresa Tinkle has recently argued,

> Through the figure of Jesus the play develops an edgy commentary on the royal politics of the time: it holds claims of kingship up to scorn as well as reverence,

---

[8] William Tydeman, "An Introduction to Medieval English Theatre," in Richard Beadle, ed., *Cambridge Companion to Medieval English Theatre* (Cambridge University Press, 1994), 26–7.

[9] James Forse, "Love and Marriage on the Medieval English Stage: Using the English Cycle Plays as Sources for Social History," *Quidditas* 32 (2011): 233.

[10] Daniel Baraz, *Medieval Cruelty: Changing Perceptions, Late Antiquity to the Early Modern Period* (Ithaca: Cornell University Press, 2003), 140–1.

and it grants redemptive potential to a so-called traitor's suffering. The playwrights subvert royal propaganda that seeks to legitimize kings and delegitimize traitors.[11]

The following pages deconstruct the various depictions of Christ as silent defendant in the hopes of grasping fully contemporary perceptions of standing mute as a strategy of resistance to royal authority.[12]

Plays in the vernacular that dramatize stories drawn from scripture date back to at least the 1100s, although the earliest evidence for the mystery cycles as they exist today comes from the late fourteenth century.[13] The purpose of undertaking these enormous annual spectacles was multiple. The locality of the plays was pivotal. Above all, they were a celebration of the cities in which they were hosted, by the guildsmen of those very same cities, many of whom were often involved deeply in local government and saw the plays as a means to model appropriate communal values. Thus, it should come as no surprise that the plays tend to promote a message of respect and obedience to local rather than central authorities, and literary critics have had little trouble uncovering ways in which the plays evoke local events to make the drama come alive for its audiences.[14] The guildsmen who produced these plays saw their work as an act of charity to those living in their communities.[15] At a time when copies of the Bible were few and far between, "[c]ycle plays were among the most common media through which ordinary Christian workers encountered the Bible and their religion in late medieval England."[16] A proclamation from the city of Chester in 1532 underscores this perspective. The city authorities viewed the plays as being critical "for the augmentation & increased faith in our [Lord]+Jesus Christ & to exhort the minds of the

---

[11] Theresa Tinkle, "York's Jesus: Crowned King and Traitor Attainted," *Speculum* 94.1 (2019): 98.

[12] This trope existed throughout the era and appears repeatedly in sermons and hagiography. Clifford Davidson, "Suffering and the York Plays," *Philological Quarterly* 81 (2002): 1.

[13] Forse, "Love and Marriage," 232.

[14] Emma Lipton, "Space and Culture of Witnessing in the York *Entry into Jerusalem*," *Journal of Medieval and Early Modern Studies* 49.2 (2019): 296.

[15] Davidson, "Suffering and the York Plays," 3.

[16] Susan Nakley, "On the Unruly Power of Pain in Middle English Drama," *Literature and Medicine* 33.2 (2015): 6.

common people."[17] The interactive nature of the drama transformed its meaning for the audience. When Christ, nailed and hanging on the cross, called out to those spectators walking by and spoke to them directly, the realness of his ghastly suffering hit home in a way that it did not for an audience listening to church dogma preached in the weekly mass. The contemporary staging enhanced the illusion, in which "Christ becomes one of the local citizens, convicted and crucified through the English judicial system, by which he redeems them all."[18]

The York Cycle offers the most comprehensive exploration of the legal setting in which Christ is hauled before three courts in one night: ecclesiastical, royal, and local, all cooperating and competing for jurisdiction in the trial of Christ the King. The night begins with the church's consistory court, in which Bishop Caiaphas presides attended by Annas, one of his prelates, both men styled with the honorific "sir" usually reserved for knights and clerics.[19] Caiaphas opens by informing his audience that he is "a lord, learned leally in your lay" (a lord, deeply learned in your law. 139, line 4),[20] but that he is about to give them a lesson in canon law. He orders his knights to bring in the "boy that is bound" (146, line 202) who dabbles in sorcery (precisely, false healing and raising from the dead), who defies church law by working on the Sabbath, and who blasphemes God by calling himself His son. Bound and shackled, Christ is dragged before the bishop. The first indication of his unwillingness to acknowledge the bishop's jurisdiction is that he does not bow down in deference to the bishop's respected status. His insolence so enrages the knights that he would have been beaten if Bishop Caiaphas had not stepped in. Almost

[17] Lawrence M. Clopper, ed., *Records of Early English Drama: Chester* (University of Toronto Press, 1979), 27; as cited in Forse, "Love and Marriage," 27.

[18] Elza Tiner, "English Law in the York Trial Plays," *The Early Drama, Art, and Music Review* 18.2 (1996): 103.

[19] The Chester play refers specifically to Caiaphas and Annas as "Sir Bishops." David Mills, ed., "Play 16, Part 1: The Trial and Flagellation of Christ," *The Chester Mystery Cycle: A New Edition with Modernised Spelling* (East Lansing: Colleagues Press, 1992), 271, line 1. In the Wakefield play, he is referred to as a "man of holy kirk." Martial Rose, ed., *The Wakefield Mystery Plays* (London: Evan Brothers, 1961), 362.

[20] Richard Beadle and Pamela King, eds., *York Mystery Plays: A Selection in Modern Spelling* (Oxford University Press, 1984), 139. In what follows, parenthetical line references refer to the York play, unless specifically indicated otherwise.

immediately, Jesus delivers a confession, but with such elusive language any erudite canon lawyer would feel compelled to reject its validity. Going right to the heart of the matter, Caiaphas inquires if he is indeed Christ, God's son (150, line 292), to which the defendant replies "Sir, thou says it thyself, and soothly I say / That I shall go to my Father that I come fro / And dwell with him winly in wealth alway" (Sir, you say it yourself, and truly I say that I shall go to my father, from whom I come, and dwell with him pleasingly, always in happiness. 150, lines 293–5).

Reinforcing the impression that Jesus does not recognize Caiaphas' jurisdiction, the prisoner announces his impatience with the process by remarking that they annoy him "by night, and also for nothing" (150, line 319). The courts' intimate, nighttime setting, signaled by the fact that Caiaphas (like Pilate soon after) is raised from slumber in order to sit as judge, was intended to underscore the illegality of the trial.[21] This characteristic is replicated in all of the mystery cycles. Medieval audiences knew full well that lawful trials take place by day, in public venues, attended by large swathes of the local population. Caiaphas then orders the knights to castigate Christ for his disrespect with a beating (often referred to as the "buffeting of Christ"). In terms of punishment for his crimes, however, Caiaphas' powers are limited. As a bishop, he can order Christ's execution, but he cannot carry it out because of the papal prohibition against clerical participation in the shedding of blood. He must rely instead on the secular arm of the law to do his bidding. Accordingly, he commands his knights to bring Jesus to Sir Pilate of Pontus, "prince of our laws" (164, line 253), called "the High Justice" in the Chester play (275, line 127), representative of Caesar the king. In the Townley play, they refer to him as "a juge sett / Emang men of state" (a judge set among men of state; 260, lines 616–17).[22] There is no question that Pilate is intended to represent one of the king's justices, most likely England's chief justice. In fact, in John

---

[21] Pamela King, "Contemporary Cultural Models for the Trial Plays in the York Cycle," in Alan Hindley, ed., *Drama and Community: People and Plays in Medieval Europe* (Turnhout: Brepols, 1999), 207. As it states in the *Mirror of Justices*, "for after the hour of noon or by night no one can hold plea so that it will be stable." William Whittaker, ed., *The Mirror of Justices* (SS, vol. VII, 1893), 93.

[22] Garrett Epp, ed., "The Buffeting," *The Townley Plays* (Kalamazoo: Medieval Institute Publications, 2017), 260.

Mush's hagiography of Margaret Clitheroe, he makes an explicit comparison between Pilate and Judge Clinch when he writes that the judge was thinking to "wash his hands with Pilate."[23]

Pilate is not as easily manipulated as the bishop had hoped he would be. He simply refuses to put Jesus to death without a proper trial in a king's court. He asks the beadle to bring Jesus in and calls out "oyez" (168, lines 367–70), the customary exclamation to signal the opening of court. He counsels Jesus "[t]o the bar draw near / To thy judgement here, / To be deemed for thy deeds undue" (draw near to the bar to your judgment here, to be judged for your illegal deeds. 168, lines 377–9). Caiaphas and Annas present their evidence, sweetening the deal by inserting that because Christ calls himself king, he is in fact also a traitor, usurping the emperor's authority, a crime punishable by death under Roman (and English) law. Yet, as Pilate points out, their evidence is virtually nonexistent and Pilate fails to obtain a sound confession from Jesus, who speaks haltingly and only when addressed. Finally, Pilate concludes that his is not the proper court to hear Christ's case. Rather, as a man from Galilee, it is Herod, the local authority, who is responsible for trying Jesus. The defendant is whisked away to his third trial of the night.

Christ also declines to bow down before Herod, a gesture that does not go unnoticed. Herod brusquely comments that he is treating him as "it were to a man of their own town" (183, line 179). In all of the plays, but York in particular, Herod appears larger than life: his is a loud, hot-tempered, and bombastic presence. As two scholars have remarked, the king is "a figure of anarchic appetite for diversion, so that when Christ fails to provide him with sport, Herod determines to have it at his expense."[24] When Herod cannot persuade Jesus to speak or perform miracles, he asks the knights who escorted him to court "where led ye this lidderon? His language is lorn" (Where have you been with this idiot? He has lost his power of speech. 183, line 190). After a thorough briefing on the accusations leveled against his silent defendant, Herod turns back to Jesus, adopting the persona of a concerned judge, resolved to discover whether Christ stands mute out of malice, or by visitation of

---

[23] John Mush, "A True Report of the Life and Martyrdom of Mrs. Clitherow," in *The Troubles of Our Catholic Forefathers Related by Themselves*, ed. John Morris, 3rd ser. (London: Burns and Oats, 1877), 420.

[24] Beadle and King, eds., *York Mystery Plays*, 175.

God. He asks: "may thou not hear me? Hey, man, art thou wood? Now tell me faithfully before how thou fare. Forth, friend. By my faith, thou art a fond food" (can you not hear me? Hey, man, are you mad? Now tell me faithfully how you are. Speak, friend. By my faith, you are a mad creature. 185, lines 248–50). Redirecting his gaze towards Jesus, he counsels him privately. Herod warns in Latin: "Si loqueris tibi laus, / Pariter quoque prospera dantur; / Si loqueris tibi fraus, / Fel, fex et bella parantur" (If you speak well of yourself, you will accordingly be treated well; but if you acquit yourself badly, bitterness, filth, and violence will ensue. 186, lines 261–4).

Christ persists in his silence. Keen to see him acknowledge the court, Herod's sons begin to shout "Oyez! Oyez! Oyez!" (188, line 332). Still, nothing. Christina Fitzgerald has argued that Christ's calm, unemotional demeanor was "calculated to whip his enemies into violent frenzies."[25] If that is the case, it certainly seems to have done the trick. In the king's court of Judea, Christ's calm plays a striking contrast to Herod's thundering presence. After much prodding, Herod ultimately surmises that Christ must be mentally disabled and thus *non compos mentis*, incapable of being held accountable for his crimes. He orders him dressed in the garments of a fool and returns him to Pilate. It is noteworthy that Christ standing mute before Herod is a stock motif of England's mystery cycles. In the Chester play, Herod muses about the possibility that Christ is deaf, dumb, or frantic (277, lines 199–200).[26] In the N-Town plays, he instructs Annas and Caiaphas to beat him with scourges to force him to speak (256, lines 231–2).[27] Finally, in Wakefield, Jesus stands mute instead before Caiaphas, who interprets his silence as consent to trial, as would have been normal in an ecclesiastical court (*Et omnis qui tacet / Hic consentire videtur*).[28]

The knights return to Pilate with their prisoner. Pilate orders the beadle to "bring [Jesus] to bar," (198, line 144) where he commands "Speak, and excuse thee if thou can" (203, line 299), a patent allusion to the request for a plea. Finally, Christ addresses the court, although his

---

[25] Christina Fitzgerald, *The Drama of Masculinity and Medieval English Guild Culture* (New York: Palgrave Macmillan, 2007), 153.

[26] Mills, ed., *Chester Mystery Cycle*, 277.

[27] Douglas Sugano, ed., "Death of Judas; Trials before Pilate and Herod," in *The N-Town Plays* (Kalamazoo: Medieval Institute Publications, 2007).

[28] Rose, ed., *Wakefield Mystery Plays*, 360.

answer is insufficient. Rather than plead, he lectures Pilate on how God gave man the ability to speak and so we must use speech wisely. Exasperated, Pilate orders the knights to scourge him. Scourges reflect the biblical narrative, but the language of peine forte et dure from the jail delivery rolls infuses the dialogue. Caiaphas intones, "Platly ye be put to perpetual pine" (directly you will be put to perpetual pain. 201, line 243).

In most versions of the mystery cycles, at this point, Pilate realizes that the Jews will not be content until he sentences Christ to death, even though the defendant is unwilling to speak in his defense. He washes his hands to symbolize a cleansing of his conscience before he endeavors one last time to save Jesus' life by offering him an Easter pardon. The Jews will have none of it; Pilate sentences him to die on the cross. The *Cornish Ordinalia* stands out here. Two doctors, that is, master scholars, are present to counsel Pilate, one of whom points out that Pilate has no grounds to sentence Jesus because he refuses to plead. He states:

A legal basis for this man's condemnation does not appear nor will it ever appear. When he was accused, he made no reply, and even if in so doing he acted like a fool, the fact remains that whoever preserves silence before a judge in this country shall not be judged. Hence, for good and sufficient reason, the man should not be crucified.[29]

In what is highly reminiscent of the courtroom debates so familiar to readers of the year books, the second doctor loudly disagrees. The two dispute the nature of his crimes: fraud, destruction in the temple, contempt, heresy. Dwelling on the absence of evidence, the first doctor champions Jesus' cause: "Your enmity towards him is as clear to me as is the further consideration that it is not just to deprive an innocent person of his life. Nor have I heard that he has ever committed a single crime of any whatsoever. It would be a sad thing indeed to destroy a blameless man through error."[30] Eventually the reason for the first doctor's unwavering faith is revealed: he, too, has come to believe that Jesus is the son of God. The second doctor rallies the crowds shouting "Crucify!" Pilate washes his hands, and the torturers appear again to escort Christ to his execution.

---

[29] Markham Harris, ed., *The Cornish Ordinalia: A Medieval Dramatic Trilogy* (Washington, DC: Catholic University of America Press, 1969), 151.
[30] Harris, ed., *Cornish Ordinalia*, 153.

Christ's insolence, failing to bow before justices, ignoring questions or counsel, as well as his refusal to plead through silence and insufficiency, represent his rejection of the authority of these three distinct courts to try him. None of these courts have proper jurisdiction because no earthly authority can judge the divine. Christ is subject only to God's law.[31] The Townley play has him say as much. Pilate summons Christ, crying: "Herk, felow, com nere. / Thou knowes I have powere / To excuse or to dampne here, / In bayll to abyde" (Hark, fellow, come near. You know I have the power to acquit, or condemn [you] to abide in misery. 264, lines 140–3), to which Jesus replies: "Sich powere has thou noght / To wyrk thi will thus with me, / Bot from my Fader that is broght, / Oonefold God in persons thre" (You do not have such power to work your will thus with me, but [that power] belongs to my father, [who is] one God in person three. 264, lines 144–7). As Robert Sturges writes, Christ's silence must be interpreted as "an infuriating sign of resistance to sovereign power."[32] Christ's dramatic heroism shines brightest during his quiet courage as he tolerates the buffeting, the scourges, and the mockery of the knights and Jews. The Townley Pilate asks, "Thou man that suffurs all this yll, / Why wyll thou us no mercy cry?" (You man that suffers all this ill, why will you not cry out to us in mercy? 267, lines 248–9). During the scourging, Christ endures his punishment with such patience that one of his torturers believes he has fallen asleep, prompting them to beat him harder. One cannot watch this play without gaining "an immense admiration for those who were able to sustain their identity in the face of torture, whether saints or others unjustly tyrannized."[33]

The depiction of Pilate as reluctant judge is particularly striking. The Townley play sees Pilate as insufferably corrupt. He takes pride in his nickname, "mouthpiece of the devil" (*Os Malleatoris*, line 13), and brags of profiting from the law through corrupt practices: "All fals endytars, / Quest-gangars, and jurars, / And thise outrydars / Ar welcom to me." (All false accusers, questmongers, and jurors, and

---

[31] King, "Contemporary Cultural Models," 200–16.

[32] Robert Sturges, "Wols-hede and Outhorne: The Ban, Bare Life, and Power in the Passion Plays," in Bonnie Wheeler, ed., *Mindful Spirit in Late Medieval Literature* (New York: Palgrave, 2006), 102.

[33] Davidson, "Suffering and the York Plays," 14.

these tax-collectors are welcome to me, lines 23–6). And yet, Pilate is relieved of blame. He does not wish to condemn Jesus to death, but he caves when faced with the persistence of Christ's Jewish accusers. Pamela King has argued that the York play, which presents Pilate in an especially favorable light, was inspired in part by the 1405 trial of Archbishop Richard Scrope, executed for his participation in the Percy Rebellion against King Henry IV. Determined to see him beheaded, the king would not recognize his plea of clergy. With the strong support of York's population, who later campaigned for Scrope's canonization, England's Chief Justice William Gascoigne declared the process illegal and refused to sit in judgment on the case. King sees that Gascoigne may have acted as a recognizable model for a York audience to make sense of the enigmatic Pilate, muddying further the distinction between biblical drama and political reality.[34] The fact that Scrope's trial took place just days before the annual performance of the play, his co-conspirators' heads likely still posted at Micklegate Bar on the day the wagons started to roll, imbued Christ's resistance to an unjust power with local relevance.[35] Scrope and his trial will be discussed in further depth in Chapter 7.

Silence acted as a vehicle to transform defendant into dissident. Through Christ's example, silence signaled to the audience a defendant's status as righteous rebel against an intrusive government. Tinkle sees this as a product of the plays' scripting and performance: "the playwrights' idea of King Jesus emerges from a context of local dissatisfaction with monarchs and from a desire to enact a model of kingship that responds to people's needs – a bottom-up rather than top-down conception of governance, suitable for the guilds that possessed the play."[36] The means of performance also provided medieval men and women a model for dissemination and reinforcement of this ideal. Entire town populations turned out to watch the drama with up to thirty-two separate plays. The performance took multiple days to complete. Because the pageant was carted on wagons in procession throughout the town, actors performed their scene multiple times, at up to twelve pre-established stations, reaching as broad an audience as possible. As a result, the

---

[34] King, "Contemporary Cultural Models," 214.   [35] Tinkle, "York's Jesus," 107.
[36] Tinkle, "York's Jesus," 105.

plays had great potential beyond entertainment as a teaching tool. This is not only a reflection of penal injustice, it is also a lens through which medieval audiences viewed their judicial system.[37] When an audience imagined the pains of peine forte et dure, the graphic representations of violence enacted against Christ during the buffeting and scourging proffered a visual mnemonic. At the same time, the mystery plays train their audiences "to see execution victims as suffering Christs and to weep for them."[38]

Medieval spectators would have seen nothing fictional about the performance of the Passion of Christ. The fact that a pilgrim can visit the specific locations of Christ's imprisonment in the Holy Land attests to the authenticity of the Passion. Late medieval travel literature talks at length about the "grett hous of Chayphas," also known as the "Carcer Domini" (prison of the Lord) located at the Church of Saint Savior on Mount Zion and said to be the prison where Christ was held during his interrogation by Annas and Caiaphas. The "Prison of Christ," a small chapel at the rear of the Church of the Holy Sepulcher in Jerusalem, where Christ was imprisoned in preparation for the crucifixion, was a "canonical pilgrimage site," "much visited by Latin Christians," "a mainstay of medieval pilgrims' itineraries."[39] Pilgrims also visited the Chapel of the Repose, where Christ was incarcerated the night of his arrest at Gethsemane; the pillar to which Christ was bound during the scourging, and the house of Annas, another imprisonment site. They could also handle a piece of the chain used to bind Christ. All of this heightened the realism of the Passion and reinforced the notion of Christ as prisoner in the collective imagination.

Further enhancing the relatability of the plays, Christ's background resonates with our typical defendant. Those who stood mute before the king's justices were almost always male, and they were rarely members of the upper rank. While the Bible might describe Christ as a king, his training was in carpentry; to a medieval audience, that indicated a guildsman. Christina Fitzgerald sees that Christ, as he is depicted in the cycle plays, is the "ideal urban male subject." Even his "extraordinary

---

[37] David Eshelman, "'Great Mowrning and Mone': Modeled Spectatorship in the Towneley Scourging," *Baylor Journal of Theatre and Performance* 2.1 (2005): 23–34.

[38] Eshelman, "Great Mowrning," 24.

[39] Anthony Bale, "God's Cell: Christ as Prisoner and Pilgrimage to the Prison of Christ," *Speculum* 91.1 (2016): 3, 27, and 11.

silence" typifies the manners recommended for members of the burgher class. The conduct books warn that being quick to anger will only get a man in trouble; better "to hold his 'owne tonge' and remain 'deef & dombe'."[40] Christ's passive resistance was a nod to his class values. While violence is often thought to have been one of the two dominant traits of medieval masculinity, by the late Middle Ages licit violence had been firmly appropriated by the knightly class. Violence enacted by anyone else was perilous and anti-social, not quintessentially masculine. Nonviolence extends also to collective resistance. As the English Rising of 1381 confirms, the people were entirely capable of staging organized violence on a grand scale, but it was a rare and unusual circumstance. More frequently, popular strategies of resistance to lordship took the form of "passive noncooperation," such as the poor performance of labor services, rent strikes or tax evasion, nonattendance at court, failure to act as suitors. Refusal to bear witness against one's neighbors in criminal suits was another sound tactic.[41] This "feet-dragging" and noncooperation was not unreliability or apathy, it was in fact a "political gesture."[42] Recognizing this helps us to better appreciate how a medieval audience would have interpreted Christ's pacifism. It was not a sign of weakness: rather, his was dignified silence, rejecting an unlawful authority.

As Chapter 2 made clear, from the Crown's vantage point, standing mute was readily linked to treason. The mystery cycles, however, turn that narrative on its head. Christ's example exposes the impudence of many a treason accusation: the Crown falsely accuses its political enemies of treason in order to eliminate them as rivals. Through silence and passivity, Christ becomes the hero of the story, revealing the Crown's hypocrisy; through martyrdom, he is victorious. Defendants who stood mute at their arraignments must have taken heart in emulating Christ's example. For those who hoped to repent of their sins, standing mute before the king's justices gave them an opportunity to voice their discontent with royal overreach, at the same time as they engaged in *imitatio Christi*.

---

[40] Fitzgerald, *Drama of Masculinity*, 151, 148, and 150.
[41] Jamie Taylor, *Fictions of Evidence: Witnessing, Literature, and Community in the Later Middle Ages* (Columbus: Ohio State University Press, 2013), 112–13.
[42] Phillipp Schofield, *Peasant and Community in Medieval England 1200–1500* (Basingstoke: Palgrave Macmillan, 2003), 160.

The emphasis on Christ's pain was also a unifying feature of the passion plays. As Esther Cohen writes, medieval men and women related to Christ through "the one sensation they surely shared with Christ: pain."[43] The cult of the Passion is key to understanding the late medieval culture of pain; yet, it is critical to understand that some late medieval theologians advocated seeing Christ's life as a series of moments of suffering. Indeed, the circumcision, Christ's first brush with pain, was merely a prefiguration of the crucifixion. Understanding Christ without also tasting pain was unfathomable from the medieval mindset. Of course, Christ's experience of pain was supernatural. As the Dominican Albert the Great (d.1280) acknowledged, "Christ's pain was the greatest that was known or would ever be known."[44] The exceptionality of his body – evident in his ability to walk on water – combined with his unique position as a sacrifice to atone for the sins of all humanity, meant his experience of pain was also unique. Thus, his suffering was not only more severe than that of mere mortals, as Aquinas (d.1274) argued he also suffered "according to every corporeal sense."[45]

The mystery cycles do not follow up to explain how God took vengeance on Pilate for ordering the death of his only son. The *South English Legendary* picks up the story, instructing its audience that the judge who judges falsely must suffer the same false punishment. Soon after the death of Christ, Saint Veronica goes to Rome to see the emperor to whom she relays the story of the crucifixion, described here as a "stronge deþe" (strong death, line 148). The emperor is incensed: he had originally sent Pilate to the edges of the empire as punishment for killing first his half-brother (son of King Tyrus), then his foster-brother (a French prince). The emperor had hoped that a job with responsibility might turn Pilate around, but Saint Veronica's story only confirms that Pilate is up to his old tricks. The emperor immediately summons Pilate to Rome to account for his actions. Attempting to win the emperor over, Pilate first sends a letter explaining that he bears no guilt for Jesus' death, that the Jews

---

[43] Esther Cohen, *The Modulated Scream: Pain in Late Medieval Culture* (University of Chicago Press, 2010), 209.

[44] As cited in Donna Trembinski, "[Pro]passio Doloris: Early Dominican Conceptions of Christ's Physical Pain," *Journal of Ecclesiastical History* 59.4 (2008): 645.

[45] Trembinski," [Pro]passio Doloris," 649.

carried it out of their own accord; but the letter does not have the intended impact on the emperor. When Pilate arrives in Rome, the emperor stands as judge at his trial, proudly wearing the kerchief (*sudarium*) that Veronica used to sponge the sweat from Christ's face. In his defense, Pilate claims that he was merely the judge in the matter; a jury found Christ guilty, and as judge he simply passed sentence. But the emperor again sees through the lies. He declares that "to strong deþ he wolde him bringe" (to strong death, he would him bring, line 180). The emperor casts Pilate in "stronge prison & deork" (a strong and dark prison, line 213), where he is bound and left "in honger & in pyne" (in hunger and in pain, line 215). He lays there so long that his limbs waste away. "He hadde leuere his deþe þan his lyf so he clonge to nouȝt" (he would rather his death than his life, so he clung to nothing, line 217). Finally, he begs the jailer to take pity on him and give him an apple to eat. The jailer does; Pilate asks also for a paring knife to slice it, which he then uses to slay himself.[46]

The epilogue to the anti-saint's *vita* makes two points clear. First, even the Roman emperor saw Christ's trial as unjust, so much so that it resulted in the condemnation of Pilate to a death that sounds eerily similar to the conditions imposed in hard prison. This is key. Late medieval Europeans held Rome up as the exemplar of all that is learned, cultured, and (somewhat ironically) modern. Placing the blame on an individual exonerates the empire for which he stands. Second, the *vita* makes an explicit comparison between the crucifixion and Pilate's punishment, both described as "strong death" and reminiscent of English hard prison. That popular audiences already associated Christ's torments with peine forte et dure is reinforced by Langland's *Piers Plowman* (1376), which makes the comparison overt when he speaks of "Þe penaunce þat Pilatus wrouȝte To iesu þe gentil" (The penance [i.e. peine forte et dure] that Pilate wrought to gentle Jesus).[47] This particular analogy is made in a number of other works of

---

[46] Charlotte d'Evelyn and Anna Mill, eds., *The South English Legendary*, 2 vols. (EETS, vols. ccxxxv and ccxxxvi, 1956), vol. II, 701–6.

[47] From Langland, *Piers Plowman* (1960) (B.10.34). Alford was the first to recognize that "penance" in this instance implies peine forte et dure. See John Alford, *Piers Plowman: A Glossary of Legal Diction* (Cambridge: D. S. Brewer, 1988), 113, headword "penaunce." Langland made numerous references to peine forte et dure in the various versions of his epic poem.

literature from the late medieval era. The Northern Homily Cycle writes how Christ underwent "Harde pyne apon the rude tree" (hard pain upon the cross).[48] A late medieval poem has Jesus deriding all mankind because while He sacrificed everything for man, man is unwilling to sacrifice for Him. In a graphic description of the pains he suffered on the cross, the poem unambiguously associates the experience with hard prison: "Ful longe in harde prison lyng." (Full long in hard prison lying, line 58).[49] Finally, a Good Friday sermon explains that while Christ was on the cross, "Cold, thirst, hunger, and everything possible for those imprisoned assaulted him."[50] These various analogies point to a popular association between crucifixion and peine forte et dure. For those who stood mute in court, then, surely this was strong confirmation that they did so in emulation of Christ, a fellow martyr who also endured a great sacrifice on behalf of those whom he loved.

Meekness Made God [a] Man[51]

Christ is not the singular example of silence and passivity; rather, after Christ's crucifixion, these qualities became the model for those faced with an unjust system of law. Civil disobedience through silence and passivity has been a core principle of the Christian church from the moment of its inception. The Roman state prohibited Christian worship for over three hundred years, producing an illustrious array of pacifist martyrs branded enemies of the Roman state, allowing themselves to be sacrificed for their faith in bizarre and spectacular ways that never ceased to impress admiring medieval audiences. Among these martyrs, silence and passivity came to represent resistance to tyranny. By the late Middle Ages, these stories had lost none of their allure; through

---

[48] Anne Thompson, ed., *The Northern Homily Cycle* (Kalamazoo: Medieval Institute Publications, 2008), 104.

[49] "Mercy Passes all Things," in Carleton Brown, ed., *Religious Lyrics of the XIVth Century*, 2nd edn. (Oxford: Clarendon Press, 1952), 127.

[50] Holly Johnson, ed. and trans., *The Grammar of Good Friday: Macaronic Sermons of Late Medieval England* (Turnhout: Brepols, 2012), 261.

[51] "Mekenes made [god] man" (*humilitas hominem deum*). Attributed to Saint Augustine. Gustaf Holmstedt, ed., *Speculum Christiani: A Middle English Religious Treatise of the Fourteenth Century* (EETS, vol. CLXXXII, 1933), 58.

retellings by John Capgrave,[52] the authors of the *South English Legendary*, the *North English Legendary*,[53] as well as the *Golden Legend*,[54] and even Geoffrey Chaucer, many of these martyr-saints went on to gain celebrity status in English culture.

Storytellers and sermon-writers celebrated the creative ways in which these pious luminaries employed passivity as a weapon. Sermons, which were circulated throughout European society to foster a standard Christianity, were a key tool in the dissemination of ideals of martyrdom. A sermon for the feast of Saint Laurence included in John Mirk's *Festial* makes this amply clear. The writer praises the martyr for showing "mekenesse aȝeynus malys" (meekness against malice, line 19). Even when the emperor orders him cast into prison and "done hym alle þe peyne þat þei mythe til he wold fayne ȝeu vp þe tresoure" (have done to him all the pain that they might, until he would give up the treasure, lines 50–1) – that is, the alms entrusted to him by Pope Sixtus and intended to go to the poor, the sick, and the blind – Laurence remains unaffected by his tormentors' cruelty. The emperor ups the ante by having Laurence "constraynid ... wyth grete penaunce to bring forth þis tresoure" (constrained ... with great penance[55] to bring forth this treasure, lines 79–80); the North English Legendary states simply that he was "in preson strang" (strong prison).[56] Laurence still does not protest. Instead, he directs his energies to healing the ailments of his fellow prisoners. Laurence is subjected to all manner of torments: "ȝardus, skorges, staves, ewles, hokus, pannus wyth colus, fyre-brondus, brennyng schaftes of yron, salte, pyche, code, brynston, molton lede, fyr-forkys, barrus, and a grete gryderen" (rods, scourges, staves, awls, hooks, pans with coals, fire brands, burning shafts of iron, salt, pitch, coal, brimstone, molten lead,

[52] John Capgrave, *The Life of St. Katharine of Alexandria*, trans. Karen Winstead (South Bend, IN: University of Notre Dame Press, 2011).

[53] Carl Horstmann, ed., "Die nordenglische Legendensammlung," in *Altenglische Legenden: Neue Folge* (Heilbronn: Henninger, 1881), 3–173.

[54] Jacobus de Voragine, *The Golden Legend: Readings on the Saints*, trans. William Ryan (Princeton University Press, 2012). Jacobus particularly delighted in pain culture. As Esther Cohen notes, he fabricated stories of pain for his saints. In his version of the life of Augustine, for example, Augustine "suffered extravagantly." Cohen, *Modulated Scream*, 236.

[55] It is entirely possible that this is a reference to pressing with irons.

[56] Horstmann, ed., "Die nordenglische Legendensammlung," 107, line 1 of "De sco Laurencio historia."

fire-forks, bars, and a great grid-iron, lines 100–3). Even when his tormentors cook him on the griddle, Laurence "schewod aʒeynus malys mekenesse .... And aʒeynus passion he scheweed louyng and swetnesse, for þe swetnesse þat he hadde of þe love of God in his herte wythinneforth made hym to sette noght be þe passion and þe tormenting þat he suffred wythouteforth (showed meekness against malice .... And against suffering, he showed loving and sweetness, for the sweetness that he had of the love of God within his heart made him see the suffering and the tormenting that he suffered on his body as nothing, lines 138–44). The only time he breaks his silence is to issue a comical reprimand to those operating the griddle: "Wreche, þis on syde is enogh – turne and ette whylle þat other syde rosteth" (Wretch, this one side is [cooked] enough – turn and eat while that other side roasts, lines 131–2).[57]

A sermon for Good Friday spells out exactly what is to be learned from Christ's example. Astutely, the sermon-writer explains that Christ could not fight "using the power of his deity," because no one on earth could have resisted it if he had. Thus, he fought with his humanity, "[a]nd that mode of fighting consisted wholly in suffering and forbearance." This is the "craft" that he taught his disciples; they in turn learned it so "perfectly that afterwards they gained the whole world with it, and they conquered emperors and kings and tyrants." Christ's "shield of suffering" allows "a girl alone" to conquer "a king with the entire army he knew how to assemble"; such is the case in the examples of Saint Katherine, who vanquished the Emperor Maxentius, and Saint Agnes when she took on the tyrants of Rome.[58] The benefits of silence and passivity are summed up best by a fourteenth-century poem: "With mekenes þou may heuene purchase" (through meekness you may buy heaven, line 117).[59]

Susannah: Type of Christ, and Silent Exemplar

Saint Augustine's spirited defense of the Old Testament in response to the dualist heresy of his own age inaugurated an allegorical reading of the Bible intended to knit more closely its Jewish and Christian

57 Susan Powell, ed., *John Mirk's Festial*, 2 vols. (EETS, vols. cccxxxiv and cccxxxv, 2009–11), vol. ii, 195–200.
58 Johnson, ed., *Grammar of Good Friday*, 191.
59 From the poem "Mercy Passes All Things," in Brown, ed., *Religious Lyrics*, 129.

halves.[60] From a Christian perspective, his approach gave a new purpose to the Old Testament, which otherwise risked supersession; it also came to dominate medieval exegesis. After Augustine it was simply not possible to read the Bible merely in a literal way; indeed, Augustine identified literal reading of the Old Testament as one of the central flaws of the Jewish people. Christian superiority rested in part on the ability to read on multiple levels.[61] Under Augustine's guidance, reading the Old Testament allegorically, Christ's Passion is prefigured everywhere. In the story of Cain and Abel, Abel is a figure of Christ, while Cain stands in for the Jews; Abel's murder then is in anticipation of Christ's Passion. Noah, too, is a type of Christ; this time his rebellious son Ham represents the Jews, who see Noah's/Christ's nakedness and thus consent to his death.

Recognizing the centrality of allegorical readings of scripture also helps us to make sense of the significance of another story beloved in late medieval England, Susannah and the Elders, which originates in the Greek version of the Book of Daniel. Susannah is presented as a type of Christ. The English retelling of her trial appears in the fourteenth-century anonymous *The Pistil of Swete Susan*, which includes a similar analogy to those who stand mute. The poem conveys the story of Susan, "sotil and sage" (subtle and wise. 82, line 14), and her husband Joachim, described as being "so lele in his lawe ther lived non him liche" (so learned in his law, there lived no one like him. 82, line 3), two Jews living in Babylon during the exile. Her wealthy husband's home serves as a hall of justice for the Babylonian Jewish community. One day, while bathing privately in the garden, two judges who regularly "haunted" (83, line 31) their home, betray Joachim's hospitality by spying on Susan and then propositioning her. Slyly they offer to teach the naked wife their law under the laurel tree. They urge her to satisfy their needs, threatening to accuse her falsely with adultery to an imaginary young man if she does not cooperate, but Susan refuses to play their game. Knowing the danger that attends her, she cries out to alert her servants, who find her in a compromising position with two well-respected men of the community. The judges

---

[60] Saint Augustine, *Reply to Faustus the Manichean.*

[61] Augustine's allegorical reading of the Bible is beautifully described in Jeremy Cohen, *Living Letters of the Law: Ideas of the Jew in Medieval Christianity* (Berkeley: University of California Press, 1999), Chapter 1.

carry through with their threat: Susan is charged with adultery, and thrown into a dungeon to await trial, confined with manacles and deprived of food (87–8, lines 175–8).[62]

While *The Pistil of Swete Susan* is set in Babylon, the court it depicts is emphatically English. The courts' judges are referred to both as "domesmen" (lawmen. 86, line 131), as well as "justices of the bench" (line 183); they preside over court in the guildhall (91, line 293); Susan is summoned to the "barre" (line 189) to listen to her appellors' "playnt" (88, line 202). In court, Susan is silent; her appellors spin their yarn, and the judges instantly sentence her to death. Susan's prayers as she leaves the courtroom are met when God intervenes and instructs Daniel, a lawyer, to come to her defense. Daniel calls once again to the guildhall, where he declares that he will "by proces apert disprove this apele" (by an open process disprove this appeal. 91, line 294). He examines the elders separately in hopes of exposing their lies. Daniel begins by impugning the first elder's reputation, recounting how he "on benche brewed muche bale" (on bench, concocted much evil. 91, line 307) and delivered "fals domes" (false judgments. 91, line 310). Hoping to catch the elder in a lie, Daniel asks him under what tree he spied Susan committing adultery. A hawthorn, he replies, before being carted off to prison. Then the second elder is brought in. He does not escape Daniel's wrath unscathed. Daniel greets him as "Canaan sede" (Cain's seed. 92, line 330), and reminds him that it is his covetousness that has brought him before the court. When asked under what tree Susan cavorted with her lover, this elder pronounces "Thei pleied bi a prine" (They played by a holm-oak. 92, line 342). The inconsistency in their stories revealed, the elders are ordered to be "drawen to the dethe" (93, line 346), in England a traitor's death.

Susannah's muteness before the court is not the focal point of the drama in *The Pistil of Swete Susan* as Christ's is in the mystery cycles. The judges do not comment on her silence; nor do they seem to expect her to speak.[63] The lack of emphasis on her silent repose does not mean

---

[62] Russell Peck, ed., "The Pistil of Swete Susan," in *Heroic Women of the Old Testament in Middle English Verse* (Kalamazoo: Medieval Institute Publications, 1991), 87–8.

[63] From a legal standpoint, one cannot help but wonder whether the fact that she stood silent on appeal, rather than being indicted at the king's suit, had any impact on the narrative of the poem. See Chapter 2.

that it goes unnoticed. Indeed, commentators on the striking parallel between Christ's silence and Susannah's surprisingly date back as far as the fourth century. On a sermon about the Gospel of Luke, Ambrose (d.397) wrote admiringly:

> The Lord is accused and is silent. And the one who does not lack a defense can certainly be silent: let those who are afraid of being conquered solicit sympathy to be defended. For by keeping silent one does not confirm an accusation; he scorns it by not refuting it. For what should one who does not seek his release fear? [Christ] would acquire the salvation of all, and that [purpose] thrusts out [concern for] his own [safety]. But why should I speak of God? Susanna was silent and she conquered; and her case was better, for she did not defend herself and she was proven [innocent].[64]

As victims of corrupt judicial systems, both betrayed in vulnerable circumstances in garden settings, vilely mistreated by the courts, and standing silent in their own defense, Susannah and Christ provoked frequent and favorable comparison. As such, Susannah was presented as both a prefiguration of Christ and a type of Christ. Catherine Tkacz has traced the theme of Susannah as Christ in over forty-four works of art, as well as a wide variety of literature (including works by Bede, Alcuin, Henry Suso, Peter Abelard, and Martin Luther) from the fourth through to the seventeenth centuries to demonstrate just how familiar it was. Good Friday sermons also regularly picked up on this allegory. Recounting Christ's trial, one late medieval sermon laments "Where are you now, Daniel, who freed Susanna who had been falsely accused and handed over to death? Daniel 13. And now the Son of God, falsely accused and handed over to death, you do not free nor speak a word on his behalf."[65] In another, the sermon's author puts words attributed to Susannah into Christ's mouth: "You know how they bore false testimony against me, and behold I die although I did none of these things" (Daniel 13:43).[66]

In medieval England, readers also interpreted Susan's courtroom silence as a "model of resistance."[67] As Lynn Staley attests, in English hands "Susanna is radicalized."[68] Again, there are plenty of examples to

---

[64] Ambrose, *In Psalmo David CXVIII expositio* (PL *15: 1494*), as cited in Catherine Brown Tkacz, "Susanna as a Type of Christ," *Studies in Iconography* 20 (1999): 103.
[65] Johnson, ed., *Grammar of Good Friday*, 269.
[66] Johnson, ed., *Grammar of Good Friday*, 393.   [67] Taylor, *Fictions of Evidence*, 84.
[68] Lynn Staley, "Susanna and English Communities," *Traditio* 62 (2007): 56.

demonstrate that the story of Susannah was well known in an English context. In 1395–6, a Leicestershire man named John Belgrave employed Susannah as a vehicle to express his displeasure with the archdeacon's court. Before the session opened for the day, he laid a forged bill "written in text hand" in the seat of the archdeacon's official, Walter Bamak. The bill explained that Bamak "might well compare with the judges who condemned Susannah, giving unrighteous judgements, oppressing the innocent, and suffering the evil-doers."[69] *The Examination of William Thorpe*, a Lollard treatise dating to the year 1407, indicates how Susannah's decision to stand mute before royal justices provided inspiration to England's proto-Protestant movement. When Archbishop Arundel demands that Thorpe recant his Wycliffite beliefs and name his accomplices, Thorpe responds with "Angwischis ben to me on ech side" (Anguish [has] been to me on each side), the same words that Susannah utters when the elders first approach her. Thorpe continued: "heerynge þese wordis þouʒte in myn herte þat þis was an vnleeful askynge, and I demed mysilf cursid of God if I consentid herto; and I þouʒte how Susanne seid 'Angwysschis ben to me on euery side,' and forþi ʒat I stood stille musynge and spak not" (hearing these words, [I] thought in my heart that this was an unlawful request, and I deemed myself cursed of God if I consented hereto; and thought how Susannah said 'Anguish [has] been to me on every side,' and for that I stood still musing and spoke not.)[70] Thorpe's silence is power: he "frustrates Arundel's attempts to turn his testimony into a self-accusing document."[71] The influence of Thorpe's example of passive disobedience on later audiences was augmented by republication of excerpts from his testimony, including this passage, in Foxe's *Book of Martyrs* (published first in 1563), presented by Foxe as an example to be emulated.

While Daniel's intervention prevented Susannah from suffering martyrdom, her willingness to sacrifice everything kept her closely aligned with that category. In this respect, the value of martyrdom in medieval culture needs to be recognized. The *Speculum Christiani* includes a discussion of the "Seven ways to release sin," of which

[69] TNA C 1/68/63 (1395–6).
[70] Anne Hudson, ed., "Testimony of William Thorpe, 1407," in *Two Wycliffite Texts* (EETS, vol. CCCI, 1993), 35, lines 365–8.
[71] Taylor, *Fictions of Evidence*, 81.

martyrdom ranks second only to baptism. Third is confession and penance – thus, the silent defendant who was not quite as heroic in his refusal to plead might still hope for release.[72] A convict's death brought enduring shame to one's family, but a martyr's death – stoic acceptance of great pain and suffering at the hands of an unjust authority, modeled on the behavior of Christ and numerous saints – points instead to heroism. Indeed, such a death might even redeem one's soul in God's eyes.

An Ironic Early Modern Post-script

Silence as a rejection of political authority was a concept that greeted Englishmen and women at every turn: in sermons and homilies, literature, communal drama, and artwork of all kinds. This association was deeply and irrevocably entrenched in medieval religious and political culture. Proving that this idea was culturally meaningful in the context of literature and drama is one thing: but how do we *know* that the defendant who stood mute had internalized these notions and thus did so in imitation of Christ? That the defendant recognized the correlation between silence and resistance to a corrupt government, and saw standing mute as a last chance for redemption, transforming infamy into glory?

King Charles I's behavior at his infamous trial (1649) firmly cements the Christological overtones of standing mute. In the months leading up to his execution, Charles brushed up on the literature of martyrdom, requesting copies of Foxe's *Book of Martyrs* and also *The Crown of Thorns* to peruse while incarcerated.[73] A poem that he wrote during that time implies that he acknowledged features of Christ's Passion in his own experience: "The crown is crucified . . . / Herod and Pontius Pilate are agreed." This is echoed also in *Eikon Basilike*, attributed to Charles but almost certainly written by someone else. The book depicts Charles petitioning God "to give me . . . the Honour to imitate His Example in suffering for Righteousness sake."[74]

Admittedly, Charles always had a flair for the dramatic. At his trial and execution, the actor in Charles must have felt that he "had at last

---

[72] Holmstedt, ed., *Speculum Christiani*, 214.
[73] Daniel Klein, "The Trial of Charles I," *Journal of Legal History* 18.1 (1997): 7.
[74] As cited in Klein, "Trial of Charles I," 7.

got the opportunity of playing a part worthy of his genius before a nation-wide audience."[75] Charles commenced the trial by disputing the court's authority, reminding them that they had no legal warrant, either scriptural or by the laws and constitutions of the realm, to try a king – not as preposterous an assertion as one might imagine. Despite frequent attempts to curb royal absolutism, English justices throughout the Middle Ages had persistently maintained the belief that the king is in fact above the law.[76] The first two sessions of court were spent attempting to extract a plea from the king; not recognizing the presence of a legitimate authority, the king refused utterly to do so. At the opening of the third day, when asked to plead, the king stated simply "For me to acknowledge a new court that I never heard of before … indeed I know not how to do it."[77] From Charles' perspective, recognizing the validity of the court would have made it impossible for him to continue being king, as he understood the term.

In total, Charles appeared before the high courts of justice four times before he was finally sentenced. At each appearance, he was asked two to three times how he wished to acquit himself of the charges against him. Thus, rather than the usual three chances to plead, Charles was granted somewhere between nine and twelve opportunities.[78] Finally, Lord President Bradshaw affirmed that it was time for the court to act. He explained the necessary course of action,

according to the known rules of the law of the land, that, if a prisoner shall stand as contumacious in contempt and shall not put in an issuable plea, guilty or not guilty of the charge given against him, whereby he may come to a fair trial, that as by an implicit confession it may be taken *pro confesso*, as it has been done to those who have deserved more favour than the prisoner at the bar has done. But besides, my Lord, I shall humbly press your Lordship upon the whole fact. The House of Commons, the supreme authority and jurisdiction of the kingdom, they have declared that it is notorious that the matter of the

---

[75] Esmé Wingfield-Stratford, *King Charles the Martyr* (London: Hollis and Carter, 1950), 337.
[76] David Seipp, "Magna Carta in the Late Middle Ages: Overmighty Subjects, Undermighty Kings, and a Turn away from Trial by Jury," *William and Mary Bill of Rights Journal* 25.2 (2016): 665–88.
[77] As cited in Klein, "Trial of Charles I," 10.
[78] Sean Kelsey, "The Trial of Charles I," *EHR* 118.477 (2003): 586.

charge is true; and it is in truth, My Lord, as clear as crystal, and as the sun that shines at noon day.[79]

In his speech, Bradshaw attempts to manipulate the law to justify interpreting Charles' uncooperativeness as a confession of guilt, even though by rights he should have died unconvicted, pressed with weights. Of course, subjecting Charles to peine forte et dure was out of the question. Such an undignified and secretive manner of death would have demonized parliament and made it seem as if they were trying to outsmart the people of England. The king was sentenced four days later. Three days after his sentence, he was executed. In his scaffold speech, the king once again returned to the theme of martyrdom: "I tell you, and I pray God it be not laid to your charge, that I am the martyr of the people."[80]

Charles' conduct at court was designed to invite comparison with Christ's. Two kings, both accused of treason, both (rightfully) refused to acknowledge the authority of the court to sit in judgment upon them. In doing so, both recognized that their actions would undoubtedly lead to their deaths. Here, it is worth noting that some historians have emphasized that Charles' fate at trial was not predetermined. In this case, a plea of not guilty might have bought time: in order for Royalists in England or Ireland to plan an attack, foreign princes to intervene, or even for the Parliamentarians to come to their senses. It was well known that Sir Thomas Fairfax (d.1671) was vehemently opposed to trying the king; so, too, was Henry Vane (d.1662), a prominent figure among Independents in the House of Commons. Time was a valuable commodity that might have allowed them to muster support against such an unprecedented and unpopular action. Yet, Charles chose not to plead, knowing the consequences, because he wanted to align himself with Christ in memory eternal. A late medieval preacher claimed that Christ stood mute before Herod because speaking would have hindered his Passion: "if Herod were satisfied concerning him, he and Pilate together would not have allowed Christ to be put to death."[81] Like Christ, Charles did not wish to derail his fate by speaking out in his defense. As Daniel Klein

[79] Kesselring, ed., *The Trial of Charles I*, 47.
[80] As cited in Klein, "Trial of Charles I," 10.
[81] Johnson, ed., *Grammar of Good Friday*, 209.

has remarked, "[i]dentifying himself as a martyr enabled the defeated and humiliated King to be restored as someone to whom it was worth listening."[82]

Publications from the period clarify that the English public had no trouble connecting the dots. The anonymous *An Elegy upon the most Incomparable King Charles the 1* (1649) refers to "Pilate Bradshaw with his pack of Jews."[83] Klein also highlights a sermon given several months after Charles' death in which the bishop made an overt comparison between the two. He explained "that the trials of Charles and Christ were so similar that 'it may seeme but ... the Stage onely changed and new actors entered upon it.'"[84] That the cult of King Charles the Martyr arose in the wake of the execution should come as no surprise.[85]

Hard Prison and the Castle of Love

The literature of the era also offers a window into common perceptions of hard prison. Royal authorities had a multi-faceted vision of prison/ peine forte et dure: most often, it was a coercive device intended to force submission to royal law; at times, it was a death penalty for those whose disregard for the king was flagrant; and always it was a form of penance, intended to mimic the pains of purgatory in order to right the disordered mind. Interpreting peine forte et dure as a form of penance justified the act; but did the English people share this vision? English sermons and poems drew regularly on the imagery associated with prison forte et dure, and they do not present it in such a magnanimous light. Indeed, the literary representation of prison forte et dure implies instead saw that Englishmen and women saw it as evidence of corrupt leadership.

---

[82] Klein, "Trial of Charles I," 3.

[83] *An Elegy upon the Most Incomparable King Charles the I* (1649), as cited in Klein, "Trial of Charles I," 15.

[84] *The Martyrdome of King Charles or, His Conformity with Christ in his Sufferings* (1649), as cited in Klein, "Trial of Charles I," 15.

[85] Surely it is ironic that when Colonel Thomas Harrison, one of the regicides, came to trial in October of 1660, he made every effort to avoid pleading. The clerk of the court asked him almost twenty times how he wished to plead, finding Harrison's response insufficient again and again. Rather than risk standing mute, Harrison eventually pleaded not guilty. See Kesselring, ed., *The Trial of Charles I*, 121–5. Many thanks to Krista Kesselring for bringing this point to my attention.

Robert Grosseteste (d.1253)'s Anglo-Norman *Chasteau d'Amour* (Castle of Love) is particularly pertinent here because it lays claim to hard prison as a universal experience, endured by all of humankind after the fall. Based on Saint Bernard of Clairvaux's allegory of God's four daughters (Truth, Justice, Peace, and Mercy), Grosseteste's *Chasteau d'Amour* and its many Middle English variants, present a highly anglicized version of the story, dominated by the language and process of the common law.[86] By creating a more familiar setting, Grosseteste hoped to instruct the laity about the centrality of redemption in Christianity in a more meaningful way.

The poem is set first in the Garden of Eden. God creates Adam a free man, seised of Paradise, with Eve at his side as a companion. He has only two codes of laws, which Adam must respect: first, natural law, which requires all men obey God; and second, positive law, which prohibits Adam from eating the fruit from the forbidden tree. God explains to Adam that through obedience, he will maintain his status as lord of Paradise;[87] transgression (*trespassa*), however, would be punished by death.[88] Of course, "for lufe of hys wyfe" (for love of his wife) Adam breaks both laws and becomes mortal.[89] He is not immediately punished, however; the poem dwells on his "defaute" (default)[90] making it clear to an English audience that when summoned to court to answer for his crimes, he fails to appear. Doing so eventually leads to both outlawry and felony forfeiture. Adam is exiled from the garden. At the same time, he loses his status as a free man and becomes a serf: "[h]e had no franches or herytage" (he has no franchise or heritage).[91] The poem prophesies that the only

---

[86] Many thanks to Jennifer Jahner for bringing this poem to my attention. "Castle of Love" (MS. English Poetry a.1., fols. 293r–296v and Additional MS. B. 107, Bodleian Library, fols. 37r–45v); "King and Four Daughters" (MS. Bodleian Library, Ashmole 61, fols. 78v–83r); "Myrour of Lewed Men" (MS. British Museum, Egerton 927, fols. 1–28); and "Foure Doughters" (MS. British Museum, Cotton Appendix VII, fols. 112v) are four versions of the text that Kari Sajavaara has identified in his *The Middle English Translations of Robert Grosseteste's* Chateau d'Amour (Helsinki: Société Néophilologique, 1967). As well, the Latin *Rex et Famulus*, which is most likely a translation and adaptation of Grosseteste's allegory.

[87] Robert Grosseteste, *Le chateau d'amour*, ed. Jessie Murray (Paris: Champion, 1918), line 126.

[88] Grosseteste, *Le chateau d'amour*, line 136.

[89] "King and Four Daughters," line 149.

[90] "King and Four Daughters," line 179.   [91] "King and Four Daughters," line 192.

way he will regain his former status is with the assistance of another man, free and of "ry3t lynage" (right lineage), who has not broken the laws of Paradise by eating from the forbidden tree.[92]

At this point in the story, the poem shifts abruptly to a heavenly setting, focusing instead on a wise king (who is unmistakably God) and his four daughters (Truth, Justice, Peace, and Mercy), each of whom contribute in their own unique and vital way to the administration of the kingdom. When one of the king's servants (Adam) breaks the law, he is submitted to a trial. For "his gult strong and gret," (his guilt strong and great) he is given over to his enemies who place him in "prison dure."[93] In that "prison of dethe," his jailers confiscate his goods, subject him to torture without measure, and refuse him food and drink.[94] The Latin *Rex et Famulus* as well as a number of the Middle English versions elaborate on the nature of the torments to which he is subjected. The serf's tormentors mirror the number of daughters, although while the daughters represent the four cardinal virtues, his tormentors have no such redeeming qualities. As Sister Mary Immaculate explains it, "the first, the Exile of Earthly Life ... casts the servant in prison; the second, the Misery of Life ... flays him alive; the third, Death ... slaughters him; and the fourth, Corruption ... devours him."[95] The term "flay" (*decoriaret* in *Rex et Famulus*), in this instance, probably takes on its alternate meaning of "to strip of everything," as is suggested by the Middle English translation "depriuen faste."[96]

Aghast, Mercy begs her father to intervene: the prisoner, "al start naked, / Of mi3t and strengþe al bare imaked" (all stark naked, powerless of might and strength), must be ransomed from his jailers.[97] Her plea launches a moral debate between the sisters concerning the circumstances in which it is appropriate for the king to show mercy. Incapable of enduring strife, Peace flees the kingdom; in her absence, the king is convinced by Truth and Justice to punish

---

[92] "King and Four Daughters," line 203.

[93] "Castle of Love," lines 309 and 312; Grosseteste, *Le chateau d'amour*, line 247.

[94] "Castle of Love," lines 312–318; Grosseteste, *Le chateau d'amour*, lines 242 and 247–8.

[95] Sister Mary Immaculate, "The Four Daughters of God in the *Gesta Romanorum* and the Court of Sapience," *PMLA* 57.4 (1942): 955.

[96] Immaculate, "Four Daughters," 952 n.8; "King and Four Daughters," line 267.

[97] "Castle of Love," lines 431–2.

humanity with the Flood, leaving only Noah and his family to survive. Overhearing this quarrel, and moved by the pleas of Mercy, the king's son (at this point he is not named Jesus, but his identity is abundantly clear) puts himself forward as a solution: he will don the thrall's "weden" (clothes) and suffer in his place.[98] The son's ransom promises to see Peace return, quarreling come to an end, and Adam (as a representative for all mankind) saved and returned to his status as a free man.

The next part of the poem is dedicated to the building of the Castle of Love (the Virgin's pure body), through which Christ descends to the earthly kingdom. At his birth, Peace comes back to stand by her father's side, exchanging a kiss with Justice, and the king begins to listen to Mercy's counsel once more. Meanwhile, on earth, the son must take on the Devil, who sees himself as "prince and lord of þis londe, / And in þe seisyne habbe long ibe" (prince and lord of this land, and in its seisin have long I been).[99] Indeed, the fiend argues that God himself granted him ownership, and God would not fail to keep up his end of the bargain. Christ responds by explaining that it was not God breaking the contract, but that the devil had done so himself when he "þorw treson to monkuynde speke" (through treason to mankind spoke) and told Eve that by eating from the forbidden tree, she would have the "miht of Gode" (might of God) and live forever.[100] "A, ich am bitrayȝed!" (Ah, I am betrayed!), exclaims the fiend; he refuses to release the prisoner unless he is paid a ransom "deore" (dear).[101] Jesus declares boldly "al my bodi for his raunsoun, / But ichul him habbe out of prisoun" (all my body for his ransom, but I shall have him out of prison).[102] Thinking that he has won, the devil will settle for nothing less than Christ's execution: but though "Cryst honged" (Christ hanged) on "þe croys" (the cross), God punishes the "traytour" (traitor) casting him down "Into helle and ibounden fast" (into Hell [where] he bound him fast).[103] The poem concludes with a sermon on the theme of Christ as Prince of Peace at the Last Judgment, and a glimpse of the joys of Heaven.

---

[98] "Castle of Love," line 547.   [99] "Castle of Love," lines 1048–9.
[100] "Castle of Love," lines 1068 and 1070.
[101] "Castle of Love," lines 1078 and 1094.
[102] "Castle of Love," lines 1015–16.   [103] "Castle of Love," lines 1333, 1335, 1337–8.

With a broad variety of formats and recensions, the storyline of *Chasteau d'amour* was widely known in medieval England. Ecclesiastical authorities were "deliberately fostering the broad dissemination of certain key texts," like the *Chasteau d'amour*, in its efforts to improve lay doctrinal literacy. As a result, Andrew Taylor suggests "tentatively" that one might even call the poem a "bestseller" for the period.[104] It is quite possible that one of the versions was put to music to make it more memorable for the laity, and Richard Southern argues that the story was typically performed for household and guests.[105] The net result, one suspects, is that when Englishmen and women thought about prison dure, they imagined Adam after his expulsion from the Garden of Eden. While other sermons[106] from the era make the analogy expressly between hard prison and Adam's experience of Hell, the Castle of Love stories suggest that life on earth under the dominion of Satan shared similar qualities, and this experience of incarceration lasted either 4,000[107] or 5,000 years,[108] depending on your source. As such, it becomes part of a universal heritage of all humankind. It also stands as a potent warning to Christians about the dangers of pride. The poem implies also the possibility that pride and hard prison remained linked in the medieval imagination, as is suggested by the cases of silent traitors who died an ignominious death in hard prison.

Grosseteste's version of the story sends a powerful message about hard prison. Yes, Adam deserved to be punished; but his was not a just punishment because punishment without mercy was simply not just. As a late medieval sermon-writer explained, "mercy and justice cannot be separated, neither one can be far away from the other."[109] The king is the ultimate judge within a realm, and even he must rule with the hand of mercy. As *Bracton* writes: "A king ought not only to be wise

---

[104] Andrew Taylor, "Manual to Miscellany: Stages in the Commercial Copying of Vernacular Literature in England," *The Yearbook of English Studies* 33 (2003): 8–9.

[105] Taylor, "Manual to Miscellany," 8. Richard Southern, *Robert Grosseteste: Growth of an English Mind* (Oxford: Clarendon Press, 1992), 225.

[106] A sermon for "Septuagesima Sunday" from the *Northern Homily Cycle* notes that until Christ's incarnation, after death man lived in "prisone strange" (*strong prison*) (lines 292–4). Thompson, ed., *Northern Homily Cycle*, 89.

[107] Richard Morris, ed., *Old English Homilies of the Twelfth Century, from the Unique MS. B. 14. 52 in the Library of Trinity College* (EETS, vol. LIII, 1873), 60.

[108] Holthausen, ed., *Vices and Virtues*, 6.

[109] Horner, ed., *A Macaronic Sermon Collection*, 268.

but merciful, his justice tempered with wisdom and mercy."[110] Peter Lombard's *Sentences*, the foundational textbook on canon law, glosses "justice" as "mercy."[111] Surely, Grosseteste adopted the experience of hard prison to explain life under the rule of the devil in familiar terms to his parishioners; but in doing so, he questions the validity of the punishment. The message he imparts is that if God had been listening to all of his daughters (especially Mercy!), he never would have devised such a cruel sentence.

Did Grosseteste intend to associate hard prison with humanity's fall from grace in a manner that openly criticized royal implementation of the practice? As bishop of the largest diocese in England, home to eight archdeaconries and over 2,000 parishes, Grosseteste felt he had a personal responsibility to intervene in political affairs when they jeopardized the souls of his parishioners.[112] Nor did the intrepid bishop shy away from criticizing the king. Twice over the course of his career, he spearheaded movements to compel the monarchy to reform its relationship with the church. In 1237, Grosseteste was responsible for composing and presenting a list of the episcopacy's complaints (*gravamina*) to the king regarding royal overreach into ecclesiastical affairs, specifically the legal treatment of criminous clerks. Grosseteste argued that the king's courts had no right to try clergymen, even if they did eventually hand them over to episcopal jurisidiction for a second trial and judgment. In 1253, Grosseteste again bumped heads with Henry III. In this set of *gravamina*, the episcopacy complained of the king's inability to adhere to both natural and common law (specifically, the Magna Carta and the Charter of the Forests). Grosseteste boldly christened the king "a murderer for potentially squandering souls"; in failing to adhere to the dictates of the law, "he risked the damnation of [his subjects'] souls."[113] While Grossesteste's own confrontations with the king were largely unsuccessful, his influence had larger repercussions through his personal relationship with the de Montfort family. He was

---

[110] *Bracton*, vol. II, 306.

[111] Philippa Byrne, *Justice and Mercy: Moral Theology and the Exercise of Law in Twelfth-century England* (Manchester University Press, 2019), 20.

[112] Richard Southern, "Robert Grosseteste (c. 1170–1253)," *ODNB* (September 23, 2004).

[113] Philippa Hoskin, "Robert Grosseteste, Natural Law and Magna Carta: National and Universal Law in 1253," *International Journal of Religion and Local History* 10.2 (2015): 127.

tutor to two of Simon de Montfort's sons, and private confessor to
Simon and his wife Eleanor. Through his religious instruction,
Grosseteste's political theory had a direct impact on the English
barons' program for monarchical reform.[114] As the first to translate
Aristotle's *Nichomachian Ethics* into Latin, Grosseteste held a definite
position on the difference between kingship and tyranny. In fact, he
supplied Simon with an abbreviated copy of a memorandum he wrote
specifically on the subject.[115] While Sophie Ambler maintains that
Grosseteste would never have supported grand-scale rebellion (all of
which transpired after his death), he did advocate in favor of "selective
disobedience of royal commands."[116]

Given his background, it is hard to imagine that Grosseteste's
characterization of prison forte et dure in the *Chasteau d'Amour* was
anything but deliberate. Justice lay at the heart of Grosseteste's theory
of pastoral care, as Philippa Hoskin writes, "because the careful and
just correction – secular and ecclesiastical – of men and women was
what led them to repent of and confess their wrongdoing, and to focus
upon doing right, so leading them to salvation."[117] With the *Chasteau
d'Amour*, Grosseteste sought to teach that "justice, that is just
punishment, was itself a form of mercy. While lenience was not good
in itself, too harsh a punishment, wrongly meted out, caused
resentment, not personal reflection."[118] This would seem to be the
wisdom he imparts on the subject of prison forte et dure.

Hard Prison and Unjust Authorities

While God's punishment may not have been just in this scenario, there
is no way that He can be depicted as an unjust authority, as was the
case in the various trials of Christ above. However, more often than
not, when hard prison was employed in English literature, it was

---

[114] Philippa Hoskin, *Robert Grosseteste and the 13th-Century Diocese of Lincoln: An
English Bishop's Pastoral Vision* (Leiden: Brill 2019), 198.
[115] Sophie Ambler, "On Kingship and Tyranny: Grosseteste's *Memorandum* and its
Place in the Baronial Reform Movement," in Janet Burton, Phillipp Schofield, and
Björn Weiler, eds., *Thirteenth Century England* XIV: *Proceedings of the Aberystwyth
and Lampeter Conference* (Woodbridge: Boydell, 2013), 116.
[116] Ambler, "On Kingship and Tyranny," 121.
[117] Hoskin, "Robert Grosseteste, Natural Law," 9–10.
[118] Hoskin, *Robert Grosseteste*, 70.

painted in a negative light by virtue of the fact that the authority commanding its usage was not only unjust, but unChristian. As such, the moral conveyed is that hard prison is a tool employed chiefly by cruel and tyrannical foreign authorities with no integrity or sense of due process. Three tales drive home this point.

John Mirk's *Festial* includes an illuminating sermon for the feast of saints Philip and James, giving us much insight into peine forte et dure as a form of punishment so horrific only a cruel and tyrannical ruler would command its usage. As one might expect, the sermon presents James as the ideal Christian. The sermon-writer informs us that James was so holy that he never drank wine or ale; he never ate meat or shaved his head; he never bathed or wore linen clothes; and he kneeled in prayer so much that his knees were worn with thick calluses that looked like camel skin. He was the first man ever to sing mass wearing vestments as a priest; and he was the bishop of the city of Jerusalem after the slaying of Christ, during a trying time in the history of the city. The city was "so cumbrud in synne þat þei haddon no grace off amendemente" (so encumbered with sin that they had no hope of redemption, line 58). Shocked and horrified by what he saw around him, Saint James set himself up in a high place and began to preach the faith of Christ, warning the city's inhabitants that if they did not love Jesus, they would be "dampned at þe day off dome" (damned on Judgment Day, line 65). When the Jewish magistrates saw what he was doing, they cast him down from on high, and "wit stonus punned hym so þat he was neghe dede" (with stones pinned him so that he was close to death, lines 67–8) – an English audience would have immediately associated this form of torment with the pressing of peine forte et dure. James did not have to suffer long. A cursed man with a walker's staff struck James on the head so that his brain burst out, and "so 30lde up þe goste" (so he gave up his soul, lines 70–1). Naturally, God took his vengeance "ffor þe synne of þis holy mannus deth (for the sin of this holy man's death, lines 72–3): the city was destroyed so utterly, that each stone of the wall was turned "vp-so-downe" (line 74), the Jews were driven into diverse countries and cities and "disparpullud" (dispersed, line 78) so that the kingdom was destroyed.[119]

Mirk's *Festial* ties peine forte et dure closely with the rule of an autocratic authority: rather than put James on trial for his crimes, he

---

[119] Powell, ed., *John Mirk's Festial*, vol. I, 124.

was convicted through summary justice without the benefit of a jury and forced to die in a horrific and highly public manner in order to deter other Christians with missionary leanings. Yet, it is noteworthy that not only was the rule of the Jewish magistrates tyrannical, it was both unChristian and anti-Christian. Something similar is apparent also in *The Seven Sages of Rome*, a story originally of Persian origin that made its way into Middle English by the fourteenth century. It is a collection of *exempla* tied together by a central plotline involving Florentine, son of Emperor Diocletian from his first marriage. The author tells us that the emperor's second wife is keen to have Florentine removed as heir so that her own sons (not yet born) might someday inherit the empire. After they marry she insists that Diocletian summon his son home from school so that she can become acquainted with him. Diocletian meets with the boy's teachers, the seven sages of the poem's title, and requests that they escort the boy home. Before their departure, Florentine and his teachers consult the moon and stars in order to see the outcome of their journey. Their astrological reading leads them to a startling revelation: Florentine must remain silent for the next seven days, or risk death. Unnerved by the reading, Florentine instantly vows silence.[120]

When he arrives at the emperor's home, Florentine convenes with the empress in private, where she informs him that he is going to become her lover. When it becomes clear that Florentine's consent to her plan is not going to be forthcoming, the empress raises the hue and cry, musses her hair, scratches her face, and rips her clothes, all so that she might accuse him of having attempted treasonously to seduce her. Holding firm to his vow, Florentine stands mute in response to the allegations. Enraged by his son's silence, the emperor has Florentine thrown into prison, knowing that the right conditions will pry open his mouth. Florentine is kept naked, without food or drink, and beaten at intervals with scourges, and there he remains for the next seven days, during which time his stepmother artfully entertains her husband with

---

[120] In the Scottish version, there is an inquisition of sorts into his dumbness. When the son and father meet once more, the father cannot get a word out of the son. He asks one of the teachers how he lost his voice. Rather than tell Diocletian about the impending threat to his son's life, the teacher responds "Schir, be this buke / All the athis that may be sworne, / He spak full weile the day at morne." ("Sir, by this book and all the oaths that may be sworn, he spoke full well this day in the morning"; lines 203–5). Catherine Van Buuren, ed., *The Buke of the Sevyne Sagis: A Middle Scots Version of The Seven Sages of Rome* (Leiden: Leiden University Press, 1982), 243.

stories illustrating the perils of sons who hope to usurp their fathers' position. Each night the enraged emperor condemns his son to death, but the next morning the seven sages undo the damage of the night before by offering up tales of wicked and deceitful wives. Despite the difficulties of his imprisonment, the son holds fast to his vow and utters not a word until the eighth day, at which point he brashly proclaims his innocence. He tells his father everything that had transpired between him and his stepmother, inciting a reluctant confession from the emperor's new wife. Diocletian declares her guilty of treason and witchcraft, and the poem concludes with her burning at the stake.[121]

Florentine's experience as it is relayed in the poem adheres to the common-law model: his refusal to plead prevents the court from proceeding to trial. He is sent to hard prison as a coercive measure, and only once he has agreed to speak is he released from incarceration. There are multiple warning signs embedded in Florentine's tale, signaling to an English audience that his experience was wholly unjust. First, while he was appealed properly of the crime, the appeal came from a woman, and as Magna Carta articulates clearly, no one is to be imprisoned on the appeal of a woman alone. Indeed, one might argue that this tale is a perfect justification for why that should be the case. Second, his judge is biased: why does the emperor immediately side with his new wife rather than his philosopher son and heir? Third, there is good reason to believe that he is laboring under her spell – witchcraft is a running theme throughout the poem. And, fourth, where is the jury?

Most damning of all, the audience is abundantly aware that the emperor is Diocletian, not only a pagan emperor, but the man who led one of the greatest persecutions of Christians in Roman history. He ordered the churches of Rome razed to the ground, scripture burned, the clergy tortured into martyrdom. He had Christian believers rounded up, and if they refused to recant their beliefs, slaughtered. At least 3,000 Christians lost their lives in the Great Persecution and all of this was written about in detail by Eusebius of Caesarea in his *Church History* and thus was well known to a medieval audience.[122]

---

[121] Killis Campbell, ed., *The Seven Sages of Rome* (Boston: Ginn and Company, 1907).
[122] Eusebius of Caesaria, *Eusebius: The Church History*, ed. and trans. Paul Maier (Grand Rapids, MI: Kregel Academic and Professional Printing, 2007).

Associating hard prison with Diocletian transforms what had been explained to the English people as an expedient coercive measure, administered in the best interests of the defendant to ensure that he had a fair trial, into a weapon wielded by a sadist, one of the greatest villains in Christian history. The transition into a Christian morality tale is complete with an analysis of the story's hero, young Florentine. To a medieval audience adept with allegorical readings, the similarity of his predicament to Susannah's was easily recognizable, the one major difference being that this time there were seven Daniels keen to take up the cause and argue his case. As such, Florentine functions as a type of Christ. The last few lines of the poem recount how he went on to great honor. Not only did he became a glorious emperor after his father, but the poem relates that he lived out his life in "Goddes seruyse" (God's service, line 4326), even though God and Christianity had both been noticeably lacking in the poem up to that point.

In *Bevis of Hampton*, the message conveyed by the use of hard prison is not as straightforward, in large part because of the character development of the central figure. While Bevis develops into a heroic knight by the end of the tale, his behavior prior to incarceration in hard prison is troubling. Admittedly, Bevis' childhood was tragic, and presumably left him with some serious psychological baggage. At the age of seven, his mother has his father, the Earl of Hampton, murdered. She also orders Bevis' death, which he survives only thanks to the quick thinking of a loyal servant who slaughters a pig instead and smears the pig's blood on clothes that he brought to the earl's wife as proof of the child's slaying. But Bevis manages to re-enter his father's castle, threaten his mother and her lover, the Emperor of Germany, and declare his intention eventually to avenge his father's death.

In response, his mother sells him to Saracen merchants boarding a ship for the realm of King Ermin, to whom the merchants present the young earl's son as a gift. The Saracen king is charmed by the boy, and eager to see him become his heir someday through marriage with his daughter Josian, but the seven-year-old rejects the notion on the grounds that he could never renounce his Christian identity. He grows to manhood in the Saracen kingdom, and by the time he is fifteen years old, he has become a formidable although arrogant knight. This is made clear through an encounter with a group of Saracens ribbing him about his devotion to Christ, which leads Bevis to slaughter mercilessly the entire group. The king is enraged, and prepared to condemn Bevis to the gallows, but his daughter begs him to listen to Bevis' side of the story. Bevis pleads self-defense and the king permits him to rest up, with the aid of his daughter's healing touch, while he thinks further on the matter. During Bevis' period of recovery, a colossal boar with five mighty tusks terrorizes the kingdom. Determined to show that he is once again the picture of health, Bevis takes on the boar single-handedly, and slays it, slicing off two tusks and the snout as trophies to bring back to his king. The king's steward, who has always despised Bevis, takes this opportunity to attack Bevis with his men. Even unarmed, Bevis remains victorious: using the boar's tusks, he slays the steward and every single one of his men.

Killing the boar may have redeemed him in the king's eyes, but Bevis' total lack of Christian mercy makes him an unlikely hero. Every victory is a massacre. This remains true even when Brademond holds the kingdom hostage, threatening to lay waste to it if Josian does not marry him. Bevis and his army of knights pursue and attack Brademond and his followers, and by sunset they have slain 60,000 of the enemy troops. After the battle, Josian opens her heart to Bevis, but he scorns her because of her Saracen background until she promises to renounce her "false gods" and become a Christian. Hearing this, her incensed father is impatient to seek revenge for his daughter's apostasy. He sends Bevis to meet with Brademond in Damascus; his letter to Brademond, however, instructs him to throw Bevis into a deep, dark pit, which he immediately does.

Bevis is cast into a pit 120-feet deep, where he is given a quarter of a loaf of bread each day, and told that "Yif thow wilt drinke, thegh it be nought swet" (if you will drink, then it will not be sweet, line 1421). (An unmistakable reference to hard prison.) Bevis is bound to a great stone that weighs the equivalent of seven quarters of wheat, and he is surrounded by a mass of poisonous snakes, newts, and toads, coming close to perishing when he is bitten on the forehead by a flying adder. Bevis "lein in bendes / seve yer in peines grete, / Lite idronke and lasse iete" (lay in bonds for seven years, in great pain. Little he drank and less he ate). Close to death, Bevis finally cries out to Jesus Christ and "seinte

Marie" for help. His jailers overhear his pitiful plaint. One of them uses a rope to slide down into the pit and strike Bevis on the head with a sword; but Bevis immediately turns things around. He breaks the jailer's neck, then disguises his voice so that the other jailer mistakenly pulls him partway up before he realizes his error. He drops Bevis back into the dungeon and slips down himself to cow Bevis back into submission, but he too loses his life to the malnourished knight. Bevis lays there for three days, still in chains and tied to the stone, but without food or drink because the jailers who had once brought it to him are now all dead. After another round of prayers to Jesus, his chains shatter and the great stone falls from his waist. He climbs the rope and makes his escape. Much more happens in the poem after this, including a trip to Jerusalem where Bevis confesses all his sins; an earnest fight for the hand of his beloved Josian, who in his absence had married a Saracen king; grappling with lions, a dragon, and a thirty-foot giant; seeing Josian baptized a Christian; and eventually Bevis even managing to avenge his father's death, become a king, produce a worthy heir, and die arm-in-arm with his true love after a life of joy and happiness.

Once again, in this poem hard prison functions as the weapon of an unjust authority – this time a Saracen, rather than a Jew or a pagan emperor – and the justification of its use is equally unlawful. The king deceitfully betrays Bevis while he is carrying out royal business. Nonetheless, in some ways, Bevis' illicit incarceration seems partly justified. His unmerciful and inhumane treatment of his fellow subjects (despite their Saracen nature) is disturbing to the reader; at the very least, the numerous massacres he initiates make it clear that he is in no way ready to take up the mantle of the Christian knight. It is only through Josian's (ironically Christian) love, and his seven years of suffering in hard prison, that he matures spiritually and emotionally, finally growing into the role of England's great Christian hero. Bevis' spiritual journey means that hard prison takes on a different meaning in this poem from the one it had in *The Seven Sages of Rome*. Despite being wielded by an unChristian and anti-Christian tyrant, the poem showcases the value of hard prison as a redemptive experience: through sacrifice of worldly goods and suffering of physical pain, the spoiled and pampered knight, who cares chiefly for himself, transforms into a caring human being. In *Bevis of Hampton*, prison forte et dure is unmistakably a vehicle for *imitatio Christi*.

Conclusion

In 1222, so Ralph of Coggeshall tells us, a delinquent youth and two women were hauled before a council at Oxford under the aegis of Archbishop Stephen Langton. The archdeacon claimed that the young man had committed a most criminal unbelief (*crimine pessimo incredulitatis*). He would not enter a church, nor would he participate in the sacraments, or listen to the advice of the Catholic Father. Instead, he had permitted himself to be crucified, the five wounds still visible on his body, and the women who accompanied him called him Jesus, to his delight. The older woman was also accused of having used magical arts (*suis magicis artibus*) to bring the youth to this height of madness (*dementia*). The younger woman, who was the man's sister, was permitted to go free because she had revealed the impious deed. However, the older woman and the youth were convicted for their crimes, and sentenced to incarceration between two walls until they died (*jussi sunt inter duos muros incarcerati quousque deficerent*).[123]

The theatrics of this Oxonian youth and his accomplices speak to the emotional impact of the Passion in medieval circles. That is not to suggest that do-it-yourself crucifixions were a normal practice in the era, but that Jesus was envisioned as a heroic figure whose experience of the Passion was worthy of emulation. Chapter 5 explored the various reasons why defendants may have opted for silence at their arraignment. The literature of the era recommends one more possibility: that they did so in emulation of Christ. When Christ was arraigned before Herod, he stood silent to indicate his refusal to recognize Herod's jurisdiction. The late medieval English were intimately familiar with this model, which rests on scriptural precedent and is repeated time and again not only in play-form, but also in poems, sermons, and even art, about Christ and others who stand in as a type of Christ, such as Susannah and even Florentine in *The Seven Sages of Rome*. These works, and others,

---

[123] Ralph de Coggeshall, *Chronicon Anglicanum*, ed. Joseph Stevenson (London: Longman, 1875), 191. Admittedly, I don't know what it means to be sentenced to incarceration between "two walls" rather than four. Was this a form of punishment similar to the pressing of peine forte et dure?

cemented the association between silence and protest against injustice. For defendants who knew their end was near, standing mute in *imitatio Christi* permitted them to turn scandal into heroism, in the hopes that a martyr's death might permit them to die with grace. The strong cultural ties between standing mute and Christ's trial before Herod is evidenced by Charles I's behavior at his own trial, although it is ironic that a method of protest designed to target unlawful rule was eventually embraced by the ruler himself. Yet, for Charles, there was no clearer way to draw attention to the similarity of his predicament to Christ's.

Medieval trial records are typically synthetic documents, terse, including only the barest of detail required by law, and often lacking the insights into those aspects of the process in which historians are most interested, such as motive, dialogue, physical gesture, emotional reaction. The contemporaneity of legal processes and settings in the medieval literature, therefore, help us to begin the process of sketching in the gaps left by the legal record. At the same time, it is critical to acknowledge that the court cases, as they are presented in the literature, are not intended to be a truthful reflection of contemporary practice and jurisprudence. Literature provides its authors and audience an opportunity to explore and resolve existing tensions within and surrounding contemporary legal practices. Accordingly, as Rebecca Kastleman has argued, literature "generates its own institutional history of legal thinking," which may reinforce, complement, or challenge the official narrative.[124] Indeed, the same literary work might perform multiple functions simultaneously, speaking to different political constituencies through the various voices of its characters. Nor does authorial intent necessarily shape the audience's reception. William Langland was horrified by the impact of *Piers Plowman* on the rising dissidents of 1381; he had no idea that his essentially conservative-minded message would be filtered through the lens of the living conditions and social experiences of its listeners to become a rallying cry for revolution.[125] To be sure, he spent the rest of his life rewriting the poem (the C-text) to confirm that it was never used in that way again.

---

[124] Rebecca Kastleman, "Impersonating the Law: The Dramaturgy of Legal Action in the York Corpus Christi Pageant and John Bale's *Three Laws*," *Theatre Journal* 68.1 (2016): 39.

[125] Carl Schmidt, ed., *Piers Plowman: A New Translation of the B-Text* (Oxford University Press, 2009), xv.

This example highlights the challenges of appreciating wholly the politics of any text, tied not only to the society that produced it but also to the individual social conditions of those listening to it being read.

Wendy Matlock reminds us that "vernacular texts, even fictional ones, can participate in contemporary legal discourse and disseminate, normalize, or critique official discourse."[126] The literary works examined in this chapter thus not only provide the historian much-needed insight into contemporary perceptions of standing mute and hard prison, they also showcase active inquiry into and communal resistance of multiple aspects of English legal procedure relating to standing mute and peine forte et dure from the perspective of the commoner. The hero of the mystery cycles, Jesus Christ, was backed into a corner by an unjust and corrupt legal process, his sentence imposed by out-of-touch elites operating for their own nefarious purposes. Nonetheless, his story is one of triumph against the venality of human government: "Christ has silently pitted himself against and defeated a raucous homosocial body of men representative of violent, martial masculinity and the discipline and punishment of law."[127] Moreover, while government officials may have appreciated prison forte as a coercive measure intended to preserve the integrity of the judicial system, ensure that all those undergoing trial had consented to trial, and had embarked on the penitential process, the literature demonstrates that the English people were not so easily convinced. Rather, they saw hard prison as an unjust sentence, employed by unmerciful and distinctly unChristian rulers. The persistence of the measure's association with foreign rule may also have led them to believe that the highly unsavory practice had alien and anti-Christian origins.

---

[126] Matlock, "Law and Violence in *The Owl and the Nightingale*," 449.
[127] Fitzgerald, *Drama of Masculinity*, 148.

7

Rejecting the Jury, Rejecting the Common Law, Rejecting the King

> The king and the pope do not think of anything else than how
> they may take away our goods and our money.
>
> MS. Douce, 137.[1]

When we think about protest, we think about noise. As Michael Sizer
has astutely observed, there is a "soundscape" to revolt.[2] It begins
quietly with whispers, chatter, buzz, nattering; then bit by bit it builds
into muttering, humming, murmuring, rumbles swelling, amplifying,
growing louder and louder. Manifested appropriately, together these
noises coalesce into the "voice of the people" (*vox populi*), that
nebulous entity sometimes credited with being the impetus behind
changes in law. When the grousing and griping goes unanswered, it
risks erupting into the unspeakable: cries, roars, clamor, and tumult –
the soundscape of revolt. Inescapably, that noise is tied to class. When
the elite wishes to speak out against the king and his policies, its
members do not speak at all: they write. They petition parliament
with parchment and ink, and because the government is replete with
other like-minded individuals who can sympathize with their
grievances, they know the likelihood of making their voices heard.

---

[1] *Le rei ne l'apostoille / Ne pensent autrement, / Fors ke il nus toillent / Nos biens e nostre
argent.* "MS. Douce 137," Isabel Aspin, ed., *Anglo-Norman Political Songs* (Anglo-
Norman Text Society, vol. IX, 1953), 45-6.

[2] Michael Sizer, "Murmur, Clamor, and Tumult: The Soundscape of Revolt and Oral
Culture in the Middle Ages," *Radical History Review* 2015.121 (2015): 9-31.

When the Crown ignores the complaints of the upper ranks, driving them to violence, it is not classified as revolt but civil war. For the rest of England's subjects, who cannot write and have no hope that the privileged lot in parliament will instinctively commiserate with their concerns, noise is their most potent weapon. Noise *is* protest.

In order to quell the voices of the dissident, parliamentary statutes and local legislation in towns and cities across later medieval England targeted the production of disruptive noise. Scolding, unlawful raising of the hue and cry, treason by words, cursing, blasphemy, rumor-mongering, gossip, barratry, false appeals, false preaching, riot – all were subject to legislation in this unquiet era. As Christian Liddy writes, "[s]peech was toxic because of its dynamic and incremental potential to fuel rumour and gossip, inspire conspiracy, and provoke insurrection."[3] Through legislation, authorities hoped to control words, or put the right words in people's mouths, and avoid the kind of deafening outburst that was heard around the kingdom in May and June of 1381. And as the rising of 1381 proved to everyone, revolt has its risks. When popular protest erupts into revolt, it might well result in a plethora of executions in retaliation: in the case of 1381, at least 1,500 rebels punished with death. It also did little to advance their cause. Revolt did not bring change; it merely hardened hearts.

Revolt, with all its accompanying shouts, barks, and bellows, remains the focus of historians eager to trace the dissonant voices of the populace. Knowing that inquiries into popular protest are grounded in the crowd studies of George Rudé and Mikhail Bakhtin's carnivalesque, in which laughter (more noise!) serves as the only viable substitute for all-out revolt, it is easy to understand why protest of the noisy kind prevails.[4] However, the emphasis on sound overlooks the ingenuity of a people who were accustomed to working within a highly regimented social hierarchy, and had discovered imaginative ways to defy the system when it worked against their

---

[3] Christian Liddy, "Cultures of Surveillance in Late Medieval English Towns: The Monitoring of Speech and the Fear of Revolt," in Justine Firnhaber-Baker and Dirk Schoenaers, eds., *Routledge History Handbook of Medieval Revolt* (New York: Routledge, 2016), 320.

[4] George Rudé, *The Crowd in the French Revolution* (Westport: Greenwood Press, 1959); Mikhail Bakhtin, *Rabelais and His World*, trans. Hélène Iswolsky (Bloomington: Indiana University Press, 1984).

best interests. It also gives us a false impression of medieval modes of resistance. Not long ago, Samuel Cohn attempted to grapple with this fallacy by attacking what he describes as the premodern paradigm of revolt. In the traditional historiography, premodern revolt is thought to be spontaneous – there are no "assemblies, secret meetings, confederations, organization or plans," rather it explodes impulsively after long-simmering tensions. It is also conservative: the people are looking backward to restore lost rights; it is masculine, as evidenced by the degree of violence; and it usually ends in brutal repression. Nonetheless, revolt in the modern world is seen as being "creative." The rebels seek "new means and issues to advance their political rights and economic advantage against the threats of industrialization and abuses of the state."[5]

Cohn's objective in sketching these contrary visions is to subvert the traditional historiography and draw out the modernity of medieval revolt. Revisionists, like Eliza Hartrich, are keen to demonstrate that premodern "rebellion was not necessarily the desperate action of a poverty-stricken peasantry or proletariat whose options had run out, but more typically a strategic demonstration made by people fully integrated into the political life of the realm or city."[6] With this renewed insight, Cohn and Hartrich, among others, are trying to restore strategic thinking and organization to the medieval protest, as well as an appreciation for gradations of resistance. This chapter hopes to add to this conversation by enlarging the category of activities that constitute protest. For medieval men and women zealous for change, full-scale revolt like the English Rising of 1381 was not the first stage of protest; neither was it the second nor the third. Violence was an act of anger and frustration, but only after everything else had failed. After centuries of dealing with entitled, over-privileged elites, the English people had developed an entire arsenal of weapons of resistance and demonstration, just as creative as anything witnessed in the modern era, that had to be exhausted before turning to physical violence. With their ears straining to hear the soundscape of riot or rebellion,

---

[5] Samuel Cohn, Jr., "The 'Modernity' of Medieval Popular Revolt," *History Compass* 10.10 (2012): 732.

[6] Eliza Hartrich, "Rebellion and the Law in Fifteenth Century English Towns," in Firnhaber-Baker and Schoenaers, eds., *Routledge History Handbook of Medieval Revolt*, 190.

however, historians of resistance have simply missed the more usual tactics of protest in the medieval context.

Strategies of protest are not timeless; rather, they are culturally dependent. Medieval men and women sometimes protested in ways that seem unfathomable to us. This is exemplified best in the fact that poverty in emulation of the apostles was one of the most common forms of protest in the era, adopted by countless heretics (the Waldensians and the Cathars immediately leap to mind), but also among the orthodox, such as the Cistercians and the friars and a whole cornucopia spilling over with mystics. Poverty was a "powerful symbolic protest" meant to help Christians visualize the stark contrast between the simplicity of Christ's example, and his legacy in the "wealthy and worldly" church.[7] Sally Smith argues that when English peasants wore buckles, brooches, and pins of good quality metal, they, too, were staging a protest. The peasantry was investing its meager resources to challenge the visual symbolism of hierarchy imposed by the sumptuary laws of the later medieval period.[8] Many of the other methods adopted by medieval men and women to protest the unreasonable demands of authorities may seem just as unorthodox to us today. As this chapter will detail, sometimes not showing up to work or failing to pay a *multure* fine were acts of protest. So, too, was ignoring a summons for jury trial, or marrying without the lord's permission. On its own, each of these "small guerilla actions" carried out by individuals may seem inconsequential; but they had their benefits. The ambiguity of their passive-aggressive actions meant that the perpetrators could protect themselves in an open confrontation. When pressed, failure to pay a toll can be explained away as the result of a faulty memory rather than an act of protest, although the astute landlord confronted with a contagion of memory lapses on his manor should be able to interpret the message as it was intended. It was "[o]nly when these little acts of resistance failed to budge the lord did the peasants move on to more open tactics."[9] Yet, they were still a long way off from revolt. As

---

[7] Rebecca Jean Emigh, "Poverty and Polygyny as Political Protest: The Waldensians and Mormons," *Journal of Historical Sociology* 5.4 (1992): 479.

[8] Sally Smith, "Materializing Resistant Identities among the Medieval Peasantry: An Examination of Dress Accessories from English Rural Settlement Sites," *Journal of Material Culture* 14.3 (2009): 309–32.

[9] Peter Larson, *Conflict and Compromise in the Late Medieval Countryside: Lords and Peasants in Durham, 1349–1400* (New York: Routledge, 2014), 231.

these acts suggest, passive, nonviolent, noncooperation typifies the medieval peasantry's strategies of resistance.

In the past, historians have explained standing mute as denunciation of the trial jury as a foreign mechanism imposed from above. This chapter adopts the approach that it was not the mechanism itself that was the problem. Rather, it was what it represented: the advance of an ever more powerful centralized governance. This is reflected in the taxonomy: when consenting to jury trial, defendants placed their fate in the hands of the "country." While those jurors might be drawn from the locality, when it came to a trial in the courts of common law, they stood for the kingdom and its king. Let there be no mistake: common law was the king's law, regularly issued in the king's name, and announced by the king's cryers. While trial juries were not the foreign institution legal historians once believed, in this instance, they were an instrument of royal justice, representing the expanding power of a newly centralized Crown. This reading of events is captured in the Statute of Westminster that sanctioned hard prison: it explained that silent defendants were to be treated as "they which refuse to stand to the common Law of the Land."[10] Similar statements are made repeatedly in the legal record. Defendants are regularly described as refusing the common law (*refusavit communem legem*), refusing good law (*refusavit bonem legem*), renouncing the common law (*legem commune[m] renunciavit*) or refusing the common law of England (*refutantes communem legem Angliae*).[11] When reading these notations in the legal record, one cannot help but wonder whether justices merely interpreted the defendants' behavior as a rejection of the law, or if defendants themselves made a statement to this effect. Unfortunately, the records on their own give us no indication either way. In this respect, standing mute was another nonviolent strategy of resistance for English subjects who chose to give their deaths meaning, knowing that the commons would appreciate their silence as a symbolic objection to the growing power of an increasingly bureaucratic authority.

Standing mute very much belongs to the category of a "'bottom up' manifestation of political community."[12] This is significant. Popular protest, especially of the well-thought-out, nonviolent kind, is typically

---

[10] Statute of Westminster I, 3 Edw. I, c. 12 (1275); *SR*, vol. 1, 29.
[11] TNA JUST 3/1/6, m. 4d (Felise Duffeld and Isote la Smale, 1334).
[12] Marc Boone, "The Dutch Revolt and the Medieval Tradition of Urban Dissent," *Journal of Early Modern History* 11.4/5 (2007): 365.

associated with the modern era.[13] As such, "modern readers do not feel called to read medieval criticism as ideological when there is no outward sign of rupture or difference."[14] However, there is no need to wait for the deafening cries and bloodshed of a revolt to see the English people express their dissatisfaction with "the predatory nature" of English "royal governance."[15] Medieval men and women expressed their discontent with royal authority in a multitude of ways, including standing mute, because the king was not keeping up his end of the bargain. A king was supposed to protect his subjects: when he failed to do so, sometimes the people spoke out. Sometimes, they were silent.

Giving Juries a New Meaning

The transition to jury trial is often envisioned as the beginning of a new phase in legal history, when in fact it arrives at the tail-end of another. England's Norman kings grasped English law as a vehicle to ingratiate themselves to their conquered subjects. Law is an integral part of national identity: thus, sanctioning the preservation of English law as well as the Anglo-Saxon court system permitted King William I (d.1087) to masquerade as a legitimate heir. In this line of thinking, better to appropriate existing procedures, evincing respect for English tradition and institutions, than to act as a disruptive force by creating new processes or importing foreign ones from home. This administrative finesse facilitated a (relatively) smooth transition in leadership. The Normans inherited an impressively centralized kingdom, that is, relative to coexisting kingdoms on the European continent, in which the Crown "exercised close control of crime and disorder."[16] Under the Angevin kings, with Henry II especially, coming in as he did in the wake of the Anarchy (1135–53), the goal was to first restore, then accelerate

---

[13] Charles Tilly, "How Protest Modernized in France, 1845–1855," in William Aydelotte, Allan Bogue, and Robert Fogel, eds., *The Dimension of Quantitative Research* (Princeton University Press, 1972), 380–455.

[14] Rita Copeland, "Introduction: Dissenting Critical Practices," in Rita Copeland, ed., *Criticism and Dissent in the Middle Ages* (Cambridge University Press, 1996), 4.

[15] Ralph Turner, "England: Kingship and the Political Community, c.1100–1272," in Rigby, ed., *A Companion to Britain*, 184.

[16] Paul Hyams, "Feud and the State in Late Anglo-Saxon England," *JBS* 40.1 (2001): 30.

this process, removing much of the responsibility for law-keeping from communal membership into the hands of individuals appointed by or explicitly working on behalf of royal authorities.[17]

The jury was the apparatus by which Angevin rulers hoped to achieve an unprecedented expansion of royal authority. If jury trial was not the great innovation that Maitland once envisioned, neither was it considered by the English people to be "a great bulwark of liberty against the crown," as it is often imagined today.[18] Sworn inquests were a long, time-honored feature of Germanic society. Yet, beginning in the era of Henry II, they were deployed on a grand scale for a wide variety of new purposes, such that they were "transformed from occasional devices for exceptional problems into regular and recurring elements of legal process."[19] English monarchs were precocious in their astute recognition of the value of jurors as both leaders and representatives of their communities, harnessing the powers of the jury for their own political objectives. As a result, the English Crown came to rely "on an exceptionally high level of popular participation, more marked than in any other European polity." The expansion of the jury system that took place over the course of the twelfth and thirteenth centuries established England as a kingdom that functioned on a "system of self-government at the king's command,"

---

[17] This view entails a rejection of the maximalist view of the Anglo-Saxon state, as proposed most comprehensively by James Campbell. Campbell sees that late Anglo-Saxon England was a "nation state" in the fullest sense of the term. See James Campbell, *The Anglo-Saxon State* (London: Hambledon 2000), 10. Much of Anglo-Saxon political history has arisen in response to Max Gluckmann's *Custom and Conflict in Africa* (Oxford University Press, 1955), in which he argued that feud cultures thrive best in stateless societies. Anglo-Saxon England, while certainly a feud culture, was far from a stateless society. In the century and a half before the Norman Conquest, in particular, English kings had a firm grip on many aspects of law and order. However, as both Simon Keynes and Richard Abels have observed, kings were often incapable of maintaining the rule of law and order when an aggressive lord with an inflated ego refused direct commands. See Simon Keynes, "Crime and Punishment in the Reign of King Æthelred the Unready," in Ian Wood and Niels Lund, eds., *People and Places in Northern Europe 500–1600: Essays in Honour of Peter Hayes Sawyer* (Woodbridge: Boydell, 1996), 69; Richard Abels, "'The Crimes by Which Wulfbad Ruined Himself with his Lord': The Limits of State Action in Late Anglo-Saxon England," *Reading Medieval Studies* 40 (2014): 50–2.

[18] Thomas McSweeney, "Magna Carta and the Right to Trial by Jury," in Randy Holland, ed., *Magna Carta: Muse and Mentor* (Eagen, MN: Thomson Reuters, 2014), 145–6.

[19] James Masschaele, *Jury, State, and Society in Medieval England* (New York: Palgrave Macmillan, 2008), 46.

or what has also been described as "government by jury."[20] The establishment of the trial jury after 1215 further entrenched the notion of the locality in service to the Crown. The trial jury thus marks the apex of this expansion not its conclusion; rather, juries proliferated at all levels of society and for a wide assortment of reasons, swiftly becoming the normal means of undertaking inquiries, resolving disputes, disseminating and collecting information, and constructing communal values. Accordingly, while juries were not a novel feature of English society, they acquired new meaning under Angevin rule. Where sworn inquests once signified communal resolution of communal problems, under the Angevins, the jury came to represent the ever-increasing expansion of royal authority across England.

Under Henry II, juries were accorded new responsibilities that had the effect of regularizing juries as a legal instrument, dramatically expanding the frequency of their usage. When it comes to the criminal law, the Assizes of Clarendon (1166) and Northampton (1176) mark the origins and expansion of the jury of presentment. Prior to 1166, crime reporting was the preserve of the victim or his/her family through the process of appeal. Henry had no intention of tampering with that system. However, in order to clamp down on rising crime rates and fulfil his commitment to his subjects as England's foremost peacekeeper, he sought to supplement appeals with a presenting jury. Described in the Assize of Clarendon as an assembly of twelve of the more lawful men drawn from each hundred, as well as groups of four lawful men from each village within the hundred, the jury's objective was to furnish sheriffs with information on local criminal activity. Such a simple reimagining of the purpose of the jury had a transformative effect on the nature of governance and the relationship between center and periphery. First, the introduction of a means of anonymous indictment led to a much more efficient system of criminal justice. Victim intimidation was pointless when jurors were required to present on private crimes; and incentive to do so, even if it meant angering one's neighbors, was enhanced by the institution of fines for failing to present, imposed on the hundred as a collective.

---

[20] John Maddicott, "The Oath of Marlborough, 1209: Fear, Government and Popular Allegiance in the Reign of King John," *EHR* 126. 519 (2011): 307–8.

Second, as outlined in Chapter 3, the Assize of Clarendon had the effect of forcing through a radical redefinition of felony. The assize stipulated that jurors were to present on robbery, homicide, theft, and any criminal collaboration (including harboring and receiving). Ten years later, the Assize of Northampton expanded that category to include also forgery and arson.[21] In doing so, Henry enacted a reconceptualization of crime as a public construct. Under the Anglo-Saxon kings, homicide was not a crime, but an offense perpetrated by one individual against another; if the victim (or his/her family) did not seek royal intervention, the king (or officials on his behalf) did not get involved because it was considered a private matter. When the Crown did get drawn in, it was usually because the offending party refused to pay up; the king mediated payment of an appropriate compensation. Compensation acted as a means of buying the right to reinstate the peace ruptured by the culprit's antisocial behavior. Thus, the offender paid *wergeld* to the victim's family, as well as *manbot* to the victim's lord (for the loss of a laborer), and *fihtwite* to the king for violating his peace. In this scenario, while the king and his peace were visualized as victims, they were secondary.[22] With the Assize of Clarendon, breach of the king's peace moved from secondary to primary importance, drawing homicide into the category of serious crime, alongside theft and robbery. For so many reasons, this was a brilliant move. Being able to curb feud and private warfare was critical to both the stability of the kingdom and Henry's reputation as peace-keeper. However, the real gains were in the financial benefits. With this shift, formal means of compensation to the victim's family vanished altogether, an event of such significance that Pollock and Maitland refer to it as "the most marvelous revolution . . . in the law of homicide."[23] In essence, homicide became what had once been known as a *bótleas* offense; like theft, it was punished not by

---

[21] Assize of Clarendon, William Stubbs, ed., *Select Charters and Other Illustrations of English Constitutional History*, 9th edn., rev. H. W. Carless Davis (Oxford: Clarendon Press, 1913), 143. The Assize of Northampton expanded the number of crimes that it must report. Stubbs, ed., *Select Charters*, 179–81.

[22] *Bótleas* (or unemendable) crimes did exist in which execution rather than compensation, theoretically, was the punishment. Yet, because execution cemeteries from the era indicate a burial rate of one felon per decade, executions would seem to have been rare. Tom Lambert, "Theft, Homicide and Crime in Late Anglo-Saxon Law," *P&P* 214.1 (2012): 38.

[23] P&M, vol. II, 459.

compensation, but by execution and felony forfeiture, payable directly to the king. The profits derived from felony forfeiture built a solid financial future for an ambitious monarchy. The scope of those profits improved with the creation of the coroner and his fellow keepers of the peace in 1194 during the reign of Henry's son, Richard I. The coroner's job was to investigate any sudden or unusual deaths, expanding the king's purview also over deaths by misadventure (again, traditionally resolved by compensation). Deaths by misadventure brought the added benefit of confiscation of the *deodand*, that is, an object or animal which caused the death of one of the king's subjects. Accordingly, the Crown justified the confiscation of his subjects' errant pigs, horses, carts, and ships laden with goods (and so forth). While this may not seem like a great boon, collection of *deodand* was often substantial enough that it was granted by the king in alms to specific churches or monasteries to fund rebuilding or expansion efforts.

More important still, Henry made sure that all of these profits came directly to his coffers and his alone: by recategorizing serious crimes as pleas of the Crown (*placita coronae*), matters in which the king held an especial interest, all felony indictments had to be tried in the king's court, rather than one's lord.[24] Not only did this redirect the profits of criminal justice into Henry's purse, but also removing the right to try crimes from his nobles diminished their prestige and authority in the social hierarchy. The Crown's sole possession of the right to try crime was reinforced visually throughout England with the prisons built under Henry II's command, also mandated by the Assize of Clarendon. Local and customary courts were still permitted to try petty crimes, such as assault or the drawing of blood; but these, too, ultimately came into the hands of the king's justices in the thirteenth century as the dominion of the king's courts expanded to encompass also trespass litigation.

Third, the jury of presentment was a direct means of funneling information from the locality to the center. As such, the jury of presentment served the Crown by providing a method with which "to keep tabs on the country with its limited resources by compelling members of the community to work for the king." The emphasis on trial jurors as royal informants meant that, contrary to modern

---

[24] Julius Goebel, Jr., *Felony and Misdemeanour: A Study in the History of Criminal Law* (Philadelphia: University of Pennsylvania Press, 1976), 401.

perceptions, medieval juries "served not so much as protection against royal power, but as extensions of it."[25] It also meant that those elite, law-worthy men who acted as jurors of presentment were in a position of great power. Jurors presumably spent weeks investigating in preparation for presentment. In this capacity, they were capable of making allegations without any evidential support disappear before the sheriff even arrived in town. At the same time, the information they chose to report might well lead to the incarceration of one of their neighbors; in the event of conviction, also risk to life and limb.

Over time, the jurors' role became even more central to the king's finances, as the articles of the eyre multiplied. By 1244, for example, the king requested that jurors report not only on the usual criminal activity, but also: unpaid debts owed to the king; recently orphaned minors who should be wards of the Crown and the value of their lands; the value of the king's sergeanties and who holds them; churches that should be in the king's gift; escheats that should have returned to the Crown; unlawful enclosure of royal property; corrupt officials and bribery; treasure troves; the estates of recently deceased Jews or Christian usurers; minting without license; properties of fugitives or outlaws; new customs; unpaid defaults; unwarranted jail deliveries; and escape of thieves.[26] This vast miscellany of seemingly arbitrary matters are all united in the fact that they represent monies owed to or withheld from the king. The articles of the eyre thus hammer home the vivid transformation in the nature of the jury. Where once the sworn inquest had been a mechanism for communal problem-solving, after Henry II it became a tool for ratting out the bad behavior of one's neighbors. It is noteworthy that the remarkable success of the jury of presentment at common law inspired bishops to adopt the same model. Thirteenth-century episcopal visitations began the process of issuing articles of visitation (eerily similar in nature to the articles of the eyre), addressed by a panel of law-worthy men from the parish expected to report all sinners from their community, as well as monies withheld, corrupt officials, and so forth.[27] The magnitude of the responsibility involved meant that only the most trustworthy were eligible to participate on the

---

[25] McSweeney, "Magna Carta and the Right to Trial by Jury," 145–6.

[26] A sample version of the "Articles of the Eyre" can be found in Helena Chew and Martin Weinbaum, eds, *London Eyre of 1244* (London Record Society, 1970), 5–10.

[27] See Ian Forrest, "The Transformation of Visitation in Thirteenth Century England," *P&P* 221 (2013): 3–38. Forrest's book, *Trustworthy Men: How Inequality and Faith*

panel. Presumably there was substantial overlap between the sworn men of the visitation panel and a hundred's jurors of presentment.

As its precursor, the presenting jury also paved the way for the eventual adoption of jury trial. Long before Lateran IV (1215), English litigants were becoming more and more comfortable with trusting juries of men to indict suspected criminals. In doing so, jurors of presentment were required to pass a preliminary verdict on whether they believed the individual to be guilty of the crime. In many respects, what they were doing was not so very different than what trial juries were later asked to do.

The jury of presentment represents the beginning of Henry's expansion of the jury system. The most notable changes in fact transpired in civil procedure, in which Henry and his government made juries primarily responsible for adjudicating disputes revolving around land claims. At the signing of the Treaty of Winchester (1153), Henry promised to restore inheritances to all those who lost them during the Anarchy. This rash assurance caused widespread confusion and resentment about property and its ownership. The Crown's eventual solution was to devise the Grand Assize, also known as the Assize of Windsor, established in 1179, a jury of twelve knights drawn from the locality and thus presumably in full possession of the history of the land or privilege under dispute. Tasked with delivering a verdict on possessory actions (such as the newly created assizes of *novel disseisin, darrein presentment,* and *mort d'ancestor*), the Grand Assize was the first example of a trial jury, although in the civil rather than criminal setting. It also met with prodigious success. This should come as no surprise given that in most instances, the alternative means of proof for litigants was battle. Few plaintiffs were willing to risk their lives to reclaim stolen property, especially since reliance on a jury of one's peers whose intimate knowledge of the circumstances and personalities involved was generally deemed to

---

Made the Medieval Church (Princeton University Press, 2018) elaborates on this thesis, arguing that by the late Middle Ages, juries of trustworthy men did the majority of the heavy lifting of governance within the dioceses in England. Admittedly, it should be noted that Helmholz suggests that the inspiration actually runs in the reverse, that is, that the use of synodal witnesses in church courts led the king's courts to fashion the jury of presentment. See Richard Helmholz, "The Early History of the Grand Jury and the Canon Law," *University of Chicago Law Review* 50 (1983): 613–27.

offer a fair solution to the problem. Judicial combat had several other strikes against it. Even as a legal resolution, combat was popularly associated with violence and conflict. While this might seem appropriate in felony trials, litigants in civil suits preferred a more peaceful means of resolution.[28] The Grand Assize, with its peaceful and impartial resolution, saw the jury implemented to address new problems in a manner that routinized the use of juries and familiarized Englishmen and women with the prospect of juries of men who handed down a final verdict.

The possessory assizes, in many respects, share the same grander objective as the redefinition of homicide as a crime in Henry's larger strategy: these legal tactics worked hand-in-hand to divert authority from local magnates to the Crown, drawing business away from the old hundred and county courts that had once reigned supreme. The end result was a gradual upending of the existing balance of power. While these local, public courts were a relatively effective means of keeping the peace, the profits of justice stuck to magnates' hands, and power and authority accrued to the sheriff, not the king. Controlling justice was profitable, providing the funds necessary to build a strong, centralized monarchy. As Robert Bartlett once expressed wryly, "[t]he king was the fount of justice but his waters did not run freely."[29] Beginning in Henry II's time, justice was implemented on a business model: he sold royal justice as the superior product: swifter and more effective than that of the local courts. In an effort to wrest petitioners away from their competitors, when it comes to civil suits, the king's courts were "pro-plaintiff," as evidenced by the gradual proliferation of venues and options. As Daniel Klerman writes, "since plaintiffs chose the forum, courts competed by making the law more favourable to plaintiffs."[30] The abundance of

---

[28] Tenants who preferred jury trial over battle had to purchase what was known as a "writ of peace" (*breve de pace habenda*) from Chancery. Combat was also problematic when one of the litigants was a member of the clergy, as was often the case. Clergymen were prohibited from participating in duels. Michael McNair has discussed this in his "Vicinage and the Antecedents of the Jury," *L&HR* 17.3 (1999): 582.

[29] Robert Bartlett, *England under the Norman Angevin Kings 1075–1225* (Oxford: Clarendon Press, 2000), 168.

[30] Daniel Klerman, "Jurisdictional Competition and the Evolution of the Common Law: An Hypothesis," in Anthony Musson, ed., *Boundaries of the Law: Geography, Gender and Jurisdiction in Medieval and Early Modern Europe* (Aldershot: Ashgate, 2005), 149.

judicial venues brought plaintiffs an array of choice. Disappointment in the county court, for example, did not necessarily bring to an end a plaintiff's quest for justice. It was merely an invitation to have one's case removed to King's Bench, or eventually to submit a bill to Chancery. In this way, the Crown did not have to strong-arm plaintiffs in order to poach business from the local courts. They came willingly, even though a writ to initiate a case in the king's courts cost at least six shillings, because royal law was superior law. Over time, this led to the subordination of the county courts to the needs of the Crown: the county court eventually became a forum where local officials sifted through royal writs in order to cooperate with itinerant justices in fulfilling the articles of the eyre. Royal justice had much to offer, including familiarity. Englishmen and women were already accustomed to the procedures implemented there, because they, too, had been borrowed from the county courts: compurgation, the ordeals, even combat. Very occasionally, royal justice adopted and repurposed also process. For example, Henry I's justices removed outlawry as a tool of power from the hands of lesser authorities and retooled it so that it transitioned from a punishment into a process to compel attendance at the *king's* court.[31] It is no wonder that local and feudal courts eventually went into a decline, helped along by the 1267 Statute of Marlborough, releasing the general duty of freemen to attend court under pain of fine.[32]

The ultimate goal of these various repurposings of the jury was to draw law and order clearly and definitively into the ambit of royal authority, and to place the king firmly at the center of its administration. Thus, while jury trial might sometimes look to a modern readership like communal resolution, justice flowed from the king: it was the king's law, administered by the king's representatives in the king's name, and emphasizing crime as a breach of the king's peace. When King's Bench was the trial venue, the king also made an effort to put in regular appearances, reinforcing the centrality of his position.[33]

---

[31] Goebel, *Felony and Misdemeanour*, 423.

[32] See Maureen Mulholland, "Trials in Manorial Courts in Late Medieval England," in Maureen Mulholland and Brian Pullen, eds., *Judicial Tribunals in England and Europe, 1200–1700: The Trial in History, Volume I* (Manchester University Press, 2003), 84.

[33] W. Mark Ormrod, "Law in the Landscape: Criminality, Outlawry and Regional Identity in Late Medieval England," in Anthony Musson, ed., *Boundaries of the*

Thus, the continuation of long-held traditions did not conceal who was actually in control: common law belonged to royal jurisdiction, and the trial jury worked at the king's behest.

The normalization and multiplication of the jury primarily furthered the best interests of the king; however, it also worked to the benefit of the small pool of local men eligible to stand as jurors. Not just anyone could be a juror: women, children, the elderly, and the infirm were automatically excluded from membership. Because jury service was intimately connected with property ownership, so, too, were the vast majority of those healthy, able-bodied men in the prime of their lives.[34] For those few, jury service was empowering. It was a path to royal privilege, recognition of one's local standing and authority, indeed a stepping stone to greater office-holding. Of course, the allure of participating in jury service did not always outweigh its disadvantages. The English Crown had astutely developed a model in which jurors were expected to undertake time-consuming work of weighty responsibility without any financial remuneration. It is no surprise that "burdensome" and "oppressive" are the two most common descriptors used by historians to explain medieval jury service. The articles of the eyre highlight the burden of investigation that fell on the shoulders of the presentment jury. We see something similar also with the advent of the trial jury. Criminal investigations were not a major priority when it was left to God to determine whether a man should hang. Trial by jury, however, relied on human industriousness to uncover evidence. Not only was this onerous for the jurors, the intrusiveness of an investigation meant that no one could be impartial. Witnesses were asked to come forward and present sworn testimony: doing so meant either snitching on neighbors or taking sides in local disputes. Either way, witnesses were being asked to put their lives in jeopardy. James Whitman impresses upon us the magnitude of this transition. He writes, "the new common law of the late twelfth and early thirteenth century was revolutionary partly because it compelled witnesses to testify where they would previously have refused to do

Law: Geography, Gender and Jurisdiction in Medieval and Early Modern Europe (Aldershot: Ashgate, 2005), 10.
[34] Anthony Musson, "Lay Participation: The Paradox of the Jury," _Comparative Legal History_ 3.2 (2015): 252–3.

so."[35] Naturally, Henry II recognized that there would be resistance. He declared that if witnesses chose not to testify then jurors would do it for them. It is no wonder that early jurors had to be forced into participation with threats of hell fire and damnation.[36] Raoul van Caenegem credits Henry's forceful personality with the system's success. He writes, "[t]he terror inspired by a royal master like Henry II . . . would make them speak up."[37]

Jury participation also implied cooperation, perhaps even collusion, with the king and the implementation of his overarching vision of royal authority. Here, it is useful to remember that the Angevin kings were not beloved by the English people. While many historians hold Henry II in high esteem, his subjects had trouble moving past the role he played in the martyrdom of Thomas Becket (d.1170), England's pre-eminent saint. They tended to see Henry as their "oppressor and as the English Church's oppressor."[38] Ralph Turner reinforces this perspective. He speaks of the "predatory nature" of royal governance in this era, singling out Henry II in particular, whom he contends viewed the kingdom as "a vast treasure trove to supply funds for his French conflicts."[39] His son John (d.1216), best known for murdering his own nephew, losing his empire's Continental holdings, and then thrusting England into needless conflict with the pope that resulted in a kingdom-wide interdict, has been described as "licentious, cruel, impious, suspicious, cunning and graceless."[40] Even Henry III (d.1272), whose piousness sometimes merits a kind word, was described by Matthew Paris (d.1259) as a "vigilant and indefatigable searcher after money."[41] For jurors, being associated with the king had its advantages if one was hoping for royal favor; within the community, however, the institution of

---

[35] James Whitman, *The Origins of Reasonable Doubt: Theological Roots of the Criminal Trial* (New Haven: Yale University Press, 2008), 77.
[36] Whitman, *Origins of Reasonable Doubt*, 76–7.
[37] Raoul van Caenegem, *Public Prosecution of Crime in Twelfth-Century England*, 30; as cited in Whitman, *Origins of Reasonable Doubt*, 77.
[38] Ralph Turner, "England in 1215: An Authoritarian Angevin Dynasty Facing Multiple Threats," in Janet Senderowitz Loengard, ed., *Magna Carta and the England of King John* (Woodbridge: Boydell, 2010), 14.
[39] Turner, "England: Kingship," 186.
[40] David Carpenter, *The Minority of Henry III* (Berkeley: University of California Press, 1990), 6.
[41] David Carpenter, "King, Magnates, and Society: The Personal Rule of King Henry III, 1234–1258," *Speculum* 60.1 (1985): 40.

the jury of presentment served to alienate jurors from the rest of the populace who once would have played a role as compurgators or sworn men in traditional means of dispute resolution. As Vincent Challet and Ian Forrest write, the jury system transformed the elite into "collaborators with outside authority, sometimes acting as representatives of their excluded neighbours in secular and ecclesiastical courts, and sometimes acting as the agents of authority in the same contexts."[42]

Of course, invitations to collude sometimes backfired on the Crown and its administrators. As Paul Hargreaves notes, the rebel leaders of the 1381 Great Rising tended to be those very same reeves and jurors who saw their office-holding experience as a training ground for rebellion.[43] Jean Birrell also observes that jurymen played a key role in all of the various protests emanating from fourteenth-century Alrewas (Staffordshire).[44] With so much riding on the medieval jury, failing to turn up for jury service itself could be an effective form of resistance by local elites to the encroachment of a powerful, centralizing authority. When sheriffs failed to muster enough eligible hundredmen to empanel a jury, the court was hamstrung: justices were obliged to send the defendant back to prison to await the next jail delivery when an appropriate jury drawn from the locality might be available to try the case. This happened more often than one might think. For example, the court roll that records the jail deliveries for the counties of Norfolk and Suffolk from 1324 to 1326 (TNA: JUST 3/117) includes 471 court appearances by individuals, of which 35 (or 13.45 percent) could not be tried because of defects in the jury. Others were so eager to be released from jury service that they paid the king for exemption: between the years 1233 and 1272, Henry III issued more than 1,200 exemptions from jury service and office holding to nearly 1,130 individuals.[45]

---

[42] Vincent Challet and Ian Forrest, "The Masses," in Christopher Fletcher, Jean-Philippe Genet, and John Watts, eds., *Government and Political Life in England and France, c.1300–c.1500* (Cambridge University Press, 2015), 281.

[43] Paul Hargreaves, "Seignorial Reaction and Peasant Responses: Worcester Priory and its People after the Black Death," *Midland History* 24.1 (1999): 54.

[44] Jean Birrell, "Confrontation and Negotiation in a Medieval Village: Alrewas before the Black Death," in Richard Goddard, John Langdon, and Miriam Müller, eds., *Survival and Discord in Medieval Society: Essays in Honour of Christopher Dyer* (Turnhout: Brepols, 2010), 199.

[45] Scott Waugh, "Reluctant Knights and Jurors: Respites, Exemptions, and Public Obligations in the Reign of Henry III," *Speculum* 58.4 (1993): 966.

Angevin leadership fostered the rise of the juries. During this era, the jury proliferated: it became the normal means of resolution for just about any problem the Crown might envision. It also became a mechanism for information-gathering, which the Crown used as a conduit for creating an efficient, centralized government. The limited membership of juries, however, had the unfortunate impact of aligning jurymen more closely with the Crown than with their localities. In this climate, when a defendant stood mute before a jury, he or she did so as a rejection of the king and his law.

A "Tradition of Rebellion"

Peasants are seldom imagined to be political actors. Generally considered to have been ultra conservative, peasants are more often thought to be a "hindrance to revolutionary progress or at best followers and indirect participants."[46] Paul Freedman expresses it most clearly when he writes:

Modern attitudes towards the peasantry in a curious way parallel those of the Middle Ages that saw peasants as hapless, inarticulate, capable of dangerous but irrational and unfocused rebellions, but lacking in any sense of program or progress. Peasant resistance was thus regarded as frequent but futile, an instinctual rage rather [than] the expression of any sort of organized plan.[47]

Nothing could be farther from the truth. Rather, as Christopher Dyer has argued, in England, the peasantry of the later Middle Ages were engaged in a continuous struggle against oppressive lordship that led to the creation of a deeply engrained "tradition of rebellion."[48] Their means of resistance was not a series of spontaneous outbursts of rage, but an accumulation of small deliberate acts of passive noncompliance in coordination with their fellow villagers. Moreover, to label their approach as "conservative" is simply the wrong descriptor. When the peasantry seemed to be harking back to "the good old law," they were not seeking a return to the past; instead, they were holding up the past

---

[46] Paul Freedman, "Peasant Resistance in Medieval Europe: Approaches to the Question of Peasant Resistance," *Filozofski vestnik* 18.2 (1997): 179.
[47] Freedman, "Peasant Resistance," 181.
[48] Christopher Dyer, "Small-Town Conflict in the Later Middle Ages: Events at Shipston-on-Stour," *Urban History* 19.2 (1992): 209.

as a reminder to those in authority of their broken promises.[49] For example, Rosamund Faith provides the example of the "great rumour" of the summer of 1377. Hoping for alleviation from financial distress, a total of forty villages from across Wiltshire, Hampshire, Surrey, Sussex, and Devon sought exemplifications of the Domesday Book in the hopes of uncovering evidence of ancient demesne status, so that they might justifiably withdraw from an array of customary duties.[50] In this instance, their actions might appear backward-looking; but the goal was in fact to delegitimize the oppressive exactions of manorial lordship by asserting the greater authority of a three-hundred-year-old document. Challet and Forrest explain that "the expression of rebel demands in terms of ancient liberties and privileges" is not "necessarily conservative." "They were not turning back the clock but making imaginative use of law and documents to secure privileges for the future."[51] Indeed, they believe that the ultimate goal of peasant resistance in the late medieval era was to have themselves more fully integrated into the state as political actors.

The actions of the Angevin rulers themselves surely emboldened the peasantry to see themselves as political actors. As Paul Hyams has argued, "the villein as subject was created out of the needs of Angevin government."[52] For much of the central Middle Ages, a compelling argument could be made for seeing villeins as chattels of their lord. They had no direct contact with the king. The king did not tax villeins; nor did he expect them to participate in peace-keeping, or military service. If the king needed to convey a message to the English villeinage, he did so through their lords, who had the power of life and death over them. Under Henry II, however, the Crown steadfastly recognized the unfree as English subjects. The need to expand sources of royal revenue led Henry to "conscript the contributions of social classes previously untouched except through the mediation of

---

[49] Freedman, "Peasant Resistance," 188.

[50] Rosamund Faith, "'The Great Rumour' of 1377 and Peasant Ideology," in Rodney Hilton and Trevor Aston, eds., *The English Rising of 1381* (Cambridge University Press, 2007), 42–73.

[51] Challet and Forrest, "Masses," 306.

[52] Paul Hyams, *King, Lords and Peasants in Medieval England: The Common Law of Villeinage in the Twelfth and Thirteenth Centuries* (Oxford: Clarendon Press, 1980), 152.

their lords."[53] The 1166 Assize of Clarendon made no distinction according to rank when it comes to crime: all homicides and thefts, regardless of the status or freedom of the perpetrator, were to be tried in the king's courts, undermining a lord's authority over the body of his serfs. The 1176 Assize of Northampton demanded that an oath of fealty "should be taken by all, to wit, barons, knights, freeholders and even villeins *(rustici)*."[54] This process continued under Henry's sons. The 1198 *carucage* – a landtax based on the size of the taxpayer's estate – was the first royal taxation conceived to apply also to the villeinage.[55] Effectively, the Angevin kings ignored the distinction between "free" and "unfree" when it comes to the peasantry. Hyams writes that "[t]hirteenth-century government distributed its burdens on a means test and left legal unfreedom on the whole to the lords."[56] By collapsing that distinction, the Angevins made room for the unfree to take their place alongside the free as political subjects.

The literature of Chapter 6 undoubtedly emanates from the tradition of rebellion about which Dyer has written. In the mystery cycles, Christ is the ultimate rebel. His silent refusal to recognize the authority of those who stood in false judgment against him is the ideal justification for righteous acts of passive noncompliance by the peasantry. Moreover, the continuous adaptation and replication of this theme in the stories of the early Christian martyrs reveals a long, enduring tradition of civil disobedience through silence and passivity. This running thread throughout the Christian religion is critical to acknowledge. In academic circles, Catholicism has traditionally been interpreted as an obstacle rather than a boon to ideologies of peasant resistance. Given that "obedience" (to God, king, lord, priest, father, and husband) lay at the very heart of medieval Christianity and its teachings, it is easy to understand how Catholic doctrine may sit uneasily within the realm of political ideology. As John Arnold observes, from Rodney Hilton to Samuel Cohn, even *medieval*

---

[53] Hyams, *King, Lords and Peasants*, 151–2.
[54] Stubbs, ed., *Select Charters and Other Illustrations*, 179–81.
[55] Hyams, *King, Lords and Peasants*, 152.
[56] Hyams, *King, Lords and Peasants*, 160.

historians of peasant resistance prefer to believe that "meaningful peasant rebellion" requires release from the yoke of orthodoxy.[57]

This viewpoint, however, negates the power of the Passion and its hold on medieval audiences that we witnessed in Chapter 6. Further, it disregards the often radical political ideologies embedded in holy scripture regarding government and taxation, which motivated what Mark Ormrod has described as a "conscious tradition of clerical resistance to the medieval English state."[58] The depiction of Christ before the law in the mystery cycles is one example of this clerical tradition. While the plays were performed by local guilds, they were written by priests, the only men with the education and intimate familiarity with scripture needed to write the story of the Bible from creation to Passion. Robert Grosseteste's *Chasteau d'Amour*, which subtly but unmistakably criticizes the state's use of prison forte et dure as an unjust punishment, is another example of clerical resistance. Literary endeavors of this nature by England's impassioned clergymen sustained a popular struggle against corrupt and tyrannical lordship in a variety of other ways. At mass, the clergy preached resistance through exempla and vitae drawn from the kingdom's long tradition of saints who worked to undercut sovereign power over the body of English subjects by releasing the imprisoned. Saints Edward Martyr, Æthelwold, Dunstan, Erkenwold, Mildreth, and Cuthbert were all celebrated for such miracles.[59] The thirteenth century in particular represents the heyday of the cult of Saint Leonard of Noblac, "erstwhile patron of inmates," chief among the saints known for liberating those suffering in royal prisons.[60] No barometer exists to measure the impact of this sermonizing. Yet, one might well ask, is it mere chance that the two best known large-scale revolts of the era (the Jacquerie of 1358 and the English Rising of 1381) both coincided with Corpus Christi celebrations? John Arnold posits

---

[57] John Arnold, "Religion and Popular Rebellion, From the Capuciati to Niklashausen," *Cultural and Social History* 6.2 (2009): 150.

[58] W. Mark Ormrod, "The Rebellion of Archbishop Scrope and the Tradition of Opposition to Royal Taxation," in Gwilym Dodd and Douglas Biggs, eds., *The Reign of Henry IV: Rebellion and Survival, 1403–1413* (York Medieval Press 2008), 163.

[59] Katherine O'Brien O'Keefe, "Body and Law in Late Anglo-Saxon England," *Anglo-Saxon England* 27 (1998): 223.

[60] Megan Cassidy-Welch, *Imprisonment in the Medieval Imagination, c. 1150–1400* (London: Palgrave Macmillan, 2011), and see Chapter 2.

that the "symbolic associations" of the feast which emphasize the "remaking of the body, community and salvation" may have prompted aspiring rebels to turn their sights also on healing the wounds of the kingdom's body politic.[61]

English clergymen who championed the rights of their struggling congregants helped to open the eyes of England's royal subjects to recognize the oppression of their king's actions. The inflammatory rhetoric of William of Pagula (d.1332)'s *Speculum Regis Edwardi III* ("Mirror of King Edward III"), written in the final years of his life, is the prime example of a tradition of clerical resistance. His mirror is a scathing attack on the custom of purveyance, which permitted the king to take the goods or labor of his subjects free of charge on the grounds that he needed it to support his household. Prior to the fourteenth century, the custom was rarely enacted; but the financial toll of continuous warfare under Plantagenet rule meant that after 1300 it became a routine form of arbitrary indirect taxation. Because the wealthy were able to obtain exemptions from purveyance, the custom's burden fell chiefly on poor rural villagers.[62] As perpetual vicar in the community of Winkfield (Berkshire), William was well aware of how purveyance victimized his parishioners, and his mirror lays it out shamelessly for the king. He writes:

When someone of your household comes to a village to provide for your arrival with geese and hens, among other geese and hens he takes from one poor woman a hen from which she could have four or five eggs to maintain herself and her children; he gives her one denarius, or at most one and a half denarii, and sometimes nothing. This poor woman did not want that hen to be sold for three denarii. This hen, since she is fat, is prepared for your mouth. You are happy from eating that hen, the poor woman is sad; you laugh, she cries; you fill your stomach with the hen which you have unjustly acquired, she is hungry and begs her bread; you feast splendidly on many ill-gotten foods, she has virtually nothing to eat. You are in the fullness of riches, she in dire poverty; you are in golden clothes, she in shabby garments; you have much, she has need; you display hospitality with knights and others by enjoying delicacies, she displays hospitality tearfully with her children crying for lack of bread. I ask you:

---

[61] Arnold, "Religion and Popular Rebellion," 153.

[62] Cary Nederman, "Property and Protest: Political Theory and Subjective Rights in Fourteenth-Century England," *Review of Politics* 58.2 (1996): 334.

by what audacity, what boldness, what impulse, do you dare to eat such a hen?[63]

Yet, as the mirror clarifies, the people are not without power. The king has his subjects to thank for his position of authority: it is through their love that he came into power, and the "love of the people" must set limits on his power.[64] William hints that Edward may also live to regret failing to respect the property rights of his people. Building on the popular theme of the body politic, William taunts Edward with the risks of malcontent subjects: "The people are not of one mind with you, although they seem to be of one body with you, and indeed, if they had another head, they would rise against you, just as they did against your father [Edward II]."[65] William's warning is fitting: even the authors of *Bracton* (*c.*1220s–60s) argued in favor of revolt when a king failed to uphold his duty. *Bracton* writes: "as long as he does justice he is the vicar of the Eternal King, but the devil's minister when he deviates into injustice, for he is called *rex* not from reigning but from ruling well, since he is a king as long as he rules well but a tyrant when he oppresses by violent domination the people entrusted to his care."[66]

William of Pagula's mirror was written in Latin; as a result, it is unlikely that many (or any) of his parishioners were able to read it. Of course, a man this fervent on a subject in writing is not going to keep his emotions bottled up inside. What did he say to his parishioners when he preached to them at mass? Or in confidence during confession? Or at the local alehouse after a couple of beers when he was relaxing in the evening? It is hard to imagine that those to whom he ministered were unaware of his seething anger at the king's exploitation of the custom of purveyance – a fury that saw him through the writing of two different versions of this mirror, which occupy sixty-six typeface pages in a modern edition. Assuredly, William of Pagula's goal was reform, not rebellion. Yet, clerics like William of Pagula surely helped to foment some of that simmering anger that led to the prolonged campaign of noncooperation by England's most lowly subjects.

---

[63] Cary Nederman, ed., *Political Thought in Early Fourteenth-Century England: Treatises by Walter of Milemete, William of Pagula, and William of Ockham* (Turnhout: Brepols, 2002), 131.
[64] Nederman, "Property and Protest," 338.
[65] Nederman, ed., *Political Thought*, 83–4.
[66] *Bracton*, vol. II, 305.

Both William of Pagula and *Bracton* adopt the same tack when criticizing the king: by reminding him that he represents the divine here on earth, they hope to humiliate him into abandoning his immoral behavior and resuming the magnificently paternal relationship that should exist between a king and his subjects. John Arnold sees that this was a common tactic of the era. When a "spiritual elite" is demanding excessive taxation, for example, disputing their right to do so is often best accomplished by undermining or "circumventing their claim to spiritual authority."[67] This is particularly pertinent in the case of those who refused to plead. If standing mute was a form of *imitatio Christi*, when turned against the king, the vicar of Christ, did standing mute continue to have the same meaning as rebellion against an unjust authority? Or, through his flawless mimicry of God incarnate – essentially outdoing the king in his resemblance to Christ – was the defendant hoping to shame the king into living up to the expectations of both God and his subjects?

The example of Richard Scrope (d.1405), Archbishop of York, who died defending the rights and purses of the people of York is especially pertinent to the theme of clerical resistance to royal tyranny. Scrope's rebellion was prompted by the king's abuse of taxation to support his opulent lifestyle. When he stood mute at his trial – because his judges chose to deny him the right of reply – his northern supporters construed him as following Christ's example through silent martyrdom for the good of his people. In 1399, when Henry IV snatched the throne away from his cousin Richard II, who died "mysteriously" in prison sometime thereafter, Scrope initially supported the usurper king.[68] Yet, six short years later, Scrope donned armor in order to lead a massive insurrection against the king, with the active support of key members of York's municipal government.[69] An anonymous chronicle reports that Scrope's protest centered on the actions of a king who disregarded the welfare of his subjects.

---

[67] Arnold, "Religion and Popular Rebellion," 155.

[68] The accession of Henry IV saw a revival in popularity of Thomas of Lancaster's cult. See John McKenna, "Popular Canonization as Political Propaganda: The Cult of Archbishop Scrope," *Speculum* 45.4 (1970): 610.

[69] James Riddle, "The Playing of the Passion and the Martyrdom of Archbishop Scrope," *Mediaevalia* 28.2 (2007): 18.

[He] exhorted and stirid the peple to be assistent and helpyng to the correccioun and amendement of the myschiefs and mysgouernaunce3 of the reme, hauyng in consideracioun the grete pouerte of the marchauntis in whom was wont to be the substaunce of the riche3 of alle the land: and also the grete reisynges of taxe3, tallages and custum3 vnder colour of borowyng: and also, that due paiement be maad for the kinge3 vitaille3: and that the clergie and the comune peple were not vexid ne charged with importable chargis of taxis and talagis as thay hadde longe tyme be: and that the heiris of noble men and of lordis of the lond my3te be restorid to their enheritaunce hoolli, euery man aftir his degre and birthe: and also that suche covetous men as were of the kyngis counsel, that took away and turned to thair owen vse suche godis as were ordeyned to the comune help of the lond, and make thaym self riche withalle, be remeued and put away fro the king.[70]

(He exhorted and stirred the people to assist in helping with the correction and amendment of the mischiefs and misgovernances of the realm, having in consideration the great poverty of the merchants in whom was supposed to be the substance of the riches of all the land: and also the great raisings of taxes, tallages and customs under color of borrowing: and also, that due payment be made for the king's vittles: and that the clergy and the common people were not vexed nor charged with importable charges of taxes and tallages as they have done for a long time: and that heirs of noblemen and of lords of the land might be restored to their whole inheritances, every man after his degree and birth: and also that such covetous men as were of the king's counsel, that took away and turned to their own use such goods as were ordained for the common help of the land, and make themselves rich with it, be removed and put away from the king.)

The myriad grievances detailed here and appearing also in Scrope's manifesto were written in English and pinned to each of the city's gates and the doors of the city's churches, as well as distributed to all diocesan curates with instructions to preach openly about them, and as Doug Biggs has recently observed, they were entirely legitimate. Henry's rash, crowd-pleasing promises at the beginning of his reign to live off his own income and abolish all taxation never came to

---

[70] John Davies, ed., *An English Chronicle of the Reigns of Richard II, Henry IV, Henry V, and Henry VI, Written before the Year 1471* (Camden Society, series 1, vol. LXIV, 1856), 31. The complaint about noble inheritances in the chronicle above was likely in reference to the concerns of Scrope's young compatriot in this uprising, Thomas Mowbray, Earl of Nottingham and Norfolk. His father had been Earl Marshal, a title and position that had always been hereditary, but Henry permitted Mowbray to keep the title only on an honorary basis while the actual position instead went to Ralph Neville, Earl of Westmorland, as a reward for supporting the new king.

fruition. Instead, the English were subject to "regular, heavy and seemingly endless taxation," not to mention a series of forced loans in order to pay for the king's household expenses.[71] Parliament pushed through a special income tax in 1404, although the House of Commons stipulated that it must not be used as precedent for future taxation – they even went so far as to order the destruction of all records relating to the tax to ensure that that was the case.[72] Nor was the church exempt: it was also subject to excessive and frequent requests for taxation during the first six years of Henry's reign. The extent of Henry's tax abuses is meaningful in large part because during Richard II's time, opponents used his forced loans and burdensome taxes as justification for his removal from office.[73] Another manifesto grievance singled out by Clement Maidstone's *Martyrium Richardi Archiespiscopi* was increased royal control over the elections of sheriffs, justices of the peace, and knights of the shire, positions normally chosen through free election. However, during Henry's reign Ricardian officials were "quietly dropped from office and replaced by men of royalist sympathy." Scrope and others soon discovered that these "freshmen sheriffs" were not only inept but corrupt.[74]

Thus, Scrope had plentiful reason to feel justified in his protest against the king. Along with Thomas Mowbray, Earl of Nottingham and Norfolk, they gathered a great host of people. Parliament's "Process and Record" after the fact concluded that the rebel army comprised somewhere between 8,000 and 9,000 supporters, at a time when the city of York's population was 12,000 or 13,000.[75] Together, this formidable force marched toward the manor home of the Earl of Westmorland. At a parlay between the earl, Scrope, and Mowbray, the

---

[71] Douglas Biggs, "Archbishop Scrope's *Manifesto* of 1405: 'Naïve nonsense' or Reflections of Political Reality?," *Journal of Medieval History* 33 (2007): 365.

[72] Biggs, "Archbishop Scrope's *Manifesto*," 363.

[73] Biggs, "Archbishop Scrope's *Manifesto*," 362.

[74] Biggs, "Archbishop Scrope's *Manifesto*," 360 and 365. Three versions of Maidstone's manuscript appear in James Raine, ed., "Miscellanea Relating to the Martyrdom of Archbishop Scrope," in *Historians of the Church of York*, 3 vols. (RS, vol. LXXI, 1886).

[75] Danna Piroyansky, "'Martyrio pulchro finitus': Archbishop Scrope's Martyrdom and the Creation of a Cult," in Jeremy Goldberg, ed., *Richard Scrope: Archbishop, Rebel, Martyr* (Donington: Shaun Tyas, 2007), 106.

rebels' political inexperience led them to make a fatal error. While the three leaders met to hammer out a treaty, the earl's men deceitfully notified the rebel forces that they had already come to an agreement. They reported that the archbishop "comaundeth every man forto go hoom agayne, for he shall this nyʒt sowpe with the erlle" (commanded every man to go home again, for he shall this night dine with the earl). The rebel forces promptly dispersed and the earl brought Scrope and Mowbray in captivity to meet with the king at Pontefract. Soon after, the citizens of York realized how easily the Earl of Westmorland had duped them and began to fear for their lives. When Henry IV entered the city days later, he was greeted with a stunning performance: the city's rebel population appeared as a contingent of penitents, barefoot and unbelted, with halters about their necks as if they were prepared to be hanged, begging the king for mercy.[76]

Having spent most of his reign already battling popular rebellions, and fearing that Scrope's rebellion was coordinated also with the more successful rebellion under the leadership of Henry Percy, Earl of Northumberland, the king was eager to make an example of Scrope and Mowbray. However, Scrope's clerical status made expedience problematic. In England, no king had ever before ordered the execution of a bishop – thus, Henry risked a dangerous precedent and ensuing legacy. As soon as Thomas Arundel, the Archbishop of Canterbury, learned of Scrope's arrest, he rode night and day in order to reach York and beg the king to spare Scrope's life. He presented Henry with multiple licit options. The proper means of trying an archbishop is to hand him over to papal authorities; but if the king wanted a local resolution, Arundel proposed that parliament might be entreated to try the archbishop. In this way, Henry could keep his "handis vndefoulid from his blood" (hands undefouled from his blood). Henry was not so easily convinced. He fretted that rumor of Scrope's activities might encourage further revolt in an already politically fragile climate.[77] Thomas Dawtrey's account of the trial

---

[76] Davies, ed., *An English Chronicle*, 32–3. Adam Usk presents an alternative account in which "the citizens of York had to take off their trousers and prostrate themselves naked on the ground, almost as if it were another judgment day, in order to beg the king's pardon – which they were granted." Chris Given-Wilson, ed., *The Chronicle of Adam Usk 1377–1421* (Oxford: Clarendon Press, 1997), 203.

[77] Davies, ed., *An English Chronicle*, 32.

tells us that the king first summoned William Gascoigne (d.1419), England's chief justice, to try the archbishop, but Gascoigne utterly refused, cautioning the king that he had "no law to kill any bishop, and insofar as you in this matter [have no jurisdiction], I am not able to be such a judge."[78] Gascoigne was dismissed. Henry had him replaced with the less scrupulous (or perhaps simply more ambitious) William Fulthorpe, a knight not a judge, who dispensed with a trial altogether and condemned the rebel leaders to death.[79] At his beheading, Scrope continued to assert his commitment to good governance, saying "Lo! I shalle die for the laweӡ and good rewle of Engelond" (Lo! I shall die for the laws and good rule of England). Scrope did everything in his power to heighten the visual comparison with Christ at his martyrdom. Like Christ upon his entry into Jerusalem riding a mule, Scrope rode to his execution on a horse without a saddle. He kissed the executioner three times in commemoration of the Trinity, forgave him for what he was about to do, requesting that he apply five strokes in his beheading, in honor of the five wounds of Christ. Then, he knelt down before the executioner and commended his soul to God. His death was a good death: as Thomas Walsingham reports, "his severed head was seen to smile serenely."[80]

Most chroniclers wrap up the tale with God's vengeance: at the very same hour as Scrope's execution, the king was struck with leprosy.[81] John Capgrave (d.1464) presents a particularly vivid account. Immediately after the beheading of Scrope, he writes: "The kyng aftir þat tyme lost þe beuté of his face, for, as þe comoun opinion went, for þat tyme onto his deth he was a lepir, and euyr fowler and fowler; for in his deth, as þei recorded þat sey him, he was contracte þat his body was scarse a cubite of length" (The king after that time lost the beauty of his

---

[78] Thomas Dawtrey, "An Account of the Proceedings against Archbishop Scrope," in Raine, ed., *Historians of York*, vol. III, 290.

[79] In instances of martial law, summary justice of this sort is legitimate. Certainly, in the case of Thomas Mowbray, a knight, this may well have been a "battlefield" implementation of the law of arms. However, Archbishop Scrope was not a knight; the law of arms in no way could be applied to his situation. Refusing to hold a proper trial for the archbishop was both illegal and an abuse of power.

[80] Thomas Walsingham, *The St Albans Chronicle: The 'Chronica maiora' of Thomas Walsingham*, vol. II: 1394–1422, ed. John Taylor, Wendy Childs, and Leslie Watkiss (Oxford: Clarendon Press, 2011), 455.

[81] Davies, ed., *An English Chronicle*, 33.

face, for, as the common opinion went, for that time until his death he was a leper, and ever fouler and fouler; for in his death, as they recorded that saw him, he was so contracted that his body was scarcely a cubit in length.)[82] While the addition of the king's illness transforms the incident into an instructive morality tale in good governance, no evidence confirms that Henry actually suffered from Hansen's disease.

Outrage at the execution of a prelate rocked both England and Europe, leading Pope Innocent VII (d.1406) to excommunicate the king. Henry had no choice but to accept blame and perform the spectacle of penance, appearing at the archbishop's palace in York barefoot and bareheaded, promising to found three religious houses in satisfaction for his sins – a promise still unfulfilled at his death.[83] Indeed, on his deathbed, Henry was still trying to wash the blood from his hands by denying that he had anything to do with the death.

Henry's act of political expediency catapulted Scrope into instant martyrdom: Henry "gave York its own Thomas Becket."[84] Once Scrope's body had been buried in the Minster at York, it became a popular site of pilgrimage and offerings, much to the Crown's chagrin. In December of 1405, Arundel, Archbishop of Canterbury, on order of the king wrote to the dean of York Minster forbidding the veneration of Scope or belief in his "pretended miracles."[85] Yet, nothing could stop the tides of pilgrims. From this era survives a four-verse carol in Scrope's honor;[86] multiple books of hours with Scrope devotions, and stained glass images of Scrope. Not long after that a keeper of the Scrope Tomb was appointed; then, a chapel dedicated to the bishop was erected in the field where he had been executed.[87] It is

---

[82] John Capgrave, *Abbreuiacion of Cronicles*, ed. Peter Lucas (EETS, o.s. vol. CCLXXXV, 1983), 229.

[83] Richard Davies, "After the Execution of Archbishop Scrope: Henry IV, the Papacy and the English Episcopate, 1405–8," *Bulletin of the John Rylands Library* 59.1 (1976): 70.

[84] Jeremy Goldberg, "St Richard Scrope, the Devout Widow, and the Feast of Corpus Christi: Exploring Emotions, Gender, and Governance in Early Fifteenth-Century York," in Susan Broomhall, ed., *Authority, Gender and Emotions in Late Medieval and Early Modern England* (Basingstoke: Palgrave Macmillan, 2015), 68.

[85] As discussed in McKenna, "Canonization as Political Propaganda," 614.

[86] Anon., "The Bishop Scrope That Was So Wise," in Stephen Wright, ed., *Richard Scrope: Archbishop, Rebel, Martyr*, 113–14.

[87] McKenna, "Canonization as Political Propaganda," 618 and 621.

noteworthy that Scrope was strictly a popular saint: despite efforts by the northern convocation in 1462, he was never formally canonized. Of course, this mattered little: the people believed he had been acclaimed a saint.[88] Enthusiasm for Scrope's cult lasted well over a century.[89]

Can visiting the shrine of a political martyr like Scrope be considered an act of political criticism in itself? Robert Swanson answered this question with a definitive "no." He contends that when it comes to political martyrs, pilgrimage cannot be read as a political act. While partisanship may have prompted visits by the shrine's original pilgrims, over time, politics are forgotten and pilgrims arrive only in search of a cure.[90] In some cases, surely that was the case. Yet, medieval Englishmen and women did not venerate saints in ignorance of their vitae. Saints' lives were familiar through sermons, exempla, popular literature, and oral histories. Saints were imbued with special qualities inspired by the events of their lives, or in the case of martyrs, their deaths. Thomas More is patron saint of attorneys and diplomats because it was his work in this capacity that got him killed. Throughout the Middle Ages, Thomas Becket was popularly venerated for standing up in defense of the church against the Crown; indeed, the memory of his political activism is exactly what Henry VIII (d.1547) hoped to obliterate when he had the shrine dismantled, his reliquary destroyed, and his bones burned before Becket was "unsainted" by proclamation.[91] As Ormrod writes, when it comes to Richard Scrope, "the cult was accompanied by a process of political mythologizing that cast Scrope as a bulwark of the liberties of the church and people against the threat of royal tyranny."[92] Veneration of political martyrs is a collective form of protest: those who turned to

---

[88] As Adam Usk wrote in his chronicle fifteen years after Scrope's martyrdom, he has "now been acknowledged as a saint on account of his numerous miracles." Given-Wilson, ed., *Chronicle of Adam Usk*, 203.

[89] Piroyanksy, "'Martyrio pulchro finitus'," 109.

[90] Robert Swanson, "Political Pilgrims and Political Saints in Medieval England," in Antón Pazos, ed., *Pilgrims and Politics: Rediscovering the Power of the Pilgrimage* (Farnham: Ashgate, 2012), 29–46.

[91] Robert Scully, "The Unmaking of a Saint: Thomas Becket and the English Reformation," *The Catholic Historical Review* 86.4 (2000): 579–602.

[92] W. Mark Ormrod, "An Archbishop in Revolt: Richard Scrope and the Yorkshire Rising of 1405," in *Richard Scrope*, 28–44.

Scrope did so knowing that they were honoring a man who stood up to the king and died for it, and they believed he earned a place in heaven alongside the saints because of it. The widespread acceptance of the archbishop's sanctity meant that his protest against royal abuse of power continued long after his death through the crowds of Englishmen and women who visited his shrine in reverence.

Scrope's chroniclers reinforced the "saint's" holiness by drawing attention to the remarkable similarities with Christ's Passion not only in Scrope's performance at the gallows, but also in the absence of a proper trial. Both Maidstone and Gascoigne, in their accounts of his execution, quote from Isaiah 53:7, a passage which prophecies Christ's martyrdom at the hands of unjust authorities, emphasizing especially his silence: "He was oppressed, and he was afflicted, yet he opened not his mouth."[93] The Dawtrey account also draws attention to Scrope's calm quiet: we are told that he had little to say in response to Henry's public accusations of his treachery.[94] Frankly, for a man as vocal and articulate as Scrope, this silent behavior seems out of character, and leads us to ponder whether the chroniclers consciously fabricated their depictions on a Christological model. Regardless, his Christ-like behavior was instantly recognizable. As James Riddle writes, "the archbishop's performance is characterized by the silence and stillness that critics have often remarked in the Christ of the York Passion plays"; as such, "Scrope's quiet acceptance of death becomes a powerful act of symbolic resistance."[95] The celebrity of Scrope's execution served also to cement the connection between silence and resistance to royal authority in the popular imagination.

Christianity represents just one thread of the kingdom's tradition of rebellion. Parallel to the growth of monarchy was an explosion in outlaw literature, a genre dedicated to "satirizing the judicial system."[96] Outlaws were a useful reminder of the limits of the king's authority: "those who remained at large cast doubt on the king's ability to keep the peace."[97] While most readers today think instantly of

---

[93] As noted in Piroyansky, *Martyrs in the Making*, 59–60.
[94] Raine, ed., *Historians of York*, vol. III, 290.
[95] Riddle, "Playing of the Passion," 24.
[96] Piroyansky, *Martyrs in the Making*, 47.
[97] Richard Gorski, "Justices and Injustice? England's Local Officials in the Later Middle Ages," in John Appleby and Paul Dalton, eds., *Outlaws in Medieval and Early*

Robin Hood, his *geste* arrives at the end of a long-lasting tradition. More commonly, medieval audiences cheered on tales of Hereward the Wake, Eustache the Monk, Fouke fitz Waryn, and Gamelyn. These anti-heroes share little in common with the Robin Hood of the modern era. Typically, they were not "mistakenly" accused of crimes, nor did they steal from the rich and give to the poor. They were criminals, plain and simple, robbing, murdering, and defrauding whenever they had a chance. Their choice of victims is what endeared them to their listeners. They attacked chiefly those who oppressed the peasantry: law enforcement officials, tax collectors, and members of the clergy. As such, this was fantasy literature, glorifying criminals as "an expression of regional resistance to the apparatus and agenda of a centralising state," prompted by "the crown's periodic programmes of crime control."[98] Many of these fictional characters were based on actual rebels. Hereward the Wake (*c.*1035–72) was the Lincolnshire nobleman who led a fierce uprising against England's Norman conquerors.[99] Eustache the Monk was loosely based on Eustace Busquet (*c.*1170–1217), a northern Frenchman who worked as a mercenary for King John, but during the civil war of 1215 sided instead with John's nobles and the king of France. In the midst of a sea battle for the English chapter, John's forces captured Eustace, and he was beheaded on the spot.[100] Fouke le Fitz Waryn was inspired by Fulk III FitzWarin (*c.*1160–1258), who rebelled against King John in a dispute over his ancestral lands. In reality, Fulk survived as an outlaw for only a few years and was eventually pardoned by the king, but the "strong anti-royalist sentiment" that embodied his experience takes center stage in the outlaw tale, which includes a distinctly unfavorable portrait of King John, described as a "man without conscience, wicked, cross, and hated by all good people."[101] The literature expressed frustration not only with the king but also with his law. The *Tale of Gamelyn*, for example, takes issue with the

Modern England: Crime, Government and Society, c.1066-c.1600 (Farnham: Ashgate, 2009), 55.

[98] Ormrod, "Law in the Landscape," 11.

[99] John McGurk, "Hereward the Wake," *History Today* 20.5 (1970): 331–7.

[100] Thomas Kelly, ed., "Eustache the Monk," in Ohlgren, ed., *Medieval Outlaws*, 61–98.

[101] Thomas Kelly, ed., "Fouke Fitz Waryn," in Ohlgren, ed., *Medieval Outlaws*, 106.

absence of procedures at common law to attaint jurors in criminal trials for delivering a false verdict; *Fouke le Fitz Waryn* provides an extensive commentary on the new Forest Charter and the punishments imposed on poachers and their dogs.[102] Again, the authors themselves were not representative of the population at large. Their literacy places them among the elite, but the scads of Englishmen and women at all levels of society who delighted in listening to outlaw tales participated in a fantasy of revenge against an excessively powerful Crown and its administrators.

The Everyday Resistance of the Peasantry

In his 1985 landmark publication, *Weapons of the Weak: Everyday Forms of Peasant Resistance*, James Scott issued a call to historians to refocus the lens on peasant resistance by looking to everyday acts of resistance rather than large-scale rebellion. Scott explains that peasant rebellion is in fact an infrequent occurrence: "the circumstances that favor large-scale peasant uprisings [are] comparatively rare, but when they do appear the revolts that develop are nearly always crushed unceremoniously" – giving us solid insight into why the peasantry resorted to revolt only when no other option was available.[103] The emphasis of historians on rebellion, then, is misplaced. If we want to understand the normal means of peasant resistance our gaze must shift instead to the "silent and anonymous forms of class struggle that typify the peasantry," such as "passive non-compliance, subtle sabotage, evasion and deception."[104] Scott's own research on class struggle within the Malaysian village brings to light the difficulties of studying peasant resistance which inevitably must be "disguised, muted, and veiled for safety's sake." He writes, "the realities of power for subordinate groups mean that much of their political action requires interpretation, precisely because it is intended to be cryptic and

---

[102] Musson, "Lay Participation," 252; Sarah Harlan-Haughey, "Forest Law through the Looking Glass: Distortions of the Forest Charter in the Outlaw Fiction of Late Medieval England," *William and Mary Bill of Rights Journal* 25.2 (2016–2017): 549–89.

[103] James Scott, *Weapons of the Weak: Everyday Forms of Peasant Resistance* (New Haven: Yale University Press, 1985), 29.

[104] Scott, *Weapons of the Weak*, 36–7 and 31.

opaque."[105] Finally, he explains that noncompliance is the most appropriate form of resistance for the peasantry.

Being a diverse class of 'low classness,' scattered across the countryside, often lacking the discipline and leadership that would encourage opposition of a more organized sort, the peasantry is best suited to extended guerrilla-style campaigns of attrition that require little or no coordination. Their individual acts of foot-dragging and evasion are often reinforced by a venerable popular culture of resistance.[106]

Scott's findings align with what historians of the English manor have uncovered in recent studies. The power relationship between manorial lord and his tenant population was one of continuous renegotiation. Resistance to oppressive taxation and customary services typically came in the form of "passive noncooperation," which Phillipp Schofield describes as "the most immediate tactic" for resistance to lordship adopted by the medieval peasantry.[107] Thus, "they quietly evaded as many dues as they could, shirked work, and managed not to hear summons to do otherwise."[108] Resistance strategies adopted many guises, including: rent strikes; evasion of fines, or challenging an authority's right to collect it; marrying without paying the *merchet*; brewing without summoning the ale-taster; letting buildings fall into disrepair; poaching rabbits from the lord's warren; refusing to take their corn to the lord's mill; defaulting on obligations to provide the steward with food, hay, and lodging; or, suddenly remembering ancient customs that favored the tenant over his landlord.[109] Miriam Müller has argued that refusing to allow one's sheep to pasture on the lord's fields in order to raise his soil fertility (to the detriment of one's own fields) might also be a form of resistance: she recorded thirty-two instances that resulted in amercements between the years 1325 and 1335 at the manor of Brandon in Suffolk.[110] In this case, the peasantry involved were customary

---

[105] James Scott, *Domination and the Arts of Resistance: Hidden Transcripts* (New Haven: Yale University Press, 1990), 137.

[106] Scott, *Weapons of the Weak*, 35.

[107] Phillipp Schofield, *Peasant and Community in Medieval England 1200–1500* (Basingstoke: Palgrave Macmillan, 2003), 160.

[108] Peter Larson, *Conflict and Compromise in the Late Medieval Countryside: Lords and Peasants in Durham, 1349–1400* (New York: Routledge, 2014), 118.

[109] Larson, *Conflict and Compromise*, 118–20.

[110] Miriam Müller, "Conflict and Revolt: The Bishop of Ely and his Peasants at the Manor of Brandon in Suffolk c. 1300–81," *Rural History* 23.1 (2012): 4.

tenants – most likely of villein (unfree) status, or those who, while free under the law, held some villein land for which customary services were due to the lord. While often thought to have been powerless at the hands of their exploitative feudal lords, Müller demonstrates that the unfree developed their own tools to resist lordship. Similarly, Peter Franklin has identified a sustained campaign of resistance by the unfree peasantry on the fourteenth-century manor of Thornbury (Gloucestershire). In the period between 1328 and 1352, the court rolls record 759 instances in which tenants refused to perform labor services, or deliberately performed them badly.[111]

While individual instances of poor performance of labor services might be dismissed as the consequence of laziness or a poor work ethic, as the peasants of Thornbury demonstrate, collectively it functioned as a recognizable political act. The power of the collective is exhibited also in the escalation of the practice of noncompliance by the community of Holywell-cum-Needingworth (Cambridgeshire). Between 1288 and 1339, the manor rolls record twenty-one refusals by individuals to perform labor services. In comparison, 191 *groups* of tenants on the same manor refused to perform labor in the period 1353 to 1403.[112] Villagers were aware of just how effective passive noncooperation might be and they reserved it for those times when they needed to strike back against the aggressive opportunism of lordship. Here, it seems likely that this protest was directed against the oppressive dictates of the Ordinance and Statute of Laborers (1349–51), sporadically enforced over the course of the second half of the fourteenth century, which attempted to regulate wages, expenses of necessities, and the movements of the peasantry.

Studies of peasant resistance uncover creative means of pushing back against aggressive lordship. The selection of the reeve on the manor of Alrewas (Staffordshire) saw its tenants undermine the process through feigned compliance. Typically, every autumn the customary tenants there were asked to put forward two names for selection. The manor's lord would choose one of those two to be reeve;

---

[111] Peter Franklin, "Politics in Manorial Court Rolls: The Tactics, Social Composition, and Aims of a Pre-1381 Peasant Movement," in Zvi Ravi and Richard Smith, eds., *Medieval Society and the Manor Court* (Oxford University Press, 1996), 162–98.

[112] Mark Bailey, *The Decline of Serfdom in Late Medieval England: From Bondage to Freedom* (Woodbridge: Boydell, 2014), 73.

the other was then fined not to serve. However, in the 1330s, he began fining the rejected candidates exorbitant sums not to serve, from six shillings and six pence to a full mark. The tenants' response was to forward the names of candidates who were ineligible for the position. In 1333, they put forward a cottager and a free sokeman, "an act of subversion for which they were amerced the sum of £2." In 1339 they proposed two free sokemen.[113] The actions of the medieval peasantry also undermine the impression that they were "deeply suspicious" of the technology of writing. At Alrewas, the tenants saw the writing of a *customal* as the means to promote their own needs and concerns, while reining in the unwanted expansion of their manor's lordship.[114] Villeins also made plentiful use of the legal instruments available under the common law to free peasants. Customary tenants regularly transferred lands and leases by charter, although the charters had no validity at common law because of their status.[115]

Perhaps what is most important to recognize is that pressure from below often achieved a measure of success. As Müller explains, "[m]anorial custom could and did change as a result of tenant pressure." She sees the introduction of leasehold as a direct response to the withholding of labor services by the customary tenants, who realized that every hour they spent working the lord's field was one less hour for their own fields. The logical solution was to transform how he made his money, by abandoning villein tenancy and instead leasing out the lord's demesne lands altogether.[116]

Resisting the King

David Carpenter sees that the manor was a "training ground" for the peasantry. There they honed their tactics of resistance to an oppressive authority as a warm-up for taking on the king.[117] When it comes to addressing the Crown's toleration of corruption in its institutions and law-enforcement officers, their approach was not always as silent and invisible as what we see on the manor. This is especially true of the civil

---

[113] Birrell, "Confrontation and Negotiation," 200.
[114] Birrell, "Confrontation and Negotiation," 209.
[115] Müller, "Conflict and Revolt," 9.
[116] Müller, "Conflict and Revolt," 2.
[117] David Carpenter, "English Peasants in Politics 1258–1267," *P&P* 136 (1992): 19.

war waged by the barons of England against Henry III (d.1272). The "Monfortian Revolution," as Sophie Ambler has termed it, was "the greatest assault on royal power in England before the 17th century civil war."[118] While it is usually envisioned as an exclusively baronial movement, Simon de Montfort framed their project as a "common enterprise," which the English people of all ranks found appealing. In the years 1258 and 1259, when the baronial lords seized central government from Henry III's control and used it to impose a legislative reform, their attempts to root out dishonesty were met with great appreciation by the peasantry, who found that their appeals to the king had long gone unacknowledged. Indeed, when the reformers approved commissions of eyre in 1258 under Hugh Bigod, they were inundated with complaints about oppressive lords who had attempted to appropriate royal power for themselves.[119] The Provisions of Westminster issued in October of 1259, intended to set into law the reforms of the rebels, responded directly to two concerns springing primarily from peasant grievances: (1) The provisions commanded that justices of the eyre cease fining those neighboring vills who fail to produce every male adult over the age of twelve for the coroner's inquest. Rather, they preferred representation only by the reeve and four men. (2) The provisions sought to see the *murdrum* fine restricted to instances of felony, rather than having it apply also in cases of death by misadventure.[120] The overall goal was to reduce dramatically the amount owed by a vill in procedural fines with each visit of the eyre in those instances in which the amercements appear to be nothing more than a "money-grab" by the Crown. The legislation proved to the English peasantry that the reformists made the welfare of the peasantry a greater priority than did their king.

While the leaders of the reformist movement belonged to the elite, they relied heavily on popular backing. Although the peasants do not figure largely in the chronicles or the legal documents of the era, they participated actively in the rebellion in a multitude of ways. Peasants, both free and unfree, played a key role in raids on the property of the leading royalists. They also assumed roles as foot soldiers in the rebel

---

[118] Sophie Ambler, "Simon de Montfort and King Henry III: The First Revolution in English History, 1258–1265," *History Compass* 11.12 (2013): 1076.
[119] Ambler, "Simon de Montfort," 1082.
[120] Carpenter, "English Peasants in Politics," 28.

armies; indeed, they "probably formed the largest element among both the combatants and the causalities."[121] The records of the trials after the fact suggest that some peasants participated only upon the command of their lords, although many others did so voluntarily, or in defiance of their lords.[122]

General support for the reformist cause is attested also by its afterlife. Even though Simon de Montfort fell in battle in 1265, his popularity did not wither away as Henry III's faction had hoped it would. The monks of Evesham collected the trunk of his desecrated corpse from the ditch where it had been disposed and had it entombed at the abbey where they studiously recorded the miracles credited to Simon's intercession: 191 in total.[123] Chroniclers eagerly reported the divine commentary on Simon de Montfort's death: Arnald FitzThedmar noted that at the hour of his fall, a great tempest arose in London with thunder and lightning, expressing God's anger with his anointed representative (that is, King Henry III).[124] Music sprang up mourning Simon's loss. The "Lament for Simon de Montfort" confirms for his audience that he was heaven-bound: "Sir Simon, the just man, and his company joyfully go to Heaven above, to everlasting life."[125] While the effort to canonize the rebel ultimately foundered, monastic chronicles regularly referred to him as a martyr, "praising his work for the reform of the realm," and at least two accounts link his death with Thomas Becket's, a saint best known for standing up to a tyrannical king.[126] Even in death, Simon rested in good company: he was surrounded by a group of men referred to as the Montfortian saints, Richard Wich, Bishop of Chichester

[121] Carpenter, "English Peasants in Politics," 11.

[122] Carpenter, "English Peasants in Politics," 42.

[123] John Theilmann, "Political Canonization and Political Symbolism in Medieval England," *JBS* 29.3 (1990): 247.

[124] Ian Stone, ed., "The Book of Arnold Fitz Thedmar," (PhD Diss., King's College London, 2015), 253.

[125] Isabel Aspin, ed., *Anglo-Norman Political Songs* (Anglo-Norman Text Society, vol. IX, 1953), 32–3.

[126] Philippa Hoskin, "Holy Bishops and Political Exiles: St Richard's Cult and Political Protest in the Late Thirteenth Century," in Paul Foster, ed., *Richard of Chichester: Bishop 1245–1253; Canonized 1262* (Chichester Cathedral Press, 2009), 23. William Stubbs, ed., *The Continuation of the Chronicle of Gervase of Canterbury, to 1327*, in *The Historical Works of Gervase of Canterbury*, 2 vols. (RS, 1879–80), vol. II, 188; and "A Song on the Death of Simon de Montfort," in Herbert Fisher, ed., *The Collected Papers of Frederic William Maitland*, 3 vols. (Cambridge University Press, 1911), vol. III, 47; both cited in Theilmann, "Political Canonization," 247, note 17.

(d.1253); Edmund of Abingdon, Archbishop of Canterbury (d.1240); and Robert Grosseteste, Bishop of Lincoln (d.1253), all supporters of the dissident reformer. Veneration of these saints, and miracles at their tombs "were all ways in which the spirit of the rebellion was kept alive and its aims could be, and were, expressed."[127]

All of these actions demonstrate that the people did not shy away from criticizing royal authority when it was important to them.

Standing Mute in Protest

Standing mute needs to take its place alongside failing to turn up for jury service and veneration of a political martyr as a weapon in the arsenal of popular resistance to unwanted encroachment by royal authority. Standing mute is the very paradigm of passive noncompliance. The real question, of course, is that if a refusal to plead was intended as a form of protest against royal authority, exactly what were they protesting? At times, the answer to that question depends very much on the individual, and with such brief and formulaic records, it is difficult to determine definitively why a particular defendant chose to remain silent. However, Table 7.1, which presents an analysis of patterns over time, can help to align defendants' actions with popular grievances of the era to create a likely hypothesis.

The data from Table 7.1 indicate that the era 1300–29 was a contentious one; while the 1340s once again sees a rise in antipathy towards the Crown that falls off for the last time in the 1350s. How do these figures tie in with events from the era? First, it must be acknowledged that the growth of monarchy did not stop with the Angevin monarchs. Scott Waugh has argued that the era 1272–1377 "witnessed profound changes in English politics and institutions" in which "royal government expanded and reached deeper into local communities than it ever had."[128] Nicknamed the "English Justinian" for the abundance of statutes produced during his reign, Edward I oversaw a shift in judicial administration that left villagers feeling more and more alienated from the workings of the law. In particular,

---

[127] Hoskin, "Holy Bishops," 22
[128] Scott Waugh, "England: Kingship and the Political Community, 1272–1377," in Rigby, ed., *A Companion to Britain*, 208.

TABLE 7.1 *Numbers of defendants who stood mute in fourteenth-century England by decade*

Decade	Defendants who stood mute
1300–9	75
1310–19	76
1320–9	67
1330–9	41
1340–9	74
1350–9	24
1360–9	23
1370–9	17
1380–9	18
1390–9	18

with the final demise of the eyre in 1294, there was a transition to targeted commissions of assize, peace, and trailbaston, in which local landlords, sometimes the very same men whose judgment local villagers were hoping to avoid, assumed the role of justices of the peace.[129] This era also coincides with the rise of an emerging professional corps of pleaders, which complicated the system immensely, making it near impossible for a litigant to represent one's own interests in court and engendering an increasingly "bureaucratic and rule-bound" system of law.[130] Finally, this era saw the decline of the county courts, making the king's court the only option for resolution in most civil litigation and trespass disputes. Any one of these changes might have been grounds for concern by the king's subjects.

A series of natural crises exacerbated the challenges of daily subsistence. Where once historians claimed the Little Ice Age began in 1300, now they recognize that the Medieval Warm Period finally drew to a close at that time, bringing an end to the elevated temperatures that fostered a thriving English wine industry. This global drop in temperature was accompanied by years of erratic weather, with severe winters and summers plagued by rain and cold.

[129] Schofield, *Peasant and Community*, 178.
[130] Robert Palmer, "England: Law, Society and the State," in Rigby, ed., *A Companion to Britain*, 251.

The result was a succession of bad harvests: 1294–5 was especially arduous for the medieval English;[131] so, too, was 1310–11 and 1321–2.[132] However, the crop failures of 1315 and 1316 must be singled out for the virulence of their impact. Those years witnessed three bad harvests in a row, a disaster of catastrophic proportions that happened only three times in the years between 1268 and 1480, inciting the following remark from two economists: "[i]n climatically temperate England, this was as bad as it could get."[133] The year 1315 marks the beginning of the Great European Famine (1315–22), when the price of grain rose to unparalleled heights.[134] The soaring cost of grain was particularly devastating for the peasantry, whose diet was grain-dependent: they subsisted chiefly on bread, pottage, and ale. Wages declined in proportion to the rising price of grain, such that for farm laborers, real wages "sank to [their] lowest recorded point ever" in the years 1315–16.[135] To make matters worse, 1316–21 saw farmers struggling also with the European cattle panzootic, which only served to aggravate the agricultural crisis. With a 63 percent loss in bovine animal production, the panzootic had a pervasive impact, affecting dairy production, manure output for fertilizing fields and, because of the loss of oxen in particular, the haulage and ploughing of fields. All of this meant a more painful and prolonged agricultural recovery, worsened by a second famine that struck in 1321.[136] The *Vita Edwardi Secundi* and the *Annals of Bermondsey* document villagers surviving by eating whatever they could lay their hands on: "many people were not able to buy the food they needed to survive. The poor frequently fed themselves as best they could, by eating dogs, cats, the dung of doves [that is, carob pods], and even their own

---

[131] John Maddicott, "Poems of Social Protest in Early Fourteenth-Century England," in W. Mark Ormrod, ed., *England in the Fourteenth Century* (Woodbridge: Boydell, 1986), 143.

[132] Mavis Mate, "High Prices in Early Fourteenth-Century England: Causes and Consequences," *Economic History Review* 28.1 (1975): 8.

[133] Bruce Campbell and Cormac Ó Gráda, "Harvest Shortfalls, Grain Prices, and Famines in Preindustrial England," *Journal of Economic History* 71.4 (2011): 869.

[134] Philip Slavin, *Experiencing Famine in Fourteenth-Century Britain* (Turnhout: Brepols, 2019).

[135] Campbell and Gráda, "Harvest Shortfalls," 871.

[136] Buchanan Sharp, "Royal Paternalism and the Moral Economy in the Reign of Edward II: The Response to the Great Famine," *Economic History Review* 66.2 (2013): 629.

children."[137] While tales of cannibalism were most likely fictionalized along biblical lines in order to heighten the sense of crisis, the chronicles bring to light the sheer desperation of the times: the English, along with many other Europeans, were slowly starving to death.

Desperation often leads to an increase in crime. If the commissions that initiated the trailbastons of 1304–7 are to be believed, the early years of the fourteenth century were already experiencing heightened levels of violent crime: "bandits, murderers, and other dangerous malefactors roamed the countryside and terrified honest men." The trailbastons, which were targeted commissions of itinerant justices assigned to address felony and violent trespass in particular regions, were the "special measures" that Edward I proposed as "necessary to restore order."[138] The crop failure of 1315, however, marks the beginning of a nationwide crime spree, with men and women turning frantically to unlawful means to support their families. Barbara Hanawalt documents an increase of over 200 percent in recorded crimes for the period 1315–19 over the average for 1300–14.[139] Thus, the English people were not only starving, they were subject to an unusual level of criminal activity, presumably making it difficult to hold on to what little a family had to support themselves.

And what policies did the English government pursue to relieve the anxieties of its subjects and assist them in their time of need? Understandably, the English government was a long way off from the development of the welfare state; yet, the Christian model of kingship, dating back to the time of Saint Augustine, emphasized a king's "responsibility to God for his subjects as if he were their parent or guardian."[140] As *Bracton* writes: "the heart of the king ought to be in the hand of God."[141] This ideology had long seen the English Crown

---

[137] Mate, "High Prices," 15. "Doves' dung" was a colloquial term for "carob pods." See Julia Marvin, "Cannibalism as an Aspect of Famine in Two English Chronicles," in Martha Carlin and Joel Rosenthal, eds., *Food and Eating in Medieval Society* (London: Hambledon, 1998), 81.

[138] Amy Phelan, "Trailbaston and Attempts to Control Violence in the Reign of Edward I," in Richard Kaeuper, ed., *Violence in Medieval England* (Woodbridge: Boydell, 2000), 130.

[139] Hanawalt, *Crime and Conflict*, 238–60.

[140] Jane Whittle and Stephen Rigby, "England: Popular Politics and Social Conflict," in Rigby, ed., *A Companion to Britain*, 84.

[141] *Bracton*, vol. II, 305.

involved in regulating the sale and distribution of bread and ale, as well as a variety of other foodstuffs, to ensure that even the most vulnerable were guaranteed availability.[142] Edward II was the first to issue a formal governmental response to the famine, although it was far from adequate, given the abject misery of his subjects. As one might expect, he forbade grain export and encouraged grain import (although given that the rest of Europe was also experiencing the Great Famine, this was not a particularly valuable measure); and for a period, he forbade also the use of wheat in brewing. The king's most substantive act was to write a general letter to all bishops across Europe, dated to April 24, 1316, requesting that they remind parishioners who hoarded grain that their actions would result in deaths by starvation, for which they would have to account on Judgment Day.[143] That is it. He did nothing to hunt down grain hoards and force equitable distribution. Nor did his own charitable activities increase in this era. What is most disconcerting is that his correspondence insinuates that he was chiefly concerned about the impact of the grain shortage on his own well-being. In December of 1321, he asked the sheriffs of Gloucestershire, Worcestershire, and Wiltshire, three counties where he believed grain hoards existed, to assist his servants in locating grain to buy at a reasonable price, and then deliver it to bakers and brewers so that they might sell their finished products to the king and his nobles.[144]

Adding insult to injury, the English were struggling with exceptional levels of taxation in order to fund the wars with France and the Scots begun by Edward I and continued by his son. Since 1298, the Crown had spent roughly £60,000 per year on the maintenance of armies and the provisioning of castles in Wales and Scotland.[145] With the changing nature of warfare, prolonged wars were unduly burdensome. War was fought "on a new scale, by paid troops massed in large armies, and they increased immensely the burdens of taxation and military service imposed by the king on the people."[146] Taxation was the backbone supporting these endeavors. Edward I was

---

[142] James Davis, *Medieval Market Morality: Life, Law and Ethics in the English Marketplace, 1200–1500* (Cambridge University Press, 2011), 467–70.
[143] Sharp, "Royal Paternalism," 635.
[144] *CPR*, Edward II, vol.IV (1321–4), 43; as cited in Sharp, "Royal Paternalism," 639.
[145] Mate, "High Prices," 9.   [146] Maddicott, "Poems of Social Protest," 142.

particularly creative in developing new fiscal policy. For example, 1294–7 saw the creation of what came to be known as the *maltolt* ("bad tax"), a new scheme for the taxation of sacks of wool that saw the Crown's profit rise from six shillings and eight pence per sack to forty shillings. The extortionate nature of the tax prompted widespread protest that culminated in the Remonstrance of 1297, a set of complaints penned by English nobility and directed to the king that eventually quashed this enterprise. Between 1275 and 1332, the Crown also levied nineteen lay subsidies, that is, a national direct tax on movable goods, including livestock, grain, utensils, raw materials, and manufactured goods.[147] Nor did the Crown refrain from levying subsidies in the years where its subjects were worst affected by the famine: both 1315 and 1316 witnessed lay subsidies mandated and collected by the Crown. Taxation was just one means of supporting the war effort. As William of Pagula's treatise discussed above implies, the early fourteenth century also witnessed "an energetic employment of purveyance and prise."[148] Even if a family was lucky enough to grow or purchase sufficient grain to feed its members, they might well see it confiscated by the king to feed his household or his armies, without hope of compensation for their loss.

What this means is that not only was the king failing to assist his people in times of need, he was making their situation even worse with his unrealistic tax expectations and military ambitions. While the upper ranks were capable of petitioning the king with their grievances, potentially ameliorating an untenable situation, what options were available to the rest of England's subjects? During the famine years, there was widespread local resistance to paying the subsidies; and in the 1320s and early 1330s, localities organized attacks on collectors.[149] Standing mute may also have been one way in which defendants, backed into a corner by poverty, protested against a monarch who neglected his struggling subjects. A starvation

---

[147] For the years: 1275, 1283, 1290, 1294, 1295, 1296, 1297 (twice), 1301, 1306, 1307, 1309, 1313, 1315, 1316, 1319, 1322, 1332, and 1334. See Stuart Jenks, "The Lay Subsidies and the State of the English Economy (1275–1334)," *Vierteljahrschrift für Sozial- und Wirtschaftsgeschichte* 85.1 (1998): 1–39, Appendix I at 29–30; Richard Britnell, "England: Towns, Trade and Industry," in Rigby, ed., *A Companion to Britain*, 52.

[148] Schofield, *Peasant and Community*, 172.

[149] Whittle and Rigby, "England: Popular Politics and Social Conflict," 74.

diet was not much of a threat when a person was already severely malnourished and knew well that his or her family could not afford to feed a prisoner anyway. Looking at the numbers, it is striking that the vast majority of those who chose silence rather than plead in the early fourteenth century were accused of some form of stealing (theft, larceny, robbery).[150] In the interval 1300–9, fifty of the seventy-five defendants (or 67 percent) were accused of thieving; over the course of 1310–19, seventy of the seventy-six defendants (or 92 percent) were similarly indicted; and for the period 1320–9, fifty-five of the sixty-seven defendants (or 83 percent) fell into the same category, although six defendants were described merely as "felons," and so they may also have been accused of theft. It is hard not to imagine that many of these men resented the king for failing to help his subjects; as they may have seen it, the king's inactivity left them no choice but to turn to crime to feed their families.

Some of those who refused to plead made their protests collectively, implying some coordination in prison along the lines of an organized strike. For example, on August 17, 1301 at Norwich castle, seventeen men stood mute (sixteen of whom stood indicted as accomplices in the same crime);[151] on August 30, 1305 at Newgate, London, six stood mute;[152] and on November 6, 1306 at the Staffordshire jail delivery, another six stood mute.[153] For the 1310s, the same kind of group patterns do not exist; however, of the seventy-six who stood mute, surely it is relevant that forty-seven of them (or 62 percent) did so during the worst years of the famine, 1315–16, when they were likely most desperate to send a message to the king about his inability to protect his subjects. It is striking also that thirty-three of those seventy-six (or 43 percent) performed their silence at Norwich castle, as did those seventeen men in 1301, hinting that standing mute may have had a special regional significance in oral history as a means of resistance. Given the small percentage of those who stood mute at court (0.8 percent), these group protests are meaningful. As Miriam Müller

---

[150] Some were accused simultaneously with other crimes, such as homicide or prison-break; however, if some form of stealing was included in the indictment, I have included that defendant in the statistics above.

[151] TNA JUST 3/47/3, m. 5d (1301).   [152] TNA JUST 3/39/1, m. 22 (1305).

[153] George Wrottesley, ed., "Gaol Delivery for Staffordshire: 34 Edward I," in *Staffordshire Historical Collections* (London: Harrison and Sons 1886), vol. VII, pt. I, 154–72.

has emphasized, collective action was what "lords feared most." While [p]ersistently troublesome and disobedient villeins could prove a nuisance … it was through collective acts of resistance by the peasantry that a lord saw the rightful and divinely sanctioned order of society turned upside down."[154]

By the 1330s, life had mostly returned to normal. Agricultural recovery was sufficient that the price of most goods had dropped considerably.[155] The political drama of the 1320s came to an abrupt end with the execution of Roger Mortimer in November of 1330; because Edward II's deposition had merely resulted in the early succession of his direct heir, Edward III, it left no lingering bad taste in his subjects' mouths, nor did the deposition create rival usurpers for the throne. All of this surely produced some sense of security in the era. Yet, of course, disaster was looming in the distance with the 1340s, another calamitous era. The decade began and ended with crop failure: 1340 saw a disastrous harvest, while 1349–51 was a repeat of 1315–16, with England undergoing one of the rare three-in-a-row crop failures, leading to a nationwide famine in 1351.[156] Sandwiched in between that, of course, was the first outbreak of the Black Death (1348–9), and the opening phase of the Hundred Years' War (1337–1453), when taxation was especially oppressive.

The Crown's response followed the standard set by Edward II during the Great European Famine. His subjects' reactions are documented best in the poems of social protest which developed as a genre during this era.[157] The poems underscore growing frustration with the king's lack of empathy for the plight of his subjects. Not only were they undergoing hardship because of the agricultural conditions, Edward III's zealous drive to resuscitate his grandfather's military agenda was swiftly leading to the impoverishment of his people. The "Song of the Husbandman" (1340) focuses chiefly on the evils of taxation, lamenting that "[g]ode ȝeres and corne bothe beth a-gon" (good years and corn [that is, grain] are both gone), and every "furthe peni mot to the kynge" (fourth penny must go to the king). To be sure,

---

[154] Miriam Müller, "The Aims and Organisation of a Peasant Revolt in Early Fourteenth-Century Wiltshire," *Rural History* 14 (2003): 1.

[155] Mate, "High Prices," 14.

[156] Maddicott, "Poems of Social Protest," 143; Campbell and Gráda, "Harvest Shortfalls," 869.

[157] Maddicott, "Poems of Social Protest," 133.

"[t]o seche selver to the kyng y mi seed solde, / Forthi mi lond leye lith ant leorneth to slepe" (to seek silver for the king, I sold my seed, wherefore my land lies fallow and learneth to sleep.)[158] These themes are echoed in the "Song against the King's Taxes" (1340), which directs the blame not at the king because he is too young ("the king is a young bachelor, and is not of an age"), but rather his advisors. The poem attacks the fifteenth (a tax on movables at the rate of one-fifteenth), grousing that "it obliges the common people to sell both cows, vessels, and clothes." Similarly, the author derides the wool tax – the *maltolt* of his grandfather's era had been revived in 1337 to raise funds for war against France. He writes, the tax "drives them commonly to sell their property ... It is not sound law, which gives my wool to the king." The poem does much more than just complain, though. The author targets corrupt officials who fail to turn over all of the taxes collected to the king. He also opines that the poor should be exempt from taxation: "Since the king is determined to take so much, he may find enough among the rich; and he would get more and do better, as it appears to me, to have taken a part from the great, and to have spared the little. He sins who takes the money of the needy without cause." The poem winds up with a warning: conditions are so dire that rebellion is imminent. "People are reduced to such ill plight, that they can give no more; I fear, if they had a leader, they would rise in rebellion. Loss of property often makes people fools."[159]

Given the burdens of the era, and the king's failure to take the welfare of his people into account, once again, the upswing in numbers of those who stood mute in the 1340s seems reasonable. Many of the suspected felons were indicted of theft-related crimes: fifty out of seventy-four (or 68 percent), and thus again may speak to crimes of desperation. There were also a number of synchronized protests. On July 27, 1340, six men stood mute at Salisbury castle. On July 23, 1345, ten men chose silence at York castle. A Wednesday in the middle of Lent in 1348 saw another six men stand mute at York. For this decade, it is Yorkshire that stands out from the other counties: thirty-seven out of the seventy-four (or 50 percent) of the defendants

---

[158] "Song of the Husbandman," in Thomas Wright, ed., *The Political Songs of England, from the Reign of John to that of Edward II* (London: Camden Society, 1839), 149–53.
[159] "Song against the King's Taxes," in Wright, ed., *Political Songs of England*, 182–7.

who refused to plead did so at their arraignments at York castle, again hinting at a regional culture of resistance.

Of course, one might well ask whether standing mute was a successful strategy of protest. After all, it does not seem to have brought about any meaningful change in the king's actions. One suspects that the king was entirely unaware that six men stood mute at Salisbury in July of 1340, for example. Whether the protest reached its target is not always what is most important. Sometimes protest is about expressing communal solidarity and building consensus. Sometimes it is about dignity in the face of tyranny. Sometimes it is about action, so that the dissident feels he is at least doing *something* to express his discontent. For a villager living in an era defined by a rigid class structure, it was also an opportunity to announce to the world that one was still in control of one's own destiny. Standing mute was a form of protest against royal authority, but it would be a mistake to assume that this message was intended exclusively for the king. The defendant may have intended it instead for the members of the defendant's own community to remind them that they also have power in the face of tyranny. The fact that the king's justices were incapable of proceeding to trial when confronted by uncooperative defendants boldly exposes the limits of royal authority. And all it took was one of the king's lowly subjects to make the point. Of course, standing mute is also a conservative maneuver intended to express the defendant's dissent without provoking an outbreak of large-scale conflict. Those present at the arraignment understood the defendant's position; and one can assume that knowledge about the defendant's resistance traveled speedily through news networks to become part of a larger oral history of resistance. The fact that instances of standing mute made their way into the chronicles tells us that Englishmen and women imbued that silence with power. And each time a king was forced to recognize that an individual who had survived for so long in hard and strong prison had done so miraculously, he had to admit publicly that God was on the side of the dissident.

Why do instances of standing mute seem to fall off after the 1350s? Peasant resistance is a measured response to the actions of those in authority. Before the Black Death, small guerilla acts of passive noncompliance were all that was deemed necessary to resist the encroachment of royal authority. The passage of the Ordinance and Statute of Laborers (1348–51), and its unprecedented aspiration of social control, ushered in a new era of protest. As Lawrence Poos writes, there was a "rising crescendo of resistance ... in part in the form of individual acts of defiance but also, it would appear, increasingly in the form of group actions," in which villagers were more "open and self-conscious" in their opposition to authority.[160] Their anger surely was fed by the lords who hoped to place the financial burden of the Black Death on the backs of their customary tenants by increasing or reintroducing labor services, raising rents, and increasing customary dues and fines.[161] The rising demands of the peasantry for relief "continually thwarted," they were no longer willing to keep quiet.[162] By 1381, the conditions were such that they had no choice but to turn to rebellion.

Conclusion

While historians have often assumed that England's uncooperative defendants were protesting the trial jury, it was not the mechanism itself that so disturbed English subjects, but rather what the jury stood for: the intrusive regulation of an expanding monarchy. From the time of Henry II, the jury became the apparatus through which the Crown expanded its authority over the kingdom. Recognizing the value in such a versatile instrument, Henry oversaw the expansion of the jury through its regularization and proliferation, such that by the fourteenth century, England was governed at all levels by a wide variety of juries. In this atmosphere, juries were not seen as a "pillar of freedom," as they have come to be recognized in the modern West today. Rather, the jury represented the grasping hand of the Crown, seeking to better control its people, and squeeze the last pennies from their purses. Standing mute in the king's court, then, became an effective strategy of royal resistance, and one that highlighted the defendant's agency: silence rendered the king's justices powerless.

---

[160] Lawrence Poos, *A Rural Society after the Black Death: Essex, 1350–1525* (Cambridge University Press, 1991), 240; Christopher Dyer, "The Social and Economic Background to the Rural Revolt of 1381," in Rodney Hilton and Trevor Aston, eds., *The English Rising of 1381* (Cambridge University Press, 2007), 30.

[161] Hargreaves, "Seigniorial Reaction and Peasant Responses," 53.

[162] Müller, "Conflict and Revolt," 2.

Acts of passive noncooperation were the most potent weapons the peasantry could wield against figures of authority. Outright violence would get them killed; but noncooperation made a point about who was really in charge. Every failure to perform labor services or to attend court demonstrated to the lower ranks that while they were subordinate, they were still necessary. The metaphor of the body politic here is apt: as head, the king is far superior to his humble subjects; but the body isn't going anywhere without its feet. John of Salisbury expressed the sentiment more eloquently in his *Policraticus* when he wrote: "Remove from the fittest body the aid of the feet; it does not proceed under its own power, but either crawls shamefully, uselessly, and offensively on its hands or else is moved with the assistance of brute animals."[163] When a defendant stood mute, even if he or she eventually succumbed and agreed to trial, for a moment in time the defendant had succeeded in exposing the Crown's vulnerability. Without a cooperative defendant, the Crown could not assert its authority.

The silent defendant's court performance had the added benefit of constructing bonds of solidarity. Historians have often overlooked medieval acts of resistance, largely because of their ambiguity. Yet, that is exactly why the men and women of medieval England adopted strategies of passive noncooperation. A failure to perform labor services might be intended as an expression of opposition to lordship; the offenders' fellow laborers might interpret it that way; but in all likelihood, his lord would dismiss it merely as laziness. Ambiguity was safe. Admittedly, the same was not true of standing mute. The legal records make it clear that a defendant's inaction was interpreted as rejecting the king and his law; however, because it is not a recognizable form of protest today, historians have simply missed the symbolism.

---

[163] John of Salisbury, *Policraticus: Of the Frivolities of Courtiers and the Footprints of Philosophers*, ed. Cary Nederman (Cambridge University Press, 1990), book v, c. 2, 67.

Conclusion

> Pryson properly ys a sepulture
> Of lyvyng men with strong lokkes thereon,
> Fortyfyed without any rupture,
> Of synners a great castigacion,
> Of feythfull frendes a probacion,
> Of fre liberté a sharp abstinence,
> Lackyng volunté for theyre dew penance.
>   *George Ashby, "Complaint of a Prisoner in the Fleet, 1463."*[1]

During much of October, 2017, newspapers and Twitter feeds across the United Kingdom were abuzz with news of the mini-series *Gunpowder*'s graphic depiction of death by peine forte et dure.[2] *Gunpowder* is a *Game of Thrones*-esque version of the Guy Fawkes story, in which a group of Catholics plotted to blow up parliament, removing the already paranoid King James I and VI, his heir, as well as the Houses of Lords and Commons all in one fell swoop, a plot that thankfully went horribly awry. Reactions to the peine forte et dure scene ranged from the suitably horrified to utter revulsion, with *The*

---

[1] (Prison properly is a tomb of living men with strong locks thereon, fortified without any breach, a great castigation to sinners, a probation from faithful friends, a sharp abstinence of free liberty, lacking will for their due penance.) Linne Mooney and Mary-Jo Arn, eds., *The Kingis Quair and Other Prison Poems* (Kalamazoo: Medieval Institute Publications, 2005), 163, lines 344–50.

[2] "Gunpowder," created by Ronan Bennett, Kit Harrington, and Daniel West (London, 2017).

Sun gleefully reporting that queasy viewers were vomiting in response to watching an elderly woman crushed to death on screen.[3] Historical consultants for the television show, Hannah Greig and John Cooper, were inspired by the death of Saint Margaret Clitheroe of York, whose March 25, 1586 execution opened this book. They drew on the details recorded in the account by her confessor John Mush in his "True Report" in order to capture appropriately the minutiae of the experience. Despite their impassioned plea that the show's violence was necessary in order to highlight the gritty reality of early modern England's brutal treatment of Catholics, many would agree that the directorial decision strains the limits of good taste.[4] *Gunpowder*'s gory portrayal of peine forte et dure is relevant chiefly because it perpetuates all the worst parts of the practice's mythology for a whole new generation of history buffs and historians.

Much of what this book has done is to sift through assumptions about peine forte et dure to separate fact from fallacy. Above all, it hopes to emphasize the fluidity of the medieval judicial system. Nothing was yet set in stone. There was no boilerplate. Although examples of pressing can be traced all the way back to the time of King Henry II (with the death of Robert de Seilhac), at no point in this era did it become a mandatory facet of peine forte et dure. Rather, pressing, a fasting diet, nakedness, isolation, deprivation of comforts – all of these tactics belonged to a corpus of prison practices that might or might not be imposed, depending on the will and instruction of the king's justices. This pliancy was typical of the era: the nature of the punishment was tailored to align with the gravity of the offense and the offender's character. Pressing, as the most severe form of the practice, was reserved for those deemed most contemptuous by authorities. The fact that many of these deaths made their way into the chronicles of the era means that those stories have dominated the narrative. The legal record,

---

[3] Ellie Genower, "Gruesome: Horrified Gunpowder Viewers Left 'Throwing Up' at Extreme Violence and Torture Scenes on BBC1 New Drama," (October 22, 2017), www.thesun.co.uk/tvandshowbiz/4748669/horrified-gunpowder-viewers-left-throwing-up-at-extreme-violence-and-horror-torture-scenes-on-bbc1-new-drama/ (accessed November 20, 2017).

[4] Hannah Greig and John Cooper, "The Bloody Truth – Why BBC's Gunpowder Had to Be So Violent," *The Conversation* (October 31, 2017), https://theconversation.com/the-bloody-truth-why-bbcs-gunpowder-had-to-be-so-violent-86264 (accessed November 20, 2017).

however, demonstrates that fasting and hard-prison conditions were the more common tools employed to coerce a suspected felon into pleading.

Malleability existed also in the multi-functionality of peine forte et dure. Most often it existed as a coercive measure. From distraint to excommunication, coercion abounds in the practice of medieval law. Even though incarceration's primary function was to hold prisoners until trial, the English also regularly employed it as a coercive measure to secure repayment of debts, to guarantee an appellor's presence at court, and to persuade the excommunicate to rejoin the Christian community. As a coercive measure, peine forte et dure met with great success: a period of a few days was generally enough to persuade a silent defendant to plead. The efficacy and adaptability of the practice led to judicial experimentation over the course of the period, such that, in some situations, hard prison was imposed punitively. For idlers, heretics, or petty thieves, the austere conditions of hard prison provided time to contemplate their sinful lives, purifying their souls, and inciting them to spiritual reform. At times, peine forte et dure also functioned as a form of capital punishment, and here it can be assumed that justices deemed the world a safer place without the defendant in it. It is also clear that when justices wished to use peine forte et dure as a threat to persuade an indecisive defendant into pleading during the arraignment process, they were quick to describe it in the worst possible light. What is important for us to recognize is that peine forte et dure did not experience a transition from coercive measure to means of execution during the medieval period. These were not distinct stages in the evolution of a practice. Rather, it continued to have multiple uses throughout the era. Andrea McKenzie's study of the early modern evidence gives us good reason to believe that the practice's versatility never entirely disappeared. She discovered eighteenth-century examples in which peine forte et dure continued in its role as coercive device.[5]

In some respects, the greater abundance of early modern evidence has led us to misunderstand the severity of pressing in the medieval period. Margaret Clitheroe's execution on Good Friday of 1583 was truly horrific: iron and stones weighing seven- or eight-hundred

---

[5] Andrea McKenzie, "This Death some Strong and Stout-Hearted Man doth Choose': The Practice of *Peine Forte et Dure* in Seventeenth- and Eighteenth-Century England," *L&HR* 23.2 (2005): 292.

pounds resting on a door balanced on her chest, a rock positioned directly under her spine. It is no wonder that the graphic brutality of her death has made such an impression on scholars. Yet, there is no evidence to suggest that anything comparable took place in the medieval context. The fact that it took days, weeks, even months for medieval prisoners to die compared to the saint's fifteen minutes lays bare the yawning disparity between the two. McKenzie's study, once again, is instrumental: she demonstrates that Clitheroe's experience was not representative of the early modern era either. Margaret Clitheroe's experience was very much an aberration: authorities intended to make an example of her to deter others from following suit. In doing so, they intensified the brutality of an (albeit already violent) act for public performance.

One of the long-standing myths perpetuated by historians of the common law is that peine forte et dure was a uniquely English practice. Looking beyond England and English history undermines this supposition. Rather, the practice itself is foreign: its origins lie in *murus strictus*, a form of public penance practiced by the medieval church across Europe for recalcitrant sinners, chiefly of the clerical variety. The English were not the only ones to borrow and adapt this practice for their own purposes. In Normandy, hard prison was imposed on those who refused to plead. It also functioned as a punishment in circumstances where the crime was not severe enough to warrant the death penalty. Its application was restricted to a year and a day, thus it was intended to be dreadful but finite. For the Swedes, its usage was also short-term and strictly coercive; much like judicial torture, it was used to extract a confession from a suspected felon. There is also good reason to believe the Scottish "sore and fulle harde presune" sprang from the same tradition, although more research needs to be done to discover the circumstances that generally warranted its usage. There is no way to be certain that "national" varieties of hard prison resembled the experiences of those held in the jails of medieval England; although, because no one felt the need to define hard prison, there is a good possibility that the term had a universal cultural significance that made definition unnecessary.

Peine forte et dure, then, was not unique to England. Conceding this fact is an important step towards deconstructing the myth of English exceptionalism.[6] English legal history is typically studied in isolation from canon law or Continental legal history. Susan Reynolds still felt the need to bemoan the "detachment of English legal history" in her 2003 article pleading for more comparative history.[7] That the journal *Comparative Legal History* launched only in 2013 suggests that we still have a long way to go in recognizing the benefits of comparative analysis. Placing hard prison in a larger context helps us to understand the penitential ideology at the foundation of the practice. It also unravels the mystery of why peine forte et dure was not considered torture by its practitioners; although it may be difficult for us to appreciate, the medieval world drew a thick line between asceticism and torture, and peine forte et dure clearly fell into the former category. That is not to say that through abuse and wrong intention asceticism did not at times transition into torture: *The Seven Sages of Rome* and *Bevis of Hampton* both outline how that might happen. When imposed correctly, with the defendant's soul as priority, peine forte et dure was about spiritual healing, not cruelty. This fact is apparent only when the practice is examined in context. Without it, the English practice looks unique, but is incomprehensible. An insistence on English exceptionalism will have us missing half the picture time and time again. In general, the firm margins drawn between systems by historians do not reflect the medieval mentality. As Thomas McSweeney writes,

medieval people did not create the kinds of impermeable boundaries between fields of knowledge that we do today. Different bodies of knowledge, such as law and theology, were not as firmly divided as our modern academic disciplines, and, in the absence of the nation-state, medieval people did not draw the kinds of national boundaries around legal systems that we see in the modern world. Law was law, and universal principles that happened to come out of the discourses of Roman and canon law would not have been rejected by people who served in the

---

[6] See Daniel Klerman and Paul G. Mahoney, "English Legal Exceptionalism," (University of Pittsburgh, 2006), www.pitt.edu/~dmberk/KlermanMahoney.pdf (accessed March 5, 2020). Tamar Herzog has also recently taken a step in this direction by including the English in defining "European" with her *A Short History of European Law: The Last Two and a Half Millennia* (Cambridge, MA: Harvard University Press, 2019).

[7] Susan Reynolds, "The Emergence of Professional Law in the Long Twelfth Century," *L&HR* 21.2 (2003): 347–8.

English royal courts simply because they came from Roman and canon law.[8]

English justices happily borrowed from canon law when it made sense to do so. Indeed, because all law emanates from God's law, gaps in common law *should* be filled by looking to canon law or Roman law.

Just as much variety existed when it comes to standing mute. The phrase applied not only when an accused felon was silent, but also when he or she answered insufficiently or challenged an excessive number of jurors. An analysis of the various meanings of silence across England's multiple judicial systems suggest that some who stood mute probably did so out of confusion. Trying to determine precisely when silence meant a refusal to plead as opposed to an admission of guilt is not an easy task for the historian, let alone for an unlearned person of the Middle Ages, devising a defense plan without the benefit of paid counsel. Venue (ecclesiastical vs. royal), jurisdiction (Crown vs. civil pleas vs. the law of arms), means of prosecution (private vs. public), and severity of the crime (whether it constituted a trespass or a felony) all mattered; or at least, they *might* matter. Whether a defendant was permitted to stand mute on appeal or when charged with treason would seem to have been an issue for judicial discretion, and there was little consistency in the application of a judicial ban even in the later part of the period. Judicial inconsistency may have thrown an axe into the works for some defendants hoping to buy time with a strategic defense.

What is unique to the English context is the insistence that a defendant must plead when indicted on felony charges. In both the church and in the courts of Continental Europe, silence was an admission of guilt, not a refusal to plead. It is only in England that justices were unwilling to proceed to trial without the defendant's consent. Endeavoring to understand exactly why that was the case is not an easy task. James Masschaele proposes that concern about consent was a byproduct of the move from a system focused on compensation to an individual victim, towards one which classifies crime as a threat to public order. Jurors would embrace this mentality and accept the heightened responsibilities of jury trial only

---

[8] Thomas McSweeney, *Priests of the Law: Roman Law and the Making of the Common Law's First Professionals* (Oxford University Press, 2019), 10.

if they understood that the defendant was eager for reintegration into society.[9] This thesis makes sense; for both jurors and justices alike, having the defendant's consent must have alleviated concern that they were passing judgment on an individual unwilling to abide by it. "Buy-in" from all concerned meant less ill will within the community. We already know that both justices and jurors were anxious about the spiritual implications of sentencing a man to his death. However, it also seems clear that the need for consent, encapsulated in the response to the long-standing question regarding how the defendant wished to acquit himself, was central to the English judicial system and had been even before this transition took place. In this particular instance, the English system had evolved distinctly from the rest of Europe. Thus, it should not be surprising that some defendants protested the removal of a right that was so fundamental for such a long time. Moreover, while standing mute became a recurrent problem after the demise of the ordeal, it was likely not an entirely "new" predicament.

The English prioritized a defendant's consent above all else. This is evident not only in the reluctance of the king's justices to proceed without it, but in myriad other ways, such as the experimentation with the writ *de bono et malo*, the court's insistence that the deaf and dumb cannot participate in the law, and the interrogation into muteness by the king's justices. As the *Leges Henrici Primi* indicates, this provision existed in part to ensure an accused felon had a fair trial; however, it was just one among many similar provisions. When theologians of the long twelfth century embraced the concept of natural rights, they fostered a proliferation of changes in procedure and jurisprudence all intended to safeguard the rights of the accused. Many of these newly recognized human liberties are captured best in the legal maxims of the era: "innocent until proven guilty"; "it is better to leave a crime unpunished than to condemn an innocent person"; "the burden of proof lies with the accuser, not the defendant"; "in doubtful matters the defendant is favored, not the plaintiff"; and "the law is more inclined to absolve than to condemn." It is no wonder that this era gave birth to a multitude of bold proclamations of fundamental rights, of which the Magna Carta may be the most well known, but is just one example. The

---

[9] James Masschaele, *Jury, State, and Society in Medieval England* (New York: Palgrave Macmillan, 2008), 83.

revolutionary fervor of the Magna Carta is captured equally in the Statutes of Pamiers (1212), the Hungarian Golden Bull (1222), the German *Statutum in favorem principum* (1231), Frederick II's Constitutions of Melfi (1231), and in what eventually became known as the Fueros de Aragón (1247). Again, history explains best why England was such a stickler for consent; as the *Leges Henrici Primi* hints, the English were precocious when it comes to the development of protections to ensure a suspected felon had the right to a fair trial. Penned around the year 1108, the *Leges* incorporated already a multitude of provisions to protect the rights of the accused, including the right to confront one's accuser and to offer a defense; and if the case is doubtful or the accuser is absent, no judgment shall be given. The era's passionate advocacy of natural rights is also our best evidence to explain why peine forte et dure was not a manifestation of "medieval barbarity"; nor was it evidence of a medieval inclination to violence. Rather, when justices remanded a silent defendant to prison to suffer peine forte et dure, they did so because they believed it was in his best interests.

Proceeding to trial with an unwilling defendant prevented justices and jurors from accomplishing their mission. If the purpose of a criminal trial was only punishment or revenge, then it would not have mattered whether the defendant consented. The era's high acquittal rates – even when jurors knew that the accused was in fact guilty of the crime – clarify that, while both punishment and revenge were relevant and meaningful, neither was the primary objective. Jurors were much more intent on reconciliation: a penitent sinner's reconciliation with the community one had offended by one's criminal acts, but ultimately also with God. Reconciliation required the defendant's cooperation, signaled by a plea. If one was not yet ready to admit one's guilt and embrace the penitential process, time in prison fasting and subjecting one's body to the austerity of prison conditions would only pave the way for one's eventual acceptance. This paradigm prioritized the defendant's soul. As canonist Huguccio of Pisa (d.1210) explained in his *Summa*, "we must not cease in the disciplining of the wicked, and by all those means according to which we are able to compel them so that they return to the Church, even though they may not wish to and refuse to."[10]

---

[10] As cited in Edward Peters, "Destruction of the Flesh – Salvation of the Spirit: The Paradoxes of Torture in Medieval Christian Society," in Alberto Ferreiro, ed., *The*

What jurors needed to see in order to produce a verdict of "not guilty" was remorse, repentance, and reform. This is exactly what justices and jurors alike hoped a defendant might find in the duress of hard prison: the inner peace necessary for them to acquit so that they did not have to take on the spiritual burden of sentencing a man to death. Putting the soul first meant that authorities granted prisoners permission to go to mass; convicted felons had an opportunity to confess and take last rites; and their bodies were given Christian burials, even if a traitor's body had been dismembered and dispersed throughout the kingdom. As God's vicar, the king was doing everything in his power to make sure his subjects had an opportunity to go to heaven: it was up to God to make the final judgment.

While the harsh conditions imposed on the accused in peine forte et dure constituted violence it was not violence in the Foucauldian sense. There was no public spectacle designed to inscribe the authority of the Crown on the defendant's body. In this instance, violence must be understood in its historical context. Christian theology altered the meaning of pain: pain was thought to be spiritually curative. Punishing the body righted the disordered mind. "[D]estruction of the flesh in order to save the spirit."[11] Most importantly, it was universally understood that penance could not be accomplished without pain. Imposed asceticism of this nature was indeed violence, but a form of praiseworthy violence that aided spiritually both the defendant and the Christian community. The church's positioning on this matter only reinforces the notion that medieval society was a culture of violence; however, that violence was not barbarous; medieval men and women were not delighting in the pain of others, nor were they desensitized to another human's pain. Violence in this context was a path to salvation.

The larger context of the era's embrace of natural rights causes us also to rethink the position of accused felons in general in medieval criminal trials. Traditional legal history has often depicted the defendant in a premodern trial as helpless prey, doomed to conviction.[12] Once

---

Devil, Heresy and Witchcraft in the Middle Ages: Essays in Honor of Jeffrey B. Russell (Leiden: Brill, 1998), 143.

[11] Peters, "Destruction of the Flesh," 147.

[12] John Baker, *An Introduction to English Legal History*, 5th edn. (Oxford University Press, 2019), 550–1; John Beattie, *Crime and the Courts in England, 1660–1800* (Oxford: Clarendon Press, 1986), 341.

again, anachronistic thinking has gotten in our way. The criminal trial had not yet become the cut-throat chess game between lawyers that we have come to expect today. While accused felons did not typically have the option to seek advice from legal counsel, nor did the prosecution, thus the defendant was not at the disadvantage one might imagine. Justices of jail delivery also emphatically believed it was their responsibility to act as legal counsel for the accused. That does not, in any way, imply that they helped the defendant plan a strategic defense. Rather, they explained clearly the legal options so that one was fully aware of the consequences of one's actions before deciding how to proceed, and when justices feared that the defendant might not be competent enough to stand trial, they ordered an inquisition to determine whether that was the case. Most importantly, in the medieval system of justice, conviction was not inevitable. Instead, there is plenty of reason to believe that medieval jurors saw the indictment process itself as sufficient penalty for most criminals. All of this confirms that suspected felons were in a much better position than has often been assumed. No one was riding roughshod over the rights of the accused.

Above all, this study demonstrates that it is time to jettison the established historical narrative in which justice developed from reliance on irrational proofs to rational procedures. This recognition is key principally because "irrational" as a term of the historians' trade is a not-so-veiled euphemism for "religious." God did not retreat from the practice of the law after the 1215 abandonment of the ordeals. Nor was there any sort of secularization of the law. To be sure, an English judiciary that sees God's law as the base of all law is far from secular. The word "God" appears 136 times in the treatise *Bracton*: its authors speak candidly of Judgment Day, referring repeatedly to the king as the vicar of God. Our eyes may gloss right over this terminology when we read *Bracton*, but theirs did not. Even the eventual development of a separate system of ecclesiastical courts does not signal a secularization of the law. God's presence and mandate hung over all courts, regardless of their purview. The view of a strict separation of church and state has been super-imposed on the medieval past by historians whose discomfort with religion has prevented them from being able to reconcile faith with modernity. Medieval jurisdictions, as historians have long recognized, were fuzzy; the blurring of lines between a sin and a crime, between penance and punishment is a product of God's omnipresence. Across the board, medieval justice was penitential justice. While punishment, revenge, and deterrence were all laudable goals adopted by this system, the ultimate goal was reconciliation with God and penance was the indispensable conduit to reach that goal.

Medieval authorities referred to peine forte et dure as penance (*penitentia*) because, to them, it was a form of penance. Certainly, the practice boasts all the characteristics normally associated with penance: fasting, isolation from family and friends, denial of comforts including clothing and shoes, even pressing with irons and stones – the lifestyles of the era's ascetics are marked by all of these practices. Moreover, the language of the age makes it clear that prison was supposed to be a form of earthly purgatory, a penitential haven where a soul in jeopardy could work off sin through deprivation and serious contemplation. In the medieval imagination, "incarceration of the body" meant "liberation of the soul."[13] When used as a coercive measure, peine forte et dure replicated the experience of the early desert fathers – the celebrated icons of the Middle Ages – and prepared the defendant to face the twelve good and true men of the jury with a genuine sense of repentance. Of course, not everyone bought into this perception. The literature of medieval England, particularly Robert Grosseteste's *Chasteau d'Amour*, reveals a degree of criticism by king's subjects on the king's resort to hard prison. Certainly, when overused, they believed peine forte et dure was an unmerciful punishment, best associated with the kind of justice meted out by unChristian, even anti-Christian, authorities.

Acknowledging the penitential edge to the medieval judicial system is the only way to truly make sense of peine forte et dure. At the same time, it leads to a sharper appreciation of what the medieval system of justice had to offer. This is especially true when it comes to spiritual reform. The colorful language used to describe medieval prisons highlights popular history's perceptions of penal culture in the medieval context: a "prototype of Hell," "dungeons of despair," and "mansions of misery."[14] Such dire perceptions are a byproduct

---

[13] Megan Cassidy-Welch, *Imprisonment in the Medieval Religious Imagination, c. 1150–1400* (London: Palgrave Macmillan, 2011), 15.
[14] Stephen Halliday, *Newgate: London's Prototype of Hell* (Stroud: Sutton, 2006); David Thomas, "Dungeons of Despair," *Ancestors* 41 (2005): 1474–2470; and

of the prison-reform movement. Nineteenth-century reformers who exposed English sensibilities to the over-crowding, disease, and filth of prisons, workhouses, and asylums shocked the public into pressuring government for reform.[15] Much of the historiography works on the premise that if prisons were that terrible in the nineteenth century, they must have been much worse hundreds of years before that. Reform sprang from new ideas about penology, which witnessed a "gradual transition from repression to governance, understood in terms of abandoning actions targeting the body in favor of a rational regime aimed at training the mind or soul."[16] Thus, nineteenth-century prison wardens prioritized rehabilitation over revenge. Religious instruction within the prison was intended to prompt moral reform in the hopes that through rehabilitation they might see fewer criminals relapse into old habits and eventually return to prison. This book does not intend to quibble with this history, except to suggest that rehabilitation was not the preserve of nineteenth-century reformers. Spiritual and moral reform were equally important in the medieval mindset. Acquitted felons were the neighbors, business associates, and fellow parishioners of the jurors who were responsible for their release, making moral reform a personal issue for all concerned. The importance of rehabilitation in the medieval setting has been overlooked simply because it was accomplished by different means. Prisoners did not take "classes" in religious instruction, nor did they spend their spare time reading state-supplied religious books – unless they were wealthy inmates who brought their own books to prison. The incarcerated did receive religious instruction through attendance at mass, but rather than place the emphasis on formal training, for them, it was enduring an ascetic lifestyle that initiated spiritual reform.

The view of medieval justice as penitential process put forward by this book is not an anomaly. Richard Helmholz has spent much of his career explaining the various ways in which the canon law shaped and

---

Jerry White, *Mansions of Misery: A Biography of the Marshalsea Debtor's Prison* (London: The Bodley Head, 2016).

[15] Victor Bailey, "English Prisons, Penal Culture, and the Abatement of Imprisonment, 1895–1922," *JBS* 36.3 (1997): 285.

[16] Guy Geltner, *Flogging Others: Corporal Punishment and Cultural Identity from Antiquity to the Present* (Amsterdam University Press, 2014), 19.

influenced English common law.[17] Helmholz's mantle has been taken up most recently by a new generation of scholars eager to break down the barriers between law and religion. Elizabeth Papp Kamali's *Felony and the Guilty Mind* (2019) views the boundaries between law and religion as permeable, resorting to theological works in order to illuminate our legal perceptions of *mens rea*.[18] Works by Philippa Byrne (2019) and Thomas McSweeney (also 2019) attempt to reconcile canon and common law through an analysis of its practitioners, the prelates appointed as king's justices who also penned the leading treatises on the law.[19] The crossover in personnel and ideology had real implications on the application of the law. Trisha Olson sees this chiefly in terms of the ordeal and punishment process, which she examines through a penitential lens. When it comes to execution, for example, she argues that "medieval punishment even in its most excruciating and sanguinary forms," is informed by belief in "bodily pain . . . as a divine gift, as a sacrificial offering that allowed the one suffering to share in Christ's passion, or as sign of purgatory that offered the hope of man's redemption."[20] Esther Cohen has also argued in favor of pain as a vehicle for spiritual reform, even in the judicial process: pain has "a salutary effect upon the condemned person's soul, completing what repentance and confession had earlier achieved. What punishment criminals took on earth they would be spared in Purgatory."[21] For the spectator, viewing an execution was also a transformative process, although deterrence was just one of the several lessons they learned. Christian audiences watched "the

---

[17] See Richard Helmholz, *Canon Law and English Common Law* (SS, 1983) and *The ius commune in England: Four Studies* (Oxford University Press, 2001).

[18] Elizabeth Papp Kamali, *Felony and the Guilty Mind in Medieval England* (Cambridge University Press, 2019).

[19] Philippa Byrne, *Justice and Mercy: Moral Theology and the Exercise of Law in Twelfth-Century England* (Manchester University Press, 2019); McSweeney, *Priests of the Law*.

[20] Trisha Olson, "Medieval Blood Sanction," 66. See also Trisha Olson, "Of the Worshipful Warrior: Sanctuary and Punishment in the Middle Ages," *St Thomas Law Review* 16 (2004): 473–549; and "Of Enchantment: The Passing of the Ordeals and the Rise of the Jury Trial," *Syracuse Law Review* 50 (2000): 109–96.

[21] Esther Cohen, "The Expression of Pain in the Later Middle Ages: Deliverance, Acceptance and Infamy," in Florike Egmond and Robert Zwijnenberg, eds., *Bodily Extremities: Preoccupations with the Human Body in Early Modern European Culture* (New York: Routledge, 2003), 216.

spectacle of punitive death through the magnifying lens of 'penitential vision'," as the steadfast criminal became one with Christ through the execution experience.[22] Penance was not reserved exclusively for the execution process. Works by Catherine McKenna and Cynthia Neville on Wales and Scotland respectively have proposed ways in which penance played a larger role in the punishment process more generally, from the penance-infused elegies performed by court poets, to judicial mandates for payment of compensation prior to remission of sins.[23] These works signal a critical turning point in the study of the common law. It is time to put the Middle Ages, warts and all, back into medieval law. The culture of medieval England was steeped in Christianity. There was no way for the people of the era to separate God out from the law, so why should we when we study it?

This book has also attempted to explain what standing mute and peine forte et dure meant for the suspected felon. Initially, standing mute functioned as a protest against radical transformations in the criminal justice system that reduced the accused's control over his or her trial. There were many other reasons to opt for silence, however. Some of those who stood mute may have intended to preserve their lands for their heirs, as has long been asserted. Fear of death was certainly another justification, although given the tendency of medieval jurors to acquit, their fears may not have been well grounded. There was little correlation between guilt and a jury's verdict. For others, standing mute was a defense strategy intended to buy time. In this respect, it falls into the same category as failing to obtain the proper paperwork (a writ *de bono et malo*), benefit of clergy, turning approver, and pleading the belly – all means exploited by suspected felons in the hopes of extending their lives. Indeed, the skillful defendant employed a whole array of delaying tactics in succession. Given the impressive speed with which medieval justice sometimes worked, this was not a bad strategy. It provided the

---

[22] Mitchell Merback, *The Thief, the Cross, and the Wheel: Pain and the Spectacle of Punishment in Medieval and Renaissance Europe* (University of Chicago Press, 1999), 149.

[23] Catherine McKenna, "Performing Penance and Poetic Performance in the Medieval Welsh Court," *Speculum* 82.1 (2007): 70–96; Cynthia Neville, "'No Remission without Satisfaction': Canonical Influences on Secular Lawmaking in High Medieval Scotland," in Jonathan Wooding and Lynette Olson, eds., *Prophecy, Fate and Memory in the Early and Medieval Celtic World* (Sydney University Press, 2020), 208–45.

defendant time for tempers to cool, witnesses and evidence to disappear or to surface, and to apply for a pardon. Others may have simply appreciated the time in an earthly purgatory fasting and praying in preparation to meet their maker.

Silence was also sometimes a means of protest. To be sure, it was the ideal mode of complaint in an era steeped in Christian mythology. Christianity is built around a central figure who does not open his mouth or raise a finger to save his life when faced with an unjust authority. The fact that English plays from the era depict Christ standing mute in a distinctly medieval court of law tell us just how closely he was associated with this practice. One suspects that he was the inspiration for those who refused to plead; and if they persisted in their silence, he was also their consolation, knowing that they followed in good footsteps. If such close imitation of Christ at the Passion was not the path to salvation, then what was?

How effective was their protest? Presumably, the eerie silence of the political martyrs haunted the king's dreams. That Henry IV on his deathbed was still denying having played a part in Scrope's beheading lends some credence to this perspective. When an ordinary person stood mute, doubtless word of his or her silence never even reached the king's ears. Yet, within that individual's community, silence was the vehicle to transform an everyday criminal into a martyr. The dearth of martyrs in late medieval Europe left devout Christians eager to find "new options for perfection in other types of death."[24] Self-mortification, crusading, missionary deaths all provided updated forms of martyrdom for an era in which Christianity was the dominant form of religion. *Hali Meðhad* even claimed that "virginity could be the equal of any ancient martyr's death."[25] In this atmosphere, standing mute gave meaning to an otherwise disreputable death, but not necessarily the meaning that historians once thought. Historians have focused chiefly on the silent defendant as a martyr for one's family, dying unconvicted to keep one's heir's inheritance intact. While some few medieval defendants fall into this category, the medieval evidence reveals an entirely different form of martrydom. When times were desperate because of famine, plague, and

---

[24] Miri Rubin, "Choosing Death? Experiences of Martyrdom in Late Medieval Europe," *Studies in Church History* 30 (1993): 156.
[25] Rubin, "Choosing Death?," 156.

over-taxation, while the king stood idly by doing nothing to protect his people, standing mute in protest of the monarch's unkingly behavior was a means of dying with dignity, in *imitatio Christi*. That these silent defendants often inspired others to follow suit tells us that at least some of them became legends in their villages. Silence, then, was awe-inspiring martyrdom, but it was also a powerful expression of communal solidarity.

The example of these individuals standing mute in protest turns the tables on traditional studies of popular resistance, readjusting our expectations of a noisy soundscape. In the right time and the right place, protest can be silent. This finding has us rethinking also our understanding of silence and its political role. More typically, silence is the end goal, it is what Crown authorities hope to return to after the turmoil and commotion of a revolt has died out. Silence represents acquiescence, obedience, deference. Silence is consent. This medieval example, however, demonstrates that sometimes silence is not consent, but defiance. Although he is speaking about the nineteenth century, Alain Corbin makes a relevant point when he argues that silence is the traditional tactic of the peasantry: "[a]n ancestral fear of saying too much might be fostered by the traps laid during inquisitions, by tax officials, by the police or by the magistrates." Strategic silence, then, was a safety measure in "a milieu where plans, ambitious or tragic, were slow to come to fruition, which meant that it was essential not to show your hand."[26] Similarly, these conclusions imply that historians of revolt need to expand their vision of the topography of protest. They have had us looking to alehouses, fields, parishes, friaries – it is time now to add also the courtroom and the prison to that grouping.[27]

The defendant standing mute is a reminder that ordinary people are "political actors in their own right, actors who usually lacked formal political power, but none the less found many ways of making their interests and ideas known."[28] The purpose of this study is to recognize the agency of the defendants, to single out their concerns, their

---

[26] Alain Corbin, *A History of Silence: From the Renaissance to the Present Day*, trans. Jean Birrell (New York: Polity, 2018), 70.

[27] Samuel Cohn, Jr., "The Topography of Medieval Popular Protest," *Social History* 44.4 (2019): 390.

[28] Jane Whittle and Stephen Rigby, "England: Popular Politics," in Stephen Rigby, ed., *A Companion to Britain in the Later Middle Ages* (Malden: Wiley-Blackwell, 2009), 83.

grievances from their political acts, even if historians have not as of yet regarded those actions as political. When standing mute first developed as a practice, likely the protest was directed at the king because of the dramatic changes in the criminal justice system that were not in the best interests of the defendant. In a relatively short span of time, church and Crown tossed aside traditional means of proof, compurgation and the ordeals. Much has been written on the subject of the changes wrought by the twelfth century legal revolution and its impact on the populace's relationship with the law. Susan Reynolds explains that law became "more complex and rule-bound."[29] The rise in a professional corps of lawmen arose precisely at this moment because negotiating the legal system became too complicated for those without training. As Anders Winroth writes, "[i]n systematizing legal procedure, the twelfth century removed control of the law from local communities and gave it to professional, educated judges, who represented the disciplinary interests of both church and state."[30] For Continental histories, the emphasis rests on the loss of collective judgment, as university-trained judges and lawyers assumed control of the system. The same cannot be said for England. There, the centralization of royal authority and the growth of monarchy were the driving force behind a transition in the law that began long before the 1215 council that mandated the abandonment of ordeals. For the ordinary subject, loss of these proofs had a monumental impact on his ability to defend himself against criminal allegations. Unlike on the Continent, the English system continued to rely on collective judgment: however, it was now to be the *right* collective judgment, that is, judgment by one's social betters. The king envisioned the "country" as his eyes in the community. Of course, jurors themselves may have had a different vision of their role. Nevertheless, the emergence of presenting and trial juries meant that the defendant was no longer able to handpick witnesses/judges, as one might do with compurgation; nor was the defendant able to choose the method of proof. Effectively, the defendant lost agency: any measure of control over one's fate had vanished.

---

[29] Reynolds, "Emergence of Professional Law," 366.
[30] Anders Winroth, "The Legal Revolution of the Twelfth Century," in Thomas Noble, John Van Engen, Anna Sapir Abulafia, and Sverre Bagge, eds., *European Transformations: The Long Twelfth Century* (South Bend, IN: University of Notre Dame Press, 2011), 351.

Standing mute was a means of regaining agency, taking back control over one's life, even if it was only for a short time before the defendant succumbed and agreed to jury trial. In many respects, these findings echo what Andrea McKenzie has had to say for those who refused to plead in the eighteenth century. She credits their noncooperation to "a more generalized resistance to a form of trial that tended to deny the accused an active voice, placing more emphasis on the discretion of prosecutors, judges, juries, and character witnesses than the testimony of the defendant."[31] The defendant's alienation from the system of judgment that she outlines so precisely here was just beginning in the twelfth and thirteenth centuries, and medieval accused felons were just as disturbed by this unwanted transformation. For the defendants McKenzie studies, noncooperation at court was the perfect tool because it was a direct violation of a "culture of deference."[32] This statement is equally true of medieval England.

Rejection of the jury is how court scribes frequently interpreted and recorded the actions of our silent defendants; yet, the jury as a mechanism of resolution is not what provoked their resistance. Rather, it was what the jury represented: the ever-expanding reach of the king at the expense of his subjects. In times of dearth and hardship, silence was also a reminder to the king of his duties. A king was expected to act *in loco parentis* to his subjects; but what kind of father extorted money from his starving child? The rise in numbers of defendants who stood mute in the early fourteenth century reflects growing distaste with kings flirting with absolutist fantasies who abuse their position and ignore the needs of the people who rely upon them. Typically, the peasantry fought back against tyranny with the "weapons of the weak": passive noncompliance, feigned compliance, sabotage, evasion, and desertion. On the manor, this took the form of rent strikes; tax evasion; and a failure to do suit of court (among other options). When the king was the target, standing mute was the weapon of choice.

[31] McKenzie, "This Death," 296.   [32] McKenzie, "This Death," 298.

Bibliography

Manuscript

The National Archives (Kew, Surrey)

C 1, Court of Chancery, Early Proceedings: select
C 144, Chancery, Criminal Inquisitions: select
JUST 1, Justices in Eyre, of Assize, of Oyer and Terminer, and of the Peace: select
JUST 2, Coroners' Rolls and Files, with Cognate Documents: select
JUST 3, Justices of Jail Delivery: Jail Delivery Rolls and Files: all 14th-century rolls, and some 15th-century
SC 8, Special Collections, Ancient Correspondence of the Chancery and Exchequer: select

Printed Primary

Aquinas, Thomas. *Summa Theologica*, translated by the Fathers of the Dominican Province. New York: Benzinger Brothers, 1947.

Arnold, Thomas, ed. *Memorials of St. Edmund's Abbey*, 2 vols. London: Eyre and Spottiswoode, 1892.

Aspin, Isabel, ed. *Anglo-Norman Political Songs*. Anglo-Norman Text Society, vol. IX, 1953.

Aungier, George, ed. *Croniques de London, depuis l'an 44 Hen. III jusqu'à 17 Edw. III*. London: Camden Society, 1844.

Baker, John, ed. "Criminal Justice at Newgate 1616–1627: Some Manuscript Reports in the Harvard Law School." *Irish Jurist* 8 (1973): 307–22.

ed. *Reports of Cases by John Caryll*, 2 vols. SS, vols. CXV and CXVI, 1998.

Bateson, Mary, ed. *George Ashby's Poems, Edited from Two Fifteenth-Century Manuscripts from Cambridge.* EETS, e.s., vol. LXXVI, 1899.

Beadle, Richard, and Pamela King, eds. *York Mystery Plays: A Selection in Modern Spelling.* Oxford University Press, 1984.

Blackstone, William. *Commentaries on the Laws of England,* 4 vols. (1723–80). In "The Avalon Project: Documents in Law, History and Diplomacy." New Haven, https://avalon.law.yale.edu/subject_menus/blackstone.asp

Bracton, Henri de. *De Legibus et Consuetudinibus Angliae,* edited by George Woodbine and Samuel Thorne. 4 vols. SS, 1968–76.

Brie, Friedrich, ed. *The Brut or the Chronicles of England,* 2 vols. EETS, vols. CXXXI and CXXXVI, 1908.

Brown, Carleton, ed. *Religious Lyrics of the XIVth Century.* 2nd edn. Oxford: Clarendon Press, 1952.

Brown, William, ed. *Yorkshire Inquisitions.* York: Yorkshire Archaeological Society, 1898.

Bullard, John, and Chalmer Bell, eds. *Lyndwood's Provinciale: The Text of the Canons Therein Contained, Reprinted from the Translation Made in 1534.* London: Faith Press, 1929.

Calendar of Close Rolls, 1273–1485, 45 vols. London: HMSO, 1911–63.

Calendar of Fine Rolls, 1272–1509, 22 vols. London: HMSO, 1911–62.

Calendar of Inquisitions Post Mortem, 26 vols. London: HMSO, 1898–2009.

Calendar of Patent Rolls, 1216–1509, 55 vols. London: HMSO, 1891–1916.

Cam, Helen, ed. *Year Books of Edward II, v. 26, pt. 1: The Eyre of London, 14 Edward II (1321).* SS, vol. LXXXV, 1968.

Campbell, Killis, ed. *The Seven Sages of Rome.* Boston: Ginn and Company, 1907.

Capgrave, John. *Abbreuiacion of Cronicles,* edited by Peter Lucas. EETS, o.s. vol. CCLXXXV, 1983.

The Life of St. Katharine of Alexandria, translated by Karen Winstead. South Bend, IN: University of Notre Dame Press, 2011.

Chew, Helena, and Martin Weinbaum, eds. *London Eyre of 1244.* London Record Society, 1970.

Childs, Wendy, ed. *Vita Edwardi Secundi: The Life of Edward the Second.* Oxford: Clarendon Press, 2005.

Childs, Wendy, and John Taylor, eds. *The Anonimalle Chronicle, 1307–34.* Yorkshire Archaeological Society Record Series, vol. CXLVII, 1991.

Cigman, Gloria, ed. *Lollard Sermons.* EETS, vol. CCXCIV, 1989.

Clopper, Lawrence, ed. *Records of Early English Drama: Chester.* University of Toronto Press, 1979.

Cockburn, James, ed. *Calendar of Assize Records. Home Circuit Indictments, Elizabeth I and James I: Introduction.* London: HMSO, 1985.

Coke, Edward. *Institutes of the Lawes of England,* 4 vols. London: E. and R. Brooke, 1797.

Connelly, Margaret, ed. "The Dethe of the Kynge of Scotis: A New Edition."
    The Scottish Historical Review 71.191/192, parts 1 &2 (1992): 46–69.
Davies, John, ed. *An English Chronicle of the Reigns of Richard II, Henry IV,
    Henry V, and Henry VI, Written before the Year 1471.* Camden Society,
    series 1, vol. LXIV, 1856.
Dawtrey, Thomas. "An Account of the Proceedings against Archbishop
    Scrope," in Raine, ed., *Historians of York*, vol. III, 290.
de Coggeshall, Ralph. *Chronicon Anglicanum*, edited by Joseph Stevenson.
    London: Longmans, 1875.
d'Evelyn, Charlotte, and Anna Mill, eds. *The South English Legendary.* 2 vols.
    EETS, vols. CCXXXV and CCXXXVI, 1956.
de Gruchy, William, ed. *L'Ancienne Coutume de Normandie.* Jersey: Charles
    le Feuvre, 1881.
de Vigeois, Geoffrey. *Chronica.* In *Recueil des Historiens des Gaules et de la
    France*, edited by Martin Bouquet, et al., 24 vols. Paris: Victor Palmé.
    1734–1904.
de Voragine, Jacobus. *The Golden Legend: Readings on the Saints*, translated
    by William Ryan. Princeton University Press, 2012.
Downer, Leslie, ed. *Leges Henrici Primi.* Oxford: Clarendon Press, 1972.
Epp, Garrett, ed. *The Townley Plays.* Kalamazoo: Medieval Institute
    Publications, 2017.
Eusebius of Caesaria. *Eusebius: The Church History*, edited and translated by
    Paul Maier. Grand Rapids, MI: Kregel Academic and Professional
    Printing, 2007.
Fehr, Bernhard, ed. *Die hirtenbriefe Ælfrics in altenglischer und lateinischer
    fasung.* Hamburg: Verlag von Henri Grand, 1914.
Fitzherbert, Anthony. *La Graunde Abridgement.* London: John Rastell and
    Wynkyn de Worde, 1516.
Foliot, Gilbert. *The Letters and Charters of Gilbert Foliot, Abbot of
    Gloucester (1139–48), Bishop of Hereford (1148–63), and London
    (1163–87),* edited by Zachary Brooke, Adrian Morey, and
    Christopher Brooke. Cambridge University Press, 1967.
Fortescue, John. *De Laudibus Legum Angliae*, edited by Stanley Chrimes, 2nd
    edn. Cambridge University Press, 2011.
Friedberg, Emil, ed. *Corpus iuris canonici*, 2 vols. Graz: Akademische Druck,
    1959.
Given-Wilson, Chris, ed. *The Chronicle of Adam Usk, 1377–1421.* Oxford:
    Clarendon Press, 1997.
Gower, John. *Mirour de l'Omme (The Mirror of Mankind)*, translated by
    William Wilson. East Lansing: Colleagues Press, 1992.
Grosseteste, Robert. *Le chateau d'amour*, edited by Jessie Murray. Paris:
    Champion, 1918.
Hall, George, ed. *The Treatise on the Laws and Customs of the Realm of
    England Commonly Called Glanvill.* Oxford: Clarendon Press, 1993.

Harris, Markham, ed. *The Cornish Ordinalia: A Medieval Dramatic Trilogy.* Washington, DC: Catholic University of America Press, 1969.

Hawkins, William. *A Treatise on Pleas of the Crown,* 2 vols. London: Elizabeth Nutt, 1721.

Henderson, Ernest, ed. "The Dialogue Concerning the Exchequer, circa 1180." In *Select Historical Documents of the Middle Ages,* 20–134. London: George Bell and Sons, 1910.

Henle, Robert, ed. *Saint Thomas Aquinas. The Treatise on Law [Being Summa Theologiae, I–II, QQ.90 through 97].* South Bend, IN: University of Notre Dame Press, 1993.

Henry of Ghent, *Quodlibet IX,* edited by Raymond Macken. *Henrici de Gandavo Opera Omnia,* vol. XIII. Leuven: Brill, 1983.

Hoccleve, Thomas. *Hoccleve's Works.* III.*The Regement of Princes* AD 1411–12, *from the Harleian MS. 4866, and Fourteen of Hoccleve's Minor Poems from the Egerton MS. 615,* edited by Frederick J. Furnivall. EETS, e.s., vol. LXI, 1897.

Holmstedt, Gustaf, ed. *Speculum Christiani: A Middle English Religious Treatise of the Fourteenth Century.* EETS, vol. CLXXXII, 1933.

Holthausen, Ferdinand, ed. *Vices and Virtues, Being a Soul's Confession of its Sins with Reason's Description of the Virtues.* EETS, vol. LXXXIX, 1888.

Horner, Patrick, ed. *A Macaronic Sermon Collection from Late Medieval England: Oxford MS Bodley 649.* Toronto: PIMS, 2006.

Horstmann, Carl, ed. "Die nordenglische Legendensammlung." In *Altenglische Legenden: Neue Folge,* 3–173. Heilbronn: Henninger, 1881. *Early South-English Legendary.* EETS, vol. LXXXIX, 1887.

Horwood, Alfred, ed. *Year Books of the Reign of Edward the First: Years XX and XXI (1292–1293).* RS no. 31, part A, vol. I, 1866.

Horwood, Alfred, ed. *Year Books of the Reign of Edward the First: Years XXX and XXXI (1302–1303).* RS no. 31, pt. A, vol. III, 1863.

Howell, Thomas, ed. *A Complete Collection of State Trials,* 21 vols. London: T. C. Hansard, 1816.

Hudson, Anne, ed. *Two Wycliffite Texts.* EETS, vol. CCCI, 1993.

John of Salisbury. *Policraticus: Of the Frivolities of Courtiers and the Footprints of Philosophers,* edited by Cary Nederman. Cambridge University Press, 1990.

Johnson, Holly, ed. *The Grammar of Good Friday: Macaronic Sermons of Late Medieval England.* Turnhout: Brepols, 2012.

Kaye, John, ed. *Placita Corone, or La Corone Pledee devant Justices.* SS, supplementary series, vol. IV, 1966.

Kelly, Thomas, ed. "Eustache the Monk." In Ohlgren, ed., *Medieval Outlaws,* 61–98. Stroud: Sutton, 1998.

"Fouke Fitz Waryn." In Ohlgren, ed., *Medieval Outlaws,* 106–67.

Kesselring, Krista, ed. *The Trial of Charles I.* Toronto: Broadview Press, 2016.

Kiralfy, Alfred, ed. *Source Book of English Law*. London: Sweet and Maxwell Limited, 1957.

Langland, William. *Piers Plowman*, translated by Talbot Donaldson, edited by Elizabeth Robertson and Stephen Shepherd. New York: W. W. Norton and Company, 2006.

Leadam, Isaac, ed. *Select Cases before the King's Council in the Star Chamber, Commonly Called the Court of Star Chamber* AD *1477–1509*, 2 vols. SS, vol. XVI and vol. XXV, 1903–11.

List of Sheriffs for England and Wales from the Earliest Times to A.D. 1383, Compiled from Documents in the Public Record Office. London: HMSO, 1898; repr. Kraus, 1963.

Luard, Henry, ed. "Annales Prioratus de Dunstaplia (AD 1–1297)." In Henry Luard, ed., *Annales Monastici*, 3 vols. London: Longmans, 1866, vol. III, 3–420.

Bartholomaei de Cotton, Monachi Norwicensis, Historia Anglicana. RS, vol. XVI, 1859.

Flores Historiarum, 3 vols. RS, 1886–9.

Luders, Alexander, T. E. Tomlins, John France, William Taunton, John Raithby, eds. *Statutes of the Realm*, 11 vols. London: Record Commission, 1810–27.

Maitland, Frederic, ed. *Bracton's Note Book: A Collection of Cases Decided in the King's Courts during the Reign of Henry the Third*. London C. J. Clay and Sons, 1887.

Pleas of the Crown for the County of Gloucester. London: Macmillan, 1884.

Select Pleas of the Crown, Vol. 1: AD *1200–1225*. SS, vol. I, 1888.

Year Books of Edward II, v. 1: 1 & 2 Edward II (AD *1307–1309*). SS, vol. XVII, 1903.

Mannyng, Robert, of Brunne. *Handlyng Synne*, edited by Idelle Sullens. Binghamton: Medieval and Renaissance Texts and Studies, 1983.

Maxwell, Herbert, ed. *The Chronicle of Lanercost, 1372–1346: Translated with Notes*. Glasgow: J. Maclehose, 1913.

Michaud-Quantin, Pierre, ed. "Un manuel de confession archaïque dans le manuscrit Avranches 136." *Sacris Erudiri* 17.1 (1966): 5–54.

Mills, David, ed. *The Chester Mystery Cycle: A New Edition with Modernised Spelling*. East Lansing: Colleagues Press, 1992.

Mont, Charles B., ed. *Chartes des libertés anglaises (1100–1305)*. Paris: Alphonse Picard, 1892.

Mooney Linne, and Mary-Jo Arn, eds. *The Kingis Quair and Other Prison Poems*. Kalamazoo: Medieval Institute Publications, 2005.

Morris, Richard, ed. *Old English Homilies of the Twelfth Century, from the Unique MS. B. 14. 52 in the Library of Trinity College*. EETS, vol. LIII, 1873.

Mush, John. "A True Report of the Life and Martyrdom of Mrs. Clitherow." In John Morris, ed., *The Troubles of Our Catholic*

Forefathers Related by Themselves, 3rd series, 360–440. London: Burns and Oats, 1877.

Musson, Anthony, with Edward Powell, eds. *Crime, Law and Society in the Later Middle Ages*. Manchester University Press, 2009.

Nederman, Cary, ed. *Political Thought in Early Fourteenth-Century England: Treatises by Walter of Milemete, William of Pagula, and William of Ockham*. Turnhout: Brepols, 2002.

Neilson, Nellie, ed. *Year Books of Edward IV: 10 Edward IV and 49 Henry VI*. SS, vol. XLVII, 1930.

Nichols, Francis, ed. *Britton: An English Translation and Notes*. 2 vols. Washington, DC: John Byrne and Co., 1901.

"Original Documents Illustrative of the Administration of Criminal Law at the Time of Edward I." *Archaeologia* 40 (1866): 89–105.

O'Brien, Bruce, ed. *God's Peace and King's Peace: The Laws of Edward the Confessor*. Philadelphia: University of Pennsylvania Press, 2015.

Ohlgren, Thomas, ed. *Medieval Outlaws: Ten Tales in Modern English*. Stroud: Sutton, 1998.

Peck, Russell, ed. *Heroic Women of the Old Testament in Middle English Verse*. Kalamazoo: Medieval Institute Publications, 1991.

Pike, Luke, ed. *Year Books of the Reign of King Edward the Third, Year* XIX. London: HMSO, 1906.

Year Books of the Reign of King Edward the Third: Year XV. RS, no. 31, part B, vol. VI, 1891.

Powell, Susan, ed. *John Mirk's Festial*, 2 vols. EETS, vols. CCCXXXIV and CCCXXXV, 2009–11.

Powicke, Frederick, and Christopher Cheney, eds. *Councils and Synods: With Other Documents Relating to the English Church*, 2 vols. Oxford: Clarendon Press, 1964.

Preest, David, ed. *The Chronica Maiora of Thomas Walsingham, 1376–1422*. Woodbridge: Boydell, 2005.

Raine, James, ed. "Miscellanea Relating to the Martyrdom of Archbishop Scrope." In *Historians of the Church of York*, 3 vols. RS, 1879–94., vol. II, 292–311.

Revard, Carter, ed. "*The Outlaw's Song of Trailbaston*." In Ohlgren, ed., *Medieval Outlaws*, 99–105.

Richardson, Henry, and George Sayles, eds. *Fleta*. SS, vol. LXXII, 1953.

Riley, Henry, ed. *Memorials of London and London Life in the 13th, 14th and 15th Centuries*. London: Longmans, Green, 1868.

Robertson, Agnes, ed. *The Laws of the Kings of England from Edmund to Henry I*. Cambridge University Press, 1925.

Roger of Wendover. *Flores historiarum*, edited by Henry Hewlett. 3 vols. RS, 1886–9.

Rogers, Elizabeth, ed. "Peter Lombard and the Sacramental System." PhD Diss., Columbia University, 1917.

Rogers, Ralph, ed. *Year Books of the Reign of King Henry the Fifth.* Wurzburg: Privately Printed, 1948.

Rose, Martial, ed. *The Wakefield Mystery Plays.* London: Evan Brothers, 1961.

Ross, Woodburn, ed. *Middle English Sermons: Edited from British Museum MS Royal 18 B.* xxiii. EETS, vol. ccix, 1940.

Saint German, Christopher. *Doctor and Student,* edited by Theodore Plucknett and John Barton. SS, vol. xci, 1974.

Sajavaara Kari, ed. *The Middle English Translations of Robert Grosseteste's Chateau d'Amour.* Helsinki: Société Néophilologique, 1967.

Sayles, George, ed. *Select Cases in the Court of King's Bench.* 7 vols. SS, 1936–71.

Schmidt, Carl, ed. *Piers Plowman: A New Translation of the B-Text.* Oxford University Press, 2009.

Scott, Samuel, ed. *The Novels of Justinian.* Cincinnati: The Central Trust Company, 1932.

Seipp, David, ed. *Medieval English Legal History: An Index and Paraphrase of Printed Year Book Reports, 1268–1535.* Boston: Boston University Law School,www.bu.edu/phpbin/lawyearbooks/search.php

Sharpe, Reginald, ed. *Calendar of Coroners' Rolls of the City of London, AD 1300–1378.* London: R. Clay and Sons, Limited, 1913.

Calendar of Letter Books of the City of London: G, 1352–1374. London: HMSO, 1905.

Smith, Thomas. *De republica Anglorum: A Discourse on the Commonwealth of England,* edited by Leonard Alston. Cambridge University Press, 1906.

Spade, Paul, ed. *Peter Abelard: Ethical Writings, Ethics and Dialogue between a Philosopher, a Jew, and a Christian.* Indianapolis: Hackett Publishing, 1995.

Staunford, William. *Les Plees del Coron.* London, 1557; reprinted by Professional Books, Ltd., 1971.

Stenton, Doris, ed. *Rolls of the Justices in Eyre Being the Rolls of Pleas and Assizes for Gloucestershire, Warwickshire and Staffordshire, 1221, 1222.* SS, vol. lix, 1940.

Rolls of the Justices in Eyre Being the Rolls of Pleas and Assizes for Lincolnshire 1218–19 and Worcestershire 1221. SS, vol. liii, 1934.

The Earliest Lincolnshire Assize Rolls, AD 1202–1209. Lincolnshire Record Society, vol. xxii, 1926.

Stone, Ian, ed. "The Book of Arnold Fitz Thedmar." PhD Diss., King's College London, 2015.

Strachey, John, et al., eds. *Rotuli Parliamentorum: ut et petitiones et placita in parliamento.* London: HMSO, 1767–77.

Stubbs, William, ed. "Annales Paulini." In William Stubbs, ed., *Chronicles of the Reigns of Edward I. and Edward II,* 253–370. London: Longman and Co., 1883.

Select Charters and Other Illustrations of English Constitutional History, 9th edn., revised by H. W. Carless Davis. Oxford: Clarendon Press, 1913.

The Continuation of the Chronicle of Gervase of Canterbury, to 1327. In William Stubbs, ed., *The Historical Works of Gervase of Canterbury*, 2 vols. RS, 1879–80, vol II, 106–324.

Sugano, Douglas, ed. *The N-Town Plays*. Kalamazoo: Medieval Institute Publications, 2007.

Sutherland, Donald, ed. *The Eyre of Northamptonshire, 3–4 Edward III (1329–1330)*. 2 vols. SS, vols. XCVII and XCVIII, 1983.

Tardif, Ernest-Joseph, ed. *Summa de Legibus Normannie in curia laicali*, 2 vols. Rouen: F. Simon, 1896.

Thompson, Anne, ed. *The Northern Homily Cycle*. Kalamazoo: Medieval Institute Publications, 2008.

Turner, George, and Theodore Plucknett, eds. *Year Books of Edward II, vol. 10: 5 Edward II (1311)*. SS, vol. LXIII, 1947.

Tymms, Samuel, ed. *Wills and Inventories from the Registers of the Commissary of Bury St Edmunds and the Archdeacon of Sudbury*. Camden Society, Original Series, vol. XLIX, 1850.

Van Buuren, Catherine, ed. *The Buke of the Sevyne Sagis: A Middle Scots Version of the Seven Sages of Rome*. Leiden University Press, 1982.

Walsingham, Thomas. *The St Albans Chronicle: The 'Chronica maiora' of Thomas Walsingham*, vol. II: 1394–1422, edited by John Taylor, Wendy Childs, and Leslie Watkiss. Oxford: Clarendon Press, 2011.

Wenzel, Siegfried, ed. *Fasciculus Morum: A Fourteenth-Century Preacher's Handbook*. University Park, PA: Pennsylvania State University Press, 1989.

Whittaker, William, ed. *The Mirror of Justices*. SS, vol. VII, 1893.

Wilkins, David, ed. *Concilia Magna Brittaniae et Hiberniae a Synodo Verulamensi anno 446 AD Londinensem 1717*. 4 vols. London: R. Gosling, et al., 1685–1745.

Wright, Stephen, ed. "The Bishop Scrope That Was So Wise." In Goldberg, ed., *Richard Scrope: Archbishop, Rebel, Martyr*, 113–14.

Wright, Thomas, ed. *The Political Songs of England, from the Reign of John to that of Edward II*. London: Camden Society, 1839.

Wrottesley, George, ed. *Staffordshire Historical Collections*. London: William Salt Archaeological Society, 1886.

Secondary

Abels, Richard. "'The Crimes by Which Wulfbad Ruined Himself with his Lord': The Limits of State Action in Late Anglo-Saxon England." *Reading Medieval Studies* 40 (2014): 42–53.

Adamson, Melitta Weiss. *Food in Medieval Times*. Westport: Greenwood Press, 2004.

Alford, John. "Literature and Law in Medieval England." *PMLA* 92.5 (1977): 941–51.

Piers Plowman: A Glossary of Legal Diction. Cambridge: D. S. Brewer, 1988.

Ambler, Sophie. "On Kingship and Tyranny: Grosseteste's *Memorandum* and its Place in the Baronial Reform Movement." In Janet Burton, Phillipp Schofield, and Björn Weiler, eds., *Thirteenth Century England* XIV: *Proceedings of the Aberystwyth and Lampeter Conference*, 115–28. Woodbridge: Boydell, 2013.

"Simon de Montfort and King Henry III: The First Revolution in English History, 1258–1265." *History Compass* 11.12 (2013): 1076–87.

Ames, Christine Caldwell. "Does Inquisition Belong to Religious History?" *AHR* 110.1 (2005): 11–37.

Amussen, Susan Dwyer. "Punishment, Discipline, and Power: The Social Meanings of Violence in Early Modern England." *JBS* 34.1 (1995): 1–34.

Appellàniz, Francisco. "Judging the Franks: Proof, Justice, and Diversity in Late Medieval Alexandria and Damascus." *Comparative Studies in Society and History* 58.2 (2016): 350–78.

Arnold, John. "Religion and Popular Rebellion, From the Capuciati to Niklashausen." *Cultural and Social History* 6.2 (2009): 149–69.

Austin, Greta. "Vengeance and Law in Eleventh-Century Worms: Burchard and the Canon Law of Feuds." In Wolfgang Müller and Mary Sommar, eds., *Medieval Church Law and the Origins of the Western Legal Tradition*, 66–76. Washington, DC: Catholic University of America Press, 2012.

Bailey, Mark. *The Decline of Serfdom in Late Medieval England: From Bondage to Freedom.* Woodbridge: Boydell, 2014.

Bailey, Victor. "English Prisons, Penal Culture, and the Abatement of Imprisonment, 1895–1922." *JBS* 36.3 (1997): 285–324.

Baker, John. *An Introduction to English Legal History*, 5th edn. Oxford University Press, 2019.

"Human Rights and the Rule of Law in Renaissance England." *Northwestern University Journal of International Human Rights* 2 (2004): 1–17.

Manual of Law French, 2nd edn. Aldershot: Scholar Press, 1990.

The Reinvention of Magna Carta 1216–1616. Cambridge University Press, 2017.

Bakhtin, Mikhail, *Rabelais and His World*, translated by Hélène Iswolsky. Bloomington: Indiana University Press, 1984.

Bale, Anthony. "God's Cell: Christ as Prisoner and Pilgrimage to the Prison of Christ." *Speculum* 91.1 (2016): 1–35.

Baraz, Daniel. *Medieval Cruelty: Changing Perceptions, Late Antiquity to the Early Modern Period.* Ithaca: Cornell University Press, 2003.

Barrington, Candace, and Sebastian Sobecki, eds. *The Cambridge Companion to Medieval English Law and Literature.* Cambridge University Press, 2019.

Bartlett, Robert. *England under the Norman Angevin Kings, 1075–1225.* Oxford: Clarendon Press, 2000.

The Hanged Man: A Story of Miracle, Memory, and Colonialism in the Middle Ages. Princeton University Press, 2004.

Bassett, Margery. "The Fleet Prison in the Middle Ages." *The University of Toronto Law Journal* 5 (1944): 383–402.

"Newgate Prison in the Middle Ages." *Speculum* 18.2 (1943): 233–46.

Bassett, William. "Canon Law and the Common Law." *Hastings Law Journal* 29 (1977–8): 1383–1420.

Baum, Jacob. "Sensory Perception, Religious Ritual and Reformation in Germany, 1428–1564." PhD Diss., University of Illinois at Urbana-Champaign, 2013.

Beattie, John. *Crime and the Courts in England, 1660–1800.* Oxford: Clarendon Press, 1986.

Bedingfield, Brad. "Public Penance in Anglo-Saxon England." *Anglo-Saxon England* 31 (2002): 223–55.

Behrmann, Carolin. "On *actio*: The Silence of Law and the Eloquence of Images." *Zeitschrift für Kunstgeschichte* 76.1 (2013): 51–70.

Bellamy, John. *Crime and Public Order in England in the Later Middle Ages.* University of Toronto Press, 1970.

The Criminal Trial in Later Medieval England. University of Toronto Press, 1998.

Bellomo, Manlio. *The Common Legal Past of Europe, 1000–1800,* translated by Lydia G. Cochrane. Washington, DC: Catholic University of America Press, 1995.

Berger, Benjamin. "*Peine Forte et Dure*: Compelled Jury Trials and Legal Rights in Canada." *Criminal Law Quarterly* 18.2 (2003): 205–48.

Berman, Harold. *Law and Revolution: The Formation of the Western Legal Tradition.* Cambridge, MA: Harvard University Press, 1983.

Biggs, Douglas. "Archbishop Scrope's *Manifesto* of 1405: 'Naïve nonsense' or Reflections of Political Reality?" *Journal of Medieval History* 33 (2007): 358–71.

Biller, Peter. "'Deep is the Heart of Man, and Inscrutable': Signs of Heresy in Medieval Languedoc." In Helen Barr and Ann Hutchison, eds., *Text and Controversy from Wyclif to Bale: Essays in Honour of Anne Hudson,* 267–80. Turnhout: Brepols, 2005.

Birrell, Jean. "Confrontation and Negotiation in a Medieval Village: Alrewas before the Black Death." In Richard Goddard, John Langdon, and Miriam Müller, eds., *Survival and Discord in Medieval Society: Essays in Honour of Christopher Dyer,* 197–211. Turnhout: Brepols, 2010.

Boone, Marc. "The Dutch Revolt and the Medieval Tradition of Urban Dissent." *Journal of Early Modern History* 11.4/5 (2007): 351–75.

Booth, Paul. "The Enforcement of the Ordinance and Statute of Labourers in Cheshire, 1349 to 1374." *Archives* 127 (2013): 1–16.

Brand, Paul. "Henry II and the Creation of the English Common Law." In Christopher Harper-Bill and Nicholas Vincent, eds., *Henry II: New Interpretations*, 215–41. Woodbridge: Boydell, 2007.

    The Origins of the English Legal Profession. Oxford: Blackwell, 1992.

    "'To None Will We Sell, to None Will We Deny or Delay Right or Justice': Expedition and Delay in Civil Proceedings in the English Medieval Royal Courts." In Remco van Rhee, ed., *Within a Reasonable Time: The History of Due and Undue Delay in Civil Litigation*, 57–71. Berlin: Duncker and Humblot, 2010.

Brewer, Jennifer. "Let Her Be Waived: Outlawing Women in Yorkshire, 1293–1294." In Alexander Kaufman, ed., *British Outlaws of Literature and History: Essays on Medieval and Early Modern Figures from Robin Hood to Twm Shon Catty*, 28–43. Jefferson, NC: MacFarland, 2011.

Britnell, Richard. "England: Towns, Trade and Industry." In Stephen Rigby, ed., *A Companion to Britain in the Later Middle Ages*, 47–64. Malden: Wiley-Blackwell, 2009.

Brown, Peter. "Society and the Supernatural: A Medieval Change." *Daedalus* 104.2 (1975): 133–51.

Bull, Marcus. "Pilgrimage." In John Arnold, ed., *The Oxford Handbook of Medieval Christianity*, 201–14. Oxford University Press, 2014.

Burke, Bernard. *A Genealogical History of the Dormant, Abeyant, Forfeited and Extinct Peerage of the British Empire*. London: Harrison, 1866.

Burton, David W. "Requests for Prayers and Royal Propaganda under Edward I." In Peter Coss and Simon Lloyd, eds., *Thirteenth Century England*, vol. III, 25–35. Woodbridge: Boydell, 1989.

Butler, Sara. *Forensic Medicine and Death Investigation in Medieval England*. New York: Routledge, 2015.

    "Pleading the Belly: A Sparing Plea? Pregnant Convicts and the Courts in Medieval England." In Sara Butler and Krista Kesselring, eds., *Crossing Borders: Boundaries and Margins in Medieval and Early Modern Britain. Essays in Honour of Cynthia J. Neville*, 131–52. Leiden: Brill, 2018.

    The Language of Abuse: Marital Violence in Medieval England. Leiden: Brill, 2007.

Bynum, Caroline Walker. *Holy Feast and Holy Fast: The Religious Significance of Food to Medieval Women*. Berkeley: University of California Press, 1988.

Byrne, Philippa. *Justice and Mercy: Moral Theology and the Exercise of Law in Twelfth-Century England*. Manchester University Press, 2019.

"Medieval Violence, the Making of Law and the Historical Present." *Journal of the British Academy* 8.s3 (2020): 133–54.

Campbell, Bruce, and Cormac Ó Gráda. "Harvest Shortfalls, Grain Prices, and Famines in Preindustrial England." *Journal of Economic History* 71.4 (2011): 859–86.

Campbell, James. *The Anglo-Saxon State*. London: Hambledon, 2000.

Campbell, William. "Theologies of Reconciliation in Thirteenth-Century England." In Kate Cooper and Jeremy Gregory, eds., *Retribution, Repentance, and Reconciliation*, 84–94. Woodbridge: Boydell, 2004.

Cappelli, Adrian. *The Elements of Abbreviation in Medieval Latin Paleography*. Lawrence: University of Kansas Libraries, 1982.

Carpenter, David. "English Peasants in Politics 1258–1267." *P&P* 136 (1992): 3–42.

"King, Magnates, and Society: The Personal Rule of King Henry III, 1234–1258." *Speculum* 60.1 (1985): 39–70.

The Minority of Henry III. Berkeley: University of California Press, 1990.

Carrel, Helen. "The Ideology of Punishment in Late Medieval English Towns." *Social History* 34.3 (2009): 301–20.

Carroll, Stuart. "Thinking with Violence." *History and Theory* 55 (2017): 23–43.

Cartlidge, Neil. "Treason." In Barrington and Sobecki, eds., *The Cambridge Companion to Medieval English Law and Literature*, 83–94.

Cassidy-Welch, Megan. *Imprisonment in the Medieval Religious Imagination, c. 1150–1400*. Basingstoke: Palgrave Macmillan, 2011.

"Incarceration and Liberation: Prisons in the Cistercian Monastery." *Viator* 32 (2001): 23–42.

Cavill, Paul. "Heresy, Law and the State: Forfeiture in Late Medieval and Early Modern England." *EHR* 129.537 (2014): 270–95.

Caviness, Madeline. "Giving the 'Middle Ages' a Bad Name: Blood Punishments in the *Sachenspiegel* and Town Law Books." *Studies in Iconography* 34 (2013): 175–235.

Challet, Vincent, and Ian Forrest. "The Masses." In Christopher Fletcher, Jean-Philippe Genet, and John Watts, eds., *Government and Political Life in England and France, c.1300–c.1500*, 279–316. Cambridge University Press, 2015.

Clanchy, Michael. *From Memory to Written Record: England 1066–1307*, 3rd edn. Malden: Wiley-Blackwell, 2012.

Clarke, Peter. "Canon and Civil Law." In Barrington and Sobecki, eds., *The Cambridge Companion to Medieval English Law and Literature*, 30–41.

Classen, Albrecht, and Connie Scarborough, eds. *Crime and Punishment in the Middle Ages and Early Modern Age: Mental Historical Investigations of Basic Human Problems and Social Responses*. Berlin: de Gruyter, 2012.

Codling, Debbi. "Henry IV and Personal Piety." *History Today* 57.1 (2007): 23–9.

Cohen, Esther. *The Crossroads of Justice: Law and Culture in Late Medieval France*. Leiden: Brill, 1993

"The Expression of Pain in the Later Middle Ages: Deliverance, Acceptance and Infamy." In Florike Egmond and Robert Zwijnenberg, eds., *Bodily Extremities: Preoccupations with the Human Body in Early Modern European Culture* 195–219. New York: Routledge, 2003.

The Modulated Scream: Pain in Late Medieval Culture. University of Chicago Press, 2010.

"Towards a History of European Sensibility: Pain in the Later Middle Ages." *Science in Context* 8.1 (1995): 47–74.

Cohen, Jeremy. *Living Letters of the Law: Ideas of the Jew in Medieval Christianity*. Berkeley: University of California Press, 1999.

Cohn, Samuel, Jr. "The 'Modernity' of Medieval Popular Revolt." *History Compass* 10.10 (2012): 731–41.

"The Topography of Medieval Popular Protest." *Social History* 44.4 (2019): 389–411.

Colman, Rebecca. "Reason and Unreason in Early Medieval Law." *Journal of Interdisciplinary History* 4.4 (1974): 571–91.

Copeland, Rita. "Introduction: Dissenting Critical Practices." In Rita Copeland, ed., *Criticism and Dissent in the Middle Ages*, 1–23. Cambridge University Press, 1996.

Corbin, Alain. *A History of Silence: From the Renaissance to the Present Day*, translated by Jean Birrell. New York: Polity, 2018.

Corblet, Jules. *Histoire du sacrament de l'eucharistie*, 2 vols. Paris: Paris société générale de librarie Catholique, 1885.

Courtney, Francis. *Cardinal Robert Pullen: An English Theologian of the Twelfth Century*. Rome: Pontifical Gregorian University, 1954.

Cubitt, Catherine. "Bishops, Priests and Penance in Late Saxon England." *Early Medieval Europe* 14.1 (2006): 41–64.

Dale, Johanna. "*Christus Regnat*: Inauguration and Images of Kingship in England, France, and the Empire c.1050–c.1250." PhD Diss., University of East Anglia, 2013.

Damaška, Mirjan. "Rational and Irrational Proof Revisited." *Cardozo Journal of International and Comparative Law* 5.25 (1997): 25–39.

Daniel, Anasseril, and Phillip Resnick. "Mutism, Malingering, and Competency to Stand Trial." *Bulletin of the American Academy of Psychiatry and the Law* 15.3 (1987): 301–8.

Daniell, Christopher. *Death and Burial in Medieval England, 1066–1550*. London: Routledge, 1996.

Davidson, Clifford. "Suffering and the York Plays." *Philological Quarterly* 81 (2002): 1–31.

Davies, Richard. "After the Execution of Archbishop Scrope: Henry IV, the Papacy and the English Episcopate, 1405–8." *Bulletin of the John Rylands Library* 59.1 (1976): 40–74.

Davis, James. *Medieval Market Morality: Life, Law and Ethics in the English Marketplace, 1200–1500.* Cambridge University Press, 2011.

de Jong, Mayke. "Monastic Prisoners, or Opting Out? Political Coercion and Honour in the Frankish Kingdoms." In Mayke de Jong, Frans Theuws, and Carine van Rhijn, eds., *Topographies of Power in the Early Middle Ages*, 291–328. Leiden: Brill, 2001.

The Penitential State: Authority and Atonement in the Age of Louis the Pious, 814–840. Cambridge University Press, 2009.

"What was Public about Public Penance? *Paenitentia Publica* and Justice in the Carolingian World." *Settimane di Studio del Centro Italiano di Studi Sull'Alto Medioevo* 44 (1997): 863–904.

Derbes, Anne. *Picturing the Passion in Late Medieval Italy: Narrative Painting, Franciscan Ideologies, and the Levant.* Cambridge University Press, 1996.

Dodd, Gwilym. "Reason, Conscience and Equity: Bishops as the King's Judges in Later Medieval England." *History* 99.335 (2014): 213–40.

Duch, Anna. "Chasing St Louis: The English Monarchy's Pursuit of Sainthood." In Elena Woodacre, Lucinda Dean, Chris Jones, Zita Rohr, Russell Martin, eds., *The Routledge History of Monarchy*, 330–51. London: Routledge, 2019.

Dunbabin, Jean. *Captivity and Imprisonment in Medieval Europe, 1000–1300.* New York: Palgrave, 2002.

Dyer, Christopher. "Small-Town Conflict in the Later Middle Ages: Events at Shipston-on-Stour." *Urban History* 19.2 (1992): 183–210.

"The Social and Economic Background to the Rural Revolt of 1381." In Rodney Hilton and Trevor Aston, eds., *The English Rising of 1381*, 9–42. Cambridge University Press, 2007.

Eckert, Raphaël. "Peine judiciare, pénitence et salut entre droit canonique et théologie (XIIe s. – début du XIIIe s.)." *Revue de l'histoire des religions* 228.4 (2011): 483–568.

Edwards, John. "The Cult of 'St.' Thomas of Lancaster and its Iconography." *Yorkshire Archaeological Journal* 64 (1992): 103–21.

Eichbauer, Melodie. "Medieval Inquisitorial Procedure: Procedural Rights and the Question of Due Process in the Thirteenth Century." *History Compass* 12.1 (2014): 72–83.

Emigh, Rebecca Jean. "Poverty and Polygyny as Political Protest: The Waldensians and Mormons." *Journal of Historical Sociology* 5.4 (1992): 462–84.

Enders, Jody. *The Medieval Theater of Cruelty: Rhetoric, Memory, Violence.* Ithaca: Cornell University Press, 1999.

Eshelman, David J. "'Great Mowrning and Mone': Modeled Spectatorship in the Towneley Scourging." *Baylor Journal of Theatre and Performance* 2.1 (2005): 23–34.

Faith, Rosamund. "'The Great Rumour' of 1377 and Peasant Ideology." In Hilton and Aston, eds., *English Rising of 1381*, 42–73.

Farris, Charles. "The Pious Practices of Edward I, 1272–1307." PhD Diss., Royal Holloway College, University of London, 2013.

Fisher, Herbert, ed. *The Collected Papers of Frederic William Maitland*, 3 vols. Cambridge University Press, 1911.

Fitzgerald, Christina. *The Drama of Masculinity and Medieval English Guild Culture*. New York: Palgrave Macmillan, 2007.

Forrest, Ian. "The Transformation of Visitation in Thirteenth Century England." *P&P* 221 (2013): 3–38.

Trustworthy Men: How Inequality and Faith Made the Medieval Church. Princeton University Press, 2018.

Forse, James H. "Love and Marriage on the Medieval English Stage: Using the English Cycle Plays as Sources for Social History." *Quidditas* 32 (2011): 227–52.

Foucault, Michel. *Discipline and Punish: The Birth of the Prison*, translated by Alan Sheridan. New York: Vintage Books, 1995.

Fox, John. "The Nature of Contempt of Court." *Law Quarterly Review* 37.2 (1921): 191–202.

Franklin, Peter. "Politics in Manorial Court Rolls: The Tactics, Social Composition, and Aims of a Pre-1381 Peasant Movement." In Zvi Ravi and Richard Smith, eds., *Medieval Society and the Manor Court*, 162–98. Oxford University Press, 1996.

Frantzen, Allen. "Spirituality and Devotion in the Anglo-Saxon Penitentials." *Essays in Medieval Studies* 22 (2005): 117–128.

Freedman, Paul. "Peasant Resistance in Medieval Europe: Approaches to the Question of Peasant Resistance." *Filozofski vestnik* 18.2 (1997): 179–211.

French, Katherine. "Localized Faith: Parochial and Domestic Spaces." In John Arnold, ed., *The Oxford Handbook of Medieval Christianity*, 166–82. Oxford University Press, 2014.

Friedland, Paul. *Seeing Justice Done: The Age of Spectacular Capital Punishment in France*. Oxford University Press, 2012.

Gabel, Leona. *Benefit of Clergy in England in the Later Middle Ages*. New York: Octagon Books, 1969.

Gatrell, Vic. *The Hanging Tree: Execution and the English People*. Oxford University Press, 1994.

Geltner, Guy. *Flogging Others: Corporal Punishment and Cultural Identity from Antiquity to the Present*. Amsterdam University Press, 2014.

"Medieval Prisons: Between Myth and Reality, Hell and Purgatory." *History Compass* 4.2 (2006): 261–74.

The Medieval Prison: A Social History. Princeton University Press, 2008.

Genower, Ellie. "Gruesome: Horrified Gunpowder Viewers Left 'Throwing Up' At Extreme Violence and Torture Scenes on BBC1 New Drama." October 22, 2017.

Geremek, Bronislaw. *The Margins of Society in Late Medieval Paris.* Cambridge University Press, 2006.

Gibbs, Spike. "Felony Forfeiture at the Manor of Worfield, c.1370–c.1600." *Journal of Legal History* 39.3 (2018): 253–77.

Gillingham, John. "Enforcing Old Law in New Ways: Professional Lawyers and Treason in Early Fourteenth Century England and France." In Per Anderson, Mia Münster-Swendsen, and Helle Vogt, eds., *Law and Power in the Middle Ages*, 199–220. Copenhagen: Djoef Publishing, 2008.

Given, James. *Inquisition and Medieval Society: Power, Discipline, and Resistance in Languedoc.* Ithaca: Cornell University Press, 1997.

Society and Homicide in Thirteenth-Century England. Stanford University Press, 1977.

Given-Wilson, Chris. "Service, Serfdom and English Labour Legislation, 1350–1500." In Anne Curry and Elizabeth Matthew, eds., *Concepts and Patterns of Service in the Later Middle Ages*, 21–37. Woodbridge: Boydell, 2000.

Glucklich, Ariel. *Sacred Pain: Hurting the Body for the Sake of the Soul.* Oxford University Press, 2001.

Gluckmann, Max. *Custom and Conflict in Africa.* Oxford University Press, 1955.

Goebel, Julius, Jr. *Felony and Misdemeanour: A Study in the History of Criminal Law.* Philadelphia: University of Pennsylvania Press, 1976.

Goering, Joseph. "Chobham, Thomas of." *ODNB.* September 23, 2004.

"The Internal Forum and the Literature of Penance and Confession." *Traditio* 59 (2004): 175–227.

"The Scholastic Turn (1100–1500): Penitential Theology and Law in the Schools." In Abigail Firey, ed., *A New History of Penance*, 219–37. Leiden: Brill, 2008.

"The 'Summa de penitentia' of John of Kent." *Bulletin of Medieval Canon Law* 18 (1988): 13–31.

Goldberg, Jeremy, ed. *Richard Scrope: Archbishop, Rebel, Martyr.* Donington: Shaun Tyas, 2007.

"St Richard Scrope, the Devout Widow, and the Feast of Corpus Christi: Exploring Emotions, Gender, and Governance in Early Fifteenth-Century York." In Susan Broomhall, ed., *Authority, Gender and Emotions in Late Medieval and Early Modern England*, 66–83. Basingstoke: Palgrave Macmillan, 2015.

Gorski, Richard. "Justices and Injustice? England's Local Officials in the Later Middle Ages." In John Appleby and Paul Dalton, eds., *Outlaws in Medieval and Early Modern England: Crime, Government and Society, c.1066-c.1600*, 55–74. Farnham: Ashgate, 2009.

Green, Richard Firth. *A Crisis of Truth: Literature and Law in Ricardian England*. Philadelphia: University of Pennsylvania Press, 2002.

"Medieval Literature and the Law." In David Wallace, ed., *Cambridge History of Medieval English Literature*, 407–31. Cambridge University Press, 1999.

Green, Thomas. *Verdict According to Conscience: Perspective on the English Criminal Trial Jury, 1200–1800*. University of Chicago Press, 1985.

Greig, Hannah, and John Cooper. "The Bloody Truth – Why BBC's Gunpowder Had to Be So Violent." *The Conversation*, October 31, 2017.

Groot, Roger. "Teaching Each Other: Judges, Clerks, Jurors and Malefactors Define the Guilt/Innocence Jury." In Jonathan Bush and Alain Wijffels, eds., *Learning the Law: Teaching and the Transmission of Law in England 1150–1900*, 17–32. London: Hambledon, 1999.

"The Jury of Presentment before 1215." *AJLH* 26.1 (1982): 1–24.

Halliday, Stephen. *Newgate: London's Prototype of Hell*. Stroud: Sutton, 2006.

Hamil, Frederick. "The King's Approver: A Chapter in the History of English Criminal Law." *Speculum* 11.2 (1936): 238–58.

Hamilton, Bernard. *The Medieval Inquisition*. New York: Holmes and Meier Publishers, Inc., 1989.

Hamilton, Sarah. "Penance in the Age of Gregorian Reform." *Studies in Church History* 40 (2004): 47–73.

"Rites for Public Penance in Late Anglo-Saxon England." In Helen Gittos and Bradford Bedingfield, eds., *The Liturgy of the Late Anglo-Saxon Church*, 65–103. Woodbridge: Boydell, 2005.

"The Unique Favour of Penance: The Church and the People, c. 800-c. 1100." In Peter Linehan and Janet Nelson, eds., *The Medieval World*, 229–45. New York: Routledge, 2001.

Hanawalt, Barbara. *Crime and Conflict in English Communities, 1300–1348*. Cambridge, MA: Harvard University Press, 1979.

"The Female Felon in Fourteenth-Century England." *Viator* 5 (1974): 253–68.

Hargreaves, Paul. "Seignorial Reaction and Peasant Responses: Worcester Priory and its People after the Black Death." *Midland History* 24.1 (1999): 53–78.

Harlan-Haughey, Sarah. "Forest Law through the Looking Glass: Distortions of the Forest Charter in the Outlaw Fiction of Late Medieval England." *William and Mary Bill of Rights Journal* 25.2 (2016–17): 549–89.

Hartrich, Eliza. "Rebellion and the Law in Fifteenth Century English Towns." In Justine Firnhaber-Baker and Dirk Schoenaers, eds., *The Routledge History Handbook of Medieval Revolt*, 189–207. New York: Routledge, 2016.

Heckman, Christina. "*Imitatio* in Early Medieval Spirituality: The Dream of the Rood, Anselm, and Militant Christology." *Essays in Medieval Studies* 22 (2005): 141–53.

Helmholz, Richard. *Canon Law and English Common Law*. SS, 1983.

"Crime, Compurgation and the Courts of the Medieval Church." *L&HR* 1.1 (1983): 1–26.

"Fundamental Human Rights in Medieval Law." *Fulton Lectures*. University of Chicago Press, 2001.

"Magna Carta and the *ius commune*." *Chicago Law Review* 66.2 (1999): 297–371.

"Natural Law and Human Rights in English Law: From Bracton to Blackstone." *Ave Maria Law Review* 3.1 (2005): 1–22.

"The Early History of the Grand Jury and the Canon Law." *University of Chicago Law Review* 50 (1983): 613–27.

The Ius Commune *in England: Four Studies*. Oxford University Press, 2001.

"The Privilege and the *Ius Commune*: The Middle Ages to the Seventeenth Century." In Richard Helmholz, et al., eds., *The Privilege against Self-Incrimination: Its Origins and Development*, 17–46. University of Chicago Press, 1997.

The Spirit of Classical Canon Law. Athens: University of Georgia Press, 1996.

Herzog, Tamar. *A Short History of European Law: The Last Two and a Half Millennia*. Cambridge, MA: Harvard University Press, 2019.

Hillner, Julia. *Prison, Punishment and Penance in Late Antiquity*. Cambridge University Press, 2015.

Hilton, Rodney, and Aston, Trevor, eds. *The English Rising of 1381*. Cambridge University Press, 2007.

Hollister, C. Warren. "Royal Acts of Mutilation: The Case against Henry I." *Albion* 10.4 (1978): 330–40.

Holsinger, Bruce. "Vernacular Legality: The English Jurisdiction of the *Owl and the Nightingale*." In Emily Steiner and Candace Barrington, eds., *The Letter of the Law: Legal Practice and Literary Production in Medieval England*, 154–84. Ithaca: Cornell University Press, 2002.

Holt, James. *Magna Carta*, 3rd edn. Cambridge University Press, 2015.

Hoskin, Philippa. "Holy Bishops and Political Exiles: St Richard's Cult and Political Protest in the Late Thirteenth Century." In Paul Foster, ed., *Richard of Chichester: Bishop 1245–1253; Canonized 1262*, 22–7. Chichester Cathedral Press, 2009.

Robert Grosseteste and the 13th-Century Diocese of Lincoln: An English Bishop's Pastoral Vision. Leiden: Brill, 2019.

"Robert Grosseteste, Natural Law and Magna Carta: National and Universal Law in 1253." *International Journal of Religion and Local History* 10.2 (2015): 120–32.

Hough, Carole. "Penitential Literature and Secular Law." *Anglo-Saxon Studies in Archaeology and History* 11 (2000): 133–41.

Hudson, John. *The Formation of the English Common Law: Law and Society in England from King Alfred to Magna Carta*, 2nd edn. London: Routledge, 2018.

"Maitland and Anglo-Norman Law." *Proceedings of the British Academy* 89 (1996): 21–46.

Hurnard, Naomi. "The Anglo-Norman Franchises." *EHR* 64.252 (1949): 289–327.

The King's Pardon for Homicide Before AD *1307*. Oxford: Clarendon Press, 1969.

Hyams, Paul. "Feud and the State in Late Anglo-Saxon England." *JBS* 40.1 (2001): 1–43.

King, Lords and Peasants in Medieval England: The Common Law of Villeinage in the Twelfth and Thirteenth Centuries. Oxford: Clarendon Press, 1980.

Rancor and Reconciliation in Medieval England. Ithaca: Cornell University Press, 2003.

"The Legal Revolution and the Discourse of Dispute." In Andrew Galloway, ed., *The Cambridge Companion to Medieval English Culture*, 43–65. Cambridge University Press, 2011.

Immaculate, Sister Mary. "The Four Daughters of God in the *Gesta Romanorum* and the Court of Sapience." *PMLA* 57.4 (1942): 951–65.

Ireland, Richard. "Law in Action, Law in Books: The Practicality of Medieval Theft Law." *C&C* 17.3 (2002): 309–31.

"The Presumption of Guilt in the History of English Criminal Procedure." *Journal of Legal History* 7.3 (1986): 243–55.

Jahner, Jennifer. "The *Mirror of Justices* and the Arts of Archival Invention." *Viator* 45.1 (2014): 221–46.

Jenks, Stuart. "The Lay Subsidies and the State of the English Economy (1275–1334)." *Vierteljahrschrift für Sozial- und Wirtschaftsgeschichte* 85.1 (1998): 1–39.

Johnston, Michael. "William Langland and John Ball." *YLS* 30 (2016): 29–74.

Jurasinski, Stefan. *The Old English Penitentials and Anglo-Saxon Law*. Cambridge University Press, 2015.

Jurkowski, Maureen. "Henry V's Suppression of the Oldcastle Revolt." In Gwilym Dodd, ed., *Henry V: New Interpretations*, 103–30. York Medieval Press, 2013.

Kamali, Elizabeth Papp. "*Felonia felonice facta*: Felony and Intentionality in Medieval England." *Criminal Law and Philosophy* 9.3 (2015): 397–421.

Felony and the Guilty Mind in Medieval England. Cambridge University Press, 2019.

"The Devil's Daughter of Hell Fire: Anger's Role in Medieval English Felony Cases." *L&HR* 35.1 (2017): 155–200.

Kamali, Elizabeth Papp, and Thomas A. Green. "A Crossroads in Criminal Procedure: The Assumptions Underlying England's Adoption of Trial by Jury for Crime." In Travis Baker, ed., *Law and Society in Later Medieval England and Ireland: Essays in Honour of Paul Brand*, 51–81. New York: Routledge, 2018.

Kantorowicz, Ernst. *The King's Two Bodies: A Study in Medieval Political Theology*. 1957; repr. Princeton University Press, 2016.

Kastleman, Rebecca. "Impersonating the Law: The Dramaturgy of Legal Action in the York Corpus Christi Pageant and John Bale's *Three Laws*." *Theatre Journal* 68.1 (2016): 37–56.

Kaye, John. "Gaol Delivery Jurisdiction and the Writ *de Bono et Malo*." *The Law Quarterly Review* 93 (1977): 259–72.

Keen, Maurice. *Nobles, Knights and Men-at-Arms in the Middle Ages*. London: Hambledon, 1996.

Kelly, Ansgar. "The Right to Remain Silent: Before and After Joan of Arc." *Speculum* 68.4 (1993): 992–1026.

Kelsey, Sean. "The Trial of Charles I." *EHR* 118.477 (2003): 583–616.

Kerr, Margaret, et al. "Cold Water and Hot Iron: Trial by Ordeal in England." *Journal of Interdisciplinary History* 22.4 (1992): 573–95.

Kesselring, Krista. "Felony Forfeiture in England, *c.* 1170–1870." *Journal of Legal History* 30.3 (2009): 201–26.

  Making Murder Public: Homicide in Early Modern England, 1480–1680. Oxford University Press, 2019.

  "Marks of Division: Cross-border Remand after 1603 and the Case of Lord Sanquhar." In Sara Butler and Krista Kesselring, eds., *Crossing Borders: Boundaries and Margins in Medieval and Early Modern Britain. Essays in Honour of Cynthia J. Neville*, 258–79. Leiden: Brill, 2018.

  "No Greater Provocation? Adultery and the Mitigation of Murder in English Law." *L&HR* 34.1 (2016): 199–225.

Keynes, Simon. "Crime and Punishment in the Reign of King Æthelred the Unready." In Ian Wood and Niels Lund, eds., *People and Places in Northern Europe 500–1600. Essays in Honour of Peter Hayes Sawyer*, 67–81. Woodbridge: Boydell, 1996.

King, Andy. "False Traitors or Worthy Knights? Treason and Rebellion against Edward II in the *Scalacronica* and the Anglo-Norman Prose *Brut* Chronicles." *Historical Research* 88.239 (2015): 34–47.

King, Pamela. "Contemporary Cultural Models for the Trial Plays in the York Cycle." In Alan Hindley, ed., *Drama and Community: People and Plays in Medieval Europe*, 200–16. Turnhout: Brepols, 1999.

Klein, Daniel. "The Trial of Charles I." *Journal of Legal History* 18.1 (1997): 1–25.

Klerman, Daniel. "Jurisdictional Competition and the Evolution of the Common Law: An Hypothesis." In Anthony Musson, ed., *Boundaries of the Law: Geography, Gender and Jurisdiction in Medieval and Early Modern Europe*, 149–68. Aldershot: Ashgate, 2005.

"Settlement and the Decline of Private Prosecution in Thirteenth-Century England." *L&HR* 19.1 (2001): 1–65.

"Was the Jury Ever Self-Informing?" *Southern California Law Review* 77 (2003): 123–49.

Klerman, Daniel, and Paul G. Mahoney. "English Legal Exceptionalism." University of Pittsburgh, 2006, www.pitt.edu/~dmberk/KlermanMahoney .pdf (accessed March 5, 2020).

Kross, Jerome, and Bernard Bachrach. *The Mystic Mind: The Psychology of Medieval Mystics and Ascetics*. New York: Routledge, 2005.

Kuskowski, Ada Maria. "*Lingua Franca Legalis?* A French Vernacular Legal Culture from England to the Levant." *Reading Medieval Studies* 40 (2014): 140–58.

Kuttner, Stephan. "The Revival of Jurisprudence." In Robert Benson, Giles Constable, and Carol Lanham, eds., *Renaissance and Renewal in the Twelfth Century*, 299–323. University of Toronto Press, 1982.

Lacey, Helen. *The Royal Pardon: Access to Mercy in Fourteenth-Century England*. York Medieval Press, 2009.

Lake, Peter, and Michael Questier. *The Trials of Margaret Clitherow: Persecution, Martyrdom and the Politics of Sanctity in Elizabeth England*. London: Continuum, 2011.

Lambert, Tom. *Law and Order in Anglo-Saxon England*. Oxford University Press, 2017.

"Theft, Homicide and Crime in Late Anglo-Saxon Law." *P&P* 214.1 (2012): 3–43.

Lander, Jack. "Attainder and Forfeiture, 1453–1509." *Historical Journal* 4.2 (1961): 119–51.

Langbein, John. "Bifurcation and the Bench: The Influence of the Jury on English Conceptions of the Judiciary." In Paul Brand and Joshua Getzler, eds., *Judges and Judging in the History of the Common Law and Civil Law: From Antiquity to Modern Times*, 67–82. Cambridge University Press, 2013.

"The Historical Origins of the Privilege against Self-Incrimination at Common Law." *Michigan Law Review* 92. 5 (1994): 1047–85.

The Origins of the Adversary Criminal Trial. Oxford University Press, 2005.

"The Prosecutorial Origins of Defence Counsel in the Eighteenth Century: The Appearance of Solicitors." *Cambridge Law Journal* 58.2 (1999): 314–65.

Torture and the Law of Proof: Europe and England in the Ancien Régime. University of Chicago Press, 1977.

Larson, Peter. *Conflict and Compromise in the Late Medieval Countryside: Lords and Peasants in Durham, 1349–1400*. New York: Routledge, 2014.

Liddy, Christian. "Cultures of Surveillance in Late Medieval English Towns: The Monitoring of Speech and the Fear of Revolt." In Justine Firnhaber-Baker and Dirk Schoenaers, eds., *Routledge History Handbook of Medieval Revolt*, 311–29. New York: Routledge, 2016.

Linehan, Peter, Janet Nelson, and Marios Costambeys, eds. *The Medieval World*. Milton Park: Routledge, 2018.

Lipton, Emma. "Space and Culture of Witnessing in the York *Entry into Jerusalem*." *Journal of Medieval and Early Modern Studies* 49.2 (2019): 295–317.

Lists of Sheriffs for England and Wales from the Earliest Times to AD 1383, Compiled from Documents in the Public Record Office. London: HMSO, 1898; reprinted by Kraus, 1963.

Maddicott, John. "Poems of Social Protest in Early Fourteenth-Century England." In Ormrod, ed., *England in the Fourteenth Century*, 130–44. Woodbridge: Boydell, 1986.

"The Oath of Marlborough, 1209: Fear, Government and Popular Allegiance in the Reign of King John." *EHR* 126.519 (2011): 281–318.

"Thomas of Lancaster, Second Earl of Lancaster, Second Earl of Leicester, and Earl of Lincoln, (c. 1278–1322)." *ODNB* (accessed January 3, 2008).

Maitland, Frederic. *The Constitutional History of England. A Course of Lectures*. Cambridge University Press, 1909.

Mäkinen, Virpi, and Heikki Pihlajamäki. "The Individualization of Crime in Medieval Canon Law." *Journal of the History of Ideas* 65.4 (2004): 525–42.

Mansfield, Mary. *The Humiliation of Sinners: Public Penance in Thirteenth-Century France*. Ithaca: Cornell University Press, 1995.

Marafioti, Nicole. "Earthly Justice and Spiritual Consequences: Judging and Punishing in the Old English *Consolation of Philosophy*." In Jay Paul Gates and Nicole Marafioti, eds., *Capital and Corporal Punishment in Anglo-Saxon England*, 113–48. Woodbridge: Boydell, 2014.

Marks, Alfred. *Tyburn Tree: Its History and Annals*. London: Brown, Langham, and Co., 1908.

Martin, Charles Trice. *The Record Interpreter* 2nd edn. 1892; reprinted Chichester: Phillimore and Co., Ltd., 1999.

Marvin, Julia. "Cannibalism as an Aspect of Famine in Two English Chronicles." In Martha Carlin and Joel Rosenthal, eds., *Food and Eating in Medieval Society*, 73–86. London: Hambledon, 1998.

Masschaele, James. *Jury, State, and Society in Medieval England*. New York: Palgrave Macmillan, 2008.

Mate, Mavis. "High Prices in Early Fourteenth-Century England: Causes and Consequences." *Economic History Review* 28.1 (1975): 1–16.

Matlock, Wendy. "Law and Violence in *The Owl and the Nightingale*." *Journal of English and Germanic Philology* 109.4 (2010): 446–67.

McDougall, Sara. *Bigamy and Christian Identity in Late Medieval Champagne*. Philadelphia: University of Pennsylvania Press, 2012.

McGlynn, Margaret. "Ecclesiastical Prisons and Royal Authority in the Reign of Henry VII." *Journal of Ecclesiastical History* 70.4 (2019): 750–66.

McGurk, John. "Hereward the Wake." *History Today* 20.5 (1970): 331–7.

McHardy, Alison. "Church Courts and Criminous Clerks in the Later Middle Ages." In Michael Franklin and Christopher Harper-Bill, eds., *Medieval Ecclesiastical Studies in Honour of Dorothy M. Owen*, 165–183. Woodbridge: Boydell, 1995.

McKenna, Catherine. "Performing Penance and Poetic Performance in the Medieval Welsh Court." *Speculum* 82.1 (2007): 70–96.

McKenna, John. "Popular Canonization as Political Propaganda: The Cult of Archbishop Scrope." *Speculum* 45.4 (1970): 608–23.

McKenzie, Andrea. "'This Death Some Strong and Stout Hearted Man Doth Choose': The Practice of Peine Forte et Dure in Seventeenth- and Eighteenth-Century England." *L&HR* 23.2 (2005): 279–313.

McLane, Bernard. "Juror Attitudes toward Local Disorder: The Evidence of the 1328 Lincolnshire Trailbaston Proceedings." In James Cockburn and Thomas Green, eds., *Twelve Good Men and True: The Criminal Trial Jury in England, 1200–1800*, 36–64. Princeton University Press, 1988.

McNair, Michael. "The Early Development of the Privilege against Self-Incrimination." *Oxford Journal of Legal Studies* 10.1 (1990): 66–84.

"Vicinage and the Antecedents of the Jury." *L&HR* 17.3 (1999): 537–90.

McSheffrey, Shannon. "Men and Masculinity in Late Medieval London Civic Culture: Governance, Patriarchy and Reputation." In Jacqueline Murray, ed., *Conflicted Identities and Multiple Masculinities: Men in the Medieval West*, 243–78. New York: Garland, 1999.

"Sanctuary and Legal Topography of Pre-Reformation London." *L&HR* 27.3 (2009): 483–514.

Seeking Sanctuary: Crime, Mercy, and Politics in English Courts, 1400–1550. Oxford University Press, 2017.

McSweeney, Thomas. "Magna Carta and the Right to Trial by Jury." In Randy Holland, ed., *Magna Carta: Muse and Mentor*, 139–157. Eagen, MN: Thomson Reuters, 2014.

Priests of the Law: Roman Law and the Making of the Common Law's First Professionals. Oxford University Press, 2019.

"The King's Courts and the King's Soul: Pardoning as Almsgiving in Medieval England." *Reading Medieval Studies* 40 (2014): 159–75.

Meens, Rob. *Penance in Medieval Europe, 600–1200*. Cambridge University Press, 2014.

Merback, Mitchell. *The Thief, the Cross and the Wheel: Pain and the Spectacle of Punishment in Medieval and Renaissance Europe*. University of Chicago Press, 1998.

Milsom, S. F. C. *Historical Foundations of the Common Law*. London: Butterworths, 1969.

Morris, Colin. *The Discovery of the Individual, 1050–1200*. University of Toronto Press, 1987.

"William I and the Church Courts." *EHR* 82.324 (1967): 449–63.

Morris, Marc. *King John: Treachery, Tyranny and the Road to Magna Carta*. London: Hutchinson, 2015.

"Starved to Death." *History Today* (January 29, 2016), www .historytoday.com/starved-death (accessed June 25, 2019).

Mulholland, Maureen. "Trials in Manorial Courts in Late Medieval England." In Maureen Mulholland and Brian Pullen, eds., *Judicial Tribunals in England and Europe, 1200–1700: The Trial in History, Volume I*, 81–101. Manchester University Press, 2003.

Müller, Miriam. "Conflict and Revolt: The Bishop of Ely and his Peasants at the Manor of Brandon in Suffolk c. 1300–81." *Rural History* 23.1 (2012): 1–19.

"The Aims and Organisation of a Peasant Revolt in Early Fourteenth-Century Wiltshire." *Rural History* 14 (2003): 1–20.

Musson, Anthony. "Lay Participation: The Paradox of the Jury." *Comparative Legal History* 3.2 (2015): 245–71.

Medieval Law in Context: The Growth of Legal Consciousness from Magna Carta to the Peasant's Revolt. Manchester University Press, 2001.

Public Order and Law Enforcement: The Local Administration of Criminal Justice, 1294–1350. Woodbridge: Boydell, 1996.

"Turning King's Evidence: The Prosecution of Crime in Late Medieval England." *Oxford Journal of Legal Studies* 19.3 (1999): 467–79.

"Wergeld: Crime and the Compensation Culture in Medieval England." Video lecture, Gresham College, October 5, 2009.

Nakley, Susan. "On the Unruly Power of Pain in Middle English Drama." *Literature and Medicine* 33.2 (2015): 302–25.

Nederman, Cary. "Property and Protest: Political Theory and Subjective Rights in Fourteenth-Century England." *Review of Politics* 58.2 (1996): 323–44.

Nemeth, Charles. *Aquinas on Crime*. South Bend, IN: St Augustine's Press, 2008.

Neville, Cynthia. "Common Knowledge of the Common Law in Later Medieval England." *Canadian Journal of History* 28 (1994): 1–18.

"'No Remission without Satisfaction': Canonical Influences on Secular Lawmaking in High Medieval Scotland." In Jonathan Wooding and Lynette Olson, eds., *Prophecy, Fate and Memory in the Early and Medieval Celtic World*, 208–45. Sydney University Press, 2020.

Violence, Custom and the Law: The Anglo-Scottish Border Lands in the Later Middle Ages. Edinburgh University Press, 1998.

O'Brien, Bruce. "From *Morðor* to *Murdrum*: The Preconquest Origin and Norman Revival of the Murder Fine." *Speculum* 71.2 (1996): 321–57.

O'Keefe, Katherine O'Brien. "Body and Law in Late Anglo-Saxon England." *Anglo-Saxon England* 27 (1998): 209–32.

Olson, Trisha. "Medieval Blood Sanction and the Divine Beneficence of Pain: 1100–1450." *Journal of Law and Religion* 22.1 (2006–7): 63–130.

"Of Enchantment: The Passing of the Ordeals and the Rise of the Jury Trial." *Syracuse Law Review* 50 (2000): 109–96.

"Of the Worshipful Warrior: Sanctuary and Punishment in the Middle Ages." *St Thomas Law Review* 16 (2004): 473–549.

Oppenheim, Chesterfield. "Waiver of Trial by Jury in Criminal Cases." *Michigan Law Review* 25.7 (1927): 695–734.

Ormrod, W. Mark. "An Archbishop in Revolt: Richard Scrope and the Yorkshire Rising of 1405." In Goldberg, ed., *Richard Scrope: Archbishop, Rebel, Martyr*, 28–44.

England in the Fourteenth Century. Woodbridge: Boydell, 1986.

"Law in the Landscape: Criminality, Outlawry and Regional Identity in Late Medieval England." In Anthony Musson, ed., *Boundaries of the Law: Geography, Gender and Jurisdiction in Medieval and Early Modern Europe*, 7–20. Aldershot: Ashgate, 2005.

"The English Monarchy and the Promotion of Religion in the Fourteenth Century." In Ludger Körntgen and Dominik Waßenhoven, eds., *Religion and Politics in the Middle Ages*, 205–18. Berlin: De Gruyter, 2013.

"The Personal Religion of Edward III." *Speculum* 64.4 (1989): 849–77.

"The Politics of Pestilence: Government in England after the Black Death." In W. Mark Ormrod and Phillip Lindley, eds., *The Black Death in England*, 147–81. Stamford: Paul Watkins, 1996.

"The Rebellion of Archbishop Scrope and the Tradition of Opposition to Royal Taxation." In Gwilym Dodd and Douglas Biggs, eds., *The Reign of Henry IV: Rebellion and Survival, 1403–1413*, 162–79. York Medieval Press, 2008.

Page, William. *A History of the County of York North Riding: Volume 1*. London: Constable, 1914.

Painter, Sidney. "Norwich's Three Geoffreys." *Speculum* 28.4 (1953): 808–13.

Palmer, Robert. "England: Law, Society and the State." In Rigby, ed., *A Companion to Britain*, 242–60.

Penman, Michael. "'Sacred Food for the Soul': In Search of the Devotions to Saints of Robert Bruce, King of Scotland, 1306–1329." *Speculum* 88.4 (2013): 1035–62.

Pennington, Kenneth. "Innocent until Proven Guilty: The Origins of a Legal Maxim." *Jurist* 63 (2000): 106–24.

The Prince and the Law, 1200–1600: Sovereignty and Rights in the Western Legal Tradition. Berkeley: University of California Press, 1993.

Peters, Edward. "Destruction of the Flesh – Salvation of the Spirit: The Paradoxes of Torture in Medieval Christian Society." In

Alberto Ferreiro, ed., *The Devil, Heresy and Witchcraft in the Middle Ages: Essays in Honor of Jeffrey B. Russell*, 131–48. Leiden: Brill, 1998.

Torture. Philadelphia: University of Pennsylvania Press, 1996.

Phelan, Amy. "Trailbaston and Attempts to Control Violence in the Reign of Edward I." In Richard Kaeuper, ed., *Violence in Medieval England*, 129–40. Woodbridge: Boydell, 2000.

Philipps, Katie. "Devotion by Donation: The Alms-Giving and Religious Foundations of Henry III." *Reading Medieval Studies* 43 (2017): 79–98.

Pihlajamäki, Heikki. "The Painful Question: The Fate of Judicial Torture in Early Modern Sweden." *L&HR* 25.3 (2007): 557–92.

Pike, Luke. *A History of Crime in England: Illustrating the Changes of the Laws in the Progress of Civilisation*, 2 vols. London: Smith, Elder, and Co., 1876.

Piroyansky, Danna. "'Martyrio pulchro finitus': Archbishop Scrope's Martyrdom and the Creation of a Cult." In Goldberg, ed., *Richard Scrope: Archbishop, Rebel, Martyr*, 100–114.

Martyrs in the Making: Political Martyrdom in Late Medieval England. New York: Palgrave Macmillan, 2008.

Plucknett, Theodore. *Concise History of the Common Law*, 2nd edn. London: Butterworths, 1936.

Pluta, Olaf. *Abbreviationes* (1993–2015), https://abbreviationes.net

Pollock, Frederick, and Frederic Maitland. *The History of English Law before the Time of Edward I*. 2 vols. Cambridge University Press, 1898.

Poos, Lawrence. *A Rural Society after the Black Death: Essex, 1350–1525*. Cambridge University Press, 1991.

"The Social Context of Statute of Labourers Enforcement." *L&HR* 1.1 (1983): 27–52.

Porter, Jean. "Responsibility, Passion, and Sin: A Reassessment of Abelard's *Ethics*." *Journal of Religious Ethics* 28.3 (2000): 367–94.

Poschmann, Bernard. *Penance and the Anointing of the Sick*. Freiburg: Herder and Herder, 1964.

Powell, Edward. "Arbitration and the Law in Late Medieval England." *TRHS* 33 (1983): 49–67.

"Jury Trial at Gaol Delivery in the Late Middle Ages: the Midland Circuit, 1400–1429." In James Cockburn and Thomas Green, eds., *Twelve Good Men and True*, 78–116. Princeton University Press, 1988.

Pryce, Huw. *Native Law and the Church in Medieval Wales*. Oxford University Press, 1993.

Pugh, Ralph. "The Duration of Criminal Trials in Medieval England." In Eric Ives and Anthony Manchester, eds., *Law, Litigants and the Legal Profession*, 104–15. London: RHS, 1983.

Imprisonment in Medieval England. Cambridge University Press, 1968.

"The Knights Hospitallers of England as Undertakers." *Speculum* 56.3 (1981): 566–74.

"The Writ de Bono et Malo." *The Law Quarterly Review* 92 (1976): 258–67.

Putnam, Bertha. *The Enforcement of the Statutes of Labourers: During the First Decade after the Black Death, 1349–1359*. New York: Longmans, Green and Co., 1908.

Radding, Charles. *The Origins of Medieval Jurisprudence: Pavia and Bologna 850–1150*. New Haven: Yale University Press, 1988.

Rentz, Ellen. *Imagining the Parish in Late Medieval England*. Columbus: Ohio State University Press, 2015.

Reynolds, Susan. "Medieval Law." In Linehan, ed., *The Medieval World*, 485–502.

"The Emergence of Professional Law in the Long Twelfth Century." *L&HR* 21.2 (2003): 347–66.

Riddle, James. "The Playing of the Passion and the Martyrdom of Archbishop Scrope." *Mediaevalia* 28.2 (2007): 17–31.

Rigby, Stephen., ed. *A Companion to Britain in the Later Middle Ages*. Malden: Wiley-Blackwell, 2009, 47–64.

Roach, Andrew. "Penance and the Making of the Inquisition in Languedoc." *Journal of Ecclesiastical History* 52.3 (2001): 409–33.

Robinson, James. "Pilgrimage and Protest: Badges at the British Museum Relating to Thomas of Lancaster and Isabella, Queen of Edward II." In Sarah Blick, ed., *Beyond Pilgrim Souvenirs and Secular Badges: Essays in Honour of Brian Spencer*, 170–81. Oxford: Oxbow Books, 2007.

Rogers, Nicholas. "Appendix: The Continuation of the Cult in the Fifteenth Century." *Yorkshire Archaeological Journal* 67 (1995): 189–91.

Rose, Jonathan. "*Feodo de Compedibus Vocato le Sewet*: The Medieval Prison 'oeconomy'." In Paul Brand, Andrew Lewis, and Paul Mitchell, eds., *Law in the City*, 72–94. London: Four Courts Press, 2005.

Royer, Katherine. *The English Execution Narrative, 1200–1700*. London: Pickering and Chatto, 2014.

Rubin, Miri. "Choosing Death? Experiences of Martyrdom in Late Medieval Europe." *Studies in Church History* 30 (1993): 153–83.

Rudé, George. *The Crowd in the French Revolution*. Westport: Greenwood Press, 1959.

Russell, Michael. "I. Trial by Battle and the Writ of Right." *Journal of Legal History* 1.2 (1980): 111–34.

"II. Trial by Battle and the Appeals of Felony." *Journal of Legal History* 1.2 (1980): 135–64.

Sadler, Gregory. "Non modo verbis sed et verberibus: Saint Anselm on Punishment, Coercion, and Violence." *Cistercian Studies Quarterly* 45.1 (2010): 35–61.

Scase, Wendy. *Literature and Complaint in England, 1272–1553*. Oxford University Press, 2007.

Schofield, Phillipp. *Peasant and Community in Medieval England 1200–1500.* Basingstoke: Palgrave Macmillan 2003.

Scott, James. *Domination and the Arts of Resistance: Hidden Transcripts.* New Haven: Yale University Press, 1990.

Weapons of the Weak: Everyday Forms of Peasant Resistance. New Haven: Yale University Press, 1985.

Scully, Robert. "The Unmaking of a Saint: Thomas Becket and the English Reformation." *The Catholic Historical Review* 86.4 (2000): 579–602.

Seabourne, Gwen. "'It is Necessary That the Issue Be Heard to Cry or Squall within the Four [Walls]': Qualifying for Tenancy by the Curtesy of England in the Reign of Edward I." *Journal of Legal History* 40 (2019): 44–68.

Seipp, David. "Magna Carta in the Late Middle Ages: Overmighty Subjects, Undermighty Kings, and a Turn away from Trial by Jury." *William and Mary Bill of Rights Journal* 25.2 (2016): 665–88.

"The *Mirror of Justices.*" In Jonathan Bush and Alain Wijffels, eds., *Learning the Law: Teaching and the Transmission of the Law in England, 1150–1900,* 85–112. London: Hambledon, 1999.

"The Reception of Canon Law and Civil Law in the Common Law Courts before 1600." *Oxford Journal of Legal Studies* 13.3 (1993): 388–420.

Shack, William. "Collective Oath: Compurgation in Anglo-Saxon England and African States." *European Journal of Sociology* 20.1 (1979): 1–18.

Sharp, Buchanan. "Royal Paternalism and the Moral Economy in the Reign of Edward II: The Response to the Great Famine." *Economic History Review* 66.2 (2013): 628–47.

Shoemaker, Karl. "The Problem of Pain in Punishment: Historical Perspectives." In Austin Sarat, ed., *Pain, Death, and the Law,* 15–41. Ann Arbor: University of Michigan Press, 2001.

Sizer, Michael. "Murmur, Clamor, and Tumult: The Soundscape of Revolt and Oral Culture in the Middle Ages." *Radical History Review* 2015.121 (2015): 9–31.

Skotnicki, Andrew. "God's Prisoners: Penal Confinement and the Creation of Purgatory." *Modern Theology* 22.1 (2006): 85–110.

Slavin, Philip. *Experiencing Famine in Fourteenth-Century Britain.* Turnhout: Brepols, 2019.

Smail, Daniel Lord. "Violence and Predation in Late Medieval Mediterranean Europe." *Comparative Studies in Society and History* 54.1 (2012): 7–34.

Smith, Roderick, and L. Lim. "Experiments to Investigate the Level of 'Comfortable' Loads for People against Crush Barriers." *Safety Science* 18 (1995): 329–35.

Smith, Sally. "Materializing Resistant Identities among the Medieval Peasantry: An Examination of Dress Accessories from English Rural Settlement Sites." *Journal of Material Culture* 14.3 (2009): 309–32.

Sommerfeldt, John. *On the Spirituality of Relationship*. New York: Newman Press, 1997.

Southern, Richard. "Robert Grosseteste (c. 1170–1253)." *ODNB*. September 23, 2004.

Robert Grosseteste: Growth of an English Mind. Oxford: Clarendon Press, 1992.

Staley, Lynn. "Susanna and English Communities." *Traditio* 62 (2007): 25–58.

Steiner, Emily, and Candace Barrington. "Introduction." In Steiner and Barrington, eds., *The Letter of the Law*, 1–11.

Strohm, Paul. *Hochon's Arrow: The Social Imagination of Fourteenth-Century Texts*. Princeton University Press, 1992.

Sturges, Robert. "Wols-hede and Outhorne: The Ban, Bare Life, and Power in the Passion Plays." In Bonnie Wheeler, ed., *Mindful Spirit in Late Medieval Literature*, 93–108. New York: Palgrave, 2006.

Summerson, Henry. "Attitudes to Capital Punishment in England, 1200–1350." In Michael Prestwich, Richard Britnell, and Robin Frame, eds., *Thirteenth Century England VIII*, 123–34. Woodbridge: Boydell, 2001.

"The Criminal Underworld of Medieval England." *Journal of Legal History* 17.3 (1996): 197–224.

"The Early Development of the Peine Forte et Dure." In Eric Ives and Anthony Manchester, eds., *Law, Litigants and the Legal Profession*, 116–25. London: RHS, 1983.

"Maitland and the Criminal Law in the Age of *Bracton*." *Proceedings of the British Academy* 89 (1996): 115–44.

Swanson, Robert. "Political Pilgrims and Political Saints in Medieval England." In Antón Pazos, ed., *Pilgrims and Politics: Rediscovering the Power of the Pilgrimage*, 29–46. Farnham: Ashgate, 2012.

Tanner, Lawrence. "Lord High Almoners and Sub-Almoners 1100–1957." *Journal of the British Archaeological Association*, 3rd series, 20–21 (1957–8): 72–83.

Taylor, Andrew. "Manual to Miscellany: Stages in the Commercial Copying of Vernacular Literature in England." *The Yearbook of English Studies* 33 (2003): 1–17.

Taylor, Arnold. "Royal Alms and Oblations in the Later Thirteenth Century: An Analysis of the Alms Roll of 12 Edward I (1283–4)." In Frederick Emmison and Roy Stephens, eds., *Tribute to an Antiquary: Essays Presented to Mark Fitch*, 93–125. London: Leopard's Head Press, 1976.

Taylor, Jamie. *Fictions of Evidence: Witnessing, Literature, and Community in the Late Middle Ages*. Columbus: Ohio State University Press, 2013.

Taylor, Scott. "*Judicium Dei, vulgaris popularisque sensus*: Survival of Customary Justice and Resistance to its Displacement by the 'New' *Ordines iudiciorum* as Evidenced by Francophonic Literature of the

High Middle Ages." In Albrecht Classen and Connie Scarborough, eds., *Crime and Punishment in the Middle Ages and Early Modern Age: Mental-Historical Investigations of Basic Human Problems and Social Responses*, 109–29. Berlin: De Gruyter, 2012.

Taylor, Thomas. "Blohin: His Descendants and Lands." *The Ancestor* 9 (April, 1904): 20–8.

Theilmann, John. "Political Canonization and Political Symbolism in Medieval England." *JBS* 29.3 (1990): 241–66.

"The Miracles of King Henry VI of England." *The Historian* 42.3 (1980): 456–71.

Thiery, Daniel. *Polluting the Sacred: Violence, Faith, and the 'Civilizing' of Parishioners in Late Medieval England*. Leiden: Brill, 2009.

Thomas, Arvind. Piers Plowman *and the Reinvention of Church Law in the Late Middle Ages*. University of Toronto Press, 2019.

Thomas, David. "Dungeons of Despair." *Ancestors* 41 (2005): 1474–2470.

Thornley, Isobel. "Treason by Words in the Fifteenth Century." *EHR* 32.128 (1917): 556–61.

Tierney, Brian. *The Idea of Natural Rights: Studies on Natural Rights, Natural Law, and Church Law, 1150–1625*. Grand Rapids, MI: Eerdmans, 1997.

Tilly, Charles. "How Protest Modernized in France, 1845–1855." In William Aydelotte, Allan Bogue, and Robert Fogel, eds., *The Dimension of Quantitative Research*, 380–455. Princeton University Press, 1972.

Tiner, Elza. "English Law in the York Trial Plays." *The Early Drama, Art, and Music Review* 18.2 (1996): 103–12.

Tinkle, Theresa. "York's Jesus: Crowned King and Traitor Attainted." *Speculum* 94.1 (2019): 96–137.

Tkacz, Catherine Brown. "Susanna as a Type of Christ." *Studies in Iconography* 20 (1999): 101–53.

Tracy, Larissa. *Torture and Brutality in Medieval Literature: Negotiations of National Identities*. Woodbridge: Boydell, 2012.

Trembinski, Donna. "[Pro]passio Doloris: Early Dominican Conceptions of Christ's Physical Pain." *Journal of Ecclesiastical History* 59.4 (2008): 630–56.

Tubach, Frederic., ed. *Index Exemplorum: A Handbook of Medieval Religious Tales*. Helsinki: Suomalainen Tiedeakatemia Akademia Scientiarum Fennica, 1969.

Turberville, Arthur. *Mediaeval Heresy and the Inquisition*. London: C. Lockwood and Son, 1920.

Turner, Ralph. "Clerical Judges in English Secular Courts: The Ideal Versus the Reality." *Medievalia et Humanistica*, n.s. 3 (1972): 159–79.

"England in 1215: An Authoritarian Angevin Dynasty Facing Multiple Threats." In Janet Senderowitz Loengard, ed., *Magna Carta and the England of King John*, 10–26. Woodbridge: Boydell, 2010.

"England: Kingship and the Political Community, c.1100–1272." In Rigby, ed., *A Companion to Britain*, 183–207.

"The Origins of the Medieval English Jury: Frankish, English, or Scandinavian?" *JBS* 7.2 (1968): 1–10.

Turning, Patricia. "Competition for the Prisoner's Body: Wardens and Jailers in Fourteenth-Century Southern France." In Classen and Scarborough, eds., *Crime and Punishment in the Middle Ages*, 281–97.

"The Right to Punish: Jurisdictional Disputes between Royal and Municipal Officers in Medieval Toulouse." *French History* 24.1 (2010): 1–19.

Tydeman, William. "An Introduction to Medieval English Theatre." In Richard Beadle, ed., *Cambridge Companion to Medieval English Theatre*, 1–36. Cambridge University Press, 1994.

Vale, Brigette. "The Scropes of Bolton and of Masham, c.1300-c.1450: A Study of a Northern Noble Family with a Calendar of the Scrope of Bolton Cartulary." 2 vols. PhD Diss., University of York, 1987.

Vámbéry, Arminius. *The Story of Hungary*. New York: G. P. Putnam's Sons, 1886.

van Caenegem, Raoul. "The Modernity of Medieval Law." *Legal History Review*, 68.3 (2000): 313–330.

Van Eickels, Klaus. "Gendered Violence: Castration and Blinding as Punishment for Treason in Normandy and Anglo-Norman England." *Gender and History* 16.3 (2004): 588–602.

Vincent, Nicholas. "The Pilgrimages of the Angevin Kings of England, 1154–1172." In Colin Morris and Peter Robert, eds., *Pilgrimage: The English Experience from Becket to Bunyan*, 12–45. Cambridge University Press, 2002.

Wagner, Karen. "*Cum aliquis venerit ad sacerdotum*: Penitential Experience in the Central Middle Ages." In Abigail Firey, ed., *A New History of Penance*, 201–18. Leiden: Brill, 2008.

Warren, Wilfred. *King John*. London: Eyre and Spottiswoode, 1961.

Waugh, Scott. "England: Kingship and the Political Community, 1272–1377." In Rigby, ed., *A Companion to Britain*, 208–23.

"Reluctant Knights and Jurors: Respites, Exemptions, and Public Obligations in the Reign of Henry III." *Speculum* 58.4 (1983): 937–86.

Webster, Paul. "Faith, Power and Charity: Personal Religion and Kingship in Medieval England." In Elena Woodacre, et al., eds., *The Routledge History of Monarchy*, 196–212. London: Routledge, 2019.

Westberg, Daniel. "The Relation between Positive and Natural Law in Aquinas." *Journal of Law and Religion* 11.1 (1994–5): 1–22.

Westerhof, Danielle. "Deconstructing the Identities on the Scaffold: The Execution of Hugh Despenser the Younger, 1326." *Journal of Medieval History* 33 (2007): 87–106.

White, Edward. "Peine Forte et Dure." In his *Legal Antiquities: A Collection of Essays upon Ancient Laws and Customs*. St Louis: Nixon-Jones Printing Co., 1913.

White, Jerry. *Mansions of Misery: A Biography of the Marshalsea Debtor's Prison*. London: The Bodley Head, 2016.

Whitman, James. *The Origins of Reasonable Doubt: Theological Roots of the Criminal Trial*. New Haven: Yale University Press, 2008.

Whittle, Jane, and Stephen Rigby. "England: Popular Politics and Social Conflict." In Rigby, ed., *A Companion to Britain*, 65–86.

Wingfield-Stratford, Esmé. *King Charles the Martyr*. London: Hollis and Carter, 1950.

Winroth, Anders. "The Legal Revolution of the Twelfth Century." In Thomas Noble, John Van Engen, Anna Sapir Abulafia, and Sverre Bagge, eds., *European Transformations: The Long Twelfth Century*, 338–53. South Bend, IN: University of Notre Dame Press, 2011.

Winter, Christine. "Prisons and Punishments in Late Medieval London." PhD Diss., Royal Holloway, University of London, 2012.

Woodbine, George. Review of Doris Mary Stenton, ed., *Rolls of the Justices in Eyre for Gloucestershire, Warwickshire and Staffordshire, 1221–1222*. In *The Yale Law Journal* 50.4 (1941): 729–32.

Wormald, Patrick. "Anglo-Saxon Law and Scots Law." *Scottish Historical Review* 88.2 (2009): 192–206.

"Giving God and King their Due: Conflict and its Regulation in the Early English State." In Patrick Wormald, ed., *Legal Culture in the Early Medieval West: Law as Text, Image and Experience*, 333–47. London: Hambledon, 1999.

"Maitland and Anglo-Saxon Law: Beyond Domesday Book." *Proceedings of the British Academy* 89 (1996): 1–20.

"Neighbors, Courts, and Kings: Reflections on Michael McNair's *Vicini*." *L&HR* 17.3 (1999): 597–601.

The Making of English Law: King Alfred to the Twelfth Century, Vol. 1: Legislation and its Limits. London: Blackwell, 2001.

Index

Milton Keynes UK
Ingram Content Group UK Ltd.
UKHW010352280324
440086UK00011B/117